Accession no.
36269678

D1586665

UNLOCKING EQUITY AND TRUSTS

6th edition   Mohamed Ramjohn

LIS LIBRARY

Date
02/06/17   IW-Che

Order No
2813865

University of ......

Routledge
Taylor & Francis Group

LONDON AND NEW YORK

First published 2017
by Routledge
2 Park Square, Milton Park, Abingdon, Oxon OX14 4RN

and by Routledge
711 Third Avenue, New York, NY 10017

Routledge is an imprint of the Taylor & Francis Group, an informa business

© 2017 Mohamed Ramjohn

The right of Mohamed Ramjohn to be identified as author of this work has been asserted by him in accordance with sections 77 and 78 of the Copyright, Designs and Patents Act 1988.

First edition published by Hodder Education 2005
Fifth Edition published by Routledge 2015

All rights reserved. No part of this book may be reprinted or reproduced or utilised in any form or by any electronic, mechanical, or other means, now known or hereafter invented, including photocopying and recording, or in any information storage or retrieval system, without permission in writing from the publishers.

Trademark notice: Product or corporate names may be trademarks or registered trademarks, and are used only for identification and explanation without intent to infringe.

British Library Cataloguing in Publication Data
A catalogue record for this book is available from the British Library

Library of Congress Cataloging in Publication Data
Names: Ramjohn, Mohamed, author.
Title: Unlocking equity and trusts/Mohamed Ramjohn.
Description: Sixth edition. | New York, NY: Routledge, 2017. | Includes bibliographical references and index.
Identifiers: LCCN 2016050423 | ISBN 9781138218697 (hardback) | ISBN 9781138218710 (pbk.) | ISBN 9781315413839 (epub) | ISBN 9781315413822 (mobipocket)
Subjects: LCSH: Trusts and trustees–England. | Equity–England.
Classification: LCC KD1480.R365 2017 | DDC 346.41/004–dc23
LC record available at https://lccn.loc.gov/2016050423

ISBN: 978-1-138-21869-7 (hbk)
ISBN: 978-1-138-21871-0 (pbk)
ISBN: 978-1-3154-1385-3 (ebk)

Typeset in Palatino
by Wearset Ltd, Boldon, Tyne and Wear

Printed and bound in Great Britain by
TJ International Ltd, Padstow, Cornwall

Contents

vi

CONTENTS

Guide to the book

In the Unlocking the Law books all the essential elements that make up the law are clearly defined to bring the law alive and make it memorable. In addition, the books are enhanced with learning features to reinforce learning and test your knowledge as you study. Follow this guide to make sure you get the most from reading this book.

AIMS AND OBJECTIVES

Defines what you will learn in each chapter.

SECTION

definition
Find key legal terminology at a glance.

Highlights sections from Acts.

ARTICLE

Defines Articles of the EC Treaty or of the European Convention on Human Rights or other Treaty.

CLAUSE

tutor tip
Provides key ideas from lecturers on how to get ahead.

Shows a Bill going through Parliament or a draft Bill proposed by the Law Commission.

CASE EXAMPLE

Illustrates the law in action.

JUDGMENT

Provides extracts from judgments on cases.

Indicates that you will be able to test yourself further on this topic using the Key Questions and Answers section of this book on www.unlockingthelaw.co.uk.

QUOTATION

Encourages you to engage with primary sources.

ACTIVITY

Enables you to test yourself as you progress through the chapter.

KEY FACTS

Draws attention to essential points and information.

student mentor tip

Offers advice from law graduates on the best way to achieve the results you want.

SAMPLE ESSAY QUESTIONS

Provide you with real-life sample essays and show you the best way to plan your answer.

SUMMARY

Concludes each chapter to reinforce learning.

Acknowledgements

The author and publishers are most grateful and would like to thank the following for permission to reproduce copyright material:

Butterworths: extracts from the *All England Law Reports*;
The Incorporated Council for Law Reporting for England and Wales: extracts from the *Law Reports* and *Weekly Law Reports*;
Sweet & Maxwell: extracts from the *Property, Planning and Compensation Reports*, *The Conveyancer* and the *Law Quarterly Review*.

This book is dedicated to Farah, Nadia, James and Jemima.

Preface

Equity and Trusts is a fast-moving subject. The two years that have elapsed since the publication of the last edition of this book have been a period of rapid development in equity and the law of trusts. In the field of case law there has been a steady accumulation in the volume of significant decisions in the law of trusts. Some of these include the decisions in *King v Dubrey* [2016] 2 WLR 1 [Chapter 4, *donatio mortis causa*]; *Liden v Burton* [2016] EWCA Civ 275 [Chapter 4, proprietary estoppel]; *Challinor v Juliet Bellis* [2015] EWCA Civ 59 [Chapter 7, resulting trust]; *Patel v Mirza* [2017] 1 All ER 191 [Chapter 7, resulting trust]; *Bilta v Nazir (No 2)* [2015] UKSC 23 [Chapter 7, resulting trust]; *Breitenfeld v Harrison* [2015] EWHC 399 [Chapter 8, constructive trusts 1]; *Brudenell-Bruce v Moore* [2014] EWHC 3679 [Chapter 8, constructive trusts 1]; *Generator Development Ltd v Lidl* [2016] EWHC 814 [Chapter 8, constructive trusts 1]; *FHR European Ventures v Cedar Capital Partners* [2014] UKSC 45 [Chapter 8, constructive trusts 1]; *Henderson v Wilcox* [2015] EWHC 3469; [Chapter 8, constructive trusts 1]; *Chadwick v Collinson* [2014] EWHC 3055 [Chapter 8, constructive trusts 1]; *Barnes v Phillips* [2015] EWCA Civ 1056 [Chapter 9, constructive trusts 2]; *Erlam v Rahman* [2016] EWHC 111 [Chapter 9, constructive trusts 2]; *Estate of York* [2015] EWCA Civ 72 [Chapter 9, constructive trusts 2]; *Curran v Collins* [2015] EWCA Civ 404 [Chapter 9, constructive trusts 2]; *Capehorn v Harris* [2015] EWCA Civ 955 [Chapter 9, constructive trusts 2]; *O'Kelly v Davies* [2014] EWCA Civ 1606 [Chapter 9, constructive trusts 2]; *Arif v Anwar* [2015] EWHC 124 [Chapter 9, constructive trusts 2]; *Barclay v Smith* [2016] EWHC 210 [Chapter 13, appointment, retirement and removal of trustees]; *Allfrey v Allfrey (a child)* [2015] EWHC 1717 [Chapter 15, variation of trusts]; *A.I.B. v Redler* [2014] UKSC 58 [Chapter 16, breach of trust]; *Purrunsing v A'Court & Co* [2016] EWHC 789 [Chapter 16, breach of trust]; *Haysport Properties v Ackerman* [2016] EWHC 393 [Chapter 16, breach of trust]; *FHR European Ventures v Mankarious* [2016] EWHC 359 [Chapter 16, breach of trust]; *Federal Republic of Brazil v Durant* [2015] UKPC 35 [Chapter 16, breach of trust]; *Lawrence v Fen Tigers Ltd* [2014] 3 WLR 555 [Chapter 17, injunctions].

This new edition has been considerably revised. The publishers and I were particularly keen to reach out to as large a selection of students as possible. While a significant number of undergraduate modules comprise solely the law of trusts, we are also aware that many modules include aspects of equity and the law of trusts. Chapter 17 on the equitable remedies of injunctions and specific performance is intended to introduce the reader to the salient elements of these remedies. Each chapter has been revisited and given a more rigorous analysis of the law.

The principal objectives of writing the sixth edition of this book remain the same as stated in previous editions: namely, to produce a text that has the right balance in terms of exposition of the law in a clear, concise and simple style, and presentation of the subject in a structured and accessible manner. I have followed the structure and style of previous editions by introducing the content of each chapter, followed by an exposition of the law in a structured manner, including a summary of the main cases and extracts from significant judgments, where appropriate. Each chapter concludes with self-test questions, a summary of the main points, a sample essay question and a list of articles for further reading.

I would like to thank the reviewers of the earlier edition of this work for their constructive suggestions for improving the presentation of materials in this edition, and the staff at Routledge for their assistance in the preparation of this book. I am particularly grateful to Fiona Briden and Ruth Noble, without whose support and patience it might not have been possible to produce this edition.

I have tried to explain and summarise the relevant principles of equity and trusts law as at October 2016. As ever, the responsibility for all errors and omissions rests with me.

Mohamed Ramjohn – LLB, LLM, CIOT, JP, Barrister at law. Associate Professor in Ealing Law School at the University of West London, Visiting Senior Fellow at the Russian State University of Justice. He has written several student books and articles on revenue law, evidence and equity.

Table of cases

Table of statutes and other instruments

List of Figures

1

Historical outlines of equity

AIMS AND OBJECTIVES

equity

That separate body of rules formulated and administered by the Court of Chancery prior to the Judicature Acts 1873/75 in order to supplement the deficiency in the rules and procedure at common law.

By the end of this chapter you should be able to:

- understand the shades of meaning of the expression 'equity' as used over the centuries

- comprehend the historical development and contribution of equity to English law

- appreciate the nineteenth-century reforms responsible for the administration of law and equity

- recognise the various maxims of equity

1.1 Introduction to equity

QUOTATION

'Equity is the branch of law, which, before the Judicature Acts 1873 and 1875 was applied and administered by the Court of Chancery.'

F W Maitland, *Equity: A Course of Lectures* (ed. A H Chaytor and W J Whittaker, revd J Brunyate, Cambridge University Press, 2011)

natural justice

Rules applied by the courts and other tribunals designed to ensure fairness and good faith and affording each party the opportunity to fairly state his case.

The system of **equity** includes that portion of **natural justice** which is judicially enforceable but which for various reasons was not enforced by the courts of common law. In this context the expression 'natural justice' is used in the broad sense of recognising and giving effect to justiciable rights of aggrieved parties based on principles of fairness and conscience that were not acknowledged by the common law courts. The common law system was perceived as being too formalistic and rigid in its outlook with the result that the potential rights of certain litigants were subject to abuse. The principles which gave effect to the rights of litigants and which were not recognised by the common law courts were known as equity.

Equity, unlike the common law, was not an independent system of legal rules. It did not stand alone. It presupposed the existence of the common law, which it

conscience
This expression denotes fairness, good faith and even-handedness.

common law
That part of the law of England and Wales formulated, developed and administered by the old common law courts. The rules that were originally applied by these courts were based on the common customs of this country.

ad hoc
For this purpose or individual cases.

supplemented and modified. The rules of equity were originally based on **conscience** and principles of natural justice, and were applied on a case-by-case basis. Where there were 'gaps' in the common law rules that created injustice to one or more of the parties, the rules of equity 'filled in these gaps'. Thus it has been said that 'Equity came to fulfil the law, not to destroy it.' The two systems of rules were complementary to each other. The rules of equity were regarded as that portion of natural justice that was judicially enforceable but which for a variety of reasons was not enforced by the courts of **common law**. The effect was that although the rules of equity did not directly contradict the common law, the application of equitable rules was capable of producing an effect which was different from the common law solution. A modern example of the operation of equity is illustrated by *Cresswell v Potter* [1978] 1 WLR 255. In this case, a sale of land by a 'poor and ignorant' person (judge's expression) at a substantial undervalue and without independent legal advice was regarded as an unconscionable bargain and the transaction was set aside.

1.1.1 Terminology

Originally, the expressions 'equity' or 'rules of equity' were synonymous with rules of justice and conscience. Individual Lords Chancellor did not consciously set out to develop a system of rules, but attempted in individual cases to achieve fairness and justice **ad hoc**. Accordingly, the principles originally applied by Lords Chancellor to determine disputes were based on rules of natural justice or conscience. These principles became known as equity.

Today, it would not be accurate to correlate 'equity' with 'justice' in the sense in which these expressions were used in medieval society. After the initial period of development the rules of equity became as settled and rigid as the common law had become. New equitable principles may not be created judicially, except within the parameters laid down by the courts over the centuries. Further, it is a myth to imagine that laying down a lax collection of principles by the courts in an effort to achieve fairness on a case-by-case basis will objectively fulfil the aim of justice in the broader sense of the word. The improved machinery for law reform has resulted in the increased willingness of Parliament to modernise the law in appropriate cases. The modern approach was reflected by Bagnall J in *Cowcher v Cowcher* [1972] 1 All ER 943, thus:

JUDGMENT

'I am convinced that in determining rights, particularly property rights, the only justice that can be attained by mortals, who are fallible and are not omniscient, is justice according to law; the justice which flows from the application of sure and settled principles to proved or admitted facts. So in the field of equity the length of the Chancellor's foot has been measured or is capable of measurement. This does not mean that equity is past child-bearing; simply that its progeny must be legitimate – by precedent out of principle. It is well that this should be so; otherwise no lawyer could safely advise on his client's title and every quarrel would lead to a law suit.'

Bagnall J

1.1.2 Petitions to the Lord Chancellor

In the thirteenth century, the available writs covered a narrow umbrella of claims – even if a claim came within the scope of an existing writ, the claimant might not have gained justice before a common law court; for example in an action commenced by the writs of debt and detinue, the defendant was entitled to wage his law. This was a process whereby the defendant discharged himself from a claim by denying the claim on oath and calling 11 persons from his neighbourhood to swear that his denial was genuine. In addition, a great deal of unnecessary intricacies were attendant on the pleadings. The pleadings were drafted by experts, and the rule at this time was that an incorrect pleading invariably led to the loss of the claim. Moreover, damages was the only remedy available at law. There were numerous occasions when this remedy proved inadequate. If A proved that B had made a contract with him and had acted in breach of such contract, A was entitled to damages in the common law courts. But that may well have been inadequate satisfaction for A, who would rather have the contract performed than be solaced with damages. The subject-matter of the breach of contract may well have had inherent unique qualities such as a contract for the sale of land or a painting. What A wanted was an order from the court compelling B to perform his duties under the contract, such as an order for specific performance that was granted initially by the Chancellor and subsequently by a court of equity. Similarly, C's conduct (D's neighbour) or use of his premises may have seriously inconvenienced D's use and enjoyment of his premises. The award of damages at common law was inadequate for D needed a remedy of an injunction to forbid C from continuing with his unlawful activity. Such a remedy was originally granted by the Chancellor and became integrated within the jurisdiction of the court of equity.

An aggrieved claimant was entitled to petition the King in Council, praying for relief. These petitions were dealt with by the Lord Chancellor, who was an ecclesiastic well versed in Canon law. Later on, the petitions were addressed directly to the Lord Chancellor, who dealt personally with the more important cases. Eventually the Chancellor and staff formed a court called the Court of Chancery to deal with the overwhelming number of petitions for equitable assistance.

1.1.3 Procedure in Chancery

The petition was presented by way of a bill filed by the claimant. Since proceedings were not commenced by writ as in the common law courts, there was never any strict procedure to be followed. The intervention by the Lord Chancellor (creating new rights and remedies) did not need validation by the pretence or fiction adopted by the common law courts in declaring the law from time immemorial, but instead considered each case on its merits and applied principles in accordance with his views of justice and fairness.

In appropriate cases a **subpoena** would be served on the defendant to compel his appearance to attend and answer the petition. The defendant was required to draft his answers on oath, called 'interrogatories'.

Usually the evidence was given on **affidavit** so that proceedings were confined to hearing legal arguments on both sides, but occasionally when the testimony of a witness (including the parties) was required to be received in the court, the witness would be required to testify on oath and be subjected to cross-examination by the Chancellor and the opposing party. This process was inquisitorial in nature and permitted the Chancellor (and the Court of Chancery) to marshal the facts freed from the formalistic and rule-driven mode of admitting the facts that was adopted by the common law courts.

The relevant decree of the court was issued in the name of the Chancellor and acted '*in personam*' on the defendant. In this context the expression '*in personam*' refers to the process in equity of enforcing the decrees of the Chancellor and the court of equity. The orders of the Chancellor were addressed to the defendant personally to comply with the order. The sanction for disobeying the Chancellor's decrees was imprisonment for **contempt of court**.

The principles of equity were even applicable irrespective of whether the defendant was within or outside the jurisdiction. Lord Selbourne LC in *Ewing v Orr Ewing (No 1)* [1883] 9 App Cas 34, said:

---

subpoena
The forerunner of the witness summons. It was a writ issued in an action requiring the addressee to be present in court at a specified date and time. Failure to attend without good cause is subject to a penalty.

affidavit
A written, signed statement made on oath or subject to a solemn affirmation.

in personam
An act done or right existing with reference to a specific person as opposed to *in rem* (or in the thing).

contempt of court
A disregard of the authority of the court. This is punishable by the immediate imprisonment of the offender.

QUOTATION

'The courts of Equity in England are, and always have been, courts of conscience, operating *in personam* and not *in rem*; and in the exercise of this personal jurisdiction they have always been accustomed to compel the performance of contracts and trusts as to subjects which were not ... within the jurisdiction.'

Lord Selborne

1.1.4 The trust – a product of equity

One of the most important contributions of equity was in the field of the 'use' (the predecessor to the 'trust'). The 'use' was a mode of transferring property to another (e.g. B) to hold to the 'use' or for the benefit of another or others (e.g. C or D and E).

The 'use' (forerunner to the trust) was created in the thirteenth and fourteenth centuries, for a variety of reasons:

1. Crusades – a landowner (X) who went on the crusades and, fearing for his life and the consequences of a succession of his wealth, might adopt the strategy of conveying land to his friend (B) to hold for the use of a nominated person or group of persons (X's wife and children) whilst he was away. B was referred to as a **feoffee to use** (today, a trustee) and X's wife and children were originally referred to as the *cestuis que use* or *trust* or, in modern parlance, 'beneficiaries'. In this example, B acquired the legal title to land on the understanding that he controlled and used it for the benefit of the stated purpose. The common law recognised and gave effect only to the legal title acquired by B and did not recognise the promise made by him. Accordingly, the common law treated B as the absolute owner of the property, unrestricted by the assurance that B gave to X. If B defaulted on the promise and claimed the property as his own, equity intervened in order to uphold the promise. Before the Wills Act 1540, wills were not recognised at common law.

2. Ownership by Franciscan monks – as a result of their vow of poverty, a community of Franciscan monks might transfer the legal title to land to C and D to the use or benefit of the monks at a stated monastery. The effect was that the monks were able to enjoy the benefit of land ownership and at the same time maintain their vows. Equity recognised the interests of the monks.

3. By far the most important reason for the creation of a use was to avoid the **feudal incidents** inherent in land ownership, such as wardship and escheat (no heir). Feudal incidents were a form of taxes levied by a landlord on his tenant. Wardship involved a fine payable to the landlord on the occasion of a tenant dying leaving a male, infant heir. Escheat occurred when a tenant died without leaving an heir. The tenant's estate in these circumstances reverted back to the landlord by way of escheat. These burdens were avoided if the land was vested in a number of feoffees to use (or trustees). The feoffees were unlikely to die together or without heir. Those who died could be replaced. The feoffees to use were required to hold the land for the benefit of the *cestui que trust* (or beneficiary) and the court of equity recognised and gave effect to the interest of the *cestui que trust*.

Thus, a tenant, A, might transfer his land by the appropriate common law conveyance to B, who undertook to hold it for the benefit of (or to the 'use' of) A and his heirs. The common law courts did not recognise A's intended beneficial interest (nor his heirs). The legal ownership vested in the feoffee, B, was everything. He had control of the property and an interest that was recognised by the common law courts. If B refused to account to his *cestuis que use*, A and his heirs, for the profits, or wrongfully conveyed the estate

---

HISTORICAL OUTLINES OF EQUITY

feoffee

An expression that was used originally to describe the trustee. The full title was 'feoffee to use'.

feudal incidents

Penalties or taxes that were payable in respect of the transfer of land.

cestui(s) que trust

An expression used originally to describe the beneficiary(ies) under a trust.

to another, this was treated merely as an immoral breach of confidence on the part of B. The common law did not provide any redress, nor did the law acknowledge any right in A and his heirs to the enjoyment of the land.

1.1.5 The Chancellor's intervention

The non-recognition of the right of enjoyment of the land on the part of A and his heirs had the potential for stultifying the practice of putting lands in use, had there been no alternative means of protecting the *cestui que use*. From about 1400 the Lord Chancellor stepped in and interceded on behalf of the *cestui que use*. He did not interfere with the jurisdiction of the common law courts because the legal title was vested in the feoffees, and this title was recognised and given effect by the common law courts. The Chancellor regarded his role as that of ensuring that the feoffee acted honestly and with morality. In accordance with the principle that equity acts *in personam* (against the wrongdoer personally), the Chancellor proceeded against feoffees who disregarded the moral rights of the *cestui que use*. The ultimate sanction for disobedience of the Chancellor's order was imprisonment or sequestration of the defendant's property until the order was complied with. In other words, the wrong that a rogue feoffee committed was a breach of contract or understanding, but it was a breach for which, at that time, no remedy existed in the common law courts. The enforceability of contracts was still undeveloped and, in any event, the rules of privity of contract would have precluded a remedy to the *cestui que use*.

1.1.6 Duality of ownership

The Chancellor's intervention in the context of the 'use' of land (a concept which initiated with respect to money) created the notion of duality of land ownership, which in turn led to duality of ownership of other types of property. The method of intervention adopted by the Chancellor was to recognise that the feoffee had acquired the legal and inviolable title to the land or other property, but insisted that the feoffee carry out the terms of the understanding or purpose of the transfer as stipulated by the transferor. This required the feoffee to hold the property exclusively for the specified *cestui(s) que trust* (or beneficiary) rather than for his benefit. Thus, equity insisted that the feoffee scrupulously observed the directions imposed upon him. In other words, the Chancellor, like the common law judges, acknowledged that the feoffee was the owner of the property but the *cestui que use* was regarded as the true owner in equity. The former had the legal title but the latter acquired the equitable ownership in the same property.

Position of the feoffee

At law, the feoffee was regarded as the absolute owner of the property and liable to the incidents of tenure. 'Tenure' was an aspect of the feudal system of land ownership whereby the king was the owner of all land and his subjects held estates by some tenure. Tenures were classified in accordance with the nature of the 'incidents' or services which the tenant was required to render for his holding. In return the lord was required to protect those who acquired estates from him. For example, the tenant might be required to provide a fraction of the lord's military force, known as 'knight service', or to say masses for the soul of the grantor, known as 'frankalmoign'. The common law courts recognised only the legal title to property.

If the feoffee was required to hold the land for the benefit of the *cestui que trust* and the common law courts failed to acknowledge the possibility that the *cestui que trust* may be entitled to enjoy the property, the feoffee might be entitled to commit a fraud on the

tutor tip

'The historical foundation of equity has a significant impact in understanding the modern law of trusts.'

cestui que trust by simply ignoring his interest. But in Chancery the feoffee was compelled to carry out the obligations created by the use, i.e. to recognise the interest of the *cestui que trust* and act for his benefit. Moreover, the Chancery developed the rule that any third parties who took the land from the feoffee with knowledge of the existence of the use was bound by the use. Hence the rule which subsists today that the use (or trust) is valid against the world, except a *bona fide* transferee of the legal estate for value without notice.

Position of the cestui que use

This individual's interest was not recognised at law but was granted recognition in equity and thus acquired an equitable interest. He was entitled to petition the Court of Chancery to have his interest and rights protected against the feoffee and the world, except the *bona fide* transferee of the legal estate for value without notice.

1.1.7 Statute of Uses 1535

The principal objection to the use was the loss to the king of revenue that arose from the incidents of tenure. The king needed all the revenue he could muster during the sixteenth century and the growth of the use hindered this process. Ultimately, the Statute of Uses 1535 was passed to reduce the scope of the use.

The statute provided that:

SECTION

hereditaments

Refers to the two types of real properties that exist, namely corporeal and incorporeal. Corporeal hereditaments are visible and tangible objects such as houses and land, whereas incorporeal hereditaments refer to intangible objects attached to the land, such as easements and restrictive covenants.

'Where any person(s) shall be seised of any lands or other **hereditaments** to the use, confidence or trust of any person(s), in every such case such person(s) that shall have any such use, confidence or trust in fee simple, fee tail, term of life or for years or otherwise shall stand and be seised, deemed and adjudged in lawful seisin, estate and possession of and in the same lands in such like estates as they had or shall have in the use.'

The statute did not suppress all uses. It only applied where the feoffee was seised to the use of another. If the feoffee held only for a term of years (i.e. a leasehold estate), he would not be seised and the statute would not apply. In addition, where the feoffee had active duties to perform, the statute did not apply because the *cestui que use* acquired property only after the feoffee had collected the rents and profits or performed his duties. In any event the statute did not execute uses in respect of personal property.

1.1.8 Use upon a use

per se

By itself or on its own.

The effect of the Statute of Uses was not to abolish uses **per se**, but to execute the use, whereby the *cestui que use* became the legal owner, and the feudal dues were collected from him. Where, for example, A (feoffee) held land to the use of B (*cestui que use*), B became the legal (and beneficial) owner under the 1535 statute.

A technique was adopted in order to create 'a use upon a use', in the hope that the first use would be executed and the second use rendered effective, i.e. 'to A to the use of B to the use of C'. The first use in favour of A was executed by the statute with the effect that B held the property to the use of C.

This device did not find favour with the courts at law. The method adopted for defeating this avoidance practice was to treat the second use as repugnant to the first use, and thus void.

CASE EXAMPLE

Jane Tyrrel's Case [1557] Dyer 155

Jane Tyrrel settled land upon herself for life, remainder to her son with a gift over ('to the use of Jane Tyrrel for life remainder to her son with a gift over to the heirs of Jane Tyrrel'). The court held that the second use was repugnant and void and the son took absolutely.

The Court of Chancery at first did not disagree with this result, even though B was never intended to be the beneficial owner. By the seventeenth century the decline in the value of money had diminished the significance of feudal dues. This motivated the Chancellor to give effect to the intention of the creator of the use (settlor). All that was necessary was to leave out A altogether and transfer the property to B upon trust for C, such as 'to the use of B in trust for C'. B acquired a legal estate and a right *in rem* and was called a trustee and C acquired an equitable interest in the property *in personam*.

1.1.9 Struggle over injunctions

The Court of Chancery had adopted the strategy of issuing a 'common injunction' against the litigant who had obtained a common law remedy unjustly or indeed to prevent him resorting to the common law to obtain a remedy. The use of the common injunction had the effect of sterilising the common law order and was viewed with great dissatisfaction by common law judges.

CASE EXAMPLE

Earl of Oxford's Case [1615] 1 Rep Ch 1

An action was brought in respect of a lease. Judgment in default was entered in favour of the original plaintiff at common law. The defendant (petitioner) instituted a suit in the Chancery Court which issued a common injunction against the original plaintiff, who was served with a subpoena to appear in the Chancery Court.

The Court of Chancery held that the defendant was entitled to relief.

JUDGMENT

'The office of the Chancellor is to correct man's consciences for frauds, breach of trusts, wrongs and oppressions of whatsoever nature and to soften and mollify the extremity of the law ... When judgment is obtained by oppression, wrong and a hard conscience, the Chancellor will frustrate and set it aside, not for any error or defect in the judgment but for the hard conscience of the party.'

Lord Ellesmere LC

The controversy was eventually resolved by James I in the seventeenth century. He referred the matter to Bacon, the Attorney General and others learned in the law. They decided in favour of the Court of Chancery. Thereafter, by and large the principles of common law and equity were treated as parts of a complete body of law. This prompted Maitland to write: 'Equity came not to destroy the law but to fulfil it.'

1.2 Contributions of equity

The contributions of equity in the development of the law may be classified into three categories:

Exclusive jurisdiction (new rights). This category refers to the rights which the Court of Chancery had created and which the common law courts failed to enforce, for example trusts, mortgages, partnerships, administration of estates, bankruptcy, company law etc.

Concurrent jurisdiction (new remedies). Equity developed a wide range of remedies for the enforcement of rights, that were recognised both at law and in equity. At common law the characteristic remedy was, and still is, damages – a monetary award for the loss suffered which is claimable as of right. However, equitable remedies were more varied and imaginative but were, and still are, discretionary. Accordingly, the court of equity will not grant an equitable remedy if a legal remedy would be adequate.

Examples of equitable remedies are:
- *specific performance* – an order to force the defendant to fulfil his bargain;
- *injunctions* – an order to restrain a party from committing a wrong;
- *rectification* – an order of the court requiring the defendant to modify a document to reflect the agreement made with the plaintiff;
- *account* – an order requiring a party who has control of money belonging to the plaintiff to report on the way in which the funds have been spent.

Auxiliary jurisdiction (new procedures). Procedural rules created by the Court of Chancery are discovery of documents, testimony on oath, subpoena of witnesses and interrogatories.

1.2.1 Court of Appeal in Chancery

The eighteenth and nineteenth centuries witnessed great advances in the development of equity. Examples included a reform of the law relating to easements and mortgages, the development of the law of trusts, charities, partnerships, succession, bankruptcy and companies to mention a few. However, the personnel in the Court of Chancery proved to be corrupt: frequently such personnel were bribed in order to issue common injunctions. In addition, the Court became overloaded with petitions which resulted in delays. Until 1813 there were only two judges in the Court of Chancery: the Lord Chancellor and the Master of the Rolls. They were unhurried in arriving at their decisions.

In 1813 a Vice-Chancellor was appointed. In 1841 two more Vice-Chancellors were appointed. In 1851 two Lords Justices of Appeal in Chancery were appointed. By the early nineteenth century the Lord Chancellor had ceased to hear petitions at first instance. In 1851 the Court of Appeal in Chancery was created to hear appeals from decisions of Vice-Chancellors and the Master of the Rolls. This court consisted of the Lord Chancellor and two Lords Justices of Appeal. There was a further appeal to the House of Lords.

1.3 Nineteenth-century reforms

Before Parliament intervened, the Court of Chancery was capable of granting only equitable remedies. Likewise, common law courts could grant only the legal remedy of damages. This inconvenience was overcome by two statutory provisions:

- the Common Law Procedure Act 1854 – this Act permitted the common law courts to grant equitable remedies;
- the Chancery Amendment Act 1858 (Lord Cairns' Act) – this Act gave the Court of Chancery power to award damages in addition to, or in substitution for, an injunction or specific performance.

However, what was needed was a more radical change which would fuse the administration of law and equity. It was an unnecessary waste of time and resources to require claimants entitled to common law and equitable rights or remedies to go to the respective court to redress their wrongs.

This change was effected by the Judicature Acts of 1873 and 1875, which adopted the following policies:

- The abolition of the separate Courts of Queen's Bench, Exchequer, Common Pleas, Chancery, Probate, the Divorce Court and the Court of Admiralty. In their place, the Supreme Court of Judicature was created. The High Court was divided into Divisions, known as the Queen's Bench, Chancery and Probate, Divorce and Admiralty. (The latter was renamed the Family Division, the Admiralty jurisdiction was transferred to the Queen's Bench Division and the Probate business was transferred to the Chancery Division under the Administration of Justice Act 1970.)
- Each Division of the High Court exercises both legal and equitable jurisdiction. Thus, any point of law or equity may be raised and determined by any Division.
- It was foreseen that a court which applied rules of common law and equity would face a conflict where the common law rules produce one result and equity rules another. For example, s 4 of the Statute of Frauds 1677 (now repealed) enacted that contracts for the sale or other disposition of land must be evidenced in writing. The strict common law rule was rigidly adhered to, whether this produced unjust results or not. Equity adopted a notion of part performance which entitled the court to intervene in order to prevent fraud even though all the terms of the contract were not in writing.

Section 25(11) of the Judicature Act 1873 (now s 49 of the Senior Courts Act 1981) provides:

SECTION

'25(11) Generally, in all matters not hereinbefore mentioned in which there is any conflict or variance between the rules of equity and the rules of common law with reference to the same matter, the rules of equity shall prevail.'

A classic illustration of the statutory resolution of the conflict of the two systems of legal rules is *Walsh v Lonsdale* [1882] 21 Ch D 9. The principle affirmed by the court was that where a contract to enter into a lease was specifically enforceable in equity but not at law, because the formal requirement of a deed had not been executed, the contract will nonetheless be recognised and enforced in equity, for 'equity regards as done that which ought to be done'. The parties will be treated as having created a lease from the date of the contract.

CASE EXAMPLE

Walsh v Lonsdale [1882] 21 Ch D 9

W entered into possession of a cotton mill under a written agreement with L for seven years. One of the terms of the agreement was that a deed would be executed containing a term that rent would be payable one year in advance upon L's demand. No deed was executed. W paid rent, quarterly, in arrears for a period of one-and-a-half years. L demanded a year's rent in advance. W refused to pay and L distrained for the amount. W sued for damages for illegal distress and specific performance of the contract for the lease. W alleged that he was in possession as a tenant from year to year and such a tenancy was determinable by six months' notice. He argued that L's demand for rent a year in advance was inconsistent with a tenancy from year to year. The court held that L was entitled in law and in equity to claim one year's rent in advance. The grounds were that since W entered into possession of the premises under a specifically enforceable contract for a lease, the contract would be treated as equivalent to the execution of a formal lease under deed. The maxim that was applicable was 'equity looks on that as done that which ought to be done'. Section 25(11) of the 1873 Act resolved the conflict in favour of the equitable principle.

JUDGMENT

'There is an agreement for a lease under which possession has been given. Now since the Judicature Act the possession is held under the agreement. There are not two estates as there was formerly – one estate at common law by reason of the payment of the rent from year to year, and an estate in equity under the agreement. There is only one court, and the equity rules prevail in it. The tenant holds under an agreement for a lease. He holds, therefore, under the same terms in equity as if a lease had been granted, it being a case in which both parties admit that relief is capable of being given by specific performance. That being so, he cannot complain of the exercise by the landlord of the same rights as the landlord would have had if a lease had been granted.'

Jessel MR

Thus, rules of equity are treated as paramount in the event of a conflict of rules of law and equity.

Practitioners, academics and judges subscribe to diverse views regarding the effect of fusion by the Judicature Acts 1873/75. The predominant or orthodox view is that the 1873 Act achieved procedural fusion. This view is that the Judicature Acts only fused the administration of law and equity by extending the jurisdiction of the courts to recognise and apply legal and equitable rights and remedies. Thus, there was no longer a need for litigants to go to common law courts to enforce legal rights and courts of equity to secure equitable rights or remedies and no new causes of action or remedies may be created. This prompted Lord Selborne LC when introducing the legislation to state as follows:

QUOTATION

'It may be asked why not abolish at once all distinction between law and equity? I can best answer that by asking another question … Do you wish to abolish trusts? If trusts are to continue, there must be a distinction between what we call a legal and an equitable estate … The distinction, within certain limits, between law and equity, is real and natural, and it would be a mistake to suppose that what is real and natural ought to be disregarded.'

In commenting on the effect of s 25(11) of the 1873 Act in *Salt v Cooper* [1880] 16 Ch D 544, Jessel MR said:

JUDGMENT

'It is stated very plainly that the main object of the Judicature Act was to assimilate the transaction of Equity business and Common Law business by different Courts of Judicature. It has been sometimes inaccurately called the fusion of Law and Equity: but it was not any fusion, or anything of the kind; it was the vesting in one tribunal the administration of Law and Equity in every cause, action or dispute which should come before that tribunal. That was the meaning of the Act. Then, as to that very small number of cases in which there is an actual conflict, it was decided that in all cases where the rules of Equity and Law were in conflict the rules of Equity should prevail.'

Jessel MR

The principle may be illustrated by reference to a claim in the tort action of conversion. In *MCC Proceeds v Lehman Brothers International* [1998] 4 All ER 675, the court decided that a beneficiary under a bare trust could not rely on its equitable title in order to ground a claim in conversion against third parties. In breach of trust shares held on behalf of the claimant beneficiary were sold to a third party. The claim in conversion failed.

JUDGMENT

'The short answer to MCC Proceeds' claim is to be found rooted deep in English legal history; conversion is a common law action and the common law did not recognise the equitable title of the beneficiary under a trust.'

Mummery LJ

The second interpretation of the effect of the Judicature Act 1873 is referred to as a 'fusion fallacy' or substantive fusion. The notion here is that the rules of common law and equity have been amalgamated since 1873 into one coherent set of principles. The argument is that decisions may only be explained on the basis that the Act had changed substantive principles. Lord Diplock has been credited as the chief exponent of this approach. In *United Scientific Holdings Ltd v Burnley Borough Council* [1978] AC 904, he expressed his opinion thus:

JUDGMENT

'My Lords, if by rules of equity is meant that body of substantive and adjectival law that, prior to 1875, was administered by the Court of Chancery but not by the courts of common law, to speak of rules of equity as being part of the law of England in 1977 is about as meaningful as to speak similarly of the Statutes of Uses or of Quia Emptores ... to perpetuate a dichotomy between rules of equity and rules of common law which it was a major purpose of the Supreme Court of the Judicature 1873 to do away with is, in my view, conducive to erroneous conclusions as to the ways in which the law of England has developed in the last hundred years.'

Lord Diplock

In similar vein Lord Denning MR in *Federal Commerce and Navigation Ltd v Molena Alpha Inc* [1978] QB 927, echoed Lord Diplock's view, and decided that the approach of the courts today is to make a ruling in the case in the interests of fairness to the parties, unhindered by the constraints of law or equity.

JUDGMENT

'Over 100 years have passed since the Supreme Court of Judicature 1873. During that time the streams of law and equity have flown together and combined so as to be indistinguishable the one from the other. We no longer have to ask ourselves: what would the courts of common law or the courts of equity have done before the Supreme Court of Judicature Act 1873? We have to ask ourselves: what should we do now so as to ensure fair dealing between the parties? This question must be asked in each case as it arises for decision; and then, from case to case, we shall build up a series of precedents to guide those who come after us.'

Lord Denning MR

A third approach to the 1873 Act is that the rules of law and equity are capable of separate development into a harmonised and coherent set of rules that may be traced back to its historical origin in law or equity. *Tinsley v Milligan* [1994] 1 AC 340, illustrates this approach. The issue was whether an equitable co-owner of property was entitled to assert her interest despite her involvement in a related illegal activity. The court decided that she was entitled to rely on the presumption of resulting trust in successfully asserting her claim to an interest in the property. In doing so she did not have to rely on the unlawful transaction.

JUDGMENT

'More than 100 years has elapsed since the fusion of the administration of law and equity. The reality of the matter is that, in 1993, English law has one single law of property made up of legal and equitable interests. Although for historical reasons legal estates and equitable estates have different incidents, the person owning either type of estate has a right of property, a right *in rem* not merely a right *in personam*. If the law is that a party is entitled to a property right acquired under an illegal transaction, in my judgment the same rule ought to apply to any property right so acquired, whether such right is legal or equitable.'

Lord Browne-Wilkinson

1.4 Adaptability of equity today

It has been suggested that it might be extremely doubtful whether new rights in equity are capable of being created in modern society, except within the framework of established principles. The philosophical notions of justice may have become suppressed in terms of formal justice based on precedents.

In *Re Diplock* [1948] Ch 465, Lord Greene MR said:

JUDGMENT

'[A claim in equity] must be shown to have an ancestry founded in history and in the practice and precedents of the courts administering equity jurisdiction. It is not sufficient that because we think that the justice of the present case requires it, we should invent such a jurisdiction for the first time.'

Lord Greene MR

Of course, the limited use of some of the older precedents may justify the modern court in adapting or moulding the principles that have been laid down in ancient times. In *Re Hallett* [1880] 13 Ch D 696, Jessel MR was prompted to say:

JUDGMENT

'It must not be forgotten that the rules of Courts of Equity are not, like the rules of the Common Law, supposed to have been established from time immemorial. It is perfectly well known that they have been established from time to time. ... The older precedents in Equity are of very little value. The doctrines are progressive, refined and improved: and if we want to know what the rules of Equity are, we must look, of course, rather to the more modern than the more ancient cases.'

Jessel MR

Many commentators and judges have acceded to the view that the rules of equity are as fixed and immutable as the common law. Judicial law making may thus be treated as severely limited, if not ended, by the Judicature Acts. In *Western Fish Products v Penwith*

BC [1981] 2 All ER 204, Megarry J said, 'The creation of new rights and remedies is a matter for Parliament, not the judges.'

In *Cowcher v Cowcher* [1972] 1 WLR 425, Bagnall J issued a caution about the unrestrained extension of equitable principles in the family law context, thus:

JUDGMENT

'In any individual cases the application of these propositions may produce a result which appears unfair. So be it; in my view that is not an injustice. I am convinced that in determining rights, particularly property rights, the only justice that can be obtained by mortals, who are fallible and are not omniscient, is justice according to law; the justice which flows from the application of sure and settled principles to proved or admitted facts. So in the field of equity, the length of the Chancellor's foot has been measured or is capable of measurement. This does not mean that equity is past childbearing; simply that its progeny must be legitimate – by precedent out of principle. It is well that this should be so; otherwise no lawyer could safely advise on his client's title and every quarrel would lead to a law suit.'

Bagnall J

An alternative view concerned the extension or enlargement of the jurisdiction of equity to promote fairness in cases concerning the family home. This view may be illustrated by Lord Denning's statement in *Eves v Eves* [1975] 1 WLR 1338:

JUDGMENT

'Equity is not past the age of childbearing. One of her latest progeny is a constructive trust of a new model. Lord Diplock [in *Gissing v Gissing* [1971] AC 886] brought it into the world and we have nourished it.'

Lord Denning MR

This liberal view of the 'new model' constructive trust attracted a great deal of criticism and was eventually overruled by the courts.

Despite the restrictive view as to the development of equitable principles, the law regarding 'freezing' (*Mareva*) and 'search' (*Anton Piller*) orders have been developed by the courts within the confines of the law relating to interim injunctions. A 'freezing' order is designed to prevent a defendant from removing assets from the jurisdiction of the British courts (or dissipating assets within the jurisdiction) which, if not prohibited, would defeat the whole purpose of the litigation. 'Search' orders authorise claimants to enter the defendant's premises and view and make copies of documents that are relevant to the claimant's case because the latter can establish a *prima facie* case of fear that the defendant is likely to destroy the documents.

The contribution of equity to the development or enrichment of the law as a whole was summed up by Lord Browne-Wilkinson in *Tinsley v Milligan* [1994] 1 AC 340, in the following sentence:

JUDGMENT

'More than 100 years has elapsed since the fusion of the administration of law and equity. The reality of the matter is that, in 1993, English law has one single law of property made up of legal estates and equitable interests.'

Lord Browne-Wilkinson

┌───┐

EQUITY

SOURCES

• originally created by the Lord Chancellor and later developed by the Court of Chancery independently from the common law until the Judicature Acts 1873/75

CONTRIBUTION TO ENGLISH LAW

• exclusive jurisdiction, e.g. the trust, succession law, bankruptcy law
• concurrent jurisdiction, e.g. equitable remedies such as specific performance, injunctions etc.
• auxiliary jurisdiction such as new procedures, witness summonses, interrogatories

Figure 1.1 The origin of equity

1.5 Maxims of equity

The intervention of the court of equity over the centuries may be reduced into the following maxims. The importance of the maxims ought not to be overstated: they are far from being rigid principles, but exist as terse sentences which illustrate the policy underlying specific principles.

Equity will not suffer a wrong to be without a remedy

This maxim illustrates the intervention of the Court of Chancery to provide a remedy if none was obtainable at common law. At the same time it must not be supposed that every infringement of a right was capable of being remedied. The 'wrongs' which equity was prepared to invent new remedies to redress were those subject to judicial enforcement in the first place.

Equity follows the law

The view originally taken by the Court of Equity was that deliberate and carefully considered rules of common law would be followed. Equity only intervened when some important factor became ignored by the law. Thus, in the early stages of the development of the law of trusts, the Lord Chancellor and, subsequently, the Court of Chancery acknowledged the valid existence of the legal title to property in the hands of the feoffee (or trustee). The acquisition of this title by the feoffee was dependent on compliance with the appropriate legal requirements for the transfer of the property.

Where there is equal equity, the law prevails

Equity did not intervene when, according to equitable principles, no injustice resulted in adopting the solution imposed by law. Thus, the *bona fide* purchaser of the legal estate for value without notice is capable of acquiring an equitable interest both at law and in equity.

Where equities are equal, the law prevails

Where two persons have conflicting interests in the same property, the rule is that the first in time has priority at law and in equity: *qui prior est tempore potior est jure*.

He who seeks equity must do equity

A party claiming equitable relief is required to act fairly towards his opponent. For example, a tracing order would not be obtained in equity if the effect would be to promote injustice.

He who comes to equity must come with clean hands

The assumption here is that the party claiming an equitable relief must demonstrate that he has not acted with impropriety in respect of the claim.

Delay defeats equity (equity aids the vigilant and not the indolent)

Where a party has slept on his rights and has given the defendant the impression that he has waived his rights, the court of equity may refuse its assistance to the claimant. This is known as the doctrine of laches.

Equality is equity

Where two or more parties have an interest in the same property but their respective interests have not been quantified, equity as a last resort may divide the interest equally.

Equity looks at the intent rather than the form

The court looks at the substance of an arrangement rather than its appearance in order to ascertain the intention of the parties. For example, a deed is not treated in equity as a substitute for consideration.

Equity imputes an intention to fulfil an obligation

The principle here is based on the premise that if a party is under an obligation to perform an act and he performs an alternative but similar act, equity assumes that the second act was done with the intention of fulfilling the obligation.

Equity regards as done that which ought to be done

If a person is under an obligation to perform an act which is specifically enforceable, the parties acquire the same rights and liabilities in equity as though the act had been performed.

Equity acts in personam

Originally, equitable orders were enforced against the person of the defendant, with the ultimate sanction of imprisonment. A later equitable invention permitted an order to be attached to the defendant's property, i.e. *in rem*. Today this maxim has lost much of its importance.

Equity will not assist a volunteer

This maxim is still applicable today and reflects the principle that a party seeking equitable assistance, such as an equitable remedy, is required to demonstrate that he has provided valuable consideration. Thus, in order to enforce a contract by way of specific performance the claimant is required to be a non-volunteer.

Equity will not allow a statute to be used as an engine of fraud

This maxim refers to the inherent jurisdiction of the court to achieve justice and may suspend the operation of a statute that imposes formal requirements if strict compliance will promote a fraud on one or more litigants. Thus, if a defendant alleges that no express trust of land exists owing to the non-compliance with the formalities laid down in the Law of Property Act 1925, but the claimant establishes that strict compliance with the statute has the effect of promoting a fraud on him, the court may suspend the operation of the provision.

KEY FACTS

Development of equity
Defects in the common law writ system and inadequate remedies
Petitioning of the king for a fair solution as the 'fountain of justice'
Delegation of the task to the Lord Chancellor
Creation of a separate Court of Chancery – staffed by clerics
Solutions based on the discretion of court
Conflict in *Earl of Oxford's Case* (1615) – in the case of conflict, equity prevails
Merger of administration with the common law in Judicature Acts 1873 and 1875
New equitable remedies which addressed the claims of the parties
Injunctions – to prevent occurrences such as a breach of trust
Specific performance – to ensure a contract is carried out
Rectification – to change a document to reflect an actual agreement
Account – report on ways in which funds have been used

Equitable maxims
Equity will not suffer a wrong to be without a remedy
Equity follows the law
Where equities are equal, the law prevails
Where the equities are equal, the first in time prevails
He who seeks equity must do equity
He who comes to equity must come with clean hands
Delay defeats equity
Equity looks to intention not the form
Equity imputes an intention to fulfil an obligation
Equity regards that which should be done as being done
Equity acts *in personam*
Equity will not assist a volunteer
Equity will not allow a statute to be used as an engine for fraud

ACTIVITY

Self-test questions

1. To what extent was equity regarded as an independent system of rules?
2. What is the significance of the equitable maxims today?
3. What is the importance of the Judicature Acts 1873 and 1875?
4. How far may modern equity be regarded as innovative?

SUMMARY

The expression 'equity' was originally synonymous with justice or fairness. This was the aim of the Lord Chancellor in dealing with petitions from aggrieved parties. This role was acquired by the Court of Chancery until the Judicature Acts 1873/75. But over the centuries a wealth of precedents had been built up and the rules of equity became as settled as the common law. Today, equity may be described as a system of doctrines, remedies and procedures which, prior to the Judicature Acts 1873/75, developed side by side with the common law.

Originally the rigidity of the common law was the main contributing factor to the creation of equitable rules. Contributions of equity may be summarised as:

- the exclusive jurisdiction – new institutions created, such as the trust;
- the concurrent jurisdiction – new remedies created, such as specific performance, injunctions;
- the auxiliary jurisdiction – new procedures created such as affidavit evidence, witness summonses (subpoenas).

The nineteenth-century reforms consolidated in the Judicature Acts 1873/75:

- transferred the jurisdiction of the old Court of Chancery to the Supreme Court of the Judicature (creating three divisions of the High Court);
- all three divisions of the High Court were empowered to exercise the jurisdiction of the old Court of Chancery: to recognise and give effect to equitable rules;
- s 25(11) of the Judicature Act 1873 lays down the rule that where there is a conflict between law and equity, 'the rules of equity shall prevail'.

The maxims of equity simplify the contributions made by equity to the development of English law.

SAMPLE ESSAY QUESTION

Consider the following essay question:

Outline the historical factors that led to the creation and development of the trust.

Answer plan

- Identify some of the problems faced by litigants owing to the rigidity of the common law, e.g.:
  - Only the legal title to property was recognised by the courts of law.
  - The only remedy available at common law was damages.
  - The 'forms of action' were inflexible and limited and were the only means of commencing an action at common law.
  - The common law system of pleadings was complex.
  - Bribery and corruption were commonplace in the common law system.
  - The 'use' (precursor to the trust) was not recognised by the common law courts.

- Consider the process adopted by litigants aggrieved by limited common law solutions:
  - Aggrieved parties petitioned the king who passed these on to the Lord Chancellor.
  - Subsequently the Court of Chancery was created.

- State the response by Parliament:
  - The Statute of Uses 1535 was passed with the aim of limiting the use by executing it in favour of the *cestui que trust*.

- Consider the technique adopted to avoid the Statute of Uses 1535, e.g.:
  - By a drafting device a second use was created. This was known as a 'use upon a use' and this use later became a trust.

- Consider the nineteenth-century reforms:
  - The Judicature Acts 1873/75 fused the administration of law and equity.
  - Thus it is arguable that the creative nature of equity disappeared with the introduction of the Judicature Acts.
  - The position where rules of law and equity conflict.

CONCLUSION

Further reading

Mason, A, 'The place of equity and equitable remedies in contemporary society' (1994) 110 LQR 238.

Winder, W, 'Precedent in equity' (1941) 57 LQR 245.

2

Introduction to trusts

AIMS AND OBJECTIVES

By the end of this chapter you should be able to:

- appreciate the main legal definitions of trusts
- identify the essential characteristics of trusts
- grasp the various types of trusts that exist
- comprehend some of the more popular reasons for the creation of express trusts

2.1 Introduction

Constructing a comprehensive definition of a trust is extremely difficult, for a variety of trusts exist, and some of these do not fit into any of the traditional definitions. It is much simpler to describe a trust and identify its essential characteristics. In essence, the mechanism of the trust is an equitable device by which property is acquired and controlled by trustees for the benefit of others, called beneficiaries. These beneficiaries, subject to a few exceptions, are entitled to enforce the trust. For a variety of reasons, it may be prudent to prevent the entire ownership of property (legal and equitable) being vested and enjoyed by one person because such person would be in a position to dispose of the entire interest, perhaps for an inappropriate purpose such as gambling away the entire fund. A trust may be set up in order to advance this objective.

2.2 Trust concept

By origin, the trust was the exclusive product of the now defunct Court of Chancery, but since the Judicature Acts 1873 and 1875, trusts may be enforced in any court of law.

2.2.1 Definitions of trusts

The trust has been defined, or described, by many academics and, recently, by statute. The classic definition of a trust was stated by Underhill as follows:

QUOTATION

'A trust is an equitable obligation, binding a person (called a trustee) to deal with property over which he has control (which is called the trust property) for the benefit of persons (who are called the beneficiaries or *cestuis que trust*) of whom he may himself be one, and any one of whom may enforce the obligation.'

A Underhill and D Hayton, *Law of Trusts and Trustees* (16th edn, Butterworths, 2002), p. 1

This definition does not include charitable and private purpose trusts, but Underhill was merely defining traditional private trusts. A private purpose trust is intended to benefit objects which do not have the capacity to enforce the trust (such as maintaining a grave in a cemetery), as distinct from benefiting society as a whole or the public at large. Charitable trusts are distinct from private trusts in many ways (see Chapter 12), and the Attorney General, as a representative of the Crown, is empowered to enforce such trusts on behalf of the public. Private purpose trusts (or trusts for imperfect obligations) in any event are considered anomalous and are exceptionally treated as valid. Underhill's definition of a trust refers to an 'equitable obligation' in that originally the Lord Chancellor and later the Court of Chancery enforced moral obligations undertaken by trustees (feoffees) in the interests of natural justice and conscience. The definition refers to property under the 'control' of trustees. It is evident that the trustees have the legal title to property but the essence of a trust is that they are required to hold the property for the benefit of the beneficiaries. It is because of the **fiduciary** position of the trustees and the temptation to abuse their position that a number of duties are imposed on the trustees. Finally, the beneficiaries, by definition, are the persons who are entitled to enjoy the benefit of the trust property and who are given a *locus standi* to enforce the trust and to ensure that the trust property is properly administered.

Maitland defined a trust thus:

fiduciary
A person whose judgment and skill is relied on by another.

QUOTATION

'When a person has rights which he is bound to exercise upon behalf of another or for the accomplishment of some particular purpose he is said to have those rights in trust for that other and for that purpose and he is called a trustee.'

F W Maitland, *Equity: A Course of Lectures* (ed. A H Chaytor and W J Whittaker, revd J Brunyate, Cambridge University Press, 2011)

It may be noted that this is a vague definition of a trust, as Maitland admitted, but, on examination, it is not a definition at all, but a description of some of the elements of a trust.

In *Lewin on Trusts* a comprehensive definition set out by an Australian judge, Mayo J, in *Re Scott* [1948] SASR 193 was referred to in the text.

QUOTATION

'The word "trust" refers to the duty or aggregate accumulation of obligations that rest upon a person described as trustee. The responsibilities are in relation to property held by him, or under his control. That property he will be compelled by a court in its equitable jurisdiction to administer in the manner lawfully prescribed by the trust instrument, or where there be no specific provision written or oral, or to the extent that such provision is invalid or lacking, in accordance with equitable principles. As a consequence the administration will be in such a manner that the consequential benefits and advantages accrue, not to the trustee, but to the persons called *cestuis que trust*, or beneficiaries, if there be any; if not, for some purpose which the law will recognise and enforce. A trustee may be a beneficiary, in which case advantages will accrue in his favour to the extent of his beneficial interest.'

Mayo J, quoted in L Tucker, N Le Poidevin, J Brightwell, Lewin on Trusts (Sweet & Maxwell, 2014)

The American Restatement of the Law of Trusts (1959) declares:

QUOTATION

'A trust ... when not qualified by the word "charitable", "resulting" or "constructive" is a fiduciary relationship with respect to the property, subjecting the person by whom the property is held to equitable duties to deal with the property for the benefit of another person, which arises as a result of a manifestation of an intention to create it.'

G Thomas and A Hudson in *The Law of Trusts* (Oxford University Press, 2004) offer a definition of a trust in this form:

QUOTATION

'The essence of a trust is the imposition of an equitable obligation on a person who is the legal owner of property (a trustee) which requires that person to act in good conscience when dealing with that property in favour of any person (the beneficiary) who has the beneficial interest recognised by equity in the property. The trustee is said to "hold the property on trust" for the beneficiary. There are four significant elements to the trust: that it is equitable, that it provides the beneficiary with rights in property, that it also imposes obligations on the trustee, and that those obligations are fiduciary in nature.'

The 'equitable obligation' that is referred to in Thomas and Hudson's definition is a reference back to the historical origin of trusts which were recognised only by equity prior to the Judicature Act 1873. The obligation to carry out the terms of the trust is attached to the trustee to control his actions as a fiduciary and to allay the fears that he may be tempted to take the property or otherwise abuse his position. The trustee acquires the legal title to the property and the beneficiary, as an equitable owner, acquires the right to enjoy the property.

2.2.2 Recognition of Trusts Act 1987

Section 1 of the Recognition of Trusts Act 1987 declares that the term 'trust' possesses the characteristics detailed in Art 2 of the Hague Convention on the Recognition of Trusts, referred to in the Schedule to the Act:

SECTION

inter vivos
During the lifetime or before death.

'Section 1
For the purposes of this Convention, the term trust refers to the legal relationship created – ***inter vivos*** or on death – by a person, the settlor, when assets have been placed under the control of a trustee for the benefit of a beneficiary or for a specified purpose.'

A trust has the following characteristics:

(a) the assets constitute a separate fund and are not a part of the trustee's own estate;

(b) title to the trust assets stands in the name of the trustee or in the name of another person on behalf of the trustee;

(c) the trustee has the power and the duty, in respect of which he is accountable, to manage, employ or dispose of the assets in accordance with the terms of the trust and the special duties imposed upon him by law.

The reservation by the settlor of certain rights and powers and the fact that the trustee may himself have rights as a beneficiary are not necessarily inconsistent with the existence of a trust.

This description of a trust has been formulated by reference to the characteristics of a trust (these are discussed below).

2.2.3 Lord Browne-Wilkinson's essential characteristics of a trust

In *Westdeutsche Landesbank Girozentrale v Islington BC* [1996] AC 669, HL (for facts, see Chapter 16), Lord Browne-Wilkinson identified four fundamental principles of trusts law the existence of which he considered uncontroversial:

JUDGMENT

'(i) Equity operates on the conscience of the owner of the legal interest. In the case of a trust, the conscience of the legal owner requires him to carry out the purposes for which the property was vested in him (express or implied trust) or which the law imposes on him by reason of his unconscionable conduct (constructive trust).

(ii) Since the equitable jurisdiction to enforce trusts depends upon the conscience of the holder of the legal interest being affected, he cannot be a trustee of the property if and so long as he is ignorant of the facts alleged to affect his conscience, i.e. until he is aware that he is intended to hold the property for the benefit of others in the case of an express or implied trust, or, in the case of a constructive trust, of the factors which are alleged to affect his conscience.

(iii) In order to establish a trust there must be identifiable trust property. The only apparent exception to this rule is a constructive trust imposed on a person who dishonestly assists in a breach of trust who may come under fiduciary duties even if he does not receive identifiable trust property.

(iv) Once a trust is established, as from the date of its establishment the beneficiary has, in equity, a proprietary interest in the trust property, which proprietary interest will be enforceable in equity against any subsequent holder of the property (whether the original property or substituted property into which it can be traced) other than a purchaser for value of the legal estate without notice.

These propositions are fundamental to the law of trusts and I would have thought uncontroversial.'

Lord Browne-Wilkinson

in rem
A right that exists against the world at large as opposed to *in personam*.

The reference to the 'conscience' of the trustee concerns the original assumption of jurisdiction by the Lord Chancellor for enforcing trusts. The trustee is treated as a fiduciary with special duties imposed on him. If they abuse their position as fiduciaries by receiving unauthorised profits they become trustees of those profits. This notion of conscience requires the trustees to be aware that they are acting with impropriety. It is evident that the trust is required to attach to identifiable property, except with regard to the liability to account as an accessory. Finally, Lord Browne-Wilkinson declares that a beneficiary under a trust acquires a proprietary interest in the trust property (i.e. a right *in rem*). The effect is that the beneficiary is entitled to recover the property in either its original or substituted form, except as against a *bona fide* transferee of the legal estate for value without notice ('equity's darling').

ACTIVITY

Compare Lord Browne-Wilkinson's essential characteristics of a trust laid down in *Westdeutsche Landesbank Girozentrale v Islington BC* (1996) with those laid down in the Recognition of Trusts Act 1987.

2.3 Characteristics of a trust

The distinctive features of a trust are outlined below. It is submitted that an understanding of these features is a more practical way of recognising and distinguishing a trust from other concepts.

2.3.1 Trust property

chose(s) in action
These are personal, intangible property(ies) such as rights to have a loan repaid, the right to dividends from shares and intellectual property.

Any existing property which is capable of being assigned may form the subject-matter of a trust. Thus, the trust property may take the form of 'personalty', such as chattels or debts enforceable at law (**choses in action**), or an interest in land called 'realty' (freehold or leasehold interest in land). Moreover, the nature of the trust property may vary throughout the trust. The property may take the form of realty which is sold and the proceeds of sale reinvested in shares.

However, only subsisting property is capable of being the subject-matter of a trust. Accordingly, an **expectancy** or future property (such as a right under a will which has not vested because the testator is still alive) cannot be the subject-matter of a trust.

expectancy
These are rights that do not currently exist but may or may not exist in the future.

2.3.2 Separation of legal and equitable interests

The legal interest in property is the title which reflects the 'indicia' of ownership. The legal owner has the right to have his title to the property and the incidents of ownership respected by the rest of society. Thus he may enforce or protect his interest in the property through litigation. The equitable interest, on the other hand, is a right or an interest in property which, before the Judicature Acts of 1873 and 1875, was recognised solely by a Court of Chancery. The Judicature Acts effected a fusion of the administration of law and equity, so that in appropriate cases equitable principles may be applied in common law courts. The equitable title is the beneficial interest in property or the right to enjoy the property.

Generally, the trustee holds the legal title to property for the benefit of the beneficiary. The beneficiary enjoys the equitable interest. The rule is that whenever the two interests (legal and equitable) are separated, a trust is in existence. For example, T (a trustee) holds the legal title to shares in X Co (trust property) on trust for B, a beneficiary, absolutely. B acquires an equitable interest in the shares.

T (trustee with the legal title) → B (beneficiary with the equitable interest)

In addition, the same interests may be enjoyed jointly by the same persons under a trust. For example, T and B may hold the legal estate on trust for T and B equally.

T & B (legal interest) → T & B (equitable interest)

If, however, the legal and equitable interests are united in the hands of the same person without a separation of interest, no trust exists. Thus, no trust exists if T holds the legal estate for himself absolutely.

2.3.3 Sub-trusts

Sometimes the trustee may hold the equitable interest on behalf of a beneficiary. This would be the case where a beneficiary, who enjoys an equitable interest under a subsisting trust, creates a trust of his interest in favour of another, i.e. a beneficiary under a trust creates a sub-trust of his entire interest in favour of a sub-beneficiary. The effect of this arrangement is that the beneficiary under the original trust assigns his interest to the new beneficiary by way of a trust. In this situation the original beneficiary adopts the role of the settlor and trustee for the benefit of another:

> T (legal owner) – B (original equitable owner) – C (sub-beneficiary or new equitable owner)

Indeed, it is possible for the original equitable owner to create a sub-trust and, at the same time, remain an equitable owner of trust property. This would be the position where the original equitable owner declares a trust of part of his equitable interest. For example, T (legal owner) holds on trust for B absolutely (equitable owner). B retains a life interest in the property and declares himself a trustee of the remainder for C absolutely.

The new arrangement may be illustrated as follows:

$$T \text{(legal title)} \frac{B \text{(life interest)} - C \text{(remainder interest)}}{\text{(equitable owners)}}$$

It should be noted that in respect of the sub-trust, B will have active duties to perform on behalf of his new beneficiary, C.

locus standi

The right to be heard in court or other proceedings.

2.3.4 Obligatory

A trust is mandatory in nature. The trustees have no choice as to whether they may fulfil the intention of the settlor. Instead, the trustees are required to fulfil the terms of the trust as stipulated in the trust instrument and implied by rules of law. The beneficiaries are given a *locus standi* to ensure that the trustees carry out their duties (but note the anomalous nature of private purpose trusts – see Chapter 11).

will

A document signed by the testator and attested by two or more witnesses which disposes of the testator's assets on his death.

2.3.5 *Inter vivos* or on death

Trusts may be created either *inter vivos* (during the lifetime of the settlor) or on death, by **will** or on an **intestacy** (under the Administration of Estates Act 1925, as amended). An *inter vivos* trust may be created by deed or in writing other than by way of a deed, orally or by conduct. Irrespective of the form which the trust takes, the trust becomes effective from the date of the execution of the document or statement. On the other hand, trusts created by wills or on intestacies take effect on the death of the testator or person dying intestate.

intestacy

A person who dies without making a valid will. His estate devolves on those specified under the intestacy rules.

2.3.6 The settlor's position

The settlor is the creator of an express trust. He decides the form that the trust property may take, the interests of the beneficiaries, the identity of the beneficiaries, the persons who will be appointed trustees and the terms of the trust. Indeed, he may appoint himself one of the trustees or the sole trustee. In short, the settlor is the author of the trust. But once the trust is created, the settlor, in his capacity as settlor, loses all control or interest in the trust property. Unless he has reserved an interest for himself, he is not entitled to derive a benefit from the trust property, nor is he allowed to control the conduct of the trustees. In other words, following the creation of a trust the settlor, in his capacity as settlor, is treated as a stranger in respect of the trust.

CASE EXAMPLE

Re Bowden [1936] Ch 71

The settlor, before becoming a nun and in order to undertake the vows of poverty, chastity and obedience, transferred property to trustees on trust for specified beneficiaries. Later, she changed her mind when she left the convent and attempted to reclaim the property for her own benefit. The court held that, since the trust was created, the claimant as settlor lost all interest in the property and therefore could not recover the property.

JUDGMENT

'the persons appointed trustees under the settlement received the settlor's interest ... and, immediately after it had been received by them, as a result of her own act and her own declaration ... it became impressed with the trusts contained in the settlement.'

Bennett J

The settlor's position vis-à-vis the trust is analogous to the position of a promoter (or shareholder) of a company and his relationship with the company. The well-known, fundamental rule in company law is that a company is an artificial legal person, distinct from its members. Thus, a company is capable of enjoying rights and is subject to duties which are generally not attributable to its members. In other words a company may own property, enter into contracts, sue and be sued and open and operate bank accounts in its own name. The rights and liabilities of the company are treated separately from the rights and duties of the members or shareholders. Accordingly, even if a company is controlled by one shareholder, the company and that shareholder are treated as distinct legal persons. This is known as the doctrine in *Salomon v Salomon & Co Ltd* [1897] AC 22. A company was formed to take over Mr Salomon's business and the House of Lords ruled that, despite Mr Salomon holding 20,001 of the 20,007 shares issued by the company, the company and Mr Salomon were distinct legal entities. Lord Macnaghten expressed the general rule thus:

JUDGMENT

'The company is at law a different person altogether from the subscribers to the memorandum; and, though it may be that after incorporation the business is precisely the same as it was before, and the same persons are managers, and the same hands receive the profits, the company is not in law the agent of the subscribers or trustee for them.'

Lord Macnaghten

The same general principle of independent legal personality of a company (or corporate veil) was affirmed by the Supreme Court in *Prest v Petrodel Resources Ltd* [2013] 2 AC 415. However, the corporate veil may be lifted in limited circumstances when the notion of separate legal personality is abused for the purpose of promoting some wrongdoing. The test was stated by Lord Sumption in *Prest v Petrodel* in the following manner:

JUDGMENT

'I conclude that there is a limited principle of English law which applies when a person is under an existing obligation or liability or subject to an existing legal restriction which he deliberately evades or whose enforcement he deliberately frustrates by interposing a company under his control. The court may then pierce the corporate veil for the purpose, and only for the purpose, of depriving the company or its controller of the advantage that they would otherwise have obtained by the company's separate legal personality. The principle is properly described as a limited one.'

Lord Sumption

2.3.7 The trustees' position

The trustees bear the responsibility of controlling and managing the trust property solely for the benefit of the beneficiaries. This responsibility is treated as giving rise to a fiduciary relationship. Its characteristics are a relationship of confidence, trustworthiness to act for the benefit of the beneficiary and a duty not to act for his (the trustee's) own advantage.

The trustees are the representatives of the trust. Owing to the opportunities to abuse their position the rules of equity were formulated to impose a collection of strict and rigorous duties on the trustees. Indeed, trustees' duties are so onerous that they are not even entitled to be paid for their services as trustees, in the absence of authority.

Trustees are liable in their personal capacity for mismanaging the trust funds and in extreme cases may be made bankrupt, should they neglect their duties.

2.3.8 The beneficiaries' position

bona fide
In good faith.

The beneficiaries (as the owners of the equitable interest) are given the power to compel the due administration of the trust. They are entitled to sue the trustees and any third party for damages (joining the trustees in the action as co-defendants) for breach of trust. In addition, the beneficiaries may trace the trust property in the hands of third parties (see Chapter 16) with the exception of *bona fide* transferees of the legal estate for value without notice. Through this process the beneficiaries may be able to recover the trust property that was wrongly transferred to another or obtain a charging order representing their interests. The beneficiaries are given an interest in the trust property and are entitled to assign the whole or part of such interest to others. The beneficiaries are entitled to terminate the trust by directing the trustees to transfer the legal title to them, provided that they have attained the age of majority, and are *compos mentis* (mentally sound) and absolutely entitled to the trust property.

CASE EXAMPLE

Saunders v Vautier [1841] Cr & Ph 240, CA

Stock was bequeathed upon trust to accumulate the dividends until Vautier (V) attained the age of 25. At this age, the trustees were required to transfer the capital and accumulated income to V. V attained the age of majority (21) and claimed the fund at this age. The question in issue was whether the trustees were required to transfer the fund to V.

Held: Since the income had vested in V, the sole beneficiary (by operation of law), subject to the enjoyment of the capital being postponed (i.e. the fund that produced the income), V acquired an indefeasible interest in the capital, subject to attaining the age of 25. As V was of full age, he was entitled to terminate the trust.

JUDGMENT

'I think that principle has been repeatedly acted upon; and where a legacy is directed to be accumulated for a certain period, or where the payment is postponed the legatee, if he has an absolute indefeasible interest in the legacy, is not bound to wait until the expiration of that period, but may require payment the moment he is competent to give a valid discharge.'

Lord Langdale MR

2.3.9 Equitable proprietary interests

The trustee's interest in the trust property is legal. His interest is described as a right *in rem*. This refers to a right that attaches to the relevant property to such an extent that it is enforceable against the world. The legal owner cannot be deprived of his rights to the property by the fraud of some third person. A beneficiary's interest in the trust property is by origin and nature equitable, which traditionally has been treated as a right *in personam*. This means that the beneficiary has the right to compel the trustee to perform his duties in accordance with the law and may pursue a claim against the trustee personally. Moreover, the equitable interest is inviolable against everyone, except the *bona fide* transferee of the legal estate for value without notice of the equitable interest.

However, despite its origin, and the justification for the Chancellor's intervention to remedy injustice, on a practical level, the equitable title may be treated as a proprietary interest. The beneficiary is entitled to protect his interest against everyone, except the *bona fide* transferee of the legal estate for value without notice. To this extent his interest is regarded as proprietary or exists *in rem*, i.e. the beneficiary's rights are attached to the trust property itself. His interest may be bought, sold or gifted away in the same way as the legal title. In *Tinsley v Milligan* [1993] 3 All ER 65, Lord Browne-Wilkinson described the nature of a beneficiary's interest under a trust as a proprietary right:

JUDGMENT

'[I]n 1993 English law has one single law of property made up of legal estates and equitable interests. Although for historical reasons legal estates have differing incidents, the person owning either type of estate has a right of property, a right in rem, not merely a right in personam.'

Lord Browne-Wilkinson

Occasions when a beneficiary has the *locus standi* to maintain a claim against third parties are for knowingly receiving trust property for his own benefit and equitable proprietary claims. In the former case the beneficiary has the capacity to bring personal claim against the third party because that third party's conscience has been affected by knowledge of the trustee's breach. In these circumstances equity imposes the duties of a trustee on the third party. The effect is that the claim by the beneficiary against the third party is put on the same footing as a claim against the trustee for an account. Likewise, the process involving equitable proprietary claims by the beneficiary to follow or trace the trust funds in the hands of third parties is based on a form of ownership. Assuming the third party is not a *bona fide* purchaser of the legal estate for value without notice the claimant beneficiary is entitled to maintain the claim by virtue of his proprietary interest. The effect is that the beneficiary is treated as having some form of proprietary interest, distinct from the trustee's legal interest *in rem*, which entitles him to institute certain proceedings against third parties.

2.3.10 *Bona fide* transferee of the legal estate for value without notice

The policy here was that in the fifteenth century, when the law of trusts was being moulded, the various Chancellors interceded only against those persons who, owing to the circumstances in which they had acquired the property, ought in conscience to be held responsible. Those persons were the heirs of the trustees, those who did not provide consideration and those who provided consideration, but bought the property in bad faith. Absent from this list was the *bona fide* transferee of the legal estate for value without notice of the equitable interest. Such a person acquired the legal title in priority over the beneficiary: see James LJ in *Pilcher v Rawlins* [1871] 7 Ch App 259:

JUDGMENT

'I propose simply to apply myself to the case of a purchaser for valuable consideration without notice, obtaining upon the occasion of his purchase, and by means of his purchase deed, some legal estate, some legal right, some legal advantage; and, according to my view of the established law of this court, such a purchaser's plea of a purchase for valuable consideration without notice is an absolute, unqualified, unanswerable defence, and an unanswerable plea to the jurisdiction of this court ... but when the purchaser has satisfied the terms of the plea ... this court has no jurisdiction whatever to do anything more than to let him depart in possession of that legal estate, that legal right, that legal advantage which he has obtained whatever it may be. In such a case the purchaser is entitled to hold that which, without breach of that duty, he has had conveyed to him.'

James LJ

Each of the elements of this principle must be satisfied. The expression '*bona fide*' is not synonymous with the absence of notice but is a distinct requirement. It involves the genuineness or *mores* of the actions of the purchaser and requires him to act in good faith. In *Midland Bank Trust Co v Green* [1981] AC 513, Lord Wilberforce said:

JUDGMENT

'The character in the law known as the *bona fide* (good faith) purchaser for value without notice was the creation of equity. In order to affect a purchaser for value of a legal estate with some equity or equitable interest, equity fastened upon his conscience and the composite expression was used to epitomise the circumstances in which equity would or rather would not do so. I think that it would generally be true to say that the words in good faith related to the existence of notice. Equity, in other words, required not only absence of notice, but genuine and honest absence of notice ... it would be a mistake to suppose that the requirement of good faith extended only to the matter of notice ... Equity still retained its interest in and power over the purchaser's conscience.'

Lord Wilberforce

The third party who acquires an interest in substitution of the beneficiary under a trust is required to purchase the trust property for valuable consideration. This involves money or money's worth or marriage consideration. It is immaterial that the consideration is not adequate and may involve all forms of non-monetary consideration. Marriage consideration is limited to ante-nuptial settlements and assumes the existence of a future marriage. A promise made in relation to a past marriage (post-nuptial agreement) is not deemed to have been supported by valuable consideration.

In order to gain the benefit of this principle the innocent third party must acquire the legal estate. This will involve a contract with the trustees to sell the property to the third party. The principle is based on the assumption that as between the two innocent parties, namely, the beneficiary under the trust with the equitable interest and the third party who acquired the legal title, the court of equity favoured the latter. The approach of the court was based on the maxim, 'where the equities are equal the law prevails'. The effect was the court's insistence that the third party acquires the legal title.

The final requirement concerns the lack of notice. Notice in this context embraces actual or constructive notice. Actual notice involves knowledge, including wilful blindness, on the part of the defendant. Constructive notice is much broader and involves knowledge which would be revealed by making reasonable inquiries.

In the case of *MCC Proceeds v Lehman Bros International (Europe), The Times*, 14 January 1998, CA, the court decided that the defendants were *bona fide* transferees of the legal title to the shares for value without notice and, thus, acquired good title to the shares. The claimants' cause of action in equity was therefore extinguished.

CASE EXAMPLE

MCC Proceeds Inc v Lehman Bros International (Europe), The Times, 14 January 1998, CA

Macmillan Incorporated, a Delaware company, was taken over in 1988 by Maxwell Communications Corporation plc (MCC) and became controlled by Robert Maxwell and members of his family. Macmillan Inc placed shares in a wholly owned subsidiary (Berlitz International Inc) together with the relevant share certificates, in the name of Bishopsgate Investment Trust plc (a nominee company controlled by Mr Maxwell). An agreement was entered into declaring that Bishopsgate held the legal title to the shares as nominees for Macmillan, who retained the beneficial interest in the shares. The agreement specified that, on Macmillan's written demand, Bishopsgate would immediately transfer the shares to Macmillan. Without Macmillan's knowledge or consent, Bishopsgate pledged the certificates with the defendants as collateral under a stock lending scheme. The defendants, who were ignorant of Macmillan's interest in the shares and certificates, subsequently arranged for the cancellation of the certificates on transfer of the shares into a central depository paperless system in New York. The defendants subsequently sold the shares to an associated company, Shearson Lehman Bros Holdings plc. The claimants, who were Macmillan's successors and assignees, instituted proceedings against the defendants in conversion. The claim was based on the ground that Macmillan had a beneficial interest in the shares and certificates and was entitled to an immediate right to possession. Such interest, the claimants alleged, was sufficient to maintain an action in conversion and the defendants' lack of knowledge of Bishopsgate's wrongdoing or of Macmillan's interest was no defence to the conversion claim. The judge granted an application to the defendants to strike out the claim for conversion on the ground that no reasonable cause of action was disclosed on the facts. The claimants appealed to the Court of Appeal.

The Court of Appeal dismissed the appeal on the following grounds:

(a) The defendants, who were *bona fide* purchasers of the legal interest in the shares without notice of any breach of trust by Bishopsgate or of any claim by Macmillan, acquired good title to the shares and certificates, free from any adverse claims. Thus, the claimants' cause of action was extinguished. The claimants enjoyed an equitable interest in the shares and certificates and, in the circumstances, their interest was overreached.

A claim for (b) conversion of goods was not maintainable by a person who had only an equitable interest in the property. Conversion was a common law cause of action and the common law did not recognise the equitable interests of beneficiaries under a trust. Accordingly, the common law recognised only the title of the trustee as a person normally entitled to immediate possession of the trust property. The claimants' action in conversion could not be maintained as its predecessor in title, Macmillan, had only an equitable interest in the shares and certificates. This rule of substantive law was not altered by the Judicature Acts 1873 and 1875, which merely fused the administration of law and equity.

2.4 Trusts and other relationships

There are a variety of legal devices that may be adopted to deal with issues concerning property rights. The trust is one of these institutions which gives rise to a number of similarities with and differences from other concepts such as gifts, contracts, bailment, the status of personal representatives of a deceased estate and the agency relationship.

2.4.1 Trusts and gifts

A gift results in a donor transferring rights in the relevant property directly to the donee for no consideration. Thus, if the donor is the absolute owner of property the gift will be complete when he transfers both the legal and beneficial ownership in the property to the donee. In order to transfer the legal title to the donee, the donor will need to comply with the relevant requirements for that type of property, for instance the transfer of registered land must be done by executing a transfer document followed by registration in the land registry, the transfer of shares in a private company requires the transferor to execute a share transfer form followed by registration in the share register of the company, the transfer of tangible moveable property requires the donor to deliver the property to the donee. Once the legal formalities have been completed the beneficial interest will be transferred in accordance with the intention of the donor. The effect is that the donor retains no control over the property that has been gifted to the donee.

An express trust, as distinct from a gift, is one where the settlor assigns his legal rights over the property to trustees on condition that they control and deal with the property for the benefit of the beneficiaries. The settlor indicates the nature of the interests of the beneficiaries who, in turn, acquire equitable rights to compel the trustees to perform their duties. The transfer of the legal interest to the trustees may be by way of a gift or sale *inter vivos* or on death. On the creation of the trust the settlor loses all interest in the property save for any rights retained as trustee or beneficiary. The trustees acquire a legal interest in the property and the beneficiaries acquire equitable interests in the property. Thus, the original interest of the settlor becomes split into legal and equitable interests acquired by different parties.

2.4.2 Trusts and contracts

There are two types of contracts recognised in English law, a 'simple' contract and a 'specialty' contract or one created by deed or covenant. A simple contract is an agreement made between two parties for consideration in money or money's worth. Whereas a specialty contract is a deed, executed as such, and which incorporates the terms of the agreement in writing. There is no need to provide consideration in order to enforce the deed at common law, but this principle does not extend to enforcement in equity. The classic features of contract law, as developed at common law, are that the agreement is essentially a bilateral arrangement between the parties and the requirement of consideration (except in relation to a speciality contract) and enforcement only by the parties to the agreement.

A trust, on the other hand, had originated and was developed in accordance with the exclusive jurisdiction of equity. Before the Judicature Acts 1873/75 the common law courts had failed to recognise the institution of the trust and it was left to the Lord Chancellor, initially, and the courts of equity, subsequently, to recognise and develop the sophisticated rules that comprise the law of trusts. An express trust is created by reference to the unilateral act of the settlor in vesting the property in the hands of the trustees and setting out the terms of the trust. It is true that the vesting of the property may be achieved by way of a contract with the trustees, but such contract will be regarded as purely collateral to the trust. Once a trust is created the beneficiary may be a volunteer and will still be capable of enforcing his rights against the trustees. It would be irrelevant that the claimant beneficiary has not provided consideration. The reason being that the beneficiary acquires an equitable interest *in rem* which the court of equity was prepared to protect, irrespective of his capacity as a volunteer. If, on the other hand, an intended trust had not been created because the property had not been vested in the trustees, the transaction will operate as an agreement to create a trust and will be enforced in equity only by non-volunteers. The common law rule, subject to statutory modification, is that only parties to the contract may enforce the agreement, see *Woodar Investment Developments Ltd v Wimpey Construction (UK) Ltd* [1980] 1 All ER 571. This is the position even though the contract was made for the benefit of a third party. The Contracts (Rights of Third Parties) Act 1999 has restricted this principle where *inter alia* the contract was made for the benefit of a third party and the agreement does not prevent the third party from enforcing it. Under a trust a beneficiary may enforce the trust against the trustee despite the fact that he was not a party to the trust instrument. Indeed, the beneficiary may not even have been in existence when the trust was set up.

2.4.3 Trusts and bailment contracts

A bailment contract involves the specific delivery of tangible, moveable property to another (called the bailee) for a specific purpose, on condition that it is to be returned to the bailor when the stated purpose had been achieved, e.g. the delivery of clothes to a laundry for cleaning and ironing and to be returned on a specific day.

The confusion with trusts law was created by the definition of bailment by Blackstone. In his *Commentaries* he defined bailment as 'a delivery of goods in trust, upon a contract expressed or implied, that the trust shall be faithfully executed on the part of the bailee'. However, this elaborate definition has very little significance in the law of trusts for the two concepts, bailment and trusts, have very little in common. A bailment contract, as distinct from the trust, is a common law device. The bailee, as opposed to the trustee, does not acquire control over the property and the bailee, generally, does not have the power to transfer ownership of the property. Further, bailment is restricted to one type of property, namely chattels, whereas, any form of property may be the subject-matter of a trust.

2.4.4 Trustees and personal representatives

Personal representatives include both 'executors' and 'administrators'. An executor is a person nominated under the will of a deceased person to collect in the assets of the deceased, pay his debts and distribute the estate in accordance with the will. An administrator achieves the same objectives but is appointed where there is no will. The similarities between personal representatives and trustees are that the representatives owe fiduciary duties to the creditors and those interested in the deceased's estate, whereas the trustees owe similar duties to the beneficiaries under the trust. Differences between the two groups of fiduciaries include their respective functions, the interests of the beneficiaries and the limitation periods.

The function of the personal representatives is to wind up the estate by paying the debts of the deceased and distributing the net estate to those entitled under the will or in accordance with the intestacy rules. The duty of trustees is to administer the trust for the benefit of the beneficiaries and this may involve a prolonged period of time. The beneficiaries under a trust acquire an equitable proprietary interest as soon as the trust is created which they can sell, exchange or give away. Whereas those interested in the estate of the deceased do not acquire an interest in the assets, instead they acquire the right to ensure that the estate is duly administered by the personal representatives. The limitation period for actions against the personal representatives is 12 years, whereas the limitation period for actions for breach of trust is six years, subject to fraud and actions for the recovery of trust assets in the hands of the trustees.

Wills sometimes include a clause to the effect that personal representatives may also act as trustees. In this event, it not easy to determine when the personal representatives cease to act as personal representatives and become trustees. The test is when the personal representatives have completed their functions of winding up the estate and have taken on the mantle of trusteeship. Once the residuary estate has been established and remains undistributed, this is the time that the personal representatives are likely to become trustees for the beneficiaries.

2.4.5 Trusts and agency

In some respects the duties imposed on a trustee are broadly similar to the duties imposed on an agent. Both institutions impose fiduciary duties on the trustee and agent. Accordingly, the trustee and the agent are not allowed to profit from their position except with authority. Similar remedies may be exercised by a beneficiary against his trustee as exist by a principal against his agent. Generally, trustees and agents may not delegate their responsibilities. However, there are differences between the two relationships. The essence of the agency relationship is based on an agreement between two parties, the principal and the agent, on the understanding that the agent acts on behalf of the principal. Thus the agent is under the control of the principal. In addition the relationship is treated as one of creditor and debtor. Whereas the relationship between the trustee and beneficiary is different in that the trustee is not under the control of the beneficiary, the trustee has legal title to the trust property and the beneficiary has an equitable proprietary interest.

2.5 Classification of trusts

The various forms of trusts may be classified into express and implied trusts. Express trusts are created in accordance with the express intention of the settlor. The term 'implied trusts' is a generic expression which includes resulting, constructive and statutory trusts.

The following is an indication of the various methods of classifying express trusts.

2.5.1 Private/public trusts

The broadest division is that between private and public (charitable) trusts.

Private trusts exist for the benefit of persons, or benefit a narrow section of the public, for instance a gift on trust for the education of the children of the settlor. There are a number of anomalous trusts in respect of which the beneficiaries are private purposes. These beneficiaries are obviously incapable of enforcing such trusts: for instance a trust for the benefit of the testator's pets or a trust for the execution and maintenance of a monument in memory of the testator. These are called 'hybrid' trusts, or trusts for imperfect obligations. Charitable trusts are public trusts which benefit the public as a whole in a number of specified ways such as the relief of poverty, the advancement of education, the propagation of religion and other purposes which are beneficial to society within the spirit and intendment of the preamble to the Charitable Uses Act 1601. The Charities Act 2011 (re-enacting the Charities Act 2006) creates a fairly detailed list of charitable purposes. This Act creates a statutory definition of charities for the first time in English law.

Private trusts may be sub-divided into various categories, namely express, resulting, constructive and statutory trusts. An express trust is one that is created intentionally by a settlor or testator for the benefit of a person or group of persons (including purposes).

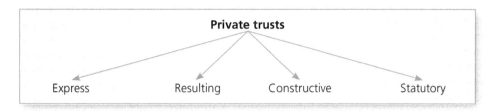

Figure 2.1 Classification of private trusts

2.5.2 Fixed/discretionary trusts

Express trusts may be sub-divided into 'fixed' and 'discretionary' trusts. A fixed trust is one where the beneficiaries have settled and identifiable interests in the property which they are entitled to enjoy and protect. For instance: on trust for A for life, remainder to B absolutely. A enjoys the interest or income for as long as he lives, whereas B has a vested interest in the capital or the entire property subject to A's interest.

A discretionary trust is one whereby the trustees are given a duty to exercise their discretion in order to distribute the property in favour of a selected group of persons. The beneficiaries, individually considered, do not have an interest in the property but have only a hope ('*spes*') of acquiring an interest in the property, prior to the exercise of the discretion by the trustees. For instance: 'For a period of 21 years from the date of the transfer to hold on trust to apply the income to such of the settlor's children as the trustees may decide in their absolute discretion.' The settlor's child or children do not have an interest in the property before the exercise of the discretion by the trustees, but each potential beneficiary has a *locus standi* to sue the trustees for breach of trust in the event of the trustees improperly exercising their fiduciary duties.

Discretionary trusts may be 'exhaustive' or 'non-exhaustive'. An 'exhaustive' discretionary trust is one where the trustees are required to distribute the income and/or capital to the objects. The trustees are given a discretion to select which objects may benefit and the 'quantum' of the benefit.

A 'non-exhaustive' discretionary trust is one where the trustees are not required to distribute the entirety of the income and/or capital but may retain or accumulate the relevant property at their discretion (see Chapter 6).

2.5.3 Resulting trusts

student
mentor tip

'Understand the difference between the types of trusts!'

A 'resulting trust' is a trust created by the courts in accordance with the presumed intention of the settlor. The settlor or his estate is presumed to be the equitable owner. An occasion giving rise to this presumption is the purchase of property in the name of another. For instance, B purchases shares and directs the vendor to transfer the shares in the name of T. T is presumed to hold the shares on trust for B.

In addition, a resulting trust may be created when there is a surplus of trust funds left over after the trust purpose has been achieved. For instance, a surplus of trust funds is left over after the testator's pet, the sole beneficiary, dies. This surplus is held on resulting trust for the testator's estate.

2.5.4 Constructive trusts

A 'constructive trust' is one created by the courts in the interests of justice and conscience. Thus, whenever a trustee abuses the confidence of the settlor by realising an unauthorised profit derived from trust property, that profit is held on constructive trust for the beneficiaries. The constructive trust extends beyond express trustees and may attach to strangers who intermeddle with trust property with notice that they are dealing with trust property. This is a subject that is in the process of development by the courts.

2.5.5 Statutory trusts

Statutory trusts are created by Parliament in special circumstances. For example, the Administration of Estates Act 1925 (as amended) created a statutory trust for the benefit of the deceased's heirs.

Section 33 of the Trustee Act 1925 created a protective trust, namely a determinable life interest in favour of the principal beneficiary coupled with a discretionary trust in favour of a specified class of objects, including the principal beneficiary, on the occurrence of the determining event.

2.6 Reasons for the creation of express trusts

There are a variety of reasons why a settlor may wish to create an express trust. These may be loosely classified as 'family situations', to undertake commercial transactions or to promote charitable or non-charitable purposes. Some of the popular reasons for such creation are:

- to provide for secret beneficiaries after the death of the testator;
- to create a marriage settlement for the benefit of the parties to a marriage and their issue, if any;
- to obtain fiscal advantages by way of tax planning;
- to protect property from spendthrift beneficiaries by means of discretionary or protective trusts;
- to promote commercial arrangements and protect lenders and customers;
- to provide an incentive to the workforce through employee trusts of various kinds;
- to enable charitable objects to be carried out;
- to make provision for a limited number of non-human objects such as pets and the maintenance of monuments;
- to benefit minors who may not have the capacity to acquire the legal interest.

KEY FACTS

The characteristics and classification of trusts

Trust concept
Underhill's definition
Section 1 of the Recognition of Trusts Act 1987
Lord Browne-Wilkinson's essential characteristics of a trust: *Westdeutsche Landesbank Girozentrale v Islington BC* [1996]

Characteristics of trusts
▣ Trust property
▣ Separation of legal and equitable interests
▣ Sub-trusts
▣ Mandatory duties imposed on the trustee
▣ *Inter vivos* or on death
▣ Settlor's position: *Re Bowden* (1936)
▣ Trustee's position (fiduciary; legal interest): *Westdeutsche Landesbank* [1996]
▣ Beneficiary's position (equitable interest): *Saunders v Vautier* [1841]
▣ Equitable proprietary interests
▣ *Bona fide* transferee of the legal estate for value without notice: *Pilcher v Rawlins* [1871]; *MCC Proceeds Inc v Lehman Bros Int* [1998]

Classification of trusts
▣ Private/public trusts
▣ Fixed/discretionary trusts
▣ Resulting trusts
▣ Constructive trusts
▣ Statutory trusts: s 33 of the Trustee Act 1925

Reasons for the creation of express trusts
▣ To provide for secret beneficiaries
▣ To create marriage settlements
▣ To implement tax avoidance schemes
▣ To protect spendthrift beneficiaries
▣ To create commercial arrangements
▣ To create employee trusts
▣ To promote charitable activities
▣ To provide for a limited number of non-human objects

Express		Resulting		Constructive		Statutory
private/ public	fixed/ discretionary	automatic	presumed	fiduciary	strangers	e.g. s 33 TA 1925

Figure 2.2 Classification of trusts

ACTIVITY

Self-test questions

1. What difficulties are posed by any attempt to define a trust?
2. Identify the fundamental characteristics of trusts.
3. What essential features distinguish the various types of trusts that exist?

SUMMARY

▣ There have been several legal definitions or descriptions of trusts. The main ones mentioned in this chapter were provided by:
  ● Maitland;
  ● Lewin;

- Underhill;
- the American Restatement of the Law of Trusts;
- the Recognition of Trusts Act 1987.

The essential characteristics of a trust are:
- Lord Browne-Wilkinson's four essential characteristics laid down in *Westdeutsche Landesbank Girozentrale v Islington BC* [1996] – operates on the conscience of the owner of the legal title to property, this is based on awareness of the factors affecting his conscience, the property is required to be identifiable and the beneficiary acquires a proprietary interest in the trust property;
- separation of the legal and equitable interests;
- obligatory nature of the trust relationship;
- the beneficiary acquires a proprietary interest in the trust property which he may assert against anyone except the *bona fide* transferee of the legal estate for value without notice;
- the trustee is regarded as a fiduciary and is prohibited from acquiring a benefit from the trust property by virtue of his position as a fiduciary.

The various types of trusts that may exist are:
- express – these are trusts created in accordance with the express intention of the settlor. This intention may be expressed orally or in writing or affirmed by the conduct of the parties;
- resulting – these are trusts that arise in accordance with the implied intention of the transferor or where a transfer of property fails or does not exhaust the entire property;
- constructive – these are trusts created by the courts in the interests of justice and conscience;
- statutory – these are trusts that are created by Parliament;
- fixed trusts – these are trusts that are created by the settlor in which the beneficiaries and their interests are ascertained or are ascertainable on the date of the creation;
- discretionary trusts – these are express trusts whereby the settlor has imposed an obligation on the trustees to exercise their discretion in favour of a class of objects;
- private trusts – a private trust exists for the benefit of a defined class of objects;
- public trusts – a public or charitable trust is designed to benefit society as a whole or a large section of society in a way that the law recognises as charitable;
- bare trusts – these are trusts in which the trustees have no active duties to perform.

Some of the more popular reasons for the creation of a trust include:
- to obtain fiscal advantages by way of tax planning;
- to promote commercial arrangements and protect lenders and customers;
- to provide an incentive to the workforce through employee trusts of various kinds;
- to enable charitable objects to be carried out;
- to make provision for a limited number of non-human objects such as pets and the maintenance of monuments.

SAMPLE ESSAY QUESTION

Consider the following essay question:

Explain how versatile trusts are capable of being.

Answer plan

Refer to the various legal definitions of the expression, 'trust'.

Consider the description of 'trusts' adopted by the Recognition of Trusts Act 1987.

Classify the various types of trusts that may exist.

State some of the popular reasons why an express trust may be created.

Elaborate on each of the following concepts:

- separation of the legal and equitable interests;
- mandatory nature of duties imposed on trustees;
- proprietary nature of interests acquired by the beneficiaries;
- creation of trusts *inter vivos* or on death;
- the prominence of the *bona fide* transferee of the legal estate for value without notice;
- the irrevocable nature of trusts;
- the types of property that may be subject to a trust;
- the significance of the rule in *Saunders v Vautier* (1841).

CONCLUSION

Further reading

Blackstone, W, *Commentaries on the Laws of England* (ed. W Morrison, Vol. 2, Cavendish Publishing, 2001).

Goodhart, W, 'Trust law for the 21st century' (1996) 10(2) Tru LI 38.

Hargreaves, E, 'The nature of beneficiaries' rights under trusts' (2011) 25(4) Tru LI I63.

Hayton, D, 'Developing the law of trusts for the 21st century' (1990) 106 LQR 87.

Millett, P, 'Equity: the road ahead' (1995) 9(2) Tru LI 35.

3

The 'three certainties' test

AIMS AND OBJECTIVES

By the end of this chapter you should be able to:

- appreciate the distinctions between trusts and powers of appointment
- understand the three certainties test and appreciate its significance in the creation of an express trust
- comprehend, define and distinguish between linguistic (conceptual) and evidential uncertainty and administrative unworkability
- recognise the various ways in which the courts have approached the 'any given postulant' test for certainty of objects

3.1 Introduction

The creation of an express trust may be achieved by one of two modes. The first involves the transfer of the relevant property to the trustees subject to a declaration of trust in favour of the beneficiaries (a transfer and declaration). The second mode requires the settlor to declare himself a trustee of the relevant property for the beneficiaries (self-declaration). It is of crucial importance that the transferor/settlor and the transferee/trustee recognise their obligations. The transferor/settlor loses all interests, as settlor, on the creation of the trust. He is treated as a complete stranger in regard to the trust property and is incapable, as settlor, of bringing or defending a claim concerning property subject to an express trust. The transferees, in this context, involve the trustees and the beneficiaries. These are the parties who are entitled to bring proceedings in respect of the trust property.

The importance to the trustees of ascertaining whether a trust has been created is in respect of their duties. The trustees are the individuals who have control of the property and are required to comply with their fiduciary responsibilities to avoid litigation for breach of trust. The beneficiaries acquire equitable interests in the property on the creation of the trust and are given a bundle of rights in order to protect their interests.

It is imperative that the parties to a trust are familiar with their respective duties and rights. Equally, the courts are required to apply a rational set of rules in order to determine whether a trust has been validly created or not. The courts have formulated a test to determine this question, known as the 'three certainties' test laid down by Lord Langdale MR in *Knight v Knight* [1840] 3 Beav 148:

JUDGMENT

'First, if the words were so used, that upon the whole, they ought to be construed as imperative; secondly, if the subject of the recommendation or wish be certain; and thirdly, if the objects or persons intended to have the benefit of the recommendation or wish be also certain.'

Lord Langdale MR

Thus, the 'three certainties' are:

- certainty of intention (words);
- certainty of subject-matter;
- certainty of objects (beneficiaries).

3.2 Certainty of intention

The requirement here is that the obligations of trusteeship are intended in respect of the property. This issue is determined by reference to all the circumstances of the case. Thus, oral and written statements, as well as the conduct of the parties, are construed by the courts to determine whether a trust relationship has been created.

3.2.1 Intention – a question of fact and degree

The test is a mixed subjective and objective issue, in that the focus of attention involves the settlor's genuine intention as construed by the courts. The question is whether the settlor has manifested a present, unequivocal and irrevocable intention to create a trust. Oral statements, the conduct of the parties and documentary evidence, if any, will be construed by the courts. Accordingly the issue is whether objectively a trust was intended, by reference to the relevant facts of each case. The maxim 'Equity looks at the intent rather than the form' is applicable in this context. The word 'trust' need not be used but if used by the settlor is construed in its context. Alternative expressions will be construed by reference to the surrounding circumstances for the purpose of ascertaining whether the trust concept is intended. The doctrine of binding precedent is not applicable here and each case is determined on its own facts.

In *Shah v Shah*, the issue was whether a letter signed by a shareholder, coupled with the signing of a share transfer form, amounted to sufficiently clear evidence of an intention to create a trust.

CASE EXAMPLE

Shah v Shah [2010] EWCA Civ 1408, CA

The claimant, D, executed and delivered a letter to his brother, M, the defendant, declaring that, 'as from today' he was holding 4,000 shares in a specified company for M as 'from the date of this declaration and letter.' In addition, D executed and delivered transfer forms for 4,000 shares in the same company in favour of M. The share certificates, however, were not delivered to M. The transfer of the legal title to the shares was duly completed and M was registered as the new owner. D now claimed that between the date of the delivery of the letter and the legal transfer of the shares no trust had been created. The letter acknowledged an intention to make a gift, which was ineffective unless and until the gift was complete. In the interim period he had changed his mind and revoked his intention to donate the shares, and equity does not perfect an imperfect gift. The defendant argued that on construction of the letter and the execution of the share transfer form the claimant had declared a trust. The High Court decided in favour of the defendant. The claimant appealed to the Court of Appeal.

Held: Dismissing the appeal, the Court decided that on construction of the letter and the execution of the share transfer form, D had declared a trust of the shares in favour of M. The question of intention to create a trust was to be judged objectively by reference to the wording of the letter and the facts. The terms of the letter indicated an intention from the date of its execution that D was holding the shares for M. The use of the words 'as from today' and 'declaration' had that effect. These words conveyed an intention to hold the beneficial interest in the shares for M until registration.

JUDGMENT

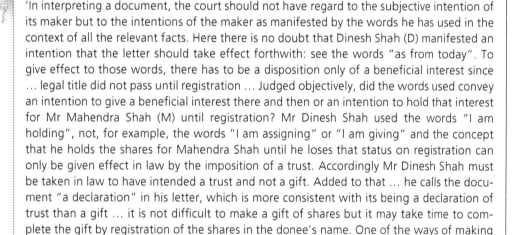

'In interpreting a document, the court should not have regard to the subjective intention of its maker but to the intentions of the maker as manifested by the words he has used in the context of all the relevant facts. Here there is no doubt that Dinesh Shah (D) manifested an intention that the letter should take effect forthwith: see the words "as from today". To give effect to those words, there has to be a disposition only of a beneficial interest since ... legal title did not pass until registration ... Judged objectively, did the words used convey an intention to give a beneficial interest there and then or an intention to hold that interest for Mr Mahendra Shah (M) until registration? Mr Dinesh Shah used the words "I am holding", not, for example, the words "I am assigning" or "I am giving" and the concept that he holds the shares for Mahendra Shah until he loses that status on registration can only be given effect in law by the imposition of a trust. Accordingly Mr Dinesh Shah must be taken in law to have intended a trust and not a gift. Added to that ... he calls the document "a declaration" in his letter, which is more consistent with its being a declaration of trust than a gift ... it is not difficult to make a gift of shares but it may take time to complete the gift by registration of the shares in the donee's name. One of the ways of making an immediate gift is for the donor to declare a trust. In my judgment that is what happened in this case.'

Arden LJ

3.2.2 Intention to benefit distinct from intention to create a trust

An intention to create a trust is fundamentally different from the broader concept of an intention to benefit another simpliciter. There are many modes of providing a benefit to another, such as gifts, exchanges and sales of property. But the requirement here is whether the settlor intended to benefit another solely by creating a trust. The trust mode of providing a benefit concerns a specific and ancient regime. The trust involves the separation of the legal and equitable interests and imposes fiduciary duties on the trustees with correlative rights in the hands of the beneficiaries. Decided cases are used merely for illustrative purposes.

CASE EXAMPLE

Jones v Lock [1865] LR 1 Ch App 25

Robert Jones placed a cheque for £900 (drawn in his favour) into the hand of his nine-month-old baby, saying 'I give this to baby and I am going to put it away for him.' He then took the cheque from the child and told his nanny: 'I am going to put this away for my son.' He put the cheque in his safe. A few days later, he told his solicitor: 'I shall come to your office on Monday to alter my will, that I may take care of my son.' He died the same day. The question in issue was whether the cheque funds belonged to the child or to the residuary legatees under Robert Jones's will.

Held:
(a) No valid gift of the funds was made in favour of the child, for the funds were not paid over to him.
(b) No trust had been declared in favour of the child, for Robert Jones had not made himself a trustee for his child.

JUDGMENT

'[T]he case turns on the very short question whether Jones intended to make a declaration that he held the property in trust for the child; and I cannot come to any other conclusion than that he did not. I think it would be a very dangerous example if loose conversations of this sort, in important transactions of this kind, should have the effect of declarations of trust.'

Lord Cranworth LC

Likewise, in the unusual case of *Duggan v Full Sutton Prison, The Times*, 13 February 2004, the court decided that no trust was created. In this case the claimant, a serving prisoner, contended that a trust was imposed on a prison governor to retain as a trustee and invest cash sums surrendered by prisoners. The Court of Appeal decided that only a debtor/creditor relationship had been created and it would have been impractical to impose a trust relationship on the prison authorities.

In *Paul v Constance* [1977] 1 WLR 527, CA, the court considered the oral statements and conduct of the parties and concluded that there was sufficient evidence of an intention to create a trust. The court, however, acknowledged that this was a borderline case because it was not easy to pinpoint the specific time of the declaration of trust.

CASE EXAMPLE

Paul v Constance [1977] 1 WLR 527, CA

Ms Paul and Mr Constance lived together as man and wife. Mr C received £950 compensation for an industrial injury and both parties agreed to put the money in a deposit account in Mr C's name. On numerous occasions, both before and after the opening of the account, Mr C told Ms P that the money was as much hers as his. After Mr C's death, Ms P claimed the fund from Mrs C, the administrator.

Held: Mr C, by his words and deeds, declared himself a trustee for himself and Ms P of the damages. Accordingly, 50 per cent of the fund was held upon trust for Ms P.

JUDGMENT

'In this court the issue becomes: was there sufficient evidence to justify the judge reaching that conclusion of fact? When one looks to the detailed evidence to see whether it goes as far as that – and I think that the evidence does have to go as far as that – one finds that from the time that Mr Constance received his damages right up to his death he was saying, on occasions, that the money was as much the plaintiff's as his. [The words] This money is as much yours as mine, convey clearly a present declaration that the existing fund was as much the plaintiff's as his own. The judge accepted that conclusion. I think he was well justified in doing so and, indeed, I think he was right to do. It might, however, be thought that this was a borderline case, since it is not easy to pinpoint a specific moment of declaration … The question … is whether in all the circumstances the use of those words on numerous occasions as between Mr Constance and the plaintiff constituted an express declaration of trust. The judge found that they did. For myself, I think he was right so to find.'

Scarman LJ

An express trust may be successfully created in a commercial context before a company becomes insolvent. Insolvency involves claims from creditors, both secured and unsecured, but with the prospect of some creditors receiving very little funds or nothing from a sale of the company's assets, the temptation to claim the existence of a trust of the company's funds may prove attractive. The trust concept was successfully employed in *Re Kayford Ltd* [1975] 1 All ER 604, HC.

CASE EXAMPLE

Re Kayford Ltd [1975] 1 All ER 604, HC

A mail-order company received advice from accountants as to the method of protecting advance payments of the purchase price or deposits for goods ordered by customers. The company was advised to open a separate bank account to be called 'Customer Trust Deposit Account' into which future sums of money received for goods not yet delivered to customers were to be paid. The company accepted the advice and its managing director gave oral instructions to the company's bank but, instead of opening a new account, a dormant deposit account in the company's name was used for this purpose. A few weeks later the company was put into liquidation. The question in issue was whether the sums paid into the bank account were held upon trust for customers who had paid wholly or partly for goods which were not delivered or whether they formed part of the general assets of the company.

Held: A valid trust had been created in favour of the relevant customers in accordance with the intention of the company and the arrangements effected. The position remained the same even though payment was not made into a separate banking account.

JUDGMENT

'[I]t is well settled that a trust can be created without using the words trust or confidence or the like: the question is whether in substance a sufficient intention to create a trust has been manifested. The whole purpose of what was done was to ensure that the moneys remained in the beneficial ownership of those who sent them, and a trust is the obvious means of achieving this. No doubt the general rule is that if you send money to a company for goods which are not delivered, you are merely a creditor of the company unless a trust has been created. The sender may create a trust by using appropriate words when he sends the money (though I wonder how many do this, even if they are equity lawyers), or the company may do it by taking suitable steps on or before receiving the money. If either is done, the obligations in respect of the money are transformed from contract to property, from debt to trust.'

Megarry VC

In *Re Ahmed & Co* [2006] EWHC 480 (Ch), the High Court decided that a trust was created where the Law Society was obliged to create a fund to hold moneys when exercising its regulatory powers over solicitors. The funds were held on trust for the Society's statutory purposes and for the benefit of those entitled to the moneys.

Similarly, a trust may be created between two parties in order to promote a commercial venture in circumstances where the parties did not have the capacity to transfer property to each other by way of a contract. The trust property may take the form of a chose in action, i.e. an intangible personal property right. This was the approach of the court in *Don King Productions Inc v Warren* [1999] 2 All ER 218, CA.

CASE EXAMPLE

Don King Productions Inc v Warren [1999] 2 All ER 218, CA

The claimant, Don King Productions Inc (DKP), was owned by Don King, the leading boxing promoter in the USA. The first defendant, Frank Warren (W), was the leading boxing promoter in the UK. The other defendants were Mr Warren's business associates. In 1994, the parties entered into two partnership agreements intended to deal with the boxing, promotion and management interests of the two promoters. One of the agreements declared that the two parties would hold all promotion and management agreements relating to the business for the benefit of the partnership. Some of the promotion agreements contained non-assignment clauses. But none of the agreements contained a prohibition on the partners declaring themselves as trustees. The issue before the court was whether the benefit of the promotion and management agreements was capable of being the subject-matter of a trust, despite the express clause prohibiting the assignment of rights.

Held: A valid trust of a chose in action was created in favour of the claimant. This was created in accordance with the intention of the parties. Accordingly, W's entry into the 'multi-fight agreement' intended for his benefit was in breach of the duties owed to the claimant.

JUDGMENT

'In principle, I can see no objection to a party to contracts involving skill and confidence or containing non-assignment provisions from becoming trustee of the benefit of being the contracting party as well as the benefit of the rights conferred. I can see no reason why the law should limit the parties' freedom of contract to creating trusts of the fruits of such contracts received by the assignor or to creating an accounting relationship between the parties in respect of the fruits.'

Lightman J

In *Charity Commission for England and Wales v Framjee* [2014] EWHC 2507, Henderson J referred to a number of factors that may give rise to a trust. These are as follows:

JUDGMENT

'(a) In order for a trust to be established, it is not necessary for a settlor to use the word "trust" or any other formal language, or to have any knowledge of trusts law, so long as the traditional "three certainties" (of words, subject-matter and objects) are satisfied, see *Paul v Constance* [1977] 1 WLR 527.

(b) Where money is transferred to a recipient to be paid to a third party, and that money is not intended to be at the free disposal of the recipient, it is likely that a trust will arise, per Lord Millett in *Twinsectra Ltd v Yardley* [2002] UKHL 12. [See Chapter 8.]

(c) Although not a pre-requisite, if there is a requirement for the money to be held by the recipient in a separate account, that will be a strong pointer in favour of the existence of a trust, per Lord Millett in *Twinsectra Ltd v Yardley*.

(d) The court is more likely to find that a trust was intended in a charitable context than in a commercial context, per Brightman J in *Jones v AG* (9 November 1976) unreported.

(e) Whether the trust is an express trust for a third party, or a Quistclose trust (1970) [see Chapter 7] in favour of the transferor with a power to apply the money in accordance with the stated purpose, will depend in particular upon whether it was contemplated that there was a real risk that the purpose for which the money was paid might fail.'

Henderson J

In *Charity Commission for England and Wales v Framjee* [2014] EWHC 2507, the High Court decided that the operations of a website by a charity inviting donors to make contributions to charities of their choice, created express trusts in favour of the nominated charities. Members of the public who contributed to the charitable website organisation entered into binding contractual relations with that organisation that imposed fiduciary obligations to transfer the funds to named charities, thus creating trust obligations along the lines of *Quistclose* trusts in favour of the intended charities.

CASE EXAMPLE

Charity Commission for England and Wales v Framjee [2014] EWHC 2507 (HC)

The applicant, Charity Commission, sought a declaration and directions concerning donations by members of the public to an unincorporated charity called the Dove Trust. The claim was brought against the interim manager, Mr Framjee. The Dove Trust operated a website which invited members of the public to make donations to charities of their choice. Following complaints, the Charity Commission initiated an inquiry and on 6 June 2013 an interim manager was appointed. No distributions were made to recipients after 6 June but the charity received further donations. The issues before the court were to determine the status of the receipts in the accounts of the Dove Trust and the mode of distribution of the remaining funds. The High Court relied on the principles laid down by Lord Millett in *Twinsectra v Yardley* [2002] 2 All ER 377, and decided that the donations were subject to contracts along the Quistclose lines which imposed fiduciary duties on the officers of Dove Trust. Accordingly, the surplus funds were held on trust in favour of the intended charities to be distributed on a pro rata basis. The beneficiaries suffered a common misfortune for which they were not responsible and were required to be treated *pari passu*.

JUDGMENT

'It seems clear to me that the donations, once received by the Dove Trust, were subject to a trust, and were not merely the subject of contractual obligations. At this point I find the observations of Lord Millett in *Twinsectra* compelling.

> "It is unconscionable for a man to obtain money on terms as to its application and then disregard the terms on which he received it. Such conduct goes beyond a mere breach of contract … The duty is not contractual but fiduciary. It may exist despite the absence of any contract at all between the parties … and it binds third parties as in Quistclose case itself. The duty is fiduciary in character because a person who makes money available on terms that it is to be used for a particular purpose only and not for any other purpose thereby places his trust and confidence in the recipient to ensure that it is properly applied. This is a classic situation in which a fiduciary relationship arises, and since it arises in respect of a specific fund it gives rise to a trust."

The trustees came under a fiduciary duty to ensure that each donation would be used only for the purpose specified by the donor, because those were the terms on which the donation had been solicited. There is no reason in principle why a single transaction cannot give rise to both a trust and a contract. As Lord Wilberforce said in *Quistclose Investments v Rolls Razors* [1970] AC 567, there is "no difficulty in recognizing the co-existence in one transaction of legal and equitable rights and remedies." See too *Twinsectra*. Thus the existence of a trust in the present case does not preclude the simultaneous existence of a contract between the donor and the trustees of the Dove Trust.'

Henderson J

Counsel for the claimants contended that each donation of funds had created separate trusts with the effect that there were a multitude of charitable trusts created by each donor. The court rejected this argument as unnecessarily complex and instead decided that establishment of the website inviting donations to charitable bodies created a sub-trust within the Dove Trust. The justification for this analysis was declared by Henderson J in *Framjee* in the following manner:

JUDGMENT

'The attraction of such an analysis, it seems to me, is that it makes due allowance for the important fact that the Dove Trust was an established charitable trust with general objects when the website was established, and the fact that it was the Dove Trust to which donations were made. Against that background, an analysis which posits the creation of a multitude of separate trusts, each of which has a separate settlor and is wholly divorced from the terms of the Trust Deed, strikes me as unnecessarily complex … I prefer to view that trust as a global sub-trust established by the trustees under the aegis of the Dove Trust itself, and not as an arrangement which gave rise to literally thousands of wholly separate trusts.'

Henderson J

3.2.3 Precatory words

These are extremely ambiguous expressions used in wills, such as expressions of hope, desire, wish, recommendation or similar expressions which impose a moral obligation on the transferee. The issue here is whether such words impose a legal obligation on the recipient of property. For instance, a testator declares in his will: 'I leave all my property to my widow feeling confident that she will act fairly towards our children in dividing the same.' Did the testator create a trust?

student mentor tip

'Make sure you know the basics well enough in order to read further around the subject.' *Gayatri, University of Leicester*

The position today is that such words may or may not create a trust, depending on the wording of the will and surrounding circumstances. There was a time during the development of the law of trusts when such words did not impose a trust, with the effect that the executor of the will was entitled to retain the property beneficially. This was the approach of the ecclesiastical courts. When the Court of Chancery was formed, it was believed that the solution allowing the executor to take the property beneficially was unacceptable. Thus, the Court of Chancery made strenuous efforts to avoid such a conclusion and decided that precatory words artificially created trusts (precatory trusts). The introduction of the Executors Act 1830 declared that the executor will be entitled to an interest under the testator's will, if this accords with the clear intention of the testator. This paved the way for the modern approach to precatory words, namely to construe them in their context of the will and surrounding circumstances.

In *Re Adams and Kensington Vestry* [1884] 27 Ch D 394 the court decided that on construction of the words used in the will, no trust was intended.

CASE EXAMPLE

Re Adams and Kensington Vestry [1884] 27 Ch D 394

A testator left his property by will 'unto and to the absolute use of my wife … in full confidence that she will do what is right as to the disposal thereof between my children'. The issue was whether a trust had been created.

Held: No trust had been created for the children, so the wife was entitled to the property absolutely.

JUDGMENT

'[C]onsidering all the words which are used, we have to see what is their true effect, and what was the intention of the testator as expressed in his will. In my opinion, here he has expressed his will in such a way as not to shew an intention of imposing a trust on the wife, but on the contrary, in my opinion, he has shewn an intention to leave the property, as he says he does, to her absolutely.'

Cotton LJ

A similar conclusion was reached in *Lambe v Eames* [1871] 6 Ch App 597.

In contrast, in *Comiskey v Bowring-Hanbury* [1905] AC 84 the court concluded that on construction of the facts of the case, a trust was intended by the testator.

CASE EXAMPLE

Comiskey v Bowring-Hanbury [1905] AC 84

The testator transferred his property by his will to his widow, subject to the following terms:

in full confidence that she will make such use of it as I should have made myself and that at her death she will devise it to such one or more of my nieces as she may think fit and in default of any disposition by her thereof by her will. I hereby direct that all my estate and property … shall at her death be equally divided among the surviving said nieces.

The widow asked the court to determine whether she took the property absolutely or subject to a trust in favour of the nieces.

Held: The intention of the testator was to transfer the property absolutely to his widow for life and, after her death, one or more of his nieces was or were entitled to benefit, subject to a selection by his widow. Failing such selection, the nieces were entitled equally.

JUDGMENT

'[E]ven if you treat the words in confidence as only expressing a hope or belief, the will would run thus: I hope and believe that she will give the estate to one or more of my nieces, but if she does not do so, then I direct that it shall be equally divided between them. I think that is a perfectly good limitation. The true antithesis I think is between the words such one or more of my nieces as she may think fit and the words equally divided between my surviving said nieces.'

Lord Davey

3.2.4 Effect of uncertainty of intention

Where the intention of the transferor is uncertain as to the creation of a trust, no express trust is created. The person who is in control of the property is entitled to retain it beneficially. Accordingly, if the transferor disposes of the property to the transferee and no trust is intended, the transferee takes it beneficially. Thus, in *Re Adams and Kensington Vestry* [1884] the testator's widow was entitled to the property absolutely, and in *Jones v Lock* [1865], because of a failure to transfer the property the deceased's estate was entitled to the £900.

KEY FACTS

Certainty of intention

Question of fact	Whether the settlor's words and conduct indicate an irrevocable intention to create a trust	*Re Kayford* [1975]; *Paul v Constance* [1977]; contrast *Jones v Lock* [1865]; *Duggan v Gov of Full Sutton Prison* [2004]
Precatory words		*Comiskey v Bowring-Hanbury* [1905]; contrast *Lambe v Eames* [1871]; *Re Adams and Kensington Vestry* [1884]

3.3 Certainty of subject-matter

The term 'subject-matter', on its own, is ambiguous and inherently deals with two concepts: namely the trust property and the beneficial interest. Although the same test is applicable to both, it is important to distinguish each type of uncertainty. If the trust property is uncertain because the settlor did not specify it with sufficient clarity, the intended trust will fail. This has a reflex action on the transferor's intention, with the effect that the transferee retains the property beneficially. For instance, if A transfers 50,000 BT plc shares to X to hold 'some' of the shares upon trust for Y, the intended trust will fail and X will retain the property beneficially. This is because A has abandoned all interest in the property.

On the other hand, where the trust property is certain but the beneficial interest is uncertain, although the intended express trust will fail, a resulting trust for the transferor will arise. Thus, the legal owner will be required to hold the property on implied trust for the transferor. For instance, A transfers 50,000 BT plc shares to X on trust to provide some of the shares for Y and the remainder of the shares on trust for Z. The trust property is certain (50,000 shares), but the beneficial interest is uncertain, i.e. the number of shares to be held on trust for Y and the balance on trust for Z. The effect is that X cannot take the property beneficially and is required to hold on resulting trust for A.

The test for certainty of subject-matter is whether the trust property and the beneficial interests are ascertained or are ascertainable to such an extent that the court may attach an order on the relevant property or interest. This is a question of law for the judge to decide and this issue is determined objectively.

3.3.1 Certainty of trust property

The issue here is whether the property that is subject to the trust is capable of satisfying the test for certainty. The determining factor is whether the formula or mode of ascertainment of the trust property specified by the settlor is sufficiently precise to enable the courts to identify the trust property.

CASE EXAMPLE

Sprange v Barnard [1789] 2 Bro CC 585

A testatrix transferred property by her will to Thomas Sprange for his sole use, and added that at his death the remaining part of what was left that he did not want for his own use was to be divided equally between two named persons. The court decided that Thomas Sprange was not a trustee, and took the property beneficially.

JUDGMENT

'[T]he question is whether he may not call for the whole; and it seems to be perfectly clear on all the authorities that he may. It is contended that the court ought to impound the property; but it appears to me to be a trust which would be impossible to be executed. I must, therefore, declare him to be absolutely entitled to the £300, and decree it to be transferred to him.'

Lord Arden

The following examples illustrate the approach of the courts and highlight the principle that each case is to be determined by reference to its own facts.

CASE EXAMPLE

Re Sheldon and Kemble [1885] 53 LT 527

A testator bequeathed, in substance, all his real and personal estate to his wife, but added the desire that, at her death, what might remain of his property should be equally divided among his surviving children. The issue involved the nature and extent of the interest that was acquired by the widow and consequently the children.

Held: The court decided that the children were entitled equally to the property on the death of the widow.

JUDGMENT

'If there is any sort of ambiguity, the court ought to adopt that construction, which most effectively regards the testator's intention, reading the whole will together.'

Kay J

CASE EXAMPLE

Re Jones [1898] 1 Ch 438

A testator gave all his property to his wife 'for her absolute use and benefit, so that during her lifetime … she shall have the fullest power to sell and dispose of my said estate absolutely. After her death, as to such parts … as she shall not have sold or disposed of … I give devise and bequeath unto my brother … and to my wife's sister … upon trust to … divide' among certain persons. The question in issue was whether the widow took an absolute interest or enjoyed the interest for life.

Held: On construction of the will the widow acquired an absolute interest in the testator's real and personal estate. Byrne J discussed the rules of construction of wills:

JUDGMENT

'It is clear that if a gift is made in terms to a person absolutely, that can only be reduced to a more limited interest by clear words cutting down the first estate. There is a principle also … that although the words are absolute in the first instance, you may find subsequently occurring words sufficiently strong to cut down the first apparent absolute interest to a life interest.'

Byrne J

The court came to a different conclusion in the *Estate of Last*. The approach adopted by the court was to construe the will of the testatrix by reference to the wording of the will and surrounding circumstances. If it was clear, based on an objective view of the evidence, that the testatrix intended the claimants to inherit an interest, the court will give effect to that intention.

CASE EXAMPLE

Estate of Last [1958] P 137

A testatrix disposed of her estate by a will in the following terms: 'I give and bequeath unto my brother … All property and everything I have money and otherwise. At his death anything, that is left, that came from me to go to my late husband's grandchildren.' The brother duly proved the will and died intestate leaving no persons interested on his intestacy. The husband's grandchildren claimed the relevant property on the death of the testatrix's brother on the ground that the latter had only a life interest with remainder in favour of the claimants. The Treasury Solicitor opposed the application and argued that the estate was acquired by the brother absolutely and may be taken by the Crown on a *bona vacantia*.

Held: On construction of the will as a whole and the surrounding circumstances the intention of the testatrix was sufficiently clear to cut down the brother's interest from an absolute to a life interest and the claimants were entitled to the estate in equal shares on the death of the testatrix's brother.

JUDGMENT

'The testatrix was very unlikely to have wished to benefit the Crown by the will, and that, therefore, the court should lean against a construction which would produce a result wholly inconsistent with the testatrix's wishes. It may well be that the testatrix did not intend the

Crown to be the object of her testamentary bounty. It may be even more likely that such a possibility never even entered her mind. But if the true construction of this will warrants the conclusion that it gave the whole estate to T. G. Cotton absolutely [the testatrix's brother], I cannot avoid such a conclusion only because it may produce a result which the testatrix did not clearly foresee and may not at all have desired.

I find the difficulty stems from the use of the words anything that is left. But for the introduction of these words I should have felt little difficulty in deciding that the testatrix intended to give a life interest only to T. G. Cotton. But the introduction of these words does not prevent the cutting down of an absolute interest to a life interest if the will itself supports such a construction.

In this case, looking at the will as a whole, I have come to the conclusion that the words used are sufficiently clear to cut down T. G. Cotton's interest from an absolute to a life interest. Clearly there is an ambiguity, but I have attempted to read the will as a whole, and then to reach that construction which most effectively, in my view, expresses the intentions of the testatrix. Weight may be given to the consideration that it is better to effectuate than to frustrate the testator's intentions.'

Karminski J

CASE EXAMPLE

Palmer v Simmonds [1854] 2 Drew 221

A transfer by will to Thomas Harrison declared that, subject to a number of stipulations, he should leave the bulk of this property by will equally to four named persons. The court decided that no trust was intended and Thomas Harrison acquired the property beneficially.

JUDGMENT

'What is the meaning then of bulk? When a person is said to have given the bulk of his property, what is meant is not the whole but the greater part, and that is in fact consistent with its classical meaning. I am bound to say she has not designated the subject as to which she expresses her confidence; and I am therefore of the opinion that there is no trust created; that Harrison took absolutely, and those claiming under him now take.'

Kindersley VC

In the context of insolvency law it may be advantageous for some creditors to promote the trust concept in an effort to gain priority over the other creditors. On an insolvency or liquidation the company's assets are available to pay its creditors. If a claimant is successful in establishing that some of the company's assets are subject to a trust these assets will not be available for distribution to its creditors. Such trust assets belong to the beneficiaries and not the company. The success of such a claim varies with the facts of each case.

In *MacJordan Construction Ltd v Brookmount Erostin Ltd*, the Court of Appeal decided that the failure to carry out a contractual obligation imposed on a property developer to set up a retention fund for the benefit of a building company was insufficient to constitute a trust in favour of the building company. An equitable interest in a notional fund involving the property developer's assets could not have been created when the company went into liquidation.

CASE EXAMPLE

MacJordan Construction Ltd v Brookmount Erostin Ltd, The Times, 29 October 1991, CA

A building contract provided for interim payments to be made against interim architects' certificates but entitled the developer to make a retention of 3 per cent from each certified amount. By January 1991 the retentions made by the developer amounted to £109,247 but no fund was appropriated and set aside by the developer. The company suffered financial difficulties and a receiver was appointed. On 4 March 1991 the bank's floating charge crystallised. The builder argued that a trust had been created in its favour in a notional fund, which ranked in priority of the bank's interest under its floating charge because the building contract pre-dated the charge. The court decided that the contractual right did not relate to any specific asset impressed with a trust and therefore the claim failed. The short answer to the builder's claim was that it had no equity as against the bank to require the bank to make available assets over which the bank had an equitable interest under the charge simply because no identifiable asset was created in favour of the building company.

A similar result was reached in *Re London Wine Co* because property in the goods had not passed to the claimant. There was no means of identifying which property was acquired by the claimant from the mass of similar property in the possession of the company before its liquidation.

CASE EXAMPLE

Re London Wine Co Ltd [1986] PCC 121

Customers bought wine from a wine company and contracted with the company to store the wine in its warehouse. On a liquidation of the company these customers claimed that a trust existed in their favour. The court decided that no property passed to the customers under the Sale of Goods Act 1979 because the customers' goods were not separated from the bulk and no valid trust was created because of uncertainty of trust property.

JUDGMENT

'It seems to me any such trust must fail on the ground of uncertainty of subject-matter. It seems to me that in order to create a trust it must be possible to ascertain with certainty not only what the interest of the beneficiary is to be but to what property it is to attach.

A farmer could, by appropriate words, declare himself to be a trustee of a specified proportion of his whole flock and thus create an equitable tenancy in common between himself and the named beneficiary, so that a proprietary interest would arise in the beneficiary in an undivided share of all the flock and its produce. But the mere declaration that a given number of animals would be held upon trust could not, I should have thought, without very clear words pointing to such an intention, result in the creation of an interest in common in the proportion which that number bears to the number of the whole at the time of the declaration. And where the mass from which the numerical interest is to take effect is not itself ascertainable at the date of the declaration, such a conclusion becomes impossible.

In the instant case, even if I were satisfied on the evidence that the mass was itself identifiable at the date of the various letters of confirmation I should find the very greatest difficulty in construing the assertion that you are the sole and beneficial owner of 10 cases of such and such a wine as meaning or being intended to mean you are the owner of such proportion of the total stock of such and such a wine now held by me as 10 bears to the total number of cases comprised in such stock.'

Oliver J

The principle in *Re London Wine* was applied in *Re Stapylton Fletcher* [1994] 1 WLR 1181 (wines kept in warehouses) and *Re Goldcorp Exchange Ltd* [1995] 1 AC 74 (gold bullion purchased by customers but retained by a broker). The Sale of Goods (Amendment) Act 1995 introduced a significant change in the law. The position today is that multiple purchasers of goods are deemed to acquire interests as tenants in common in the subject-matter.

Where the trust property consists of shares, or property other than goods which is indistinguishable, the quantification of the interest on its own may be sufficient to satisfy the test. Thus, one fully paid-up BT plc share is the same as any other BT share of the same description. There may be no need to identify the relevant property by means of the share certificate numbers.

CASE EXAMPLE

Hunter v Moss [1994] 1 WLR 452

The defendant declared himself trustee for the claimant of 5 per cent of the issued share capital of a company. (One thousand shares of one denomination were issued.) The issue was whether the test for certainty of trust property was satisfied even though the defendant did not identify the share certificate numbers of the relevant shares. The court held that a valid trust was created.

Dillon LJ referred to the case of *Re London Wine* [1986] and distinguished it thus:

JUDGMENT

'It seems to me that that case is a long way from the present. It is concerned with the appropriation of chattels and when the property in chattels passes. We are concerned with a declaration of trust, accepting that the legal title remained in the defendant and was not intended, at the time the trust was declared, to pass immediately to the plaintiff. The defendant was to retain the shares as trustee for the plaintiff.

…just as a person can give, by will, a specified number of his shares of a certain class in a certain company, so equally, in my judgment, he can declare himself trustee of 50 of his ordinary shares in MEL or whatever the company may be and that is effective to give a beneficial proprietary interest to the beneficiary under the trust. No question of a blended fund thereafter arises and we are not in the field of equitable charge.'

Dillon LJ

A similar result was reached by the High Court in *Re Harvard Securities Ltd, The Times*, 18 July 1997, in respect of shares sold to clients but retained by nominees on their behalf.

3.3.2 Beneficial interests

Where the trust property is certain, but the interest to be acquired by the beneficiaries is uncertain, the express trust will fail and the property will be held on resulting trust for the transferor. This may be the case where the trustees acquire the trust property but some individual is required to divide the property between two or more beneficiaries. If that individual fails to allocate the relevant portions to the respective beneficiaries, and the issue cannot be resolved by the courts, the intended express trust will fail, thus giving rise to a resulting trust. This is the position where the settlor imposes a personal obligation on an individual to specify the relevant interests to be acquired by the beneficiaries.

CASE EXAMPLE

Boyce v Boyce [1849] 16 Sim 476

A testator devised two houses to trustees on trust to provide one for Maria, whichever she might choose, and the other to Charlotte. Maria died before the testator and had failed to make a selection. The question in issue was whether Charlotte might acquire one of the properties. The court decided that a personal obligation to select was imposed on Maria. No other person could have made the selection and the intended express trust failed but a resulting trust was set up for the testator's estate.

However, if no mode of distribution is provided in the trust instrument, the court may resolve the difficulty by adopting an arbitrary but fair means of distributing the property to the beneficiaries. This may take the form of equal division (if appropriate) or some other method of distribution.

CASE EXAMPLE

Re Knapton [1941] 2 All ER 573

The testatrix in her will provided for a number of houses to be distributed 'one each to my nephews and nieces and one to Nellie Hird one to Florence Knapton one to my sister one to my brother'. The will did not contain a method of distribution. The court decided that the beneficiaries had the right to choose a house in the order in which they were listed in the will and in the event of a failure to agree then the allocation would be by drawing lots.

JUDGMENT

'The clear intention of the testatrix is that each of the nephews and nieces should have a house. I think that it is equally clear that each of those nephews and nieces is to have a choice in priority to those devisees named later in the will. Accordingly, I construe this as a devise of: A house to each of my nephews and nieces, a house to Nellie Hird, and my nephews and nieces are to have a choice before Nellie Hird. How are they to choose? If they cannot agree, then, by the principle of the civil law, the choice must be determined by lot.'

Simonds J

3.3.3 Effect of uncertainty of subject-matter

The consequences of uncertainty of subject-matter vary with the nature of the subject-matter. If the trust property is uncertain, then no express trust could have been intended by the settlor, for no trust may attach on property that has not been identified. The effect is that the transferee of the property retains the property beneficially. No resulting trust arises.

If, on the other hand, the trust property is certain but the beneficial interest is uncertain, the intended express trust will fail but a resulting trust will arise in favour of the transferor. In these circumstances, although the intention to create a trust is clear, the scope or division of the trust property is incapable of being resolved and thus a resulting trust will arise, see *Boyce v Boyce* (above).

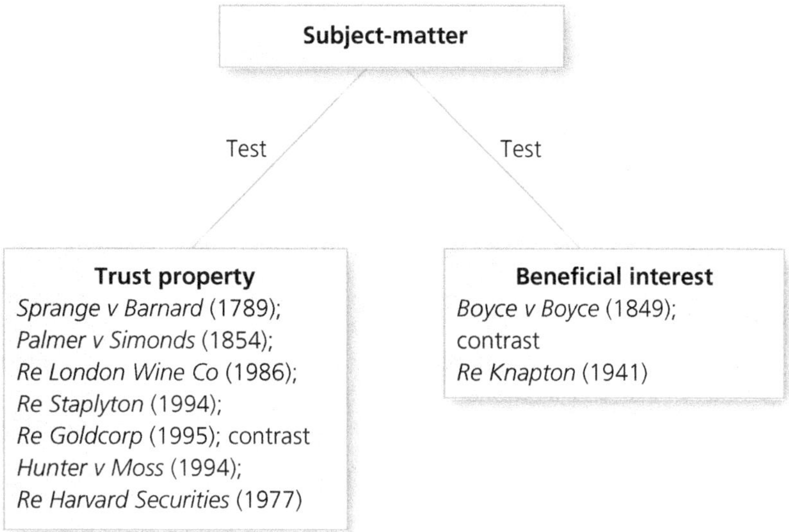

Figure 3.1 Certainty of subject-matter

3.4 Certainty of objects

The trustees owe their duties to, and are required to exercise the same for the benefit of, the beneficiaries under the trust. Accordingly, there is an obvious need for the trustees to be able to ascertain the beneficiaries under an express trust. The test for certainty of objects varies with the type of express trust created. There is a narrow test for certainty of objects for fixed trusts and a broader test for discretionary trusts. If the intended settlor fails to satisfy the relevant test for certainty of objects, the express trust will fail and a resulting trust will arise in his favour.

3.4.1 Fixed trusts

A fixed trust is one where the settlor has attempted to specify the number of beneficiaries and the extent of their interests in the trust instrument, for example a trust in favour of 'my children equally'. The trustees do not have a discretion to distribute the funds to the intended beneficiaries: on the contrary, in a fixed trust each of the intended beneficiaries acquires a vested interest in the trust property on the date of the creation of the trust. Thus, the beneficiaries may sell, exchange or give away their interests as they wish. This enjoyment of their interests is not dependent on the trustees exercising their discretion in favour of the beneficiaries. On the contrary, the beneficiaries enjoy their interests as of right. The test for certainty of objects is whether the objects are ascertained or are ascertainable with clarity, so that the courts may, if necessary, execute the trust. This is known as the 'list' test in the sense that the trustees are required to draw up a comprehensive list of all the beneficiaries. The test is sometimes also referred to as the 'class ascertainability' test. The settlor is required to identify the beneficiary or a group of beneficiaries with such precision that the court may be able to attach an order on the property only in favour of the relevant beneficiaries and no others. If the beneficiaries are not referred to by name, they are required to be identified by reference to a clear formula amounting to a complete class of objects, such as the 'children' or 'relatives' of the settlor: see *IRC v Broadway Cottages Trust* [1955] Ch 20.

CASE EXAMPLE

IRC v Broadway Cottages Trust [1955] Ch 20

A settlement was created whereby trustees held property upon trust to apply the income for the benefit of all or any of a class of objects including, *inter alia*, the settlor's wife, specific relations of the settlor and the Broadway Cottages Trust, a charitable institution. The trustees paid income to the Broadway Cottages Trust and claimed exemption from income tax in respect of this. It was not possible to ascertain all the objects who might fall within the class of objects but it was possible to determine with certainty whether a particular person was a member of the class. The question in issue was whether the trust was valid or void. The court decided that the trust was void for uncertainty of objects, and the claim for a repayment of income tax failed.

In a more recent case, *OT Computers Ltd v First National Tricity Finance Ltd and Others* [2003] EWHC 1010 (Ch), HL, the question arose as to whether the *Broadway Cottages* (1955) test was satisfied. One set of beneficiaries ('urgent suppliers') was defined in an inconclusive manner.

CASE EXAMPLE

OT Computers Ltd v First National Tricity Finance Ltd and Others [2003] EWHC 1010 (Ch), HL

The claimant (company) traded as 'Tiny Computers' and was a retailer of computer products and accessories. In 2000 it started to make substantial losses. On 23 January 2002 the company instructed its bank to open two separate trust accounts for the payment of customer deposits and of moneys due to 'urgent suppliers'. The company transferred sums from its current account into each of the trust accounts. The company created two schedules; one contained the names of customers and the other reflected some of the names of its suppliers, who were potential beneficiaries. The company was subsequently put into receivership. The bank later demanded repayment of a loan from the company. One of the defendants was an unpaid supplier whose name did not appear on the company's schedule.

The question in issue was whether valid trusts had been created for customers and 'urgent suppliers'.

Held:
1. It was clear that the directors of the company intended to create trusts in favour of its customers and 'urgent suppliers'.
2. There was a valid declaration of trust in favour of the customers.
3. However, it was not possible to identify each member of the class of 'urgent suppliers'. Accordingly, this trust failed and a resulting trust for the company's creditors was created.

JUDGMENT

'The question immediately arises what can be meant by urgent suppliers. Mr Mann submits with considerable justification that the term urgent is simply too vague to define any class of beneficiary. It is important to remember that the trust which is proposed is a fixed trust. Accordingly, it must be possible to identify each member of the class of beneficiaries.

In my judgment it is essential to distinguish clearly between the Suppliers Trust on the one hand and the Customers Trust on the other. So far as the Customers Trust is concerned, there is no such difficulty about identification of the beneficiaries as is presented by the Suppliers Trust. In my judgment, the requirement for certainty of beneficiaries for the latter is plainly not met. It follows that the Suppliers Trust was imperfectly constituted.'

Pumfrey J

Before 1971 the narrow test laid down in *Broadway Cottages* was applicable to all types of express private trusts – fixed and discretionary. Today, the 'list' test is applicable to fixed trusts only (see *OT Computers,* above). Discretionary trusts, since 1971, have been subject to a much broader test.

3.4.2 Discretionary trusts

A discretionary trust is an express trust whereby the trustees are required to exercise their discretion to select the beneficiaries from among a class of objects and/or to determine the quantum of interest that the beneficiaries may enjoy. In other words, the trustees decide who, when and how much funds a beneficiary may enjoy. For example, £50,000 capital is transferred to trustees A, B and C to be held on trust to distribute the income for a period of 15 years to such of the relatives and dependants of the settlor as the trustees may decide in their absolute discretion. The effect is that the trustees are obliged to distribute the income only to members of the class or classes of objects. Prior to the exercise of the trustees' discretion the objects do not have an interest in the income, but merely a hope or '*spes*' of acquiring an interest.

The modern test for certainty of objects in respect of discretionary trusts is known as the 'individual ascertainability' test, or the 'is or is not' test, or the 'any given postulant' test. This test was laid down by the House of Lords in *McPhail v Doulton* (*sub nom Re Baden*) [1971] AC 424.

CASE EXAMPLE

McPhail v Doulton [1971] AC 424

The settlor, Bertram Baden, transferred property to trustees to apply the net income, in their absolute discretion, to the officers, ex-officers, employees and ex-employees of a company or their relatives or dependants. The question in issue was whether the trust was valid as satisfying the test for certainty of objects. At this time the test for certainty of objects for all private trusts was the 'list' test as stated above. The trust objects were too broad to satisfy this narrow test. The House of Lords decided that the trust was valid and changed the test for certainty in respect of discretionary trusts. The new test for such trusts is whether the trustees may say with certainty that any given postulant is or is not a member of a class of objects, and there is no need to draw up a list of the objects.

JUDGMENT

'[I]t necessary to consider whether … the court should proceed on the basis that the relevant test is that laid down in the *Broadway Cottages* case [1955] Ch 20 or some other test. That decision gave the authority of the Court of Appeal to the distinction between cases where trustees are given a power of selection and those where they are bound by a trust for selection. In the former case the position, as decided by this House, is that the power is valid if it can be said with certainty whether any given individual is or is not a member of the class and does not fail simply because it is impossible to ascertain every member of the class (the *Gulbenkian* case [1970] AC 508). But in the latter case it is said to be necessary, for the trust to be valid, that the whole range of objects (I use the language of the Court of Appeal) should be ascertained or capable of ascertainment.

The conclusion which I would reach, implicit in the previous discussion, is that the wide distinction between the validity test for powers and that for trust powers, is unfortunate and wrong, that the rule recently fastened on the courts by the *Broadway Cottages* case [1955]

Ch 20 ought to be discarded, and that the test for the validity of trust powers ought to be similar to that accepted by this House in *Re Gulbenkian's Settlement Trusts* [1970] AC 508 for powers, namely that the trust is valid if it can be said with certainty that any given individual is or is not a member of the class.'

Lord Wilberforce

The effect of the 'any given postulant' test is that the class or classes of objects are required to be defined by reference to a clear formula without necessarily drawing up a list of all the persons who are within the class or classes. Thus, the test is very much a 'definitional' exercise in order to determine the validity of the trust. The members of the class or classes of objects alone may benefit from the trust and the trustees who wish to distribute the property need to know whether the person selected for benefit falls within the class or classes of objects.

3.4.3 Powers of appointment

A mere power of appointment or power collateral is an authority to dispose of property in favour of members of a class of objects. Unlike a discretionary trust, a power of appointment does not impose an obligation on the donee of the power, or appointor, to distribute the property, but merely empowers him to distribute the property in his discretion. The only similarity with a discretionary trust lies in the fact that the discretion concerns a class of objects, rather than beneficiaries under a fixed trust. The individual members of the class of objects do not enjoy an interest prior to the exercise of the discretion but acquire a hope of enjoying an interest in the property.

The donee of the power may be granted either a personal or a fiduciary power of appointment in favour of the objects. A personal, or non-fiduciary, power is a power of appointment granted to a donee of the power in his capacity as an individual, such as the testator's widow. There is no duty to consider exercising the authority, nor is there a duty to distribute the property in favour of the objects. In short, the donee of the power is given almost complete freedom in exercising his discretion. Indeed, the donee of the power may release the power even if this would mean that he will benefit from the release; for instance a testator may transfer property by will to his widow, W, for life with the remainder to such of his children A, B and C as W may appoint by will. In *Re Hay's Settlement Trust* [1982] 1 WLR 202, Megarry VC described the scope of the authority given to a non-fiduciary donee of the power thus: 'If he does exercise the power, he must, of course, confine himself to what is authorised, and not go beyond it … A person who is not in a fiduciary position is free to exercise the power in any way he wishes unhampered by any fiduciary duties.'

A fiduciary power, unlike a personal power, is a power of appointment granted to an individual *virtute officio*, such as a trustee. The fiduciary power is similar to a personal power in only one respect in that there is no obligation to distribute the property. But, unlike a personal power, the trustees are required to deal with the discretion in a responsible manner. Accordingly, a number of duties are imposed on the trustees, which were summarised by Megarry VC in *Re Hay's Settlement Trust* (1982):

virtute officio
By virtue of his office.

JUDGMENT

'The duties of a trustee which are specific to a mere power seem to be threefold. Apart from the obvious duty of obeying the trust instrument, and in particular of making no appointment that is not authorised by it, the trustee must, first, consider periodically whether or not he should exercise the power; second, consider the range of objects of the power; and third, consider the appropriateness of individual appointments. I do not assert that this list is exhaustive; but as the authorities stand it seems to me to include the essentials, so far as relevant to the case before me.'

Megarry VC

Because of the lack of any obligation to distribute the property, the appointor is entitled to release the power and the beneficiaries entitled on an express gift over in default of appointment or a resulting trust may become entitled to the property. This rule is subject to one exception, namely a 'fiduciary power in the full sense'. A fiduciary power which is exercisable in respect of a pension fund is treated as a unique power which cannot be released. If the trustees fail to distribute the property the court is required to exercise the discretion. This type of fiduciary power was created by Warner J in *Mettoy Pension Trustees Ltd v Evans* [1990] 1 WLR 1587.

CASE EXAMPLE

Mettoy Pension Trustees Ltd v Evans [1990] 1 WLR 1587

Mettoy Co Ltd launched an occupational pension scheme on 1 January 1968. The claimant, a wholly owned subsidiary of Mettoy, became the sole trustee of the scheme. In 1980, with the introduction of new legislation, new scheme rules were made. Rule 13(5) provided as follows:

Any surplus of the trust fund remaining after securing all the aforesaid liabilities in full may, at the absolute discretion of the employer be applied to secure further benefits within the limits stated in the rules, and any further balance thereafter remaining shall be properly apportioned amongst the principal employer and each participating employer.

Mettoy experienced financial difficulties and receivers were appointed in 1983. The company was wound up in 1984. As a consequence, the scheme was required to be liquidated. The claimant asked the court for directions in respect of a surplus of funds.

Warner J held that r 13(5) created a fiduciary power which could not be released or exercised by a receiver or liquidator. Accordingly, the court was required to decide what method of exercise would be appropriate.

JUDGMENT

'Category 2 comprises any power conferred on the trustees of the property or on any other person as a trustee of the power itself: per Romer LJ in *Re Mills* [1930] 1 Ch 654 at p. 669. I will, as Chitty J did in *Re Somes* [1896] 1 Ch 250 at p. 255, call a power in this category a fiduciary power in the full sense. Mr Walker suggested as an example of such powers vested in persons other than the trustees of the property the powers of the managers of a unit trust. A power in this category cannot be released; the donee of it owes a duty to the objects of the power to consider, as and when may be appropriate, whether and if so how he ought to exercise it; and he is to some extent subject to the control of the courts in relation to its exercise: see, for instance, *Re Abrahams' Will Trust* [1969] 1 Ch 463 at p. 474, per Cross J; *Re Manisty's Settlement* [1974] Ch 17 at p. 24 per Templeman J; and *Re Hay's Settlement Trusts* [1982] 1 WLR 202 at p. 210 per Sir Robert Megarry VC.'

Warner J

Certainty of objects (1)

Fixed trusts	The 'list' test (whether the trustees are capable of drawing up a comprehensive list of all the objects)	*IRC v Broadway Cottages* [1955]
Discretionary trusts (post-1971)	The 'any given postulant' test	*McPhail v Doulton* [1971]
Powers of appointment (personal, fiduciary, fiduciary powers in the full sense)	The 'any given postulant' test	*Re Gestetner* [1953] (see below); *Re Gulbenkian* [1970] (see below); *Mettoy Pension Trustees v Evans* [1990]

3.4.4 Analysis of the 'any given postulant' test

The test for certainty of objects in respect of powers has always been whether the donee of the power may say with certainty that any given individual (postulant) is or is not a member of a class of objects. This test was laid down by Harman J in *Re Gestetner's Settlement* [1953] 1 Ch 672:

JUDGMENT

'The trustees as I see it, have a duty to consider whether or not they are to distribute any and, if so, what part of the fund and if so, to whom they should distribute it ... if therefore, there be no duty to distribute, but only a duty to consider, there is no difficulty in ascertaining whether any given postulant is a member of the specified class. Of course, it can be easily postulated whether John Doe or Richard Roe is or is not eligible to receive the settlor's bounty. It is not necessary that the trustees worry their heads to survey the world from China to Peru when there are perfectly good objects of the class in England.'

Harman J

In essence, the 'any given postulant' test will be satisfied if the boundaries concerning the identification of the classes of objects are clearly drawn and it is unnecessary to name each member of the class of objects, for example if a power of distribution is given in favour of the relatives of the settlor. The gift will be valid if the expression 'relatives' is capable of a legal definition so that the trustees may be able to distinguish the objects from the non-objects. It is unnecessary for the trustees to identify each object.

Prior to the House of Lords' decision in *Re Gulbenkian's Settlement* [1970] AC 508, the courts adopted a diluted approach to the 'any given postulant' test, namely whether at least one person fell within the class of objects, even though it may not be possible to say whether others come within the class or fall outside it. The House of Lords in *Re Gulbenkian's Settlement* (1970) overruled this approach and reiterated the strict 'any given postulant' test.

CASE EXAMPLE

Re Gulbenkian's Settlement [1970] AC 508

A special power of appointment was granted to trustees to appoint in favour of Nubar Gulbenkian, 'any wife and his children or remoter issue ... and any person ... in whose house or apartment or in whose company or under whose care and control or by or with whom he may from time to time be employed or residing' subject to a gift over in default of appointment. The House of Lords overruled the diluted approach to the test adopted by the Court of Appeal and held that the gift created a valid power of appointment within the strict *Gestetner* (1953) test.

JUDGMENT

'My Lords ... Lord Denning MR [in the Court of Appeal] propounded a test in the case of powers collateral, namely that if you can say of one particular person meaning thereby, apparently, any one person only that he is clearly within the category the whole power is good though it may be difficult to say in other cases whether a person is or is not within the category, and he supported that view by reference to authority. Moreover, Lord Denning MR expressed the view that the different doctrine with regard to trust powers should be brought into line with the rule with regard to conditions precedent and powers collateral.

... with all respect to the contrary view, I cannot myself see how consistently with principle, it is possible to apply to the execution of a trust power the principles applicable to the permissible exercise by the donees, even if the trustees of mere powers; that would defeat the intention of donors completely.

But with respect to mere powers, while the court cannot compel the trustees to exercise their powers, yet those entitled to the fund in default must clearly be entitled to restrain the trustees from exercising it save among those within the power. So the trustees, or the court, must be able to say with certainty who is within and who is without the power. It is for this reason that I find myself unable to accept the broader position advanced by Lord Denning MR and Winn LJ, mentioned earlier, and agree with the proposition as enunciated in Re Gestetner [1953] 1 Ch 672 and the later cases.'

Lord Upjohn

The point was made earlier that, prior to the decision in *McPhail v Doulton* [1971], the test for certainty of objects in respect of private trusts was the narrower *Broadway Cottages* [1955] 'list' test. The justification for this narrow test in respect of discretionary trusts concerned the notion of facilitating the court in the exercise of the discretion if the trustees failed to exercise their discretion. A discretionary trust is obligatory and any omission to exercise the discretion is required to be remedied by the court. It was believed that equal division of the funds in favour of the members of the class of objects would discharge the jurisdiction of the courts, hence the need, at this time, to equate the test for certainty of objects in respect of fixed and discretionary trusts. It was subsequently recognised by the courts that equal division of the funds in favour of the class of objects was merely one option. Other options included the appointment of new trustees or representative members of the classes of objects to prepare a scheme of distribution. Accordingly, there was no longer a need to adopt the same test for certainty of objects in respect of both fixed and discretionary trusts. The modification in the test for certainty of objects for discretionary trusts was adopted in *McPhail v Doulton* [1971] (see above). Lord Wilberforce reasoned that it was striking how narrow and in a sense artificial is the distinction between discretionary trusts and powers. He recognised there were differences, but felt that such differences between discretionary trusts and powers of appointment did not justify the fundamentally different tests for certainty of objects. Accordingly, the test for certainty of objects in respect of powers was extended to discretionary trusts.

Certainty of objects (2)

Two separate tests	
Fixed trusts ('list' test)	*IRC v Broadway Cottages Ltd* [1955]
Discretionary trusts ('any given postulant' test)	*McPhail v Doulton (Re Baden)* [1971]; *R v District Auditors, ex p W Yorkshire MCC* [1986] (see below)

Three limitations

In *McPhail v Doulton* [1971] Lord Wilberforce laid down three limitations to the 'any given postulant' test – semantic uncertainty, evidential uncertainty and administrative unworkability.

Per Lord Wilberforce in *McPhail v Doulton* [1971] AC 424:

JUDGMENT

'I desire to emphasise the distinction clearly made and explained by Lord Upjohn (in *Re Gulbenkian* [1970] AC 508) between linguistic or semantic uncertainty which, if unresolved by the court, renders the gift void, and the difficulty of ascertaining the existence or whereabouts of members of the class, a matter with which the court can appropriately deal on an application for directions. There may be a third case where the meaning of the words used is clear but the definition of beneficiaries is so hopelessly wide as not to form anything like a class so that the trust is administratively unworkable or in Lord Eldon LC's words one that cannot be executed (*Morice v Bishop of Durham* [1805] 10 Ves 522). I hesitate to give examples for they may prejudice future cases, but perhaps all the residents of Greater London will serve. I do not think that a discretionary trust for relatives even of a living person falls within this category.'

Lord Wilberforce

Semantic uncertainty. This is also referred to as linguistic or conceptual uncertainty. This involves uncertainty or vagueness in defining the class or classes of individuals in respect of whom the trustees are entitled or required to exercise their discretion: for example, a distribution by the trustees, in their discretion, in favour of anyone in respect of whom the trustees may consider to have a moral claim on the settlor, or 'old friends of the settlor' (see *Brown v Gould* [1972] Ch 53). This restriction or proviso is applicable to both powers and trusts. If the gift suffers from such uncertainty, it is void.

Evidential uncertainty. This principle applies to both powers and trusts but does not invalidate either if the class is not conceptually uncertain. This limitation concerns uncertainty in ascertaining the existence or whereabouts of objects. In this event, the trustees may apply to the courts for directions, referred to as a Benjamin order, and the courts may make such order as is appropriate in the circumstances.

Administrative unworkability. This involves situations where the testator or settlor expressed the class of objects so broadly that it is difficult for the court to ascertain any sensible exercise of the discretion. In the event of the trustees failing to exercise their discretion, the court may find it difficult to exercise the discretion in a rational manner: for example, a duty to distribute a fund in favour of such of the residents of Greater London as the trustees may decide in their absolute discretion. This type of uncertainty does not affect the validity of powers of appointment but may invalidate discretionary trusts. In *R v District Auditors, ex p West Yorkshire Metropolitan County Council* [1986] 26 RVR 24, the Divisional Court decided that a settlement of £400,000 on trust for the purposes of benefiting 'any or all or some of the inhabitants' of West Yorkshire (population approximately 2.5 million) was void as a discretionary trust, because of administrative unworkability owing to the size of the class of objects. Accordingly, a resulting trust had arisen. In *Re Manisty's Settlement* [1974] Ch 17, a settlement gave a power of appointment to the trustees to use a fund for the benefit of the settlor's relations, excluding those inserted in an excepted class. Templeman J held that the clause was valid, but in an *obiter* pronouncement stated that problems could arise if the identification of the class of objects was so 'capricious' that the courts may be incapable of resolving the difficulty, such as a class of objects including 'residents of Greater London'. Templeman J's view of capriciousness, as laid down in *Manisty*, requires the court to determine whether the extent of the trustees' discretion 'negatives any sensible intention on the part of the settlor' (determined objectively) and authorises the court to invalidate the gift on this ground. In *Brown v Burdett* [1882] 21 Ch D 667, the court decided that a gift of a house on trust to block up its windows and doors for 20 years was void for the gift provided no obvious benefit to anyone. The effect of Templeman J's approach would require the court to exercise a value judgment as to the purpose of the gift. If the court decides that the gift is nonsensical or a waste of resources it may invalidate the gift on this ground. This is essentially different from the approach towards administrative unworkability, as laid down by Lord Wilberforce in *McPhail v Doulton*, with regard to the width of the class of objects.

3.4.5 Distinct approaches to the 'any given postulant' test

The House of Lords in *McPhail v Doulton* [1971], after reforming the test for certainty of objects in respect of discretionary trusts, remitted the case (*Re Baden (No 2)* [1972] 3 WLR 250) to the High Court to decide whether the new test was satisfied on the facts of the case. The High Court decided that the gift was valid and an appeal was made to the Court of Appeal which affirmed the decision of the High Court. However, each Lord Justice of Appeal adopted a different approach to the test.

The 'question of fact' approach

This approach is based on the assumption that the gift is conceptually certain (that is, linguistically certain). It then becomes a question of evidence or fact as to whether an individual proves to be within the class. Failure to discharge this burden of proof means that he is outside the class. In this respect it makes no difference whether the class is small or large. It is submitted that this approach concerns the practicalities of exercising the discretion as opposed to a test of validity of the gift. This mode of applying the test was laid down by Sachs LJ in *Re Baden (No 2)* [1972], thus:

JUDGMENT

'Once the class of persons to be benefited is conceptually certain it then becomes a question of fact to be determined on evidence whether any postulant has on enquiry been proved to be within it; if he is not so proved then he is not in it.'

Sachs LJ

The 'substantial number' approach

This approach advocated by Megaw LJ in *Re Baden (No 2)* [1972] is to the effect that in terms of validity of the gift, the test for certainty of objects is whether a substantial number of objects is within the class of objects, and it is immaterial whether it is not possible to say with certainty that other objects are within or outside the class of objects. What is a substantial number of objects is for the courts to decide. Accordingly, the 'any given postulant' test is diluted to a 'substantial number of objects' test.

JUDGMENT

'To my mind, the test is satisfied if, as regards at least a substantial number of objects, it can be said with certainty that they fall within the trust; even though, as regards a substantial number of other persons, if they ever for some fanciful reason fell to be considered, the answer would have to be, not they are outside the trusts, but it is not proven whether they are in or out. What is a substantial number may well be a question of common sense and of degree in relation to the particular trust.'

Megaw LJ

The advantage of this approach is that the gift remains valid despite the fact that the classes of objects are incapable of definition. To a limited extent, the broad objective of the settlor will be fulfilled. But this approach attracts a number of objections such as the striking similarity with the now-defunct 'one person' approach, which had been over-ruled by the House of Lords in *Re Gulbenkian* [1970]. The 'substantial number' test seems to be a variant of the outdated approach. In addition, this diluted approach to the 'any given postulant' test creates a class within a class. The class as laid down by the settlor is varied to include only a substantial number of objects.

The 'strict' approach

In *Re Baden (No 2)* [1972] Stamp LJ subscribed to the view that the 'any given postulant' test requires the trustees to say of any individual that he either is clearly within or outside the class of objects. Accordingly, everyone is classified as being within or outside the class of objects. This requires clarity and precision in defining the qualifying class or classes of objects without listing the objects who fall within the class or classes. If such precise definitions are not forthcoming, the gift is void.

JUDGMENT

'Validity or invalidity is to depend on whether you can say of any individual and the accent must be on that word any, for it is not simply the individual whose claim you are considering who is spoken of – that he is or is not a member of the class, for only thus can you make a survey of the range of objects or possible beneficiaries.'

Stamp LJ

In addition, in *Re Tuck's Settlement Trust* [1978] Ch 49, the courts developed two further approaches that have a bearing on the 'any given postulant' test. The approaches involve conditional gifts and the 'dictionary' meaning of objects.

Gifts subject to conditions precedent and subsequent

Property law draws a distinction between two types of conditional gifts: conditions precedent and subsequent. In the case of gifts subject to conditions precedent, the requirement of certainty is less strict, as opposed to gifts subject to conditions subsequent. A gift subject to a condition precedent is one where the donee does not acquire an interest in the property until he satisfies the relevant condition, for example a gift of £500 to A provided that he passes his year one LLB examinations. A does not obtain the property until he passes the relevant examination. The approach of the courts is that the claimant donee needs to establish, if he can, that he satisfies the condition or qualification whatever be the appropriate test. If the formula is such as to involve questions of degree or description the uncertainty of the description or event contemplated will not necessarily invalidate the gift in the case of a condition precedent. What is required is that the claimant be able to convince the court by reference to any reasonable test that he satisfies the description or condition.

CASE EXAMPLE

Re Allen [1953] Ch 810

A testator by his will left property to the eldest of his nephews 'who shall be member of the Church of England and an adherent to the doctrine of that Church'. The question in issue was whether the qualification was valid or void. The Court of Appeal held that the qualification created a condition precedent and, to satisfy it, it was not necessary that the condition be capable of exact definition. The claimant was required to prove that he, at least, satisfied the limitation.

Similarly, in *Re Tuck's Settlement Trust* [1978] Ch 49, the Court of Appeal in an *obiter* pronouncement decided that a gift subject to an ambiguous condition precedent may be valid by way of a benevolent construction of the condition. This approach has the added advantage of giving effect to the intention of the settlor.

CASE EXAMPLE

Re Tuck's Settlement Trust [1978] Ch 49

The settlor, Sir Adolf Tuck, the first baronet, executed a settlement in 1912 with the intention of ensuring that each baronet in succession would marry an 'approved wife'. The settlement provided for the payment of income to the baronet for the time being so long as he should be of the Jewish faith and married and living with an 'approved wife'. An 'approved wife' was identified in the settlement as 'a wife of Jewish blood by one or both of her parents and who has been brought up in and has never departed from and at the date of her marriage continues to worship according to the Jewish faith'. The settlor then added an arbitration clause to the effect that in the event of 'any dispute ... the decision of Chief Rabbi in London ... shall be conclusive'. Sir Adolf died in 1926. He was succeeded by his eldest son, Sir William Tuck, who married an approved wife. Sir William died in 1954 and was succeeded by his eldest son, Sir Bruce Tuck. Sir Bruce first married an approved wife but was divorced in 1964. In 1968, he married a lady who was not an approved wife. The question in issue was whether the limitation was valid or void.

The Court of Appeal held that the limitation was not void, on the grounds that the restriction created a condition precedent which was not wholly uncertain, and the Chief Rabbi clause constituted a valid delegation of decision-making power on the relevant questions of fact, in the event of a dispute. The clause was similar to an arbitration clause in contract law.

JUDGMENT

'There is another distinction to be found in the cases. It is between conditions precedent and conditions subsequent. Conceptual uncertainty may avoid a condition subsequent, but not a condition precedent. I fail to see the logic of this distinction. Treating the problem as one of construction of words, there is no sense in it. If the words are conceptually uncertain – so as to avoid a condition subsequent – they are just as conceptually uncertain in a condition precedent – and should avoid it also. But it is a distinction authorised by this court in *Re Allen* [1953] Ch 810 and acknowledged by Lord Wilberforce in *Blathwayt v Baron Cawley* [1976] AC 397.'

Lord Denning MR

The same principle was applied in *Re Barlow's Will Trust* [1979] 1 All ER 296.

CASE EXAMPLE

Re Barlow's Will Trust [1979] 1 All ER 296

A testatrix, by her will, directed her executor to sell her collection of valuable paintings subject to the provision that 'any member of my family and any friends of mine' be allowed to purchase any of the paintings at a catalogue price compiled in 1970 (which was substantially below their market value on the date of death). The executors applied to the court to ascertain whether the direction was void for uncertainty and for guidance as to the appropriate method for identifying members of the testatrix's family.

The court held that the direction as to 'friends' was valid, for the properties were to be distributed in specie and the quantum of the gifts did not vary with the class. Despite the expression 'friend' being conceptually uncertain, the transfer by will amounted to a series of individual gifts to persons who satisfied a specific description. The court also gave guidelines on the identification of friends, namely:

(a) The relationship with the testatrix was required to be of long standing.
(b) The relationship must have been social as opposed to business or professional.
(c) When circumstances permitted they met frequently. The expression 'family' meant a blood relationship with the testatrix.

JUDGMENT

'Counsel for the fourth defendant, who argued in favour of the validity of the gift, contended that the tests laid down in the *Gulbenkian* case, and *McPhail v Doulton* were not applicable in this case. The test, he says, is that laid down by the Court of Appeal in *Re Allen* [1953] Ch 810 as appropriate in cases where the validity of a condition precedent or description is in issue, namely that the gift is valid if it is possible to say of one or more persons that he or they undoubtedly qualify even though it may be difficult to say of others whether or not they qualify.

…if the nature of the gift was such that it was legally necessary to draw up a complete list of friends of the testatrix or to be able to say of any person that he is not a friend, the whole gift would probably fail even as to those who, by any conceivable test, were friends. But in the case of a gift of a kind which does not require one to establish all the members of the class (for example, a gift of £10 to each of my friends), it may be possible to say of some people that, on any test, they qualify.

The recent decision of the Court of Appeal in *Re Tuck's Settlement Trust* [1978] Ch 49 establishes that the test in *Re Allen* is still the appropriate test in considering such gifts, notwithstanding the *Gulbenkian* and *McPhail v Doulton* decisions.

Accordingly, in my judgment, the proper result in this case depends on whether the disposition in clause 5(a) is properly to be regarded as a series of individual gifts to persons answering the description friend (in which case it will be valid), or a gift which requires the whole class of friends to be established (in which case it will probably fail).

The effect of clause 5(a) is to confer on friends of the testatrix a series of options to purchase. Although it is obviously desirable as a practical matter that steps should be taken to inform those entitled to the options of their rights, it is common ground that there is no legal necessity to do so. Therefore, each person coming forward to exercise the option has to prove that he is a friend; it is not legally necessary, in my judgment, to discover who all the friends are. In order to decide whether an individual is entitled to purchase, all that is required is that the executors should be able to say of that individual whether he has proved that he is a friend. The word friend therefore is a description or qualification of the option holder.'

Browne-Wilkinson J

In *Re Barlow* [1979] the court drew a distinction between gifts where the quantum of the interest varies with the class of beneficiaries, such as 'a gift of £1,000 to my friends to be divided equally'. In such a case if the class of beneficiaries is conceptually uncertain, the gift will fail. Whereas, as the facts of the case suggest, the quantum of the interest to be enjoyed by the beneficiaries did not vary with the class but involved a finite number of paintings. In such a case there was no need to identify the beneficiaries with precision, but instead the claimant was required to convince the trustees that he satisfied the description. The position would be the same if the testator had bequeathed £10 (from a pool of say £1,000) for 'each of my friends'.

A condition subsequent, on the other hand, operates to divest or determine a gift that had previously vested in the donee. If the condition is void, the gift or beneficial interest will remain in the donee. The courts are generally hesitant about divesting gifts or estates that have already vested and will hold a condition subsequent void only if its terms are such that it cannot clearly be known in advance or from the beginning what circumstances will cause the divesting or determination of the gift or estate: for instance an endowment to B until he is called to the Bar. Here, B obtains a vested interest which is determined when he is called to the Bar. Query whether the condition would be satisfied if B was called to the New York Bar. In *Clayton v Ramsden* [1943] AC 320, HL the court decided that a condition subsequent attached to a gift was so vague that the restriction was void.

CASE EXAMPLE

Clayton v Ramsden [1943] AC 320, HL

A testator bequeathed a legacy and a share of the residue of his estate upon trust for his daughter, Edna, for life with remainder on trust for her issue equally. The gift was subject to forfeiture (expressly inserted by the testator), if she should marry a person 'not of Jewish parentage and of the Jewish faith'. Edna married the appellant, Harold Clayton, who was an English Wesleyan who was admittedly not of Jewish parentage. The question in issue was whether the forfeiture clause was valid or void.

The House of Lords held that, on construction, the clause created a composite set of conditions subsequent which were void for uncertainty. The testator had given no indication of the degree of attachment or adherence to the faith which he required on the part of his daughter's husband. The forfeiture conditions were too vague to enable it to be said with certainty that a particular individual complied with the requirement.

The 'dictionary' approach

The 'dictionary' approach is based on the notion that the settlor may adopt a definition of the class or classes of objects specifically in a clause in the trust instrument. The effect is that there is likely to be little doubt as to the category of objects intended to benefit. For example, the settlor may give the trustees a discretion to distribute in favour of such of my 'old friends' as they may decide. He may then define the expression 'old friends' in any way he considers appropriate. In this way the class of objects which would otherwise have failed may be rescued by the settlor provided that the description offered by the settlor is clear enough for the courts to supervise. A variation on this theme entitles the settlor to appoint a third person as sole arbiter of the definition of the class of objects and perhaps all issues incidental to the exercise or non-exercise of the discretion. Difficulties have arisen if the arbitrator appointed by the settlor or testator happens to be the trustee. It must be observed that a settlor or testator cannot deprive a beneficiary of his right of access to the courts, at any rate on questions of law. Such clauses are void on the grounds of repugnancy to the beneficiary's rights and also public policy as an attempt to oust the jurisdiction of the courts, except in cases where the arbitrator has acted in bad faith.

CASE EXAMPLE

Re Raven [1915] 1 Ch 673

A provision in the testator's will giving the trustees the final say as to the identity of the beneficiary in the event of doubt was void on grounds of repugnancy and public policy because the province of the trustees' power involved a question of law.

On the other hand, in *Re Coxen* [1948] 2 All ER 492, the opinion of the trustees was treated as one of fact and the clause was treated as valid. However, in *Dundee General Hospital Board of Management v Walker* [1952] 1 All ER 896, the House of Lords appeared to suggest that a clause in a will making the trustees' decision final on questions of law was valid. Moreover, in *Re Tuck* [1978] (see above), Lord Denning MR decided that the arbitration clause requiring the Chief Rabbi to determine any dispute as to whether the beneficiary satisfied the descriptions 'of Jewish faith' and married to an 'approved wife' was valid on analogy with arbitration clauses in the law of contract:

JUDGMENT

'I see no reason why a testator or settlor should not provide that any dispute or doubt should be resolved by his executors or trustees, or even a third person. To prove this, I will first state the law in regard to contracts. Here the general principle is that whenever persons agree together to refer a matter to a third person for decision, and further agree that his decision is to be final and binding upon them, then, so long as he arrives at his decision honestly and in good faith, the two parties are bound by it. They cannot reopen it for mistakes or errors on his part, either in fact or law, or for any reason other than fraud or collusion.'

Lord Denning MR

It ought to be observed that in *Re Tuck* [1978], the testator gave a partial definition of the description of the restrictive conditions, namely an 'approved wife'. It is unclear whether this was a significant feature of the case and what effect the absence of such definition or description may have had on the outcome of the case. In any event the court is entitled to admit extraneous evidence of the intention of the settlor.

It would appear that the application of the test for certainty of objects is far from clear although the modern approach attempts, to some extent, to give effect to the intention of the settlor or testator.

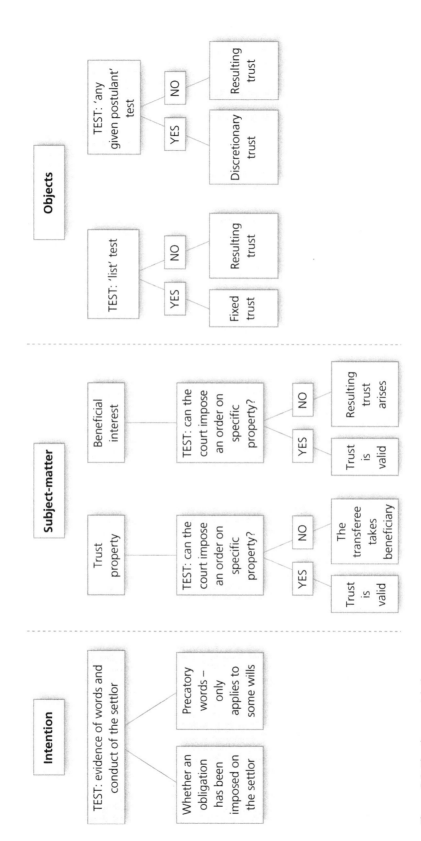

Figure 3.2 The three certainties

KEY FACTS

Judicial approaches to the 'any given postulant' test

Strict approach	Question of fact	Substantial number	Conditional gifts	Dictionary
Lord Upjohn in *Re Gulbenkian*; Stamp LJ in *Re Baden (2)*	Sachs LJ in *Re Baden (2)*	Megaw LJ in *Re Baden (2)*	Lord Denning in *Re Tuck*	Lord Denning in *Re Tuck* Browne-Wilkinson J in *Re Barlow*

ACTIVITY

Applying the law

1. The Bargain Basement Co Ltd runs a mail-order business. Finding itself in financial difficulties, it takes advice and as a result begins to pay all money as it is received from customers into a separate account (The Bargain Basement No 2 Deposit Account). Mrs
Prudence orders £500 worth of goods and sends a deposit of £100 to the company which
is paid into the No 2 account. Before the goods are delivered, Bargain Basement Co goes
into liquidation. Is Mrs Prudence entitled to the return of her deposit and/or the interest it
has earned in the account?

2. T, a testator, leaves a will containing the following gifts:

    (a) 'My three freehold houses to X and Y, my trustees, to hold two of the properties on
    trust for my daughter, to be selected by her, and the other on trust for my son.' The
    daughter survived the testator but died before making a selection.

    (b) £5,000 to my wife, Harriet, knowing that she will employ a reasonable amount for the
    benefit of my aged housekeeper, Camilla.'

Comment on the validity of these gifts.

SUMMARY

- An express trust is required to satisfy the three certainties test, namely, certainty of
intention, subject-matter and objects.

- Certainty of intention involves the manifestation of a clear intention on the part of
the settlor to impose a trust obligation in respect of specific property for the benefit
of a beneficiary or a group of beneficiaries. In cases of dispute the court will consider
all the circumstances to determine whether a trust was intended.

- The test for certainty of subject-matter will be satisfied if the trust property and the
beneficial interest are sufficiently clear so that the court may attach an order in respect
of the property and the beneficial interest.

- A trust assumes the existence of an obligation on the trustees to distribute the rel-
evant property to the appropriate beneficiaries.
  - The trust may be 'fixed' or 'discretionary'.
  - A 'fixed' trust is one where the trustees do not have a discretion as to how, when
    and to whom to distribute the property. A 'discretionary' trust, in contrast, is one

where the trustees are obliged to distribute the property in favour of a member or members of a class of objects.

- The test for certainty of objects varies with the type of trust created.
- In respect of fixed trusts, the test is whether the objects are identified or are identifiable by reference to a clear formula. The test for certainty of objects in respect of discretionary trusts is the 'any given postulant' formula.
- A power of appointment is an authority to distribute property in favour of members of a class of objects.
- The test for certainty of objects concerning a power of appointment is similar to the test for certainty of objects in respect of discretionary trusts, namely the 'any given postulant' test.
- There are three types of powers – personal, fiduciary and fiduciary powers in the full sense.

- Fundamental to the creation of an express trust is the three certainties test – certainty of intention, subject-matter (i.e. property and beneficial interest) and objects. If the test for certainty of intention and trust property is not satisfied the intended express trust fails and the transferee takes the property beneficially. But if the test for certainty of beneficial interest or objects is not satisfied then, despite the failure of the intended express trust, a resulting trust for the transferor arises.

- Linguistic (or conceptual) uncertainty, evidential uncertainty and administrative unworkability were limitations to the 'any given postulant' test laid down by Lord Wilberforce in *McPhail v Doulton (sub nom Re Baden)*.

  - Linguistic uncertainty arises when the class or classes of objects cannot be legally defined. The gift, as a trust or a power of appointment, fails and a resulting trust may arise.
  - Evidential uncertainty arises when the whereabouts of an object (or objects) is unknown. The gift does not fail but the trustees may apply to the court for directions.
  - Administrative unworkability is a concept that invalidates trusts but not powers of appointment. This is the case where the class of objects is so huge as to defy any sensible exercise of the discretion, see *R v District Auditors ex p W. Yorkshire CC* [1986].

- There have been five judicial approaches to the 'any given postulant' test for certainty of objects. These are:

  - Sachs LJ's question of fact approach advocated in *Re Baden (No 2)*;
  - Megaw LJ's substantial number of objects approach in *Re Baden (No 2)*;
  - Stamp LJ's strict or traditional approach in *Re Baden (No 2)*;
  - the dictionary approach adopted by Lord Denning MR in *Re Tuck*;
  - the liberal approach in construing conditions in respect of gifts subject to conditions precedent, see *Re Tuck* and *Re Barlow*.

SAMPLE ESSAY QUESTION

Consider the following essay question:

To what extent is it necessary to be able to distinguish between a discretionary trust and a power, particularly when considering the need for certainty of objects under a discretionary trust or power of appointment?

Answer plan

Define a discretionary trust and contrast this with a power of appointment.

Classify and distinguish the various types of powers of appointment, e.g. general, special, hybrid, personal, fiduciary and fiduciary powers in the full sense, see *Mettoy Pension Trustees v Evans*.

Outline the complexities with the list test, e.g. identify the difficulties in satisfying the test for certainty of objects with regard to discretionary trusts before 1971, see *IRC v Broadway Cottages* and consider the extent to which *McPhail v Doulton* addressed the problem.

Identify the main duties imposed on trustees in respect of discretionary trusts and compare these with the duties imposed on fiduciaries in respect of powers of appointment, see *Re Hay's WT*.

Outline the extent to which the 'any given postulant' test differs with regard to discretionary trusts and powers of appointment, e.g. administrative unworkability, see *R v District Auditors ex p West Yorkshire County Council*.

Outline the main approaches to the 'any given postulant' test, see *Re Baden (No 2)*, *Re Tuck* and *Re Barlow*.

Identify the main duties imposed on trustees in respect of discretionary trusts and compare these with the duties imposed on fiduciaries in respect of powers of appointment, see *Re Hay's WT*.

CONCLUSION

Further reading

Battersby, G, 'A reconsideration of property and title in the Sale of Goods Act' (2001) JBL 1.

Emery, C, 'The most hallowed principle: certainty of beneficiaries in trusts and powers of appointment' (1982) 98 LQR 551.

Gardner, S, 'Fiduciary powers in Toytown' (1991) 107 LQR 214.

Goodhart, W and Jones, G, 'The infiltration of equitable doctrine into English commercial law' (1980) 43 MLR 489.

Grbich, Y, 'Baden: awakening the conceptually moribund trust' (1974) 37 MLR 643.

Hayton, D, 'Certainty of objects: what is heresy?' (1984) Conv 307.

Hayton, D, 'Uncertainty of subject-matter of trusts' (1994) 110 LQR 335.

Jones, A, 'Creating a trust over an unascertained part of a homogeneous whole' (1993) Conv 466.

McKay, L, 'Re Baden and the third class of uncertainty' (1974) 38 Conv 269.

Martin, J, 'Certainty of objects: what is heresy?' (1984) Conv 304.

Martin, J, 'Validity of trust of unidentified shares' (1996) Conv 223.

Worthington, S, 'Sorting out ownership interests in a bulk: gifts, sales and trusts' (1999) JBL.w

4

Constitution of an express trust

AIMS AND OBJECTIVES

By the end of this chapter you should be able to:

- identify the essential tests in *Milroy v Lord* for the constitution of an express trust
- appreciate that the law in this chapter involves gifts and the creation of trusts
- distinguish between a perfect and an imperfect trust and understand the consequences of constitution
- grasp the principle in *Fletcher v Fletcher*
- understand and apply the maxims, 'Equity will not assist a volunteer' and 'Equity will not perfect an imperfect trust'

4.1 Introduction

A settlor who wishes to create an express trust is required to adopt either of the following methods:

(a) a self-declaration of trust; or

(b) a transfer of property to the trustees, subject to a direction to hold upon trust for the beneficiaries.

This is known as the rule in *Milroy v Lord* [1862] 31 LJ Ch 798, HC. The effect of the perfect creation of a trust is that the beneficiary, who may be a volunteer, may enforce the trust. However, if the trust is incompletely constituted, the transaction involving an intended trust operates as an agreement to create a trust. Subject to the Contracts (Rights of Third Parties) Act 1999, this agreement may be enforced by a person who has provided consideration.

Alternatively, a donor may make a perfect gift to the donee by transferring the legal and equitable interests directly to the desired donee. This involves a gift, as opposed to an intended trust. But a difficulty arises if the intended donor fails to transfer the legal title to the intended donee. The latter may be tempted to argue that the intended donor retains the legal title as an express trustee for the disappointed intended donee, and thus the imperfect transfer, by way of intended gift, constitutes the creation of an express trust. Such an argument, without any additional evidence, has been consistently rejected by the courts.

There are two maxims that summarise the approach of the courts: 'Equity will not assist a volunteer' and 'Equity will not perfect an imperfect gift'.

4.2 The rule in *Milroy v Lord* [1862]

The principle laid down by Turner LJ in *Milroy v Lord* [1862] identifies the various modes of creating an express trust. Generally, there are two modes of constituting an express trust and the onus is on the settlor to execute one (or in exceptional circumstances both) of these modes for carrying out his intention.

CASE EXAMPLE

Milroy v Lord [1862] 31 LJ Ch 798, HC

The settlor executed a deed purporting to transfer shares to Mr Lord on trust for Mr Milroy. The shares were only capable of being transferred by registration in the name of the transferee in the company's books. The settlor failed to complete the transfer, although Mr Lord held a power of attorney as agent for the settlor. On the settlor's death, Lord gave the share certificates to the settlor's executors and the question arose whether the shares were held upon trust for the claimant.

Held: There was no gift of the shares to the objects nor was there a transfer of the shares to the intended trustee. The settlor having failed to transfer the shares to the trustee, the court will not infer that he is a trustee for the claimant.

JUDGMENT

'[I]n order to render a voluntary settlement valid and effectual, *the settlor must have done everything which, according to the nature of the property comprised in the settlement, was necessary to be done* in order to transfer the property and render the settlement binding upon him. He may, of course, do this … if *he transfers the property to a trustee* for the purposes of the settlement, or *declares that he himself holds it in trust* for those purposes … but, in order to render the settlement binding, *one or other of these modes* must … be resorted to, for there is no equity in this court to perfect an imperfect gift. The cases go further to this extent, that if the settlement is intended to be effectuated by one of the modes to which I have referred, the court will not give effect to it by applying another of those modes. If it is intended to take effect by transfer, the court will not hold the intended transfer to operate as a declaration of trust, for then every imperfect instrument would be made effectual by being converted into a perfect trust.' [Emphasis added]

Turner LJ

On analysis, the court decided the following:

- There was no gift of the shares to Mr Milroy.
- The settlor did not have an intention to create a trust.
- In order to create a trust or to transfer the property (legal title), the settlor or transferor is required to do everything expected of him in order to vest the property in the name of the intended transferee.

- The requirements necessary to be complied with in order to transfer the property vary with the type of property involved.
- The settlor may transfer the property to the trustee subject to a valid declaration of trust.
- The settlor may declare himself a trustee.
- If the trust is intended to be created by one of these modes the court will not automatically adopt another mode of creating the trust.

These are the primary rules concerning the constitution of a trust.

4.2.1 Transfer and declaration mode

A settlor may wish to create a trust by transferring the property to another person (or persons) as trustee(s), subject to a valid declaration of trust. In this context the settlor must comply with two requirements, namely a transfer of the relevant property or interest to the trustees complemented with a declaration of the terms of the trust (see the 'three certainties' test above). If the settlor intends to create a trust by this method and declares the terms of the trust, but fails to transfer the property to the intended trustees, it is clear that no express trust is created. The ineffective transaction will amount to a conditional declaration of trust but without the condition (the transfer) being satisfied. For instance, S, a settlor, nominates T1 and T2 to hold 50,000 BT plc shares upon trust for A for life with remainder to B absolutely (the declaration of trust). In addition, S is required to transfer the property in the shares to T1 and T2. The declaration of trust on its own without the transfer is of no effect.

The formal requirements, if any, concerning the transfer of the legal title to property vary with the nature of the property involved. There are broadly two types of properties that exist – realty and personalty. In order to transfer the legal title to registered land the settlor is required to execute the prescribed transfer form and register the transfer in the names of the trustees at the appropriate Land Registry. The transfer of tangible moveable property requires the settlor to deliver the property to the trustees, accompanied by the appropriate intention to transfer; the transfer of the legal title to shares in a private company involves the execution of the appropriate transfer form and registration of the transfer in the company's share register. The various requirements for the transfer of the most common forms of properties can be summarised as follows:

- Legal estates and interests in land must be transferred by deed under s 52(1) of the Law of Property Act 1925.
- Equitable interests in either land or personalty must be disposed of in writing: see s 53(1)(c) of the Law of Property Act 1925.
- Choses in action (intangible personal property such as debts or intellectual property) may be assigned in law in writing in accordance with s 136 of the Law of Property Act 1925. As an alternative, an assignment may be executed in equity.
- Tangible moveable property (chattels) may be transferred by delivery accompanied by clear and unequivocal intention that the transferor intends to transfer property to the recipient, or by deed of gift. In *Re Cole* [1964] Ch 175, a husband showed his wife the furniture in a house and said that it was all hers. The question in issue was whether a transfer of the legal title had taken place. **Held:** no transfer had taken place, as the words spoken were too loose to reflect an intention to donate.
- Shares in a private company will be transferred when the transfer procedure laid down in the Companies Act 2006 has been complied with.

4.2.2 Transfer of shares in a private company

The owner of the legal title to shares in a private company is the person whose details are registered in the company's books. Thus, a new transferee acquires the legal title when he is registered with the company. The Companies Act 2006 outlines the procedure that is required to be followed in order to transfer shares in a private company. The transferor is required to execute a stock transfer form, issued under the Stock Transfer Act 1963, and send this, along with the share certificates, to the registered office of the company for registration. The company usually has an absolute discretion to decide whether to register the new applicant without giving reasons for its decision. In addition, the company deals only with the registered legal owner of the shares.

tutor tip

'It is instructive to analyse the judgment of Turner LJ in *Milroy v Lord* [1862] 31 LJ Ch 798.'

In accordance with the *Milroy v Lord* [1862] principle, if the transferor has done everything required of him and the only things remaining to be done are to be performed by a third party, the transfer will be effective in equity. This is known as the 'last act' principle. The donor has completed the last act that may be achieved by him. This will be sufficient to transfer the equitable interest in the property to the donee. In these circumstances the donor who retains the legal title to the property holds it as a trustee for the donee. The type of trust is constructive and is thus created by operation of law. In short, at the point where the transfer of the legal title is imperfect at law for want of registration, the court of equity will nonetheless perfect the imperfect gift by declaring a constructive trust in favour of the transferee provided that the transferor has done everything required of him. The effect is that dividends declared at any time after the transferor has completed his duties in respect of the transfer, and before the new owner is registered, will be held on trust for the new transferee. Likewise, votes attaching to the shares are required to be cast as trustee for the new owner. Whether the transferor has done everything required of him to transfer the shares is essentially a question of fact.

CASE EXAMPLE

Re Rose [1952] Ch 499, CA

Mr Rose executed two transfers of shares on 30 March 1943. He died more than five years after executing the transfers, but less than five years (the claw-back period at this time) after the transfers were registered in the company's books, on 30 June 1943. For estate duty purposes it was necessary to know when the donee had received the shares.

Held: The shares were transferred on 30 March 1943. At this time the transferor had done everything in his power to transfer the shares, and all that remained was for the directors of the company to consent to the transfer and register the new owner.

JUDGMENT

'[I]f a document is apt and proper to transfer the property – is, in truth, the appropriate way in which the property must be transferred – then it does not seem to me to follow from the statement of Turner LJ [in *Milroy v Lord* [1862]] that, as a result, either during some limited period or otherwise, a trust may not arise, for the purpose of giving effect to the transfer. Whatever might be the position during the period between the execution of this document and the registration of the shares, the transfers were, on 30th June 1943, registered. After registration, the title of Mrs Rose was beyond doubt complete in every respect, and if Mr Rose had received a dividend between execution and registration and Mrs Rose had claimed to have that dividend handed to her, what would Mr Rose's answer have been? It could no longer be that the purported gift was imperfect; it had been made perfect. I am not suggesting that the perfection was retroactive.'

Lord Evershed MR

The *Re Rose* principle is to the effect that once the legal owner of shares delivers to his donee the share certificates and a properly executed share transfer form relating to those shares, he will have done all within his own power to transfer the shares to the donee. The donee will only become their *legal* owner upon being later registered as a member, a matter commonly outside the donor's control; and until such registration, the donor will remain the legal owner. But once the donor has done all in his power to transfer the shares, he will be regarded as holding the legal title upon trust (constructive trust) for the donee, who will thereupon become their beneficial owner.

A similar conclusion was reached in *Mascall v Mascall* [1984] 49 P&CR 119, in respect of the execution of a transfer concerning registered land. Browne-Wilkinson LJ explained the justification of this principle.

JUDGMENT

'The basic principle underlying all the cases is that equity will not come to the aid of a volunteer. Therefore, *if a donee needs to get an order from a court of equity in order to complete his title, he will not get it. If, on the other hand, the donee has under his control everything necessary to constitute his title completely without any further assistance from the donor, the donee needs no assistance from equity and the gift is complete.* It is on that principle, which is laid down in *Re Rose*, that in equity it is held that a gift is complete as soon as the settlor or donor has done everything that the donor has to do, that is to say, as soon as the donee has within his control all those things necessary to enable him, the donee, to complete his title.' [Emphasis added]

Browne-Wilkinson LJ

In contrast to the *Re Rose* [1952] principle, if the transferor has not done everything required of him, the transfer will not be effective in equity. This may be illustrated by *Re Fry* [1946].

CASE EXAMPLE

Re Fry [1946] Ch 312, HC

The donor of shares was domiciled in the USA, and needed the consent of the Treasury (under the Emergency Regulations (Defence (Finance) Regulations 1939)) to transfer shares in a British company. He sent the necessary forms to the company for registration of the new owner, save for Treasury approval. This he had applied for, but had not been granted at the time of his death. The question in issue was whether a transfer in equity had been made at the time of the donor's death.

Held: The shares had not passed to the donee at the time of the donor's death, for he had not done everything required of him: he had not obtained Treasury consent.

JUDGMENT

'Had they, however, arrived at the position which entitled them, as against that company, to be put on the register of members? Had everything been done which was necessary to put the transferees into the position of the transferor? If these questions could be answered affirmatively, the transferees would have had more than an inchoate title; they would have had it in their own hands to require registration of the transfers. Having regard, however, to the Defence (Finance) Regulations 1939, it is impossible, in my judgment, to answer the questions other than in the negative. The requisite consent of the Treasury to the transactions had not been obtained, and, in the absence of it, the company was prohibited from registering the transfers. In my opinion, accordingly, it is not possible to hold that, at the date of the testator's death, the transferees had either acquired a legal title to the shares in question, or the right, as against all other persons (including Liverpool Borax Ltd) to be clothed with such legal title.'

Romer J

The court decided that the donor had not done everything required of him to secure registration of the shares, despite his death after his application for Treasury approval was made. The logic of the *Re Fry* [1946] decision may be understood on the ground that the donor might have been required to furnish more information to the Treasury before consent was obtained. In any event, the company was not entitled legitimately to consider registering the new owner until Treasury consent was obtained. The court came to a similar decision on the facts of *Milroy v Lord* [1862] (see above).

In the case of *Pennington v Waine* [2002] All ER (D) 24, CA the Court of Appeal decided that where the donor had manifested an immediate and irrevocable intention to donate shares to another, signed a transfer form to this effect and instructed her agent to complete the transfer of the legal title to shares in a private company, the transfer of the equitable title to shares will be complete at this point and the donor will not be permitted to deny the interest acquired by the donee.

CASE EXAMPLE

Pennington v Waine [2002] All ER (D) 24, CA

The donor, Ada, was the owner of a number of shares in a company and was also one of its directors. Under instructions from Ada, one of the company's auditors, Mr Pennington, prepared a transfer form for 400 shares which was duly executed by Ada and returned to Mr Pennington (rather than being sent to the company's registered office to secure the registration of the new owner). The transfer was intended for Ada's nephew, Harold, to secure his appointment as a director as a 51 per cent holder of shares. Ada informed Harold of her intention to transfer the shares into his name. The form was placed on the company's file. Mr Pennington assured Harold that he was appointed a director and nothing more was required to be done by him. No further action was taken in relation to the transfer. Ada died and by her will left her estate to others. The question in issue was whether a transfer in equity was made by Ada before her death in favour of Harold, or whether the shares passed to her heirs under her will.

Held: A transfer to Harold in equity was made during Ada's lifetime. Ada intended an immediate and irrevocable transfer in favour of Harold. The court considered that the test here was whether Ada had done everything required of her to secure the transfer, as distinct from whether she had done everything short of registration. The main ground for the decision was the fact that it would have been unconscionable for Ada and her heirs to deny the interest acquired by Harold. As an alternative ground the court decided that Ada and Mr Pennington were agents for Harold to submit the form to the company. The court also decided that the interim trust that arose, pending registration, was a constructive trust.

JUDGMENT

'There was a clear finding that Ada intended to make an immediate gift. It follows that it would also have been unconscionable for Ada to recall the gift. It follows that it would also have been unconscionable for her personal representatives to refuse to hand over the share transfer to Harold after her death. If Ada had procured the registration of Harold as the owner of the shares in the books of the company, the legal title to the shares would have passed to him. In these circumstances I can see no reason for holding that there was no valid equitable assignment to him without delivery of the transfer or shares to him. *In those circumstances, in my judgment, delivery of the share transfer before her death was unnecessary so far as perfection of the gift was concerned.* I would also decide this appeal in favour of the respondent on this further basis … the words used by Mr Pennington should be construed as meaning that Ada and, through her, Mr Pennington became agents for Harold for the purpose of submitting the share transfer to the Company.' [Emphasis added]

Arden LJ

It should be noted that the *Pennington v Waine* [2002] principle is distinct from the traditional *Re Rose* [1952] principle. In the former case, the court proceeded on the basis of 'unconscionability' on the part of the donor to prevent her from denying that no transfer took place. This is a fairly broad concept and involves a question of law for the court to decide in its discretion, as opposed to the narrow *Re Rose* [1952] question of fact, as to whether the donor had done everything required of him to effect the transfer. Unconscionability is a relatively vague concept and may be akin to an estoppel. This involves a promise made by the donor, relied on by the donee to his detriment. In these circumstances the court will prevent the donor from denying the promise and reclaiming the property as his own. Equally, the court will prevent the personal representatives of the donor from the transfer in equity. But what factors would prompt a court to rule that it would be unconscionable for a donor to change his mind about the gift? Although the underlying circumstances will vary with the facts of each case, in *Pennington*, Arden LJ identified a number of factors that made it unconscionable for Ada to deny the gift.

JUDGMENT

'A donor will not be permitted to change his or her mind if it would be unconscionable, in the eyes of equity, vis a vis the donee to do so, what is the position here? There can be no comprehensive list of factors which makes it unconscionable for the donor to change his or her mind: it must depend on the court's evaluation of all relevant considerations. What then are the relevant factors here? Ada made the gift of her own free will: there is no finding that she was not competent to do this. She not only told Harold about the gift and signed a form of transfer which she delivered to Mr Pennington for him to secure registration: her agent also told Harold that he need take no action. In addition Harold agreed to become a director of the Company without limit of time, which he could not do without the shares being transferred to him. If Ada had changed her mind … the court could properly have concluded that it was too late for her to do this as by that date Harold signed the form, the last of the events identified above to occur.'

Arden LJ

The difficulty with this analysis is that Arden LJ's attempt to restate the rationale of equity's involvement to perfect an imperfect gift is based not only on the flexible concept of unconscionability but concentrates on the *intention* of the donor rather than her *conduct*. It is questionable whether a donor's clear intention to transfer property to a donee without complying with the formal requirements ought to be sufficient to pass the equitable interest. Arden LJ decided that in certain circumstances the delivery of the share transfer form to the company could be dispensed with. This would be the case where it would be unconscionable for the donor to renege on his promise. In any event Arden LJ decided that the auditors could have been treated as the agent of the donee

(Harold) for the purpose of submitting the form to the company. On this basis delivery to Harold's agent may be treated as a delivery of the form to Harold (the donee). In addition the status of the third party who decides on the registration of the legal title to the shares is required to be taken into account. If the third party has a formal role to play in deciding on the registration of the legal interest, then the constructive trust will be terminated on the date of the complete transfer of the legal title. But if the third party plays a more active role and has the power to refuse to register the transfer of the legal title the question arises as to whether the constructive trust will continue or be terminated. In *Pennington v Waine* the court in an *obiter* pronouncement decided that the constructive trust will continue to operate despite the refusal to register the new owner. On this basis it could be argued that the court has created another exception to the rule that 'Equity will not perfect an imperfect gift.'

In summary, Briggs J in *Curtis v Pulbrook* (2011) (see later) analysed Arden LJ's judgment in *Pennington* and concluded that she identified three routes whereby a court of equity may come to the aid of a donee and assist him in the acquisition of an *equitable* interest in shares (or other property). These are, first, where the donor has done everything required of him to dispose of the interest to such an extent that the donee does not require the assistance of the donor to complete the transfer (*Re Rose* (1952)). Second, where the donee may establish detrimental reliance on a representation of the donor to such a degree that it would be unconscionable on the part of the donor to deny the transfer. This involves the constructive trust (the ratio in *Pennington v Waine* (2002)). Third, where the court is entitled to adopt a benevolent construction of the circumstances and may conclude that a purported gift of the property may be interpreted as a valid self-declaration of trust, as decided in *Choithram v Pagarani* (2001) (see later).

In respect of the *Re Rose* method of effecting a transfer of property to the donee, the cases were all concerned with the transfer of the *legal title*. An additional complication arises where the donor has only the *equitable title* to the shares (or other property) and wishes to dispose of the relevant property in favour of the donee. In these circumstances the equitable owner is not in a position to deal with the legal title and accordingly the *Re Rose* principle will not be applicable. If he wishes to dispose of the equitable interest he is required to comply with s 53(1)(c) of the Law of Property Act 1925 and 'dispose' of his interest in writing by way of an assignment, declaration of trust or direction to the trustees in favour of the donee (see Chapter 5). In *Zeital v Kaye* (2010), the Court of Appeal decided that a purported transfer of an equitable interest in shares was ineffective where the intended donor delivered a 'blank' share transfer form (undated and without inclusion of the transferee's name) to the intended donee unaccompanied by the share certificate. The delivery of the incomplete transfer form manifested merely a donative intent but was insufficient to transfer the equitable interest in the share.

CASE EXAMPLE

Zeital v Kaye [2010] EWCA Civ 159, CA

The appellants (Zeitals) are the widow and daughters of Raymond Zeital (Raymond). The Zeitals are the administrators and sole beneficiaries of the estate of Raymond who died intestate. Prior to his death Raymond had incorporated Dalmar Properties Ltd (Dalmar), a property investment company with two issued shares vested in the names of the formation agents, Mr and Mrs Kumar, but the equitable interest was retained solely by Raymond. The Kumars signed an undated blank stock transfer form in relation to each share and left blank the transferee boxes. These forms were delivered to Raymond. Raymond formed a relationship with his partner, Stefka, who testified that Raymond had transferred beneficial ownership in the two shares to her prior to his death. The trial judge found that Raymond had completed the stock transfer form in relation to one share, naming Stefka as the transferee, which transferred the beneficial interest to her. He also found that although Raymond had given Stefka the transfer form relating to the second share without adding her name as transferee and dating the form, the beneficial interest in this second share was transferred to Stefka on the ground that Raymond had done everything required of him to transfer the beneficial interest to Stefka. The appellants appealed to the Court of Appeal.

Held: allowing the appeal in respect of the second share. The judge had misdirected himself in deciding that, consistent with Raymond's donative intention, the delivery of the 'blank' transfer form to Stefka satisfied the *Re Rose* principle and was sufficient to transfer Raymond's equitable interest in the second share. The only way that he could have transferred his interest to Stefka was by declaring himself a trustee for her or by assigning his interest in writing to her or to a trustee for her in compliance with s 53(1)(c) of the Law of Property Act 1925, and he had not done so. Accordingly, Raymond retained the beneficial ownership in the second share and after his death his personal representatives became entitled to the share.

JUDGMENT

'...so far as I am aware the only way in which he could do so was by (i) declaring himself a trustee for Stefka of his equitable interest, thus creating a sub-trust; (ii) assigning his interest to her by "writing signed by [him], or by his agent thereunto lawfully authorised in writing..." so as to comply with section 53(1)(c) of the Law of Property Act 1925; or (iii) making a like written assignment of his interest to a trustee for Stefka.

He did none of these things. He did not purport to declare a trust (which, had he wanted to, he could have done orally). Nor did he effect a written assignment either to Stefka or to a trustee for her. I would not regard the stock transfer form signed by Mrs Kumar as constituting such an assignment. That was a document she had signed for the purpose of enabling a future transfer of the legal title to the second share. It did not purport to assign Raymond's equitable interest in the share.'

Rimer LJ

In any event where an intended donor fails to comply with any of the formal requirements necessary to transfer the legal title to shares in a company and, without authority, merely issues new share certificates to the intended donee, the legal title to the shares will not be acquired by the intended donee. Equally, there will be no grounds on which a court of equity may assist the intended donee even by adopting the most benevolent construction of the circumstances. Thus the bare intention of the donor to transfer the property to the donee will be of no effect in equity. The court so held in *Curtis v Pulbrook*.

CASE EXAMPLE

Curtis v Pulbrook [2011] EWHC 167, High Court

The defendant, Mr Pulbrook, until his retirement was the director and substantial shareholder of Farnham Royal Nurseries Ltd (FRN) and trustee of three family settlements. Owing to discontent among the beneficiaries of Mr Pulbrook's handling of the affairs of the family settlement resulting in litigation, Mr Pulbrook in breach of trust procured the withdrawal of trust funds which was used for his own purposes. In addition, Mr Pulbrook, without authority, issued 314 new share certificates in FRN in favour of his wife (300 shares) and daughter (14 shares) and secured their registration on the share register of the company. One of the issues before the court was whether there had been valid gifts of the shares in favour of Mr Pulbrook's wife and daughter.

Held: The gifts were invalid at law and equity. Since Mr Pulbrook was not authorised by FRN to issue share certificates to his wife or daughter or to record them as shareholders in FRN's register, the legal title to the shares had not been effectively transferred. None of the three routes identified by Arden LJ in *Pennington* in order to gain equitable assistance to effect the transfer of the equitable interest in shares was satisfied in the present case. Mr Pulbrook failed to comply with the proper means to transfer the shares to his wife and daughter by delivering an executed share transfer form and relevant share certificates to them. Moreover, there was no detrimental reliance by Mr Pulbrook's wife and daughter sufficient to justify a constructive trust. In addition, no amount of benevolent construction of the circumstances was capable of rendering an ineffective gift into a valid declaration of trust on Mr Pulbrook's part. Accordingly, the intended gifts of the shares were void.

JUDGMENT

'In my judgment Henry Pulbrook was not authorised by FRN either to issue share certificates to his wife and daughter, or to record them as shareholders in the company's Register. There is no evidence of a delegation of that function by the board to him as managing director. It follows that legal title to the shares did not pass either to Alice [daughter] or Anucha Pulbrook [wife].

All that his wife and daughter received were documents purporting to be new share certificates in their names which Mr Pulbrook had created without FRN's authority. The result was that, without his assistance in making available the duly completed stock transfer forms, neither his wife nor his daughter could perfect the intended gifts without further assistance from Mr Pulbrook.'

Briggs J

It may be noted that Briggs J in *Curtis* expressed his opinion that, as a result of the litigation in *Pennington v Waine*, the boundaries as to when equity will and will not perfect an imperfect gift of shares remain unclear. The uncertainty may stem from the notion that in *Pennington* the Court of Appeal focused more on the intentions of the donor rather than his actions, as in *Re Rose*, in delivering the relevant share transfer form to the donee.

In addition to the transfer of the relevant property to the trustees, the settlor is required to declare the terms of a trust. In other words, the requirement here is that in order to constitute the trust the settlor must transfer the property to the trustees and, either before or after the transfer, declare the terms of the trust. A transfer of the property to the trustees unaccompanied by a declaration of trust by definition will not create an express trust. Such a transfer may create a resulting trust for the settlor. For example S, an intended settlor, purports to create an express trust of 10,000 BT plc shares by transferring the legal title to the shares to T1 and T2 as trustees, but failed to declare the terms of the trust. The intended beneficiary of the shares was his son, B, absolutely, but S failed to indicate the terms of the trust. Since T1 and T2 acquire the shares as trustees without a declaration of the terms of the trust, the intended express trust fails and a resulting trust for S will arise. Likewise, a declaration of trust of 10,000 BT plc shares in favour of B absolutely with the intention that T1 and T2 will acquire and hold the shares as trustees for B will fail if T1 and T2 did not acquire the relevant shares.

A declaration of trust involves a present, irrevocable intention to create a trust. This involves the 'three certainties' test: certainty of intention to create a trust, certainty of subject-matter and certainty of objects (see Chapter 3).

4.3 Self-declaration of trust

An alternative mode of creating an express trust is by way of a self-declaration. A settlor declares that he presently holds specific property on trust, indicating the interest, for a beneficiary. The settlor is the creator of the trust and the trustee. He simply retains the property as trustee for the relevant beneficiaries. Clear evidence is needed to convert the status of the original owner of the property to that of a trustee. This form of creating an express trust is as effective as the transfer and declaration mode. In the absence of specific statutory provisions to the contrary, no special form is required as long as the intention of the settlor is sufficiently clear to constitute himself a trustee, for 'Equity looks at the intent rather than the form'. Thus, the declaration of trust may be in writing or may be evidenced by conduct or may take the form of a verbal statement or a combination of each of these types of evidence: see *Paul v Constance* [1977] 1 WLR 527 (above); contrast *Jones v Lock* [1865] LR 1 Ch App 25 (above). What is required from the settlor is a firm commitment on his part to undertake the duties of trusteeship in respect of the relevant property for the benefit of the specified beneficiaries (see the 'three certainties' test, above). In this respect there is no obligation to inform the beneficiaries that a trust has been created in their favour. The effect of this mode of creation is to alter the status of the settlor from a beneficial owner to that of a trustee. For instance, S, the absolute owner of 50,000 shares in BP plc, declares that henceforth he holds the entire portfolio of shares upon trust for B, his son, absolutely. In these circumstances an express trust is created. S retains the legal title to the shares, but B acquires the entire equitable interest in the shares.

4.4 No self-declaration following imperfect transfer

The court will not automatically imply the self-declaration mode of creating a trust if there has been an imperfect gift or transfer of the property to the intended recipient. A gift is created when the donor transfers both legal and equitable interests to the donee. As distinct from a trust, the gift does not involve the separation of the legal and equitable interests. If, therefore, the donor intended to create a gift but fails to transfer the relevant property to the donee, the court will not assist the intended donee to order that the intended gift be perfected. Equally the intention to give is fundamentally different from an intention to create or declare a trust. Accordingly, an imperfect transfer will not be construed as a valid declaration of trust. This rule applies to imperfect gifts of property (see *Jones v Lock* [1865] above) as well as imperfect transfers to trustees, for 'Equity will not perfect imperfect gifts'. The reason for the rule is that, despite the transferor's intention to benefit another by means of a transfer (whether on trust or not), the transferor ought not to be treated as a trustee if this does not accord with his intention: see *Richards v Delbridge* [1874] LR 18 Eq 11.

CASE EXAMPLE

Richards v Delbridge [1874] LR 18 Eq 11

A grandfather attempted to assign a lease of business premises to his grandson, R, by endorsing the lease and signing a memorandum: 'This deed and all thereto I give to R from this time henceforth with all stock in trade.' He gave the lease to R's mother to hold on his behalf. On the death of the grandfather it was ascertained that his will made no reference to the business premises. The question in issue was whether the lease was acquired by the grandson, R, during the grandfather's lifetime, or was transferred to the residuary beneficiaries under the grandfather's will.

Held: There was an imperfect gift *inter vivos*, as the assignment, not being under seal, was ineffectual to transfer the lease. Further, no trust had been created, as the grandfather did not declare himself a trustee of the lease for the grandson. The court will not construe an ineffectual transfer as a valid declaration of trust.

JUDGMENT

'[F]or a man to make himself a trustee there must be an expression of intention to become a trustee, whereas words of present gift show an intention to give over property to another, and not retain it in the donor's own hands for any purpose, fiduciary or otherwise.'

Jessel MR

The principle has been summarised in a passage from F W Maitland's *Equity: A Course of Lectures* (1909):

QUOTATION

'I have a son called Thomas. I write a letter to him saying "I give you my Blackacre estate, my leasehold house in the High Street, the sum of £1,000 Consols standing in my name, the wine in my cellar." This is ineffectual – I have given nothing – a letter will not convey freehold or leasehold land, it will not transfer Government stock, it will not pass the ownership in goods. Even if, instead of writing a letter, I had executed a deed of covenant – saying not I do convey Blackacre, I do assign the leasehold house and the wine, but I covenant to convey and assign – even this would not have been a perfect gift. It would be an imperfect gift, and being an imperfect gift the court will not regard it as a declaration of trust. I have made quite clear that I do not intend to make myself a trustee, I meant to give. The two intentions are very different – the giver means to get rid of his rights, the man who is intending to make himself a trustee intends to retain his rights but to come under an onerous obligation. The latter intention is far rarer than the former. Men often mean to give things to their kinfolk, they do not often mean to constitute themselves trustees. An imperfect gift is no declaration of trust. This is well illustrated by the case of *Richards v Delbridge*.'

4.5 The settlor may expressly adopt both modes of creation

The settlor may expressly manifest an intention to transfer the relevant property to third party trustees (transfer and declaration mode) and, prior to completing the transfer, to declare himself a trustee for the beneficiaries (self-declaration mode). In this event, the trust will be perfect, provided that the third party trustee acquires the property during the settlor's lifetime. In other words, the self-declaration of trust is regarded as conditional on an effective transfer of the property to the third party trustee. This condition may only be satisfied during the lifetime of the settlor. The court has also decided that it is immaterial how the third party trustee acquires the property: see *Re Ralli's Will Trust* [1964] Ch 288, HC.

CASE EXAMPLE

Re Ralli's Will Trust [1964] Ch 288, HC

In 1899, a testator died, leaving the residue of his estate upon trust for his wife for life with remainder to his two children, Helen and Irene, absolutely. In 1924, Helen covenanted in her marriage settlement and under clause 7 to settle all her 'existing and after acquired property' upon trusts which failed, and ultimately on trust for the children of Irene. The settlement declared that all the property comprised within the terms of the covenant will, under clause 8, 'become subject in equity to the settlement hereby covenanted to be made'. Irene's husband was appointed one of the trustees of this marriage settlement. In 1946, Irene's husband was also appointed a trustee of the 1899 settlement. In 1956, Helen died and, in 1961, Helen and Irene's mother died. The question in issue was whether Helen's property from the 1899 settlement was held upon the trusts of Helen's marriage settlement, or subject to Helen's personal estate.

Held: By virtue of the declaration in Helen's settlement in 1924, Helen and, since her death, her personal representative (Irene's husband), held her share of the 1899 settlement subject to the trusts of Helen's settlement. This was the position even though the vesting of the property in Irene's husband came to him in his other capacity as trustee of the 1899 settlement. The same conclusion could be reached by applying the rule in *Strong v Bird* [1874] LR 18 Eq 315 (see below).

JUDGMENT

'In my judgment the circumstance that the plaintiff holds the fund because he was appointed a trustee of the will is irrelevant. He is at law the owner of the fund and the means by which he became so have no effect on the quality of his legal ownership. The question is: for whom, if any one, does he hold the fund in equity? In other words, who can successfully assert an equity against him disentitling him to stand on his legal right? It seems to me to be indisputable that Helen, if she were alive, could not do so, for she has solemnly covenanted under seal to assign the fund to the plaintiff and the defendants can stand in no better position.'

Buckley J

In this case it is worth noting the fortuitous event in 1946 when Irene's husband was appointed a trustee of the 1899 settlement. This meant that the third party trustee acquired the trust property, and since it was during Helen's lifetime, the trust became perfect.

4.6 Multiple trustees including the settlor

In the case of *Choithram International v Pagarani* [2001] 1 WLR 1, PC, the Privy Council decided that where the settlor appoints multiple trustees, including himself, and declares a present, unconditional and irrevocable intention to create a trust for specific persons, a failure to transfer the property to the nominated trustees is not fatal, for his (settlor's) retention of the property will be treated as a trustee. Trusteeship for these purposes is treated as a joint office so that the acquisition of the property by one trustee is equivalent to its acquisition by all the trustees. For example, S nominates himself and T1 and T2 as trustees of property and specifies the terms. If S manifests an irrevocable and unconditional intention to create a trust, his failure to transfer the property to T1 and T2 is not fatal because S retains the property as a trustee. His retention of the property as one of the trustees is equivalent to all the trustees acquiring a right to acquire the property. Thus the trust is perfect.

CASE EXAMPLE

T Choithram International SA v Pagarani [2001] 1 WLR 1, PC

The settlor, Mr Choithram Pagarani (CP), intended to set up a foundation to serve as an umbrella organisation for four charitable bodies which he had already established. CP and the other trustees executed the foundation trust deed, despite CP's rapidly failing health. The trust deed was made between CP, as settlor, and CP and seven other named individuals as trustees.

CP transferred £1,000 to the trustees as the initial subject-matter of the trust, with further property to be placed under the control of the trustees. The deed also set out the terms of the trust. Immediately after signing the documents CP said words to the effect that 'I have given all my wealth to the trust.' He then told his accountant, who was present at the time of signing, to transfer all his balances with the companies and his shares to the foundation trust. At a subsequent meeting of the trustees, CP reported that the foundation had been established and all his wealth had been given to the trust. The relevant documents were prepared, but CP refused to sign. Evidence was adduced that CP had an aversion to signing such documents and had been advised that it was not necessary to do so. However, CP repeatedly declared that he had done his 'bit': he had given all his wealth to the foundation and there was nothing more for him to do. In the end, CP had failed to execute the forms which were necessary to carry out the formal transfer of the further assets before his death.

The claimants, CP's first wife and her children, commenced proceedings in the British Virgin Islands for a part of CP's estate. The claim was made on the ground that the intended gifts to the foundation were ineffective because CP had failed to transfer the relevant properties, namely CP's shares and deposit balances in the companies, to the foundation. The trial judge found that CP intended to make immediate gifts of the relevant properties, but his intention was not irrevocable. In addition, the judge found that, despite CP's intention to make immediate gifts to the foundation, he had failed to vest the properties in the hands of all the trustees of the foundation. This decision was affirmed by the Caribbean Court of Appeal. The defendants (executors of CP) appealed to the Privy Council.

Held: Effective transfers *inter vivos* had been made to the trustees subject to the trusts, on the following grounds:

1. CP's intention was to make a present, immediate, unconditional and irrevocable gift to the foundation. This was manifested by the execution of the foundation deed, verbally declaring his intention upon signing the document and instructing his accountant to transfer all his balances with the companies and his shares to the foundation trust.

2. Although the words used by CP were appropriate to an outright gift, 'I give to X', on a benevolent construction, those words were intended to create a gift to the trustees of the foundation on trust for the foundation. This was partly attributed to the fact that the foundation had no legal existence apart from the trust declared by the foundation trust deed. Accordingly, the *Milroy v Lord* [1862] principle for the creation of an express trust had been satisfied.

3. Since the property was vested in one of the trustees, namely CP himself, the express trust was constituted. Accordingly, there was a duty to transfer the property to all of the trustees of the foundation trust. In principle there was no distinction between a case where a settlor declared himself to be a sole trustee for a beneficiary and the case where he declared himself to be one of the trustees for that beneficiary. In both cases the trust was perfect and the beneficiary acquired an equitable proprietary interest in the property.

4. The subject-matter of the trust comprised all of CP's wealth in the British Virgin Islands, namely CP's deposit balances and shares in the four companies. This was in accordance with CP's statements and conduct.

JUDGMENT

'The foundation has no legal existence apart from the trust declared by the foundation trust deed. Therefore *the words, "I give to the foundation" can only mean "I give to the trustees of the foundation trust deed to be held by them on the trusts of the foundation trust deed".* Although the words are apparently words of outright gift they are essentially words of gift on trust ...

What is the position here where the trust property is vested in one of the body of trustees, viz TCP? In their Lordships' view there should be no question. TCP has, in the most solemn circumstances, declared that he is giving (and later that he has given) property to a trust which he himself has established and of which he has appointed himself to be a trustee. All of this occurs at one composite transaction taking place on 17 February. There can in principle be no distinction between the case where the donor declares himself to be sole trustee for a donee or a purpose and the case where he declares himself to be one of the trustees for that donee or purpose. In both cases his conscience is affected and it would be unconscionable and contrary to the principles of equity to allow such a donor to resile from his gift.'

Lord Browne-Wilkinson

It ought to be emphasised that a clear distinction between an intention to transfer property to another and an intention to declare oneself a trustee for another had been recognised by the courts over the centuries. The latter intention involved the exclusive jurisdiction of equity before the Judicature Acts 1873/75 and has the effect of converting the transferor from an absolute owner of property to one burdened with the office of trusteeship on behalf of another. As a corollary to this distinction the courts have established that an ineffective transfer of property will not be construed as automatically creating a trust with the intended donor being treated as a trustee for the intended donee, see *Richards v Delbridge* (1874). However, Lord Browne-Wilkinson in *Pagarani* advocated a benevolent construction of the circumstances of that case in order to convert an intention to transfer property to an intention to declare a trust. This conclusion was reached because the donee (foundation) had no legal personality and therefore the capacity to receive the property directly, but may only enjoy the property as beneficiaries under a trust. Accordingly, the intended gift was to the trustees of the foundation and as the settlor was one of the nominated trustees the legal title had already vested in one of the trustees and therefore the trust was perfect. This is a bold construction of the facts and admittedly a novel decision.

4.7 No trust of future property

It is not possible to create an express trust of property that does not exist or property that may or may not be acquired by the settlor simply because there is no property that is capable of being subject to an order of the court. Such property is referred to by a variety of names but the principle remains the same. Examples of terms used are 'future' or 'after-acquired' property or an 'expectancy' or a '*spes*' (or hope of acquiring property). Thus, it is not possible to create a trust of lottery winnings in the future.

CASE EXAMPLE

Re Ellenborough [1903] 1 Ch 697, HC

An intended beneficiary under a will voluntarily covenanted to transfer her inheritance to another upon trusts as declared. Before the testator had died the intended beneficiary (covenantor) changed her mind. The covenantee brought an action claiming that the covenantor was under a duty to transfer the relevant property.

Held: No trust of the covenant had been created, because the property was not owned by the covenantor at the time of the covenant. In addition, the covenantee could not bring an action to enforce the agreement for he had not provided consideration.

JUDGMENT

'The question is whether a volunteer can enforce a contract made by deed to dispose of an expectancy. It cannot be and is not disputed that if the deed had been for value the trustees could have enforced it … Future property, possibilities, and expectancies are all assignable in equity for value: *Tailby v Official Receiver* [1888] 13 App Cas 523. But when the assurance is not for value, a court of equity will not assist a volunteer.'

Buckley J

It should be noted that although a trust cannot be created in respect of future property, a contract is capable of being created in respect of such property.

4.8 Trusts of choses in action

A chose in action is a right to intangible personal property such as a right to dividends attaching to shares, intellectual property and the creditor's right to have a loan repaid by the debtor. A trust is capable of being created in respect of any type of existing property, including a chose in action. The chose may be assigned to the trustees in accordance with the intention of the settlor.

CASE EXAMPLE

Don King Productions Inc v Warren [1999] 2 All ER 218, CA

K and W (two well-known boxing promoters) entered into partnership agreements in which W purported to assign the benefit of promotion and management agreements to the partnership. However, several of the contracts contained express prohibitions against assignment. The question in issue was whether a trust of the benefit of the agreements (choses in action) was created.

Held: The benefit of promotion and management agreements was capable of being the subject-matter of a trust in accordance with the intention of the parties.

JUDGMENT

'[I]n principle, I can see no objection to a party to contracts involving skill and confidence or containing non-assignment provisions from becoming trustee of the benefit of being the contracting party as well as the benefit of the rights conferred. I can see no reason why the law should limit the parties' freedom of contract to creating trusts of the fruits of such contracts received by the assignor or to creating an accounting relationship between the parties in respect of the fruits.'

Lightman J

Similarly, the court may construe the subject-matter of a covenant as creating a chose in action, namely the benefit of the covenant. This intangible property right may be transferred to the trustees on trust for the relevant beneficiaries. What is needed to assign such a right or chose is a clear intention on the part of the assignor to dispose of the chose to the transferee. Accordingly, A may execute a covenant with B to transfer £10,000 to B upon trust for C. If the subject-matter of the trust is treated as the cash, namely £10,000, it becomes a question of fact as to whether the sum has been transferred to B. If we assume that A did not transfer the sum to B it is still possible that the trust may be treated as perfect. The court may construe the trust property as the 'benefit of the covenant' or the 'right to the cash', i.e. a chose in action. This chose may be transferred by operation of law in accordance with the intention of the parties. Therefore, in a sense the trust is perfect in that B has the trust property even though A did not transfer £10,000 in cash to B. B having acquired the right to the cash is entitled to claim the cash from A. This difficult principle is known as the rule in *Fletcher v Fletcher* [1844] 4 Hare 67.

CASE EXAMPLE

Fletcher v Fletcher [1844] 4 Hare 67

The settlor, Ellis Fletcher, covenanted (for himself, his heirs, executors and administrators) with trustees (their heirs, executors, administrators and assigns) to the effect that if either or both of his natural issue (illegitimate children), Jacob and John, survived him and attained the age of 21, Ellis's executors would pay to the covenantees (or heirs etc.) £60,000 within 12 months of his death, to be held on trust for the relevant natural issue. In the circumstances, Jacob alone survived the settlor and attained the age of 21. The surviving trustees (covenantees) declined to act in respect of the trust of the covenant, unless the court ordered otherwise. Jacob brought an action directly against the executors, claiming that he become solely entitled in equity to the property.

Held: A trust of the covenant was created in favour of Jacob, the claimant, who was entitled to enforce it as a beneficiary.

JUDGMENT

'[W]here the relation of trustee and *cestui que trust* is constituted, as where property is transferred from the author of the trust into the name of a trustee, so that he has lost all power of disposition over it, and the transaction is complete as regards him, the trustee, having accepted the trust, cannot say he holds it, except for the purposes of the trust, if it is not already perfect. This covenant, however, is already perfect. The covenantor is liable at law, and the court is not called upon to do any act to perfect it.'

Wigram VC

On analysis, in *Fletcher v Fletcher* [1844], the court decided that:

(a) On construction of the terms of the covenant, the intended trust property was the 'benefit of the covenant' or a right to the cash sum, i.e. a chose in action, and not the cash sum of £60,000.

(b) Since the sum had existed in Ellis Fletcher's estate at the time of the covenant, this chose in action was transferred to the covenantees, trustees, on the date of the creation of the covenant.

(c) The covenantees therefore became trustees, subject to the achievement of the stipulated conditions, surviving the settlor and attaining the age of 21.

(d) Since Jacob satisfied these conditions he became a beneficiary unconditionally and was therefore entitled to protect his interest.

It is questionable who had the 'benefit of the covenant'. Was it Ellis Fletcher or the covenantees, trustees? Did Ellis Fletcher have the benefit of the covenant? He was the covenantor. He (or his estate) was under a duty to transfer the sum to the covenantees, trustees. He (or his estate) therefore had the burden of transferring the sum to the covenantees, trustees. It is true that Ellis Fletcher had the cash in his estate at the time of the covenant, but this did not derive from the covenant. This sum existed independently of the covenant.

Alternatively, it could be argued that the covenantees, trustees had the 'benefit of the covenant' as covenantees. They were nominated as the recipients of the sum of £60,000, albeit in a representative capacity. In other words, between the two parties to a voluntary covenant – the covenantor and the covenantees – only the covenantees may be treated as acquiring the 'benefit of the covenant'. If this is the true position, then only the covenantees may create a trust of this chose or benefit: i.e. only the covenantees may become the settlors of the chose in action. On the facts of *Fletcher v Fletcher* [1844], this was clearly not the intention of the covenantees, trustees.

A separate analysis of the *Fletcher v Fletcher* [1844] rule which is consistent with the *Milroy v Lord* [1862] principle is to identify the trust property as the cash sum of £60,000, and not the 'benefit of the covenant' or the chose in action. The issue then is whether the covenantees, trustees, acquired, or were entitled to acquire, the cash sum and, if so, when. It could be argued that the terms of the covenant were unique and imposed a positive duty, not on Ellis Fletcher, but his personal representatives to transfer £60,000 to the covenantees as trustees for Jacob. Under the covenant Ellis Fletcher merely had a duty to retain the cash sum in his estate at the time of his death. If he had done this at the time of his death then Ellis Fletcher would have done everything in his power, barring his death, to perfect the trust under the *Re Rose* (1952) principle. He was merely required to die (an issue outside his control), leaving the cash sum in his estate. This he had done. At this point a positive duty would be imposed on Ellis Fletcher's personal representatives to transfer the property to the covenantees, trustees.

4.8.1 *Fletcher* restricted to debts enforceable at law

Owing to the difficulties posed by the *Fletcher v Fletcher* [1844] principle and the opportunities for intended beneficiaries under an imperfect trust, it is not surprising that the principle has been restricted by the courts to one type of chose in action, namely debts enforceable at law. A debt enforceable at law involves a legal obligation to pay a quantified amount of money. It does not concern an obligation to transfer shares or paintings. In addition the obligation involves existing, and not future, property. This restriction was imposed in an *obiter* pronouncement in *Re Cook's Settlement Trust* [1965] Ch 902, HC.

CASE EXAMPLE

Re Cook's Settlement Trust [1965] Ch 902, HC

A number of valuable paintings were gifted by his father to Sir Francis Cook, who covenanted with trustees to the effect that if any of the paintings was sold during his lifetime, the net proceeds of sale were required to be settled on trust for stated beneficiaries. Sir Francis gave one of the paintings to his wife who wanted to sell it. The question in issue was whether the covenant may be enforced as an agreement to create a trust or as a trust.

Held:
(a) The parties to the agreement were volunteers who could not enforce the covenant.
(b) The intended trust was imperfect for the subject-matter concerned future property, i.e. the proceeds of sale in the future. For this reason the *Fletcher* [1844] principle was not applicable. In any event the *Fletcher* principle was applicable to debts enforceable at law.

JUDGMENT

'The covenant with which I am concerned did not, in my opinion, create a debt enforceable at law, that is to say, a property right, which, although to bear fruit only in the future and on a contingency, was capable of being made the subject of an immediate trust, as was held to be the case in *Fletcher v Fletcher* … this covenant on its true construction is, in my opinion, an executory contract to settle a particular fund or particular funds of money which at the date of the covenant did not exist and which might never come into existence. It is analogous to a covenant to settle an expectation or to settle after acquired property.'

Buckley J

KEY FACTS

Constitution of express trusts

Rule in *Milroy v Lord* [1862] (a) self-declaration of trusts (b) transfer to trustees and declaration	Settlor is the trustee ('three certainties' test) *Re Kayford* [1975]; *Paul v Constance* [1977] Vesting of property in the hands of the trustees accompanied by a valid declaration of trust
Transfer of the legal title – nature of the property	Land – registration under the LRA 1925 Chattels – deed of gift or delivery *Re Cole* [1964] Shares in a private company – execution of a stock transfer form and registration in the company's share register choses in action – assignment at law under s 136 LPA 1925
Transfer of the equitable interest Whether the transferor has done everything required of him to effect the transfer	Writing under s 53(1)(c) of the LPA 1925 *Re Rose* [1952]; *Mascall v Mascall* [1984]; *Pennington v Waine* [2002]; *Zeital v Kaye* [2010]; *Curtis v Pulbrook* [2011]
Where there are multiple trustees nominated by the settlor (including the settlor) and the latter has manifested an irrevocable intention to create a trust, the trust is valid even though the other named trustees have not acquired the property	*Choithram v Pagarani* [2001]
An imperfect transfer to the trustees will not automatically be treated as a valid declaration of trust	*Richards v Delbridge* [1874]; *Jones v Lock* [1865]
A settlor may expressly declare himself a trustee pending a transfer to the third party trustees. If the transfer takes place during the lifetime of the settlor the trust will be perfect	*Re Ralli* [1964]
The benefit of a covenant (chose in action of a debt) may be the subject-matter of a trust	*Fletcher v Fletcher* [1844]

4.9 Consequences of a perfect trust

sui juris
A person who is under no disability, such as mental illness, affecting his power to own or transfer property.

If a trust is perfect or completely constituted, the beneficiary acquires an equitable interest and before 1873/75 was entitled to enlist the assistance of the Court of Chancery to protect this interest.

- If the beneficiary is **sui juris** and absolutely entitled to the property he may terminate the trust by directing the trustees to transfer the legal title to him (see Chapter 2).

- The beneficiary is given a right *in rem* (in the thing), i.e. a right that is inherent in the trust property and is entitled to trace his property against anyone except the *bona fide* transferee of the legal estate for value without notice (see Chapter 2). This right to trace is exempt from the limitation period.

- The result is that it is immaterial whether the beneficiary is a volunteer or not (see below). He is given a right or a *locus standi* to enforce the trust, simply by proving that he is an authorised equitable owner of the property. He may bring the claim in his own name and is entitled to join the trustee as a co-defendant. In the normal course of events the trustees bring the claim on behalf of the trust. If, however, the intended trust is imperfect the transaction operates as an agreement to create a trust and, subject to the Contracts (Rights of Third Parties) Act 1999, may only be enforced by parties who have provided consideration: see *Jeffreys v Jeffreys* [1841] Cr & Ph 138.

CASE EXAMPLE

Jeffreys v Jeffreys [1841] Cr & Ph 138

A father voluntarily conveyed a freehold property to trustees upon trust for the benefit, *inter alia*, of his daughters. He also covenanted with the trustees to surrender copyhold property to the trustees upon the same trusts. He died without surrendering the copyhold property and by his will devised both the freehold and copyhold properties to his widow. After the father's death, the daughters sought to have the trusts of the deed carried into effect and to compel the widow to surrender her interest under the will to the freehold and copyhold properties.

Held: As far as the freehold property was concerned, the trust was completely constituted and the daughters, as beneficiaries, succeeded in the claim. In respect of the copyhold property the trust was imperfect and because the daughters were volunteers, they were not entitled to compel the widow to part with the legal interest, which she acquired under her deceased husband's will.

4.10 Incompletely constituted trusts

If the intended trust is imperfect by reference to the *Milroy v Lord* [1862] rule, the transaction operates as an agreement to create a trust. This involves the law of contract, as opposed to the law of trust. An agreement to create a trust may only be enforced in equity by non-volunteers. The rule is that 'Equity will not assist a volunteer' and 'Equity will not perfect an imperfect gift'. To obtain an equitable remedy, the claimant is required to establish that he has furnished consideration. For instance, if A agrees to transfer specific property to B upon trust for C, a volunteer, and A has failed to transfer the relevant property to B, the trust is imperfect. The question in issue is whether C may enforce the agreement to create a trust. The general rule is that if C is a volunteer he cannot enforce the agreement in equity. It is of great importance to classify C's status (volunteer or non-volunteer) if the trust is imperfect.

A 'volunteer' is one who has not provided valuable consideration. Valuable consideration refers either to common law consideration in money or money's worth or marriage consideration. Common law consideration is the price by each party to an agreement. 'Marriage consideration' takes the form of an ante-nuptial settlement made in consideration of marriage, or a post-nuptial settlement made in pursuance of an ante-nuptial agreement. A post-nuptial settlement *simpliciter* is not within the marriage consideration. An ante-nuptial agreement is one made before or at the time of a marriage, on condition that the marriage takes place, on the occasion of the marriage and for the purpose of facilitating the marriage. The persons who are treated as providing marriage consideration are the parties to the marriage and the issue of the marriage, including remoter issue. Any other children affiliated to the parties to the marriage are volunteers. Thus, illegitimate, legitimated and adopted children as well as children of a subsequent marriage are volunteers. Such volunteer children may derive an incidental benefit if their interests are intertwined with the interests of the non-volunteers, i.e. in special circumstances, the non-volunteers in bringing a claim may be required to acknowledge the interests of the volunteers. This was stated in an *obiter* pronouncement in *Attorney General v Jacob-Smith* [1895] 2 QB 341. Good consideration such as natural love and affection is insufficient for these purposes.

4.10.1 Agreements enforceable by non-volunteers

It follows that if the trust is imperfect and the claimant wishes to obtain equitable assistance, he is required to demonstrate that he has furnished valuable consideration. If this is the case, the imperfect trust will be treated to all intents and purposes as though it was perfect. In other words, the claimant who has furnished valuable consideration will derive from the agreement to create a trust all the benefits accorded to a beneficiary under a perfect trust. Thus, the non-volunteer will be entitled to bring a claim directly against the reluctant settlor for an equitable remedy in order to have the agreement enforced and the limitation period will not operate.

CASE EXAMPLE

Pullan v Koe [1913] 1 Ch 9

By a marriage settlement made in 1859, a wife covenanted to settle after-acquired property of £100 and over. In 1879, she received a gift of £285 but did not transfer the relevant sum to the trustees. Instead, the money was paid into her husband's bank account and he later invested it in bonds, which remained in his estate at the time of his death in 1909. The trustees of the marriage settlement claimed the securities from the husband's executors on behalf of the children of the marriage. The executors pleaded the Statute of Limitations as a defence.

Held: The trustees, as representatives of non-volunteers, were entitled to trace the intended trust assets on behalf of the non-volunteers. The claim was treated as equivalent to an action brought in respect of a perfectly created trust.

JUDGMENT

'In my opinion as soon as the £285 was paid to the wife it became in equity bound by and subject to the trusts of the settlement ... the property being thus bound, these bonds became trust property, and can be followed by the trustees and claimed from a volunteer ... the trustees are entitled to come into a court of equity to enforce a contract to create a trust, contained in a marriage settlement, for the benefit of the wife and the issue of the marriage, all of whom are within the marriage consideration.'

Swinfen Eady J

4.10.2 Covenants to create trusts before the Contracts (Rights of Third Parties) Act 1999

Assume that A voluntarily promises (i.e. without consideration) to transfer 10,000 BP plc shares to B to hold on trust for C, a volunteer and non-party, absolutely. A fails to transfer the shares to B. The trust is therefore imperfect. Since B and C are volunteers, neither may bring an action in equity against A to enforce the promise. The rule that only persons who have provided consideration may claim rights under a promise to create a trust, is subject to one limitation, namely that a party to a voluntary covenant (i.e. a deed) may claim the common law remedy of damages for breach of covenant. The rule at common law is that in a 'specialty' contract (i.e. a deed) the absence of consideration does not prevent a party from enforcing the contract at law by claiming damages. In this respect 'Equity follows the law' and does not prevent the party from enforcing his legal rights. At the same time, the volunteer is not entitled to claim equitable assistance, for 'Equity will not assist a volunteer'. In the above example if the voluntary promise between A (an intended settlor) and B (an intended trustee) is incorporated in a deed for the benefit of C (an intended beneficiary), although B and C are volunteers, B, in theory, is entitled to claim damages at common law for breach of contract. This was decided in *Re Cavendish-Browne's Settlement Trust* [1916] WN 341 (substantial damages were awarded). However, the court came to a different conclusion in *Re Kay's Settlement* [1939] 1 All ER 245 (B was prevented from bringing an action for damages on behalf of C), applying the principle laid down in *Re Pryce* [1917] 1 Ch 234 (C was not entitled to apply to the court for directions to force B to bring a claim for damages on behalf of C, because the volunteer ought not to obtain by indirect means, relief that he cannot obtain by direct procedure). The quantum of damages may or may not pose a problem depending on the circumstances. The approach in *Re Pryce* [1917] and *Re Kay* [1939] appears to be based on the premise that if B were to succeed in the claim for damages and obtain substantial damages he may be required to hold the damages on trust for the volunteer, non-covenantee, C. Thus, C may obtain a remedy indirectly.

A different solution is adopted if C, a volunteer, is also a party to the covenant. He will be entitled to claim damages in his own right, but of course will not be entitled to an equitable remedy because of his status as a volunteer.

CASE EXAMPLE

Cannon v Hartley [1949] Ch 213

A deed of separation made between the defendant, his wife (non-volunteer) and his daughter (volunteer) contained a clause requiring the defendant to settle future property. The daughter brought a claim for damages against her father for breach of covenant.

Held: The daughter was entitled to substantial damages because she was a party to the deed.

JUDGMENT

'In the present case the plaintiff, although a volunteer, is not only a party to the deed of separation but is also a direct covenantee under the very covenant upon which she is suing. She does not require the assistance of the court to enforce the covenant for she has a legal right herself to enforce it. She is not asking for equitable relief for damages at common law for breach of covenant.'

Romer J

It would appear that if the claimant has provided consideration, he may bring a claim in equity (perhaps specific performance) on behalf of a volunteer who was entitled to benefit from the agreement: see *Beswick v Beswick* [1968] AC 58, HL.

CASE EXAMPLE

Beswick v Beswick [1968] AC 58, HL

Peter Beswick executed a deed with his nephew to transfer his business in return for a salary payable to Peter during his life and after his death an annuity payable to his widow. After Peter's death the nephew refused to pay his aunt the annuity. She brought a claim for specific performance against her nephew in the capacity of her deceased husband's personal representative.

Held: The aunt was entitled to succeed in her claim.

JUDGMENT

'It is argued that since the widow personally had no rights which she personally could enforce the court will not make an order which will have the effect of enforcing those rights. I can find no principle to this effect. The condition as to payment of an annuity to the widow personally was valid. The estate (though not the widow personally) can enforce it. Why should the estate be barred from exercising its full contractual rights merely because in doing so it secures justice for the widow who, by a mechanical defect of our law, is unable to assert her own rights? Such a principle would be repugnant to justice and fulfil no other object than that of aiding the wrongdoer. I can find no ground on which such a principle should exist.'

Lord Pearce

4.10.3 Effect of the Contracts (Rights of Third Parties) Act 1999

Under the Contracts (Rights of Third Parties) Act 1999, the decisions in *Re Pryce* [1917] and *Re Kay* [1939] are reversed. Under Section 1 of the Act, a third party to a contract is entitled 'in his own right' to enforce a term of the contract if, *inter alia*, a 'term of the contract purports to confer a benefit on him'. This is clearly covered by a contract to create a trust for the benefit of C. Section 1(5) enacts the policy of treating the volunteer third party C as 'if he had been a party to the contract'. The effect is that even though C is not a party to the contract, he will be treated as if he is a party. Today, C would be entitled to claim substantial damages from A, even though he is not a party to the contract. The statutory changes endorse the principle in *Re Cavendish-Browne* [1916] and equate the process with the method

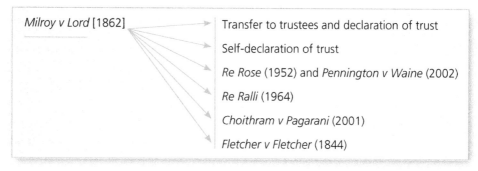

Figure 4.1 Perfect trusts

in *Cannon v Hartley* [1949] (see above). At the same time, the Act has reversed the decisions in *Re Pryce* [1917] and *Re Kay* [1939]. However, notwithstanding the reforms enacted in the 1999 Act, C, a volunteer, would not be entitled to an equitable remedy of specific performance. Such a remedy would not have been available to him even if he had been a party to the contract, for 'Equity will not assist a volunteer.'

ACTIVITY

Self-test questions

1. Explain and illustrate the maxim 'Equity will not perfect an imperfect gift'.
2. What is meant by marriage consideration?
3. What changes has the Contracts (Rights of Third Parties) Act 1999 introduced by way of assistance to a volunteer in enforcing an agreement to create a trust?

SAMPLE ESSAY QUESTION

Consider the following essay question:

When would a trust be perfectly constituted?

Answer plan

> Define a completely constituted trust and identify the essential requirements for the creation of such a trust, see *Milroy v Lord*.

> If there has not been a perfect transfer of the property to the trustee would the court imply a self-declaration of trust on the part of the settlor? See *Re Ralli* contrast *Jones v Lock* and *Richards v Delbridge*.

> If the transferor has not completed the transfer of the legal title to the transferee, consider whether the transfer is effective in equity. This will be the position where he (the transferor) has done everything required of him to transfer the property to the intended trustee, see *Re Rose*. State the test laid down in *Mascall v Mascall* (whether the donee needs the assistance of the court to complete the transfer). Consider the extension of this principle in *Pennington v Waine* to unconscionable conduct, but distinguished in *Zeital v Kaye* (delivery of a blank transfer form to the intended donee) and *Curtis v Pulbrook* (unauthorised issue of new share certificates to the intended donee).

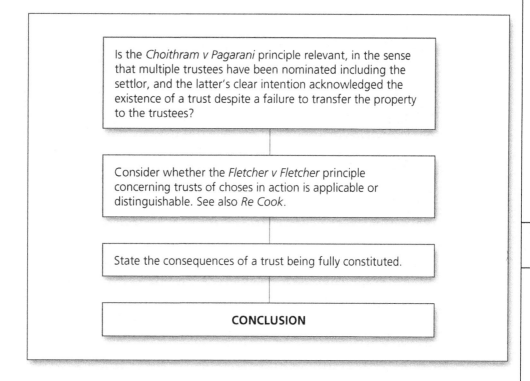

Is the *Choithram v Pagarani* principle relevant, in the sense that multiple trustees have been nominated including the settlor, and the latter's clear intention acknowledged the existence of a trust despite a failure to transfer the property to the trustees?

Consider whether the *Fletcher v Fletcher* principle concerning trusts of choses in action is applicable or distinguishable. See also *Re Cook*.

State the consequences of a trust being fully constituted.

CONCLUSION

4.11 Introduction to exceptions to the rule that equity will not assist a volunteer

There are a number of occasions when, although a gift or trust is imperfect, equity would give assistance to volunteers and force the defendant to complete the intended gift or trust. These exceptions are:

- the rule in *Strong v Bird*;
- *donatio mortis causa*;
- proprietary estoppel.

4.11.1 The rule in *Strong v Bird*

The rule in *Strong v Bird* [1874] LR 18 Eq 315 is that if an *inter vivos* gift is imperfect by reason only of the fact that the transfer to the intended donee is incomplete, the incomplete gift will become perfect when the donee acquires the property in the capacity of executor of the donor's estate. This rule is applicable to both personal and real property.

In probate law, a deceased's estate devolves on his executor as appointed in his will; the executor's function is to administer the estate of the deceased. The executor is treated in law as the *alter ego* of the deceased. All that is needed to transfer the estate to the executor is:

- the valid execution of a will in which an executor is appointed; and
- the acquisition of probate by the nominated executor. The probate document has the effect in law of vesting the estate of the deceased in the executor. Third parties wishing to deal with the estate of the deceased are required to act through the executor.

The donee/executor will take the property beneficially in accordance with the *inter vivos* intention of the donor, even though he acquires the asset in a different capacity. In short, the defective gift, because of the failure to transfer the property *inter vivos*, will be cured by operation of law when the donee/executor obtains probate.

CASE EXAMPLE

Strong v Bird [1874] LR 18 Eq 315

The defendant's stepmother became a lodger and agreed to pay for her board and lodging. The defendant borrowed £1,000 from her and it was agreed that the sum would be repaid by reductions from each quarter's rent. After £200 had been repaid the stepmother generously refused to hold the defendant to the loan and paid the full rent. This new arrangement was not binding at law, for lack of consideration, but the intention to release the debt continued until her death. The defendant was appointed her executor until her will. The next of kin claimed that the defendant was required to repay the balance of the loan.

Held: The intended gift of the balance of the loan became perfect on the death of the testatrix.

JUDGMENT

'[W]hen a testator makes his debtor executor, and thereby releases the debt at law, he is no longer liable at law. It is said that he would be liable in this court: and so he would, unless he could shew some reason for not being made liable. Then what does he shew here? Where he proves to the satisfaction of the court a continuing intention to give; and it appears to me that there being the continuing intention to give, and there being a legal act which transferred the ownership or released the obligation – for it is the same thing – the transaction is perfected.'

Jessel MR

4.11.2 The nature of the donor's intention

The donor's intention is of paramount importance. The claimant is required to establish that the donor manifested a present, continuous intention to make an *inter vivos* gift to him. The *Strong v Bird* [1874] rule concerns only intended *inter vivos* gifts or transfers. The rule was never intended for purely testamentary transfers. Such transfers are required to be made by wills. Accordingly, there is no contradiction of the requirements under the Wills Act 1837.

Present intention of the donor

In order to activate the rule, the intended **transferee is required to prove** that the donor had the intention to transfer the property **immediately and not in the** future. Thus, if the donor promised to transfer the property **after he had modified the property** and he fails to modify the property, the test will not be **satisfied. Moreover, if the** modification of the property has been completed, the donor is required to make a further promise to transfer the property to the donee.

CASE EXAMPLE

Re Freeland [1952] 1 Ch 110

The claimant alleged that the testatrix promised to transfer her car to the claimant after it was repaired. The car was repaired but was not delivered to the claimant; instead the defendant, who had borrowed the car from the testatrix, kept possession of it until the testatrix's death. The claimant was appointed executor of the deceased's estate. The issue was whether the imperfect gift was completed.

Held: The *Strong v Bird* [1874] rule was not applicable to these facts, for the intention of the testatrix was to transfer the car in the future.

JUDGMENT

'There was no room for the application of the principle [in *Strong v Bird* [1874]] where there was an intention to give which was not completed because the intended donor desired first to apply the subject matter of the gift to some other purpose. In such a case the intended donee when appointed executor could not say that nothing remained to complete his gift.'

Evershed MR

Continuous intention

The claimant is required to prove that the donor manifested an intention to transfer the relevant property to him and that this intention remained unaltered up to the time of the donor's death. Any break in the continuity of the intention would disentitle the transferee of the property. The date of the execution of the will may offer some evidence of the inconsistency of the intention of the testator. If a will is executed after a declaration of intent by the testator and the will transfers the relevant property to another donee, this may be sufficient to break the continuity of the testator's intention. This is a question of fact. It follows that if the donor had forgotten his intention to donate the property to the donee and treated the property as his own, the requisite intention would not be satisfied.

CASE EXAMPLE

Re Wale [1956] 1 WLR 1346

The testatrix, Elizabeth Wale, declared her intention in 1939 to make a transfer of shares to trustees subject to a trust in favour of her daughter. The testatrix had taken no steps to transfer the shares to the trustees and for the remainder of her life showed no indication of remembering the 1939 settlement. By her will she left her estate to her two sons. Her daughter was appointed one of the executors. The issue was whether the imperfect gift of the shares was perfected on Elizabeth Wale's death.

Held: The rule in *Strong v Bird* [1874] was not applicable, for the donor's intention was not continuous until her death.

The rule was originally intended to perfect an imperfect gift in favour of the transferee, beneficially. But the principle has been extended to transfers to trustees to hold on trust for beneficiaries. There ought to be no reason in principle to prevent such an extension. It is not an essential part of the rule that the transferee is required to be a beneficial owner of the property. Instead, the purpose of the rule is merely to complete an imperfect transfer when probate of the will is obtained by the intended transferee/executor. The donee's status is immaterial. Accordingly, the rule is applicable where the donor intends to transfer property to X (executor) as trustee for Y: see *Re Ralli* [1964] Ch 288, HC (see above).

Extension to intestacies

The *Strong v Bird* [1874] principle has been extended to transfers to the administrator of a deceased's estate on his death intestate. A person dies intestate when he dies without making a will. The deceased's next of kin is entitled to administer his estate. His function is to distribute the deceased's estate in accordance with the intestacy rules. He is treated as the equivalent to the executor in the case of a person dying testate. In *Re James* [1935] Ch 449, the court extended the *Strong v Bird* [1874] rule to transfers on an intestacy.

CASE EXAMPLE

Re James [1935] Ch 449

A inherited his father's house on the latter's death intestate. A 'gave' the house to his father's housekeeper, handing her the title deeds, but he did not convey the house to her. She occupied the house as donee and A had a continuing intention to give her the house until his own death intestate, nine years later. The housekeeper was appointed one of two administratrixes of A's estate. The legal interest in the house therefore vested in the housekeeper jointly with the other administratrix. The issue was whether the claimant was entitled to enlist the assistance of equity to complete the transfer beneficially to the housekeeper.

Held: The imperfect transfer was required to be perfected under the *Strong v Bird* [1874] rule.

obiter

A principle of law stated by a judge but not directly applicable to the facts of the case before him.

However, in *Re Gonin* [1979] Ch 16, the High Court in an **obiter** pronouncement, severely criticised the *Re James* [1935] solution. The tenor of this criticism was that although the donor promised to transfer the relevant property to the donee, his appointment as the deceased's next of kin did not constitute a conscious effort of the deceased, but a fortuitous event. Accordingly, the court ought not to intervene to assist such a volunteer.

CASE EXAMPLE

Re Gonin [1979] Ch 16

A mother who wanted to make a gift of her house to her daughter erroneously believed that she could not do so because the daughter was illegitimate. As an alternative, she wrote a cheque for £33,000 in the daughter's favour. This cheque was found after the mother's death. At this time it was too late to cash the cheque as the funds in the account of the deceased became frozen. The daughter became the administratrix of her mother's estate and claimed the house in accordance with the *Strong v Bird* [1874] rule.

Held: That the rule in *Strong v Bird* [1874] was not applicable as there was no continuing intention to give the house to the daughter.

JUDGMENT

'The appointment of an administrator is not the act of the deceased but of law. It is often a matter of pure chance which of many persons equally entitled to a grant of letters of administration finally takes them out. Why, then, should any special tenderness be shown to a person so selected by law and not the will of the testator. It would seem an astonishing doctrine of equity that if the person who wishes to take the benefit of the rule in *Strong v Bird* manages to be the person to obtain a grant then he will be able to do so.'

Walton J

Gilbert Kodilinye, in an article entitled 'A fresh look at the rule in *Strong v Bird*' [1982] Conv 14, analyses the attack by Walton J on *Re James* [1935] and suggests that his criticisms were unfounded. The policy of the *Strong v Bird* [1874] rule is simply to vest the property in the hands of the legal representative of the deceased. In this respect, it makes no difference whether during the intended donor's lifetime the transferee was, or was not, consciously appointed to act as his representative on death. The material issue is whether the defective transfer *inter vivos* is cured by the transfer to the intended donee by operation of law on the death of the donor.

4.12 *Donatio mortis causa*

donatio mortis causa

A deathbed gift or gift made *inter vivos* in contemplation of and conditional on the death of the donor.

A ***donatio mortis causa*** (DMC) involves an *inter vivos* transfer of control over property by the donor whilst contemplating his impending death but on condition that the gift will become perfect on death. The principle here is that immediately on the death of the donor the transfer becomes perfect or if at the point of death the gift is incomplete the donee is placed in a position of having the imperfect transfer perfected on the donor's death. The transferor may make a 'complete' delivery of the property but conditional on death, as would suffice in the case of an *inter vivos* gift. For example the delivery of a watch or bracelet to the donee before undergoing surgery. In these circumstances the donee's title will become unconditional on the death of the donor and no action on the part of the donor's personal representatives is needed to perfect the donee's title. The donee will simply retain the property beneficially. Alternatively, there could be a valid DMC even though the delivery or transfer does not vest the donor's title in the donee. For example, the transfer of a chose in action, such as a passbook to funds in the donor's building society account in contemplation of and conditional on death, does not vest the funds in the account to the donee on the death of the donor. The donee will be required to convince a court of equity that he has better title to the relevant property than those entitled under the donor's will or intestacy. This may be achieved by means of a DMC. In this event, the donor's personal representatives are required to hold the legal title to the property on trust for the donee. This is a true case of 'equity perfecting an imperfect gift', or 'equity assisting a volunteer'.

In a significant number of cases the court may be asked to determine whether the doctrine has been satisfied based on the testimony of the claimant and in some cases without corroborative evidence. Accordingly, the approach of the courts has always been one of caution, requiring strict proof of the elements of a DMC in order to filter out the unscrupulous claimant. In *Cosnahan v Grice* [1862] 15 Moo PC 215, Lord Chelmsford stressed the importance of clear evidence in the following terms:

JUDGMENT

'Cases of this kind demand the strictest scrutiny. So many opportunities, and such strong temptations, present themselves to unscrupulous persons to pretend these deathbed donations, that there is always a danger of having an entirely fabricated case set up. And, without any imputation of fraudulent contrivance, it is so easy to mistake the meaning of persons languishing in a mortal illness, and, by a slight change of words, to convert their expressions of intended benefit into an actual gift of property, that no case of this description ought to prevail, unless it is supported by evidence of the clearest and most unequivocal character.'

Lord Chelmsford

A DMC has been described by Buckley J in *Re Beaumont* [1902] 1 Ch 889 as a 'singular form of gift', something between an unconditional *inter vivos* gift and a gift on death. It is a transfer of property *inter vivos*, but conditional on death.

JUDGMENT

'A *donatio mortis causa* is a singular form of gift. It may be said to be of an amphibious nature, being a gift which is neither entirely *inter vivos* nor testamentary. It is an act *inter vivos* by which the donee is to have absolute title to the gift not at once but if the donor dies. If the donor dies the title becomes absolute not under the will but as against the executor. In order to make the gift valid it must be made so as to take complete effect on the donor's death. The court must find that the donor intended it to be absolute if he died, but he need not actually say so.'

Buckley J

The classical statement of the elements necessary in order to create a DMC were laid down by Farwell J in *Re Craven's Estate* [1937] Ch 423, in the following terms:

JUDGMENT

'The conditions which are essential to a donatio mortis causa are, firstly, a clear intention to give, but to give only if the donor dies, whereas if the donor does not die then the gift is not to take effect and the donor is to have back the subject matter of the gift. Secondly, the gift must be made in contemplation of death, by which is meant not the possibility of death at some time or other, but death within the near future, what may be called death for some reason believed to be impending. Thirdly, the donor must part with dominion over the subject matter of the donation.'

Farwell J

The subject will be analysed by reference to the following elements:

- the donor is required to contemplate his impending death;
- an *inter vivos* delivery of the relevant property must be conditional on death;
- the donor is required to transfer dominion over the property during his lifetime;
- certain types of property are incapable of forming the subject-matter of a DMC.

4.12.1 Contemplation of death

The requirement here is that the donor contemplates impending death or death in the near future from a specific health condition, such as incurable cancer, or an event, such as major surgery or undertaking a dangerous journey. It is not sufficient for the donor to contemplate the mere possibility of death from natural causes. The requirement is much more specific than that, as we will all die some day. However, the donor need not contemplate immediate death or be on his deathbed in order to satisfy this principle. The test here is essentially subjective and involves a question of fact. In the recent case *King v Dubrey* [2016] 2 WLR 1, the Court of Appeal reviewed the law relating to the DMC concept and decided that such a claim is required to be construed with considerable caution to avoid unscrupulous treasure hunters adjusting their recollections in order to gain huge rewards. It is not a popular doctrine and serves little useful purpose except to validate deathbed gifts. This doctrine is distinct from, and takes precedence over, a carefully drafted will drawn up by a solicitor in the absence of beneficiaries. In addition there are little safeguards to the recollection of claimants during deathbed conversations. Accordingly, the courts ought to proceed with unequivocal evidence of the requirements of a DMC. The first requirement is that the donor contemplates his impending death in the near future *from an identified cause*. In each of the classic cases where the claim succeeded the donor was contemplating death from a specific cause, in *Re Craven's Estate* [1937] Ch 423, the donor was about to undergo serious medical surgery; in *Birch v*

Treasury Solicitor [1951] Ch 298, the donor was in hospital having suffered a serious accident; in *Sen v Headley* [1991] Ch 425, the donor was in hospital suffering from pancreatic cancer. However, in *Vallee v Birchwood* [2013] EWHC, the High Court made a wrong turn in deciding that a valid DMC was created where the elderly donor was approaching the end of his natural life but was not suffering from a perceived specific life-threatening condition and had ample opportunity to take legal advice and make a will. Accordingly, the Court of Appeal overruled *Vallee*.

CASE EXAMPLE

King v Dubrey [2016] 2 WLR 1, Court of Appeal

The testatrix was the claimant's aunt who made a valid will in 1998 leaving the bulk of her estate, including her house, to various animal charities. In 2007 the claimant went to live with his aunt and, owing to her declining health, became her carer. The claimant testified to the effect that on several occasions his aunt told him that the house and property will be his after her death. In November 2010 she signed a note stating that she left him her house and property in the hope that he will care for her animals until their death. On another occasion, about four months before her death, the aunt presented the claimant with the title deeds to her house saying, 'This will be yours when I go.' The claimant said that his aunt knew her health was failing and that her death was approaching. In March 2011 the claimant prepared a so-called 'will' for his aunt to sign, leaving him her wealth, but the aunt's signature was not duly attested. Accordingly this document was invalid as it did not comply with s 9 of the Wills Act 1837. In April 2011 the aunt died and the pets were found homes. The will of 1998 took effect but the claimant argued *inter alia* that a valid *donatio mortis causa* (DMC) had been created by the deceased which then took priority over the will. The trial judge found in favour of the claimant. The charities appealed.

Held: The Court of Appeal allowed the appeal, reviewed the law relating to DMCs and decided that the trial judge had misdirected himself in concluding that the gift of the house was made in contemplation of impending death. The trial judge had relied on *Vallee v Birchwood* in deciding that this condition had been satisfied; but the evidence demonstrated that when the aunt gave the claimant the deeds she had not been contemplating her impending death from a specific cause but merely her natural death. If she was dissatisfied with her 1998 will and suddenly wished to leave her estate to her nephew the obvious thing for her to do was to see her solicitors and make a new will to that effect.

In addition, the gift was not made on the condition of her death.

JUDGMENT

'It is clear, on the authorities, that the donor must have good reason to anticipate death in the near future from an identified cause. It is also clear, on the authorities, that the death which the donor is anticipating need not be inevitable. The illness or event which the donor faces can be one which he may survive. In *Re Craven's Estate* (1937), for example, if the operation had been successful the donor would have recovered.

In my view it cannot be said that June (aunt) was contemplating her impending death … at the relevant time. She was not suffering from a fatal illness. Nor was she about to undergo a dangerous operation or to undertake a dangerous journey. If June was dissatisfied with her existing will and suddenly wished to leave everything to the claimant the obvious thing for her to do was to go to her solicitors and make a new will. June was an intelligent retired police officer. There is not the slightest reason why she should not have taken that course.'

Jackson LJ

The Court of Appeal decision in *King v Dubrey* is regarded as a significant restatement of the law relating to the doctrine of DMC. Besides reviewing the leading authorities on the subject, overruling the controversial decision in *Vallee v Birchwood* and reasserting the need for unequivocal evidence on this subject, Jackson LJ made a number of *obiter* pronouncements which may require further judicial analysis. One such observation is the usefulness of the doctrine in modern society. He states that the doctrine 'serves little useful purpose today, save possibly as a means of validating death bed gifts'. At the same time he pointed out that the doctrine is not restricted solely to donors on their deathbeds, although this may be the context in which the doctrine may serve a useful purpose in modern society. A factor that appeared to have influenced his decision was the possibility that the donor had sufficient time and capacity to see her solicitor and execute a valid will in order to consolidate her wishes in favour of her nephew. This factor has never been a requirement for a valid DMC and may be too restrictive as a policy objective.

The donor need not express his personal sentiments as to his impending death: very often, in the appropriate environment, the courts will infer this condition from the surrounding circumstances. The donor may contemplate death as a result of undertaking a dangerous mission (see *Agnew v Belfast Banking* [1896] 2 IR 204, contemplation of military service) or undergoing surgery. Contemplation of death by suicide may also suffice, since suicide is no longer a crime.

4.12.2 Conditional on death

tutor tip

'After reading each chapter, compile a list of the legal definition of terms with relevant authorities.'

The donor must intend the gift to become absolute only on his death. In the meantime the gift is revocable. There can be no DMC if the donor intends to make an immediate gift *inter vivos*. In that case the gift stands or falls as an ordinary gift *inter vivos*. Likewise, there can be no DMC if the donor intends to make a gift by will, i.e. he intends his wishes to take effect on his death but he does not wish to part with dominion over the asset *inter vivos*. To satisfy this condition the donor is required to part with dominion over the asset *inter vivos* but with the intention that the gift will become complete on death. Each case is determined on its own facts. In *King v Dubrey* (2016) the Court of Appeal decided that an aunt who gave her nephew the title deeds to her house saying, 'This will be yours when I go' did not satisfy this test. The court said that these words were more consistent with a statement of testamentary intent rather than a gift conditional on the aunt's death within a limited period of time. In addition, the subsequent execution of void intended wills purporting to transfer her estate to her nephew were inconsistent with the proposition that the aunt felt had already disposed of her estate by way of a DMC.

During the donor's lifetime the transfer of the asset is required to be revocable. This is a question of fact. Revocation is automatic if the donor recovers from the illness which he contemplated leading to death. Alternatively, the donor may expressly revoke the transfer by resuming dominion over the property. There is no revocation of the transfer by will, for the will speaks from the date of death and the time of death makes the transfer perfect. In *King v Dubrey* (2016), Jackson LJ affirmed this principle in the following manner:

JUDGMENT

'The charities suggest that those actions (the subsequent execution of void wills purporting to transfer the relevant property to her nephew) constituted a revocation of the DMC, if previously made. I doubt that that is the correct analysis. June (aunt) prepared and signed the two invalid wills with the assistance of the claimant. The steps which they were both taking were based on the shared assumption that June had the ability to dispose of her house by will. That would not be the case if June had made a DMC.'

Jackson LJ

In exceptional circumstances, the donor may specify that death alone from a specific ailment will make the gift complete. If that be the case then only death from that source will suffice. In the ordinary course of events, if the donor contemplates death from a specific condition then death from any condition will be sufficient to satisfy this requirement.

CASE EXAMPLE

Wilkes v Allington [1931] 2 Ch 104

The donor knew that he was suffering from cancer and had no hope of recovery. He did not know how long he had to live when he transferred property to the donee. One month later he caught a cold on a bus journey and died from pneumonia.

Held: A valid DMC of the property had been made.

4.12.3 Parting with dominion

The donor is required to part with dominion or control over the property during his lifetime. Mere intention to make a gift to the donee is insufficient for these purposes. What is needed is some overt act of physical transfer to the donee during the lifetime of the donor. It is required to be established that the donor has lost control over the asset during his lifetime and, at the same time, the donee has acquired control over the subject-matter of the gift. With regard to tangible moveable property (chattels) this condition will be satisfied if the donor has delivered the chattel to the donee with the intention that property in the chattel will be transferred on death. This test will not be satisfied where the donor has merely transferred custody over the property to the donee.

CASE EXAMPLE

Reddel v Dobree [1834] 10 Sim 244

The donor, in declining health, delivered a locked ash box to X, telling her that the box contained money for her. He insisted that the box be returned to him for inspection every three months during his lifetime and that, on his death, X would be entitled to obtain the key from his son. The question was whether a valid DMC had been created.

Held: No valid DMC was created, for the donor had retained dominion over the property.

It is immaterial whether the delivery of the chattel is made before or after the donor expresses his intention to make the transfer.

CASE EXAMPLE

Cain v Moon [1896] 2 QB 283

A daughter delivered a deposit note to her mother for safe custody. Two years later, when the daughter was seriously ill, she told her mother: 'The bank note is for you if I die.' The issue was whether a valid DMC was created. The court held that the antecedent delivery sufficed and it was not necessary for the mother to hand back the note and for the daughter to redeliver it when she expressed her intention. Thus, a valid DMC was created.

Delivery of the property may even be effected constructively as when a key is delivered to the donee to enable him to acquire the subject-matter of the gift. However, in *Re Craven's Estate* [1937] 1 Ch 423, Farwell J in an *obiter* pronouncement declared broadly that the retention of a spare set of keys by the donor is inconsistent with the test of parting with dominion over the property. However, in *Woodard v Woodard* [1995] 3 All ER 980, CA the Court of Appeal refused to follow this statement and, instead, considered the circumstances responsible for the donor retaining a spare set of keys. If the donor consciously and deliberately retained the spare set of keys in order to maintain control over the property, this is inconsistent with his parting with dominion. However, if the spare set of keys was retained by the donor through absent-mindedness, or without a deliberate effort to retain control over the property, dominion may be transferred. The retention of the spare set of keys would be irrelevant in these circumstances.

CASE EXAMPLE

Woodard v Woodard [1995] 3 All ER 980, CA

A father who was dying from cancer was admitted to hospital. He was driven to the hospital by his son (the defendant) in the father's car. The father told the defendant, in the presence of the claimant, the defendant's mother, that he might keep the keys as he (the father) would not be driving his car any more. The father died three days later. The defendant sold the car and the claimant, as administrator and sole beneficiary of her deceased husband's estate, brought an action against the defendant for the recovery of the proceeds of sale. The defendant argued that his father had made either an outright *inter vivos* gift or a DMC. The trial judge decided that the father had made an outright gift to his son. The claimant appealed to the Court of Appeal.

Held: A valid DMC had been created in favour of the son.

▪ It was clear from the evidence that the defendant would have had to give the car back if his father had recovered. There was therefore no outright gift of the car, but a transfer conditional on the death of the father.

▪ It was also clear that the transfer was made in contemplation of death owing to the surrounding circumstances.

▪ It was irrelevant that the defendant already had possession of the car and set of keys. There was no need for the defendant to return the car and keys to the father and for the latter to re-transfer the car and keys to the defendant; reliance was placed on *Cain v Moon* [1896] 2 QB 283 and *Re Stoneham* [1953] Ch 59.

Likewise, in *Re Lillingston* [1952] 2 All ER 184 the test was satisfied where the subject-matter of the gift is transferred, or the means of acquiring the asset is transferred to the donee.

CASE EXAMPLE

Re Lillingston [1952] 2 All ER 184

D, a donor in contemplation of death, handed X a collection of jewellery and the keys to her trunk, telling her that the trunk contained the key to her Harrods safe deposit, which in turn contained the key to her city safe deposit. D said that she wished X to have all her jewellery and that, after her death, X could go and get the jewellery in these safe deposits. D and X agreed that the jewellery should be kept in the trunk, which was in D's room and X placed the collection of jewellery in the trunk, whereupon D said: 'Keep the key, it's now yours.' On D's death the issue arose as to whether valid DMCs were created in favour of X.

Held: There were valid DMCs of the collection of jewellery and of the jewellery in the two safe deposits.

JUDGMENT

'[It did not matter] in how many boxes the subject of a gift may be contained or that each, except the last, contains a key which opens the next, so long as the scope of the gift is made clear.'

Wynn-Parry J

Transfer of dominion over choses in action

In the case of a chose in action which cannot be transferred by delivery, the donor is required to transfer the legal title to the donee by complying with the relevant formalities. Alternatively, the donor is required to deliver a document of title or essential evidence of title concerning the chose in action in order to secure a transfer of the property. The latter test was laid down in *Birch v Treasury Solicitor* [1951] 1 Ch 298, CA.

CASE EXAMPLE

Birch v Treasury Solicitor [1951] 1 Ch 298, CA

A, a donor, in contemplation of death, delivered to the donee, B, her Post Office Savings Bank book, London Trustee Savings Bank book, Barclays Bank deposit passbook and Westminster Bank deposit account book, intending that the money in these accounts should belong to B on A's death. The issue was whether valid DMCs were created. Expert evidence was tendered on behalf of the Trustee Savings Bank that the passbook was essential evidence of title to the funds in the account.

Held: There was sufficient delivery of documents to establish valid DMCs of the funds in each of the bank accounts.

JUDGMENT

'[W]e think that the real test is whether the instrument amounts to a transfer as being the essential *indicia* or evidence of title, possession or production of which entitles the possessor to the money or property purported to be given … We think, accordingly, that in the case of both banks the condition stated on the face of the deposit books must be taken to have remained operative, i.e., that the book was, and is, the essential *indicia* of title and that delivery of the book amounted to transfer of the chose in action.'

Evershed MR

In *King v Dubrey* (2016) Jackson LJ summarised the test for regarding the transfer of dominion thus:

JUDGMENT

'From a review of the cases I conclude that "dominion" means physical possession of

(a) the subject matter or
(b) some means of accessing the subject matter (such as the key to a box), or
(c) documents evidencing entitlement to possession of the subject matter.'

Jackson LJ

4.12.4 The types of property

In general, most properties are capable of being the subject-matter of a DMC. However, there are a number of properties that may not be suitable to be transferred by a DMC: cheques, land, and stocks and shares.

 Cheques. The cheque of the donor, drawn on his own bank, is a revocable mandate which is revoked on his death. During the donor's lifetime the cheque may be cashed by the donee. In this event, the issue is whether the donee is entitled to retain the funds or not. This is not related to a DMC. Alternatively, the payee of the cheque may present the cheque for payment after the death of the payer. In this event the gift is imperfect and cannot be perfected by a DMC. The donor's cheque is incapable of being the subject-matter of a DMC: see *Re Beaumont* [1902] 1 Ch 889, HC.

 Land. Lord Eldon in *Duffield v Elwes* [1827] 1 Bli NS 497, in an *obiter* pronouncement, took the view that land cannot be the subject-matter of a DMC. It was widely believed that this view was too broad for the test is whether the essential indicia of title had been transferred during the donor's lifetime. The fact that the donor may still be empowered to deal with the subject-matter of the transfer, despite the transfer of the essential indicia of title, is not inconsistent with the test of dominion. For example in the case of unregistered land the donor may have delivered the title deeds to the donee and retained the capacity to declare a trust of the land without departing from the dominion principle. In *Sen v Headley* [1991] 2 WLR 1308, CA, the Court of Appeal decided that Lord Eldon's view could not be supported in respect of unregistered land.

CASE EXAMPLE

Sen v Headley [1991] 2 WLR 1308, CA

The deceased, while suffering from inoperable cancer, was looked after by the claimant, with whom he lived. The claimant visited him in hospital every day. Three days before he died, he told the claimant that 'The house [was hers] … You have the keys … The deeds are in the steel box.' The sole key to the box was given to her. In addition, the claimant had her own house keys. The issue was whether there was a valid DMC of the house (unregistered land).

Held: The transfer of the title deeds to the house was a sufficient parting with dominion over the house, but the retention of the house keys, on its own, was insufficient to transfer the house. Further, a DMC operates by way of a constructive trust.

JUDGMENT

'It cannot be doubted that title deeds are the essential *indicia* of title to unregistered land. Moreover, on the facts found by the judge, there was here a constructive delivery of the title deeds of 56 Gordon Road equivalent to an actual handing of them by Mr Hewett to Mrs Sen. And it could not be suggested that Mr Hewett did not part with dominion over the deeds … We hold that land is capable of passing by way of a *donatio mortis causa* and that the three general requirements for such a gift were satisfied in this case.'

Nourse LJ

Likewise in *Vallee v Birchwood* [2013] EWHC Civ 1449, Jonathan Gaunt QC (sitting as Deputy High Court judge) reiterated this principle thus:

JUDGMENT

'A gift by way of *donatio* does not become effective until the death of the donor, so the property remains both at law and in equity the property of the donor. There seems to be no reason why acts of continued enjoyment of his own property should be regarded as incompatible with his intention to make a gift effective on his death … There is no doubt that the concept of dominion in this context is a slippery one. Its fundamental rationale appears to be that something must be done by way of delivery of the property or indicia of title sufficient to indicate that what is intended is a conditional gift and not something that falls short of that. There does not have to be a delivery or transfer which would suffice at law to effect a gift *inter vivos*.'

Jonathan Gaunt QC

Stocks and shares. The question of whether shares are capable of being the subject-matter of a DMC is the subject of a number of contradictory judicial rulings.

CASE EXAMPLE

Ward v Turner [1752] 2 Ves Sen 431

The court decided that the delivery of receipts for the purchase price of South Sea annuities was not a sufficient delivery of the annuities to the donee by way of a DMC.

JUDGMENT

'[A DMC of company stock could not be made] without a transfer, or something amounting to that. The receipts were nothing but waste paper.'

Lord Hardwicke

CASE EXAMPLE

Staniland v Willott [1850] 3 Mac & G 664

The donor, in contemplation of death, made a valid legal transfer of shares in a public company to the donee, but the transfer was revoked by the recovery of the intended donor from his illness. Accordingly, there was no DMC, but the court decided that, had the facts been different, shares were capable of being the subject-matter of a DMC.

In *Moore v Moore* [1874] LR 18 Eq 474, the court decided that railway stock could not be the subject-matter of a DMC. This decision was followed in *Re Weston* [1902] 1 Ch 680, where the court decided that building society shares were an inappropriate subject of a DMC.

The effect of these cases is that an unattractive distinction between shares in a public company and shares in a private company has been drawn. The decision in *Staniland v Willott* [1850] seems difficult to justify, for share certificates are not documents of title. With regard to shares in a private company, if the donor has executed a share transfer form in favour of the transferee (so that he has done everything required of him), the transfer may be effective in accordance with the *Re Rose* [1952] Ch 499, CA principle (see above). There will be no need to seek equitable assistance in order to perfect the gift, for the gift will already be perfect in equity.

4.13 Proprietary estoppel

Proprietary estoppel is a right given to a volunteer whenever a landowner stands by and allows the volunteer to improve his property by incurring expenditure on the property on the assumption that there will be a transfer to him. The landowners and successors in title are estopped from denying the interest acquired by the volunteer. Unlike promissory estoppel, which may be used only 'defensively', proprietary estoppel may be used 'offensively' (as a cause of action) in order to perfect the imperfect gift or complete an incompletely constituted trust. This principle is sometimes referred to as the rule in *Dillwyn v Llewellyn* [1862] 4 De GF & J 517.

CASE EXAMPLE

Dillwyn v Llewellyn [1862] 4 De GF & J 517

A father, wishing his son to live nearby, offered him a farm so that he could build a house on the land. The son accepted the offer, expended a sum of money and built a house on the land, to the knowledge and approval of the father. The father died before a conveyance of the legal estate was ever made to the son. The son claimed to have the land conveyed to him.

Held: The father's actions gave the son the impression that the land would be conveyed to him. Thus, it would have been unconscionable to deny the son an interest in the property. Likewise, the father's personal representatives were estopped from denying the interest acquired in the property. They were obliged to convey the fee simple to the claimant, the son.

JUDGMENT

'If A puts B in possession of a piece of land and tells him I give it to you that you may build a house on it, and B, on the strength of that promise, with the knowledge of A expends a large sum of money in building a house, I cannot doubt that the donee acquires a right from the subsequent transaction to call on the donor to perform that contract and complete the imperfect donation which was made.'

Lord Westbury

The principle was explained in the dissenting speech of Lord Kingsdown in *Ramsden v Dyson* [1866] LR 1 HL 129, thus:

JUDGMENT

'[I]f a man, under a verbal agreement with a landlord for a certain interest in the land, or, what amounts to the same thing, under an expectation, created or encouraged by the landlord, that he shall have a certain interest, takes possession of such land, with the consent of the landlord, and upon the faith of such promise or expectation, with the knowledge of the landlord, and without objection by him, lays out money upon the land, a court of equity will compel the landlord to give effect to such promise or expectation.'

Lord Kingsdown

4.13.1 Five probanda

In *Willmot v Barber* [1880] 15 Ch D 96, Fry J set out the requirements in more detail:

JUDGMENT

'It has been said that the acquiescence which will deprive a man of his legal rights must amount to fraud, and in my view that is an abbreviated statement of a very true proposition. A man is not to be deprived of his legal rights unless he has acted in such a way as would make it fraudulent for him to set up those rights. What then are the elements necessary to constitute fraud? In the first place, the plaintiff must have made a mistake as to his legal rights. Secondly, the plaintiff must have expended some money or must have done some act (not necessarily upon the defendant's land) on the faith of his mistaken belief. Thirdly, the defendant, the possessor of the legal right must know of the existence of his own right which is inconsistent with the right claimed by the plaintiff. Fourthly, the defendant must know of the plaintiff's mistaken belief of his rights ... Lastly, the defendant must have encouraged the plaintiff in his expenditure of money or in the other acts which he has done, either directly or by abstaining from asserting his legal right. Where all these elements exist, there is fraud of such a nature as will entitle the court to restrain the possessor of the legal right from exercising it, but nothing short of this will do.'

Fry J

probanda
Proof of specified
elements.

These five *probanda*, as they are called, have not been applied consistently by the courts. Some courts refer to the propositions as factors as opposed to essential requirements in order to establish the principle. The test laid down by Fry J was endorsed by Scarman LJ in *Crabb v Arun District Council* [1975] 3 All ER 865:

JUDGMENT

'If the plaintiff has any right, it is an equity arising out of the conduct and relationship of the parties. In such a case I think it is now well settled law that the court, having analysed and assessed the conduct and relationship of the parties, has to answer three questions. First, is there an equity established? Secondly, what is the extent of the equity, if one is established? And thirdly, what is the relief appropriate to satisfy the equity?'

Scarman LJ

In *Greasley v Cooke* [1980] 3 All ER 710, CA, the Court of Appeal decided that the claimant is not obliged to incur expenditure in order to succeed in the claim; instead the claimant is required to suffer a detriment in reliance on the promise made by the defendant, to such an extent that it would be unjust and inequitable for the promissor to go back on his promise. The notion of reliance is presumed in favour of the claimant.

CASE EXAMPLE

Greasley v Cooke [1980] 3 All ER 710, CA

The claimant had given assurances to the defendant, a maid, to the effect that she was entitled to remain in the house for as long as she wished. The defendant remained in the house, caring for the family (including a mentally retarded child), without payment. Possession proceedings were brought against the maid.

Held: That an equity in the defendant's favour was raised and an order was made entitling her to occupy the house rent free for as long as she wished to stay there. Further there is a presumption of reliance once the claimant has established a promise.

JUDGMENT

'There is a presumption that [she remained in the house] relying on assurances given to her ... The burden is not on her but on them to prove that she did not rely on their assurances. They did not prove it, nor did their representatives. So she is presumed to have relied on them ... It so happens that in many of these cases of proprietary estoppel there has been expenditure of money. But that is not a necessary element.'

Lord Denning MR

4.13.2 Unconscionability

The modern approach to proprietary estoppel is to broaden its scope and to focus on the defendant's unconscionability, rather than strict, rigid rules. This test was laid down by Oliver J in *Taylors Fashions Ltd v Liverpool Victoria Friendly Society* [1981] 1 All ER 897:

JUDGMENT

'The more recent cases indicate that the application of the *Ramsden v Dyson* principle ... requires a very much broader approach which is directed rather at ascertaining whether it would be unconscionable for a party to be permitted to deny that which, knowingly or unknowingly, he has allowed or encouraged another to assume to his detriment than to inquiring whether the circumstances can be fitted within the confines of some preconceived formula serving as a universal yardstick for every form of unconscionable behaviour. So regarded, knowledge of the true position by the party alleged to be estopped becomes merely one of the relevant factors (it may even be a determining factor in certain cases) in the overall inquiry. This approach, so it seems to me, appears very clearly from the authorities.'

Oliver J

The claimant is required to establish the following four elements: first, an assurance by the owner of land or an interest therein. Second, reliance on that assurance by the person to whom it was addressed (usually the claimant). Third, some unconscionable detriment by the person to whom the assurance was made. Fourth, a remedy designed to satisfy the minimum equity necessary in order to do justice or prevent unconscionable conduct.

4.13.3 Assurance or expectation

The assurance made by the defendant may be express or implied, but is required to induce the claimant into believing that he will obtain an interest or entitlement in land. This may be illustrated in *Crabb v Arun District Council*.

CASE EXAMPLE

Crabb v Arun District Council [1975] 3 All ER 865, CA

The claimant and defendant (the council) reached an understanding, not amounting to a contract, whereby the claimant could access the defendant's land in order to gain entry on to his own land. The defendant encouraged the claimant to use its land. On a sale of the claimant's land, the issue was whether the defendant became estopped from asserting the right of way. The court held that the claimant was entitled to the right of way, as the defendant by its conduct had led him to believe that it would grant him such right of way.

CASE EXAMPLE

Re Basham Decd [1986] 1 WLR 1498

The claimant and her husband had helped her mother and her stepfather in all sorts of ways throughout the claimant's adult life. She received no remuneration but understood that she would inherit her stepfather's property when he died. After her mother's death in 1976, and until her stepfather's death in 1982, she and her husband lived near the cottage to which her stepfather had moved (but never lived in the cottage). The claimant was told by her stepfather that 'she would lose nothing' by her help and (a few days before his death) that she was to have the cottage. The stepfather died intestate. The claimant sought an interest in the estate of her stepfather. The court decided that she was entitled to the whole of the estate of the stepfather by way of an estoppel.

In *Cobbe v Yeoman's Row Management Ltd*, the House of Lords decided that a proprietary estoppel claim required clarity as to the terms of the representation or expectation and the interest in the property in question that the estoppel is designed to defeat. Clearer evidence of the expectation is required in the context of commercial transactions than is needed in a domestic context. In this case the evidence of an expectation was far from clear.

CASE EXAMPLE

Cobbe v Yeoman's Row Management Ltd [2008] UKHL 55 (HL)

Y Ltd owned land with potential for residential development and entered into negotiations with C for the sale of the land to C. They reached an oral 'agreement in principle' on the core terms of the sale, but no written contract, or even a draft contract for discussion, was made. The structure of the agreement between Y and C was that C, at his own expense, would draw up plans for the residential development and that, if planning permission was obtained, Y would sell the land to C, for an agreed up-front price of £12 million. C would then, again at his own expense, develop the land in accordance with the planning permission, sell off the residential units, and divide the proceeds equally between himself and Y, provided that the gross proceeds of sale exceeded £24 million. Pursuant to this agreement C made the application for planning permission at his own expense. C was encouraged by Y to do so. The application was successful and the desired planning permission was obtained. Y then sought to re-negotiate the core financial terms of the sale, asking, in particular, for a substantial increase in payments. C was unwilling to commit himself to the proposed new financial terms, and Y was unwilling to proceed on the original terms. C commenced legal proceedings against Y.

Held: The House of Lords decided that there was insufficient evidence of a proprietary estoppel. The claimant's expectation was not an expectation that he would, if the planning application succeeded, become entitled to a 'certain interest in land', but involved an expectation of a contingency that in the future contractual terms will be agreed and incorporated into a formal written contract. His expectation was therefore always contingent. The court would not have been able to infer the contractual terms that further negotiations would or might have produced so as to make complete the inchoate agreement. But in a restitutionary claim the court awarded compensation to the claimant, to prevent the unjust enrichment of the defendant.

JUDGMENT

'When he [Mr Cobbe] made the planning application his expectation was, for proprietary estoppel purposes, the wrong sort of expectation. It was not an expectation that he would, if the planning application succeeded, become entitled to a certain interest in land. His expectation was that he and Mrs Lisle-Mainwaring, [on behalf of Yeoman's Row Ltd] or their respective legal advisers, would sit down and agree the outstanding contractual terms to be incorporated into the formal written agreement, which he justifiably believed would include the already agreed core financial terms, and that his purchase, and subsequently his development of the property, in accordance with that written agreement would follow. This is not, in my opinion, the sort of expectation of a certain interest in land that Oliver J in the *Taylor Fashions* case or Lord Kingsdown in *Ramsden v Dyson* had in mind.'

Lord Scott

In *Thorner v Major* the court decided that the claimant is required to establish that the terms of the representation or expectation and the nature of the property and interest are sufficiently clear that the court may ascertain the extent of the injustice to the claimant that warrants the imposition of a court order. In this context the court is required to assess the question of clarity and certainty practically and sensibly. This principle may be applied more flexibly in a domestic context.

CASE EXAMPLE

Thorner v Major [2009] 1 WLR 776 (HL)

The claimant was the nephew of the deceased, who owned a dairy farm. The claimant helped the deceased on the farm for approximately 30 years, but was not paid. In 1997, the deceased made a will under which the claimant would inherit the residue of his estate, subject to some legacies. The deceased later revoked his will, because of a desire to exclude from benefit one of the legatees. The deceased did not make another will, and died intestate. The deceased's next of kin were his siblings, the defendants. The claimant brought proceedings against the defendants, alleging that the deceased's estate was bound by conscience to give him the farm on the basis of a proprietary estoppel. The House of Lords decided that the nature of the interest to be received by the claimant was clear: it was the farm as it had existed on the deceased's death. The discretion of the court could not be fettered so as to require the precise extent of the property the subject of the alleged estoppel to be strictly defined in every case.

JUDGMENT

'The analysis of *Cobbe's* case was against the background of different facts. The relationship between the parties in that case was entirely arm's length and commercial, and the person raising the estoppel was a highly experienced businessman. The circumstances were such that the parties could well have been expected to enter into a contract, however although they discussed contractual terms, they had consciously chosen not to do so. They had intentionally left their legal relationship to be negotiated, and each of them knew that neither of them was legally bound. In this case, by contrast, the relationship between Peter (the deceased) and David (the claimant) was familial and personal, and neither of them, least of all David, had much commercial experience. Further, at no time had either of them even started to. Peter contemplate entering into a formal contract as to the ownership of the farm after Peter's death made what were, in the circumstances, clear and unambiguous assurances that he would leave the farm to David and David reasonably relied on, and reasonably acted to his detriment on the basis of those assurances over a long period. In these circumstances, I see nothing in the reasoning of Lord Scott in *Cobbe's* case which assists the defendants in this case. It would represent a regrettable and substantial emasculation of the beneficial principle of proprietary estoppel if it were artificially fettered so as to require the precise extent of the property, the subject of the alleged estoppel to be strictly defined in every case.'

Lord Neuberger

In *Liden v Burton* [2016] EWCA Civ 275, the Court of Appeal affirmed the decision of the trial judge to the effect that a payment by a wife of £500 per month to her husband was objectively considered in the context to amount to a clear assurance sufficient to found a proprietary estoppel. There was some dispute between the parties as to whether the payment was rent, as the husband contended, or a payment towards the ownership of the house, as the wife contended. The judge objectively considered the intentions of the parties were sufficiently clear and pointed towards a proprietary estoppel.

4.13.4 Detrimental reliance

The second and third requirements of a proprietary estoppel may be taken together. These requirements involve detrimental reliance on the assurance made by the defendant to such an extent that it would amount to unconscionable conduct on his part if the assurance is not enforced. Frequently the detriment may involve expenditure on the part of the claimant which enhances the defendant's property, but in the domestic context may involve making a personal sacrifice based on an assurance by the defendant, see *Greasley v Cooke* above. In *Gillett v Holt* the Court of Appeal reviewed the principles of proprietary estoppel and decided that reliance and detriment are often intertwined and the fundamental principle that permeates the doctrine is to prevent unconscionable conduct. In the end the court is required to look at the matter in the round.

CASE EXAMPLE

Gillett v Holt [2001] Ch 210, CA

The claimant spent his working life as farm manager for and as a friend of the first defendant, a landowner of substantial means. The first defendant made repeated promises and assurances over many years that the claimant would succeed to his farming business, including the farmhouse in which the claimant and his family had lived for over 25 years. After 1992 relations between the claimant and the first defendant deteriorated rapidly. In 1995 the claimant was dismissed and the first defendant made lifetime dispositions to the second defendant and altered his will, making no provision for the claimant. The claimant brought a claim based on proprietary estoppel.

Held: The Court of Appeal allowed the claim and decided that the defendant's conduct had given rise to an estoppel, and the minimum equity to do justice to the claimant was for the first defendant to convey to him the freehold of the farmhouse together with a sufficient sum of money to compensate for his exclusion from the rest of the farming business. The defendant's repudiation of the assurance was unconscionable in all the circumstances.

JUDGMENT

'[I]n this case Mr Holt's assurances were repeated over a long period, usually before the assembled company on special family occasions, and some of them (such as it was all going to be ours anyway) were completely unambiguous. I find it wholly understandable that Mr and Mrs Gillett, then 10 years married and with two young sons, may have been worried about their home and their future depending on no more than oral assurances, however emphatic, from Mr Holt. The bitterly fought and ruinously expensive litigation which has ensued shows how right they would have been to be worried. But Mr Gillett, after discussing the matter with his wife and his parents, decided to rely on Mr Holt's assurances because Ken was a man of his word. Plainly the assurances given on this occasion were intended to be relied on, and were in fact relied on. In any event reliance would be presumed: see *Greasley v Cooke*.'

Walker LJ

4.13.5 Nature of the interest acquired

The fourth requirement accords to the court a considerable degree of flexibility in structuring the remedy to avoid the unconscionable behaviour of the defendant. The basic principle here is that the remedy will not exceed that which was promised or 'the minimum equity to do justice'. Once it is established that a right, by way of a proprietary estoppel, exists in favour of the claimant, the court will strive to find the most appropriate way of giving effect to the claimant's interest. This will depend on all the circumstances of the case. Solutions adopted by the courts include a transfer of the freehold estate, a decree of specific performance of the renewal option in a lease, a lien for the amount expended by the claimant, the creation of a licence for the claimant and a financial award. In this regard the Court of Appeal will rarely reverse the decision of the trial judge, provided that he had directed himself correctly in law and gave due consideration to the evidence presented at the trial. The issues that are determined by the trial judge are fact sensitive and the judge is best placed to deal with such matters.

KEY FACTS

Exceptions to the rule that equity will not assist a volunteer

Rule in *Strong v Bird* – proof of present, continuous intention to make an inter vivos gift
☐ appointment of intended donee as executor (would the next of kin have this effect?)

Donato mortis causa – transfer of dominion over the property *inter vivos*
☐ in contemplation of death ☐ conditional on death

Proprietary estoppel – voluntary promise
☐ reliance ☐ detriment ☐ nature of the estate

ACTIVITY

Essay writing

In his judgment on *Re Beaumont* [1902], Buckley LJ said:

> A *donatio mortis causa* is a singular form of gift. It may be said to be of an amphibious nature, being a gift which is neither entirely *inter vivos* nor testamentary. It is an act *inter vivos* by which the donee is to have absolute title to the gift not at once but if the donor dies. If the donor dies the title becomes absolute not under the will but as against the executor.

Explain and analyse this statement by reference to decided cases.

SUMMARY

- The essential tests for the constitution of express trusts as laid down by Turner LJ in *Milroy v Lord* require either a self-declaration of trust by the settlor or a transfer to the trustees followed by a declaration of trust. Alternatively, where the transferor has done everything required of him in order to transfer the property to the trustees, but some aspect of the legal title remains outstanding, the transfer may be effective in equity, see *Re Rose, Mascall v Mascall, Pennington v Waine, Zeital v Kaye, Curtis v Pulbrook*.

- The law in respect of gifts may, to some extent, overlap with trusts law. Gifts, like trusts, may be created *inter vivos* or on the death of the donor. The express trust may be created without consideration being furnished by the trustee or the beneficiary. The position remains the same where the gift or trust has not been completed.

- A perfect trust is one where the trustee has received the trust property subject to the valid declaration of trust, see *Milroy v Lord*. The effect is that the beneficiary acquires rights *in rem* to the trust property and it is immaterial that he is a volunteer; equity will assist a volunteer in these circumstances. On the other hand, where the trust is imperfect, the intended beneficiary does not necessarily acquire an interest in the property. The imperfect trust operates as an agreement to create a trust and only those who have provided valuable consideration may obtain a remedy. This principle is subject to exceptions created by equity and statute.

- The principle in *Fletcher v Fletcher* is to the effect that a trust may be constituted in respect of the benefit of a covenant or a chose in action. In *Re Cook* the court decided that the *Fletcher* rule is restricted to one type of chose, namely debts enforceable at law.

- The maxims 'Equity will not assist a volunteer' and 'Equity will not perfect an imperfect gift' are applicable when the settlor or donor has failed to create an express trust or gift and the intended beneficiary or donee wishes to enforce the arrangement. A volunteer is one who has not provided valuable consideration. In these circumstances the claimant will not be entitled to an equitable remedy.

- The relevance of the exceptions to the maxims that 'Equity will not assist a volunteer' or 'Equity will not perfect an imperfect gift' is based on the assumption that the trust or gift is imperfect, the claimant is a volunteer and in exceptional circumstances he (the claimant) will be entitled to equitable assistance.

- The rationale of the rule in *Strong v Bird* is that the imperfect gift *inter vivos* will become perfect by operation of law when the intended donee becomes the executor of the donor's estate provided that the donor manifests the requisite intention.

- The rationale of the *donatio mortis causa* exception is that the transfer of dominion over the relevant property *inter vivos* in contemplation and conditional on death will take effect immediately on the death of the donor. It has been reiterated by the courts on many occasions that clear evidence of the relevant conditions must be provided before a DMC will arise. In these circumstances equity will regard the gift as complete even though the proper mode of transfer was not used.

- The rationale behind the principle of proprietary estoppel is to prevent unjust enrichment where a gift is imperfect and the intended donee, in reliance on a promise made by the donor, expends money improving the property to the knowledge and acquiescence of the donor. The court will grant an equitable remedy to the donee that will give effect to the promise made by the donor.

- Each of the exceptions to the rule that 'Equity will not assist a volunteer' is subject to limits laid down judicially so as to avoid conflict with well established doctrines that are applicable to both *inter vivos* gifts and those arising after death.

- The methods of granting equitable assistance vary with each exception. The gift may be complete when the appropriate contingencies take place or, alternatively, the court may empower the volunteer donee to sue the donor (or his estate) to ensure that the imperfect gift is perfected.

SAMPLE ESSAY QUESTION

Consider the following essay question:

In what circumstances will equity perfect an imperfect gift?

Answer plan

> Ascertain when a gift becomes perfect.

> What are the requirements for a perfect gift? Consider the *Re Rose* principle.

> State the consequences of a gift being treated as perfect.

> The donee, despite being classified as a volunteer, acquires an interest in the property which the court will protect.

> Where the gift is imperfect but the intended donee has provided valuable consideration he will be entitled to support a claim in equity, see *Pullan v Koe*.

Alternatively, where the gift is imperfect the intended donee, subject to exceptions, will not obtain equitable assistance, see *Jones v Lock* and *Richards v Delbridge*.

The aggrieved donee, despite being a volunteer, is entitled to sue the donor for damages by virtue of the Contracts (Rights of Third Parties) Act 1999.

The court will grant equitable assistance to a volunteer in the exceptional circumstances that exist in:

- the rule in *Strong v Bird*;
- the doctrine of the *donatio mortis causa*;
- proprietary estoppel.

CONCLUSION

Further reading

Baker, P, 'Land as a *donatio mortis causa*' (1993) 109 LQR 19.

Barton, J, 'Trusts and covenants' (1975) 91 LQR 236.

Bright, S and Macfarlane, B, 'Proprietary estoppel and property rights' (2005) CLJ 449.

Cumber, H, 'Donationes mortis causa: a doctrine on its deathbed?' (2016) Conv 56.

Delany, D and Ryan, D, 'Unconscionability: a unifying theme in equity' (2008) Conv 401.

Dixon, M, 'Proprietary estoppel: a return to principle?' (2009) Conv 260.

Dixon, M, 'Confining and defining proprietary estoppel: the role of unconscionability' (2010) 30 LS 408.

Etherton, Sir Terence, 'Constructive trusts and proprietary estoppel: the search for clarity and principle' (2009) Conv 104.

Gardner, S, 'The remedial discretion in proprietary estoppel: again' (2006) 1222 LQR 492.

Garton, J, 'The role of the trust mechanism in the rule in *Re Rose*' (2003) Conv 364.

Halliwell, M, 'Perfecting imperfect gifts and trusts: have we reached the end of the Chancellor's foot?' (2003) Conv 192.

Jaconelli, J, 'Privity: the trust exception examined' (1998) Conv 88.

Jaconelli, J, 'Problems in the rule of *Strong v Bird*' (2006) Conv 432.

Kodilinye, G, 'A fresh look at the rule in *Strong v Bird*' (1982) Conv 14.

Luxton, P, 'In search of perfection: the *Re Rose* rule rationale' (2012) Conv PL 70.

Maitland, F W, *Equity: A Course of Lectures* (eds A H Chaytor and W J Whittaker, revd J Brunyate, Cambridge University Press, 2011).

Martin, J, 'Casenotes on *Sen v Headley* and *Woodard v Woodard*' (1992) Conv 53. Pawlowski, M, 'Death bed gifts' (1994) 144 NLJ 48.

Piska, N, 'Hopes, expectations and revocable promises in proprietary estoppel' (2009) 72 MLR 998.

Rickett, C, 'Completely constituting an inter vivos trust: property rules' (2001) Conv 515.

Robertson, A, 'The reliance basis of proprietary estoppel remedies' (2008) Conv 295.

Roe, T, 'Contractual intention under s 1(1)(b) and s 1(2) of the Contracts (Rights of Third Parties) Act 1999' (2000) 63 MLR 887.

Samuels, A, '*Donatio mortis causa* of a share certificate' (1966) 30 Conv 295.

5

Formalities for the creation of express trusts

AIMS AND OBJECTIVES

By the end of this chapter you should be able to:

- ascertain the rationale governing the statutory formalities referred to in this chapter
- recognise when the formalities are relevant in a problem question
- analyse and apply the appropriate formal requirement in answering an examination question

5.1 Introduction

As a general rule, equity does not insist on special formal requirements in order to create an express trust: 'Equity looks at the intent rather than the form.' However, occasionally Parliament has intervened and has imposed a number of formal requirements. These formalities vary with the subject-matter of the trust, such as land, the nature of the interest involved, such as an equitable interest, and the mode of creation, such as *inter vivos* or by will. These formalities are distinct from the necessary pre-conditions (see Chapter 4) needed to be satisfied in order to transfer the property to the trustees and so constitute the trust. Many of these formalities were originally enacted in the Statute of Frauds 1677. This was a statute passed in order to prevent fraud and require writing in appropriate circumstances. This chapter will consider the formal requirements for the creation of an *inter vivos* trust of land and the *inter vivos* transfer of an equitable interest by a beneficiary under a subsisting trust.

5.2 Declaration of a trust of land

Section 53(1)(b) of the Law of Property Act 1925 (originally s 7 of the Statute of Frauds 1677) enacts that:

SECTION

'A declaration of trust respecting any land or any interest therein must be manifested and proved by some writing signed by some person who is able to declare such trust or by his will.'

personalty
Personal property.

The subsection is only applicable to *inter vivos* trusts concerning land and not personal property, thus, a trust concerning one square inch of land is subject to the subsection, but a trust of £1 million of **personalty** may be declared orally.

5.2.1 'Land or an interest in land'

'Land', under Sched 1 to the Interpretation Act 1978, 'includes buildings and other structures, land covered with water, and any estate, interest, easement, servitude or right in or over land'.

Section 205(1)(ix)–(x) of the Law of Property Act 1925 enacts:

SECTION

' "land" includes (ix) land of any tenure, and mines and minerals, whether or not held apart from the surface, buildings or parts of buildings (whether the division is horizontal, vertical or made in any other way) and other corporeal hereditaments; also a manor, an advowson, and a rent and other incorporeal hereditaments, and an easement, right, privilege, or benefit in, over, or derived from land; and "mines and minerals" include any strata or seam of minerals or substances in or under the land, and powers of working and getting the same; and "manor" includes a lordship, and reputed manor or lordship; and "hereditament" means any real property which on an intestacy occurring before the commencement of this Act might have devolved upon an heir; "legal estates" (x) mean the estates, interests and charges, in or over land (subsisting or created in law) which are by this Act authorised to subsist or to be created as legal estates; "equitable interests" mean all the other interests and charges in or over land; and equitable interest "capable of subsisting as a legal estate" means such as could validly subsist or be created as a legal estate under this Act.'

Thus, included in the definition of 'land' are all rights to the land. In addition, s 2(6) of the Law of Property (Miscellaneous Provisions) Act 1989 defines an 'interest in land' as 'any estate, interest or charge in or over the land'. Thus, a mortgagee's right over the land is treated as an interest in land.

5.2.2 'Declarations of trusts'

Section 53(1)(b) of the Law of Property Act 1925 is only applicable in respect of declarations of trusts as the means of benefiting another. A declaration of trust was examined in Chapters 3 and 4. The test is whether a present, irrevocable intention to create a trust was manifested by the settlor. This requires the settlor to comply with the 'three certainties' test: certainty of intention, subject-matter and objects.

5.2.3 'Manifested and proved by some writing'

The requirement here is that the declaration of trust is only required to be *proved* by writing. It is not required to be *made* in writing. The trust is merely required to be evidenced in writing for the purposes of enforcement. The trust may validly be declared orally, but it simply would not be enforceable in a court. Thus, the writing need not be contemporaneous with the declaration but may be adduced some time after the declaration of trust and may enforce the trust retrospectively.

For instance, on Day 1, S, a settlor orally declares a trust in respect of land in favour of B, absolutely. This declaration is within s 53(1)(b) of the LPA 1925 and, because it is not supported by writing, it is unenforceable. However on Day 2, S executes a document endorsing the terms of the trust declared on Day 1. The trust is now enforceable, not from Day 2, but retrospectively, from Day 1.

The effect of non-compliance with s 53(1)(b) is to render unenforceable the valid declaration of trust.

5.2.4 'Writing'

'Writing' for these purposes does not assume any special mode and has taken the most diverse set of forms, ranging from recitals in an instrument to affidavits, answers to interrogatories, telegrams and even letters to third parties. In short, writing may take any form that may be appropriate for the Land Registry. The test is whether the material terms of the trust are included in a document (or series of documents) signed by the settlor. The material terms, of course, involve the 'three certainties' test.

In the law of evidence a 'document' has been defined in s 13 of the Civil Evidence Act 1995 as 'anything in which information of any description is recorded'. Thus, a document for these purposes may include an audio or video cassette, and even information stored in electronic form. But this notion of a document may be too broad to constitute 'writing' for the purposes of the Law of Property Act 1925. The objective under the 1925 Act assumes the delivery of the terms of the trust to the Registrar, for the purposes of registration in the Land Registry.

The material terms of the trust need not be contained in one document but may be contained in a variety of documents. There is a need for each document to refer to the other to such an extent that the documents, taken as a whole, form a complete memorandum of the terms of the trust.

For instance, Document 1 may manifest the settlor's intention to create a trust and be signed by him, Document 2 may contain the subject-matter of the trust and Document 3 may contain the objects of the trust. Provided that all three documents are joined, a complete memorandum of the terms of the trust may exist. In this event, the documents may refer to each other with sufficient certainty to identify them. Each document or at least one of the documents is required to be signed by the settlor.

This requirement is fundamentally different from the test enacted in s 2(1) of the Law of Property (Miscellaneous Provisions) Act 1989 concerning contracts for the sale or other dispositions of land. Under this Act the terms of the contract are required to be included in one document.

5.2.5 Signature

Section 53(1)(b) of the Law of Property Act 1925 requires the person able to declare the trust to sign the document(s). The requirement here is that the settlor must endorse the document containing the terms of the trust. The signature need not be the full, formal signature of the settlor but may take the form of some mark attributed to the settlor and intended by him to authenticate the document(s). Thus, initials or the thumbprint of the settlor will be sufficient. Section 1(4) of the Law of Property (Miscellaneous Provisions) Act 1989 enacts that ' "sign" in relation to an instrument includes making one's mark on the instrument and "signature" is to be construed accordingly'. Likewise, the settlor's voice or image on a recording may amount to a signature.

However, the signature of the settlor's agent is not effective for these purposes.

5.3 Exclusion

Section 53(2) of the Law of Property Act 1925 (replacing s 8 of the Statute of Frauds 1677) provides that 'This section shall not affect the creation or operation of implied, resulting and constructive trusts.' Resulting and constructive trusts are types of implied trusts that are created by the courts. These trusts are exempt from the above formal requirement.

Accordingly, an *inter vivos* resulting trust of land may arise without the terms being reduced into writing.

CASE EXAMPLE

Hodgson v Marks [1971] Ch 892

Mrs Hodgson (Mrs H), a widow aged 83, owned a house in Edgware, London. She took a lodger, Mr Evans, whom she trusted, but who was disliked by her nephew who also lived in the house. In order to prevent her nephew turning Mr Evans out of the house, Mrs H voluntarily transferred the house to Mr Evans, who was duly registered as the legal owner of the property. Mrs H had orally declared that the house was to remain hers. Mr Evans later attempted to transfer the house to Mr Marks. When Mrs H discovered this, she claimed that she was entitled in equity to the house. Mr Marks argued that no trust was created in favour of Mrs H because the oral statement by Mrs H was not reduced into writing signed by her.

Held: Mrs H had retained the absolute equitable interest in the house by way of a resulting trust. This trust was enforceable by virtue of s 53(2) of the LPA 1925.

JUDGMENT

'[T]he evidence is clear that the transfer [to Mr Evans] was not intended to operate as a gift, and, in those circumstances, I do not see why there was not a resulting trust of the beneficial interest to the plaintiff, which would not, of course, be affected by s 53(1). It was argued that a resulting trust is based upon implied intention, and that where there is an express trust for the transferor intended and declared – albeit ineffectively – there is no room for such an implication. I do not accept that. If an attempted express trust fails, that seems to me just the occasion for implication of a resulting trust, whether the failure be due to uncertainty, or perpetuity, or lack of form. It would be a strange outcome if the plaintiff were to lose her beneficial interest because her evidence had not been confined to negativing a gift but had additionally moved into a field forbidden by s 53(1) for lack of writing. I remark in this connection that we are not concerned with the debatable question whether on a voluntary transfer of land by A to stranger B there is a presumption of a resulting trust. The accepted evidence is that this was not intended as a gift, notwithstanding the reference to love and affection in the transfer, and s 53(1) does not exclude that evidence.'

Russell LJ

In *Hodgson v Marks* (1971) it would have been ironic that the precursor to s 53(1)(b) of the LPA 1925, namely s 7 of the Statute of Frauds 1677, a statute passed to prevent fraud, could have been used to perpetrate a fraud, but for s 53(2) of the LPA 1925. In any event, a similar conclusion could have been reached by adopting the constructive trust institution, namely to prevent a fraud being committed on Mrs Hodgson. In such a case the court could have applied the maxim, 'Equity will not allow a statute to be used as an engine for fraud' as illustrated in *Rochefoucauld v Boustead* [1897] 1 Ch 196 (see later in Chapter 8).

5.4 Dispositions under s 53(1)(c) of the Law of Property Act 1925

Section 53(1)(c) of the LPA 1925 (substantially, but not completely, reflecting the terms of s 9 of the Statute of Frauds 1677) provides as follows:

SECTION

'A disposition of an equitable interest or trust subsisting at the time of disposition, must be in writing signed by the person disposing of the same, or by his agent thereunto lawfully authorised in writing or by will.'

Section 9 of the Statute of Frauds 1677, before its repeal, provided:

SECTION

'all grants and assignments of any trust or confidence shall be in writing signed by the party granting or assigning the same or by such last will or devise or else shall be utterly void and of no effect.'

Rationale of the provision

The policy underlying the enactment is to:

(i) prevent fraud by prohibiting oral hidden transfers of equitable interests under trusts. For example, assume that A holds the legal title to property upon trust for B and B disposes of his equitable interest in writing in favour of C. On the same day B, without writing, purports to sell the same property to D. Who will acquire B's equitable interest? Clearly C will acquire the equitable interest because B has complied with the requirements of s 53(1)(c). If D has been defrauded he may be able to bring a personal claim against B for damages.

(ii) assist trustees by enabling them to identify the whereabouts of the equitable interest subsisting under a trust. In the example above the issue is in whose favour will A, the trustee, be required to hold the property upon trust? There is a potential conflict of equitable ownership and A will be required to hold the relevant property upon trust for C because B has validly transferred the property to C. The requirement of writing permits A to verify the true ownership of the property.

See Lord Upjohn in *Vandervell v IRC* [1967] 2 AC 291:

JUDGMENT

'[T]he object of the section [53(1)(c)], as was the object of the old Statute of Frauds, is to prevent hidden oral transactions in equitable interests in fraud of those truly entitled, and making it difficult, if not impossible, for the trustees to ascertain who are in truth his beneficiaries.'

Lord Upjohn

Effect of non-compliance

The effect of non-compliance with this provision is that the purported disposition is void. This is distinct from s 53(1)(b): see above. The wording of the statutory provision (s 53(1)(c)) is mandatory in nature. The operative words are 'must be in writing'.

Subsisting equitable interest

An essential restriction on the operation of s 53(1)(c) is that it is applicable only to subsisting equitable interests. In other words, the provision is applicable to the interest of a beneficiary under a subsisting trust. The subsection is not applicable to *the original creation of a trust*, but is activated only when a beneficiary under a trust seeks to dispose of his interest. For instance, S, a settlor, transfers property to the trustees, A and B, to hold property upon trust for C absolutely. Thus, A and B hold the legal title to property and C enjoys the equitable interest. The formalities that S will need to comply with, if any, will depend on the type of property concerned. But this arrangement does not involve s 53(1)(c). If C wishes to dispose of his equitable interest (subsisting) he is required to comply with the statutory provision. A subsisting equitable interest may exist under any type of trust, express, resulting, constructive or statutory.

Land and personalty
The subsection is applicable to subsisting equitable interests in realty or personalty and contains no restriction as to the type of property. Indeed, the provision focuses on the type of *interest*, and not the type of property in which that interest is enjoyed. This is the position despite the definition of 'equitable interests' under s 205(1)(x) of the Law of Property Act 1925, which states that 'equitable interests mean all the other interests and charges in or over land'.

Writing
Writing is not required to be included in a formal document but within this limitation may take a variety of paper forms such as letters and telegrams. The test is whether a permanent form of representation exists of the transfer of the relevant interest (see earlier regarding s 53(1)(b)).

Signature
The signature of the disponer or his agent may take any form which endorses the document, including thumb prints, initials and perhaps the disponer's voice on a tape recording: see above.

Agent's signature
The section authorises the signature of an agent, provided the agent was lawfully authorised in writing. The position here is different from s 53(1)(b): see above.

Disposition
The key feature of s 53(1)(c) is the meaning of the term 'disposition'. This has not been defined in the statute. But the term 'conveyance' has been defined in s 205(1)(ii) of the Law of Property Act 1925 as including a disposition. The subsection provides as follows:

SECTION

'Conveyance includes a mortgage, charge, lease, assent, vesting declaration, vesting instrument, disclaimer, release and every other assurance of property or of an interest therein by any instrument, except a will; convey has a corresponding meaning; and disposition includes a conveyance and also a devise, bequest, or an appointment of property contained in a will; and dispose of has a corresponding meaning.

In *Timpson's Executors v Yerbury* [1936] 1 KB 645, Romer LJ described a disposition thus:

JUDGMENT

'The equitable interest in property in the hands of the trustee can be disposed of by the person entitled to it in favour of a third party in any one of four different ways. The person entitled to it:

(1) can assign it to the third party directly;
(2) can direct the trustees to hold the property in trust for the third party;
(3) can contract for valuable consideration to assign the equitable interest to him; or
(4) can declare himself to be a trustee for him of such interest.'

Romer LJ

5.4.1 Direction to trustees

Romer LJ, in his second classification of a disposition in *Yerbury* (1936), declared that a direction by a beneficiary under a subsisting trust to the trustees (holding the legal title) to hold upon trust for another beneficiary is within s 53(1)(c). For instance, S creates a trust of 50,000 shares in BT plc to T1 and T2, as trustees, by transferring the legal title to the shares for the benefit of B absolutely. If B directs T1 and T2 to hold the property on trust for C, this intended disposition would be within s 53(1)(c). Thus, B is required to issue the direction in writing otherwise it is void.

In *Grey v IRC* [1960] AC 1, HL, the House of Lords decided that an oral direction by an equitable owner to the trustees of a trust fund to hold the property upon trust for another was a purported disposition and void for non-compliance with s 53(1)(c).

CASE EXAMPLE

Grey v IRC [1960] AC 1, HL

In 1949, Mr Hunter (the settlor) transferred shares of a nominal sum to trustees upon trust for his six grandchildren. In 1955, the settlor transferred 18,000 £1 shares to the same trustees upon trust for himself. In an attempt to avoid *ad valorem* stamp duty (payable on instruments which transfer any property or interest in property), the settlor verbally instructed the trustees to hold the shares upon trust for the grandchildren. The trustees subsequently executed confirmatory documents affirming the oral instructions. The Revenue assessed the documents to *ad valorem* stamp duty.

Held: The oral instructions by Mr Hunter were ineffective and void for non-compliance with s 53(1)(c), but the confirmatory documents had the effect of transferring the equitable interests to the grandchildren. Accordingly, the documents were stampable.

JUDGMENT

'If the word disposition is given its natural meaning it cannot, I think, be denied that a direction given by the beneficiary whereby the beneficial interest in the shares theretofore vested in another or others is a disposition.'

Lord Simonds

JUDGMENT

'[T]he short question [is] whether the oral direction that Mr Hunter gave to his trustees on 18 February 1955, amounted in any ordinary sense of the words to a disposition of an equitable interest or trust subsisting at the time of the disposition, I do not feel any doubt as to my answer. I think that it did. Whether we describe what happened in technical or in more general terms, the full equitable interest in the eighteen thousand shares concerned, which at that time was his, was (subject to any statutory invalidity) diverted by his direction from this ownership into the beneficial ownership of the various equitable owners, present and future, entitled under his six existing settlements.

Moreover, there is warrant for saying that a direction to his trustee by the equitable owner of trust property prescribing new trusts of that property was a declaration of trust. But it does not necessarily follow from that that such a direction, if the effect of it was to determine completely or pro tanto the subsisting equitable interest of the maker of the direction, was not also a "grant or assignment" for the purposes of s 9 [of the Statute of Frauds 1677] and therefore required writing for its validity. Something had to happen to that equitable interest in order to displace it in favour of the new interests created by the direction: and it would be at any rate logical to treat the direction as being an assignment of the subsisting interest to the new beneficiary or beneficiaries or, in other cases, a release or surrender of it to the trustees.'

Lord Radcliffe

Mr Hunter, the settlor, would have been better advised, from the point of view of avoiding stamp duty, to have omitted the transaction involving the transfer of the legal title to the 18,000 shares to the trustees and, as the absolute legal and equitable owner of the shares, orally declare himself a trustee in favour of his six grandchildren. This would have amounted to a self-declaration of trust of 18,000 shares with Mr Hunter holding the legal title as trustee for the beneficiaries. The effect of such a declaration would have been to create an original trust and would have been outside s 53(1)(c). No writing would have been required. Further, if Mr Hunter wanted the original trustees to hold on trust, he could have transferred the legal title to the shares to them in a subsequent transaction. This would have attracted only nominal stamp duty.

Section 53(1)(c) did not consolidate s 9 of the Statute of Frauds 1677

In *Grey v IRC* (1960), counsel for the taxpayer argued that the Law of Property Act 1925 is a consolidating Act and, in effect, consolidated s 9 of the Statute of Frauds 1677. It was submitted that a consolidating Act does not change the law and as this transaction would have been effective under the 1677 Statute, it ought to be equally effective under the 1925 legislation. This argument was rejected by the House of Lords. Lord Radcliffe pointed out that s 9 of the Statute of Frauds was repealed and replaced (or consolidated) by the Law of Property Act 1922. The 1922 Act was amended by the Law of Property (Amendment) Act 1924 by the introduction of the broad concept of 'disposition', as opposed to the old narrower expressions 'grants or assignments'. The 1925 Law of Property Act then consolidated the law that existed after 1924. Thus, the link between the 1677 Statute and the 1925 Act was broken by the 1924 Act.

JUDGMENT

'The Law of Property Act 1925 itself was, no doubt, strictly a consolidating statute. But what it consolidated was not merely the Law of Property Act 1922, a statute which had itself effected massive changes in the law relating to real property and conveyancing, but also the later Law of Property (Amendment) Act 1924. The Statute of Frauds sections had not been touched by the Act of 1922, but they were, in effect, repealed and re-enacted in altered form by the operation of s 3 of the Act of 1924. This new wording is what is carried into s 53 of the Act of 1925. For these reasons I think that there is no direct link between s 53(1)(c) of the Act of 1925 and s 9 of the Statute of Frauds.'

Lord Radcliffe (in *Grey v IRC*)

5.4.2 Transfer of both the legal and equitable titles to a third party

In *Vandervell v IRC* [1967] 2 AC 291, HL, the House of Lords decided that s 53(1)(c) has no application where the equitable owner, under a subsisting trust, directs the legal owner to transfer his title to a third party, and in the same transaction, the equitable owner, without writing, transfers his interest to the same third party. In other words, the effect of the transaction is to terminate the trust by uniting both the legal and equitable interests in the hands of the third party. Clearly, such a transaction is outside the mischief of s 53(1)(c): see above. There can be no fraudulent dealing with the equitable interest simply because it is now incorporated with the legal title. The trustees do not need to identify the movement of the equitable interest because this is united with the legal title and, in any event, the position of the trustee is redundant because the trust no longer subsists.

CASE EXAMPLE

Vandervell v IRC [1967] 2 AC 291, HL

In 1958, Mr Vandervell decided to donate £150,000 to the Royal College of Surgeons to found a chair of pharmacology. He decided to achieve this purpose by transferring 100,000 ordinary shares in Vandervell Products Ltd (a private company controlled by Mr Vandervell) to the College subject to an option (vested in a separate company, Vandervell Trustee Company) to repurchase the shares for £5,000. In pursuance of this scheme, Mr Vandervell orally directed the National Provincial Bank (which held the legal title to the shares on behalf of Mr Vandervell) to transfer the shares to the College, subject to the option exercisable by the Trustee Company. The bank complied with the directions. During the tax years 1958–59 and 1959–60, dividends on the shares amounting to £162,500 and £87,500 respectively were paid to the College. The Inland Revenue assessed Mr Vandervell to surtax in respect of the dividends, on two grounds:

(a) that Mr Vandervell had not absolutely divested himself from the shares, so that the dividends fell to be treated as his income within s 415 of the Income Tax Act 1952 (now s 683 Income and Corporation Taxes Act 1988);

(b) in the alternative, that Mr Vandervell had not transferred his equitable interest in the shares to the College because of his failure to comply with s 53(1)(c) of the Law of Property Act 1925.

Held:

(i) The Revenue succeeded on the first ground because Mr Vandervell had transferred only the legal title to the option to the Trustee Company. The equitable title to the option had not been consciously transferred to the Trustee Company or anyone. Accordingly, Mr Vandervell retained an interest in the option, namely an equitable interest by way of a resulting trust. Since Mr Vandervell retained an interest in the option to acquire the 100,000 shares he, therefore, retained an interest in the shares by way of a resulting trust.

(ii) Mr Vandervell won the argument on the second ground of the assessment. The court decided that in a composite transaction the transfer of both the legal and equitable interests in property to a third party is outside the mischief of s 53(1)(c).

JUDGMENT

'[W]hen the beneficial owner owns the whole beneficial estate and is in a position to give directions to his bare trustee with regard to the legal as well as the equitable estate there can be no possible ground for invoking the section [s53(1)(c)] where the beneficial owner wants to deal with the legal estate as well as the equitable estate.

Section 53(1)(c) is, in my opinion, directed to cases where dealings with the equitable estate are divorced from the legal estate and I do not think any of their Lordships in *Grey* and *Oughtred* had in mind the case before your Lordships. To hold the contrary would make assignments complicated; if there had to be assignments in express terms of both legal and equitable interests that would make the section more productive of injustice than the supposed evils it was intended to prevent.'

Lord Upjohn

JUDGMENT

'[W]hen the taxpayer instructed the bank to transfer the shares to the college, and made it abundantly clear that he wanted to pass, by means of that transfer, his own beneficial or equitable interest, plus the bank's legal interest, he achieved the same result as if there had been no separation of the interests. The transfer thus made, pursuant to his intentions and instructions, was a disposition, not of the equitable interest alone, but of the entire estate in the shares. In such a case, I see no room for the operation of s53(1)(c).'

Lord Donovan

As an additional point, in *Vandervell v IRC* (1967), instead of transferring his subsisting equitable interest in the shares to the College without writing, Mr Vandervell could have achieved the same result by first terminating the trust under the *Saunders v Vautier* (1841) 4 Beav 115 principle (termination of trust on the direction of the beneficiaries, provided that they are *sui juris* and absolutely entitled to the equitable interest, see above). The effect would have been that Mr Vandervell would then acquire the legal title. Second, armed with both the legal and equitable interests in the shares, Mr Vandervell could have created a trust for the College by orally declaring himself a trustee for the same beneficiary. This transaction would have been effective outside s53(1)(c), for there would no longer be a subsisting equitable interest and the arrangement would have involved the creation of a new trust.

5.4.3 Section 53(2) of the Law of Property Act 1925

Section 53(2) (re-enacting s8 of the Statute of Frauds 1677) provides as follows:

SECTION

'This section shall not affect the creation or operation of resulting, implied or constructive trusts.'

The issue which is considered in this section is: how far does s53(2) restrict the operation of s53(1)(c)? The groundswell of opinion is to the effect that the resulting and constructive trusts referred to in s53(2) are created by the courts. Accordingly, a court will not contradict itself by requiring a disposition under such trust (constructive) to be in writing. Either the court feels that the circumstances of the case warrant the imposition of a trust or it does not. If the court favours the creation of a trust, it ought not to be a defence that the transfer of the equitable interest has not been reduced into writing.

The relationship between s 53(1)(c) and s 53(2) was examined in *Oughtred v IRC* [1960] AC 206. In this case the House of Lords decided that a specifically enforceable contract between a mother and son to exchange their interests in shares created a constructive trust when the mother disposed of her interest to her son before he reciprocated. The purpose of the transaction was to reduce the level of estate duty payable on the mother's estate on her death and to avoid stamp duty. Despite the trust, a majority of the Law Lords decided that the document was liable to stamp duty. But only three Law Lords considered the relationship between s 53(1)(c) and s 53(2). It is believed that the opinion of Lord Denning on this issue is no longer tenable.

JUDGMENT

'I do not think the oral agreement was effective to transfer Peter's reversionary interest to his mother. I should have thought that the wording of section 53(1)(c) of the Law of Property Act, 1925, clearly made a writing necessary to effect a transfer: and section 53(2) does not do away with that necessity.'

Lord Denning

JUDGMENT

'The appellant as a result of what was done on June 26 was, as the release recognised, absolutely entitled to the settled shares, but that was not because the equitable interest was transferred to or vested in her by the transfer but because Peter, having become a constructive trustee for her of his equitable interest, could not, after his nominees had received the consideration shares, as they did on June 26, 1956, dispute the appellant's title to the settled shares.'

Lord Cohen (dissenting)

This appears to be the language of an estoppel.

JUDGMENT

'On June 18, 1956, the son owned an equitable reversionary interest in the settled shares: by his oral agreement of that date he created in his mother an equitable interest in her reversion, since the subject-matter of the agreement was property of which specific performance would normally be decreed by the court. He thus became a trustee for her of that interest *sub modo*: having regard to subsection (2) of section 53 of the Law of Property Act, 1925, subsection (1) of that section did not operate to prevent that trusteeship arising by operation of law. On June 26 Mrs Oughtred transferred to her son the shares which were the consideration for her acquisition of his equitable interest: upon this transfer he became in a full sense and without more a trustee of his interest for her. She was the effective owner of all outstanding equitable interests. It was thus correct to recite in the deed of release to the trustees of the settlement, which was to wind up their trust, that the trust fund was by then held upon trust for her absolutely. There was, in fact, no equity to the shares that could be asserted against her, and it was open to her, if she so wished, to let the matter rest without calling for a written assignment from her son.'

Lord Radcliffe (dissenting)

In respect of the relationship between ss 53(1)(c) and 53(2), in *Oughtred v IRC* (1960) only Lord Radcliffe's opinion reflected a degree of rationality and realism. A constructive trust is created by the court in order to prevent unjust enrichment. It is the conduct of the defendant that justifies the imposition of the trust. It would be unrealistic for the court to shackle its jurisdiction on the sole ground of the lack of writing, particularly if it feels that the circumstances justify the imposition of a constructive trust. Accordingly, the subsequent authorities refused to follow Lord Denning's and Lord Cohen's opinions.

In *Re Holt's Settlement* [1968] 1 All ER 470, Megarry J adopted Lord Radcliffe's judgment in *Oughtred v IRC* (1960) in the context of schemes under the Variation of Trusts Act 1958:

JUDGMENT

'Mr Millett for the tenant for life, provided … [a] means of escape from s 53(1)(c) in his helpful reply. Where, as here, the arrangement consists of an agreement made for valuable consideration, and that agreement is specifically enforceable, then the beneficial interests pass to the respective purchasers on the making of the agreement. Those interests pass by virtue of the species of constructive trust made familiar by contracts for the sale of land, whereunder the vendor becomes a constructive trustee for the purchaser as soon as the contract is made … S 53(2), he continued, provides that: "This section does not affect the creation or operation of resulting, implied or constructive trusts." Accordingly, because the trust was constructive, s 53(1)(c) was excluded … It seems to me that there is considerable force in this argument in cases where the agreement is specifically enforceable, and in its essentials I accept it.'

Megarry J

In *Chinn v Collins* [1981] AC 533, the House of Lords decided that a specifically enforceable contract was not essential in order to effect a transfer of an equitable interest. The equitable interest in the vendor was transferred to the purchaser as soon as he made the payment of the price. This opinion was expressed in the context of a tax-avoidance scheme:

JUDGMENT

'The legal title to the shares was at all times vested in a nominee and dealings related to the equitable interest in these required no formality. As soon as there was an agreement for their sale accompanied or followed by payment of the price, the equitable title passed at once to the purchaser and all that was needed to perfect his title was notice to the trustees or the nominee, which notice both had at all material times.'

Lord Wilberforce

More recently, the Court of Appeal, in *Neville v Wilson* [1996] 3 WLR 460, reviewed the diverse opinions delivered in *Oughtred v IRC* (1960) and endorsed Lord Radcliffe's view that s 53(2) restricted the operation of s 53(1)(c).

Nourse LJ in *Neville v Wilson* (1996), after referring to *Oughtred v IRC* (1960), said:

JUDGMENT

'Why then should sub-section (2) not apply? No convincing reason was suggested in argument and none has occurred to us since. Moreover, to deny its application in this case would be to restrict the effect of general words when no restriction is called for, and to lay the ground for fine distinctions in the future. With all the respect that is due to those who have thought to the contrary, we hold that sub-section (2) applies to an agreement such that we have in this case.'

Nourse LJ

In *Neville v Wilson* (1996), shares in U Ltd were held in trust for J Ltd, a family company. The shareholders in J Ltd agreed informally to liquidate J Ltd and divide the equitable interest in U Ltd shares among themselves in proportion to their existing shareholdings. The question in issue was whether s 53(1)(c) invalidated this agreement. The Court of Appeal held that each shareholder's agreement gave rise to a constructive trust so that s 53(2) exempted them from the requirements of s 53(1)(c).

In addition, s 2(5) of the Law of Property (Miscellaneous Provisions) Act 1989 exempts 'implied resulting and constructive trusts' from the requirement that a contract for the sale of land or an interest in land must be in writing.

5.4.4 Overlap between subsections 53(1)(b) and (c) of the Law of Property Act 1925

Section 53(1)(b) of the Law of Property Act 1925 concerns a declaration of trust respecting land and s 53(1)(c) deals with the disposition of a subsisting equitable interest in land or personalty. It follows that a beneficiary under a trust of land, who declares a trust of such property, will attract the requirements of both subsections. Since s 53(1)(c) is expressed in a mandatory form, no disposition of the equitable interest will take place until the transfer (or declaration) is in writing.

5.4.5 Estoppel

In the controversial case, *Re Vandervell Trusts (No 2)* [1974] Ch 269, the Court of Appeal decided *inter alia* that the doctrine of equitable estoppel creates an exception to the s 53(1)(c) requirements.

JUDGMENT

'If he (Mr Vandervell) had lived, and not died, he could not have claimed it back. He could not be heard to say that he did not intend the children's trust to have it. Even a court of equity would not allow him to do anything so inequitable and unjust.'

Lord Denning MR

In *Re Vandervell Trusts (No 2)* Mr V orally directed the trustee company, VT Ltd, to exercise the option to repurchase the shares. This was done by VT Ltd and the legal title to the shares was vested in VT Ltd. The issue here was whether the equitable interest in the shares was acquired for the benefit of the children's settlement or was retained for Mr V (and his estate following his death). The Court of Appeal decided that the equitable interest in the shares was held by VT Ltd for the children's settlement. Section 53(1)(c) was not applicable to a transaction which extinguished a resulting trust.

5.4.6 Self-declaration of trust of part of an equitable interest

A disposition may be effected by means of a self-declaration. This method was referred to by Romer LJ in the *Yerbury* decision (1936): see above. Thus, B, a beneficiary, may declare himself a trustee of his entire interest in favour of C. This arrangement is valid only if it is reduced into writing.

However, it is debatable whether a self-declaration of trust of *part* of a subsisting equitable interest amounts to a disposition within s 53(1)(c). It has been suggested that when a settlor (with a subsisting equitable interest) declares himself a trustee of *part* of his equitable interest, he retains his equitable interest but a subsidiary equitable interest becomes vested in the new beneficiary. The effect of this transaction is that a new trust may be carved out of an equitable interest that may not amount to a disposition within s 53(1)(c). For example, B, a beneficiary who enjoys an absolute equitable interest under a trust, retains a life interest and orally declares himself a trustee of the remainder interest in favour of C. It is arguable that since B has active duties to perform, the sub-trust created by B amounts to the creation of a new trust and is not a 'disposition' within s 53(1)(c). Accordingly, the policy of enacting s 53(1)(c) is not relevant and such a disposition is outside the provision: see *Grainge v Wilberforce* (1889) 5 TLR 436, *Re Lashmar* [1891] 1 Ch 258 and A Underhill and D Hayton, *Law of Trusts and Trustees* (16th edn, Butterworths, 2002). On the other hand, Lewin, in *Trusts and Trustees* (17th edn, Sweet & Maxwell, 2003), asserts that a self-declaration of trust, whether as to part of the equitable interest or the entirety, is a disposition within s 53(1)(c) and requires writing. Brian Green in an article entitled '*Grey, Oughtred* and *Vandervell*: a contextual reappraisal' (1984) 47 MLR 385 observes that the subsection draws no distinction between dealings with equitable interests carrying beneficial rights, on the one hand, and dealings with equitable interests shorn of beneficial rights, that is valuable and valueless equitable interests, on the other hand:

QUOTATION

'[Professor Hayton] expressed the view that, in deciding whether a "declaration of trust" over a subsisting equitable interest falls within s 53(1)(c), it is necessary to distinguish between declarations under which the declarant purports to reserve to himself an active role as trustee of the derivative equitable interest established by him, and declarations whereby the declarant renders himself a bare trustee for others. The former case is said to fall outside s 53(1)(c), whilst the latter is said to be within it on the basis that the declarant having no further role to play simply "drops out of the picture" from the moment of declaration onwards. Three 19th century cases are cited in support of this view, *Onslow v Wallis* (1849) 1 Mac & G 506; *Re Lashmar* [1891] 1 Ch 258; *Grainge v Wilberforce* (1889) 5 TLR 436 … this somewhat inelegant distinction between declarations within s 53(1)(c) and declarations outside it, whatever its intuitive appeal, is certainly not justified by the 19th century authorities marshalled in its support, and is inconsistent with the view adopted by the House of Lords in *Oughtred v IRC* (1960) in relation to a constructive bare trustee of an equitable interest who most definitely remained "in the picture" until the execution of a "completion document" deliberately removed him from it.'

....

**student
mentor tip**

....

'Equity and Trusts can be challenging: just stick to the reading and read the cases in full.'
Adil, Queen Mary University

In *Nelson v Greening & Sykes Ltd* [2007] EWCA Civ 1358, the Court of Appeal refused to accept that the 'intermediate trustee' ceases to be a trustee. The effect was that as a matter of law, as distinct from practicality, the bare trust continues and is not extinguished. It is submitted that this amounts to a vindication of the view of Brian Green.

JUDGMENT

'It is true that in *Grey v IRC* [1958] Ch 690 (affirmed [1960] AC 1), Lord Evershed MR (dissenting, but not on this point) said that where a person who is the owner beneficially of property (and the legal estate is vested in another as trustee for him) makes a declaration of trust the practical effect would seem, in common sense, to amount, or be capable of amounting, to the getting rid of a trust or equitable interest then subsisting. It is said in Snell, *Equity* (31st ed McGhee, 2005), para 19–11 that where property is transferred to T "on trust for B absolutely" … if B in turn becomes a bare trustee of his equitable interest for C, T will hold directly in trust for C … citing *Head v Lord Teynham* (1783) 1 Cox Eq Cas 57 (which only holds that where trustees and the beneficiary are before the court, an intermediate trustee of the equitable interest need not be made a party).

These authorities do not bind this court to hold that as a matter of law an intermediate trustee ceases to be a trustee. I accept the submission for G&S that saying (as Lord Evershed MR said) that the practical effect would seem to amount to or be capable of amounting to the getting rid of the trust of the equitable interest then subsisting, is not the same as saying that as a matter of law it does get rid of the intermediate trust. What he was saying was that in the case of a trust and sub-trust of personal property the trustees may decide that as a matter of practicality it is more convenient to deal directly with the beneficiary of the sub-trust.

But in any event it seems to me that the authorities have no application to a case where the trust property is the purchaser's interest in land created by the existence of an executory contract for sale and purchase … the bare trust continued and at the date of the hearing Mr Nelson held his beneficial interest on trust for Mrs Hanley. The contract was specifically enforceable against Mr Nelson.'

Collins LJ in *Nelson v Greening & Sykes Ltd*

5.4.7 Disclaimers

Disclaimers are exempt from s 53(1)(c), despite being included in the definition of a 'conveyance' within s 205(1)(ii). A disclaimer involves a conscious decision on the part of the individual to abandon his interest in the property. There is no positive intention on his part to transfer the interest to any specific person. The effect of the disclaimer is that the property is transferred or acquired by another, but this is distinct from a conscious decision to dispose of the property or interest to another.

JUDGMENT

'A disclaimer operates by way of avoidance and not by way of disposition. For the general aspects of disclaimer we refer briefly to the discussion in *Re Stratton's Disclaimer* [1958] Ch 42.'

Danckwerts LJ in *Re Paradise Motor Co* [1968] 1 WLR 1125

A surrender of an equitable interest, on the other hand, would appear to be a disposition within s 53(1)(c), despite academic commentary to the contrary. The argument, which is not very convincing, is that a surrender involves an extinguishment of an interest which is distinct from a disposition. If this is true it would amount to a relatively simple exercise in avoiding the rigour of s 53(1)(c).

5.4.8 Pension scheme nominations

Nominations by staff pension fund holders of the persons who will become entitled to benefits under a pension fund after the deaths of the pension holders are not dispositions within s 53(1)(c).

JUDGMENT

'The question is thus whether an instrument with this elective, contingent and defeasible quality, which takes effect only on the death of the person signing it, can fairly be said to be a disposition of an equitable interest or trust subsisting at the time of the disposition. Mr Ferris put much emphasis on the word subsisting: however wide the word disposition might be in its meaning, there was no disposition of a subsisting equity, he said, I should hesitate to describe an instrument which has a mere possibility of becoming a disposition as being in itself a disposition *ab initio*; and I agree that the word, subsisting also seems to point against the nomination falling within section 53(1)(c) … I very much doubt whether the nomination falls within section 53(1)(c).'

Megarry J in *Re Danish Bacon Co Ltd. Staff Pension Fund* [1971] 1 WLR 248

KEY FACTS

Formalities

Declarations of trusts of land (s 53(1)(b) LPA 1925)	
▦ Land or an interest in land ▦ Declarations of trusts ▦ Manifested and proved ▦ Writing ▦ Signature ▦ Exemption	s 205(1)(ix) LPA 1925; s 2(6) LP (Miscellaneous Provisions) Act 1989 'Three certainties' test Unenforceable s 13 Civil Evidence Act 1995
	Endorsement: s 2(5) LP (Miscellaneous Provisions) Act 1989 s 53(2) LPA 1925; *Hodgson v Marks* (1971)
Dispositions of subsisting equitable interests (s 53(1)(c) LPA 1925)	
▦ Disposition ▦ Subsisting equitable interest ▦ 'Must be in writing' ▦ Land or personalty ▦ Signature (inclusive of agent's signature)	*Timpson's Executors v Yerbury* (1936); *Grey v IRC* (1960); *Vandervell v IRC* (1967); *Re Vandervell Trusts (No 2)* (1974); *Oughtred v IRC* (1960); *Re Holt* (1968); *Neville v Wilson* (1996); *Re Paradise Motor Co* (1968); *Re Danish Bacon Staff Pension Fund* (1971) Intended transfer is void for non-compliance with the provision S 205 (1)(ix)–(x) LPA 1925; s 2(6) LP (Misc Prov) Act 1989

ACTIVITY

Applying the law

Peter transfers his freehold property, Blackacre, to Jason and Joseph to hold upon trust for the benefit of Anthony absolutely.

Consider the effect of the following alternative directions:

(i) Anthony orally declares himself a trustee of his interest on behalf of Hamish absolutely.

(ii) Anthony orally declares himself a trustee of his interest for himself for life with remainder to Hamish absolutely.

(iii) Anthony orally contracts with Hamish to transfer his interest to him in return for a payment of £30,000.

(iv) Anthony orally directs Jason and Joseph to transfer their legal interest to Hamish and Anthony orally promises Hamish to transfer his equitable interest to him.

(v) Anthony orally disclaims his interest which, if effective, will enable Peter to obtain his interest absolutely.

SUMMARY

▦ The rationale behind the statutory formality requirement of s 53(1)(b) of the Law of Property Act 1925 is to prevent fraud. Documentary evidence of the terms of the transaction helps to prevent fraud.

▦ The rationale behind s 53(1)(c) of the LPA 1925 is to prevent fraud and give the trustees the opportunity to identify the whereabouts of the subsisting equitable interest in both land and personalty.

- Section 53(1)(b) of the LPA 1925 is applicable in respect of express trusts concerning land, whereas s 53(1)(c) of the LPA 1925 is concerned with dispositions of equitable interests under existing trusts.

- The expression 'dispositions' was defined in *Timpson's Executors v Yerbury*.

- Section 53(1)(b) of the LPA 1925 is applicable where a person declares himself a trustee of land or interests in land. Non-compliance with the provision merely renders the trust unenforceable.

- Section 53(1)(c) of the LPA 1925 is applicable where a beneficiary under a trust assigns his equitable interest to another, or directs the trustees to hold it on trust for another, or declares himself a trustee of his equitable interest for another, or sells his interest under a contract for valuable consideration. Non-compliance with the provision results in the intended transfer being void. It is debatable whether the subsection is applicable where a subsisting equitable owner declares himself a trustee of part of his interest for the benefit of another. The subsection is not applicable where a subsisting equitable interest is disclaimed, or where a transferor is estopped from denying a transfer of an equitable interest, or where a beneficiary is nominated under a pension fund or life assurance policy.

SAMPLE ESSAY QUESTION

Consider the following essay question:

To what extent is there certainty in the law as to what may constitute a 'disposition' within s 53(1)(c) of the Law of Property Act 1925?

Answer plan

> Narrate the subsection, indicating the consequences of non-compliance and refer to the classification of transactions laid down in *Timpson's Executors v Yerbury* that may amount to 'dispositions'.

> Distinguish between the original 'creation of trusts' and 'dispositions of subsisting equitable interests' within s 53(1)(c).

> Discuss the leading cases determining whether a transaction may amount to a disposition – *Grey v IRC, Oughtred v IRC, Neville v Wilson*.

> Discuss the main cases that created limitations on the expression 'disposition' – *Vandervell v IRC, Re Vandervell Trusts No 2, Re Paradise Motor Co, Re Danish Bacon Staff Pension Fund*.

> Refer to the academic debate regarding declarations of trusts that may constitute dispositions within s 53(1)(c) and declarations of trusts of partial interests which are outside the subsection.

> Consider s 205(1)(x) of the Law of Property Act 1925 that defines 'equitable interests' in terms of realty, but the courts have broadened this definition to include personalty.

> **CONCLUSION**

Further reading

Clarke, P, 'Mr Vandervell again' (1974) 38 Conv 405.

Green, B, '*Grey, Oughtred* and *Vandervell*: a contextual reappraisal' (1984) 47 MLR 385.

Hill, G, 'Section 2 of the Law of Property (Miscellaneous Provisions) Act 1989' (1990) 106 LQR 396.

Howell, J, 'Informal conveyances and s 2 of the Law of Property (Miscellaneous Provisions) Act 1989' (1990) Conv 441.

Thompson, M, 'Disposition of equitable interests' (1996) Conv 368.

Youdan, T, 'Formalities for trusts of land and the doctrine in *Rochefoucauld v Boustead*' (1984) CLJ 306.

6

Discretionary trusts

AIMS AND OBJECTIVES

By the end of this chapter you should be able to:

- define a discretionary trust, distinguish it from a fixed trust and classify discretionary trusts
- contrast a discretionary trust with a power of appointment
- list the duties imposed on fiduciaries
- appreciate the individual and collective interests of objects under discretionary trusts and powers of appointment
- understand a protective trust under s 33 of the Trustee Act 1925

6.1 Introduction

A discretionary trust exists where the trustees are given a discretion to pay or apply property (the income or capital or both) to or for the benefit of all or anyone selected from a group or class of objects on such terms and conditions as the trustees may see fit. In tax law this type of trust is known as a trust without an interest in possession. The trust is created in accordance with the express intention of the settlor. The relevant property is transferred to the trustees and the scope of the trustees' discretion expressed in the trust instrument.

For example, S, a settlor, transfers a cash fund of £100,000 to trustees on trust to pay or apply the income and capital (including accumulations of income) to or for the benefit of any or all of the settlor's children, A, B and C, as the trustees may decide in their absolute discretion.

In this example, a discretionary trust is created in respect of both income and capital. The trustees are required to decide in whose favour the property (income and capital) may be distributed. In Year 1, the trustees may distribute the entire income to A. In Year 2, the trustees may distribute the income and a portion of the capital to B and in Year 3 the income may be distributed equally to A, B and C and the entire capital distributed to C.

Fixed trusts

trust
instrument
The instrument
setting out the
terms of an
express trust.

The alternative type of express trust that may be created is a 'fixed' trust or a trust with an interest in possession. This is the case if, on the date of the creation of the trust, the settlor has not only identified the beneficiaries under the trust but also quantified the interest vested in each beneficiary. Thus, each beneficiary is entitled to sell, exchange or gift away his interest, subject to provisions to the contrary as detailed in the **trust instrument**. In a fixed trust the trustees do not have a discretion to decide the extent of the beneficial interest which the objects may enjoy, for example trustees hold specified property on trust for the children of the settlor, D, E and F, in equal shares absolutely. On the date of the creation of the trust, each beneficiary has a fixed one-third share of the fund that he may retain or dispose of as he likes.

Discretionary trusts

Under a discretionary trust, the individual members of the class of objects have only a hope or '*spes*' of acquiring a benefit under the trust. In other words, under a discretionary trust, the members of the class of objects, prior to the exercise of the trustees' discretion, do not enjoy an interest in the trust property but are treated as potential beneficiaries and are incapable of disposing of their potential interests by way of a trust.

6.2 Exhaustive/non-exhaustive discretionary trusts

A discretionary trust may be either 'exhaustive' or 'non-exhaustive'. This is determined by reference to the intention of the settlor.

An exhaustive discretionary trust is one where, during the trust period, the trustees are required to distribute the income or capital, or both, but retain a discretion as to the mode of distribution and the persons to whom the distribution may be made. The trustees are required to distribute the income each year as it arises, but have a discretion regarding the persons who may actually benefit.

A non-exhaustive discretionary trust is one where the trustees are given a discretion as to whether or not to distribute the property (either income or capital). A non-exhaustive discretionary trust of income exists where the trustees may legitimately decide not to distribute the income and the settlor has specified the effect of non-distribution; for instance, the undistributed income may be accumulated or paid to another. In short, a non-exhaustive discretionary trust of the income is a trust for distribution of the income coupled with a power to accumulate or otherwise dispose of the undistributed income.

For example, a settlor transfers £50,000 to trustees, T1 and T2, upon trust to distribute the income in their discretion in favour of the settlor's children, A, B and C, as the trustees may decide in their absolute discretion. At this stage this is an exhaustive discretionary trust of the income in favour of the children of the settlor. But if the settlor had inserted in the trust instrument a power to accumulate the income in the trustees' discretion, the trust would become non-exhaustive with regard to the income.

It follows that the distinction between an exhaustive and non-exhaustive discretionary trust is based on the power of the trustees to refrain from distributing the property that is within the discretion of the trustees. In the ordinary course of events the trustees will be required to accumulate the income that has not been distributed. The accumulated income is treated as capitalised income or capital in both trust law and tax law. In *IRC v Blackwell Minor's Trustees* (1925) 10 TC 235, the accumulation of undistributed surplus income at the discretion of the trustees was treated as capital of the beneficiary, and not liable to income tax.

6.3 Period of accumulation

Prior to its abolition, the period of accumulation was determined by reference to a number of statutory provisions. The combined effect of s 164 of the Law of Property Act 1925 and s 13 of the Perpetuities and Accumulations Act 1964 was that the settlor became entitled to select any one (but only one) of a specified number of periods as the maximum period during which the trustees may accumulate the income. These periods were unduly complex, and outlived their usefulness.

The Perpetuities and Accumulations Act 2009 was passed, following the recommendations of the Law Commission in its report published in 1998. The Law Commission analysed the policy behind the rule against excessive accumulations and decided that the application of the current principles were disproportionate and unnecessarily complex, and ought to be abolished, except for charitable purposes, where the period ought to be modified. The reason for dealing separately with charitable trusts is that it was regarded as being in the public interest to restrict the period for which income may be accumulated. In its report, the Law Commission concluded as follows:

QUOTATION

'In relation to the rule against excessive accumulations, the Law Commission found that there was no longer a sound policy for restricting settlors' ability to direct or allow for the accumulation of income, except in the case of charitable trusts (for which there is a public interest in limiting the time for accumulations, so that income is spent for the public benefit, rather than accumulated indefinitely).'

Law Commission report 1998

Sections 13 and 14 of the Perpetuities and Accumulations Act 2009 reflected the opinion of the Law Commission. This Act came into force on 6 April 2010. Section 13 introduced the general principle and abolished the rule against excessive accumulation, except for charities. The effect is that in the case of a non-charitable trust, the trustees are entitled to accumulate the trust income for as long as they consider reasonable.

Section 13 of the Perpetuities and Accumulations Act 2009:

SECTION

'These provisions cease to have effect –

(a) sections 164 to 166 of the Law of Property Act 1925 (which impose restrictions on accumulating income, subject to qualification);

(b) section 13 of the Perpetuities and Accumulations Act 1964 (which amends section 164 of the 1925 Act).'

With regard to charitable trusts, the Law Commission's recommendation for a modification of the accumulation period was enacted in s 14 of the Perpetuities and Accumulations Act 2009. It was considered to be in the interest of the public that charitable income, including accumulated income, be distributed within a short period of time. This was considered to be a period of 21 years. Thus, income accumulated for charitable purposes is required to be distributed by the trustees within 21 years from the date that the income accrued. A power inserted in the trust instrument which exceeds the statutory period is valid for 21 years and void in respect of the excess period.

Section 14 of the Perpetuities and Accumulations Act 2009:

'(1) This section applies to an instrument to the extent that it provides for property to be held on trust for charitable purposes.

(2) But it does not apply where the provision is made by a court or the Charity Commission for England and Wales.

(3) If the instrument imposes or confers on the trustees a duty or power to accumulate income, and apart from this section the duty or power would last beyond the end of the statutory period, it ceases to have effect at the end of that period…

(4) The statutory period is a period of 21 years starting with the first day when the income must or may be accumulated as the case may be.'

6.4 Reasons for creating discretionary trusts

6.4.1 Flexibility

Where a settlor wishes to make a present disposition on trust but is uncertain as to future events and would like the trustees to react to changed circumstances and the needs of the potential beneficiaries, he may create a discretionary trust. This would require the trustees to take into consideration the circumstances, including fiscal factors surrounding individual members of the class of objects. The trustees may well take into account that the distribution of income will be more tax-efficient if paid to objects with lower income, and transfers of capital may be more beneficial to those with larger incomes. The effect is that the discretionary trust has the advantage of flexibility. The settlor may nominate himself as one of the trustees and, even if he does not, he may still be entitled to exercise some influence over the trustees.

6.4.2 Protection of objects from creditors

Since an object under a discretionary trust is not entitled to an interest in the trust property, prior to the exercise of the discretion in his favour, but is merely entitled to a hope of acquiring a benefit, the bankruptcy of such an object does not entitle the trustee in bankruptcy to a share of the trust fund. The trustee in bankruptcy is only entitled to funds paid to the object in the exercise of the discretion of the trustees. Moreover the trustee in bankruptcy is not entitled to claim funds paid to third parties (such as tradesmen and hoteliers) in discharge of obligations *bona fide* undertaken by the potential beneficiaries.

6.5 Administrative discretion

Discretionary trusts are distinct from the administrative discretions that accompany all trusts. Thus, the trustees may have a power or discretion over the type of investments that may be made by the trust, whether to appoint agents on behalf of the trust, whether to apply income for the maintenance of infant beneficiaries, whether to make an advancement on behalf of a beneficiary, whether to appoint additional trustees, etc. But these powers and discretions are of an administrative nature and do not affect the beneficial entitlement of the objects. Accordingly, the existence of such administrative powers does not create discretionary trusts but is consistent with both fixed and discretionary trusts.

6.6 Mere powers and trust powers

The settlor may authorise another or others to distribute property to a class of objects but without imposing an obligation to distribute the same. This is called a mere power of appointment (or bare power, or power collateral).

For example, S may transfer property by will to his widow, W, for life with remainder to such of his children A, B and C, as W may appoint by will. W is referred to as a donee of the power and A, B and C as the objects of the power. They are not beneficiaries but, like the objects of a discretionary trust, are potential beneficiaries or have a *'spes'* of enjoying a benefit prior to the exercise of the power in their favour. If W makes a valid appointment in favour of the objects they become beneficiaries in respect of the amount of property distributed in their favour. On the other hand, if the donee of the power fails to make an appointment, the property is held on resulting trust for the settlor or his estate.

In order to dispense with the resulting trust, it is customary for the settlor to insert an 'express gift over in default of appointment' in the trust instrument. If this clause is inserted, the objects under the 'gift over' take the property unless the donee of the power validly exercises the power. Indeed, *prima facie*, the individuals entitled on a **gift over in default of appointment** are entitled to the property subject to such interest being defeated on a valid exercise of the power.

It was pointed out in Chapter 3 that a mere power of appointment may be 'personal' or 'fiduciary'. A 'personal' power is one granted to a donee of the power in his personal capacity, such as the testator's widow in the above example. Such powers impose no duties on the donee of the power, save for a distribution in favour of the objects if the appointor wishes to exercise his discretion. Conversely, a fiduciary power is created where the appointor acquires the property in his capacity as a fiduciary or trustee. A number of fiduciary duties are imposed on the appointor. These were listed by Megarry VC in *Re Hay's Settlement Trust* [1982] 1 WLR 202, as a duty to consider periodically whether or not the power ought to be exercised, a duty to consider the range of objects of the power and a duty to consider the appropriateness of individual appointments.

Both personal and fiduciary powers may be released by the appointor, but Warner J, in *Mettoy Pension Fund Trustees Ltd v Evans* [1990] 1 WLR 1587, created a further category of powers, called 'fiduciary powers in the full sense'. The distinctive feature of this last type of power is that it cannot be released by the appointor. If the donee of the power fails to exercise his discretion the court will ensure that the discretion is exercised in favour of the objects.

prima facie

At first appearance, or on the face of it.

gift over in default of appointment

An alternative gift in the event of a failure to distribute property under a power of appointment.

6.7 Trust powers (discretionary trusts)

A trust power is in substance a discretionary trust but, in form, the gift resembles a power. The court construes the instrument and decides that, in accordance with the intention of the settlor, a discretionary trust was intended. Accordingly, the trustees may not release their discretion and if they refuse to exercise their discretion the court will intervene.

JUDGMENT

'There are not only a mere trust and a mere power, but there is also known to this court a power, which the party to whom it is given, is entrusted and required to execute; and with regard to that species of power the court considers it as partaking so much of the nature and qualities of a trust, that if the person who has that duty imposed on him does not discharge it, the court will, to a certain extent, discharge the duty in his room and place.'

Lord Eldon in *Brown v Higgs* (1803) 8 Ves 561

CASE EXAMPLE

Burrough v Philcox [1840] 5 My & Cr 72

The testator transferred property on trust for his two children for life, with remainder to his issue, and declared that if they should die without issue, the survivor should have the power to dispose by will 'among my nieces and nephews, or their children, either all to one or to as many of them as my surviving child shall think fit'. The testator's children died without issue and without any appointment having been made by the survivor. It was held that a trust was created in favour of the testator's nieces and nephews and their children. The trust was subject to a power of selection in the surviving child.

JUDGMENT

'Where there appears a general intention in favour of a class, and a particular intention in favour of individuals of a class to be selected by another person, and the particular intention fails from that selection not having been made, the court will carry into effect the general intention in favour of the class.'

Lord Cottenham

On the other hand, in *Re Weekes's Settlement* [1897] 1 Ch 289, the court, on construction of the instrument, concluded that a mere power was created.

CASE EXAMPLE

Re Weekes's Settlement [1897] 1 Ch 289

The testatrix transferred property to her husband for life with 'power to dispose of all such property by will amongst our children'. There was no gift over in default of appointment. There were children but the husband died intestate without having exercised the power. It was held that a mere power of appointment was given to the husband and not a trust power. The court was not entitled to intervene in favour of the children. Thus the property was not divided among the children equally but went to the testatrix's heir.

JUDGMENT

'[N]ow, apart from the authorities, I should gather from the terms of the will that it was a mere power that was conferred on the husband, and not one coupled with a trust that he was bound to exercise. I see no words in the will to justify me in holding that the testatrix intended that the children should take if her husband did not execute the power.'

Romer LJ

Ultimately, the question whether a 'mere power of appointment' or a 'trust power' was created varies with the intention of the settlor. This is a question of fact. Decided cases illustrate how unpredictable this question is likely to be. There are two types of gifts that are consistent with the conclusion that a mere power of appointment was intended by the settlor. These are:

■ The creation of an express gift over in default of appointment. This is an express alternative gift in the event of the donee of the power failing to exercise the power. The settlor has made provision by declaring alternative beneficiaries in the event of the failure to exercise the power, for example '50,000 is transferred to trustees to distribute the income for a period not exceeding 15 years in favour of such of the relatives of the settlor as the trustees may decide in their absolute discretion. In the event of the trustees failing to distribute any part of the income to the relatives, Mr X will be entitled to the same'. In this case the clause entitling Mr X to a beneficial interest is an express gift over in default of appointment. The material feature is that the clause is only activated if the trustees fail to distribute the property in favour of the relatives of the settlor. *Re Mills* [1930] 1 Ch 654 illustrates this principle.

A general power of appointment is incapable of being a trust power, for the courts are incapable of exercising such power. A general power of appointment is one which entitles the donee of the power to appoint in favour of anyone, including himself. Thus, there are no limits to the objects of such a power of appointment. Similarly, a hybrid power of appointment is incapable of being a trust power. A hybrid power is similar in appearance to a general power save for the disqualification of an excluded class of objects, for example 'on trust for X to appoint in favour of anyone except the settlor and his spouse'.

In *Blausten v IRC* [1972] Ch 256, the settlement gave the trustees the power to introduce any person other than the settlor as a member of a class of objects, but subject to the written consent of the settlor. It was held that a hybrid power of appointment was created.

Likewise, in *Re Manisty's Settlement* [1973] 3 WLR 341, the court decided that a hybrid power was created. In this case the trustees were given a power to add objects to a class of potential beneficiaries which excluded the settlor, his wife and certain named persons.

However, a special power of appointment may or may not create a trust power. A special power of appointment confers on the trustee an authority or a duty to distribute the fund in favour of a specific class of objects, such as the children of the settlor. If there is no express gift over in default of appointment, it is extremely difficult to know whether a special power of appointment creates a trust power or a mere power. The issue is one of construction of the terms of the gift. The absence of an express gift over in default of appointment is nothing more than an argument that the settlor did not intend to create a trust. The weight of such an argument will vary with the facts of each case.

JUDGMENT

'The authorities do not show, in my opinion, that there is a hard-and-fast rule that a gift to A for life with a power to A to appoint among a class and nothing more must, if there is no gift over in the will, be held a gift by implication to the class in default of the power being exercised. In my opinion the cases show … that you must find in the will an indication that the testatrix did intend the class or some of the class to take – intended in fact that the power should be regarded in the nature of a trust.'

Romer LJ in *Re Weekes's Settlement* (1897)

ACTIVITY

Self-test question

How would you distinguish a mere power of appointment from a trust power?

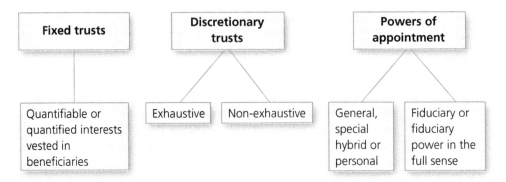

Figure 6.1 Classification of private trusts and types of discretions

6.8 Duties imposed on fiduciaries

A discretionary trust is mandatory and a power is merely permissive, but similar duties are imposed on both discretionary trustees and those exercising fiduciary powers. Thus, under a fiduciary power, the trustees are required to act responsibly and *bona fide* to consider, from time to time, whether to exercise their discretion but they may legitimately fail to exercise their discretion. In this event the gift over in default of appointment will take effect. Under a discretionary trust, however, if the discretionary trustees fail to exercise their discretion the courts will intervene and repair the omission by the trustees.

It may be recalled that there are two kinds of discretionary trusts: exhaustive and non-exhaustive discretionary trusts (see earlier). In an exhaustive discretionary trust the trustees are required to distribute the relevant property (income or capital) within a reasonable period of time. On the other hand, a non-exhaustive discretionary trust is one where the trustees may legitimately fail to distribute the property. In this event the property is retained by the trustees. For instance, in the case of a non-exhaustive discretionary trust of income, on a failure to distribute the income within a reasonable time the income will be accumulated and becomes capitalised (or capital). Thus, in such a case the discretion may be exercised by a decision to accumulate the income.

Whether the trust is exhaustive or not, the trustees are under a duty to refrain from acting capriciously, but are under a duty to act in a responsible manner, surveying the range of objects both in terms of the categories of objects and the qualifications of individual objects with a view to distribution.

JUDGMENT

'[A] trustee with a duty to distribute, particularly among a potentially very large class, would surely never require the preparation of a complete list of names, which anyhow would tell him little that he needs to know. He would examine the field, by class and category; might indeed make diligent and careful enquiries, depending on how much money he had to give away and the means at his disposal, as to the composition and needs of particular categories and of individuals within them; decide on certain priorities or proportions and then select individuals according to their needs and qualifications.'

Lord Wilberforce in *McPhail v Doulton* [1971] AC 424

If the trustees act in good faith and with due care and attention, confirming the exercise of their discretion within the terms authorised by the settlor, the courts will not interfere with the trustees' discretion.

The distinction between an exhaustive and a non-exhaustive discretionary trust becomes significant when the trustees fail to exercise their discretion. This will be evident if the trustees fail to distribute the relevant property (exhaustive) or fail to take relevant factors into consideration (non-exhaustive). In these circumstances the court will intervene and execute the unfulfilled duty of the trustees. The court has a variety of options available to it in order to execute the trust, but whichever course is adopted its objective would be to give effect to the intentions of the settlor or testator. The court is entitled to appoint new trustees able and willing to exercise the discretion or by directing the trustees to distribute the fund. Alternatively, the court may direct representatives of the classes of objects to prepare a scheme of distribution or in appropriate cases the court may order an equal division of the funds in favour of the objects. This last course of action would be appropriate in cases of family trusts of a limited class.

CASE EXAMPLE

Re Locker's Settlement [1977] 1 WLR 1323

An exhaustive discretionary trust of income was created but the trustees failed to distribute the income. They subsequently declared an intention to repair their omission by distributing accumulated income and asked the court for directions. The court granted directions to the effect that the trustees were entitled to make the distribution.

6.9 Control of trustees' discretion

A trustee is a fiduciary and under a duty to act on behalf of the beneficiaries in good faith, with reasonable care and in accordance with the terms of trust instrument. Where the trustee acts in breach of his duties he is liable to the beneficiaries in a claim for breach of trust. This is the position even if the trustee acts on the erroneous advice of a lawyer or other professionals. The liability here is strict and there is no requirement for any fault or negligence on the part of the fiduciary. In contrast, in the exercise of discretionary powers the trustee is under a duty to act in good faith, responsibly and reasonably. Before making his decision he is required to inform himself of relevant matters and not be influenced by irrelevant factors. The trustee may frequently be required to take advice from appropriate experts and ultimately make decisions that affect the trust. But where the trustee acts within the proper scope of his duties and relies on the advice of an appropriately qualified professional whose advice was negligently tendered, the decision of the trustee may have serious adverse consequences for the trust. Although claims to compensate the beneficiaries for their losses are available to the beneficiaries, they may be inclined to set aside the transaction entered into by the trustee. Indeed, the trustee himself may wish to take steps to reverse his action in order to benefit the trust. The court has a supervisory jurisdiction to act in the interests of the beneficiaries and the question in issue is whether, and if so, on what basis will the court exercise its jurisdiction to set aside a decision of the trustee? For example, the trustee may have taken advice from an expert and entered into a transaction in order to reduce the extent of the tax liability of the trust. If it turns out that the advice was inaccurate and results in a large tax liability, the trustee may be tempted to apply to the court to set aside the transaction in order to reduce the tax liability of the trust.

The starting point in exercising the jurisdiction of the court is known as the principle in *Re Hastings-Bass* [1974] 2 All ER 193. The test is where a trustee acts under a dispositive discretion (i.e. a discretion to change the beneficial interest) created by the trust instrument and enters into a contentious transaction, the court may intervene and set aside the transaction if it is clear that he would not have undertaken the transaction had he not failed to take into account factors that he ought to have taken into account, or he took into account factors that he ought not to have taken into account. The allegation is that the trustee's decision is seriously flawed because of the inadequate foundation on which the decision is based.

CASE EXAMPLE

Re Hastings-Bass [1974] 2 All ER 193, CA

Peter Hastings-Bass (P) was life-tenant of a settlement made in 1947, with power to appoint by deed or will amongst his sons or remoter male issue. By a revocable deed of appointment P appointed the fund in trust for his son William (W) born in 1948, at 25 absolutely. In 1957 P's sister made a settlement under which she gave a life interest to W and created other interests and powers. In order to save estate duty on P's death, the trustees of the 1947 settlement, under s 32(1) of the Trustee Act 1925, advanced £50,000 to the trustees of the 1957 settlement, to be held on the trusts of that settlement. Since W was not a life in being in 1947, all the limitations of the advanced fund were void for perpetuity except for W's life interest, although at the time the trustees did not appreciate that fact. P died on 4 June 1964. The trustees took out a summons to determine whether estate duty was payable on the advanced fund. It was common ground that duty would not be payable if the advancement was effective to create a valid life interest in possession in the advanced fund in favour of W. The Crown contended that the advancement was wholly void, so that the fund remained subject to the trusts of the 1947 settlement. The Court of Appeal, reversing the decision of the High Court, decided that such parts of the advanced sums as did not infringe the perpetuity rule were valid provided that the trustees addressed their minds to the appropriate considerations and the sum advanced benefited the appropriate person. On the facts there was evidence that the advancement was in accordance with the intention of the trustees and was accordingly effective in conferring a life interest on W.

JUDGMENT

'Where trustees intend to make an advancement by way of sub-settlement, they must no doubt genuinely apply their minds to the question whether the sub-settlement as a whole will operate for the benefit of the person advanced, but this does not, we think, involve regarding this benefit as a benefit of a monolithic character. It is, in our opinion, more naturally and logically to be regarded as a bundle of benefits of distinct characters. Each and all of those benefits is conferred, or is intended to be conferred, by a single exercise of the discretion under section 32. If by operation of law one or more of those benefits cannot take effect, it does not seem to us to follow that those which survive should not be regarded as having been brought into being by an exercise of the discretion. If the resultant effect of the intended advancement were such that it could not reasonably be regarded as being beneficial to the person intended to be advanced, the advancement could not stand, for it would not be within the powers of the trustees under section 32. In any other case, however, the advancement should, in our judgment, be permitted to take effect in the manner and to the extent that it is capable of doing so … where by the terms of a trust (as under section 32) a trustee is given a discretion as to some matter under which he acts in good faith, the court should not interfere with his action notwithstanding that it does not have the full effect which he intended, unless (1) what he has achieved is unauthorised by the power conferred upon him, or (2) it is clear that he would not have acted as he did (a) had he not taken into account considerations which he should not have taken into account, or (b) had he not failed to take into account considerations which he ought to have taken into account. In the present case (2) above has not, in our judgment, been established. The 1947 settlement trustees parted with the transferred assets and could not, we think, have recovered them even after William's death. They parted with the legal ownership and had no equitable interest in the transferred assets which would have enabled them to assert any claim to them at any time thereafter.'

Buckley LJ

The rule in *Hastings-Bass* (as it was called) was subject to a great deal of criticism both judicially and extra-judicially. The true *ratio* of the case was that the sum advanced, that was not void on the ground of infringing the perpetuity rule, was valid unless it could not reasonably be regarded as beneficial to the intended beneficiary. If not, the exercise of the power was unauthorised. This question called for an objective inquiry and did not involve the state of mind of the trustees. On this basis, the first limb of Buckley LJ's statement alone was relevant. Whereas, in *Mettoy Pension Trustees Ltd v Evans* [1990] 1 WLR 1587, Warner J applied an allegedly new principle in the context of an occupational pension scheme and in circumstances where the trustees' exercise of a discretionary power was within the scope of that power. His approach was to consider what the trustees would have done. This is essentially a subjective question which seems to have distorted the principle. In *Abacus Trust Co (Isle of Man) v Barr* [2003] 1 All ER 763, Lightman J, in considering the rule, addressed four issues and decided that: (1) a fundamental mistake on the part of the trustees was not necessary, (2) a breach of trustees' duty is essential in the application of the rule, (3) the rule applied on the facts of the case, (4) the consequences of applying the rule is that the transaction becomes voidable, not void. These principles were endorsed by the Supreme Court in the conjoined appeal in *Pitt v Holt* and *Futter v Futter* [2013] 2 AC 108. Lord Walker stated that 'the rule [in *Hastings-Bass*], properly understood, depends on breach of duty in the performance of something that is within the scope of the trustees' powers, not in the trustees doing something that they had no power at all to do'.

In *Pitt v Holt* and *Futter v Futter* (2013) the Supreme Court reviewed the law concerning the rule in *Hastings-Bass* and clarified the scope of the rule. The court decided that the rule is distinct from the equitable doctrine of mistake, although there are circumstances when the two principles overlap. The ratio in *Hastings-Bass* was not about mistake; it did not concern what the trustees had in their minds at the relevant time. The statement of the rule by Buckley LJ was far from clear and decisive as to when the court may intervene and set aside the transactions of the trustees. Further, trustees may still be liable for breach of trust, even if they had taken competent professional advice, but it would be contrary to principle to impose a form of strict liability where they had acted on apparently competent professional advice which turned out to be wrong.

CASE EXAMPLE

Pitt v Holt; Futter v Futter [2013] 2 AC 108, Supreme Court

In the case of Pitt, the claim was brought by Mr Pitt's personal representatives after his death in 2007. In 1990 Mr Pitt suffered very serious head injuries in a road traffic accident which resulted in his mental incapacity. His wife was appointed as his receiver under the Mental Health Act 1983. Mr Pitt's claim for damages was compromised by a structured settlement, approved by the court, in the sum of £1.2 million. A firm of financial advisers counselled the claimant's solicitors to settle the fund in a discretionary trust. This was done in 1994 with the authority of the Court of Protection. The report of the financial advisers dealt with the advantages of income and capital gains taxes of creating the settlement, but made no mention of inheritance tax. Had the trust complied with the special provisions laid down in s 89 of the Inheritance Act 1984, no inheritance tax would have been payable, as opposed to a tax bill of £100,000, with further charges on the tenth anniversary of the settlement. The personal representatives commenced proceedings to have the settlement set aside under the *Hastings-Bass* principle or on the ground of mistake.

In the case of *Futter*, solicitors advised Mr Futter and executed a scheme that was designed to avoid capital gains tax. However, the advice of the solicitors was inaccurate and resulted in a large liability to tax on Mr Futter. The trustees applied to the court to have the scheme set aside. The Supreme Court decided that the *Hastings-Bass* principle was not applicable to either of the cases. In *Pitt* the wife as Receiver had taken expert advice and followed it. There was no evidence that she failed to exercise her fiduciary duty. Similarly in *Futter* the advice from the expert was followed and was inaccurate but there was no evidence of breach of trustees' duties. However, the structured settlement in *Pitt* may be set aside on the ground of the equitable doctrine of mistake. There were no grounds to set aside the scheme in *Futter* and the transactions stood.

JUDGMENT

'If, in exercising a fiduciary power, trustees have been given, and have acted on, information or advice from an apparently trustworthy source, and what the trustees purport to do is within the scope of their power, the only direct remedy available (either to the trustees themselves, or to a disadvantaged beneficiary) must be based on mistake (there may be an indirect remedy in the form of a claim against one or more advisers for damages for breach of professional duties of care). This serves to emphasise that the so-called rule in *Hastings-Bass* was not in play in that case.

The injustice (or unfairness or unconscionableness) of leaving a mistaken disposition uncorrected must be evaluated objectively, but with an intense focus on the facts of the particular case. The court cannot decide the issue of what is unconscionable by an elaborate set of rules. It must consider in the round the existence of a distinct mistake (as compared with total ignorance or disappointed expectations), its degree of centrality to the transaction in question and the seriousness of its consequences, and make an evaluative judgment whether it would be unconscionable, or unjust, to leave the mistake uncorrected. The court may and must form a judgment about the justice of the case.'

Lord Walker

6.10 Status of objects under discretionary trusts

student
mentor tip

'Equity and Trusts can be complex so re-read textbooks to get fully acquainted with the principles.'
Pelena, University of Surrey

Under a fixed trust the beneficiaries are given quantifiable interests in the trust property which each may enjoy, sell, exchange or gift away. Each beneficiary is entitled to the protection of a court of equity and is empowered to pursue actions in order to enforce such rights.

For example, in a gift to the trustees on trust for A for life, remainder to B absolutely, A has a vested interest in possession and is entitled to the income as of right from the trust fund for life. B has a vested interest in the capital of the fund as of right and would acquire an absolute interest on A's death.

6.10.1 Individual interest

Under a discretionary trust the trustees are given a discretion to decide what interest, if any, may be distributed to the objects. The objects are dependent on the trustees exercising their discretion in their favour. In *Gartside v IRC* [1968] 1 All ER 121, a case involving a non-exhaustive discretionary trust, the House of Lords reiterated the principles that the objects have rights in competition with each other. No object is entitled to a quantifiable interest in the property. Prior to the exercise of the discretion, the objects, individually considered, have an expectation or hope of acquiring a benefit. Each object does not have a right to the income of the fund, but merely a right to require the trustees to consider whether they will distribute any property to the object. If the trustees decide to distribute property to an object, he gets it not by reason of having the right to have his case considered, but only because the trustees have decided to distribute the property to him. This is the position whether the discretionary trust is exhaustive or non-exhaustive. The same principles apply to objects under a power of appointment.

It follows that if an object assigns his rights under a discretionary trust to a third party or becomes bankrupt, the assignee or trustee-in-bankruptcy can be in no better position than the object. Accordingly, the assignee or trustee-in-bankruptcy obtains property at the discretion of the trustees and has no right to demand the income as it arises.

CASE EXAMPLE

Re Coleman [1888] 39 Ch 443

An object under a discretionary trust assigned his interest for consideration to a third party. The trustees declined to pay the income to the third party. The question in issue was whether the trustees had retained their discretion concerning the income. It was held that the third party was entitled to no interest in the income as it arose.

vis-à-vis
In relation to.

However, following an assignment of rights to third parties any income actually paid to the assignor may be claimed by the assignee or trustee-in-bankruptcy in the capacity as a representative of the assignor **vis-à-vis** the trust. But a payment in a non-traceable form by the trustees to another, on behalf of the object of the trust, may not be claimed by the assignee or trustee-in-bankruptcy.

JUDGMENT

'If the trustees were to pay an hotel-keeper to give him a dinner he would get nothing but the right to eat a dinner, and that is not property which could pass by assignment or bankruptcy.'

Cotton LJ in *Re Coleman* (1888)

Of course, income legitimately paid to an object in the exercise of the discretion of the trustees becomes the property of the beneficiary as and when the trustees exercise their discretion in his favour. Moreover, it is not accurate to say that individual objects under a discretionary trust do not have rights under the trust. Each object has the right to be considered to be entitled to the property in the exercise of the discretion of the trustees. In addition, each object has the right to require the trustees to exercise their discretion *bona fide* in a responsible manner and within the limits as laid down by the settlor.

JUDGMENT

'No doubt in a certain sense a beneficiary under a discretionary trust has an interest: the nature of it may, sufficiently for the purpose, be spelt out by saying that he has a right to be considered as a potential recipient of benefit by the trustees and a right to have his interest protected by a court of equity.'

Lord Wilberforce in *Gartside v IRC* [1968] 1 All ER 121

6.10.2 Group interest

In trusts law, if all the objects entitled to both income and capital act in unison and if they are of full age and sound mind, they are entitled to terminate the discretionary trust and acquire the property for their own benefit. This principle is applicable to both exhaustive and non-exhaustive trusts; for instance, if trustees hold property on discretionary trust to distribute the income in favour of all or any of a closed group of persons, A, B and C, for 21 years and subject thereto the capital is held on trust for D. Provided that A, B, C and D are of full age and sound mind and are in agreement, they may terminate the trust.

Similarly, the sole objects collectively are entitled to assign their interests to a third party. In these circumstances, the third party is entitled to demand the fund from the trustee.

CASE EXAMPLE

Re Smith, Public Trustee v Aspinall [1928] Ch 915

A testator gave one-quarter of the residue of his estate to trustees on trust to pay, at their absolute discretion, the income for the maintenance of Mrs Aspinall for life and/or all or any of her children. On the death of Mrs Aspinall the trustees were required to pay both income and capital, including capitalised income, to the children in equal shares. Mrs Aspinall joined with her two surviving children and the personal representative of her deceased child in executing an assignment of their interest in favour of Legal and General Assurance Company in order to secure a mortgage. The question in issue was whether the trustees were required to pay the income, as it arose, to the company until the discharge of the mortgage, or whether they were at liberty to pay the income at their discretion to Mrs Aspinall. It was held that the income was payable to the company because the sole objects of the trust were entitled to dispose of the entire income.

JUDGMENT

'What is to happen where the trustees have a discretion whether they will apply the whole or only a portion of the fund for the benefit of one person, but are obliged to apply the rest of the fund, so far as not applied for the benefit of the first-named person, to or for the benefit of a second-named person? There, two people together are the sole objects of the discretionary trust and, between them, are entitled to have the whole fund applied to them or for their benefit … you treat all the people put together just as though they formed one person, for whose benefit the trustees were directed to apply the whole of a particular fund.'

Romer J

ACTIVITY

Self-test question

What rights do objects enjoy under a discretionary trust?

6.11 Protective trusts under s 33 of the Trustee Act 1925

A protective trust under s 33(1) of the Trustee Act 1925 involves a determinable life interest in favour of the principal beneficiary and, in the event of a termination or forfeiture of the interest taking place, the establishment of a discretionary trust of the income in favour of a class of objects, including the principal beneficiary, his spouse and issue. But, if the principal beneficiary has no spouse or issue, the capital and income will be held on discretionary trust in favour of the principal beneficiary and his next of kin.

This 'ready-made' protective trust exists as a device to obviate the risk to the settlor of inadvertently creating a conditional interest instead of a determinable interest.

Section 33(1) of the Trustee Act 1925:

SECTION

'Where any income … is directed to be held on protective trusts for the benefit of any person (in this section called the principal beneficiary) for the period of his life or for any less period, then, during that period (in this section called the trust period) the said income shall … be held [on the trusts laid down in s 33(1)(i) and (ii)].'

In *Re Wittke* [1944] Ch 166, it was decided that it is unnecessary for the settlor to set out the details of the trust. All that is required is that the settlor should manifest an intention to create a protective trust. The model trust under s 33 will be adopted.

In any event, the settlor is entitled to set up his special express protective trust incorporating as much detail as he considers appropriate. Furthermore, s 33(2) entitles the settlor to adopt any variation of the structure of the protective trust as laid down in s 33(1). For example, the settlor may incorporate the s 33 trust, but exclude the discretionary trust that arises when the forfeiture event takes place and substitute a remainder interest of both capital and income in favour of the principal beneficiary's issue or, failing issue, his next of kin.

Section 33(2) of the Trustee Act 1925:

SECTION

'This section … has effect subject to any variation of the implied trusts aforesaid contained in the instrument creating the trust.'

Section 33(3) enacts what would have been implied in any event, namely, that s 33 does not validate any provision which would be liable to be set aside. Accordingly a determinable life interest in favour of the settlor is void as against his trustee in bankruptcy.

Section 33(3) of the Trustee Act 1925:

SECTION

'Nothing in this section operates to validate any trust which would, if contained in the instrument creating the trust, be liable to be set aside.'

6.11.1 Determining events (forfeiture)

Section 33(1)(i) of the Trustee Act 1925 adopts a broad formula for ascertaining the occasions when the life interest will be determined:

SECTION

'[W]hen the principal beneficiary does or attempts to do or suffers any act or thing, or until any event happens, other than an advance under any statutory or express power, whereby, if the said income were payable during the trust period to the principal beneficiary … he would be deprived of the right to receive the same on any part thereof.'

It is to be noted that an advancement under an express or statutory power (such as s 32 of the Trustee Act 1925) is excluded from the forfeiting events. An advancement involves the provision of an enduring benefit on behalf of a beneficiary such as the provision of a house or the setting up of a business.

The burden of proving a forfeiture lies on any party who claims that a determining event has taken place. In this respect, the principal beneficiary may rely on a presumption that the forfeiting event has not taken place, until the contrary is proved to the satisfaction of the court.

The determining event formula under s 33 of the Trustee Act 1925 not only includes the acts or omissions of the principal beneficiary, but also circumstances outside his control which deprive him of the right to receive the income under the trust.

CASE EXAMPLE

Re Gourju [1943] Ch 24

The principal beneficiary, an English national, became marooned in German-occupied Nice. The effect was that the income from the trust became payable to the Custodian of Enemy Property under the Trading with the Enemy Act 1939. It was decided that this event triggered a forfeiture of the beneficiary's interest.

In *Re Hall* [1944] Ch 46, however, in similar circumstances, there was no forfeiture in respect of a French national who lived in France, and was regarded as an 'enemy' under the 1939 Act. It appears that, subject to an express provision to the contrary, a positive act on the part of the beneficiary which is outside the ordinary course of events is required to be done in order to trigger a forfeiture.

Accordingly, the purported sale, gift or other disposition by the principal beneficiary of his interest, as well as his bankruptcy have the effect of activating the determining event.

6.11.2 Other examples of forfeiting events

- *Re Balfour's Settlement* [1938] Ch 928: the impounding by trustees of part of the income of the principal beneficiary in order to repair a breach of trust instigated by the beneficiary prior to the date of bankruptcy of the beneficiary.

- *Re Baring's Settlement Trust* [1940] Ch 737: a sequestration order against the beneficiary following her failure to obey a court order to return her infant children to the jurisdiction of the court.

- *Re Dennis's Settlement Trusts* [1942] Ch 283: the execution of a deed of variation releasing the principal beneficiary's right to part of the income. It seems that there is forfeiture if a representative of the principal beneficiary is appointed in order to look after the beneficiary's interests, as opposed to a transfer of property to a representative for the benefit of another.

- *Re Oppenheim's Will Trusts* [1950] Ch 633: the appointment of a receiver to handle the affairs of the beneficiary, who was certified as a person of unsound mind, did not cause a forfeiture.

- Likewise, in *Re Westby's Settlement* [1950] Ch 296: fees paid to the receiver, who was appointed in order to represent the interests of a person of unsound mind, did not cause a forfeiture.

Dispositive discretions

Mere powers	Authoritative
Personal powers Re Weekes (1897)	Yes – may be released by appointor
Fiduciary powers Blausten v IRC (1972); Re Manisty (1974)	Yes – may be released by appointor
Fiduciary powers in the full sense Mettoy Pension v Evans (1990)	Yes – but may not be released by the appointor
Discretionary trusts/trust powers (trust powers)	
Exhaustive/non-exhaustive – McPhail v Doulton (1971)	Mandatory – may not be released by trustees

SUMMARY

A discretionary trust exists where the trustees are required to exercise their discretion to distribute funds in favour of members of a class of objects. Discretionary trusts are either exhaustive or non-exhaustive. A fixed trust exists where, on the date of creation, the beneficiaries acquire or will acquire a quantified or quantifiable interest in the trust property.

A power of appointment, as distinct from a discretionary trust, is one where the trustees (or donees of the power) are entitled to distribute property in favour of members of a group of objects. Powers of appointment may be fiduciary, personal or regarded as powers in the full sense. A 'fiduciary power in the full sense' cannot be released by the appointor.

Fiduciary duties imposed on trustees include the duty to act in a responsible manner, in good faith and with due care to the objects. They are required to survey the range of objects and consider the appropriateness of distributions.

The individual interests of the objects include the right to be considered to be entitled to an interest in the property as distinct from a right to the property itself. The collective interests of the objects of both discretionary trusts and powers of appointment are similar to the individual interests as stated above. But if the objects of a discretionary trust are entitled to the property (both income and capital) they may be entitled to terminate the trust and obtain the property for their own benefit.

A protective trust under s33 of the Trustee Act 1925 involves a determinable life interest in favour of a principal beneficiary with a discretionary trust in favour of a group of persons, including the principal beneficiary, should the life interest determine. The test to ascertain whether the determining event has taken place is laid down in s33(1)(i) of the Trustee Act 1925.

SAMPLE ESSAY QUESTION

Consider the following essay question:

How may the courts decide whether a trust or a power of appointment was intended by the settlor?

Answer plan

> Define a trust and distinguish this from a power.

> A trust is by origin equitable but a power may be either legal or equitable.

> There are two types of trusts – fixed and discretionary. There are two classifications of discretionary trusts – exhaustive and non-exhaustive. There are three types of powers of appointment – personal, fiduciary and powers in the full sense. A trust is mandatory in nature but a power is permissive, save for a 'fiduciary power in the full sense'.

> Factors that determine whether a power of appointment has been created include:
> - the existence of an express gift over in default of appointment;
> - the existence of a general or hybrid power of appointment;
> - ultimately, the issue is dependent on the intention of the settlor and involves a question of construction.

> 'Administrative unworkability' does not extend to powers but will invalidate trusts.

> Since 1971 the test for certainty of objects is the 'any given postulant test' for both trusts and powers.

> **CONCLUSION**

Further reading

Etherton, T, 'The role of equity in mistaken transactions' (2013) 27(4) Tru LI 159.

Gardner, S, 'Fiduciary powers in Toytown' (1991) 107 LQR 214.

Grubb, A, 'Powers, trusts and classes of objects: *Re Hay's Settlement*' (1982) Conv 432.

Harris, J, 'Trust, power and duty' (1971) 87 LQR 31.

Sheridan, L, 'Discretionary trusts' (1957) 21 Conv 55.

Williams, G, 'The doctrine of repugnancy: conditions in gifts' (1943) 59 LQR 343.

7

Resulting trusts

AIMS AND OBJECTIVES

By the end of this chapter you should be able to:

- classify resulting trusts
- understand the *Quistclose* controversy
- recognise an unincorporated association
- comprehend the basis of distributing funds on the liquidation of unincorporated associations
- understand the rationale behind presumed resulting trusts

7.1 Introduction

So far, we have been considering various aspects of express trusts. These trusts, it may be recalled, are created in accordance with the express intention of the settlor. This intention is required to be clearly expressed to the satisfaction of the court. All the circumstances are considered by the courts including verbal and written statements as well as the conduct of the settlor. The effect is that the material terms of an express trust are complete. There are no shortcomings by the draftsperson. A resulting trust, on the other hand, is implied by the court in favour of the settlor/transferor or his estate, if he is dead. Such trusts arise by virtue of the unexpressed or implied intention of the settlor or testator. The settlor or his estate becomes the beneficial owner under the resulting trust when no other suitable claimants can be found. It is as though the settlor has retained a residual interest in the property, albeit one that is implied or created by the courts. The trust is created as a result of defective drafting. The draftsperson omitted to deal with an event that has taken place, and the court is asked to deal with the beneficial ownership of the property. The expression 'resulting trust' derives from the Latin verb *resultare*, meaning to spring back (in effect, to the original owner). Examples are the transfer of property subject to a condition precedent which cannot be achieved, the intended creation of an express trust which becomes void, or the incomplete disposal of the equitable interest in property. In *Vandervell v IRC* [1967] 2 AC 291 (see Chapter 5) the House of Lords decided that the equitable interest in the option to purchase shares was vested in Mr Vandervell by way of a resulting trust.

JUDGMENT

'If A intends to give away all his beneficial interest in a piece of property and thinks he has done so but, by some mistake or accident or failure to comply with the requirements of the law, he has failed to do so, either wholly or partially, there will, by operation of law, be a resulting trust for him of the beneficial interest of which he had failed effectually to dispose. If the beneficial interest was in A and he fails to give it away effectively to another or others or on charitable trusts it must remain in him. Early references to equity, like nature, abhorring a vacuum, are delightful but unnecessary.'

Lord Upjohn

7.2 Automatic and presumed resulting trusts

In *Re Vandervell Trusts (No 2)* [1974] 1 All ER 47, Megarry J classified resulting trusts into two categories, namely 'automatic' and 'presumed' (see below). 'Automatic' resulting trusts arise where the beneficial interest in respect of the transfer of property remains undisposed of. Such trusts are created in order to fill a gap in ownership. The equitable maxim that is applicable here is 'equity abhors a beneficial vacuum'. The equitable or beneficial interest cannot exist in the air and ought to remain with the settlor/transferor. The resulting trust here does not depend on any intentions or presumptions, but is the automatic consequence of the transferor's failure to dispose of property that was vested in him. In other words, if the transfer is made subject to an intended express trust that fails, the resulting trust that arises does not establish the trust but merely carries back the beneficial interest to the transferor. In *Vandervell v Inland Revenue Commissioners* (1967) (see Chapter 5), a settlor transferred the legal title to property (an option to purchase shares in a company) to Vandervell Trustees Ltd, but failed to identify the beneficial owner. The House of Lords decided that the beneficial interest resulted back to the settlor by way of an automatic resulting trust.

JUDGMENT

'The beneficial interest must belong to or be held for somebody; so if it was not to belong to the donee or be held in trust by him for somebody, it must remain with the donor.'

Lord Reid in *Vandervell v Inland Revenue Commissioners*

'The conclusion, on the facts found, is simply that the option was vested in the trustee company as a trustee on trusts, not defined at the time, possibly to be defined later. But the equitable, or beneficial interest, cannot remain in the air: the consequence in law must be that it remains in the settlor … he (Mr Vandervell) had, as a direct result of the option and of the failure to place the beneficial interest in it securely away from him, not divested himself absolutely of the shares which it controlled.'

Lord Wilberforce in *Vandervell v Inland Revenue Commissioners*

This notion of the 'automatic' resulting trust explains cases where the purpose of the transfer fails for one reason or another, such as where an intended express trust fails for lack of beneficiaries or where the trust purposes have been fulfilled with only part of the trust property, leaving a surplus of funds to be returned to the transferor. This type of resulting trust is not dependent on the intention of the transferor, but is a process adopted by equity to 'fill the gap' in ownership and to acknowledge that the equitable interest belongs to the most appropriate person, namely the transferor or, as a last resort, the Crown on a *bona vacantia*.

The 'presumed' resulting trust arises, in the absence of evidence to the contrary, when property is purchased in the name of another, or property is voluntarily transferred to another. For instance, A purchases property and the legal title is conveyed in the name of B, or A transfers the legal title to property in the name of B. In these circumstances B *prima facie* holds the property on resulting trust for A. This is a rebuttable presumption of law that arises in favour of A. The question is not one of the automatic consequences of a dispositive failure by A in respect of the equitable interest, but one of presumption: the legal title to the property has been transferred to B, and because of the absence of consideration and any presumption of advancement, B is presumed *not* to take the entire interest beneficially, but to hold the equitable interest on trust for A absolutely. The presumption thus establishes both that B is to take on trust and also the nature of that trust. In short, where A voluntarily transfers the legal title to property to B or purchases property in the name of B and it is unclear in whom the equitable interest vests, the courts steps in and infers or presumes an intention that A remains the beneficial owner. This trust is a resulting trust and is proprietary in nature. Megarry J in *Re Vandervell Trusts (No 2)* (1974) classified resulting trusts in the following manner:

JUDGMENT

'Where A effectually transfers to B (or creates in his favour) any interest in any property, whether legal or equitable, a resulting trust for A may arise in two distinct classes of case:

(a) the first class of case is where the transfer to B is not made on any trust, there is a rebuttable presumption that B holds on resulting trust for A. The question is not one of the automatic consequences of a dispositive failure by A, but one of presumption: the presumption thus establishes both that B is to take on trust and also what that trust is. Such resulting trusts may be called presumed resulting trusts;

(b) the second class of case is where the transfer to B is made on trusts which leave some or all of the beneficial interest undisposed of. Here B automatically holds on resulting trust for A to the extent that the beneficial interest has not been carried to him or others. The resulting trust here does not depend on any intentions or presumptions, but is the automatic consequence of A's failure to dispose of what is vested in him. Such resulting trusts may be called "automatic resulting trusts".'

Megarry J

Professor Birks advanced a theory that the resulting trust (automatic or presumed) is triggered in order to reverse unjust enrichment. His view is that where the defendant has innocently received property as a result of a mistake, or on a failure of consideration or under a void contract, a resulting trust will arise to prevent the unjust enrichment of the transferee. This view was extended by Professor Chambers who argued that in cases of mistake or failure of consideration, the resulting trust was created in accordance with the intention of the transferor *not to pass the beneficial interest* to the transferee. In short, the transfer of property to a transferee, subject to a mistake or failure of consideration, will effectively only dispose of the legal title to the transferee. These theories map out a major role for the resulting trust.

Sir Peter Millett, writing extra-judicially ('Restitution and constructive trusts' (1998) LQR 399), argued that a transfer of property based on a mistake or failure of consideration does not give rise to an immediate resulting trust. The initial transfer of property disposes of both legal and beneficial interests to the transferee in accordance with the intention of the transferor. There is no room for a resulting trust at this stage. Once the mistake or failure of the consideration has been revealed to the transferor, he obtains a 'mere equity' to rescind the contract and pursue restitutionary remedies, including a re-conveyance of the property. In other words, the transferee obtains a defeasible equitable interest which will be defeated if the contract is rescinded.

William Swadling ('A new role for resulting trusts' (1996) 16 LS 110) argues that the resulting trust is displaced by evidence of intention which is contrary to the intention to create a trust. If the transferor intended the transferee to have the equitable interest, the existence of a mistake on the part of the transferor does not change things and does not give rise to a resulting trust. The transferor will be able to recover the mistaken payment at common law on a total failure of consideration.

In *Westdeutsche Landesbank Girozentrale v Islington BC* [1996] AC 669, Lord Browne-Wilkinson rejected the notion that the resulting trust is designed to reverse unjust enrich-ment, and declared that this type of trust gives effect to the common intention of the parties. The transferor does not intend to part with the equitable interest and the recipi-ent of the property is also aware that he is not the intended beneficial owner. The trust is imposed on the basis of the conscience of the recipient of the property. In his Lord-ship's opinion this trust arises in two sets of circumstances, namely the purchase of property in the name of another and the existence of surplus trust funds after the trust purpose has been fulfilled. His Lordship disagreed with Megarry J's underlying ration-ale for the automatic resulting trust laid down in *Re Vandervell Trusts (No 2)* because of his lack of emphasis on implied intention:

JUDGMENT

'A resulting trust arises in two sets of circumstances: (A) where A makes a voluntary payment to B or pays (wholly or in part) for the purchase of property which is vested either in B alone or in the joint names of A and B, there is a presumption that A did not intend to make a gift to B: (B) Where A transfers property to B on express trusts, but the trusts declared do not exhaust the whole beneficial interest: *Quistclose Investments Ltd v Rolls Razor Ltd (In Liquida-tion)* [1970] AC 567. Both types of resulting trust are traditionally regarded as examples of trusts giving effect to the common intention of the parties. A resulting trust is not imposed by law against the intentions of the trustee (as is a constructive trust), but gives effect to his pre-sumed intention. Megarry J in *In Re Vandervell's Trusts (No 2)* [1974] Ch 269 suggests that a resulting trust of type (B) does not depend on intention but operates automatically. I am not convinced that this is right.'

Lord Browne-Wilkinson

The principle laid down in *Carreras Rothmans Ltd v Freeman Matthews Ltd* [1984] 3 WLR 1016, is to the effect that where property is transferred to the trustee for a specific purpose, to the extent that the equitable interest in the property remains with the trans-feror until the specified purpose is carried out, it would be unconscionable for the trustee to deny the existence of a resulting trust. This resulting trust will arise in accordance with the common intention of the settlor and the trustee.

JUDGMENT

'Equity fastens on the conscience of the person who receives from another property trans-ferred for a specific purpose only and not therefore for the recipient's own purposes, so that such person will not be permitted to treat the property as his own or to use it for other than the stated purpose. If the common intention is that property is transferred for a specific purpose and not so as to become the property of the transferee, the transferee cannot keep the property if for any reason that purpose cannot be fulfilled.'

Peter Gibson J

The difficulty with this rationale for the creation of a resulting trust is that the boundaries between resulting and constructive trusts become blurred.

In *Air Jamaica v Charlton* [1999] 1 WLR 1399, Lord Millett emphasised the relevance of intention in the context of a resulting trust. But he also added that the resulting trust will arise whether or not the settlor/transferor intended to retain a beneficial interest, as in *Vandervell v IRC*:

JUDGMENT

'Like a constructive trust, a resulting trust arises by operation of law, though unlike a constructive trust it gives effect to intention. But it arises whether or not the transferor intended to retain a beneficial interest – he almost always does not – since it responds to the absence of any intention on his part to pass a beneficial interest to the recipient. It may arise even where the transferor positively wished to part with the beneficial interest, as in *Vandervell v Inland Revenue Commissioners* [1967] 2 AC 291.'

Lord Millett

Essentially, a resulting trust arises as a default mechanism that returns the property to the transferor, in accordance with his presumed or inferred intention, as determined by the courts. Very often the transferor may not have contemplated the possibility of a return of the property, but this may be regarded as immaterial if, in the discretion of the court, the circumstances trigger a return of the property to the transferor.

The classification by Megarry J in *Re Vandervell Trusts (No 2)* (1974) into automatic and presumed resulting trusts, despite criticism, serves the useful purpose of simplifying the categories of resulting trusts and for the purpose of exposition we will rely on it.

7.3 Automatic resulting trusts

The rationale behind this type of resulting trust, as indicated above, is that the transfer of property is subject to a condition precedent that has not been achieved or that the destination of the beneficial interest has not been dealt with. As Megarry J declared in *Re Vandervell Trusts (No 2)* (1974), this type of resulting trust is not dependent on the intention of transferor but involves the automatic consequences of the failure of the transfer. This type of resulting trust arises in a variety of situations.

CASE EXAMPLE

Re Ames [1946] Ch 217

A transfer to trustees was made subject to a marriage settlement that turned out to be void. The court decided that the fund was held on resulting trust for the settlor's estate on the ground that the money was paid on a consideration that had failed.

A similar result was reached in *Essery v Cowlard* (1884) 26 Ch D 191, where the court decided that the contract to marry had definitely and absolutely been put to an end.

In *Vandervell v IRC* [1967] 2 AC 291, the transfer of the legal title to the share option was effectively made but the transferor omitted to deal with the destination of the equitable interest in a share option scheme.

In *Barclays Bank v Quistclose* [1970] AC 567, a resulting trust was created with regard to a loan made for a specific purpose which was not carried out. It must be emphasised that in order to implement the law of trust, the specific loan to the borrower must be such that the sum does not become the general property of the borrower. The specific purpose of the loan identified by the lender must be sufficient to impress an obligation on the borrower to use the amount solely for the purposes as stated by the lender.

CASE EXAMPLE

Barclays Bank v Quistclose [1970] AC 567

Quistclose Ltd loaned £209,719 to Rolls Razor Ltd, subject to an express condition that the latter would use the money to pay a dividend to its shareholders. Q Ltd's cheque for the relevant sum was paid into a separate account opened specifically for this purpose with Barclays Bank Ltd, which knew of the purpose of the loan. Before the dividend was paid, Rolls Ltd went into voluntary liquidation and Barclays Ltd claimed to use the amount to set off against the overdrafts of Rolls Ltd's other account at the bank.

The House of Lords held that the terms of the loan were such as to impress on the money a trust in favour of Quistclose Ltd in the event of the dividend not being paid, and since Barclays had notice of the nature of the loan, it was not entitled to set off the amount against Rolls Ltd's overdraft. Lord Wilberforce broadened the basis on which the resulting trust arose by deciding that there were two trusts posed by these facts – a primary trust to pay a dividend and a secondary trust that arises if the purpose of the primary trust has not been carried out.

JUDGMENT

'[W]hen the money is advanced, the lender acquires an equitable right to see that it is applied for the primary designated purpose ... when the purpose has been carried out (i.e. the debt paid) the lender has his remedy against the borrower in debt: if the primary purpose cannot be carried out, the question arises if a secondary purpose (i.e. repayment to the lender) has been agreed, expressly or by implication: if it has, the remedies of equity may be invoked to give effect to it, if it has not (and the money is intended to fall within the general fund of the debtor's assets) then there is the appropriate remedy for recovery of the loan. In the present case *the intention to create a secondary trust for the benefit of the lender, to arise if the primary trust, to pay the dividend, could not be carried out*, is clear and I can find no reason why the law should not give effect to it.' [Emphasis added]

Lord Wilberforce

In *Twinsectra v Yardley* [2002] 2 AC 164, Lord Millett in an *obiter* pronouncement reiterated that the duty imposed on the borrower or recipient of the funds to use the funds for the stipulated purpose was not merely contractual, but equitable, and therefore affected the interests of third parties:

JUDGMENT

'The duty is not contractual but fiduciary. It may exist despite the absence of any contract at all between the parties ... and it binds third parties as in the *Quistclose* case itself. The duty is fiduciary in character because a person who makes money available on terms that it is to be used for a particular purpose only and not for any other purpose thereby places his trust and confidence in the recipient to ensure that it is properly applied. This is a classic situation in which a fiduciary relationship arises, and since it arises in respect of a specific fund it gives rise to a trust.'

Lord Millett

A *Quistclose* type trust is a species of resulting trust that arises when property is transferred on terms which do not leave it at the free disposal of the transferee, but is transferred for a specific purpose which has not been fulfilled. The status of the receipt involves a question of construction that varies with the facts of each case. In *Challinor v Juliet Bellis* (2015), the Court of Appeal reversed the decision of the trial judge regarding the status of funds paid by disappointed investors to a firm of solicitors contracted by an investment company that went into liquidation. The Court of Appeal decided that property in the loans passed to the investment company and on liquidation became available to its creditors. There was no room for a *Quistclose* trust.

CASE EXAMPLE

Challinor v Juliet Bellis [2015] EWCA Civ 59 (Court of Appeal)

In 2007 a group of some 21 investors paid a sum of £2.28 million to a firm of solicitors, Juliet Bellis (the Firm), intending to invest in a property development scheme relating to land near an airport in Surrey, known as Fairoaks. An off-the-shelf company, known as Albermarle Fairoaks Limited (AFL), had acquired the airport land with the aid of a bridging loan from the Royal Bank of Scotland (RBS). AFL were the clients of the Firm and investors were invited to send their funds promptly to the Firm's client account. The Fairoaks scheme foundered. The Firm used the bulk of the investors' funds to pay off part of the RBS loan and a further amount was retained by the Firm for professional fees in respect of work done on behalf of AFL. AFL was placed into administration in 2010. The investors commenced proceedings seeking to recover their losses in full from the Firm based *inter alia* on a *Quistclose* type resulting trust and in restitution. The Court of Appeal reversed the decision of the High Court and ruled that the objective intention of the investors was to pay the sum to the Firm's client, AFL, by way of a general loan in return for loan notes. This objective intention was ascertained by construction of the relevant documents surrounding the payment to the Firm. The investors took the risk that AFL may become insolvent before the airport land investment scheme had materialised. Further, on the restitution claim, the Firm would have been entitled to a defence of *bona fide* change of position. The Firm had owed no duties or responsibilities to the investors because they advanced the monies by way of immediate loans to AFL. Thus, the Firm had changed its position by paying the sum on behalf of its client, AFL.

JUDGMENT

'Of course, money paid into a solicitors' client account is held on trust, but where a party to a transaction pays money at the other party's request to that other party's solicitor, then the default position is, and has been for over a century, that payment to the solicitor is equivalent to payment to the solicitor's client, so that the money is held on trust for the client: see *Ellis v Goulton* [1893] 1 QB 350. By "the default position", I mean the position in the absence of any agreement or arrangement to the contrary.

I consider that, on the judge's findings of primary fact, the Respondents made their payments to the Firm as immediate loans to AFL, paying into the Firm's client account at what they understood to be AFL's direction, and therefore lending to AFL by payment to the Firm as its agent.

[In rejecting the unjust enrichment claim, Briggs LJ continued] … from the moment of receipt the Firm held the Respondents' monies on client account trust for AFL. The Firm was, therefore, not enriched at all by the receipts.

In my view, the Firm would have had a change of position defence if a restitutionary claim had otherwise been available … Mrs. Bellis [the Firm] owed no duties or responsibilities to the Respondents [investors] at all, because they advanced their monies by way of immediate loan to her client AFL.'

Briggs LJ

In *R v Common Professional Examination Board ex p Mealing-McCleod*, the Court of Appeal decided that a *Quistclose* trust was created where a specific loan from Lloyds Bank was made to the borrower for the purpose of security for costs in respect of litigation and subject thereto, to be held on trust for the lender. The court followed the reasoning of Lord Wilberforce in *Quistclose*.

CASE EXAMPLE

R v Common Professional Examination Board ex p Mealing-McCleod, The Times, 2 May 2000

The career of Sally Mealing-McCleod (the applicant), as a student at the Bar, had been dogged by disputes and litigation involving educational institutions and the Common Professional Board (the Board). The applicant sought judicial review of two decisions of the Board to the effect that the applicant had not qualified for, or was not eligible for, the Bar Vocational Course. The Court of Appeal granted leave to appeal provided that the applicant gave security for costs in the sum of £6,000. The applicant complied with the order by borrowing £6,000 from Lloyds Bank. The loan agreement with the bank provided in clause 2(c) that: 'You must use the cash loan for the purpose specified … You will hold that loan, or any part of it, on trust for us until you have used it for this purpose.' The money was paid into court but the Board conceded that the applicant was entitled to apply for a place on the Bar Vocational Course. The applicant sought to recover the sum paid into court, on the ground that the money was subject to a trust in favour of the bank. Hidden J refused the application. The applicant appealed.

The court allowed the appeal and ordered that the relevant sum be paid to the bank. The nature of the loan and the surrounding circumstances created a *Quistclose* trust in respect of the purpose of the loan. The effect was that since the primary purpose of the loan was not carried out, a resulting trust for the lender was created.

In *Wise v Jimenez* (2013), the High Court endorsed the *Quistclose* principle and created a resulting trust for a disappointed investor who transferred funds to the defendant. The court regarded the principle of law as well established but the main issue in this case was one of fact, namely, deciding which party's version of events was to be believed.

CASE EXAMPLE

Wise v Jimenez and another [2013] Lexis Citation 84

The claimant, Dennis Wise (W), an ex-professional footballer, made a payment of £500,000 to the first defendant, Tony Jimenez (J), a close friend and co-owner of Charlton Football Club. The payment was made in December 2007 through the second defendant, CD Investments Ltd (CDI), a company set up for such a purpose and owned by W and his wife. Following the payment the company was put into liquidation. The payment was made to J as an investment for the purpose of developing a golf course in France, a project which failed to materialise.

It was agreed between the parties that W paid the relevant sum to J but it was disputed whether the sum was invested for the stated purpose. On the evidence the court preferred W's explanation of events and held in his favour. In the circumstances the recipient of the sum of money was subject to fiduciary obligations to apply the fund for the stated purpose only. Since the golf course project failed to materialise, the moneys were held on resulting trust for the claimant.

7.3.1 *Quistclose* analysis

Lord Wilberforce's reasoning in *Quistclose* (1970) has attracted a great deal of judicial and academic comment. Millett P, writing extra-judicially ('The *Quistclose* trust: who can enforce it?' (1985) 101 LQR 269), questioned whether a valid 'primary trust' had existed in *Quistclose* (1970). An express trust, subject to limited exceptions, assumes the existence of a person with a *locus standi* to enforce the trust. Without such a person the intended express trust is void (see later). The intended 'primary trust' was to pay a dividend. This lacks a beneficiary to enforce the trust. Thus, it is doubtful whether there could be a valid express trust in order to pay a dividend as Lord Wilberforce decided. In addition such a primary trust may lack precision or certainty which the law requires.

In *Twinsectra v Yardley* [2002] All ER 377 Lord Millett restated his views:

JUDGMENT

'In several of the cases the primary trust was for an abstract purpose with no one but the lender to enforce performance or restrain misapplication of the money ... It is simply not possible to hold money on trust to acquire unspecified property from an unspecified vendor at an unspecified time.'

Lord Millett

In addition there have been a variety of approaches to the 'secondary trust' in favour of the lender, as laid down by Lord Wilberforce in *Quistclose* (1970). In *Carreras Rothmans Ltd v Freeman Matthews Treasure Ltd* [1984] 3 WLR 1016, Peter Gibson J decided that this trust will affect the conscience of the borrower where the terms of the agreement had not been carried out. The justification here is based on the common intention of the parties. This is consistent with a constructive trust as distinct from a resulting trust.

CASE EXAMPLE

Carreras Rothmans Ltd v Freeman Matthews Treasure Ltd [1984] 3 WLR 1016

The claimant company (a cigarette manufacturer) engaged the services of the defendant, an advertising agency. The defendant fell into financial difficulty and needed funds to pay its production agencies and advertising media. The claimant made a special agreement with the defendant to pay such of its debts which were directly attributable to the claimant's involvement with the defendant. A large fund was paid into a special bank account established in the name of the defendant. A few months later the defendant went into liquidation. The liquidator refused to pay the claimant any sums from the special account. The court held that the funds in the account were held on resulting trust for the claimant in accordance with the *Quistclose* principle. Accordingly, the sum was not part of the defendant's assets to be distributed among its creditors.

JUDGMENT

'In my judgment the principle ... is that equity fastens on the conscience of the person who receives from another property transferred for a specific purpose only and not therefore for the recipient's own purposes, so that such person will not be permitted to treat the property as his own or to use it for other than the stated purpose. If the common intention is that property is transferred for a specific purpose and not so as to become the property of the transferee, the transferee cannot keep the property if for any reason that purpose cannot be fulfilled. In my judgment therefore the [claimant] can be equated with the lender in *Quistclose* as having an enforceable right to compel the carrying out of the primary trust.'

Peter Gibson J

A similar conclusion was reached by the Court of Appeal in *Re EVTR* [1987] BCLC 646, where the court decided that the lender retained an interest in the fund by way of a constructive trust, but if the fund was not used for its stated purpose a resulting trust arose in favour of the lender.

CASE EXAMPLE

Re EVTR [1987] BCLC 646

The claimant acquired a windfall sum of money and decided to assist the company that employed him by purchasing new equipment. He paid a sum of money to the company's solicitors to be released to the company 'for the sole purpose of buying new equipment'. The new equipment was ordered, but before it was delivered the company went into receivership. The claimant alleged that the sum of money was repayable to him in accordance with trusts law. The court held in the claimant's favour. The court applied the *Quistclose* principle and decided the sum was held on resulting trust for the claimant. However, the court also reasoned that a constructive trust was created when the sum was originally received by the defendant.

JUDGMENT

'On *Quistclose* principles, a resulting trust in favour of the provider of the money arises when money is provided for a particular purpose only, and that purpose fails … It is a long-established principle of equity that, if a person who is a trustee receives money or property because of, or in respect of, trust property, he will hold what he receives as a constructive trustee on the trusts of the original trust property. It follows, in my judgment, that the repayments made to the receivers are subject to the same trusts as the original [sum] in the hands of the company. There is now, of course, no question of the [amount] being applied in the purchase of new equipment for the company, and accordingly, in my judgment, it is now held on a resulting trust for the [claimant].'

Dillon LJ

Similarly in *Cooper v PRG Powerhouse Ltd* [2008] EWHC 498 (Ch), the High Court decided that a payment that is subject to a *Quistclose* trust makes the payee a fiduciary for the benefit of the payer. The effect is that if the payee becomes bankrupt, the payer is entitled to trace his funds in the hands of the payee and may recover his funds in priority over the creditors of the payee.

CASE EXAMPLE

Cooper v PRG Powerhouse Ltd [2008] EWHC 498 (Ch)

The claimant had been the managing director of the defendant company. He purchased a Mercedes motor car from Godfrey Davis Ltd for £37,239 pursuant to a credit agreement and the defendant company agreed to discharge the instalment payments on his (the claimant's) behalf as part of the salary which he received. Later the claimant resigned and it was agreed that the claimant might keep the car in return for a lump sum payment of £34,329 to the defendant company. It was expected that the defendant company would pay this amount to Godfrey Davis Ltd in discharge of the credit agreement. The claimant made the payment to the defendant, but before the latter could pay Godfrey Davis Ltd, the defendant company went into administration and the payment failed. The claimant brought proceedings for a declaration that the sums paid were held on trust for him and that he was entitled to a repayment of the funds. The principal issues in the proceedings were:

(i) whether a purpose trust had been created in favour of the claimant; and
(ii) if so, whether the claimant was entitled to trace his funds in the hands of the defendant company.

The court held in favour of the claimant and decided that on the evidence it was clear that the payment by the claimant was impressed with a purpose trust to pay that sum to Godfrey Davis Ltd in reduction of his loan. The effect was that the defendant company became a fiduciary in respect of the sum received. The failure to carry out the purpose meant that the claimant was entitled, in equity, to trace his funds in the hands of the defendant company.

The advantage of the constructive trust is that it avoids the 'beneficiary' principle (see Chapter 11). However, the objection to the imposition of such trust in the context of the *Quistclose* analysis is that the constructive trust is not dependent on the intention of the lender or transferor. A constructive trust is created by the courts in order to promote good conscience or to prevent unjust enrichment. The date on which the trust is created is also significant, for if the constructive trust is imposed at the time when the defendant receives the funds, then the equitable interest of the lender would appear to be created before the defendant performs an 'unconscionable' act. The same argument may be raised with regard to the resulting trust. The point here is that the claimant's (lender's) equitable interest does not leave him until the sum is applied for the purpose stipulated by the lender. Accordingly, on receipt of the relevant amount the borrower merely acquires the bare legal title to the funds to be used for the stipulated purpose. If the sum is not used for such purpose the proprietary interest of the claimant may be asserted by him. In *Twinsectra v Yardley* [2002] 2 All ER 377, Lord Millett expressed his opinion that a *Quistclose* trust is a resulting trust for the lender and the underlying basis of the trust is the fiduciary relationship that is created between the lender and borrower:

JUDGMENT

'[T]he *Quistclose* trust is a simple commercial arrangement akin (as Professor Bridge observes) to a retention of title clause (though with a different object) which enables the borrower to have recourse to the lender's money for a particular purpose without entrenching on the lender's property rights more than necessary to enable the purpose to be achieved. *The money remains the property of the lender unless and until it is applied in accordance with his directions, and insofar as it is not so applied it must be returned to him.* I am disposed, perhaps pre-disposed, to think that this is the only analysis which is consistent both with orthodox trust law and with commercial reality.

It is unconscionable for a man to obtain money on terms as to its application and then disregard the terms on which he received it. Such conduct goes beyond a mere breach of contract. The duty is not contractual but fiduciary. It may exist despite the absence of any contract at all between the parties … and it binds third parties as in the *Quistclose* case itself. The duty is fiduciary in character because a person who makes money available on terms that it is to be used for a particular purpose only and not for any other purpose thereby places his trust and confidence in the recipient to ensure that it is properly applied. This is a classic situation in which a fiduciary relationship arises, and since it arises in respect of a specific fund it gives rise to a trust.' [Emphasis added]

Lord Millett

In *Templeton Insurance Ltd v Penningtons Solicitors LLP* [2006] EWHC 685 (Ch), the High Court endorsed the resulting trust analysis to the effect that a payment subject to a *Quistclose* trust creates a resulting trust in favour of the payer, but subject to a power vested in the recipient of the fund to use it for the stated purpose.

CASE EXAMPLE

Templeton Insurance Ltd v Penningtons Solicitors LLP [2006] EWHC 685

The claimant, an insurance company, intended to invest in properties by purchasing and re-selling the same at a profit over a short period of time. The intention was that the claimant would lend Mr Johnston the fund to purchase the property. The moneys were paid to John-ston's solicitors, the defendants, subject to an express solicitor's undertaking that the defend-ant would keep the moneys in its client's account only to be used to acquire the identified property. The claimant was led to believe that the property price was £500,000 whereas in reality the purchase price was £236,000. The greater part of the balance of the fund was paid on disbursements and for other purposes unconnected to the purchase of the property. The claimant brought an action seeking compensation and a proprietary interest in the balance of the funds. The court held that the money was subject to a *Quistclose* trust and the claimant was entitled to its return.

JUDGMENT

'It is now conceded (which it was not, I believe, last November) that when Templeton paid the money to Penningtons, it was held by Penningtons on trust for Templeton and that the money was beneficially owned by Templeton. That, as it seems to me, is plain from the terms of the under-taking. Plainly, therefore, at any rate, until completion took place, the money was Templeton's money beneficially.

The terms of the trust were the classic *Quistclose* type of trust, namely, a resulting trust in favour of Templeton subject to a power on the part of Penningtons to apply the money depos-ited for the purpose of completing the purchase of 4 Aymer Close, Thorpe. It seems to me to follow that monies which were not paid out of the client account for that purpose were monies paid in breach of trust.'

Lewison J

An alternative analysis advocated by an academic, Robert Chambers, is to consider that the resulting trust is created only when the fund is not used for the stipulated purpose. Here it could be argued that the defendant receives both the legal and equitable interests in the fund subject to perhaps a contractual obligation to use the fund for the stipulated purpose. If the fund is used in accordance with the common intention of the parties the defendant acquires both the legal and equitable interests. But if the defendant fails to carry out the stipulated purpose a resulting trust automatically springs up in favour of the claimant.

The *Quistclose* principle

Quistclose trust	Lord Wilberforce	Primary express trust to pay a dividend and secondary resulting trust if primary trust fails
Ex p Mealing-McCleod		Applying *Quistclose*
Carreras Rothmans	Gibson J	Common intention – trust imposed on conscience of the recipient of funds (constructive trust?)
Re EVTR	Dillon LJ	Constructive trust for the purpose of the loan and on failure a resulting trust for the lender arises
Twinsectra	Lord Millett	Debtor has fiduciary duties regarding the purpose of the loan and on failure a resulting trust arises
Templeton Ins v Penningtons Robert Chambers	Lewison J	Resulting trust for the payer but with a power vested in the payee to use the fund for the stated purpose Defendant acquires legal and equitable interests with a resulting trust created where the fund is not used for the stated purpose

ACTIVITY

Self-test questions

To what extent is it possible to formulate a comprehensive theory regarding resulting trusts? Discuss.

7.3.2 Surplus of trust funds

Where the trust exhausts only some of the trust property, leaving a surplus of funds after the trust purpose has been satisfied, a resulting trust for the transferor or settlor may arise in respect of the surplus. This principle is based on two assumptions:

(a) the trust purpose has been satisfied; and

(b) a surplus of funds has been left over.

CASE EXAMPLE

Re Abbott [1900] 2 Ch 326

An appeal was launched to raise funds for two sisters who were destitute. The purpose of the appeal was to enable the beneficiaries to live in lodgings in Cambridge and to provide for their 'very moderate wants'. Considerable sums were raised and a surplus was left over after the ladies died. The question in issue involved the destination of this surplus. The court decided that the surplus was held on resulting trust for the subscribers. The court dismissed the assertion that the fund was intended to become the absolute property of the ladies entitling them to demand a transfer to themselves, or if they became bankrupt transferring the funds to their trustee in bankruptcy. On construction of the terms of the appeal and the surrounding circumstances, the intention of the subscribers was to give a wide discretion to the trustees as to whether any, and if so what, part of the fund ought to be applied for the benefit of the ladies. This approach was only consistent with a resulting trust.

It is to be noted that a material factor in these types of cases is the intention of the transferor. If the intention is expressed an express trust will be created for the transferor. In the absence of an express intention the court is required to consider whether there is any evidence of an implied intention that the transferor retained an interest in the property. Such evidence will vary with the facts of each case. In *Re Abbott* (1900) some of the factors that appealed to the court were that virtually all the contributors were identifiable and acquainted with the ladies, the terms of the appeal indicated that the basic needs of the ladies were to be taken care of and the trustees were given a wide discretion as to the means of caring for the ladies. These factors were sufficient to impress on the court that an implied resulting trust ought to be created in favour of the contributors.

In *Re Gillingham Bus Disaster Fund* [1958] Ch 300, the court concluded that a resulting trust is created even though the contributors were anonymous.

CASE EXAMPLE

Re Gillingham Bus Disaster Fund [1958] Ch 300

A disaster took place on the streets of Gillingham. A bus had careered into a group of marching cadets, killing several persons and maiming several more. An appeal was launched to raise funds by means of collecting boxes to be used for funeral expenses, caring for the disabled and 'for worthy causes' in memory of the dead boys (non-charitable purposes). A surplus of funds remained after the bus company admitted liability and paid substantial sums for similar purposes. The court was asked to determine the destination of the surplus. Harman J decided, on construction of the circumstances, that a resulting trust for contributors was created. The donors did not part 'out and out' with their contributions, but only for the specific purposes as stated in the appeal. In this respect, it was immaterial that the donors contributed anonymously. Accordingly, the surplus amount was held on resulting trust for the donors. The sum was paid into court to await claimants. Failing claimants, the fund was taken by the Crown on the basis of *bona vacantia*. The court took the view that the ordinary resulting trust rule ought to be followed despite the fact that the vast majority of the contributors were anonymous. The ruling of the court was to the effect that all the contributors (small and large, anonymous and identifiable) were to be treated as having the same intention. The position was analogous to trustees who could not find their beneficiaries. But the court could easily have come to the opposite conclusion, namely the donors being anonymous, manifested an intention not to have the property returned to them. They would then have parted with their funds 'out and out', leaving no room for a resulting trust. The Crown would then have been entitled to the property on the basis of *bona vacantia*. This case was heavily criticised in *Re West Sussex Constabulary Trusts* [1971] Ch 1 (see later).

No resulting trust – beneficial interest taken by the transferee

An alternative construction that may be adopted by the court is to the effect that the transferee may take the property beneficially in accordance with the implied intention of the transferor/settlor. In this event there is no room for a resulting trust. This approach may be adopted where the beneficiary is still capable of enjoying the benefit from the settlement. The issues concerning the implied intention of the transferor and whether the purpose of the transfer is still capable of being achieved remain questions of construction of the circumstances of each case.

CASE EXAMPLE

Re Andrew's Trust [1905] 2 Ch 48

The first Bishop of Jerusalem died, leaving several infant children. An appeal was launched to raise funds 'for or towards' their education. The children had subsequently completed their formal education with use of some of the funds. The question in issue concerned the destination of the remainder of the funds. The court held that the surplus was taken by the children in equal shares, in accordance with the implied intention of the contributors. There was no resulting trust for the contributors. The court was influenced by the fact that the children were still capable of deriving benefits from the fund, unlike *Re Abbott* (1900) (where the ladies had died: see above). In addition, the court was willing to construe 'education' in a broad sense and did not restrict it to formal education. In any event, the court decided that education in the narrow sense as referring to formal education was merely the motive for the gift, as distinct from the intention underlying the gift.

A similar result was reached in *Re Osoba* [1979] 1 WLR 24.

CASE EXAMPLE

Re Osoba [1979] 1 WLR 24

A testator bequeathed the residue of his estate, which comprised rents from certain leasehold properties, to his widow 'for her maintenance and for the training of my daughter up to University grade'. The widow died and the daughter completed her formal education. The testator's son claimed the remainder of the residue which had not been used for the daughter's education. The court held that the widow and daughter took as joint tenants. This joint tenancy was not severed. Thus, on the death of the widow the daughter succeeded to the entire fund. The references to maintenance and education in the will were merely declarations of the testator's motive for the gift.

JUDGMENT

'[T]he testator has given the whole fund; he has not given so much of the fund as the trustee or anyone else should determine, but the whole fund. This must be reconciled with the testator having specified the purpose for which the gift is made. This reconciliation is achieved by treating the reference to the purpose as merely a statement of the testator's motive in making the gift. Any other interpretation of the gift would frustrate the testator's expressed intention that the whole subject matter should be applied for the benefit of the beneficiary.'

Buckley LJ

An additional factor that had influenced the court was that the transfer was made in a residuary clause in the testator's will. The significance of this was the fact that any failure of the gift would have resulted in an intestacy which would have frustrated the testator's intention.

KEY FACTS

Automatic resulting trusts

Transfer of the legal title to trustees subject to an intended trust which is void	*Re Ames* (1946)
Transfer of the bare legal title to trustees without disposing of the equitable interest	*Vandervell v IRC* (1967); *Hodgson v Marks* (1971)
Disposal of property to another subject to a specific limitation which has not been achieved	*Barclays Bank v Quistclose* (1971); *Carreras Rothmans v Freeman Matthews* (1984); *Re EVTR* (1987); *Templeton Insurance v Pennington* (2006); *Wise v Jimenez* (2013); *Challinor v Juliet Bellis* (2015)
Surplus of trust funds left over after the trust purpose had been achieved	*Re Abbott* (1900); *Re Gillingham Bus Disaster Fund* (1958); contrast *Re Andrew's Trust* (1905); *Re Osoba* (1979)

ACTIVITY

Self-test questions

Consider the ownership of the equitable interests in the relevant properties, in respect of each of the dispositions made by Alfred of properties which he originally owned absolutely:

(a) A transfer of 10,000 shares in British Telecom plc to his wife, Beryl, subject to an option, exercisable by their son, Charles, at any time within the next five years, to repurchase 5,000 of the shares. The shares have been duly registered in Beryl's name and she pays 50 per cent of the dividends received to Alfred.

(b) A transfer of £50,000 to trustees 'upon trust to distribute all or such part of the income (as they in their absolute discretion shall think fit) for the maintenance and training of my housekeeper's daughter, Mary, until she graduates from university or reaches the age of 25, whichever happens earlier', subject to gifts over. Mary, aged 24, has recently graduated from the Utopia University.

7.3.3 Dissolution of unincorporated associations

An unincorporated association comprises a group of individuals joined together to promote a common purpose or purposes, not being commercial activities and creating mutual rights and duties among its members. Many sports clubs are run as unincorporated associations. Such associations vary in size and objectives; some may be long-standing or exist with a view to making profits and have open or restricted membership. They differ from incorporated associations in that they lack a legal personality – separate and distinct from those of its members. The title of the association is treated as a label to identify its members. The association may sue or be sued through its officers who act on behalf of the members collectively. The association is regulated by its rules, which have the effect of imposing an implied contract between all the members *inter se*. Thus, all the members are collectively joined together by the rules of the association. Its affairs are normally handled by a committee and its assets may be held on trust for the members of the association in order to ensure that the association's property is kept separate from that of its members.

In the leading case of *Conservative and Unionist Central Office v Burrell* [1982] 1 WLR 522, Lawton LJ defined an 'unincorporated association':

JUDGMENT

'[T]wo or more persons bound together for one or more common purposes, not being business purposes, by mutual undertakings, each having mutual duties and obligations, in an organisation which has rules which identify in whom control of it and its funds rests and upon what terms and which can be joined or left at will. The bond of union between the members of an unincorporated association has to be contractual.'

Lawton LJ

The issue in this case involved the legal status of the Conservative Party and whether it was liable to corporation tax on its profits. The court decided that the party was not an unincorporated association but an amorphous combination of various elements. The party lacked a central organisation which controlled local organisations.

In *Re Bucks Constabulary Fund (No 2)* [1979] 1 WLR 936, Walton J graphically described the structure of an unincorporated association in the following manner:

JUDGMENT

'If a number of persons associate together then, for practical purposes, some one or more persons have to act in the capacity of treasurers or holders of the property. In any sophisticated association there will accordingly be one or more trustees in whom the property which is acquired by the association will be vested. These trustees will of course not hold such property on their own behalf. If the trust deed is a shade more sophisticated it may add that the trustee holds the assets on trust for the members in accordance with the rules of the association. Now in all such cases the persons, and the only persons, interested therein are the members. Save by way of a valid declaration of trust in their favour, there is no scope for any other person acquiring any rights in the property of the association.'

Walton J

In *Hanchett-Stamford v Attorney General* [2008] All ER (D) 391 (Feb), the High Court decided the novel principle of ownership of surplus funds of a non-charitable unincorporated association, subject to only one surviving member. The court decided that the sole surviving member of the association was entitled to the assets absolutely and without restriction.

CASE EXAMPLE

Hanchett-Stamford v Attorney General [2008] All ER (D) 391

The claimant had joined the Performing and Captive Animals Defence League (the League) in the mid-1960s as a life member. The League was a non-charitable, unincorporated association whose object was to introduce legislation outlawing circus tricks and animal films depicting cruelty. The League acquired a building and had a substantial portfolio of shares. The claimant became the sole surviving member of the League and wished to transfer the assets of the organisation to an active charity supporting animal welfare and identified the Born Free Foundation as an appropriate charity to receive the assets. The Attorney General was named as the defendant.

The issues that required consideration by the court were:

(a) whether the objects of the League satisfied the tests for charitable status; and
(b) if not, to whom did the assets belong?

The court (Lewison J) decided that the objects of the League were inconsistent with charitable status because one of its main objects was to change the law. The League was a private unincorporated association and its assets were owned by the members of the association. Subject to any agreements between members of the League to the contrary, deceased members were deprived of all interests in the assets of such associations. The claimant, as sole surviving member of the association, was entitled to its assets without restriction.

The court distinguished an *obiter* pronouncement by Walton J in *Re Bucks Constabulary Fund (No 2)* [1979] 1 WLR 936, to the effect that the sole surviving member of an unincorporated association cannot say that he is or was the association, and therefore is not entitled solely to its funds. In Walton J's view the surplus assets of the association, being ownerless, are taken by the Crown on a *bona vacantia*. In the present case, Lewison J took issue with Walton J's analysis and questioned whether the Crown ought to be entitled to the assets of a defunct society, as opposed to the last surviving member. The learned judge considered the potential contradiction in Walton J's reasoning to the effect that ownership of the society's assets will be vested in its subsisting members, provided that there is a minimum of two members. But if there is one surviving member that member loses all interest in the assets. Lewison J decided that was equivalent to suggesting that the death of the last but one member deprives the last member of his interest:

JUDGMENT

'[W]hat I find difficult to accept is that a member who has a beneficial interest in an asset, albeit subject to contractual restrictions, can have that beneficial interest divested from him on the death of another member. It leads to the conclusion that if there are two members of an association which has assets of, say, £2 million, they can by agreement divide those assets between them and pocket £1 million each, but if one of them dies before they have divided the assets, the whole pot goes to the Crown as *bona vacantia*.'

Lewison J

bona vacantia
Property without an apparent owner but which is acquired by the Crown.

Likewise, the principle in *Cunnack v Edwards* [1896] 2 Ch 679 was distinguished on the ground that, in that case, there were no surviving members of the society, and on the death of the last surviving third party annuitant beneficiary, the surplus assets of the organisation were ownerless and thus taken by the Crown on a *bona vacantia*. In that case the society was established to raise funds through subscriptions etc. from its members to provide annuities for the widows of its deceased members. There were no surviving members of the association and on the death of the last widow (beneficiary) an unsuccessful claim to the surplus assets of the society was made by her personal representatives.

Lewison J in *Hanchett-Stamford* also regarded that an individual is guaranteed the right of peaceful enjoyment of possessions in Article 1 of Protocol 1 of the European Convention on Human Rights and Fundamental Freedoms 1950. To deprive the sole surviving member of an unincorporated association of his share in the assets of the association, without compensation, would be in breach of this Convention right. Accordingly, the claimant, as the sole surviving member of the League, was entitled to the assets of the society, free from any restrictions imposed by the rules of the League. The unincorporated association ceased to exist on the death of the claimant's husband. It followed that she was free to devote the funds to the Born Free Foundation if she so wished.

The rules of the association usually provide the procedure for enforcing rights and ownership of interests in respect of a distribution of the assets of the society on a dissolution. If the rules make provision for the distribution of assets on a liquidation those rules will be decisive and the court will merely give effect to such rules. But in the event that the rules are silent as to the destination of the surplus funds on dissolution, the courts are required to resolve the mode of distribution of the assets. The analysis here is twofold:

(a) What is meant by a 'dissolution'?

(b) What rules will be applied by the courts in order to ascertain ownership of the funds on the date of dissolution?

Dissolution

tutor tip

'The classification and limits of resulting trusts have been reviewed by judges and academics in order to identify the underlying rationale for such trusts.'

In the vast majority of cases the date of the dissolution of the association will not be in dispute. This will be the date when a formal resolution is passed to wind up the association. But, occasionally, an association may be dormant for a considerable period of time and the traditional formal resolution to wind up the body may not accurately identify the date of termination. If the inactivity is so prolonged, or the circumstances are exceptional, the court may infer that the association has become dissolved. In such cases there may be some difficulty in determining the precise date of dissolution. The less activity there is, the greater the difficulty of determining the specific date of dissolution. In such cases the court will choose a date somewhere between the time when the club could still be said to exist, and the time when its existence had clearly come to an end. The subsisting members of the association will then be entitled to participate in the distribution of the assets.

In *Re William Denby & Sons Ltd Sick and Benevolent Fund* [1971] 1 WLR 973, Brightman J classified four categories of cases in which an unregistered friendly society or benevolent fund should be regarded as having been dissolved or terminated so that its assets became distributable:

1. in accordance with the rules;

2. by agreement of all persons interested;

3. by order of the court in the exercise of its inherent jurisdiction;

4. when the substratum on which the society or fund was founded had gone, so that the society or fund no longer had any effective purpose.

On the facts of the case, it was held that the substratum had not gone, so that the fund was not distributable.

In *Re GKN Bolts & Nuts* [1982] 1 WLR 774 the court decided that mere inactivity, by itself, is insufficient to constitute spontaneous dissolution. The association may be treated as merely going through a dormant period.

CASE EXAMPLE

Re GKN Bolts & Nuts [1982] 1 WLR 774

In 1946 the trustees of a social club bought a sports ground for use for the benefit of employees of a company. By 1969 the club was in financial difficulties and the sports ground was no longer in use. In February 1975 the last general meeting was held. In September 1975 the stock of the club was sold. On 18 December 1975 a special meeting of the club was convened to consider an offer to buy the sports ground and the members voted unanimously to sell the property. On 18 August 1978 the sale was completed. One of the issues involved the date of dissolution. The court held that the club ceased to exist on 18 December 1975.

JUDGMENT

'The question is whether on the facts of the present case the society ceased to exist on 18th December 1975. On that date, the position was that the club had ceased to operate as a club for several months. The picture was not one of mere inactivity alone; there were positive acts towards the winding up of the club. The sale of the club's stock of drinks was one instance, and others were the ending of the registration for VAT, and the dismissal of the steward. The cessation of any club activities, the ending of the use of the sports ground and the abandonment of preparing accounts or issuing membership cards were all in one sense examples of inactivity; but I think that there was in all probability some element of deliberation in these matters, and not a mere inertia.

However that may be, the resolution to sell the sports ground seems to me to conclude the matter. Having taken all steps, active or passive, required to terminate the activities of the club, short of passing a formal resolution to wind it up or dissolve it, the general meeting of the club resolved to sell the club's last asset.'

Megarry VC

In the recent case, *Keene v Wellcom London Ltd* [2014] EWHC 134, the High Court decided that a dormant unincorporated association had not been spontaneously dissolved. Inactivity, even for a long period of time, may amount to strong evidence of spontaneous dissolution but, on its own, may be insufficient to constitute spontaneous dissolution. If there is spontaneous dissolution the court will have to decide the precise date of such liquidation with ramifications for members and third party creditors. The question of spontaneous dissolution is ultimately a question of degree to be determined by reference to the facts of each case.

CASE EXAMPLE

Keene v Wellcom London Ltd [2014] EWHC 134

The Graphic Reproduction Federation (the federation) was an unincorporated association that was formed in 1916 to further the interests of employers within the graphic trade. Its aims were stated in the federation rules. Clause 51 of the rules provided for circumstances when the federation could be dissolved and the consequences of dissolution. The trustees contended that administrative records had not been kept since 1986. No subscriptions had been called for or paid since then. There had been no annual general meetings since 1985. The management committee had not met since 1987. The only activity carried out had been the preparation of annual accounts by accountants and the storage of the records by the trustees. By 1987 most of the federation's members had resigned or been expelled for non-payment of subscriptions. The federation's assets were valued at £590,683. The claimants, trustees of the federation, applied to the court for a declaration that the federation had been spontaneously dissolved at some stage between 1987 and the present day or in the alternative, a court order pursuant to the court's inherent jurisdiction to dissolve the federation and consequential directions on distributions. The High Court refused the declaration on the ground that the federation had not been spontaneously dissolved, but granted an order dissolving the federation that would take effect on the date of the judgment. The distribution of assets was to be made to the subsisting members on the date of dissolution *pro rata* to their contributions.

JUDGMENT

'It is impossible, in my view, on the evidence to see that any particular date from 1987 can be picked for the dissolution of the Federation as argued by the trustees. Its ramification would be larger because it is quite conceivable that one could pick a date (for example) after 1998 when Mayday Reproduction (a subscriber) had already been dissolved and thus would have lost any entitlement but leave the other companies which were dissolved after the dissolution of the Federation.'

Smith J

Basis of distribution

The court initially adopted the resulting trust solution on the ground that the funds provided by the members were for the benefit of themselves. Not all the members may realistically enjoy the same benefits; some of them may get nothing whilst others may qualify and receive a good deal of benefits under the rules. But if they were all equally entitled to a contingent benefit on the happening of certain events, a resulting trust in their favour was considered to be the fairest way of distributing the fund. The division will be in favour of the subsisting members of the association on the date of dissolution.

CASE EXAMPLE

Re Printers and Transferrers Society [1899] 2 Ch 84

A trade union society was funded by weekly subscriptions to raise funds for strikes and other benefits for its members. The scale of benefits varied with the duration of membership and different conditions applied to printers as opposed to transferrers. The rules of the society were silent as to the mode of distribution of assets on a dissolution. There were assets of £1,000 and the society consisted of 201 subsisting members. On the question of the distribution of the fund, the court held that a resulting trust had existed in favour of the subsisting members on the date of distribution in proportion to the amount contributed over the years. It is to be noted in this case that the court did not discount the benefits received by those sharing in the distribution.

On the other hand, in *Re Hobourn Aero Components Ltd's Air Raid Distress Fund; Ryan v Forrest* [1946] Ch 194, the court decided that all members, both past and present, were entitled to a share in the distribution of the fund.

CASE EXAMPLE

Re Hobourn Aero Components Ltd's Air Raid Distress Fund; Ryan v Forrest [1946] Ch 194

Employees of a company voluntarily contributed to a fund for the purpose of relieving air raid losses during the Second World War. After the war a surplus of funds had existed. On the destination of the surplus, the court decided that all the subscribers were entitled to share in the distribution, because each retained an interest in the amount of his contributions, but subject to reductions in respect of benefits received from the fund.

The contemporary basis for distribution of the funds on liquidation involves the law of contract rather than the trust. Megarry J in *Re Sick and Funeral Society of St John's Sunday School v Golcar* [1973] Ch 51 (see below) explained that the law of contract is the basis of membership rights:

JUDGMENT

'[M]embership of a club or association is primarily a matter of contract. The members make their payments, and in return they become entitled to the benefits of membership in accordance with the rules. The sums they pay cease to be their individual property, and so cease to be subject to any concept of resulting trust. Instead, they become the property, through the trustees of the club or association, of all the members for the time being, including themselves. A member who, by death or otherwise, ceases to be a member thereby ceases to be the part owner of any of the club's property: those who remain continue owners. If, then, dissolution ensues, there must be a division of the property of the club or association among those alone who are owners of that property, to the exclusion of former members.'

Megarry J

It follows that if members of a society subscribe to a fund, not for their own personal benefit but to provide for a third party, perhaps their widows, the members would have parted 'out and out' with the funds subject to the hope that a surviving widow will take the property. If the members die without leaving a widow they are not entitled to recover their contributions. Likewise, when all the widows die the estates of the members are not entitled to claim the property.

CASE EXAMPLE

Cunnack v Edwards [1896] 2 Ch 679

A society was formed to provide annuities for the widows of deceased members. By 1879, all the members had died and by 1892 the last widow had died. There was a surplus of funds of £1,250. The personal representatives of the last widow claimed the fund. The court held that the Crown took the fund as *bona vacantia*. There was no room for a resulting trust in favour of past members.

A similar result was reached in *Re West Sussex Constabulary's Widows, Children and Benevolent Fund Trusts* [1971] Ch 1.

CASE EXAMPLE

Re West Sussex Constabulary's Widows, Children and Benevolent Fund Trusts [1971] Ch 1

A fund was established for providing payments to widows of deceased members of the West Sussex Constabulary. The rules provided that, with exceptions, a member who resigned would forfeit all claims to the fund. Receipts were derived from four classes of contributors, namely:

(a) identifiable donations and legacies;
(b) members' subscriptions;
(c) collecting boxes; and
(d) proceeds of entertainment, sweepstakes and raffles.

On 1 January 1968, the Constabulary was amalgamated with other police forces and the fund came to an end. The question in issue concerned the distribution of the fund. The court held that a resulting trust was created for the first category of contributors but the remainder of the fund was taken by the Crown as *bona vacantia* subject to an indemnity given by the Crown to honour continuing payments to surviving widows. The court decided that the first category contributors paid sums for a specific purpose which was no longer feasible. The second category of contributors provided funds not for their benefit but for third party widows and had therefore deprived themselves of any interest in the property. The third category of contributors, by virtue of their anonymity, had never expected the return of their funds (distinguishing *Re Gillingham Bus Disaster Fund* (1958)) and the fourth category of contributors received consideration for their payments.

In *Re Bucks Constabulary Widows' and Orphans Fund Friendly Society (No 2)* [1979] 1 WLR 936, on similar facts the court decided that on a dissolution of a friendly society the subsisting members were entitled to the funds.

CASE EXAMPLE

Re Bucks Constabulary Widows' and Orphans Fund Friendly Society (No 2) [1979] 1 WLR 936

The objects of the society included the relief of widows and orphans of deceased members of Bucks Constabulary. On an amalgamation with other societies a surplus of funds was available for distribution. Walton J held that the subsisting members were entitled to the property equally. The court was able to distinguish *Re West Sussex Constabulary Fund* (1971) on the ground that that case did not involve a friendly society. Further, the court ruled that the rights of entitlement on a dissolution of an unincorporated association are based on the law of contract as opposed to the law of trusts.

JUDGMENT

'[S]o far as the members are concerned it is a matter of pure contract, and, being a matter of pure contract, it is, in my judgment, as far as distribution is concerned, completely divorced from all questions of equitable doctrines.'

Walton J

If the rules of the association distinguish between the members in terms of entitlement, such as creating two or more forms of membership with correlative entitlement, then on a liquidation this discrimination is required to be reflected in the distribution. Thus, members who were required to pay double subscriptions while the society continued will be entitled to double the funds available for distribution.

CASE EXAMPLE

Re Sick and Funeral Society of St John's Sunday School v Golcar [1973] Ch 51

A Sunday school society was formed to provide sickness and death benefits for its members. Subscriptions were based on a sliding scale according to age; those under 13 paid half of one old penny per week and those over 12 paid one old penny. The benefits for those paying the full subscription were twice those of the younger subscribers. It was resolved to wind up the society. No further subscriptions were paid. There was some £4,000 of surplus assets. The court held that the distribution took the form of full shares for full members and half shares for the other members.

JUDGMENT

'On the footing that the rules of a club or association form the basis of the contract between all the members, I must look at the rules of the society to see whether they indicate any basis other than that of equality. It seems to me that they do. Those aged from five to 12 years old pay contributions at half the rate, and correspondingly their allowances and death benefit (rule 14) are also paid at half the rate. Where the rules have written into them the basis of inequality this ought also to be applied to the surplus property of the society.'

Megarry J

Similar principles are applicable to surplus funds within pension schemes. However, since the pension trustee holds the funds upon trust for the investors it would be logical if the resulting trusts principles were applicable in this context. In *Davis v Richards and Wallington Industries* [1990] 1 WLR 1511, the court decided that in respect of a pension fund surplus, the employers' contributions were held on resulting trust but the employees' contributions and other transferred funds were taken by the Crown as *bona vacantia*. The reason stated by Scott J for the *bona vacantia* solution concerned the difficulties in calculating the shares that would have been subject to such trusts, in view of the different benefits received by employees. In *Air Jamaica Ltd v Charlton* [1999] 1 WLR 1399, the Privy Council decided that a resulting trust of the surplus fund was created in favour of the employer and employees equally. In distinguishing *Davis v Richards* (1990), the court decided that the fact that the transferors did not intend to retain a benefit was not sufficient to militate against the imposition of a resulting trust.

JUDGMENT

'[L]ike a constructive trust, a resulting trust arises by operation of law, though unlike a constructive trust it gives effect to intention. But it arises whether or not the transferor intended to retain a beneficial interest – he almost always does not – since it responds to the absence of any intention on his part to pass a beneficial interest to the recipient. It may arise even where the transferor positively wished to part with the beneficial interest, as in *Vandervell v Inland Revenue Commissioners* [1967] 2 AC 291.'

Lord Millett in *Air Jamaica Ltd v Charlton* (1999)

KEY FACTS

Dissolution of unincorporated associations

'Unincorporated associations' – meaning		*Conservative & Unionist Central Office v Burrell* (1982) – *per* Lawton LJ
		Re Bucks Constabulary Fund (No 2) (1979) – *per* Walton J
Date of dissolution		*Re GKN Bolts & Nuts* (1982); *Keene v Wellcom* (2014)
Basis of distribution	Resulting trust	*Re Printers and Transferrers Society* (1899) (subsisting members)
	Resulting trust	*Re Hobourn Air Raid Distress Fund* (1946) (past and current members)
	Contract	*Cunnack v Edwards* (1896) (*bona vacantia*)

Contract	*Re West Sussex Constabulary Fund* (1971) (*bona vacantia*)
Contract	*Re Bucks Constabulary Fund (No 2)* (1979) (subsisting members)
Contract	*Re Sick and Funeral Society of St John's Sunday School v Golcar* (1973) (subsisting members)
	Hanchett-Stamford v AG (2008) sole surviving member entitled beneficially

ACTIVITY

Applying the law

The Dealing Tennis Club, an unincorporated association, has just been offered a substantial sum of money for its site by a property developer. The club was founded 40 years ago and derives its funds from subscriptions, fêtes, bazaars and other entertainment activities, collection boxes in respect of special tournaments and legacies. The committee of the club is minded to accept the offer to liquidate the association but wishes to know (i) on what basis the site is held and (ii) how any surplus assets following the winding-up of the association will be distributed.

Advise the committee.

7.4 Presumed resulting trusts

A presumption of law is a conclusion which the court is obliged to draw on proof of specific facts. A presumed resulting trust is a *prima facie* rule of evidence that creates a rebuttable presumption of law. It is a default mechanism that comes into play when there is a purchase of property in the name of another or the voluntary transfer of property to another, and there is no definitive evidence in the first place concerning the transferor's real intention. If there is clear evidence as to the destination of the equitable interest, either a gift or an express trust would be created and there would be no room for a presumed resulting trust. For instance, if A transfers the legal title to 500 BT plc shares to B and expresses his intention that B will retain the equitable interest in the shares, a gift is created by A in favour of B. In other words, the transaction is clear as to the location of the legal and equitable titles. B has both titles. Equally, the equitable interest is clearly identifiable when an express trust is created. For instance, C transfers the legal title to 2,000 BAA plc shares to D, subject to an express trust in favour of E absolutely. D acquires the legal title and E enjoys the equitable interest absolutely. But if the location of the equitable interest is uncertain, equity *prima facie* imposes a trust on the transferee for the benefit of the transferor. The transferor is presumed to have retained the equitable title and the transferee is presumed to obtain a nominal interest in the property. The rule is arbitrary in the sense that the two transactions mentioned below trigger the presumption. In this respect the presumption has the advantage of clarifying the ownership of the beneficial interest, subject to evidence to the contrary.

There are two types of transactions that give rise to the presumption, namely:

- a purchase of property in the name of another; and
- a voluntary conveyance of property in the name of another.

7.4.1 Purchase in the name of another

The rule is that where property (real or personalty) is vested in the name of another or in the purchaser jointly with others, a resulting trust will be presumed in favour of those who provide the purchase moneys and in proportion to the contribution made by each person. Parol evidence is admissible in order to identify the purchaser. If A and B jointly purchase a house and have it conveyed in the name of B so that B becomes the legal owner of the house, B is presumed to hold the house on trust for both A and B in proportion to the contribution made by each of them. If A provides four-fifths and B one-fifth of the purchase moneys, B is presumed to hold the house for himself beneficially as to one-fifth and the remainder on trust for A.

JUDGMENT

'The clear result of all the cases, without a single exception is that the trust of a legal estate, whether taken in the names of the purchasers and others jointly, or in the names of others without that of the purchaser, whether in one name or several; whether jointly or successive – results to the man who advances the purchase money. It is the established doctrine of a court of equity that this resulting trust may be rebutted by circumstances in evidence.'

Eyre CB in *Dyer v Dyer* (1788) 2 Cox Eq 92

In order to trigger the presumption it is essential that the provision of the money is by way of a purchase and not as a loan. If a loan is provided the relationship of the parties is that of creditor and debtor and no presumed resulting trust will arise. Likewise, it is essential that the parties contribute to the purchase of property and not merely the payment of rent. In *Savage v Dunningham* [1973] 3 All ER 429 an attempt was made to extend the presumed resulting trust to a flat-sharing arrangement. The court rejected this application and decided that rent, unlike purchase money, is not paid for the acquisition of a capital asset but merely for the right to use the property.

Members of a lottery syndicate who pay their subscriptions to nominees on behalf of the syndicate may become beneficiaries of any winnings. The members of the lottery on making a contribution acquire a chose in action or a right to the lottery winnings by way of a resulting trust: see *Abrahams v Abrahams, The Times*, 26 July 1999.

CASE EXAMPLE

Abrahams v Abrahams, The Times, 26 July 1999

Mr and Mrs Abrahams paid a weekly subscription of £1 each as members of a lottery syndicate. Mrs A left her husband but continued to make contributions on his behalf. There was no secrecy about the circumstances and extent of her contributions and no syndicate member objected. Mr A subsequently became bankrupt and later the syndicate won the jackpot. Mr A's trustee in bankruptcy claimed Mr A's share of the winnings. This was opposed by Mrs A. The court held that Mrs A had purchased a property right in the name of her husband. The right was to have winnings duly administered in accordance with the rules of the syndicate. Accordingly, Mr A's share of the winnings was held in trust for Mrs A.

In the definitive case of *Prest v Petrodel Resources Ltd* [2013] 2 AC 415, the Supreme Court reviewed the law on corporate personality and the occasions when the veil of incorporation may be lifted. In this case the court decided that the circumstances did not justify lifting the corporate veil. But the principle of the resulting trust was appropriate to deal with the wife's claim for ancillary relief from her husband following a divorce. The resulting trust was activated when the husband transferred seven residential properties to companies under his control, each for nominal consideration and before the companies had commenced trading. The court relied on the trial judge's ruling that the relevant properties were purchased by the husband before the transfer to companies under his control and the husband and the companies deliberately sought to conceal the facts and failed to comply with court orders for disclosure of evidence. In these circumstances the court is entitled to draw adverse inferences to the effect that the disclosure of the relevant evidence had the potential to reveal the husband's beneficial interest.

CASE EXAMPLE

Prest v Petrodel Resources Ltd [2013] 2 AC 415

Mrs Prest (W) claimed ancillary relief under ss 23 and 24(1)(a) of the Matrimonial Causes Act 1973 against her husband (H) who was the sole owner of a number of offshore companies, including Petrodel Resources Ltd (PRL). W's claim was in respect of the ownership of seven residential properties acquired by H but transferred to the ownership of PRL for nominal sums at a time before the company commenced trading. Section 23 of the 1973 Act conferred wide powers on the court to order ancillary relief for the benefit of W and the children of the marriage. Section 24(1)(a) of the Act empowers the court to order the transfer of property in the 'possession or reversion' of a party to the marriage for the benefit of the other. H failed to comply with a number of court orders requiring him to disclose information concerning the properties. The Supreme Court considered that the appeal raised three issues – (a) the extent to which the corporate veil may be lifted on general legal principles, (b) whether the scope of s 24(1)(a) of the 1973 Act empowered the court to order that H procure the transfer of the properties from the companies to W, (c) whether H had interests in the properties by way of resulting trusts and may be ordered by the court to transfer those properties to W. The court decided in favour of W only in respect of point (c) above, drawing such inferences as appear proper in the circumstances by virtue of H's deliberate failure to comply with orders for the disclosure of relevant facts. In addition, the court decided that the circumstances did not justify lifting the corporate veil on general principles within (a) above, and that the Family Court did not have special jurisdiction under s 24(1(a) to order H to transfer to W property to which in law he was not entitled.

JUDGMENT

'[T]he only basis on which the companies can be ordered to convey the seven disputed properties to the wife is that they belong beneficially to the husband, by virtue of the particular circumstances in which the properties came to be vested in them. The issue requires an examination of evidence which is incomplete and in critical respects obscure. A good deal therefore depends on what presumptions may properly be made against the husband given that the defective character of the material is almost entirely due to his persistent obstruction and mendacity. There is nothing to rebut the ordinary presumption of equity that PRL was not intended to acquire a beneficial interest in them. There is therefore an ordinary resulting trust back to the husband.'

Lord Sumption

7.4.2 Voluntary transfer in the name of another

Where the legal title to property is voluntarily (without consideration) transferred to another and there is no indication as to the destination of the equitable interest, the transaction may give rise to a presumed resulting trust. It is necessary to distinguish personalty from realty.

In relation to personalty, the voluntary nature of the transfer of the legal title and the uncertainty in the location of the equitable interest are sufficient to trigger the presumed resulting trust in favour of the transferor.

CASE EXAMPLE

Re Vinogradoff [1935] WN 68

A grandmother voluntarily transferred £800 worth of war loan stock into the joint names of herself and her granddaughter, then aged four. The grandmother continued to receive the dividends until her death. By her will, the grandmother transferred her interest in the stock to another. On her death, leaving her will unchanged, the question arose as to the beneficial ownership of the stock. The court held that a presumed resulting trust for the grandmother's estate was created and there was no evidence to rebut the presumption.

In respect of realty, prior to the enactment of the Law of Property Act 1925 a voluntary conveyance had the effect of creating a presumed resulting trust in favour of the grantor. To prevent the resulting trust from arising the grantor was required to insert a trust in favour of the grantee. This principle was reversed by s 60(3) of the Law of Property Act 1925:

SECTION

'In a voluntary conveyance a resulting trust for the grantor shall not be implied merely by reason that the property is not expressed to be conveyed for the use or benefit of the grantee.'

The effect of s 60(3) is to prevent the implication of a resulting trust in favour of transferor by reason only of a voluntary conveyance. However, a presumed resulting trust may still arise in accordance with the intention of the transferor: see *Hodgson v Marks* (1971) (above).

7.4.3 Presumption of advancement

The presumption of advancement was an archaic principle that was discriminatory by nature. It contravened Article 5 of the Seventh Protocol to the Convention on Human Rights, which lays down that 'spouses shall enjoy equality of rights and responsibilities of a private law character between them, and in their relations with their children, as to marriage, during marriage and in the event of its dissolution'. The presumption has been abolished by s 199 of the Equality Act 2010, which is yet to be brought into force. The effect is that in respect of transactions that take place after the commencement of the Act, the presumption of advancement will not operate, instead the presumption of resulting trust will apply.

Section 199 of the Equality Act 2010:

SECTION

'(1) The presumption of advancement (by which, for example, a husband is presumed to be making a gift to his wife if he transfers property to her, or purchases property in her name) is abolished.

(2) The abolition by subsection (1) of the presumption of advancement does not have effect in relation to –

(a) anything done before the commencement of this section, or

(b) anything done pursuant to any obligation incurred before the commencement of this section.'

What follows is a discussion of the principles that trigger the presumption of advancement, which will be of historical interest when s 199 comes into force.

In *Murless v Franklin* (1818) 1 Swanst 13, Lord Eldon enunciated the principle with regard to the presumption of advancement:

JUDGMENT

'The general rule that on a purchase by one man in the name of another, the nominee is a trustee for the purchaser is subject to an exception where the purchaser is under a species of natural obligation to provide for the nominee.'

Lord Eldon

In *Bennet v Bennet* (1879) 10 Ch D 474, Jessel MR laid down the modern version of the presumption:

JUDGMENT

'The doctrine of equity as regards presumption of gifts is this, that where one person stands in such a relation to another that there is an obligation on that person to make a provision for the other, and we find either a purchase or investment in the name of the other, or in the joint names of the person and the other, of an amount which could constitute a provision for the other, the presumption arises of an intention on the part of the person to discharge the obligation to the other; and therefore, in the absence of evidence to the contrary, that purchase or investment is held to be in itself evidence of a gift. In other words, the presumption of gift arises from the moral obligation to give.'

Jessel MR

A presumption of advancement, as distinct from a presumption of a resulting trust, is a presumption of a gift in favour of the transferee. Where a 'special relationship' exists between the transferor and transferee, a purchase of property in the name of another or the voluntary transfer of real or personal property in another's name gives rise to a presumption of a gift. Thus, the transferor is presumed to lose his beneficial interest in the property.

This presumption, like the presumption of a resulting trust, may be rebutted by evidence of the intention of the transferor.

The special relationship with the transferee produces occasions which, in the past, the courts had recognised as giving rise to an obligation on the part of the transferor to provide or support the transferee.

These are occasions where:

- the transferee is the wife of the transferor;
- a transfer is made by a father to his legitimate child;
- the transferor stands *in loco parentis patris* to the child: see *Re Paradise Motor Co* [1968] 1 WLR 1125.

Transfers by husband to his wife

A presumption of advancement arises when a husband transfers real or personal property to his wife. In other words, a husband may be construed as making a gift to his wife by purchasing property in her name or voluntarily conveying property to her.

JUDGMENT

'The law of this court is perfectly settled that where a husband transfers money or other property into the name of his wife only, then the presumption is that it is intended as a gift or advancement to the wife absolutely.'

Malins VC in *Re Eykyn's Trusts* (1877) 6 Ch D 115

The presumption does not arise if the parties are not married or where the wife transfers property in the name of her husband. In these circumstances the general rule concerning the presumption of a resulting trust will arise. The presumption of advancement has been severely weakened since the 1940s as a result of the socio-economic and cultural changes concerning married couples: see later.

Transfers by fathers to their legitimate children

A voluntary transfer of property or a purchase of property by a father in the name of his legitimate child is presumed to create a gift in favour of the child. The reason for this is that the father is under a moral obligation to care for his child.

JUDGMENT

'[T]he father is under [an] obligation from the mere fact of his being the father, and therefore no evidence is necessary to show the obligation to provide for his child, because that is part of his duty. In the case of a father, you have only to prove the fact that he is the father, and when you have done that the obligation at once arises.'

Jessel MR in *Bennet v Bennet* (1879) 10 Ch D 474

This presumption is treated as extremely weighty, and is not rebutted by slight evidence.

CASE EXAMPLE

Shephard v Cartwright [1955] AC 431

The claimants' father transferred a number of shares in the names of his legitimate children. The children, under instructions from their father, signed documents without understanding their effect. These documents permitted the father to sell the shares and ultimately withdraw and dissipate the funds from their bank accounts. Following the death of the father the children claimed an account from the estate. The court held in favour of the children. A presumption of advancement had arisen and was not rebutted.

However, the presumption of advancement does not arise where the child transfers property in the name of their father. The general rule of resulting trust operates here. The child therefore is presumed to retain the beneficial interest.

Transfers by persons who stand in loco parentis

In accordance with the general rule, a presumption of resulting trust operates when a mother transfers property in the name of her child. In *Bennet v Bennet* (1879) 10 Ch D 474, a transfer of £3,000 from a mother to her son was treated as giving rise to a loan.

JUDGMENT

'[A]s regards a child, a person, not the father of the child, may put himself in the position of one *in loco parentis* to the child, and so incur the obligation to make provision for the child … in the case of a person *in loco parentis* you must prove that he took upon himself the obligation.'

Jessel MR

But where a person stands in the shoes of a male parent (*in loco parentis patris*) and transfers property to his surrogate child, a presumption of advancement arises.

The question as to whether a person stands *in loco parentis* is a question of degree. The person is required to undertake the duties of parenthood and in particular a male parent. To this extent only a person of the male gender who undertakes the responsibility to care for the child will satisfy the test.

JUDGMENT

'A person *in loco parentis* means a person taking upon himself the duty of a father of a child to make provision for that child. It is clear that the presumption can only arise from that obligation, and therefore the doctrine can only have reference to the obligation of a father to provide for his child, and nothing else.'

Jessel MR

In *Re Paradise Motor Co* (1968), the transferor, a stepfather, treated his stepson as his own. He transferred shares to the stepson and this was treated as giving rise to a presumption of advancement.

7.4.4 Rebuttal of the presumptions

The presumptions of resulting trusts and advancement are capable of being rebutted by evidence that establish the true intention of the transferor. The party against whom the relevant presumption operates bears the legal burden of proof. The weight of the presumptions will vary with the facts of each case and the court will consider all the circumstances of the case to determine whether there is sufficient evidence to rebut the relevant presumption.

CASE EXAMPLE

Fowkes v Pascoe [1875] LR 10 Ch App 343

A testatrix bought stock which she put into the joint names of herself and Pascoe. In her will she left her residuary estate to her daughter-in-law and then to Pascoe and his sister. The question in issue was whether the stock formed part of the residuary estate. The court decided the presumption of resulting trust had arisen initially but on the facts the presumption was rebutted. The testatrix intended to make a gift to Pascoe. There was sufficient evidence that the testatrix was a wealthy woman; she was clearly fond of Pascoe and considered herself as having no near relations.

In *Lord Grey v Lady Grey* (1677) 2 Swan 594, the court decided that the presumption of advancement was not rebutted when a son allowed a father to receive income from land, the subject-matter of the transfer. Such conduct amounted to reverence and good manners.

- In *Shephard v Cartwright* (1955) (see above) the court decided that the children's conduct in signing documents under the instructions and control of their father was not admissible in order to rebut the presumption of advancement.

- In *Re Paradise Motor Co* (1968) (see above) the verbal disclaimer by a stepchild of rights to shares amounted to a rebuttal of the presumption of advancement.

ACTIVITY

Evaluate the status of the presumptions of resulting trusts and advancement in contemporary society.

7.4.5 Intended unlawful activity and rebuttal evidence

A transferor may voluntarily convey property to a nominee in an attempt to implement some unlawful activity, such as to avoid his creditors. Later the transferor repents, withdraws from the illegal purpose and wishes to claim the property back from the nominee. The issue is whether the claimant ought to be allowed to recover the property in the light of his impropriety concerning the original transfer. In effect, should the claimant be allowed to rely on the presumption of resulting trust?

In *Tinker v Tinker* [1970] 1 All ER 540, the court applied the maxim 'He who comes to equity must come with clean hands', and prohibited the adduction of evidence of the true intention of the transferor.

CASE EXAMPLE

Tinker v Tinker [1970] 1 All ER 540

A husband transferred the matrimonial home to his wife in order to defeat his creditors, should his business fail. His business flourished but his wife claimed the house as hers. The court decided that the presumption of advancement arose in favour of the wife and the husband was not entitled to rebut the presumption by adducing evidence of his own impropriety.

JUDGMENT

'The husband had the house put into his wife's name so as to avoid any risk of it being taken by his creditors in case his business was not a success. What is the result in law? In *Gascoigne v Gascoigne* [1918] 1 KB 223, it was held that, when a husband put a house in his wife's name so as to avoid it being taken by his creditors, the house belonged to the wife. The husband could not be heard to say that it belonged to him, because he could not be allowed to take advantage of his own dishonesty. That case was applied in *Re Emery's Investment Trust* [1959] Ch 410. We were invited by counsel for the husband to overrule those decisions. But in my opinion they are good law.

I am quite clear that the husband cannot have it both ways. So he is on the horns of a dilemma. He cannot say that the house is his own and, at one and the same time, say that it is his wife's. As against his wife, he wants to say that it belongs to him. As against his creditors, that it belongs to her. That simply will not do. Either it was conveyed to her for her own use absolutely; or it was conveyed to her as trustee for her husband. It must be one or other. The presumption is that it was conveyed to her as trustee for her husband. It must be one or other. The presumption is that it was conveyed to her for her own use; and he does not rebut that presumption by saying that he only did it to defeat his creditors. I think that it belongs to her.'

Lord Denning MR

In *Rowan v Dann* (1992), the Court of Appeal adopted a different approach to the issue. If the transfer creates a resulting trust in favour of the transferor so that *prima facie* he retains the equitable interest and he does not rely on his own improper conduct in order to recover the property, the court may allow him to do so. It is immaterial that the defendant raises the issue that the transferor does not have 'clean hands'.

CASE EXAMPLE

Rowan v Dann (1992) 64 P & CR 202, Court of Appeal

Rowan was the owner of farmland. He granted tenancies to Dann in order to prevent the assets falling into the hands of his creditors should he become bankrupt, and also in pursuance of an intended joint business venture. No rent was actually paid, although such payment was stipulated in the agreement. Rowan claimed that the land should revert to him under a resulting trust as the purpose of the transfer (a joint business venture) had failed to materialise. Dann claimed that Rowan could not rely on the resulting trust as he did not have 'clean hands', having created sham tenancies in order to defeat his creditors. The Court of Appeal held in favour of Rowan. A resulting trust existed in favour of Rowan by reason of the failure of the joint business venture, and this presumption was not rebutted. The improper, underlying purpose of the transfer was common to both sides. The creditors were not disadvantaged and Rowan did not have to rely on the unlawful purpose to support his claim.

JUDGMENT

'[I]f the illegal transaction had been carried out, the plaintiff himself, in my judgment, could not afterwards have recovered the goods. But the illegal transaction was not carried out; it wholly came to an end. To hold that the plaintiff is enabled to recover does not carry out the illegal transaction, but the effect is to put everybody in the same situation as they were before the illegal transaction was determined upon, and before the parties took any steps to carry it out.

In the present case, there is no evidence that the scheme to defeat creditors was put into effect. There is no evidence that any creditor was persuaded to hold his hand in the belief that Mr Rowan's land was encumbered by the tenancies and the option. In my opinion, the present case is on its facts covered by the principle expressed in *Taylor v Bowers* [1876] 1 QBD 291.'

Mellish LJ

The law was reviewed by the House of Lords in *Tinsley v Milligan* [1994] 1 AC 340 and a different approach was heralded by the court. It was decided that where a transfer of property (real or personal) to another gives rise to a resulting trust in favour of the transferor so that *prima facie* he retains the equitable interest in the property and does not have to rely on the illegality in order to establish a proprietary claim (the 'reliance' principle), the illegality is no bar to a successful action. In other words, if the claimant enjoys an equitable interest by way of a resulting trust, his subsequent illegality is not decisive. In this respect the claimant is not rewarded or does not profit from his unlawful conduct, instead he is merely allowed to recover his property. The House of Lords in *Tinsley* rejected the flexible approach adopted by the Court of Appeal of balancing the adverse consequences of granting relief against not granting relief.

CASE EXAMPLE

Tinsley v Milligan [1994] 1 AC 340

The defendant transferred property into the name of her friend, the claimant, in order to facilitate a fraud on the Department of Social Security. Both litigants were parties to the fraud, which was carried on for a few years. The parties fell out and the claimant sought to evict the defendant from the property. The defendant claimed that the property was held on trust for both parties in equal shares. The House of Lords decided in favour of the defendant. The court ruled that where a party based her claim on title to property (whether legal or equitable) that was acquired in the course of an illegal transaction, that party may recover the property so long as she was not forced to plead, or rely on, the illegality. In this case the presumption of a resulting trust applied. Consequently, the defendant did not have to rely on the illegality since she only had to establish a contribution to the purchase price.

JUDGMENT

'Neither at law nor in equity will the court enforce an illegal contract which has been partially, but not fully, performed. However, it does not follow that all acts done under a partially performed contract are of no effect. In particular it is now clearly established that at law (as opposed to in equity), property in goods or land can pass under, or pursuant to, such a contract. *If so, the rights of the owner of the legal title thereby acquired will be enforced, provided that the plaintiff can establish such title without pleading or leading evidence of the illegality.* It is said that the property lies where it falls, even though legal title to the property was acquired as a result of the property passing under the illegal contract itself [emphasis added]. [His Lordship reviewed the following common law cases: *Bowmakers Ltd v Barnet Instruments Ltd* [1945] KB 65; *Ferret v Hill* (1854) 15 CB 207; *Taylor v Chester* (1869) LR 4 QB 309; *Alexander v Rayson* [1936] 1 KB 169, and concluded:]

From these authorities the following propositions emerge:

(1) property in chattels and land can pass under a contract which is illegal and therefore would have been unenforceable as a contract;

(2) a plaintiff can at law enforce property rights so acquired provided that he does not need to rely on the illegal contract for any purpose other than providing the basis of his claim to a property right;

(3) it is irrelevant that the illegality of the underlying agreement was either pleaded or emerged in evidence: if the plaintiff has acquired legal title under the illegal contract that is enough.

The presumption of a resulting trust is, in my view, crucial in considering the authorities. On that presumption (and on the contrary presumption of advancement) hinges the answer to the crucial question "does a plaintiff claiming under a resulting trust have to rely on the underlying illegality?" Where the presumption of resulting trust applies, the plaintiff does not have to rely on the illegality. If he proves that the property is vested in the defendant alone but that the plaintiff provided part of the purchase money, or voluntarily transferred the property to the defendant, the plaintiff establishes his claim under a resulting trust unless either the contrary presumption of advancement displaces the presumption of resulting trust or the defendant leads evidence to rebut the presumption of resulting trust.'

Lord Browne-Wilkinson

In *Tinsley v Milligan* (1994) it would appear that a party may be entitled to assert his equitable interest in the property by relying on the presumption of a resulting trust, if he withdraws from the intended unlawful activity. On the other hand, if the presumption of advancement operates against the claimant so that he is required to rebut the presumption in order to establish an equitable interest in the property, the claimant may have difficulty in attempting to adduce evidence of his illegality:

JUDGMENT

'In cases where the presumption of advancement applies, the plaintiff is faced with the presumption of gift and therefore cannot claim under a resulting trust unless and until he has rebutted that presumption of gift: for those purposes the plaintiff does have to rely on the underlying illegality and therefore fails.'

Lord Browne-Wilkinson

However, in *Tribe v Tribe* [1995] 4 All ER 236, the Court of Appeal seemed to have extended *Tinsley v Milligan* (1994) by allowing the illegal purpose to be used to rebut the presumption of advancement. The court decided that where the presumption of advancement is created by a transfer of property intended to promote an unlawful purpose, *but which has not been carried into effect*, the transferor is entitled to adduce evidence of the unlawful purpose in order to rebut the presumption of advancement. *Gascoigne v Gascoigne* was distinguished on the ground that, in that case, there was sufficient evidence that the husband intended to transfer the beneficial interest in the house to his wife. Moreover, *Tinker v Tinker* was regarded as a case where the husband's evidence confirmed the presumption of advancement as distinct from rebutting it. In *Tribe*, the court's approach appears to be based on the transferor withdrawing from the transaction before any part of the illegal purpose had been carried into effect. This is the position irrespective of whether the equitable interest arises by virtue of the presumption of advancement or resulting trust. The significant factor involves the transferor repenting or withdrawing from the illegal enterprise before it comes to fruition.

CASE EXAMPLE

Tribe v Tribe [1995] 4 All ER 236

The claimant owned 459 out of 500 shares in a company. He was the tenant of a number of clothing shops which were occupied by the company as a licensee. The landlords of two of the shops served dilapidation notices on the claimant, requiring him to carry out substantial repairs to the property. He was advised that if these claims were valid, he might be forced to sell the company or dispose of his shares. In order to avoid this, he transferred the shares to one of his sons for an alleged consideration of £79,995. It was never intended that this amount would be paid. The dispute with the landlords was subsequently resolved and the claimant requested a re-transfer of the shares from his son. The son refused. The court decided in favour of the father on the ground that the intended illegal transaction was not completed. The father was therefore entitled to assert his equitable interest.

JUDGMENT

'The question whether a transferor can repudiate his fraudulent scheme before it is carried into effect and then give evidence of his dishonest intention in order to rebut the presumption of advancement did not fall for consideration in *Gascoigne v Gascoigne*, where it was arguably too late for him to do so; and it did not arise in *Tinker v Tinker*, where he was found to have had no dishonest intention. *In my opinion, the weight of the authorities supports the view that*

a person, who seeks to recover property transferred by him for an illegal purpose can lead evidence of his dishonest intention whenever it is necessary for him to do so provided that he has withdrawn from the transaction before the illegal purpose has been carried out. It is not necessary, if he can rely on an express or resulting trust in his favour; but it is necessary (i) if he brings an action at law, and (ii) if he brings proceedings in equity and needs to rebut the presumption of advancement [emphasis added].

In my opinion the following propositions represent the present state of the law:

(1) title to property passes both at law and in equity even if the transfer is made for an illegal purpose. The fact that title has passed to the transferee does not preclude the transferor from bringing an action for restitution;

(2) the transferor's action will fail if it would be illegal for him to retain any interest in the property;

(3) subject to (2), the transferor can recover the property if he can do so without relying on the illegal purpose. This will normally be the case where the property was transferred without consideration in circumstances where the transferor can rely on an express declaration of trust or a resulting trust in his favour;

(4) it will almost invariably be so where the illegal purpose has not been carried out. It may be otherwise where the illegal purpose has been carried out and the transferee can rely on the transferor's conduct as inconsistent with his retention of a beneficial interest;

(5) the transferor can lead evidence of the illegal purpose whenever it is necessary for him to do so provided that he has withdrawn from the transaction before the illegal purpose has been wholly or partly carried into effect. It will be necessary for him to do so:
(i) if he brings an action at law; or
(ii) if he brings proceedings in equity and needs to rebut the presumption of advancement;

(6) the only way in which a man can protect his property from his creditors is by divesting himself of all beneficial interest in it. Evidence that he transferred the property in order to protect it from his creditors, therefore, does nothing by itself to rebut the presumption of advancement; it reinforces it. To rebut the presumption it is necessary to show that he intended to retain a beneficial interest and conceal it from his creditors;

(7) the court should not conclude that this was his intention without compelling circumstantial evidence to this effect. The identity of the transferee and the circumstances in which the transfer was made would be highly relevant. It is unlikely that the court would reach such a conclusion where the transfer was made in the absence of an imminent and perceived threat from known creditors.'

Millett LJ

Where a party enters into an unlawful transaction and asserts an equitable interest in the property in reliance on the fraudulent transaction, the court will prevent him from establishing his alleged equitable in the property on the ground that he is not allowed to profit from an unlawful transaction. This is an illustration of the maxim, 'He who comes to equity must come with clean hands.' The court so decided in *Barrett v Barrett* (2008). The principle in *Tinsley* is distinguishable on the basis that in *Barrett*, the claimant will be required to rely on his illegal motive in an attempt to establish an equitable interest in property. Equally, *Tribe* is distinguishable because in *Barrett* the unlawful transaction had been executed.

CASE EXAMPLE

Barrett v Barrett [2008] EWHC 1061 (High Court)

The claimant (Thomas) and defendant (John) were brothers. In 1977 the claimant purchased a freehold house as sole legal and beneficial owner. In June 1993 he became bankrupt and the property became vested in the trustee in bankruptcy. The defendant offered to purchase the property from the trustee in bankruptcy and this offer was accepted. In due course the defendant became the registered proprietor of the property. In June 1996 the claimant was discharged from bankruptcy. The defendant had lived in the property from the time of its purchase until about 2000. The claimant continued to live in the property until it was sold in September 2005. The net sale proceeds were £115,000 which was paid to the defendant and he paid the same to his sister. The sister refused to repay the sum to the defendant contending that she held it on behalf of the claimant. The basis of the claimant's action was that in pursuance to an agreement in October 1994, it was agreed that the defendant would purchase the property but allow the claimant to remain in occupation. Further, it was contended that the claimant would pay all expenses relating to the property. There were no written terms (or express trust) of such arrangement and therefore the claimant was required to rely on a constructive trust. The defendant denied the existence of an agreement and contended that the claimant's case was based on pursuance of an illegal purpose as the arrangement was not disclosed to the trustee in bankruptcy as required by s 333(2) of the Insolvency Act 1986. The court held in favour of the defendant. The illegal motive behind the sale to the defendant constituted the essence of the transaction. The only purpose of the arrangement was an attempt to create a trust for the benefit of the claimant and thereby render his interest unenforceable. *Tinsley v Milligan* [1993] 3 All ER 65 was distinguished on the ground that in that case the claimant was entitled to establish her interest without reliance on the unlawful transaction.

JUDGMENT

'Given that Thomas must rely on the pleaded agreement or arrangement that he was to be the beneficial owner and was to pay the mortgage instalments, can he avoid reliance on its unlawful purpose? In my judgment, he cannot. He has in effect pleaded the unlawful purpose in his particulars of claim: the purpose of purchasing the property in the name of John was "to avoid its being repossessed by the Trustee in Bankruptcy". Without that purpose, the agreement or arrangement has no rational explanation. Thomas needs to allege and prove it in order to establish the agreement, but in doing so he relies on his own illegal purpose and thereby renders his interest unenforceable.'

Richards J

In *O'Kelly v Davies* [2014] EWCA Civ 1606, the Court of Appeal decided that in the context of the *Tinsley v Milligan* principle, it made no difference whether the claimant's beneficial interest arose by way of a resulting or constructive trust. The crucial issue is whether the claimant is required to rely on his unlawful conduct in order to establish a beneficial interest in the property. If that be the case, he will not be allowed to adduce evidence in order to establish his beneficial interest. If, on the other hand, the unlawful conduct is merely incidental to the assertion of a beneficial interest, the claimant will not be prohibited from establishing his beneficial entitlement.

In *Bilta (UK) Ltd v Nazir* (2015), the Supreme Court decided that where a company goes into liquidation, but before this event its directors became embroiled in fraudulent transactions in breach of their fiduciary duties, the liquidator of the company may be entitled to pursue claims against the directors for losses caused by their breach of duties. It would be absurd and unjust for the directors to be allowed to attribute their wrong-doing or knowledge to the company as a defence to a claim brought by the liquidators. Thus, the liquidator may not be barred by the doctrine of illegality from pursuing claims against the directors and their accessories for the losses caused by the directors' breach of fiduciary duties.

CASE EXAMPLE

Bilta (UK) Ltd v Nazir (No. 2) [2015] UKSC 23 (Supreme Court)

The defendants were directors and their accessories of Bilta (B) who caused B to enter into a series of fraudulent transactions relating to European Emissions Trading Scheme Allowances with the consequence that B had insufficient funds to pay VAT to HM Revenue & Customs. B was compulsorily liquidated and the liquidator (on behalf of the creditors) claimed damages and compensation from the defendants. The accessories to the fraud defended on the ground of the directors' illegality. The Supreme Court dismissed the defendants' appeal on the ground that the accessories were not permitted to defend the claim by attributing the co-defendants' (directors) knowledge of the illegal transactions to B.

JUDGMENT

'Where a company has been the victim of wrongdoing by its directors, or of which its directors had notice, then the wrongdoing, or knowledge, of the directors cannot be attributed to the company as a defence to a claim brought against the directors by the company's liquidator, in the name of the company and/or on behalf of its creditors, for the loss suffered by the company as a result of the wrongdoing, even where the directors were the only directors and sharehold-ers of the company, and even though the wrongdoing or knowledge of the directors may be attributed to the company in many other types of proceedings.'

Lord Neuberger PSC

In a joint judgment, Lord Toulson and Lord Hodge JJSC additionally decided that the fiduciary duties which a director owes to an insolvent company differs from his fiduciary duties owed to a solvent company. In the former case, the duties owed to the company are for the benefit of the creditors, whereas in the latter case the duties are owed to the company and its shareholders.

JUDGMENT

'It has been stated many times that the doctrine of illegality has been developed by the courts on the ground of public policy. The context is always important. In the present case the public interest which underlies the duty that the directors of an insolvent company owe for the pro-tection of the interests of the company's creditors, through the instrumentality of the dir-ectors' fiduciary duty to the company, requires axiomatically that the law should not place obstacles in the way of its enforcement. To allow the directors to escape liability for breach of their fiduciary duty on the ground that they were in control of the company would undermine the duty in the very circumstances in which it is required. It would not promote the integrity and effectiveness of the law, but would have the reverse effect. The fact that they were in sole control of the company and in a position to act solely for their own benefit at the expense of the creditors, makes it more, not less, important that their legal duty for the protection of the interests of the creditors should be capable of enforcement by the liquidators on behalf of the company.

The courts would defeat the very object of the rule of law which we have identified, and would be acting contrary to the purpose and terms of sections 172(3) and 180(5) of the Companies Act 2006, if they permitted the directors of an insolvent company to escape responsibility for breach of their fiduciary duty in relation to the interests of the creditors, by raising a defence of illegality to an action brought by the liquidators to recover, for the benefit of those creditors, the loss caused to the company by their breach of fiduciary duty. In everyday language, the purpose of the inclusion of the creditors' interests within the scope of the fiduciary duty of the directors of an insolvent company towards the company is so that the directors should not be off the hook if they act in disregard of the creditors' interests. It would be contradictory, and contrary to the public interest, if in such circumstances their control of the company should provide a means for them to be let off the hook on the ground that their illegality tainted the liquidators' claim.'

Lords Toulson and Hodge JJSC

Reform

The Law Commission in its 2010 report, 'The Illegality Defence' (Law Com. No. 320), regarded the rules involving illegality issues as complex and confused due to the wide variety of circumstances in which the issue may arise, such as unjust enrichment, property disputes and trusts law. It may not be possible to lay down rigid principles in the context of illegality issues. Instead, the courts ought to give effect to property rights, but at the same time prevent a claimant from profiting from his own wrong. In the area of trusts law the Commission recommended legislative reform, giving the courts a statutory discretion to decide the effect of illegality on trusts law. The courts will be required to take into account a list of factors, including the conduct of the parties; the value of the interest in issue; whether refusing the claim would act as a deterrent; and the interests of third parties. However, in 2012 the Ministry of Justice decided not to implement the recommendations in the Law Commission report. The Ministry was not convinced that the recommendations would have the effect of improving the current law and s 199 of the Equality Act 2010, when implemented, will have a significant impact in improving the state of the law in this area.

In *Patel v Mirza* (2017), the Supreme Court conducted an extensive review of the case law on restitution and the illegality defence, as well as the rationale underlying the *Tinsley* principle and decided that it was time for *Tinsley* to be overruled. It concluded by a majority (5:4 split) that there is an underlying need for principle, clarity and certainty in the law coupled with fairness and justice for litigants. The court recognised that it is unlikely that Parliament will enact the proposals recommended by the Law Commission for a change of the law in this area. Instead the majority of the Justices of the Supreme Court adopted the main recommendations of the Law Commission. The *Tinsley* rule was based on a procedural technicality concerning the presumption of a resulting trust and the burden of proof rather than a consideration of the merits of the case. The court decided that the integrity of the justice system was dependent in finding a right balance between two policy objectives namely, the rule that a person may not be allowed to profit from his own wrongdoing and the policy factors that make it necessary to proscribe the transaction in question. In finding the right balance a more flexible approach was needed enabling the court to weigh up a range of factors, including the seriousness of the unlawful transaction, the extent to which it is central to the contract, whether it is intentional conduct and to keep into perspective a sense of proportionality.

CASE EXAMPLE

Patel v Mirza [2017] 1 All ER 191 (Supreme Court)

The claimant paid the defendant £620,000 under an illegal agreement concerning the movement of RBS shares index but based on insider information available to the defendant. Section 52 of the Criminal Justice Act 1993 made it an offence for a person in possession of inside information to deal or encourage another to deal in securities. About two months later the defendant told the claimant that the bet was off because his expected information failed to materialise. The defendant assured the claimant that he will return his money. However, by error he paid the amount to a mutual friend, Mr Georgiou, before his bankruptcy. The claimant sued the defendant for a return of the funds. The trial judge rejected the claim because he felt that the claimant was required to prove the illegal purpose. On appeal, the Court of Appeal allowed the appeal on the ground that the illegal agreement had not been carried out, relying on *Tribe v Tribe*, and consequently the claimant was entitled to a return of his funds. On appeal, the Supreme Court unanimously dismissed the appeal but the majority of the Justices of the Supreme Court decided on different grounds from the minority. The majority of the Justices adopted the 'flexible' approach of considering the Parliamentary justification for proscribing the transaction, tempered by a range of factors. (The Supreme Court Justices in the majority were Lords Toulson, Kerr, Hale, Wilson and Hodge JJSC.)

The minority Justices relied on restitution principles involving claims where there has been a total failure of consideration provided that these principles do not give effect to the unlawful transaction but merely unpicks it or returns the parties to their positions before the unlawful transaction. It was observed that the 'flexible' approach advocated by the majority has the effect of converting a legal principle into an exercise of discretion. (These comprised Lords Neuberger, Mance, Clarke and Sumption.)

JUDGMENT

'I would say that one cannot judge whether allowing a claim which is in some way tainted by illegality would be contrary to the public interest, because it would be harmful to the integrity of the legal system, without (a) considering the underlying purpose of the prohibition which has been transgressed, (b) considering conversely any other relevant public policies which may be rendered ineffective or less effective by denial of the claim, and (c) keeping in mind the possibility of overkill unless the law is applied with a due sense of proportionality. That trio of necessary considerations can be found in the case law.'

Lord Toulson

Resulting trusts

Automatic resulting trusts	
Failure of an intended express trust	*Re Ames* (1946); *Vandervell v IRC* (1967)
Transfers subject to conditions precedent which fail to materialise	*Barclays Bank v Quistclose* (1970); *Carreras Rothmans v Freeman Matthews Ltd* (1984); *Re EVTR* (1987); *Twinsectra v Yardley* (2002); *Templeton Insurance v Pennington* (2006); *Cooper v Powerhouse* (2008); *Wise v Jimenez* (2013); *Challinor v Juliet Bellis* (2015)
Surplus of trust funds	*Re Abbott* (1900); *Re Gillingham Bus Disaster Fund* (1959)
Surplus beneficial interest acquired by beneficiary	*Re Andrew's Trust* (1905); *Re Osoba* (1979)
Dissolution of unincorporated associations:	
'dissolution'	*Re William Denby Benevolent Fund* (1971); *Re GKN Bolts & Nuts* (1982); *Keene v Wellcom* (2014)
'unincorporated associations'	*Conservative and Unionist Central Office v Burrell* (1982); *Re Bucks Constabulary Fund (No 2)* (1979)
Resulting trust	*Re Printers and Transferrers Society* (1899); *Re Hobourn Air Raid Distress Fund* (1946)
Contract	*Cunnack v Edwards* (1896); *Re West Sussex Constabulary Fund* (1971); *Re Bucks Constabulary Fund* (1979); *Re Sick and Funeral Society v Golcar* (1973); *Hanchett-Stamford v AG* (2008)
Presumed resulting trusts	
Purchase of property in the name of another	*Dyer v Dyer* (1788); *Abrahams v Abrahams* (1999); *Prest v Petrodel* (2013)
Voluntary transfer of personal property to another	*Re Vinogradoff* (1935)
Section 60(3) LPA 1925	*Hodgson v Marks* (1971)
Exception – presumptions of advancement – transfers by a husband to his wife – transfers by fathers to their legitimate children – transfers by persons who stand *in loco parentis patris*	See s 199 of the Equality Act 2010 *Tinker v Tinker* (1970) *Shephard v Cartwright* (1955) *Re Paradise Motor Co Ltd* (1968)
Rebuttal of presumptions	*Fowkes v Pascoe* (1875); *Lord Grey v Lady Grey* (1677); *Shephard v Cartwright* (1955); *Re Paradise Motor Co* (1968)
Intended unlawful activity and rebuttal evidence	*Tinker v Tinker* (1970); *Tinsley v Milligan* (1994); *Tribe v Tribe* (1995); *Patel v Mirza* (2017); *Barrett v Barrett* (2008); *O'Kelly v Davies* (2014); *Bilta v Nazir (No 2)* (2015)

ACTIVITY

Essay writing

How far are the presumptions of resulting trusts and advancement significant in the context of property transferred to another subject to the unfulfilled intention of defeating creditors? Discuss.

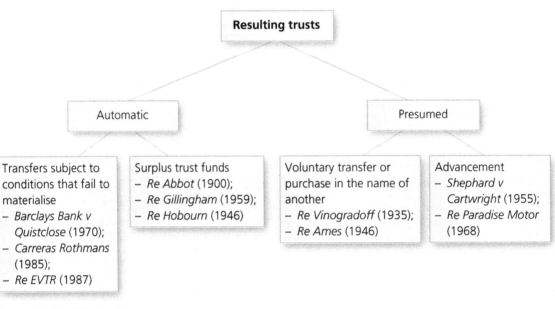

Figure 7.1 Resulting trusts

SUMMARY

- There have been various classifications of resulting trusts: automatic and presumed, common intention of the parties (purchase in the name of another and surplus of trust funds), intention of the settlor and to prevent unjust enrichment. There is also the view that the trust arises whether or not the transferor intended to retain a beneficial interest.

- The *Quistclose* controversy was created by Lord Wilberforce's analysis to the effect that where a primary purpose trust cannot be carried out a secondary trust may arise in favour of the transferor. The difficulty here is that, subject to limited exceptions, an express purpose trust is void. An alternative view is that where the common intention is that property has been transferred for a specific purpose the transferee cannot keep the property beneficially if the purpose cannot be carried out. A variation on this theme involves a transfer of property by way of a constructive trust and if the purpose cannot be achieved a resulting trust in favour of the transferor arises. A different analysis assumes that the lender transfers both legal and equitable interests in the fund to the borrower subject to an obligation to promote the stated purpose. A resulting trust for the lender will arise if the stated purpose has not been fulfilled.

- An unincorporated association involves two or more persons joined together by mutual undertakings to promote common objectives, not being a partnership. The rules of the association create a contract between the members and identify in whom control of the society subsists. The unincorporated association does not have a separate legal existence.

- On a liquidation of an unincorporated association a resulting trust would be an inappropriate solution. Instead, the solution lies in the law of contract. Thus, where the society exists for the benefit of its members the surplus funds will be distributed to its subsisting members on the date of liquidation. But if the society exists for the benefit of third parties, the subsisting members may be excluded from receiving a benefit and the Crown may take the property on a *bona vacantia*.

- The rationale behind the presumed resulting trust is that where the location of the equitable interest in the property is unclear equity will presume that such interest subsist for the benefit of the transferor. This is a rule of evidence and the presumption may be rebutted by evidence to the contrary.

- A claimant who transfers property to another with the intention of committing an unlawful purpose may be able to recover his property if he is not required to rely on the unlawful transaction, or he repents before completing the unlawful transaction.

- The flexible approach, see *Patel v Mirza*.

SAMPLE ESSAY QUESTION

Consider the following essay question:

When may a resulting trust be imposed?

Answer plan

> Give a brief definition of a resulting trust highlighting automatic resulting trusts, occasions when there are surplus trust funds left over after the trust purpose has been achieved, the presumptions of resulting trusts and advancements.

> Identify the traditional theories justifying the creation of resulting trusts.

> State when automatic resulting trusts will be created.

> Explain the *Quistclose* controversy and consider the various judicial approaches to the *Quistclose* principle.

> State the various solutions adopted by the courts on occasions when a surplus of funds is left over after the trust purpose has been achieved.

Identify the occasions when a presumed resulting trust will arise and illustrate the type of evidence that may be admissible to rebut the presumption, including occasions when a transfer is made in order to promote an intended unlawful purpose.

Briefly highlight the problem underlying unincorporated associations and the solutions adopted by the courts in identifying ownership of the surplus funds on liquidation of the association.

CONCLUSION

Further reading

Andrews, G, 'The presumption of advancement: equity, equality and human rights' (2007) Conv 340.

Cotterill, I, 'Property and impropriety: the *Tinsley v Milligan* problem again' (1999) LMCLQ 465.

Creighton, P, 'The recovery of property transferred for illegal purposes' (1997) 60 MLR 102.

Euonchong, N, 'Title clauses and illegal transactions' (1995) 111 LQR 135.

Gardner, S, 'New angles on unincorporated associations' (1992) Conv 41.

Glister, J, 'How not to abolish the presumption of advancement' (2010) 73 MLR 807.

Green, G, 'The dissolution of unincorporated non-profit associations' (1980) 45 MLR 626.

Greer, S, 'A last resort' (2007) 157 NLJ 696.

Harpum, C, 'Perpetuities, pensions and resulting trusts' (2000) Conv 170.

Ho, L and Smart, P S J, 'Reinterpreting the *Quistclose* trust: a critique of Chambers' analysis' (2001) 210 JLS 267.

Kodilinye, G, 'Resulting trusts, advancements and fraudulent transfers' (1990) Conv 213.

Lim, E, 'Tensions in private law judicial decision-making: a case study on the illegality defence' (2016) JBL 325.

Millett, P, 'The *Quistclose* trust: who can enforce it?' (1985) 101 LQR 269.

Onaram, L, 'The trust behind the veil: *Prest v Petrodel*' (2013) PCB 273.

Panesar, S, 'Surplus funds and unincorporated associations' (2000) 14(10) T&T 698.

Pawlowski, M, 'Resulting trusts, joint borrowers and beneficial shares' (2008) Fam Law 654.

Pettit, P, 'Illegality and repentance' (1996) 10 Tru LI 51.

Rickett, C, 'Unincorporated associations and their dissolution' (1980) CLJ 88.

Rickett, C and Grantham, R, 'Resulting trusts: the true nature of the failing trust cases' (2000) 116 LQR 15.

Rose, F, 'Gratuitous transfers and illegal purposes' (1996) 112 LQR 386.

Smart, P, 'Holding property for non-charitable purposes: mandates, conditions and estoppels' (1987) Conv 415.

Strauss, N, 'Ex turpi causa oritur actio' (2016) LQR 236.

Swadling, W, 'A new role for resulting trusts' (1996) 16 LS 110.

Swadling, W, 'Explaining resulting trusts' (2008) 124 LQR 72.

8

Constructive trusts I

AIMS AND OBJECTIVES

By the end of this chapter you should be able to:

- understand the shades of meaning of the expression 'constructive trust' as used over the centuries
- distinguish between an institutional and remedial constructive trust
- understand the rule in *Keech v Sandford*
- identify the occasions when a trustee may be remunerated for his work
- recognise occasions when a stranger may become a constructive trustee or be accountable for benefits acquired

8.1 Introduction

A constructive trust is an aspect of the creative jurisdiction of equity. It is an implied trust created by the courts when it is unconscionable for a defendant with the legal title to property to claim that property (or some part) beneficially to the prejudice of the claimant. The trust is created independently of the intentions of the parties. It is the conduct of the parties, and in particular the defendant, that governs the jurisdiction of the court to impose a constructive trust. This type of trust attaches to specific property, held by a person in circumstances where it would be inequitable to allow him to assert full beneficial ownership of the property.

In *Gissing v Gissing* [1971] AC 886, reference was made to the occasions when such a trust may be created:

JUDGMENT

'A constructive trust is created by a transaction between the trustee and the cestui que trust … whenever the trustee has so conducted himself that it would be inequitable to allow him to deny to the cestui que trust a beneficial interest [in the property].'

Lord Diplock

The trust is categorised as of a residuary nature that is called into play whenever the court desires to create a trust that does not correspond to any other category. The trust may be imposed on express trustees and other fiduciaries in respect of the receipt of any unauthorised benefit. In addition, the trust may be imposed on strangers or third parties who intermeddle with the affairs of the trust. Thus, a stranger or third party who receives property subject to a fiduciary relationship, and who has actual or constructive knowledge that it is trust property that has been transferred to him in breach of trust or fiduciary duties, will be a constructive trustee of that property. If the constructive trustee becomes bankrupt the property is not available for his general creditors but for the beneficiaries in whose favour the constructive trust operates. In addition, the limitation periods for bringing a claim do not operate.

In *Lonrho plc v Fayed (No 2)* [1992] 1 WLR 1, Millett J said this about the constructive trust:

JUDGMENT

'It is … the independent jurisdiction of equity as a court of conscience to grant relief for every species of fraud and over unconscionable conduct. When appropriate, the court will grant a proprietary remedy to restore to the plaintiff property of which he has been wrongly deprived, or to prevent the defendant from retaining a benefit which he has obtained by his own wrong. It is not possible, and it would not be desirable, to attempt an exhaustive classification of the situations in which it will do so. Equity must retain what has been called its inherent flexibility and capacity to adjust to new situations by reference to mainsprings of the equitable jurisdiction. [R Meagher, W Gummon and J Lehane, *Equity, Doctrines & Remedies* (2nd edn), Butterworths, 1984, p. 327.] All courts of justice proceed by analogy, but a court of equity must never be deterred by the absence of a precise analogy, provided that the principle invoked is sound.'

Millett J

8.2 Constructive trusts/duty to account

The interest of a beneficiary under a constructive trust is proprietary in nature. In other words, the beneficiary's interest exists *'in rem'*, and in the event of the bankruptcy of the trustee the beneficiary's interest prevails over the trustee in bankruptcy and the claimant will take priority over the claims of his general creditors. In respect of claims to recover the trust property, the limitation periods, as laid down in the Limitation Act 1980, do not operate against the beneficiary. If the constructive trustee retains the trust property in identifiable form, the beneficiary may recover the asset, or the relevant portion of the asset, from the defendant along with any income derived from such property. This will be the position whether the constructive trustee is solvent or not. If the asset has increased in value the beneficiary will be entitled to this increase. But if the value of the asset has fallen, the beneficiary may claim the asset and in addition assert a personal claim against the trustee for the loss suffered. If the trust asset is in the hands of a third party the beneficiary may trace his interest in the asset and claim the same, subject to any defences that may be raised by the third party, such as the defences of *bona fide* purchase of the legal estate for value without notice, and change of position. If the trust property has been dissipated the beneficiary may be entitled to pursue only a personal claim against the constructive trustee and will rank with his general creditors rather than taking priority.

In addition, the expression 'constructive trust' is sometimes used in a different sense, in that no specific property is subject to the trust. But the defendant is treated constructively as if he is a trustee so that he is personally liable to account to the claimants for any losses or gains resulting from his misconduct. The effect is that a claim *in personam* arises in favour of the beneficiary. This type of 'constructive trust' concerns, in reality, a personal liability to account such as dishonestly assisting another in a fraudulent scheme involving the trust property. The limitation periods for bringing claims apply to such actions and if the fiduciary becomes bankrupt the beneficiaries do not acquire priority over his ordinary creditors.

Lord Millett in *Paragon Finance plc v Thakerar* [1999] 1 All ER 400 referred to the two interpretations of constructive trusts and stated that the importance of distinguishing the two categories lies with regard to the non-existence or existence of the limitation period for bringing against the trustees. Allied to this principle is the process of tracing or following the beneficiary's property in cases of category 1 constructive trustees.

JUDGMENT

'The expressions constructive trust and constructive trustee have been used by equity lawyers to describe two entirely different situations. The first covers those cases where the defendant, though not expressly appointed as trustee, has assumed the duties of a trustee by a lawful transaction which was independent of and preceded the breach of trust and is not impeached by the plaintiff. The second covers those cases where the trust obligation arises as a direct consequence of the unlawful transaction which is impeached by the plaintiff.

The importance of the distinction between the two categories of constructive trust lies in the application of the statutes of limitation. Constructive trusts of the first kind are treated in the same way as express trusts and were often confusingly described as such; claims against the trustees were not barred by the passage of time. Constructive trusts of the second kind however were treated differently. They were not in reality trusts at all, but merely a remedial mechanism by which equity gave relief for fraud. The Court of Chancery, which applied the statutes of limitation by analogy, was not misled by its own terminology; it gave effect to the reality of the situation by applying the statute to the fraud which gave rise to the defendant's liability.'

Lord Millett

Recently the Supreme Court in *Williams v Central Bank of Nigeria* [2014] UKSC 10, reinforced this distinction and affirmed that a knowing recipient and a defendant lending assistance in a dishonest transaction are not genuine trustees in the orthodox sense, but are liable in a personal action to account to the beneficiaries for their wrongful actions. This principle was stated in the context of the liabilities of trustees under the Limitation Act 1980, see later (Chapter 16).

JUDGMENT

'[The second meaning of the phrase constructive trustee] comprises persons who never assumed and never intended to assume the status of a trustee, whether formally or informally, but have exposed themselves to equitable remedies by virtue of their participation in the unlawful misapplication of trust assets. Either they have dishonestly assisted in a misapplication of the funds by the trustee, or they have received assets knowing that the transfer to them was a breach of trust. In either case, they may be required by equity to account as if they were trustees or fiduciaries, although they are not. These can conveniently be called cases of ancillary liability. The intervention of equity in such cases … is purely remedial.'

Lord Sumption

'It is unreal to refer to a person who receives property dishonestly as a trustee, i.e. a person in whom trust is reposed, given that the trust is said to arise simply as a result of dishonest receipt. Nobody involved, whether the dishonest receiver, the person who passed the property to him, or the claimant, has ever placed any relevant trust and confidence in the recipient … I conclude that a trustee in s 21(1)(a) [of the Limitation Act 1980] does not include a party who is liable to account in equity simply because he was a dishonest assister and/or a knowing recipient. This is because such a party, while liable to account in the same way as a trustee, is not, according to the law laid down by the courts, a trustee, not even a constructive trustee.'

Lord Neuberger

8.3 Institutional and remedial constructive trusts

Constructive trusts are sometimes described as institutional or remedial. An institutional constructive trust is the traditional constructive trust that is declared by the courts retrospectively from the date of the misconduct by the constructive trustees. The courts merely declare the existence of such a trust.

A remedial constructive trust is imposed in order to prevent unjust enrichment. This type of trust is essentially a remedy that may be called into play whenever the claimant seeks to recover his property from a fiduciary (or his successors in title) who acts in breach of his duties. In short it is a judicial remedy that gives rise to an enforceable obligation. The court order creates the right with a correlative remedy as opposed to being simply confirmatory as to the existence of the trust.

In *Westdeutsche Landesbank Girozentrale v Islington BC* [1996] AC 669 Lord Browne-Wilkinson described the distinction between institutional and remedial constructive trusts:

JUDGMENT

'Under the institutional constructive trust, the trust arises by operation of law as from the date when the circumstances give rise to it. The function of the court is merely to declare that such trust has arisen in the past. The consequences which flow from such trust having arisen (including the possibly unfair consequences to third parties who in the interim receive trust property) are also determined by rules of law, not under discretion. A remedial constructive trust is different. It is a judicial remedy giving rise to an enforceable equitable obligation; the extent to which it operates retrospectively to the prejudice of third parties lies in the discretion of the courts.'

Lord Browne-Wilkinson

In *Thorner v Major* [2009] UKHL 18, Lord Scott attempted to draw a distinction between cases that involve proprietary estoppel on the one hand and cases that concern the remedial constructive trust. A claim to proprietary estoppel involves three main elements. First, a sufficiently clear and unequivocal representation made or assurance given to the claimant; second, reliance by the claimant on the representation or assurance; and, third, some detriment incurred by the claimant as a consequence of that reliance. In addition, the proprietary estoppel relates to representations regarding an immediate interest in the property. Whereas the remedial constructive trusts relate to inheritance cases based on the common intention of the parties, reliance and detriment, see *Gissing v Gissing* [1971] AC 886, and cases where representations are of future benefits, see *Re Basham* [1987] 1 All ER 405.

It is submitted that Lord Scott's distinction between proprietary estoppel and constructive trusts is far from being clear and is likely to create further confusion in the law in this area.

Moreover, it is equally unwarranted to equate a constructive trust with a resulting trust. In *Hussey v Palmer* [1972] 1 WLR 1286, Denning MR declared that a constructive trust exists as a remedy. In the United States of America, the constructive trust is treated as a remedy which is defined in terms of preventing unjust enrichment. In English law, quasi-contractual remedies based on the prevention of unjust enrichment are available and, traditionally, the constructive trust has been treated as a substantive right. However, Denning MR attempted to equate English law with the law in the United States of America:

JUDGMENT

'[The constructive trust] is an equitable remedy by which the court can enable an aggrieved party to obtain restitution.'

Lord Denning MR

In the UK, remedies exist in quasi-contract which are based on unjust enrichment. It is arguable that the use of the constructive trust to provide a remedy is not justifiable. This is the predominant view of the English courts. This is reflected in the judgment of Peter Gibson LJ in *Halifax Building Society v Thomas* [1996] 2 WLR 63.

CASE EXAMPLE

Halifax Building Society v Thomas [1996] 2 WLR 63

The defendant obtained a mortgage by a fraudulent misrepresentation of a building society. He fell into arrears and after the property was sold, a surplus remained. The society claimed the surplus by way of a constructive trust, in order to prevent the defendant from profiting from his fraud. The court rejected this claim, on the ground that a remedial constructive trust does not exist in English law. There was no universal principle that involved restitution of a benefit received from a wrongdoing party. The defendant was merely a debtor as opposed to being a fiduciary for the society. Thus the surplus belonged to the defendant although it could be confiscated as the proceeds of crime in separate criminal proceedings under the Proceeds of Crime Act 2002.

JUDGMENT

'English law has not followed other jurisdictions where the constructive trust has become a remedy for unjust enrichment. As is said in *Snell's Equity*, 29th edn, 1990, p. 197: In England the constructive trust has in general remained essentially a substantive institution; ownership must not be confused with obligation, nor must the relationship of debtor and creditor be converted into one of trustee and cestui que trust.'

Peter Gibson LJ

8.4 Recognised categories of constructive trusts

A constructive trust is created by an order from the court and is based on circumstances in which equity considers it unconscionable for the holder of property to deny the claimant an interest in the same. It is sometimes difficult to state exactly when the defendant's conduct may give rise to a constructive trust. In English law, the boundaries surrounding a constructive trust have not been precisely drawn, for the circumstances that may give rise to such a trust are inexhaustible. The courts reserve the right to determine when the circumstances of each case justify the creation of the constructive trust. In this respect the categories of constructive trusts are never closed.

In *Carl Zeiss Stiftung v Herbert Smith and Co (No 2)* [1969] 2 Ch 276, Edmund-Davies LJ declared that the reason why the boundaries of a constructive trust have been deliberately left vague by the courts is to empower the courts to decide on the fairness of transactions undertaken by fiduciaries, and stated that the basis for imposing a constructive trust is to satisfy the demands of justice and good conscience:

JUDGMENT

'English law provides no clear and all-embracing definition of a constructive trust. Its boundaries have been left perhaps deliberately vague, so as not to restrict the court by technicalities in deciding what the justice of a particular case may demand … The concept of unjust enrichment has its value as providing one example among many of what, for lack of a better phrase, I would call want of probity, a feature which recurs through and seems to connect all those cases drawn to the court's attention where a constructive trust has been held to exist. *Snell's Principles of Equity* expresses the same idea by saying 26th ed, 1966, p. 201 that:

> A possible definition is that a constructive trust is a trust which is imposed by equity in order to satisfy the demands of justice and good conscience, without reference to any express or presumed intention of the parties.

It may be objected that, even assuming the correctness of the foregoing, it provides no assistance, inasmuch as reference to unjust enrichment, want of probity and the demands of justice and good conscience merely introduces vague concepts which are in turn incapable of definition and which therefore provide no yardstick. I do not agree. Concepts may defy definition and yet the presence in or absence from a situation of that which they denote may be beyond doubt. The concept of want of probity appears to provide a useful touchstone in considering circumstances said to give rise to constructive trusts, and I have not found it misleading when applying it to the many authorities cited to this court. It is because of such a concept that evidence as to good faith, knowledge and notice plays so important a part in the reported decisions.'

Edmund-Davies LJ

In *Cobbe v Yeoman's Row Management Ltd* [2008] 1 WLR 1752, Lord Scott reiterated the broad jurisdiction of equity in this field. He said that it 'is impossible to prescribe exhaustively the circumstances sufficient to create a constructive trust but it is possible to recognize particular factual circumstances that will do so and also to recognize other factual circumstances that will not'.

However, despite the general reluctance of the courts to limit its jurisdiction in this context, a number of general categories may be posited as to when the trust may be imposed. These are:

(a) occasions when a trustee or fiduciary allows his interests to conflict with his duties;

(b) contracts for the sale of land;

(c) the operation of the maxim, 'Equity will not allow a statute to be used as an engine for fraud'; and

(d) occasions when it would be unconscionable for the legal owner of property to deny an interest in property in favour of another.

The nature of the remedy that may be available to the claimant would depend on whether identifiable property has been acquired by the trustee/fiduciary or not. If identifiable property has been acquired by the defendant in breach of his fiduciary duties, a constructive trust of a proprietary nature will be imposed on that property which will subsist against third parties, except as against a *bona fide* transferee of the legal estate for value without notice. In appropriate cases the claimant may follow or trace his interest in such property. On the other hand, if there is no identifiable property over which a constructive trust may attach, the claimant will be entitled to the personal remedy of an account. In *Sinclair Investment Holdings v Versailles Trade Finance Ltd (No 3)* [2007] EWHC 915, Rimer J, at first instance, expressed the point in the following terms:

JUDGMENT

'Any identifiable assets acquired by fiduciaries in breach of their fiduciary duty are, and can be declared to be, held upon constructive trust for the principal … There will in practice often be no identifiable property which can be declared by the court to be held upon such constructive trust, in which case no declaration will be made and the principal may at most be entitled to a personal remedy in the nature of an account of profits.'

Rimer J

8.4.1 Conflict of duty and interest

The rule is that a person occupying a position of confidence (such as a trustee or fiduciary) is prohibited from deriving any personal benefit by availing himself of his position, in the absence of authority from the beneficiaries, trust instrument or the court. In other words, the trustee or fiduciary should not place himself in a position where his duty may conflict with his personal interest. If such a conflict occurs and the trustee obtains an unauthorised benefit or profit, the advantage is held on constructive trust for the beneficiary. This is generally known as the rule in *Keech v Sandford*.

CASE EXAMPLE

Keech v Sandford (1726) Sel Cas Ch 61

The defendant, an express trustee, held the profits of a lease of Romford market on trust for a minor. Before the expiration of the lease, the defendant requested a renewal of the lease in favour of the beneficiary personally, but this was refused. The trustee then attempted to renew the lease in his capacity as trustee for the infant but this was also refused. The lessor agreed to renew the lease in favour of the trustee personally and this was done. A claim was brought on behalf of the beneficiaries. The court held that the profits of the renewed lease were held on constructive trust in favour of the beneficiaries. The court declared that the trustee was the only person of all mankind who was not entitled to have the benefit of the lease. But it was crucial that the rule be strictly adhered to for it was obvious what would be the consequences of letting trustees have the lease, on refusal to renew in favour of the beneficiary. The trustees were in control of the property and could, in theory, have obtained sensitive information about the property which is concealed from the public.

JUDGMENT

'I must consider this as a trust for the infant, for I very well see, if a trustee, on the refusal to renew, might have a lease to himself, few trust estates would be renewed to the cestui que use. Though I do not say there is fraud in this case, yet he should rather have let it run out than to have had the lease to himself. It may seem hard that the trustee is the only person of all mankind who might not have the benefit of the lease; but it is very proper that the rule should be strictly pursued and not in the least relaxed; for it is very obvious what would be the consequences of letting trustees have the lease, on refusal to renew to the cestui que trust.'

Lord King LC

Perhaps the reason for this harsh rule is that the courts are reluctant to run the risk of finding it difficult in many cases to ascertain accurately whether or not an unfair advantage has been taken by the trustee. Unfairness to the trustee is not the major concern; the primary consideration of the courts is to ensure that there is no possibility of injustice to the beneficiaries.

The rationale for the harsh rule in *Keech v Sandford* was stated by Lord Herschell in an *obiter* pronouncement in *Bray v Ford* [1896] AC 44.

JUDGMENT

'It is an inflexible rule of a court of equity that a person in a fiduciary position … is not, unless otherwise expressly provided, entitled to make a profit; he is not allowed to put himself in a position where his interest and his duty conflict. It does not appear to me that this rule is … founded upon principles of morality. I regard it rather as based on the consideration that human nature being what it is, there is a danger, in such circumstances, of the person holding a fiduciary interest being swayed by interest rather than duty, and thus prejudicing those he is bound to protect. It has, therefore, been deemed expedient to lay down this positive rule.'

Lord Herschell

In effect, in order to succeed in the action against the trustee or fiduciary, the claimant is required to establish each of the following three elements:

(a) the defendant holds a fiduciary position vis-à-vis the claimant; and

(b) the defendant obtained a benefit derived from the property; and

(c) there is a causal connection between the relationship and the benefit.

It is irrelevant that the trustee or fiduciary acted in good faith for the liability here is strict.

The obligation on the trustee/fiduciary to avoid conflicts of duties and interests is both preventative and restitutionary to ensure that the trustee/fiduciary acts fairly and justly in dealing with the affairs of the trust. The principle is preventative in the sense that the fiduciary is obliged to refrain from acting in circumstances where there is a possibility of conflict. It is restitutionary in the sense that any profit or advantage may be claimed on behalf of the trust. This broad principle may be sub-divided into two specific principles – the rule against 'self-dealing' and the rule of 'fair dealing'.

The rule against self-dealing is applicable where the trustee, without authority, deals with the trust property for his own benefit as illustrated by *Keech v Sandford*. The trustee is both vendor and purchaser of the property. The consequence is that the impugned purchase by the trustee or trustees is treated as a voidable transaction at the instance of the beneficiaries, even though the purchase may have the appearance of being fair. Likewise, this rule cannot be evaded by transfers to nominees with the ultimate aim of benefiting the trustee (or trustees). Such nominees, with knowledge of the circumstances, cannot acquire a better title than the trustee. In addition, any profit from the use of the property is accountable to the beneficiaries. Megarry VC in *Tito v Waddell (No 2)* [1977] Ch 106, expressed the principle thus, 'If a trustee purchases trust property from himself, any beneficiary may have the sale set aside, however fair the transaction.'

The fair-dealing rule concerns the occasion where the trustee purchases or acquires the beneficiary's interest subsisting under the trust. In these circumstances, the purchase or acquisition by the trustee will be treated as voidable at the instance of the beneficiary. The burden of proof will lie on the trustee to establish that the sale was fair, after full disclosure by the trustee and that the beneficiary exercised an independent judgment. In *Tito v Waddell (No 2)* (1977), Megarry VC said, 'if a trustee purchases the beneficial interest of any of his beneficiaries, the transaction is not voidable *ex debito justitiae*, but can be set aside unless the trustee can show that he has not taken advantage of his position and has made full disclosure to the beneficiary, and that the transaction is fair and honest'.

8.4.2 Fiduciary relationship

A fiduciary is an individual who is aware that his judgment and confidence is relied on, and has been relied on, by the claimant in some particular matter. This concept is extremely wide and is interpreted fairly flexibly by the courts. Material factors are whether the parties stand on an equal footing, whether there has been an abuse of one's position and whether there has been full disclosure between the parties. Obvious fiduciary relationships include trustee/beneficiary, principal/agent, director/company, partner/co-partners, solicitor/client, key employees with access to sensitive information belonging to their employer. Ultimately, the question is one of fact and degree to be determined on a case-by-case basis. Moreover, the categories of fiduciary relationships are never closed. Factors that are taken into account are the terms of the contract and general principles of common law and equity. The primary obligations of a fiduciary are loyalty and good faith to his principal. A collection of remedies are available to the innocent beneficiary when the fiduciary acts in breach of his duties. Any property acquired by the fiduciary may be subject to a proprietary claim by the beneficiary. In addition, the fiduciary is required to compensate the trust for any losses suffered.

In *Reading v AG* [1951] AC 507 the court decided that a uniformed officer in the Armed Forces was a fiduciary in respect of unauthorised benefits received.

Likewise, in *English v Dedham Vale Properties* [1978] 1 WLR 93 a fiduciary relationship was created in respect of a purchaser of land who abused his position by pretending to have the vendor's permission to apply for and obtain planning permission in respect of the property. But in *Swain v Law Society* [1982] 3 WLR 261, it was decided that the Law Society was not in a fiduciary relationship with respect to members of the solicitors' profession.

A fiduciary is expected to act in the interests of the other, to act selflessly and with undivided loyalty.

The distinguishing features of a fiduciary were stated by Millett LJ in *Bristol and West BS v Mothew* [1996] 4 All ER 698 as follows:

JUDGMENT

'A fiduciary is someone who has undertaken to act for or on behalf of another in a particular matter in circumstances which give rise to a relationship of trust and confidence. The distinguishing obligation of a fiduciary is the obligation of loyalty. The principal is entitled to the single-minded loyalty of his fiduciary. This core liability has several facets. A fiduciary must act in good faith; he must not make a profit of his trust; he must not place himself in a position where his duty and interest may conflict; he may not act for his own benefit or the benefit of a third person without the informed consent of his principal. This is not intended to be an exhaustive list but it is sufficient to indicate the nature of fiduciary obligations. They are defining characteristics of the fiduciary.'

Millett LJ

On analysis the fundamental characteristics of the fiduciary relationship, as laid down by Millett LJ, are as follows:

- The creation of the fiduciary relationship depends on the circumstances of each case. The issue is whether the nature of the relationship, or transaction undertaken, involve an element of trust and confidence reposed in the defendant. Although there are a number of well-established relationships that are regarded as fiduciary, such as trustee/beneficiary, solicitor/client, director/company, partner/co-partner, agent/principal relationships, ultimately the courts will decide as a question of law whether the relationship ought to be classified as fiduciary;

- The overriding duty imposed on the fiduciary is one of loyalty to his principal. This manifests itself in various forms and overlaps with other features stated below.

- The fiduciary is required to act in good faith. This is a question of fact. The defendant's motives and intention are material factors in deciding this question.

- He must not place himself in a position of conflict with his interest. This requirement has many facets such as making unauthorised profits, he may not act for himself in a way inconsistent with the trust as well as the self-dealing and fair-dealing rules.

The remainder of this chapter will focus on various aspects of the fiduciary relationship.

8.4.3 Unauthorised remuneration or financial benefit received by trustee or fiduciary

A trustee is not allowed to receive any remuneration or financial benefit, save for that authorised by the trust instrument, statute, the beneficiaries or the courts. The reason is that, owing to his status as a fiduciary, he is not allowed to receive a profit from his position in order to avoid the temptation of putting his interest before his duty. This is summarised as the 'no-profit' rule that is applicable to fiduciaries.

An individual who has not been appointed a trustee may become a fiduciary if he purports to act on behalf of a trust without authority, and obtains confidential information as a result of being an apparent representative of the trust. In this event, any profits obtained by the fiduciary in connection with the use of such confidential information are subject to the trust. Indeed, in *Boardman v Phipps* [1967] 2 AC 46, it was decided that the confidential information obtained in such circumstances may be treated as trust property. Thus, a solicitor to a trust was treated as a fiduciary and accountable to the trust in respect of unauthorised profits received.

CASE EXAMPLE

Boardman v Phipps [1967] 2 AC 46

Mr Boardman, a solicitor to a trust, was a fiduciary when he received confidential information concerning the company that assisted in him obtaining control of the company and reorganising it. Although he acted in good faith he was liable to account as a constructive trustee for the profits made. The opportunity to make the profit arose by virtue of his fiduciary relationship with the trust. On behalf of Mr Boardman it was argued that information concerning the trust was incapable of being treated as trust property. The court rejected this argument and decided that the confidential information acquired in this case which was capable of being and was turned to account can be properly regarded as the property of the trust. However, the court awarded him generous remuneration in recognition of his outstanding contribution to the trust.

JUDGMENT

'The proposition of law involved in this case is that no person standing in a fiduciary position, when a demand is made upon him by the person to whom he stands in the fiduciary relationship to account for profits acquired by him by reason of the opportunity and the knowledge, or either, resulting from it, is entitled to defeat the claim upon any ground save that he made profits with the knowledge and assent of the other person. There was a potential conflict between Boardman's position as solicitor to the trustees and his own interest in applying for the shares. He was in a fiduciary position *vis à vis* the trustees and through them *vis à vis* the beneficiaries.

Mr Boardman's fiduciary position arose from the fact that he was at all material times solicitor to the trustees of the will of Mr Phipps senior. It was as solicitor to the trustees that he obtained the information … This information enabled him to acquire knowledge of a most extensive and valuable character which was the foundation upon which a decision could, and was taken to buy the shares in Lester & Harris Ltd.'

Lord Hodson

Likewise, in *Crown Dilmun v Sutton* [2004] EWHC 52, the claimant was successful in establishing that the defendant was under a duty to account in breach of his fiduciary duties. The claimant contended that the defendant owed fiduciary duties by virtue of his capacity as a managing director and the existence of a restraint of trade clause. Thus, the defendant owed the claimant a duty to make full and frank disclosure of profit-making opportunities concerning the claimant's land.

In *Cobbetts v Hodge* [2009] EWHC 786 (Ch), the High Court decided that although the creation of the employment relationship did not per se create a fiduciary relationship, the nature of the employment might provide the context in which fiduciary duties might arise. In this case the introduction of investors was within the scope of the defendant's employment, but in carrying out these duties the defendant owed fiduciary duties to the claimants. The opportunity to acquire shares in a third party company and realise a profit had derived from his employment and amounted to a breach of his duties. Thus, the defendant bore the burden of proving that the claimants consented to the profit made by the defendant. On the facts the defendant failed to discharge this burden.

In accordance with the *Keech v Sandford* principle, a trustee or fiduciary is not entitled to receive remuneration for his services unless he can establish that the remuneration is authorised.

CASE EXAMPLE

Williams v Barton [1927] 2 Ch 9

Mr Barton, one of two trustees, received commission as a stockbroker's clerk when he introduced the trust to his firm of stockbrokers. Mr Barton took no part in the work of valuation. The co-trustee now claimed to recover the commission on behalf of the trust. The court held that despite the valuation being quite proper in the circumstances, Mr Barton was required to account for the commission, because the opportunity to earn the reward derived from his position as trustee.

JUDGMENT

'It is a well-established and salutary rule of equity that a trustee may not make a profit out of his trust. A person who has the management of property as a trustee is not permitted to gain any profit by availing himself of his position, and will be a constructive trustee of any such profit for the benefit of the persons equitably entitled to the property.

The case is clearly one where his duty as trustee and his interest in an increased remuneration are in direct conflict. As a trustee, it is his duty to give the estate the benefit of his unfettered advice in choosing the stockbrokers to act for the estate; as the recipient of half the fees to be earned by George Burnand & Co on work introduced by him his obvious interest is to choose or recommend them for the job.'

Russell J

Likewise, where a fiduciary (director) of a company allows his interests to conflict with his duties by assisting in setting up a trading company in competition with the company in which he is a director, he is liable to account for the profits made. It is irrelevant that he acts in good faith and traded on fair terms with the new company. The rationale for the general rule is based on prevention rather than fairness to the director. The court so held in *Breitenfeld (UK) v Harrison and Others* (2015).

CASE EXAMPLE

Breitenfeld (UK) v Harrison and Others [2015] EWHC 399 (High Court)

Mr Harrison ('Mr Harrison') became the managing director of Forge-Met Steel Company Ltd ('ForgeMet') in 2004. At about the same time his son, John ('John'), and subsequently his wife ('Gemma'), became employed by the same company, as Works and Office Manager and purchasing and sales assistant respectively. ForgeMet was a small German-owned company that operated in the UK and supplied high-grade steel for use in the engineering industry. It changed its name to Breitenfeld UK Ltd. During their employment in ForgeMet, John and Gemma set up a company called Harrison Special Steels Ltd ('HSS') in competition with ForgeMet with the knowledge and approval of Mr Harrison. Transactions were conducted between the two companies essentially for the benefit of HSS. Subsequently, proceedings were commenced against Mr Harrison, John, Gemma and HSS in respect of claims for accounts, equitable compensation and damages. The High Court upheld the claims.

JUDGMENT

'It all depends upon an analysis of the transaction to see whether objectively there is a real sensible possibility of conflict (not an examination of whether the fiduciary in fact succumbed to temptation). Here there plainly was a real sensible possibility of conflict even though

Mr Harrison had no direct financial interest in the counterparty to the engagements which he caused ForgeMet to enter into, because that counter-party was the creature of closely connected persons. The whole course of dealing is riddled with conflicts.'

[In rejecting the argument that John and Gemma formed HSS to assist ForgeMet to complete customers' orders, Norris J said] 'I do not accept that John Harrison or Gemma Harrison at the time believed that ForgeMet "needed" to outsource work or that Mr Harrison was acting in ForgeMet's best interests in entering into transactions with HSS.'

Norris J

Section 29 of the Trustee Act 2000 allows a professional trustee to receive remuneration for his services, but this section is not applicable to lay trustees. However, the court has an inherent jurisdiction to authorise payment or increased payment to a trustee. This power is frequently exercised where the work for which remuneration is sought has already been done so that the court will be able to assess the merits of the application with the benefit of hindsight. The focus here is to ensure the efficient administration of the trust. Although the jurisdiction is to be exercised sparingly, factors which may influence a court may include whether the trustee's efforts are of exceptional benefit to the trust, whether the services undertaken by the trustee were of an exceptionally onerous character, whether the activities undertaken by the trustee may be properly regarded as above and beyond the call of duty, whether there has been a financial gain to the trust, whether the services rendered by the trustee were wholly outside his reasonable contemplation when he accepted the post. In *Brudenell-Bruce v Moore* [2014] EWHC 3679, the High Court refused to entertain an application for the award of remuneration to a lay trustee who acted in breach of trust and was responsible for losses to the trust. Indeed, in this case the lay trustee, who agreed to act gratuitously, retained a part of the trust property for his remuneration and was ordered by the court to repay the amount to the trust.

Pallant v Morgan *equity*

A '*Pallant v Morgan* equity' derives from the case *Pallant v Morgan* [1953] Ch 43, to the effect that if A and B agree that A will acquire some specific property for the joint benefit of A and B on terms yet to be agreed, and B, in reliance on A's agreement, is thereby induced to refrain from attempting to acquire the property, equity will not permit A, when he acquires the property, to insist on retaining the whole of the benefit for himself to the exclusion of B. Unlike a proprietary estoppel, the claimant (B) has not suffered a detriment as a consequence of the defendant (A) acquiring the property. However, the defendant has obtained an advantage by keeping the claimant out of the market.

The fundamental elements of the *Pallant v Morgan* rule are, first, the existence of a common intention, arrangement or understanding between the parties to the effect that, following the acquisition of the relevant property, the claimant will be entitled to share an interest in it. This understanding need not amount to a valid contract in writing between the parties because such contract may be enforceable in its own right. Secondly, reliance on the understanding or arrangement by the claimant which confers an advantage on the defendant in that the claimant stays out of the market, or the loss of an opportunity by the claimant to acquire the relevant property. Thirdly, the defendant acts in a way that is inconsistent with the arrangement or understanding by denying the existence of the agreement. It is the unconscionable conduct of the defendant that justifies the existence of the constructive trust in this context.

CASE EXAMPLE

Pallant v Morgan [1953] Ch 43

An agreement was entered between the claimant's and defendant's respective agents that they would not compete against each other in bidding for a property at an auction. It was agreed that the defendant's agent alone should bid and if he was successful the property was to be divided between them. The basis of the division was to be subsequently agreed. Thus, the bidding by the defendant at the auction was on behalf of both parties. The defendant's bid was successful and he attempted to deny the claimant an interest in the property.

The High Court decided that, although the agreement for division was too uncertain to be specifically enforceable, the defendant was not entitled to keep the property for his sole benefit, but was required to hold the property upon trust for the parties jointly.

JUDGMENT

'In my judgment, the proper inference from the facts is that the defendant's agent, when he bid for lot 16, was bidding for both parties on an agreement that there should be an arrangement between the parties on the division of the lot if he were successful. The plaintiff and the defendant have failed to reach such an agreement, and the court cannot compel them to one. The best it can do is to decree that the property is held by the defendant for himself and the plaintiff jointly, and, if they fail to agree on a division, the property must be re-sold, either party being at liberty to bid, and the proceeds of sale being divided equally after repaying to the defendant the £1,000 which he paid with interest at 4 per cent.'

Harman J

Pallant v Morgan was reviewed by Chadwick LJ in *Banner Homes plc v Luff Developments Ltd* and the principle approved. In *Banner Homes v Luff* (2000) a constructive trust arose where two rival bidders made an arrangement concerning the purchase of property, and the defendant conducted itself in a way inconsistent with the agreement and in an inequitable manner.

Chadwick LJ in *Banner Homes* laid down the following five elements which are required to be proved in order to establish a *Pallant v Morgan* constructive trust.

JUDGMENT

First the court stated: 'By contrast with ordinary international treaties, the EC Treaty [now TFEU] has created its own legal system which on entry into force ... became an integral part of the legal systems of the member states and which their courts are bound to apply. By creating a Community of limited duration having ... powers stemming from a limitation of the sovereignty, or a transfer of powers from the states to the community, the member states have limited their sovereign rights, albeit within limited fields, and have thus created a body of law which binds both their nationals and themselves.'

It also added: 'The transfer, by member states from their national orders in favour of the [EU] order of its rights and obligations arising from the Treaty, carries with it a clear limitation of their sovereign right upon which a subsequent unilateral law, incompatible with the aims of the community cannot prevail.'

Concluding: 'It follows from all these observations that the law stemming from the Treaty, an independent source of law, could not, because of its special and original nature, be overridden by domestic legal provisions, however framed, without being deprived of its character as [EU] law and without the legal basis of the [EU] itself being called into question.'

'(1) A *Pallant v Morgan* equity may arise where the arrangement or understanding on which it is based precedes the acquisition of the relevant property by one party to that arrangement. It is the pre-acquisition arrangement which colours the subsequent acquisition by the defendant and leads to his being treated as a trustee if he seeks to act inconsistently with it. Where the arrangement or understanding is reached in relation to property already owned by one of the parties, he may (if the arrangement is of sufficient certainty to be enforced specifically) thereby constitute himself trustee on the basis that "equity looks on that as done which ought to be done"; or an equity may arise under the principles developed in the proprietary estoppel cases.

(2) It is unnecessary that the arrangement or understanding should be contractually enforceable. Indeed, if there is an agreement which is enforceable as a contract, there is unlikely to be any need to invoke the *Pallant v Morgan* equity; equity can act through the remedy of specific performance and will recognise the existence of a corresponding trust. In particular, it is no bar to a *Pallant v Morgan* equity that the pre-acquisition arrangement is too uncertain to be enforced as a contract – see *Pallant v Morgan* [1953] Ch 43 itself.

(3) It is necessary that the pre-acquisition arrangement or understanding should contemplate that one party ("the acquiring party") will take steps to acquire the relevant property; and that, if he does so, the other party ("the non-acquiring party") will obtain some interest in that property. Further, it is necessary that (whatever private reservations the acquiring party may have) he has not informed the non-acquiring party before the acquisition (or, perhaps more accurately, before it is too late for the parties to be restored to a position of no advantage/no detriment) that he no longer intends to honour the arrangement or understanding.

(4) It is necessary that, in reliance on the arrangement or understanding, the non-acquiring party should do (or omit to do) something which confers an advantage on the acquiring party in relation to the acquisition of the property; or is detrimental to the ability of the non-acquiring party to acquire the property on equal terms. It is the existence of the advantage to the one, or detriment to the other, gained or suffered as a consequence of the arrangement or understanding, which leads to the conclusion that it would be inequitable or unconscionable to allow the acquiring party to retain the property for himself, in a manner inconsistent with the arrangement or understanding which enabled him to acquire it. *Pallant v Morgan* [1953] Ch 43 itself provides an illustration of this principle. There was nothing inequitable in allowing the defendant to retain for himself the lot (lot 15) in respect to which the plaintiff's agent had no instructions to bid. In many cases the advantage/detriment will be found in the agreement of the non-acquiring party to keep out of the market. That will usually be both to the advantage of the acquiring party – in that he can bid without competition from the non-acquiring party – and to the detriment of the non-acquiring party – in that he loses the opportunity to acquire the property for himself. But there may be advantage to the one without corresponding detriment to the other. Again, *Pallant v Morgan* provides an illustration. The plaintiff's agreement (through his agent) to keep out of the bidding gave an advantage to the defendant – in that he was able to obtain the property for a lower price than would otherwise have been possible; but the failure of the plaintiff's agent to bid did not, in fact, cause detriment to the plaintiff – because, on the facts, the agent's instructions would not have permitted him to outbid the defendant. Nevertheless, the equity was invoked.

(5) That leads, I think, to the further conclusions: (i) that although, in many cases, the advantage/detriment will be found in the agreement of the non-acquiring party to keep out of the market, that is not a necessary feature; and (ii) that although there will usually be advantage to the one and correlative disadvantage to the other, the existence of both advantage and detriment is not essential – either will do. What is essential is that the

circumstances make it inequitable for the acquiring party to retain the property for himself in a manner inconsistent with the arrangement or understanding on which the non-acquiring party has acted. Those circumstances may arise where the non-acquiring party was never "in the market" for the whole of the property to be acquired; but (on the faith of an arrangement or understanding that he shall have a part of that property) provides support in relation to the acquisition of the whole which is of advantage to the acquiring party. They may arise where the assistance provided to the acquiring party (in pursuance of the arrangement or understanding) involves no detriment to the non-acquiring party; or where the non-acquiring party acts to his detriment (in pursuance of the arrangement or understanding) without the acquiring party obtaining any advantage therefrom.'

Chadwick LJ

CASE EXAMPLE

Banner Homes v Luff [2000] 2 WLR 772

Two rival bidders made an arrangement concerning the purchase of property. The defendant conducted himself in a way inconsistent with the agreement, and in an inequitable manner. The court decided that a constructive trust arose in the circumstances. It was essential that the circumstances made it inequitable for the acquiring party to retain the property for himself in a manner inconsistent with the arrangement or understanding on which the non-acquiring party had acted.

JUDGMENT

'In my view the judge misunderstood the principles upon which equity intervenes in cases of this nature. The *Pallant v Morgan* equity does not seek to give effect to the parties' bargain, still less to make for them some bargain which they have not themselves made, as the cases to which I have referred make clear. The equity is invoked where the defendant has acquired property in circumstances where it would be inequitable to allow him to treat it as his own, and where, because it would be inequitable to allow him to treat the property as his own, it is necessary to impose on him the obligations of a trustee in relation to it. It is invoked because there is no bargain which is capable of being enforced; if there were an enforceable bargain there would have been no need for equity to intervene in the way that it has done in the cases to which I have referred.

I am satisfied, also, that the judge was wrong to reject the constructive trust claim on the grounds that Banner had failed to show that it had acted to its detriment in reliance on the arrangement agreed on 14th July 1995.'

Chadwick LJ

In *Kilcarne Holdings Ltd v Targetfollow Ltd* the court decided that the *Pallant v Morgan* claim failed because there was no evidence of a joint venture between the parties.

CASE EXAMPLE

Kilcarne Holdings Ltd v Targetfollow Ltd [2005] All ER (D) 203, CA

The defendant company (TGL) was set up specifically to acquire a lease of the property in Birmingham. The amount required to complete the transaction was £2.5 million. As part of a composite transaction Kilcarne and an associated company called Rosedale Ltd together lent £2.5 million to TGL. There was evidence of some discussion concerning financial arrangements between the principal shareholder of TGL and the managing director of another company,

Sitac Ltd (which acted on behalf of the claimant companies). The claimants contended that a legally enforceable oral agreement was created between the claimants and the defendant for a joint venture for the development of the property. The judge considered the circumstances, including the minutes of the meetings held by the various companies, and decided that there was no evidence of a joint venture between the parties. The claimants further alleged that constructive trusts had been created in their favour based on the *Gissing v Gissing* and *Pallant v Morgan* principles. The judge rejected these claims and decided that the intentions of the parties were reflected in the formal legal contracts creating loan agreements between the parties. The claimants appealed to the Court of Appeal.

The court dismissed the appeal. There was ample evidence to support the judge's decision. The parties did not share a common intention to create equitable interests in relation to the lease. Such a common intention was necessary in order to establish a *Gissing v Gissing* constructive trust (see later). There was some evidence of discussions and negotiations between the parties but no concluded agreement as to a joint venture had been reached. In addition, the *Pallant v Morgan* constructive trust claim failed because the parties did not commit themselves to a joint venture or a venture whereby the claimants would obtain some interest in the property.

JUDGMENT

'Kilcarne never intended to acquire the lease itself and cannot therefore be said to have refrained from attempting to do so.

It follows that the case for a *Pallant v Morgan* constructive trust also fails at the first hurdle. There was never any agreement, arrangement or understanding between TGL and Kilcarne that the lease should be acquired for their joint benefit or that Kilcarne would obtain some interest in it.'

Sir Martin Nourse LJ

It follows that there are no grounds for a *Pallant v Morgan* equity where the claimant fails to establish the existence of a common understanding or assurances to allow the defendant to acquire property on the basis that the claimant will be entitled to a share in it. In these circumstances the defendant will be entitled to keep the property for himself. The High Court reviewed the leading authorities on the subject and came to this conclusion in *Generator Developments v Lidl* (2016).

CASE EXAMPLE

Generator Developments LLP v Lidl (UK) Gmbh [2016] EWHC 814 (High Court)

The claimants, Generator, were a property development company. The defendants, Lidl, were part of a group of companies which operated supermarkets. The issue concerned the purchase of a plot of land for development in Essex. The claimants' offer to purchase the land for £5.01 million in conjunction with the defendants was accepted 'subject to contract'. Following a series of inconclusive discussions between the parties the defendants ultimately bought the property for a sum of £6.81 million. Generator brought a claim against Lidl contending that the circumstances in which Lidl bought the property gave rise to a *Pallant v Morgan* constructive trust. The court held in favour of Lidl on the grounds that there was no understanding between the parties that was capable of giving rise to a joint venture constructive trust. Factors giving rise to this conclusion included Generator not providing any cash to fund the purchase, not assuming any obligation to contribute to a share of the loss that may be suffered if the development did not proceed and Lidl had to sell the property, Generator was in a position to decide not to proceed with the joint venture, the protracted negotiations between the parties resulted in the absence of an agreement or understanding involving a joint commercial venture.

JUDGMENT

'On the facts of the present case, the central question is whether there was an arrangement or understanding that, if Lidl acquired the Property, Generator would obtain some interest in it. Since the alleged arrangement or understanding was not a contract, it is not a question of looking for the acceptance of an offer, but rather of assessing all the relevant evidence as to what the parties said and did. Having carried out that exercise, I find that there was no such arrangement or understanding.'

Nicholas Lavender QC

Where the parties set out on a joint venture to purchase property in the name of one of the parties, as in *Pallant* and *Banner Homes*, it is clear that the understanding as to a shared interest need not amount to a contract between the parties in order to give rise to the constructive trust. Accordingly, the arrangement between the parties may be 'subject to contract'. But where the property that is the subject of a joint venture claim is already owned by one of the parties prior to the alleged joint venture transaction, the rule is that the bargain between the parties must give rise to a concluded contract before a *Pallant v Morgan* constructive trust may be created. In these circumstances, the unconscionable behaviour of the defendant is triggered when he reneges on the contract, see *London & Regional Investments Ltd v TBI plc*.

CASE EXAMPLE

London & Regional Investments Ltd v TBI plc [2002] EWCA Civ 355 (Court of Appeal)

The claimants and the defendants entered into a sale and purchase agreement for the sale of the defendants' property portfolio for £190 million. The defendants also owned land adjacent to Belfast airport and had an option to acquire land adjacent to Cardiff airport. But these plots were not included in the sale agreement. Instead, the parties promised to use their best endeavours to agree the terms of a joint venture regarding the land adjacent to Belfast and Cardiff airports. Such agreement was 'subject to contract'. The claimants alleged that there were oral assurances given by the defendants concerning the land adjacent to the airports and contended that the defendants held such land on trust for both parties. The Court of Appeal affirmed the decision of the High Court in favour of the defendants. In the circumstances there was nothing unconscionable in the defendants' subsequent refusal to proceed with the joint venture after the original sale agreement had been concluded.

JUDGMENT

'In general, it is not unconscionable for a party to negotiations, which are expressly stated to be "subject to contract" to exercise a reserved right to withdraw from the negotiations before a final agreement has been concluded. If that was the effect of the agreement between the parties on 13 May 1999 I do not see how the conduct of TBI before that date can now be relied on to establish unconscionable conduct giving rise to a constructive trust or an estoppel. For the court to hold that a constructive trust existed in those circumstances would be contrary to what the parties had expressly agreed was to be subject to the making of a future agreement.'

Mummery LJ

8.4.4 Bribes or secret profits received by fiduciaries

A 'bribe' exists when property is received by a fiduciary in order to perform a service that betrays the trust bestowed on him by his principal. The bribe may exist in the form of money or other property proffered by a third party to the fiduciary without the knowledge or approval of the principal.

When a bribe is received in money or in kind, the money or property constituting the bribe belongs in law to the recipient, i.e. the property in the bribe passes to the recipient of the bribe in accordance with the intention of the parties. For example, if T, a third party, pays a bribe of £50,000 to E, an employee of a local authority, P, in order to approve plans for a planning application, the property in the £50,000 passes to E. He acquires these funds for himself and not for the benefit of P. Equity, however, acts *in personam* and insists that it is unconscionable for a fiduciary to obtain and retain a benefit in breach of his duties. Thus, he is under a duty to pay and account for the bribe to the person to whom that duty was owed. If, however, the bribe consists of property which increases in value, or if a cash bribe is invested advantageously, should the fiduciary be accountable not only for the original amount or value of the bribe but also for the increased value of the property representing the bribe? The case law was in some disarray but the issue has now been finally placed on a firm footing by the Supreme Court decision in *FHR European Ventures v Cedar Capital Partners* (2014). On the one hand, the bulk of the authorities (*Heiron* (1880), *Lister* (1890), *Sinclair* (2011), *Cadogan* (2011)) regarded the procurement of the bribe as involving a debtor/creditor relationship as the property in the bribe had passed to the recipient. A personal claim to account lay against the recipient of the bribe. This was the initial, and now out of date, basis of liability. On the other hand, the Privy Council in *AG for Hong Kong v Reid* (1994) and the High Court in *Daraydan v Solland* (2004) decided that a proprietary claim based on a constructive trust arose in favour of the principal or claimant, as the bribe represents money or assets belonging to the principal. Ultimately, the Supreme Court in *FHR European Ventures* (2014) affirmed the approach of the court in *AG for Hong Kong* and overruled the earlier solution in *Heiron, Lister, Sinclair and Cadogan*. What follows is a brief account of the development of the law on bribes or secret profits received by fiduciaries.

CASE EXAMPLE

Metropolitan Bank v Heiron [1880] 5 Ex D 319

The Court of Appeal decided that a director of a company who received a bribe was able to plead successfully a limitation defence on the ground that the company could not treat the bribe as the property of the company. The liability of the director was personal and involved a duty to account which was subject to the limitation defence.

JUDGMENT

'The ground of this suit is concealed fraud. If a man receives money by way of a bribe for misconduct against a company or cestui que trust, or any person or body towards whom he stands in a fiduciary position, he is liable to have that money taken from him by his principal or cestui que trust. But it must be borne in mind that that *liability is a debt only differing from ordinary debts in the fact that it is merely equitable*, and in dealing with equitable debts of such a nature Courts of Equity have always followed by analogy the provisions of the Statute of Limitations.' [Emphasis added]

James LJ

In *Lister v Stubbs* (1890) the Court of Appeal decided that where a fiduciary received a bribe or secret commission, no trust arises in favour of his principal. Instead, the relationship between the recipient and payer of the bribe is that of a debtor and creditor and the recipient of the bribe is required to account to the principal for the amount of the bribe. The justification for this rule, as stated by Lindley LJ, is the undesirability of preferring the principal to the detriment of the creditors of the fiduciary in the event of the latter becoming bankrupt. In addition, if the proceeds of the bribe have been invested in assets which have appreciated in value, the court felt that it would have been too generous to the principal to require the fiduciary to account for the extra profits.

CASE EXAMPLE

Lister v Stubbs [1890] LR 45 Ch D 1

The Court of Appeal came to a conclusion similar to *Heiron* in respect of an employee who received a bribe from one of his employer's suppliers. The bribe could not be considered as the property of the employer.

JUDGMENT

'Then comes the question, as between [employer] and [employee], whether [the employee] can keep the money he has received without accounting for it? Obviously not. I apprehend that he is liable to account for it the moment that he gets it. It is an obligation to pay and account to [the employer] … But *the relation between them is that of debtor and creditor; it is not that of trustee and cestui que trust.* We are asked to hold that it is – which would involve consequences which, I confess, startle me. One consequence, of course, would be that, if [the employee] were to become bankrupt, this property acquired by him with the [bribe] would be withdrawn from the mass of his creditors and be handed over bodily to [the employer]. Can that be right? Another consequence would be that [the employer] could compel [the employee] to account to them, not only for the money with interest, but for all the profits which he might have made by embarking in trade with it. Can that be right? It appears to me that those consequences shew that there is some flaw in the argument.'

Lindley LJ

The reasoning in *Lister* has been subject to widespread academic criticism. Lindley LJ decided the debtor/creditor relationship is created 'the moment the fiduciary received [the bribe]' but he did not explain why this debt is different from ordinary debts. Implied in the judgment is that, unlike ordinary debts, this debt existed where no terms were agreed and the debt was payable immediately, whereas ordinary debts are payable on demand. The Law Commission in its Report in 1981 on 'Breach of Confidence' concluded that *Lister* does not represent the law. The relationship between the fiduciary and his principal is one of trust and confidence. The fundamental duty of the fiduciary is to serve the interest of the principal and not to place himself in a position of conflict of duty and interest. If there is such a conflict and the fiduciary obtains a profit, he is not entitled to retain the profit for himself. The intervention of equity is not only to give redress for the breach, but to enforce the duty. The constructive trust is the means by which equity is able to enforce the fiduciary duty. The policy behind the 'no conflict' 'no profit' rule is to deter the fiduciary from breaching his duties in an effort to curb the excesses of human nature and not primarily to compensate the principal. It is based on a pessimistic, but realistic, appraisal of human nature and designed to avoid temptation. The policy of equity is to require the false fiduciary to disgorge the profit he has made. Moreover, the 'startling' consequences, identified by Lindley LJ, of imposing a trust on the profits received by the fiduciary may well be misconceived. The creditors of the fiduciary ought not to be in a better position than the principal. The fiduciary is not a *bona fide* transferee of the sum, he simply ought not to have received or retained the bribe and accordingly his creditors can have no legitimate claim to the same. In short, the creditors claim through their debtor (the fiduciary) and they cannot lay claim to funds to which he is not entitled. The same arguments may be raised to justify the principal in claiming any increased profits made by the fiduciary in investing the proceeds of the bribe in an appreciating asset. If the fiduciary is not entitled to the bribe, equally he cannot be entitled to derivative profits from the bribe. The profits are part and parcel of the 'no profit' nature of the fiduciary relationship.

In contrast to the decision in *Lister*, the Privy Council in *AG for Hong Kong v Reid* decided that *Lister* was wrongly decided. The bribe and its traceable proceeds were held on constructive trust for the principal. The reasoning was that as soon as the bribe was received it should have been paid or transferred instantly to the person who suffered from the breach of duty. Equity considers as done that which ought to have been done. Thus, when the bribe was received, whether in cash or in kind, the fiduciary holds it on a constructive trust for the person injured. If the property representing the bribe decreases in value, the fiduciary must pay the difference between that value and the initial amount of the bribe, because he should not have accepted the bribe or incurred the risk of loss. If the proceeds of the bribe were invested in assets which have appreciated in value, the principal would be entitled to retain the enhanced value of the asset for his benefit. In addition, if the fiduciary becomes insolvent his unsecured creditors will be deprived of their right to share in the proceeds of that property, for the unsecured creditors cannot be in a better position than their debtor. These results were achieved in *AG for Hong Kong v Reid* [1994] 1 All ER 1.

CASE EXAMPLE

AG for Hong Kong v Reid [1994] 1 All ER 1

The DPP of Hong Kong received bribes which were invested in properties in New Zealand. The Attorney General for Hong Kong brought an action for an account in respect of bribes received by Mr Reid and a declaration that the properties in New Zealand were held on trust for the government of Hong Kong. In the meantime the value of the properties had decreased in value. The question in issue concerned the status of a fiduciary who received a bribe, in particular, whether such a fiduciary became a mere debtor for the innocent party or alternatively a trustee for the aggrieved party. The defendants mounted an argument claiming that the fiduciary became a debtor for the innocent party and had no equitable interest in the properties, relying on the Court of Appeal decision in *Lister v Stubbs* (1890) 45 Ch D 1. The claimants asserted that the decision in *Lister v Stubbs* (1890) should not be followed, as it was inconsistent with basic equitable principles. The Privy Council decided in favour of the claimant on the ground that the bribe and representative property acquired by the fiduciary were subject to the claims of the injured party. Since the representative property had decreased in value, the fiduciary was liable to account for the difference between the bribe and the undervalue.

JUDGMENT

'When a bribe is offered and accepted in money or in kind, the money or property constituting the bribe belongs in law to the recipient. Money paid to the false fiduciary belongs to him. The legal estate in freehold property conveyed to the false fiduciary by way of bribe vests in him. Equity, however, which acts *in personam*, insists that it is unconscionable for a fiduciary to obtain and retain a benefit in breach of duty. The provider of a bribe cannot recover it because he committed a criminal offence when he paid the bribe. The false fiduciary who received the bribe in breach of duty must pay and account for the bribe to the person to whom that duty was owed. In the present case, as soon as the first respondent received a bribe in breach of the duties he owed to the Government of Hong Kong, he became a debtor in equity to the Crown for the amount of that bribe ... As soon as the bribe was received it should have been paid or transferred instantly to the person who suffered from the breach of duty. Equity considers as done that which ought to have been done. As soon as the bribe was received, whether in cash or in kind, the false fiduciary held the bribe on a constructive trust for the person injured.'

Lord Templeman

Endorsing the decision in *Reid*, the High Court in *Daraydan Holdings Ltd v Solland Interiors Ltd* decided that a fiduciary who receives a bribe or a secret commission becomes a constructive trustee. Such a fiduciary or agent who makes a secret profit is accountable to his trustee or principal. The agent should not put himself in a position where his duty and interest may conflict, for such bribes deprive the principal of objective advice from the agent to which the principal is entitled. The agent and the third party who pays the bribe are jointly and severally liable to account for the bribe and each may be liable in damages to the principal for fraud or deceit or conspiracy to deceive.

In proceedings against the third party who pays the bribe, it is unnecessary for the principal to prove:

- that the third party acted with a corrupt motive;
- that the agent's mind was affected by the bribe;
- that the third party knew or suspected that the agent would conceal the payment from the principal;
- that the principal suffered any loss or that the transaction was in some way unfair.

CASE EXAMPLE

Daraydan Holdings Ltd and Others v Solland Interiors Ltd and Others [2004] EWHC 622 (Ch), HC

The claimants were a Middle Eastern consortium that purchased residential properties in London. One of the defendants, Mr Khalid, was relied on by the claimants to identify and obtain quotations from contractors for the refurbishment of the properties and make recommendations to the claimants who made the final decision. Mr and Mrs Solland, who carried on business through a design and refurbishment company, Solland Interiors Ltd, were introduced to the claimants through Mr Khalid. Ultimately Solland Interiors was contracted to refurbish the properties of the claimants. However, Solland Interiors Ltd procured the discreet payment to Mr Khalid of 10 per cent of the sums paid by the claimants to Solland Interiors Ltd in the expectation of receiving additional contracts. This additional amount was surreptitiously written into the quotations provided by Solland Interiors Ltd to the claimants. A dispute arose between the claimants and Solland Interiors Ltd and the claimants became aware of the secret commissions paid to Mr Khalid. The claimants commenced proceedings against Solland Interiors Ltd and Mr Khalid. The claim against Solland Interiors Ltd was eventually settled. The claims against Mr Khalid were for an account of all secret commissions, an order for restitution of the secret profits and a declaration that they were received on resulting or constructive trust.

The court decided in favour of the claimants on the following grounds:

1. Mr Khalid was a fiduciary who extracted substantial payments from the Sollands and their companies in return for his influence in obtaining contracts from the claimants.
2. The bribes or secret commissions received by Mr Khalid were in breach of his fiduciary duties owed to the claimants.
3. Following the Privy Council decision in *AG for Hong Kong v Reid* [1994] 1 AC 324, Mr Khalid became a constructive trustee for the claimants.

JUDGMENT

'An agent or other fiduciary who makes a secret profit is accountable to his or her principal or cestui que trust. The agent and the third party are jointly and severally liable to account for the bribe, and each may also be liable in damages to the principal for fraud or deceit or conspiracy to injury by unlawful means. Consequently, the agent and the maker of the payment are jointly and severally liable to the principal (1) to account for the amount of the bribe as money had and received and (2) for damages for any actual loss. But the principal must now elect between the two remedies prior to final judgment being entered. The third party may also be liable on the basis of accessory liability in respect of breach of fiduciary duty: *Bowstead and Reynolds*, para 8–221. The principal is also able to rescind the contract with the payer of the bribe.

I am wholly satisfied that, on any application of the concept of fiduciary, Mr Khalid was a fiduciary who extracted very substantial payments from the Sollands and their companies in return for his influence in obtaining and carrying out the contracts.'

Collins J

Moreover, Collins J in *Daraydan* expressed a preference for the decision of the Privy Council in *Reid* but, in any event, was able to distinguish *Lister v Stubbs* on two grounds. In *Daraydan*, the bribe received by Mr Khalid derived directly from the claimants' property owing to the deception practised by the former. This amounted to restitution of money extracted from the claimants. Second, the portion representing the bribe was paid as a result of a fraudulent representation of the Sollands to which Mr Khalid was a party, giving the appearance that the invoice price was the true costs when in fact the costs had been inflated to pay the bribes.

JUDGMENT

'[I]f this case were not distinguishable from *Lister & Co v Stubbs*, I would have applied *AG for Hong Kong v Reid*. There are powerful policy reasons for ensuring that a fiduciary does not retain gains acquired in violation of fiduciary duty, and I do not consider that it should make any difference whether the fiduciary is insolvent. There is no injustice to the creditors in their not sharing in an asset for which the fiduciary has not given value, and which the fiduciary should not have had.'

Collins J

In *Halifax Building Society v Thomas* [1996] 2 WLR 63, it was decided that a borrower who fraudulently induced a building society to execute a mortgage on a flat was entitled to the surplus proceeds of sale from the flat. This surplus was not held on resulting trust for the building society. Moreover, the building society had no restitutionary remedy against the borrower, whose unjust enrichment was not gained at the expense of the building society. Accordingly, the borrower was not a constructive trustee of the surplus funds for the society. On conviction of the borrower, the Crown Prosecution Service, as opposed to the society, was entitled to a charging order.

JUDGMENT

'In my judgment on the sale of the mortgaged property by the society, in 1989 Mr Thomas became entitled under s105 of the Law of Property Act 1925 to the surplus and the society could not have claimed the surplus on the ground of a further liability to account being established against him in subsequent proceedings.

On the facts of the present case, in my judgment, the fraud is not in itself a sufficient factor to allow the society to require Mr Thomas to account to it.

I would add that, in so far as the society relies on the submission that to allow a fraudster to take a profit derived from his fraud would be offensive to concepts of justice, the House of Lords in *Tinsley v Milligan* [1994] 1 AC 340, although divided in their decision, were unanimous in rejecting the public conscience test as determinative of the extent to which rights created by illegal transactions should be recognised. It is not appropriate to ask whether the allowance of a claim would be an affront to the public conscience.'

Peter Gibson LJ

In a subsequent decision, the Court of Appeal cast doubt on the reasoning in *Reid*, and decided that the receipt of unauthorised profits, obtained from property in breach of fiduciary duties, imposes only a personal liability to account, as distinct from a proprietary right over the property. This was the view taken in *Sinclair Investments (UK) Ltd v Versailles*.

CASE EXAMPLE

Sinclair Investments (UK) Ltd v Versailles Trade Finance Ltd and Others [2011] EWCA Civ 347, CA

The principal shareholder in Versailles Trade Finance Ltd (VTFL) was Mr Carl Cushnie. VTFL was the trading subsidiary of the Versailles Group PLC (VGP). The main business of VTFL required funds received from clients to be used in the purchase of goods which had been agreed for sale. VTFL acquired funds from two main sources: first, from the claimant investors through an investment company, Trading Partners Ltd (TPL); second, from loans from the third and sixth defendant banks (the banks). Sinclair Investments Ltd was one of the traders who paid money to TPL and took an assignment of all claims of TPL and of other traders.

The funds advanced by TPL and the banks were passed to VTFL but were not used in the purchase of goods. Instead, the funds were (i) used to pay profits to traders, (ii) stolen by Mr Cushnie's associate and co-conspirator, Mr Clough, or (iii) circulated around a number of other companies, also controlled by Mr Cushnie and/or Mr Clough. The purpose of this circulation of funds, referred to in the judgment as 'cross-firing', was to inflate VTFL's apparent turnover and to mask the absence of any genuine business.

As a result of the fraud and the 'cross-firing' arrangements, shares in VGP increased in value and were offered to the public. Several years later, Mr Cushnie sold 5 per cent of his total holding at a grossly exaggerated value of £29m. The proceeds of this sale were distributed to various parties, including repayments to the banks. After the fraud was discovered the companies were ordered to be wound up and liquidators were appointed. Messrs Cushnie and Clough were charged with criminal offences, convicted and sentenced to imprisonment.

As a result of the fraud, both the claimant investors and the defendant lenders suffered substantial losses. The current proceedings arose out of a dispute between the claimant investors and the defendant banks over who would be entitled to the proceeds. TPL, through Sinclair Investments Ltd, asserted a proprietary claim to the proceeds of sale of Mr Cushnie's shares, which alleged that Mr Cushnie held on constructive trust for TPL. The defendants conceded that Mr Cushnie was liable to account to TPL for the gain attributable to the misuse of TPL's moneys, but contended that this obligation was a personal liability and not a proprietary claim against Mr Cushnie. Both the High Court and the Court of Appeal disallowed the claim on the ground that the claimant was not entitled to assert a proprietary interest in the proceeds of sale of the shares sold by Mr Cushnie. Instead, the claimant was entitled to an equitable account in respect of money or assets acquired by a fiduciary in breach of his duties to the beneficiaries. The shares were neither beneficially owned by the claimant nor derived from opportunities beneficially owned by the claimant. Indeed, the shares were acquired by Mr Cushnie even before TPL was incorporated. Thus, the claimant did not have a proprietary interest in the shares, and the profits therefrom.

JUDGMENT

'The mere fact that the breach of duty enabled Mr Cushnie to make a profit should not, of itself, be enough to give TPL a proprietary interest in that profit. Why, it may be asked, should the fact that a fiduciary is able to make a profit as a result of the breach of his duties to a beneficiary, without more, give the beneficiary a proprietary interest in the profit? After all, *a proprietary claim is based on property law*, and it is not entirely easy to see conceptually how the proprietary rights of the beneficiary in the misused funds should follow into the profit made on the sale of the shares … it does not matter to the defaulting fiduciary if he is stripped of his profits because they are beneficially owned by the beneficiary, or because he has to account for those profits to the beneficiary. But the difference very much matters to the other creditors of the defaulting fiduciary, if he is insolvent. A person with a proprietary claim to assets held in the name of an insolvent person is better off than a secured creditor, and all such assets are unavailable to other creditors.' [Emphasis added]

Lord Neuberger MR

In the extract above, Lord Neuberger draws a fine distinction between a profit which the trustee makes from the unauthorised use of trust property and a profit, such as a bribe, which the trustee receives from a third party. The former line of cases concerns a constructive trust with a proprietary interest vested in the beneficiaries, as illustrated by *Boardman v Phipps*, whereas the latter type of cases concerns a personal duty to account, as illustrated by *Heiron* and *Lister*. The difficulty with this analysis is that the source of the bribe is irrelevant when the policy in equity is to discourage or prohibit the fiduciary from receiving an unauthorised benefit. Equity was capable of treating the sum paid to the fiduciary by a third party as part of the trust fund. In *Williams v Barton* (1927) (see earlier), the commission received by the trustee was treated as part of the trust fund for he had infringed the 'no profit' rule.

In addition, it is arguable that the decision in *Sinclair* is over-generous to the trustee's creditors, at the expense of the beneficiaries. According to *Sinclair*, a beneficiary's claim is treated as a personal action against the trustee to account for the amount of the unauthorised remuneration. If the trustee becomes insolvent, the beneficiary will rank with the other unsecured creditors. But significantly the trustee has acted in breach of his core or fiduciary duties owed to the beneficiaries. Two fundamental principles that are applicable to fiduciaries are the 'no conflict' and 'no profit' rules. The 'no conflict' rule, as indicated earlier, is a deterrent principle which discourages the fiduciary from putting himself in a position of conflict. The 'no profit' rule means that where such conflict occurs and the fiduciary makes an unauthorised profit by abusing his position, he is required to disgorge the profit in favour of the principal. These are strict duties which require the trustees to hold any unauthorised profits for the beneficiaries. To require an independent proprietary base for such profits may be regarded as excessively generous to the creditors and unnecessarily restrictive to the beneficiaries.

If the amount of the bribe has increased in value because it consisted of a benefit in kind that has escalated in value (e.g. a house), or the bribe consisted of money that was invested in property that has increased in value (e.g. £50,000 cash was invested in shares worth £75,000), the issue was whether the trustee could have retained the benefit which had been derived from the increased value of the bribe. In an *obiter* pronouncement Lord Neuberger MR in *Sinclair* suggested that in such a case the value of the property exceeding the amount of the bribe may be subject to a claim for equitable compensation:

Thus, Lord Neuberger in *Sinclair* recognised the importance of ensuring that the fiduciary ought to be required to disgorge any profit he had made by investing the bribe. However, unlike Lindley LJ in *Lister*, he suggested that the personal duty to account might be 'adjusted' to transfer the profits to the principal. But this suggestion fails to acknowledge that the processes of following and tracing are part of property law which require a property base, as distinct from the personal duty to account.

In *Cadogan v Tolly* [2011] EWHC 2286, the High Court applied the *Sinclair* principle in summary proceedings involving a bribe or secret commission received by a fiduciary. The court decided that such proceedings involved a personal claim, as distinct from a proprietary cause of action.

In the recent, definitive Supreme Court decision in *FHR European Ventures v Cedar Capital Partners* [2014] UKSC 45, the court reviewed the leading authorities concerning the status of bribes and secret commissions, and concluded that, in accordance with traditional equitable principles, and in the interests of practicality, clarity and consistency, bribes and secret commissions received by an agent or other fiduciary, in breach of his fiduciary duties, will be held on constructive trusts for the principal. The effect of this ruling is that the principal acquires a proprietary interest in the benefit and is entitled to exercise either a proprietary or personal remedy against the agent. Thus, the principal is required to elect between the two remedies. The advantages of the proprietary remedy are that the principal is entitled to trace the proceeds of the bribe or secret commission into other assets and follow them into the hands of knowing recipients. In addition, if the agent becomes insolvent, a proprietary claim would effectively give the principal priority over the agent's unsecured creditors, as opposed to ranking *pari passu* with other unsecured creditors where the claim is for compensation.

The court analysed the significant number of authorities on this subject and drew the following conclusions. First, where the agent or other fiduciary makes an unauthorised profit by taking advantage of opportunities, not involving bribes and secret commissions, arising by virtue of his fiduciary relationship, the 'no conflict' principle applied and the principal acquires a proprietary interest in the asset obtained by the agent. By way of illustration, in *Phipps v Boardman* (1967), agents of trustees purchased shares in circumstances where they only had the opportunity because they were agents and were required to hold the same beneficially for the trust. Second, the majority of the cases on bribes and secret commissions support the view that the same principles apply to all benefits received by the agent in breach of his fiduciary duties. In short, no distinction may be drawn between the receipt of benefits generally and bribes and secret commissions specifically. The agent is required to hold the secret commission or bribe on trust for his principal rather than simply having an equitable duty to account to his principal. Third, the House of Lords' decision in *Tyrrell v Bank of London* (1862) 10 HL Cas 26, and a number of Court of Appeal decisions, including *Lister v Stubbs* (1890) and *Sinclair v*

Versailles (2011) appeared to have created a narrower rule, rejecting the proprietary remedy of the principal and reducing the claimant's rights to the bribe or secret commission to a personal remedy for equitable compensation.

In *Tyrrell*, a solicitor, retained to act for a company that was involved in the purchase of land, had arranged to benefit from the company's acquisition of property by obtaining a 50 per cent beneficial interest in adjoining land. Following the completion of the purchase by the company, it discovered that the solicitor had secretly profited from the transaction and claimed a proprietary interest in the adjoining land. The court rejected this claim as being outside 'the limit of the agency' but decided that the solicitor was liable to account for the profit he had made on the adjoining land.

In the present case, the Supreme Court observed that a number of Court of Appeal authorities were inconsistent with the notion that the rule applies to bribes and secret commissions. In *Metropolitan Bank v Heiron* (1880) 5 Ex D 319, the issue concerned the Limitation Acts by analogy. In *Lister v Stubbs* an interlocutory injunction was refused on the ground that the relationship between the company and its agent was that of a creditor and debtor, not beneficiary and trustee. In *Sinclair Investments v Versailles* the Court of Appeal decided that it would follow *Heiron* and *Lister*. On the other hand, in *AG for Hong Kong v Reid* (1994), the Privy Council concluded that bribes received by a corrupt Director of Public Prosecutions were held on trust for his principal and could be traced into properties acquired in New Zealand. Lord Templeman disapproved of the reasoning in *Heiron* and *Lister*. The Supreme Court concluded by disapproving the House of Lords' decision in *Tyrrell* and overruling the decisions in *Heiron*, *Lister* and subsequent cases that relied on these precedents, including *Sinclair v Versailles*.

CASE EXAMPLE

FHR European Ventures v Cedar Capital Partners [2014] UKSC 45

The claimants engaged the services of the defendants, Cedar Holdings, to investigate and negotiate the purchase price of the Monte Carlo Grand Hotel. The defendants entered into a brokerage agreement with the owners of the hotel in order to facilitate the sale of the hotel in return for a commission of €10 million. The defendants failed to inform the claimants of the brokerage agreement and the receipt of the commission. Following the purchase of the hotel the claimants became aware of the secret commission and issued proceedings claiming a proprietary interest in the amount of the commission. The defendants argued that the receipt of the monetary secret commission created a debtor/creditor relationship and, despite the breach of the agent's fiduciary duties, the claimants' remedy ought to be equitable compensation and not a proprietary remedy, relying on *Tyrrell v Bank of London* (1862), *Lister v Stubbs* (1890), *Metropolitan Bank v Heiron* (1880) and *Sinclair Investments v Versailles* (2011). The trial judge made a declaration to the effect that the defendants were required to pay the amount of the commission to the claimants but refused to grant a proprietary remedy in their favour. The Court of Appeal reversed the decision of the trial judge and granted the claimants a proprietary remedy. The defendants' appeal to the Supreme Court was dismissed and a declaration was made to the effect that the secret commission of €10 million was held on constructive trust for the claimants. The court considered the wider application of the claimants' argument as to whether the creation of a proprietary interest in the bribe or secret commission in favour of the principal has the effect of prejudicing the agent's unsecured creditors. The court decided that there was limited force in this argument for the agent's creditors may only be entitled to property that the agent is lawfully entitled to retain and cannot be in better position than the agent. Further, the bribe or commission will very often deplete the benefit which the principal would otherwise have obtained and, to that extent, may fairly be attributed to the principal, as illustrated in the present case. The vendor may have sold for less than the contract price if it was not required to pay the defendant a commission of €10 million.

Tyrrell was disapproved and *Heiron, Lister* and subsequent cases that followed these authorities, including *Sinclair*, were overruled. Accordingly, the discussion of *Lister, Sinclair* and subsequent cases that relied on these authorities, see above, are only of historical interest.

JUDGMENT

'The principal is entitled to the benefit of the agent's unauthorised acts in the course of his agency, in just the same way as, at law, an employer is vicariously liable to bear the burden of an employee's unauthorised breaches of duty in the course of his employment. The agent's duty is accordingly to deliver up to his principal the benefit which he has obtained, and not simply to pay compensation for having obtained it in excess of his authority. The only way that legal effect can be given to an obligation to deliver up specific property to the principal is by treating the principal as specifically entitled to it.'

Lord Neuberger

Lord Neuberger addressed a wider point, namely, whether an agent should hold a bribe or secret commission on trust for his principal in circumstances where he could not have acquired the underlying property on behalf of his principal. The court remarked that leading authorities had decided that the principal acquired a proprietary interest in such property, see *Keech v Sandford* (1726) and *Boardman v Phipps* (1967). Lord Neuberger in *FHR Ventures v Cedar* reasoned thus:

JUDGMENT

'In each of these cases, a person acquired property as a result of his fiduciary or quasi-fiduciary position, in circumstances in which the principal could not have acquired it: yet the court held that the property concerned was held on trust for the beneficiary. In *Keech*, the beneficiary could not acquire the new lease because the landlord was not prepared to let him, and because he was an infant; in *Boardman* the trust could not acquire the shares because they were not authorised investments.'

Lord Neuberger

The Supreme Court in *FHR Ventures* had regard to the inherently artificial and absurd distinction between an unauthorised benefit received by an agent in breach of his fiduciary duties and a bribe or secret commission obtained in similar circumstances. The principle in *Heiron* and *Lister* appeared to be that where a bribe or secret commission is paid to an agent in breach of his duties the principal has a proprietary interest in the bribe if it consists of shares, but not if it consists of money. Lord Neuberger dismissed this argument in the following manner:

JUDGMENT

'[I]t would be artificial, impractical and absurd if the issue whether a principal had a proprietary interest in a bribe to his agent depended on the mechanism agreed between the briber and the agent for payment of the bribe.'

Lord Neuberger

8.4.5 Trustee-director's remuneration

The requirement of a share qualification of a director may be provided for in the articles of association. If the trustee uses the shareholding of the trust to secure his appointment as a director, he is accountable to the trust for the remuneration received, in the absence of authority. This is the position, despite the payment being made for services as director of the company. If the opportunity to receive the remuneration was gained as a result of the conduct of the trustee, then he would have put himself in a position where his interest and duty conflicted.

CASE EXAMPLE

Re Macadam [1946] Ch 73

The articles of a company provided that the trustees of a will had a power to appoint two persons to directorships. The trustees appointed themselves directors and received remuneration. The court held that they were liable to account to the trust for the directors' fees received from the company.

JUDGMENT

'Did he acquire the position in respect of which he drew the remuneration by virtue of his position as trustee? In the present case there can be no doubt that the only way in which the plaintiffs became directors was by the exercise of the powers vested in the trustees of the will under article 68 of the articles of association of the company.'

Cohen J

But if the defendant is appointed a director before he acquires the trust shares or secures his appointment as director by the use of shares held in his personal capacity, he is not accountable to the trust.

CASE EXAMPLE

Re Gee [1948] Ch 284

The issued capital of a private company, Gee & Co Ltd, was 5,000 £1 shares. Immediately before his death, Alfred Gee (the testator) was the registered holder of 4,996 shares in Gee & Co. The remaining four shareholders, who held one share each, were: Miss Gee (the testator's sister); the testator's wife; his daughter (Mrs Hunter); and his son-in-law (Mr Staples). By his will, the testator appointed his wife, Mrs Hunter and Mr Staples to be his executors and trustees after his death. After the death of the testator and before his will was probated, Mr Staples was appointed managing director of the company by the unanimous agreement of the three executors and Miss Gee, who together constituted all the registered beneficial shareholders at that time. Mr Staples agreed to act as director of the company, and received £15,721 as remuneration for the 10 years that he managed the company. The beneficiaries under the will now claimed that Mr Staples was liable to account for the profit. The court rejected the claim and decided that Mr Staples was not accountable because he was appointed a director unanimously by the shareholders for qualities independent of the trust votes. The trust votes were not brought into play to secure his appointment.

'After the death of the testator, only four persons remained on the register of this company, and they alone could attend meetings of it. As I have said before, the meeting of 6th January 1938 was attended by all the corporators. Each of them held one share, and as the resolutions were passed unanimously, they must be supposed to have voted in favour by the use of that share. If the corporators, as I think, held their shares beneficially, they were entitled to vote as they chose. If, on the other hand, they were nominees of the testator, there were still three of them whose votes outweighed the vote of Mr Staples if it was his duty to vote against his own interest. In neither event did the trust shares come into the picture at all.'

Harman J

8.4.6 Occasions when a trustee may receive remuneration

Authority in the trust instrument

Trustees may negotiate with the settlor to be paid for their services. Such clauses are frequently included where a professional trustee is appointed. Charging clauses are construed strictly against the trustee. However, s 28 of the Trustee Act 2000 introduced a degree of flexibility with charging clauses for professionals. The section enacts that in the case of an express charging clause if the trustee is a trust corporation or acts in a professional capacity, the trustee is entitled to be paid even if the services are capable of being provided by a lay person. On the occasions when trustees are entitled to be paid under charging clauses they are entitled to charge only a reasonable amount.

Statutory authority

Section 28 of the Trustee Act 2000 provides that, subject to provisions to the contrary in the trust instrument, a trust corporation or a professional trustee who is authorised to charge for services is entitled to remuneration even though the services may be provided by a lay trustee. In the case of a charitable trust, a trustee who is not a trust corporation may charge for such services only if he is not the sole trustee and a majority of the other trustees agree in writing.

Section 29 of the Trustee Act 2000 creates an implied power of payment on the part of professional trustees. A trust corporation is entitled to receive reasonable remuneration for services provided. A professional trustee who is neither a trust corporation nor a sole trustee is entitled to receive reasonable remuneration if the other trustees agree in writing. The reason for the exclusion of the sole trustee is to promote objectivity concerning this decision. The implied authority to remuneration does not apply to trustees of a charitable trust.

In addition, by virtue of s 42 of the Trustee Act 1925, where the court appoints a corporation to be a trustee it (the court) may authorise the corporation to charge such remuneration for its services as the court may think fit.

Reimbursements

Section 31 of the Trustee Act 2000 (which repeals and replaces s 30(2) of the Trustee Act 1925) entitles trustees to be reimbursed for expenses properly incurred when acting on behalf of the trust. Whether an expense was properly incurred would depend on general principles and the circumstances surrounding the expense.

Authority of the court

The court will only authorise reasonable remuneration for services performed by trustees which are of exceptional benefit to the trust. In *Boardman v Phipps* (1967), generous remuneration was awarded by the court for the efforts of the appellants.

Despite the fact that the defendant may be liable to account for profits made in breach of his fiduciary duties, the court retains a wide discretion to determine whether to grant an allowance for expenditure incurred, and work and skill applied, for the benefit of the trust. In *Phipps v Boardman* [1964] 2 All ER 187, Wilberforce J at first instance said:

JUDGMENT

'Moreover, account must naturally be taken of expenditure which was necessary to enable the profit to be realised. But, in addition, should not the defendants be given an allowance or credit for their work and skill? It seems to me that this transaction, i.e. the acquisition of a controlling interest in the company, was one of a special character calling for the exercise of a particular kind of professional skill. If Boardman had not assumed the role of seeing it through, the beneficiaries would have had to employ … an expert to do it for them … It seems to me that it would be inequitable now for the beneficiaries to step in and take the profit without paying for the skill and labour which has produced it.'

Wilberforce J

A similar rule, as well as the rationale underlying the principle, was referred to by Lord Goff in *Guinness v Saunders* [1990] 2 AC 663, thus:

JUDGMENT

'It will be observed that the decision to make the allowance was founded upon the simple proposition that it would be inequitable now for the beneficiaries to step in and take the profit without paying for the skill and labour which has produced it … The decision has to be reconciled with the fundamental principle that a trustee is not entitled to remuneration for services rendered by him to the trust except as expressly provided in the trust deed. Strictly speaking, it is irreconcilable with the rules so stated. It seems to me therefore that it can only be reconciled with it to the extent that the exercise of the equitable jurisdiction does not conflict with the policy underlying the rule. And, as I see it, such a conflict will only be avoided if the exercise of the jurisdiction is restricted to those cases where it cannot have the effect of encouraging trustees in any way to put themselves in a position where their interests conflict with their duties as trustees.'

Lord Goff

But the wide discretion of the court to grant equitable allowance to the defendant will not be exercised where the latter is guilty of dishonesty or surreptitious dealing in connection with the trust property. On this basis the court in *Cobbetts v Hodge* (see above) refused to grant an allowance to the defendant for his work and skill on the ground that his conduct was designed to mislead the claimants. However, the court allowed the defendant to recover the costs of the shares. Floyd J reasoned thus:

JUDGMENT

'It is easy to feel some sympathy for Mr Hodge, given his work for EL over a period of some three years. But it seems to me that to award him an allowance on the facts of the present case would offend against the principles stated by Wilberforce J in *Phipps v Boardman* and Lord Goff in *Guinness v Saunders*. Mr Hodge did not simply omit to disclose the arrangement with EL … he gave Mr Rimmer a misleading account of the basis of the acquisition of these shares. Moreover, to permit an allowance in these circumstances would be to encourage fiduciaries to place their own interests ahead of those whom they serve. For both those reasons I decline to order any allowance in the present case, beyond the cost of acquisition of the shares.'

Floyd J

Moreover, the court is entitled to increase the amount of the remuneration as laid down in the charging clause: see *Re Duke of Norfolk's Settlement Trusts* [1981] 3 All ER 220.

CASE EXAMPLE

Foster v Spencer, The Times, 14 June 1995

The court decided that, in the exercise of its inherent jurisdiction, trustees of a cricket club were entitled to remuneration for past services, but not to future remuneration. The trustees were extremely active in bringing about a sale of the site for a reasonable price. The decisive factors were:

(i) There were no funds out of which to pay remuneration at the time of the appointment of the trustees.
(ii) The refusal of the claim to remuneration would have resulted in the beneficiaries being unjustly enriched at the expense of the trustees.
(iii) There was no true appreciation of the extent of the task at the time of appointment. Had the trustees realised what they were in for, they would have declined to act unless remunerated in some way.

Agreement with all the beneficiaries
If all the beneficiaries are *sui juris* and absolutely entitled to the trust property, they may agree to remunerate the trustees. It is essential that the beneficiaries act independently and without any undue influence from the trustees.

The rule in **Cradock v Piper (1850) 1 Mac&G 664**
A trustee/solicitor may act as a solicitor for himself and co-trustee in litigation involving the trust and may recover the costs for acting on behalf of his co-trustee. This anomalous rule is restricted to litigious work and may not be extended beyond the relationship of trustee/solicitor.

The rule in **Re Northcote [1949] 1 All ER 442**
The principle is that English executors and trustees, who are entitled to earn a commission under a foreign jurisdiction in which the trust assets are situated, are empowered to retain such remuneration for their own benefit.

CASE EXAMPLE

Re Northcote [1949] 1 All ER 442

A testator, domiciled in England, died leaving assets in England and the United States. His executors obtained a grant of probate in England. They also obtained a grant in New York in respect of the American assets. They collected the American assets and were entitled to agency commission under the law of that state. The question in issue was whether they were accountable for the commission. The court held that the executors were not accountable.

8.4.7 Purchases of trust property (rule against self-dealing)
The courts have developed a rule prohibiting trustees and other fiduciaries, without authority, from purchasing the trust property. If the purchase takes place the transaction is treated as voidable at the instance of the beneficiaries.

JUDGMENT

'[T]he purchase is not permitted in any case, however honest the circumstances; the general interests of justice requiring it to be destroyed in every instance.'

Lord Eldon in *Ex p James* (1803) 8 Ves 337

JUDGMENT

'During ... argument, two agreed labels emerged for the two rules, I propose to refer to them as follows:

The self-dealing rule: if a trustee (1) purchases trust property from himself, any beneficiary may have the sale set aside ex debito justitiae, however fair the transaction.

The fair-dealing rule: if a trustee (2) purchases his beneficial interest, the beneficiary may have the sale set aside unless the trustee can establish the propriety of the transaction, showing that he had taken no advantage of his position and that the beneficiary was fully informed and received full value.'

Megarry VC in *Tito v Waddell (No 2)* [1977] Ch 106

Reasons commonly associated with this harsh rule are that the trustees would otherwise be both vendors and purchasers and it would be difficult to ascertain whether an unfair advantage had been obtained by the trustees. In addition, the property may become virtually unmarketable since the title may indicate that the property was at one time trust property. Third parties may have notice of this fact and any disputes concerning the trust property may affect their interest. The aggrieved beneficiary is required to act within a reasonable time in order to avoid the sale. The rule cannot be avoided by conveying the property to a nominee of the trustees for the court will consider all the circumstances to ascertain whether an unfair advantage has been acquired by the trustees.

CASE EXAMPLE

Wright v Morgan [1926] AC 788

A testator by his will gave his son, Harry Herbert, the option to purchase a plot of land provided that the price was fixed by an independent valuer. Harry was also a trustee under the will. Harry assigned the option to Douglas Wright, his co-trustee and brother, but who was not authorised to purchase the property. Douglas retired from the trust and purported to exercise the option at a price fixed by the valuers. The beneficiaries under the will brought an action to set aside the sale. The court held that the sale ought to be set aside on the ground of a conflict of duty and interest.

CASE EXAMPLE

Regal (Hastings) Ltd v Gulliver [1942] 1 All ER 378

Regal Ltd received an offer from one of its subsidiaries to sell to Regal a quantity of shares. Regal did not have the specified amount of funds but four of its directors subscribed for the shares personally and later sold them for a profit. It was found as a fact that all the transactions were *bona fide*. Regal now claimed that the directors were accountable for their profit. The House of Lords held that the directors were accountable to the company.

JUDGMENT

'I am of opinion that the directors standing in a fiduciary relationship to Regal in regard to the exercise of their powers as directors, and having obtained these shares by reason and only by reason of the fact that they were directors of Regal and in the course of the execution of that office, are accountable for the profits which they have made out of them. The equitable rule laid down in *Keech v Sandford* and *Ex p James*, and similar authorities applies to them in full force.'

Lord Russell

Lord Russell in *Regal* expressed the rationale for liability to account as being simply that the fiduciary is prohibited from taking personal profits from any activity connected with his status as a fiduciary. He is required to perform his duties selflessly and it is immaterial that he does not act with impropriety.

JUDGMENT

'The rule of equity which insists on those, who by use of a fiduciary position make a profit, being liable to account for that profit, in no way depends on fraud, or absence of *bona fides*; or upon such questions or considerations as whether the profit would or should otherwise have gone to the plaintiff, or whether the profiteer was under a duty to obtain the source of the profit for the plaintiff, or whether he took a risk or acted as he did for the benefit of the plaintiff, or whether the plaintiff has in fact been damaged or benefited by his action. The liability arises from the mere fact of a profit having, in the stated circumstances, been made.'

Lord Russell

CASE EXAMPLE

Industrial Development Consultants v Cooley [1972] 1 WLR 443

The defendant was the managing director of the claimant company. He was approached by the Chairman of the Eastern Gas Board to work for them, although at the time the claimant company was interested in a project for the Gas Board. In his capacity as managing director, he had obtained special knowledge which should have been passed on to the claimant company. Concealing this knowledge, he obtained his release from the service of the claimant, basing his request on alleged ill health. The claimant would not have released him had it known the full facts. The claimant sued the director alleging that he was a trustee of profits of his new contract on behalf of the claimant. The court held in favour of the claimant in view of the conflict of duty and interest in failing to pass on the information to the claimant.

JUDGMENT

'It seems to me plain that throughout the whole of May, June and July 1969 the defendant was in a fiduciary relationship with the plaintiffs. From the time he embarked upon his course of dealing with the Eastern Gas Board, irrespective of anything which he did or he said to Mr Hicks, he embarked upon a deliberate policy and course of conduct which put his personal interest as a potential contracting party with the Eastern Gas Board in direct conflict with his pre-existing and continuing duty as managing director of the plaintiffs.'

Roskill J

In an *obiter* pronouncement in *Murad v Al-Saraj* [2005] EWCA Civ 959, the Court of Appeal expressed the view that the *Boardman v Phipps* principle prohibiting fiduciaries from taking benefits was too inflexible to be maintained as a rule of equity. It may be recalled that Mr Boardman acted in good faith and was still accountable for breach of his fiduciary duties. Arden LJ in *Murad* expressed the sentiment that this might be perceived as being too harsh. She expressed a preference that liability to account ought to be based on fault by the defendant. However, Arden LJ conceded that this issue may be revisited by a higher court in the future.

JUDGMENT

'It may be that the time has come when the court should revisit the operation of the inflexible rule of equity in harsh circumstances, as where the trustee has acted in perfect good faith and without any deception or concealment, and in the belief that he was acting in the best interests of the beneficiary. I need only say this: it would not be in the least impossible for a court in a future case to determine as a question of fact whether the beneficiary would not have wanted to exploit the profit himself, or would have wanted the trustee to have acted other than in the way that the trustee in fact did act. Moreover, it would not be impossible for a modern court to conclude as a matter of policy that, without losing the deterrent effect of the rule, the harshness of it should be tempered in some circumstances. In addition, in such cases, the courts can provide a significant measure of protection for the beneficiaries by imposing on the defaulting trustee the affirmative burden of showing that those circumstances prevailed. Certainly the Canadian courts have modified the effect of equity's inflexible rule (see *Peso Silver Mines Ltd v Cropper* (1966) 58 DLR (2d) 1; see also the decision of the Privy Council on appeal from Australia in *Queensland Mines v Hudson* (1978) 52 AJLR 399), though I express no view as to the circumstances in which there should be any relaxation of the rule in this jurisdiction. That sort of question must be left to another court.'

Arden LJ

In *Murad,* two sisters undertook a joint business venture with the defendant to purchase a hotel. The defendant was required to contribute a specific amount towards the scheme but failed to disclose that he was entitled to earn a commission from the vendor to secure the deal. It was found that the defendant was a fiduciary and had fraudulently induced the claimants to enter into the transaction. The court decided that he was accountable to the claimants for the profits made on the transaction.

JUDGMENT

'Mr Al-Saraj was found to have made a fraudulent misrepresentation to the Murads who had placed their trust in him. I do not consider that, even if we were free to revisit the *Regal* case, this would be an appropriate case in which to do so. The appropriate remedy is that he should disgorge all the profits, whether of a revenue or capital nature, that he made from inducing the Murads by his fraudulent representations from entering into the Parkside Hotel venture.'

Arden LJ

In *Kane v Radley Kane* [1999] Ch 274, Scott VC held that the self-dealing rule applied to a personal representative who had appropriated property to satisfy a legacy to herself without the sanction of the court or the consent of the beneficiaries. It follows that the appropriation was voidable at the suit of a beneficiary.

Although the general principle of avoiding a conflict of duty and interest is applied strictly by the courts, there are exceptional circumstances when a fiduciary may retain an unauthorised benefit. Each case is determined on its own facts. In *Holder v Holder* [1968] Ch 353, the Court of Appeal found a number of exceptional circumstances that entitled an executor to retain a benefit.

CASE EXAMPLE

Holder v Holder [1968] Ch 353

The testator appointed his widow, daughter and one of his sons, Victor, to be his executors and trustees. Victor at first took a few minor steps in connection with the administration of the estate (signing cheques, etc.) but then abstained from taking any further part in the administration. One of the assets of the estate included a farm. Victor had acquired no special knowledge of the farm in his capacity as executor and all his knowledge about the farm was acquired as a tenant of that farm. The farm was then offered for sale at an auction, subject to Victor's tenancy. At the auction, Victor made a successful bid for the farm. Another son applied to the court for the sale to be set aside. The court held that the sale ought not be set aside, for the following reasons:

- Victor had not instructed the valuer nor had he arranged the auction. Thus, Victor could not be construed as both a vendor and purchaser.
- Victor had never assumed the duties of executor, for he had done virtually nothing in the administration of the estate, nor had Victor any influence on the two other executors in respect of the sale.
- In any case, Victor had made no secret of his intention to buy the farm and had paid a good price for the property.
- Victor was not relied upon by other beneficiaries to protect their interests.

JUDGMENT

'In this case Victor's … interference with the administration of the estate was of a minimal character and the last cheque he signed was in August before he executed the deed of renunciation. He took no part in the instructions for probate, nor in the valuations or fixing of the reserves. Everyone concerned knew of the renunciation and of the reason for it, namely, that he wished to be a purchaser.'

Harman LJ

A similar principle applies in respect of the purchase by the trustee of the beneficiary's interest. This is known as the 'fair dealing' rule. The test here is whether the beneficiary was capable of exercising an independent judgment after full disclosure by the trustee. The presumption is that the trustee exercised undue influence on the beneficiary. The burden of proof is therefore on the trustee to rebut this presumption. In disputed cases the trustee is required to establish that the contract with the beneficiary is distinct and clear, after a jealous and scrupulous examination of all the circumstances, proving that the beneficiary intended the trustee to purchase his interest; and that there was no fraud, no concealment, no advantage taken, by the trustee of information, acquired by him in the character of trustee. This is a question of degree.

8.5 Public policy and the Forfeiture Act 1982

The courts have adopted a principle of public policy to the effect that a person convicted of the killing of another would be prevented from benefiting from the deceased person's estate either under his will or on an intestacy. The convicted person's potential interest will be forfeited on an application to the court. In *Cleaver v Mutual Reserve Fund Life Association* [1892] 1 QB 147, Fry LJ stated, 'no system of jurisprudence can with reason include amongst the rights which it enforces rights directly resulting to the person asserting them from the crime of that person'.

The rationale for the forfeiture rule is the public policy notion that no one may benefit from his own wrong *a fortiori* as a consequence of killing another. It has been defined in s 1(1) of the Forfeiture Act 1982 as meaning 'the rule of public policy which in certain circumstances precludes a person who has unlawfully killed another from acquiring a benefit in consequence of the killing'. If the convicted killer does not acquire title to the property before the death of the victim there is no need for the courts to impose a constructive trust. The court simply forfeits the interest that he acquires under the estate of the victim. In *Re Crippen* [1911] P 108, C murdered his wife, who died intestate. C was executed and, in his will, left property to his mistress, X. The court decided that X was not entitled to the wife's estate because C was never beneficially entitled to it. Evans J reasoned: 'It is clear that the law is, that no person can obtain, or enforce, any rights resulting to him from his own crime; neither can his representative, claiming under him, obtain or enforce any such rights.'

On the other hand, if the killer acquires title to the property as a consequence of the death of the victim, there is room for the imposition of the constructive trust in order to prevent his unjust enrichment. The constructive trust principles entitle the courts to focus on the broader question whether the taking of the benefit by the wrongdoer would be so unconscionable as to attract the public policy rule disentitling the claimant from benefiting from his crime.

After a period of uncertainty, the Court of Appeal in *Dunbar v Plant* (1997), decided that the forfeiture rule is applicable to those convicted of murder, manslaughter (both voluntary and involuntary) and other unlawful killing and accessories to such offences as aiding and abetting the suicide of another. What matters, in deciding whether the forfeiture rule applies, is the nature and not the name of the crime. In *Dunbar v Plant* (1997), Phillips LJ declared:

> so far as the [forfeiture] rule is concerned, it is hard to see any logical basis for not applying it in all cases of manslaughter ... [I]n the crime of manslaughter the *actus reus* is causing the death of another. That *actus reus* is rendered criminal if it occurs in one of the various circumstances that are prescribed by law. Anyone guilty of manslaughter has *ex hypothesi*, caused the death of another by criminal conduct. It is in such circumstances that the rule ... applies. If, as I believe, the forfeiture rule applies to offences under the Suicide Act 1961 and the application of the rule is not dependent upon the degree of culpability attaching to the crime, it must follow that the rule applies to aiding and abetting the suicide of another in pursuance of a suicide pact.

This approach was treated as conclusive in *Dalton v Latham* [2003] EWHC 796, where Patten J said, '[*Dunbar v Plant*] must now be taken to be a binding statement of the law as to the application of the rule of public policy. It applies to all cases of unlawful killing, including manslaughter by reason of diminished responsibility or by reason of provocation. The only possible exception is where the defendant is found to be criminally insane, which leads to an acquittal.'

Where the property of the killer and the deceased is co-owned as joint tenants, then, in accordance with the forfeiture rule, on the death of the victim, the killer acquires the entire legal title to the property in accordance with the right of survivorship, but holds the property on trust for himself and the heirs of the deceased. In other words, the killer's interest in the property before the killing is unaffected by the forfeiture rule which, in these circumstances, deals only with the interest of the deceased, see *Re K* [1985] Ch 85, per Vinelott J, 'where one joint tenant murders the other while the entire interest vests in the survivor the law imports a constructive trust of an undivided one-half share for the benefit of the next of kin of the deceased'. The same result was reached by the High Court in *Henderson v Wilcox* [2015] EWHC 3469, per Cooke J: 'the forfeiture rule has no application to any interest now existing or in future created under either of the trusts'. However, where the interest of the killer is enjoyed in remainder with the victim as life tenant the position becomes more complicated. Although the problem has not yet arisen, it may be argued that on the one hand, the interest of the killer had become vested in the property before the unlawful killing, and accordingly the forfeiture rule does not apply in this situation. Alternatively, one commentator has argued that in such a situation the killer's remainder interest ought to be postponed for such a period as the victim may have lived and the income from the property ought to be held on constructive trust for the heirs of the victim.

In *Re DWS (deceased)* [2001] 1 All ER 97, the Court of Appeal extended the forfeiture principle to those claiming through the wrongdoer on an intestacy, such as the child of the killer. Since the killer, the parent, was still alive it followed that the killer's child could not inherit his grandparent's estate. The court decided that this solution stems from s 47 of the Administration of Estates Act 1925. The effect was that the victim ought to be treated as having died without issue, which meant that the victim's grandchildren could not inherit the property. The harshness of this solution was considered by the Law Commission in its report 'The Forfeiture Rule and the Law of Succession' in 2005 (Law Com. No. 295), which recommended its modification. This was achieved in the Estates of Deceased Persons (Forfeiture Rule and the Law of Succession) Act 2011, which added a new s 46A to the 1925 Act reversing the effect of *Re DWS*. Under the new provision the killer is to be treated as having died immediately before the victim, thus the killer's children may be eligible to inherit their grandparent's estate.

The Forfeiture Act 1982, s 2(1) authorises the court to modify the forfeiture rule in the case of a person who has unlawfully killed another (excluding convicted murderers, s 5). Section 2(2) identifies the factors which the court is required to consider in order to exercise its discretion. It enacts as follows:

SECTION

'The court shall not make an order … modifying the effect of the forfeiture rule in any case unless it is satisfied that, having regard to the *conduct of the offender* and of the *deceased* and to such *other circumstances* as appear to the court to be material, *the justice of the case* requires the effect of the rule to be so modified in that case.' [Emphasis added]

The court's approach in construing s 2(2) was analysed in *Dunbar v Plant* (1997) by Phillips and Mummery LJJ. Phillips LJ focused on the level of culpability of the claimant's conduct:

[The] first and paramount consideration must be whether the culpability attending the beneficiary's criminal conduct was such as to justify the application of the forfeiture rule at all.

Phillips LJ

Whereas Mummery LJ's approach required the court to have regard to all the material facts of the case, including a number of listed factors, and then asking the question whether the justice of the case warrants modification of the forfeiture rule:

'[The court is required to] look at the case in the round, pay regard to all the material circumstances, including the conduct of the offender and the deceased, and then ask whether "the justice of the case requires" a modification of the effect of the forfeiture rule. ... The court is entitled to take into account a whole range of circumstances relevant to the discretion, quite apart from the conduct of the offender and the deceased: the relationship between them; the degree of moral culpability for what happened; the nature and gravity of the offence; the intentions of the deceased; the size of the estate and the value of the property in dispute; the financial position of the offender and the moral claims and wishes of those who would be entitled to take the property on the application of the forfeiture rule.'

Mummery LJ

In *Dunbar v Plant* (1997) the court decided that determining whether it ought to exercise its discretion in modifying the forfeiture rule would depend on the facts of each case. There has been little guidance from the Act concerning the factors which the judge is required to take into consideration, save for the conduct of the victim and the claimant. The judge must take into consideration all the material facts of the case and his evaluation of these facts is a matter for him. The Court of Appeal will rarely interfere with the exercise of the discretion of the judge unless he misdirects himself as to the factors to be taken into account.

CASE EXAMPLE

Dunbar v Plant [1997] 3 WLR 1261, CA

Miss Plant was accused by her employer of theft and threatened with imprisonment. She discussed her fears with her fiancé and they agreed on a suicide pact by hanging themselves in the loft with bedsheets. Her fiancé was successful but the noose around her neck became loose and she survived. She then unsuccessfully attempted to end her life by cutting her throat and wrist and jumping out of the back bedroom window. Her fiancé died intestate owning a house jointly with her, various building society and bank accounts and a life assurance policy naming Miss Plant as the beneficiary. The deceased was survived by his parents who applied to the court to have Miss Plant's inheritance forfeited. Miss Plant argued that the forfeiture rule did not apply in order to preclude her from taking the entire beneficial interest in the house by survivorship. Alternatively, if the forfeiture rule did apply, the court should exercise its discretion to make a modification under the Act of 1982, so as to allow her to take the joint property and the insurance moneys. The trial judge decided that the forfeiture rule operated to deprive Miss Plant from inheriting any part of the estate of the deceased, but in exercising his discretion under the Forfeiture Act 1982 the court modified the effect of the forfeiture rule by granting Miss Plant partial relief from forfeiture. On appeal, the Court of Appeal endorsed one aspect of the decision of the trial judge, namely, the forfeiture rule operated where the defendant aided and abetted suicide, but reversed the decision of the trial judge based on the wrongful exercise of his discretion in seeking to do justice between the parties, rather than considering whether the culpability of the defendant's conduct was such as to justify the application of the forfeiture rule. The proper course was to grant full relief from forfeiture.

JUDGMENT

'The discretion is a broad one, and it is legitimate to have regard to all the consequences of the order, but it is not right to approach the exercise of the discretion as if dealing simply with an inter partes dispute. In these circumstances it is for this court to exercise afresh the discretion given by the Forfeiture Act 1982.

The first, and paramount consideration, must be whether the culpability attending the beneficiary's criminal conduct was such as to justify the application of the forfeiture rule at all. Each case must be assessed on its own facts. The desperation that led Miss Plant to decide to kill herself, and which led to the suicide pact, was an irrational and tragic reaction to her predicament. I do not consider that the nature of Miss Plant's conduct alters what I have indicated should be the normal approach when dealing with a suicide pact – that there should be full relief against forfeiture. The assets with which this case is concerned were in no way derived from Mr. Dunbar's family. They are the fruits of insurance taken out by Mr. Dunbar for the benefit of Miss Plant.'

Phillips LJ

In *Chadwick v Collinson and Others* (2014), the High Court considered the two approaches adopted in *Dunbar v Plant* and decided that, although the culpability of the claimant in committing the offence was a primary consideration, the court is required to consider other material factors as indicated by Mummery LJ. Having regard to all the evidence, the court decided that it was not in the interests of justice to modify the forfeiture rule.

CASE EXAMPLE

Chadwick v Collinson and Others [2014] EWHC 3055, HC

The claimant lived with his partner, Lisa Clay ('the deceased'), for over 10 years. They had one child, Joseph, aged six at the time of his death. The relationship between the claimant and the deceased was ostensibly stable and loving. In the early morning of 9 April 2013, the claimant unlawfully killed the deceased and Joseph by stabbing each of them repeatedly in a frenzied attack. The claimant was charged with murder but his plea to manslaughter by way of diminished responsibility was accepted by the Crown. In 2008 the deceased executed her will under which the claimant was the residuary beneficiary. The deceased and the claimant jointly owned the matrimonial home as joint tenants. The acquisition of this property was mainly funded by the deceased. The net value of the deceased's estate was £79,000 of which £60,000 was attributed to the deceased's interest in the family home. The claimant instituted proceedings asserting that the forfeiture rule did not apply in the circumstances of this case or alternatively, that the forfeiture rule should be modified pursuant to s 2(2) of the Forfeiture Act 1982. The court dismissed the claimant's application on the grounds that:

- recent case law had established that the forfeiture rule was applicable to all cases of unlawful killing whether it be murder or manslaughter (voluntary and involuntary), see *Dunbar v Plant* (1997);
- in accordance with the Forfeiture Act 1982 the justice of the case did not require the forfeiture rule to be modified. Despite the circumstances of his mental disability, which did not impact on his ability to form a rational judgment, the court decided that the claimant exhibited such a high level of culpability that the modification of the forfeiture rule would be contrary to the interests of justice;
- in addition, the nature and gravity of the offences committed by the claimant were factors that weighed against the disapplication of the forfeiture rule;
- moreover, the evidence suggested that the couple's relationship was at all times stable, loving and had been long-lasting. Further, most of the interest in the family home was funded by the deceased.

On the question of culpability for the commission of the offence, the court considered the medical evidence and noted that the expert witness testified to the effect that the claimant was aware of the nature and quality of his acts and that what he was doing was wrong.

In addition, the ferocity of the attacks, their duration, the number of times that he returned to assault each individual and his failure to take any steps to seek help in the immediate aftermath were factors that weighed heavily against granting relief.

There could be no criticism of the conduct of the deceased. There was no evidence that the relationship between the claimant and the deceased was other than stable, loving and long-lasting. She appointed the claimant to be her executor and the guardian of their child. She left the entirety of her estate to the claimant and only to her children in the event that he did not survive her for more than 28 days. Most if not all of her interest (and that of the claimant) in the property had been funded by the deceased. In addition, most of the balance of the deceased's estate was derived from the funds of the deceased. The court considered the financial needs of the claimant in the future and decided that his prospects of finding gardening work may be slim. Further, in the event of an intestacy the transmission of the deceased's estate to her aunts and cousins, who were not intended to be her beneficiaries, was yet another factor to be taken into account. But, on balance, the interests of justice did not warrant the granting of relief under the Forfeiture Act 1982.

In *Henderson v Wilcox* (2015), the High Court decided that taking into consideration all the material circumstances of the case, the claimant's conduct towards the victim, his mental state, the deceased's imputed intention to benefit the claimant and his financial circumstances, the justice of the case warranted no relief to the claimant.

CASE EXAMPLE

Henderson v Wilcox [2015] EWHC 3469

The claimant, a 62-year-old man, killed his 87-year-old mother in a severe assault in which she sustained multiple injuries. He was initially charged with murder and pleaded not guilty, but this charge was vacated by the prosecution when he pleaded guilty to manslaughter on the grounds that he had no intention to kill and at the relevant time was suffering from serious mental disorder and autism. The claimant had a history of violence towards his mother despite her evasive actions in her motive to protect him from the authorities. The defendants were the deceased's sister-in-law (joint executor with the claimant of the deceased's will), the nephew of the deceased (a default beneficiary) and two solicitors who were named as trustees of property under the deceased's will. The family home, in which the deceased and claimant lived, was subject to an *inter vivos* trust whereby the deceased and the two solicitors were appointed discretionary trustees for the benefit of the deceased, her nephew and the claimant. In addition, by her will, the deceased left her entire estate to the claimant. The claimant applied to the court for a declaration that the common law forfeiture rule did not apply to his interest under the *inter vivos* trust and relief under the Forfeiture Act 1982 in respect of his interest under the will. The High Court decided that the forfeiture rule did not apply to the claimant's interest under the *inter vivos* trust because such interests crystallised when the trust was created and not by virtue of the death of the mother. The circumstances of the case did not justify the court in exercising its discretion to modify the forfeiture rule and allow the claimant to inherit his mother's estate under her will.

Section 2(3) of the Forfeiture Act 1982 enacts that proceedings for relief are required to be brought within a period of three months beginning with the date of the conviction. Section 3 excludes the forfeiture rule in respect of applications for financial provision made pursuant to a number of specified Acts of Parliament, including the Inheritance (Provision for Family and Dependants) Act 1975. In *Land v Land* [2006] All ER (D) 71 (Oct), the High Court decided that the time period of three months laid down in s 2(3) of the Forfeiture Act 1982 was incapable of extension. However, the deceased's son was allowed to make an application under the Inheritance (Provision for Family and Dependants) Act 1975 on the basis that reasonable financial provision had not been made for his maintenance.

8.6 Contracts for the sale of land

It is a fundamental principle of property law that when a contract for the sale of land is made but the sale has not been completed, the vendor becomes a constructive trustee for the purchaser from the date of the exchange of the contract until the date of completion for 'Equity regards as done that which ought to be done'. On the date of the completion of the contract the legal title to the property is acquired by the purchaser, but in the interim period the beneficiary acquires a proprietary interest commencing on the date of the creation of the contract.

CASE EXAMPLE

Lysaght v Edwards [1876] 2 Ch D 499

Edwards agreed in writing to sell real property to the claimant but, before completion, Edwards died. By his will, he devised his real property to trustees on trust to sell and invest the proceeds of sale. On a claim by the purchaser for an order requiring the executors to complete the sale the court decided in favour of the purchaser, on the ground that on the date of the creation of the contract, the equitable title to the property was acquired by the purchaser by operation of law.

JUDGMENT

'[I]n equity, the vendor becomes the trustee for the purchaser of the real estate sold; the beneficial ownership passes to the purchaser of the estate, the vendor retaining a right to the purchase money.'

Lord Jessell MR

8.7 Equity will not allow a statute to be used as an engine for fraud

The court is entitled to suspend the operation of a statutory provision if insistence on its strict compliance will have the tendency to perpetuate a fraud. The court will not sit back and acquiesce in a defendant abusing his position by committing a fraud on the claimant in reliance on a statutory formal provision.

CASE EXAMPLE

Rochefoucauld v Boustead [1897] 1 Ch 196

The claimant was the mortgagor of several estates but found herself in financial difficulty. The defendant purchased the properties from the mortgagee and orally agreed to hold them on trust for the claimant, subject to the repayment to the defendant of the purchase price and expenses. The defendant sold the estates and later became bankrupt. The claimant sued the trustee in bankruptcy for an account. The trustee in bankruptcy alleged that the oral agreement was not enforceable as the predecessor to s 53(1)(b) of the Law of Property Act 1925 (namely s 7 of the Statute of Frauds 1677) was not complied with and the claimant had no interest in the proceeds of sale. The court decided in favour of the claimant on the ground that it will not allow s 7 of the Statute of Frauds 1677 to be used as an engine for fraud. It would be a fraud for a person to whom land is conveyed on trust, to deny the trust and claim the land as his own. Even if there was insufficient evidence to constitute a memorandum in order to satisfy s 7 of the 1677 Act, parol evidence was admissible to establish that the defendant bought the properties as trustee.

JUDGMENT

'It is established by a series of cases ... that the Statute of Frauds does not prevent the proof of a fraud; and that it is a fraud on the part of a person to whom land is conveyed as a trustee, and who knows it was so conveyed, to deny the trust and claim the land himself. Consequently, notwithstanding the statute, it is competent for a person claiming land conveyed to another to prove by parol evidence that it was so conveyed upon trust for the claimant, and that the grantee, knowing the facts, is denying the trust and relying upon the form of the conveyance and the statute, in order to keep the land himself.'

Lindley LJ

Moreover, it was clear that the Court of Appeal was enforcing an express trust that was not reduced into writing:

JUDGMENT

'The trust which the plaintiff has established is clearly an express trust ... which both plaintiff and defendant intended to create. This case is not one in which an equitable obligation arises although there may have been no intention to create a trust. The intention to create a trust existed from the first.'

Lindley LJ

In *Bannister v Bannister* [1948] 2 All ER 133, Scott LJ in the Court of Appeal explained the nature of a fraudulent transaction that would attract the constructive trust. The fraud may involve a transfer of property with the object of defeating the equitable interest or any other occasion when the defendant sets up the absolute nature of the legal title in order to defeat the beneficiary's interest. In any event, in this case the Court of Appeal regarded the *Rochefoucauld* decision as a case involving a constructive trust.

JUDGMENT

'The fraud which brings the principle into play arises as soon as the absolute character of the conveyance is set up for the purpose of defeating the beneficial interest. It is enough that the bargain should have included a stipulation under which some sufficiently defined beneficial interest in the property was to be taken by another.'

Scott LJ

KEY FACTS

Constructive trusts – duty to account

Trustee (fiduciary) making unauthorised profits (to prevent unjust enrichment)	*Keech v Sandford* (1726); *Bray v Ford* (1896); *Boardman v Phipps* (1967); *Banner Homes v Luff* (2000); *Crown Dilmun v Sutton* (2004); *Cobbetts v Hodge* (2009); *Williams v Barton* (1927); *Brudenell-Bruce v Moore* (2014); *Breitenfeld v Harrison* (2015)

Secret profits received by fiduciary	*AG for Hong Kong v Reid* (1994) [contrast *Lister v Stubbs* (1890); *Metropolitan Bank v Heiron* (1880); *Sinclair v Versailles* (2011)]; *Daraydan Holdings v Solland* (2004); *FHR European Ventures v Cedar Partners* (2014)
Pallant v Morgan equity Acquisition of property by killing and the Forfeiture Act 1982	*Pallant v Morgan* (1953); *Banner Homes v Luff* (2000); *Kilcarne Holdings v Targetfollow* (2005); *Generator Development v Lidl* (2016) *Re Crippen* (1911); *Dunbar v Plant* (1997); *Re DWS* (2001); *Chadwick v Collinson* (2014); *Henderson v Wilcox* (2015)
Unauthorised receipt of remuneration by trustee or fiduciary	*Re Macadam* (1946); *Williams v Barton* (1927); *Industrial Developments v Cooley* (1972); *Holder v Holder* (1968); *Murad v Al-Saraj* (2005); *Brudenell-Bruce v Moore* (2014)
Unauthorised purchases of trust property	*Wright v Morgan* (1926); *Regal (Hastings) Ltd v Gulliver* (1942); *Kane v Radley Kane* (1999)
Contracts for the sale of land	*Lysaght v Edwards* (1876)
Equity will not allow a statute to be used as an engine for fraud	*Rochefoucauld v Boustead* (1897); *Hodgson v Marks* (1971)

8.8 Strangers as constructive trustees

8.8.1 Introduction

Generally, third parties, strangers to a trust or agents of the trustees, do not become constructive trustees simply because of a breach of trust committed by the trustees or even a neglect of duties by the agent. The third party may be liable to the trust to pay damages for breach of contract or in the law of tort in accordance with general principles of law.

CASE EXAMPLE

Mara v Browne [1896] 1 Ch 199

A solicitor acting on behalf of the trustees unlawfully invested trust funds on certain mortgages and the trust suffered loss. The court held that the solicitor was not liable as a constructive trustee, though he would have been liable in contract for his negligence had the action not become time-barred.

An agent or stranger to a trust becomes a constructive trustee if he intermeddles with trust property. A person intermeddles in the affairs of a trust if he undertakes the mantle of a trustee. He may do so by assuming the duties of trusteeship or abusing the trust relationship reposed in him in his dealings with the trust property. Lord Selborne in *Barnes v Addy* (1874) LR 9 Ch App 244 identified the categories of constructive trusteeship as follows:

JUDGMENT

'Those who create a trust clothe the trustee with a legal power and control over the trust property, imposing on him a corresponding responsibility. That responsibility may no doubt be extended in equity to others who are not properly trustees, if they are found either making themselves trustees de son tort, or actually participating in any fraudulent conduct of the trustee to the injury of the cestui que trust ... *Strangers are not to be made constructive trustees merely because they act as agents of trustees in transactions within their legal powers,* transactions, perhaps, of which a court of equity may disapprove, unless those agents:

(a) *receive and become chargeable with some part of the trust property; or*
(b) *they assist with knowledge in a dishonest or fraudulent design on the part of the trustees.'*
[Emphasis added]

Lord Selborne in *Barnes v Addy*

CASE EXAMPLE

Barnes v Addy [1874] LR 9 Ch App 244

A solicitor advised the settlement trustees against the appointment of a beneficiary as the sole trustee of a part of the trust funds, but nevertheless prepared the necessary documents. The sole trustee misapplied the property and became bankrupt. An action was brought against a solicitor and the trustees of a trust settlement. The court held that the solicitor was not liable for the loss for he did not receive the trust property but acted honestly and within the course of his authority. The settlement trustees were liable.

trustee *de son tort*

Trustee of his own wrong, or one who intermeddles as a trustee without authority.

Thus, by reference to the judgment of Lord Selbourne, an intermeddler in the affairs of a trust becomes a constructive trustee within one of the following categories:

- a **trustee *de son tort*** (of his own wrongdoing);
- knowingly receiving or dealing with trust property for his own use;
- dishonest assistance or accessory liability (formerly 'knowingly assisting in a fraudulent or dishonest transaction on the part of the trustee/fiduciary').

However, the modern view is that the latter two categories of intermeddlers in the affairs of the trust – knowing recipients and dishonest assisters – are not trustees, not even constructive trustees. They are liable in personal actions to account to the beneficiaries for their wrongful actions. In *Williams v Central Bank of Nigeria* [2014] UKSC 10, Lord Neuberger explained the status of these individuals thus:

JUDGMENT

'It is unreal to refer to a person who receives property dishonestly as a trustee, i.e. a person in whom trust is reposed, given that the trust is said to arise simply as a result of dishonest receipt. Nobody involved, whether the dishonest receiver, the person who passed the property to him, or the claimant, has ever placed any relevant trust and confidence in the recipient ... I conclude that a trustee in s 21(1)(a) [of the Limitation Act 1980] does not include a party who is liable to account in equity simply because he was a dishonest assister and/or a knowing recipient. This is because such a party, while liable to account in the same way as a trustee, is not, according to the law laid down by the courts, a trustee, not even a constructive trustee.'

Lord Neuberger

8.8.2 Trustees *de son tort*

A trustee *de son tort* is a person who has not been appointed a trustee but such a person assumes that he has been validly appointed a trustee and acts in the capacity of a trustee. The phrase was coined on analogy with an executor *de son tort*, i.e. a person who assumes the function of an executor and intermeddles in the estate of a deceased. A trustee *de son tort* undertakes the duties of a trustee and deals with the trust property, not for his own benefit, but on behalf of the beneficiaries. This principle was stated *obiter* by Smith LJ in *Mara v Browne*.

CASE EXAMPLE

Mara v Browne [1896] 1 Ch 199

The case concerned a marriage settlement. The first defendant (HB) was a solicitor. He advised the persons who were acting as trustees, though not yet formally appointed as such. He suggested a series of investments for the trust funds. They were not proper investments for trustees to make. The investments were made and the money was lost. Lord Herschell postulated that, if the claimants had sued HB in negligence and brought the action in time, they might well have succeeded, in which case both HB and his partner would have been liable. But any such action was barred by the Statute of Limitations. Accordingly the claimants alleged that HB had intermeddled with the trust and was liable as a trustee *de son tort*. They alleged that he had laid out the trust moneys at a time when there were no trustees, and therefore must be taken to have acted as a principal in the matter and not as a mere agent for the trustees. Such a claim would not be statute-barred. The trial judge agreed with this analysis and held that both HB and his partner were liable. The Court of Appeal took a different view of the facts. They held that it was not correct to say that at the relevant dates there were no trustees. But even if there had been none, HB would not have been liable. He did not intend or purport to act as a trustee, and no one supposed that he was so acting. He purported to act throughout only as solicitor to the trustees and was understood by all concerned to be acting as such.

JUDGMENT

'[I]t was said that he had made himself a constructive trustee, which, so far as I know, is the same thing as a trustee *de son tort*. Now, what constitutes a trustee *de son tort*? It appears to me if one, not being a trustee and not having authority from a trustee, takes upon himself to intermeddle with trust matters or to do acts characteristic of the office of trustee, he may thereby make himself what is called in law a trustee of his own wrong, i.e. a trustee *de son tort*, or, as it is also termed, a constructive trustee.'

Smith LJ

In *Taylor v Davies* [1920] AC 636, Viscount Cave described a trustee *de son tort* as follows:

JUDGMENT

'[T]hough not originally trustees, [they] had taken upon themselves the custody and administration of property on behalf of others; and though sometimes referred to as constructive trustees, they were, in fact, actual trustees, though not so named.'

Viscount Cave

In *Dubai Aluminium Co v Salaam* [2003] 1 All ER 97, Lord Millett described a trustee *de son tort* thus:

JUDGMENT

'Substituting dog Latin for bastard French, we would do better today to describe such persons as de facto trustees. In their relations with the beneficiaries they are treated in every respect as if they had been duly appointed. They are true trustees and are fully subject to fiduciary obligations. Their liability is strict; it does not depend on dishonesty. Like express trustees they could not plead the Limitation Acts as a defence to a claim for breach of trust.'

Lord Millett

In *Boardman v Phipps* (1967), a solicitor mistakenly believed that he had the permission of all of the beneficiaries to take over a company in which trust shares were held. He was accountable for the profits that he had made, although generous remuneration was awarded to him by the court for his exceptional effort.

8.8.3 Knowingly receiving or dealing with trust property for his own use

The rationale behind the trustee's liability under this head is based on the premise that the stranger or agent has received the trust property with knowledge of the same, before he acts, or fails to act, for his own benefit in a manner inconsistent with the trust. The trust relationship need not necessarily derive from a formal trust, but will exist on a broader basis where there has been a transfer of property to the stranger in breach of fiduciary duties. In effect, the stranger to the trust, if he still has the trust property or its traceable assets under his control, claims a proprietary interest in the subject-matter of the trust and thus attempts to compete with the interests of the beneficiaries. But where the stranger no longer has the property or its product, maybe because the property has been dissipated, or a *bona fide* purchaser of the legal estate for value without notice has acquired the property, the claimant may pursue a personal action against the stranger or fiduciary. This claim will be to compensate the innocent party for the loss suffered. Thus, the claim against the intermeddling stranger under this head may be either proprietary or personal, depending on the circumstances.

In a claim for knowingly receiving trust property for one's own benefit, the claimant is required to prove, first, a disposal of his assets in breach of fiduciary duty; second, the beneficial receipt by the defendant of assets which are traceable as representing the assets of the claimant; and third, knowledge on the part of the defendant that the assets he received are traceable to a breach of fiduciary duty. Thus, liability may arise where the stranger:

- receives trust property knowing that his possession is in breach of trust ('receipt of property constructive trust'); or
- receives trust property initially without knowledge that his acquisition is in breach of trust, but subsequently becomes aware of the existence of the trust and acts in a manner inconsistent with the trust ('wrongful dealing constructive trust').

The elements of liability under this head were stated by Hoffmann LJ in *El Ajou v Dollar Land Holdings* [1994] 2 All ER 685 thus:

JUDGMENT

'[T]he plaintiff must show, first, a disposal of his assets in breach of fiduciary duty; secondly, the beneficial receipt by the defendant of assets which are traceable as representing the assets of the plaintiff; and thirdly, knowledge on the part of the defendant that the assets he received are traceable to a breach of fiduciary duty.'

Hoffmann LJ

CASE EXAMPLE

Belmont Finance Corporation v Williams Furniture & Others (No 2) [1980]
1 All ER 393

Belmont Co, a wholly owned subsidiary of Williams Co, entered into a scheme for the unlawful purchase of its own shares and was subsequently put into receivership. The receiver claimed damages for conspiracy and also sought to recover from the directors as constructive trustees the proceeds of sale which were still traceable. The Court of Appeal held in favour of the receiver on the ground that the participating companies and their directors were liable as constructive trustees. Liability arose by the receipt of trust moneys and the fact that the directors knew of all the circumstances, in particular the unlawfulness of the transaction, and had knowledge or ought to have known that the sum received from the sale of Belmont's shares was trust money. There was no need to prove fraud.

JUDGMENT

'The directors of a limited company are treated as if they were trustees of those funds of the company which are in their hands or under their control, and if they misapply them they commit a breach of trust … So, if the directors of a company in breach of their fiduciary duties misapply the funds of their company so that they come into the hands of some stranger to the trust who receives them with the knowledge (actual or constructive) of the breach, he cannot conscientiously retain those funds against the company unless he has some better equity. He becomes a constructive trustee of the misapplied funds.'

Buckley LJ

Test for 'knowledge'

In *Re Baden Delvaux and Lecuit v Société Générale pour Favoriser le Developpement du Commerce et de l'Industrie en France SA* [1983] BCLC 325, Peter Gibson J, in a lengthy judgment, postulated five categories of 'knowledge':

JUDGMENT

'What types of knowledge are relevant for the purposes of constructive trusteeship? … knowledge can comprise any one of the five different mental states as follows:

(i) actual knowledge;
(ii) wilfully shutting one's eyes to the obvious;
(iii) wilfully and recklessly failing to make such inquiries as an honest and reasonable man would make;
(iv) knowledge of circumstances which would indicate the facts to an honest and reasonable man;
(v) knowledge of circumstances which would put an honest and reasonable man on inquiry.

More accurately, apart from actual knowledge, they are formulations of circumstances which may lead the court to impute knowledge of the facts to the alleged constructive trustee, even though he lacked actual knowledge of those facts.'

Peter Gibson J

The first three categories of knowledge involve a subjective or partly subjective enquiry, whereas categories (iv) and (v) require a purely objective assessment of the circumstances. Actual knowledge within category (i) concerns such facts of which the stranger is aware, positively and consciously. Wilfully shutting one's eyes to the obvious within category (ii) is a common law notion involving abstinence from making enquiries because the defendant knows what the result would entail. Similarly, knowledge within category (iii) embraces circumstances when the defendant foresees or suspects the likelihood of a serious risk of loss of the trust property if reasonable enquiries are not made, but is indifferent as to the consequences of failing to make such enquiries. Knowledge within categories (iv) and (v) involves a wholly objective enquiry in that the reasonable man would have made reasonable enquiries or would have been put on enquiry. The court adopts its own standard in fixing an individual with knowledge within categories (iv) and (v). The effect is that the degree of culpability that is required to make a stranger a constructive trustee within the latter two categories, borders between fraud and negligence. It is arguable that this test is divorced from dishonesty or want of probity, which ought to be the basis of the liability to account. In other words, an innocent failure to make reasonable enquiries is distinct from acting dishonestly, or consciously acting with impropriety.

In a collection of cases the courts had decided on a variety of categories of knowledge in respect of knowingly receiving claims. The traditional notion of knowledge involved any of the *Baden Delvaux* categories. The older cases adopted this solution. Second, a series of cases adopted the idea of subjective knowledge within the first three categories of *Baden*. A third approach drew a distinction between non-commercial and commercial cases. This line of cases decided that in non-commercial transactions, such as family trusts, knowledge within any of the *Baden* categories will suffice, but with regard to commercial transactions subjective knowledge within the first three categories of the *Baden* classification was appropriate. Finally, the current touchstone of liability is now based on a broad-brush test of unconscionability, with knowledge as a key feature of this test.

In accordance with the traditional rationale for liability here, all five types of *Re Baden Delvaux* (1983) knowledge were applicable in order to impose liability on the intermeddling recipient of trust property. Such a view was laid down in a significant number of cases, for liability under this head was treated as restitution based rather than being fault based. In *Nelson v Larholt* (1948), the High Court decided that the defendant was liable as a constructive trustee because he received property belonging to a trust estate with constructive knowledge of the breach of trust, i.e. equivalent to categories (iv) and (v) of the *Baden* classification of knowledge.

CASE EXAMPLE

Nelson v Larholt [1948] 1 KB 339

An executor fraudulently drew eight cheques on the banking account of his testator's estate in favour of the defendant, a turf accountant. The total amount of the sums paid away was £135. The defendant claimed that he was unaware of the lack of authority on the part of the executor. The co-executor and three beneficiaries brought a claim against the defendant for knowingly receiving trust property.

Held: In favour of the claimant. On the facts of this case the inference was irresistible that the defendant knew or ought to have known of the executor's want of authority.

JUDGMENT

'The moneys of the estate were transferred by Potts [the executor] without any authority into the hands of the defendant. Potts had clearly no authority to draw cheques on the bank account for his own purposes. The law will therefore compel the defendant to restore the moneys to the estate unless he received the moneys in good faith and for value and without notice of the want of authority. But did he have notice of the want of authority? That depends on what amounts to notice. *He must, I think, be taken to have known what a reasonable man would have known. If, therefore, he knew or is to be taken to have known of the want of authority, as, for instance, if the circumstances were such as to put a reasonable man on inquiry, and he made none, or if he was put off by an answer that would not have satisfied a reasonable man, or, in other words, if he was negligent in not perceiving the want of authority, then he is taken to have notice of it.*' [Emphasis added]

Denning J

In *Karak Rubber Co Ltd v Burden (No 2)* [1972] 1 All ER 1210, Brightman J referred to the extent of recipient's knowledge as equivalent to either subjective or objective.

JUDGMENT

'[A person] is a constructive trustee because (although not nominated as a trustee) he has received trust property with actual or constructive notice that it is trust property transferred in breach of trust.'

Brightman J

Similarly, in *Agip Ltd v Jackson* [1990] Ch 265, Millett J endorsed the notion of all forms of knowledge in reference to a person who receives trust property for his own benefit as a result of a breach of trust.

JUDGMENT

'He is liable as a constructive trustee if he received it with notice, actual or constructive, that it was trust property and that the transfer to him was a breach of trust.'

Millett J

Likewise, in *International Sales Ltd v Marcus*, the court decided that any form of knowledge (subjective and objective) will be relevant to decide on the liability of the defendant.

CASE EXAMPLE

International Sales and Agencies Ltd v Marcus [1982] 3 All ER 551

The defendant made a personal loan of £30,000 to a major shareholder of the claimant company. After the death of the debtor, a friend and director of the claimant company repaid the loan with the company's funds, to the knowledge of the defendant. The claimant sought to make the defendant a constructive trustee of the funds. The court held in favour of the claimant.

JUDGMENT

'The knowing recipient of trust property for his own purposes will become a constructive trustee of what he receives if either he was in fact aware at the time that his receipt was affected by a breach of trust, or if he deliberately shut his eyes to the real nature of the transfer to him (this could be called imputed notice), or if an ordinary reasonable man in his position and with his attributes ought to have known of the relevant breach. This I equate with constructive notice. Such a position would arise where such a person would have been put on enquiry as to the probability of a breach of trust.'

Lawson J

In *Polly Peck International plc v Nadir and Others (No 2)* [1992] 4 All ER 769, the Court of Appeal applied the restitution-based test of liability and decided that only subjective knowledge within the first three categories of knowledge laid down in *Re Baden Delvaux* (1983) would be sufficient to impose liability on the defendant. On the evidence, the court decided that the recipient bank was not liable for money transferred in breach of trust because there was no evidence that the bank had subjective knowledge of any impropriety.

CASE EXAMPLE

Polly Peck International plc v Nadir and Others (No 2) [1992] 4 All ER 769

The administrators of the claimant's company (PPI) alleged that N and IBK (a bank controlled by him) had misapplied £142 million of PPI's funds. Part of that money had been transferred by the bank to the London account of the fourth defendant, the Central Bank of the Turkish Republic of Northern Cyprus. The Central Bank exercised the supervisory and regulatory role of a central bank in a sovereign state. The claimants contended that either the Central Bank had actual knowledge of the fraudulent scheme or, at best, was put on enquiry as to the impropriety of the scheme. Accordingly, the claimants alleged that the Central Bank was a constructive trustee, requesting a tracing order in respect of some £8.9 million standing to the Central Bank's account at the London clearing bank, and a Mareva injunction (a 'freezing' order) against the Central Bank to protect the £8.9 million. The judge (Millett J) granted the injunction subject to a proviso to enable the Central Bank to carry on its banking business in the normal way. The bank appealed against the order. The Court of Appeal allowed the appeal, discharged the order and held that there was insufficient evidence for finding that the Central Bank had knowledge of the alleged impropriety perpetrated by N and IBK. The tracing claim failed for the same reason.

JUDGMENT

'Liability as constructive trustee in a knowing receipt case does not require that the misapplication of the trust funds should be fraudulent. It does require that the defendant should have knowledge that the funds were trust funds and that they were being misapplied. Actual knowledge obviously will suffice. The various categories of mental state identified in *Re Baden*'s case are not rigid categories with clear and precise boundaries. One category may merge imperceptibly into another.

The real question, however, is whether the circumstances in which the transfers were made should have made the Central Bank suspicious of the propriety of what was being done. Millett J thought so. He thought so because of the sheer scale of the payments.

I find myself unimpressed by the sheer scale argument in so far as it is put forward as a ground for contending that the Central Bank ought to have suspected impropriety. the constructive trust test, the honest and reasonable banker being put on enquiry (if that is indeed the test), postulates inquiry as to whether or not impropriety is being committed. The test is not satisfied by the inference of no more than curiosity.'

Scott LJ

It should be noted that in *Polly Peck International plc v Nadir* the Court of Appeal identified the test of liability under the 'knowingly receiving' head as restitution based. The rationale for imposing liability on the defendant is based on the premise that he has acquired the claimant's property. Dishonesty or want of probity ought not to be the touchstones of liability. The issues in this context are: whether the defendant had acquired the claimant's property, and whether he knows that his acquisition was in breach of trust. The reverse situation, which will entitle the defendant to take free of the claimant's allegation, depends on whether he is a *bona fide* purchaser for value without notice of the breach of trust. Accordingly, 'knowledge' within the first three categories laid down in *Re Baden* will be sufficient to impose liability on the defendant.

In *Carl Zeiss Stiftung v Herbert Smith & Co (No 2)* [1969] 2 Ch 276, the court decided that the claimant failed to establish an equitable interest in the property in the first place and consequently failed in its attempt to make the defendant a constructive trustee. A 'doubtful equity' is insufficient to support a claim under this head.

CASE EXAMPLE

Carl Zeiss Stiftung v Herbert Smith & Co (No 2) [1969] 2 Ch 276

An East German firm, Carl Zeiss, brought a passing-off action against a West German firm of the same name. It was alleged that following the partition of Germany, members of the claimant firm fled to the West and had set up a competing business. Solicitors of the West German firm were paid a sum of money for work done for their clients. The East German firm claimed this money from the solicitors, contending that they had received the sum knowing that the same belonged to the claimant. The court held in favour of the defendants, for the ownership of the assets of the claimant firm was seriously in dispute on reasonable grounds. The solicitors could have no knowledge that the funds belonged to the claimants.

In *Uzinterimpex v Standard Bank* [2008] EWCA Civ 819, the Court of Appeal drew a distinction between cases where money had been paid into a bank account and the recipient of the sum acquired the same in a beneficial capacity, and, in contrast, the occasion when the recipient obtains the funds as an agent for another, i.e. in a ministerial capacity without knowledge of a breach of duty. In the latter case the defendant would not be liable to account for knowingly receiving funds because he did not receive the funds for his own benefit.

JUDGMENT

'It has long been recognised that a distinction is to be drawn between one who receives trust property merely as agent and one who receives it in a beneficial capacity: see *Snell's Equity*, 31st edn para 28–46 which is supported by the dictum of Sir James Bacon V-C in *Lee v Sankey* (1873) LR 15 Eq 204, and the decision of Bennett J in *Williams-Ashman v Price & Williams* [1942] 1 All ER 310. The ground of distinction, as I understand it, is that a person who receives property merely as an agent has no interest of any kind in it himself and must simply account to his principal for it. Receipt by him is the equivalent of receipt by the principal.'

Moore-Bick LJ

8.8.4 Alternative rationale of liability

Megarry VC, in *Re Montagu's Settlement* [1987] Ch 264, reviewed the basis of liability under this head and concluded that 'the constructive trust should not be imposed unless the conscience of the recipient is affected; this depends on knowledge, not notice; want of probity includes actual knowledge, shutting one's eyes to the obvious, or wilfully and recklessly failing to make such inquiries as a reasonable and honest man would make (subjective knowledge or *Baden*'s first 3 categories of knowledge); it does not include knowledge of circumstances which would indicate the facts to an honest and reasonable man or would put the latter on enquiry' (objective knowledge or categories 4 and 5 of *Baden*'s knowledge). In short, the test for knowledge is based only on the first three categories of *Re Baden Delvaux* (1983) knowledge because the basis of liability is dependent on want of probity, which is a subjective notion.

CASE EXAMPLE

Re Montagu's Settlement [1987] Ch 264

Under a subsisting trust, the trustees, on advice from a firm of solicitors, settled chattels in favour of the beneficiary, the tenth Duke of Manchester, absolutely. The transfer was in breach of trust but as a result of an honest mistake on the part of the solicitors and the Duke. The Duke disposed of a number of chattels during his lifetime. After his death, the eleventh Duke claimed that his predecessor had become a constructive trustee of the chattels and was liable to re-transfer the remaining assets (and traceable proceeds of sale of the disposed chattels) and was also personally liable in respect of the value of any assets disposed of and in respect of which the proceeds were not traceable. The court held that the Duke (or his estate) was not personally liable as a constructive trustee because he did not have subjective knowledge of the breach, but was liable to re-transfer to the settlement trustees undisposed trust assets and traceable proceeds as an innocent volunteer.

Megarry VC summarised the following propositions:

JUDGMENT

'(1) The equitable doctrine of tracing and the imposition of a constructive trust by reason of the knowing receipt of trust property are governed by different rules and must be kept distinct. Tracing is primarily a means of determining the rights of property, whereas the imposition of a constructive trust creates personal obligations that go beyond mere property rights.

(2) In considering whether a constructive trust has arisen in a case of the knowing receipt of trust property, the basic question is whether the conscience of the recipient is sufficiently affected to justify the imposition of such a trust.

(3) Whether a constructive trust arises in such a case primarily depends on the knowledge of the recipient, and not on notice to him; and for clarity it is desirable to use the word "knowledge" and avoid the word "notice" in such cases.

(4) For this purpose, knowledge is not confined to actual knowledge, but includes at least knowledge of types (ii) and (iii) in the *Baden* case [1983] BCLC 325, p. 407, i.e. actual knowledge that would have been acquired but for shutting one's eyes to the obvious, or wilfully and recklessly failing to make such inquiries as a reasonable and honest man would make; for in such cases there is a want of probity which justifies imposing a constructive trust.

(5) Whether knowledge of the *Baden* types (iv) and (v) suffices for this purpose is at best doubtful; in my view, it does not, for I cannot see that the carelessness involved will normally amount to a want of probity.

(6) For these purposes, a person is not to be taken to have knowledge of a fact that he once knew but has genuinely forgotten: the test (or a test) is whether the knowledge continues to operate on that person's mind at the time in question.

(7) (a) It is at least doubtful whether there is a general doctrine of "imputed knowledge" that corresponds to "imputed notice".

(b) Even if there is such a doctrine, for the purposes of creating a constructive trust of the "knowing receipt" type the doctrine will not apply so as to fix a donee or beneficiary with all the knowledge that his solicitor has, at all events if the donee or beneficiary has not employed the solicitor to investigate his right to the bounty, and has done nothing else that can be treated as accepting that the solicitor's knowledge should be treated as his own.

(c) Any such doctrine should be distinguished from the process whereby, under the name "imputed knowledge", a company is treated as having the knowledge that its directors and secretary have.

(8) Where an alleged constructive trust is based not on "knowing receipt" but on "knowing assistance", some at least of these considerations probably apply; but I need not decide anything on that, and I do not do so.'

Megarry VC

Likewise, the High Court (Knox J) in *Cowan de Groot Properties Ltd v Eagle Trust* (1992) endorsed the decision of Megarry VC in *Re Montagu*, subject to an element of refinement based on the status of the transaction. In commercial transactions a restricted interpretation of knowledge was needed which was akin to subjective knowledge. This restricted interpretation was introduced by Vinelott J in *Eagle Trust v SBC Securities* [1992] 4 All ER 488 in the context of an application to strike out a knowingly receiving claim. In *Cowan de Groot* the court decided that a stranger to a trust cannot be made liable as a constructive trustee unless he acted with 'knowledge' (categories (i) to (iii) in the *Baden* case) that his conduct was inconsistent with the trust. This was the extent of knowledge, at the very least, in respect of commercial transactions. The basis of liability under this head, in Knox J's view, was impropriety or want of probity. Accordingly, on a counterclaim by the defendant, the court decided that the claimant was not a constructive trustee under the 'knowingly receiving' category.

CASE EXAMPLE

Cowan de Groot Properties Ltd v Eagle Trust plc [1992] 4 All ER 700, HC

E plc agreed to sell three properties for a total of £900,000 to Pinepad Ltd (P Ltd) (a 100 per cent subsidiary of C Ltd) and to grant an option to purchase two other properties to P Ltd. Prior to the completion of the sale, E sought to rescind the whole agreement. Shortly thereafter, P purported to exercise the option. In various stages P sold on the three properties to C Ltd. C now brought an action against E, claiming a declaration that the notice exercising the option was valid and effective. E counterclaimed, maintaining that the agreement was defective and that P or C was liable as constructive trustee of the properties and proceeds of sale, on the ground of 'knowing receipt'. It was alleged by E that two of its directors acted fraudulently in bringing about the sale, and that C's managing director (Mr Samuelson) knew of the fraudulent breach. It was alleged that Mr Samuelson knew (subjectively within categories (i) to (iii) of *Baden*'s case) of the undervalue at which the properties were sold. In the alternative, that P Ltd or C Ltd had objective knowledge (categories (iv) and (v) in *Baden*'s case) of the impropriety.

Held: The constructive trust claim failed. C's managing director did not, on the facts, have subjective knowledge of fraudulent conduct of E's directors. The duty of directors of a purchasing company was to purchase the property as cheaply as they possibly could. It was reasonable for C's managing director to assume that E was looking for a quick sale and had no time to market the property efficiently. Objective notice was not relevant to found a claim in commercial transactions based on the 'knowingly receiving' category of constructive trust. Alternatively, if objective knowledge was relevant in such a claim, there was insufficient evidence to support the contention that C's managing director acted in a commercially disreputable manner.

JUDGMENT

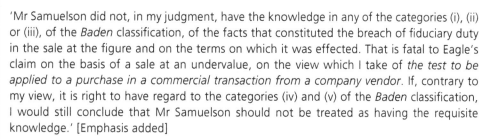

'Mr Samuelson did not, in my judgment, have the knowledge in any of the categories (i), (ii) or (iii), of the *Baden* classification, of the facts that constituted the breach of fiduciary duty in the sale at the figure and on the terms on which it was effected. That is fatal to Eagle's claim on the basis of a sale at an undervalue, on the view which I take of *the test to be applied to a purchase in a commercial transaction from a company vendor*. If, contrary to my view, it is right to have regard to the categories (iv) and (v) of the *Baden* classification, I would still conclude that Mr Samuelson should not be treated as having the requisite knowledge.' [Emphasis added]

Knox J

Judicial support for Megarry VC's view followed in a spate of other High Court decisions, including *Barclays Bank v Quincecare Ltd* [1992] 4 All ER 363 and *Lipkin Gorman v Karpnale* [1992] 4 All ER 363.

In summary, prior to the decision of the Court of Appeal in *BCCI v Akindele* (2000) (see below), there were at least three judicial approaches on the extent of knowledge that was necessary to impose liability on a knowing recipient:

1. any of the categories of *Baden* knowledge, see *Karak v Burden* (1990), *Agip v Jackson* (1990);

2. subjective knowledge within categories (i), (ii) and (iii) of *Baden*'s knowledge, see *Re Montagu* (1987);

3. subjective knowledge within *Baden*'s first three categories but only in respect of commercial transactions, see *Cowan de Groot v Eagle Trust* (1992), *Polly Peck v Nadir (No. 2)*. In respect of non-commercial transactions, any form of knowledge will be sufficient, see *obiter* in *Eagle Trust v SBC Securities* (1992).

In the Court of Appeal decision of *BCCI v Akindele* [2000] 3 WLR 1423, Nourse LJ reviewed the law with regard to liability under the head of knowingly receiving trust property. He was sympathetic with the rationale of liability adopted by Megarry VC in *Re Montagu* [1987], which he considered a seminal judgment. In *Montagu*, Megarry VC observed that the constructive trust should not be imposed unless the conscience of the recipient was affected. In this context, the Court of Appeal rejected the series of authorities that ground liability on the basis of knowledge simpliciter (whether subjective and objective or solely subjective). Instead, a different and broader test of liability based on the unconscionable conduct of the defendant will be adopted. The focus of attention should not be on knowledge or even the categorisation of knowledge, but on the conscience of the defendant. What was necessary was that the recipient's state of knowledge should be such as to make it unconscionable for him to retain the benefit of the receipt. The effect is that, in Nourse LJ's view, liability under this head is based on unconscionability, as evidenced by actual or subjective knowledge on the part of the defendant that the assets received were linked to a breach of trust. He equated liability under this head with accessory liability and doubted the utility of the five categories of knowledge laid down by Peter Gibson J in *Re Baden Delvaux* [1983]. Nourse LJ rejected the test of dishonesty and identified the basis of liability under this head as involving the conscience of the defendant, i.e. 'whether the defendant's state of knowledge is such as to make it unconscionable for him to retain the property'.

CASE EXAMPLE

BCCI v Akindele [2000] 3 WLR 1423

The defendant received $6.68 million in 1988 as profit on a payment of $10 million he had paid to the bank in 1985 under an artificial loan agreement. The transaction involved a fraudulent breach of fiduciary duties owed to the bank. It was found that the defendant had no subjective knowledge of the frauds at the time of the transaction. The claimants contended that the defendant was liable to account to them for $6.79 million as a constructive trustee. The Court of Appeal dismissed the claim on the ground that the test for liability for knowing receipt cases is whether a recipient could conscientiously retain the funds as against the company. Just as there is now a single test of dishonesty for knowing assistance, so ought there to be a single test of knowledge for knowing receipt cases. Further, it was debatable whether the fivefold categorisation of knowledge laid down by Peter Gibson J in *Re Baden Delvaux* (1983) was of any use in knowing receipt cases. The material date for determining the defendant's state of knowledge was 1985, the date of the agreement. Additional knowledge that he acquired between 1985 and 1987, press rumours of irregularities involving BCCI, warnings to him from business figures in Nigeria and him becoming aware of the arrest of BCCI officials in connection with money laundering did not make it unconscionable for him to retain the receipt. The additional knowledge went to the general reputation of BCCI. It was not sufficient to question the propriety of the 1985 transaction.

JUDGMENT

'The question is whether the recipient must have actual knowledge (or the equivalent) that the assets received are traceable to a breach of trust or whether constructive knowledge is enough. The instinctive approach of most equity judges, especially in this court, has been to assume that constructive knowledge is enough. But there is now a series of decisions of eminent first instance judges who, after considering the question in greater depth, have come to the contrary conclusion, at all events when commercial transactions are in point.

I have come to the view that, just as there is now a single test of dishonesty for knowing assistance, so ought there to be a single test of knowledge for knowing receipt. *The recipient's state of knowledge must be such as to make it unconscionable for him to retain the benefit of the receipt.* A test in that form, though it cannot, any more than any other, avoid difficulties of application, ought to avoid those of definition and allocation to which the previous categorisations [in *Baden Delvaux*] have led. Moreover, it should better enable the courts to give commonsense decisions in the commercial context in which claims in knowing receipt are now frequently made.' [Emphasis added]

Nourse LJ

The *Akindele* principle has the added attraction of a simple formulation of the requirements for liability for knowing receipt. Dishonesty has been rejected as a requirement; likewise knowledge as a fundamental basis of liability has also been rejected. Rather than considering various types of knowledge and consequential judicial inconsistencies, the *Akindele* principle has the merit of introducing a single test of unconscionability. The knowledge of the recipient is required such as to make it unconscionable for him to retain the benefit of the receipt. The idea of unconscionability is therefore linked to the extent of knowledge of the defendant and the issue is whether the defendant has such knowledge of the circumstances so as to make his retention or dealing with the property unconscionable. This is a question of law for the court to decide.

Lord Nicholls, in an extra-judicial statement entitled 'Knowing receipt: the need for a new landmark' (in W R Cornish, R Nolan, J O'Sullivan and G Virgo (eds), *Restitution Past, Present and Future: Essays in Honour of Gareth Jones*, Hart, 1998), advocated a principle of strict liability subject to the defence of change of position as the proposed test of liability in this context.

JUDGMENT

'In this respect equity should now follow the law. Restitutionary liability, applicable regardless of fault but subject to a defence of change of position, would be a better-tailored response to the underlying mischief of misapplied property than personal liability which is exclusively fault-based. Personal liability would flow from having received the property of another, from having been unjustly enriched at the expense of another. It would be triggered by the mere fact of receipt, thus recognising the endurance of property rights. But fairness would be ensured by the need to identify a gain, and by making change of position available as a default in suitable cases when, for instance, the recipient had changed his position in reliance on the receipt.'

Lord Nicholls in *Royal Brunei Airlines v Tan* [1995] 2 AC 378

However, Nourse LJ in *BCCI v Akindele* doubted whether, in this context, strict liability coupled with the defence of change of position would be preferable to fault-based liability:

JUDGMENT

'I beg leave to doubt whether strict liability coupled with a change of position defence would be preferable to fault-based liability in many commercial transactions, for example where, as here, the receipt is of a company's funds which have been misapplied by its directors. Without having heard argument it is unwise to be dogmatic, but in such a case it would appear to be commercially unworkable and contrary to the spirit of the rule in *Royal British Bank v Turquand* (1856) 6 El & Bl 327, [1843–60] All ER Rep 435, that, simply on proof of an internal misapplication of the company's funds, the burden should shift to the recipient to defend the receipt either by a change of position or perhaps in some other way.'

Nourse LJ

In *Charter plc v City Index* [2008] 3 All ER 126 (see later) the issue involved a contribution between one knowing recipient and another. Carnwath LJ endorsed the principle laid down in *Akindele*:

JUDGMENT

'City Index's liability to Charter does not depend solely on receipt of the money paid in breach of trust, but on their retaining it or paying it away in circumstances where it would be unconscionable to do so. Although the directors' legal duty arose at an earlier stage, it was only when City failed to return the money that Charter suffered any loss.'

Carnwath LJ

In the decision, *Armstrong v Winnington Networks Ltd* (2012), the High Court endorsed the *Akindele* principle and decided that the test of unconscionability was satisfied on the facts. The recipient of a chose in action had deliberately closed its eyes (Nelsonian knowledge) to the risk that the vendor may not have the authority to sell the asset in question. Accordingly, he had knowledge of the impropriety and thus it would have been unconscionable to retain the property.

CASE EXAMPLE

Armstrong v Winnington Networks Ltd [2012] EWHC 10

The claimant company (Armstrong GmbH) instituted proceedings against the defendant company (Winnington) in restitution and knowing receipt as a result of a fraudulent transfer of carbon emission allowances (EUAs). EUAs were regarded as choses in action. Armstrong operated two factories in Germany and had been credited with EUAs which were held in an account with the German registry. Winnington traded in EUAs and was contacted by a third party (Zen), offering to sell EUAs. Winnington became interested in purchasing the EUAs from this third party. Armstrong's user name and password were obtained by fraud and the EUAs were transferred from Armstrong's account in Germany to Winnington's account in the UK. When the fraud was discovered, Armstrong commenced restitutionary proceedings against Winnington, including a claim for knowingly receiving trust property. The High Court decided in favour of the claimant company, Armstrong. The defendant, Winnington, had knowingly received trust property belonging to the claimant. The receipt of the EUAs was unconscionable because the defendant had deliberately closed its eyes to the risk that the third party might not have had the authority to sell the asset.

JUDGMENT

'Despite what the Court of Appeal said in the *Akindele* case, the *Baden* classification is still useful for the purpose of determining what kind of knowledge makes it unconscionable for the defendant to retain the trust property. In my judgment, the position, in a commercial context, can be summarised as follows: (1) *Baden* types (1) to (3) knowledge on the part of a defendant render receipt of trust property 'unconscionable'. (2) Further, *Baden* types (4) and (5) knowledge also render receipt "unconscionable" but only if, on the facts actually known to this defendant, a reasonable person would either have appreciated that the transfer was probably in breach of trust or would have made inquiries or sought advice which would have revealed the probability of the breach of trust.

I conclude that the state of Winnington's knowledge of the relevant circumstances was such as to render its receipt of the EUAs unconscionable. Whilst I accept that no one at Winnington had actual knowledge of the fraud nor that the EUAs were stolen, I am satisfied that the relevant personnel at Winnington were actually aware that there was a possibility that Zen did not have title to, or authority to sell, the EUAs and they consciously and deliberately closed their eyes to that risk or possibility.'

Stephen Morris QC

8.8.5 Dishonest assistance or accessory liability

Under the head of accessory liability, the defendant (alleged constructive trustee) does not acquire control of the property, but merely assists in a dishonest breach of trust. He is under a duty to account and, strictly, he ought not to be labelled a constructive trustee, for liability is personal and not *in rem*. Provided that the defendant is solvent, there are no difficulties. But if the defendant is insolvent, the classification of his status will have important consequences. A proprietary remedy (tracing process) may subsist even though the defendant is insolvent. The same applies to the limitation period. The assertion of a right *in rem* is not subject to limitation periods. Millett LJ in *Paragon Finance v Thakerar* (1999) made reference to the importance of adopting the correct classification of this principle and declared that since the fiduciary defendant does not obtain control of the relevant property he is only liable to account:

JUDGMENT

'The expressions constructive trust and constructive trustee have been used by equity lawyers to describe two entirely different situations. The first covers those cases where the defendant, though not expressly appointed as trustee, has assumed the duties of a trustee by a lawful transaction which was independent of and preceded the breach of trust and is not impeached by the plaintiff. The second covers those cases where the trust obligation arises as a direct consequence of the unlawful transaction which is impeached by the plaintiff.

A constructive trust arises by operation of law whenever the circumstances are such that it would be unconscionable for the owner of property (usually but not necessarily the legal estate) to assert his own beneficial interest in the property and deny the beneficial interest of another. In the first class of case, however, the constructive trustee really is a trustee. He does not receive the trust property in his own right but by a transaction by which both parties intend to create a trust from the outset and which is not impugned by the plaintiff. In these cases the plaintiff alleges that the circumstances in which the defendant obtained control make it unconscionable for him thereafter to assert a beneficial interest in the property.

The second class of case is different [see *AG for Hong Kong v Reid* [1993] 3 WLR 1143]. It arises when the defendant is implicated in a fraud. Equity has always given relief against fraud by making any person sufficiently implicated in the fraud accountable in equity. In such a case he is traditionally, though I think unfortunately, described as a constructive trustee and said to be liable to account as a constructive trustee. Such a person is not in fact a trustee at all, even though he may be liable to account as if he were. He never assumes the position of a trustee, and if he receives the trust property at all it is adversely to the plaintiff by an unlawful transaction which is impugned by the plaintiff. In such a case the expressions constructive trust and constructive trustee are misleading, for there is no trust and usually no possibility of a proprietary remedy; they are nothing more than a formula of equitable relief.'

Millett LJ

Likewise, in *Dubai Aluminium Co v Salaam* [2003] 1 All ER 97, Lord Millett considered the way in which equitable relief against fraud is sometimes inaccurately expressed by judges. It is traditionally stated that a dishonest assistant is accountable in equity as a constructive trustee, but in reality he is not a trustee. In reality he does not claim to be a trustee or act on behalf of beneficiaries. In this respect the accessory does not become a fiduciary, although he commits an equitable wrong and is liable to account for the profit made. Lord Millett expressed his opinion in the following manner:

JUDGMENT

'[A dishonest assistant] is traditionally (and I have suggested unfortunately) described as a constructive trustee and is said to be liable to account as a constructive trustee. But he is *not in fact a trustee at all, even though he may be liable to account as if he were.* He never claims to assume the position of trustee on behalf of others, and *he may be liable without ever receiving or handling the trust property.* If he receives the trust property at all he receives it adversely to the claimant and by an unlawful transaction which is impugned by the claimant. He is not a fiduciary or subject to fiduciary obligations; and he could plead the Limitation Acts as a defence to the claim.' [Emphasis added]

Lord Millett

It was stated by Lord Millett in *Dubai*'s case that in the case of 'knowing assistance' ('accessory' liability) it is not a prerequisite of liability that the assistant or accessory receive or handle property belonging to another. The issue is whether the dishonest assistant or accessory provides assistance to someone else who is a fiduciary and has committed a breach of fiduciary duties. The basis of the claim against the accessory is that he committed an equitable wrong by dishonestly lending assistance to another which results in a breach of fiduciary duties owed to the beneficiaries. Thus, it is irrelevant whether the breach by the accessory involves a misapplication of trust funds.

In his judgment in *Sinclair Investment Holdings v Versailles Trade Finance Ltd* [2007] EWHC 915 (Ch), Rimer J, after referring to Millett LJ's judgment in *Paragon*, adopted the personal remedy for the dishonest accessory:

JUDGMENT

'The importance of that passage [in *Paragon*] is, first, that it is concerned with a case such as the present in which Mr Cushnie was a dishonest party to a breach of a trust of which he was not a trustee. Secondly, it confirms that even though it has become traditional to describe such a wrongdoer as a constructive trustee, he is not in fact a trustee at all, and the formula is nothing more than one intended to indicate that equitable relief will or may be available against him by reason of his participation in the breach. It is not a formula which, once applied, has the effect of turning the wrongdoer into an actual trustee.'

Rimer J

This head of liability was formerly known as 'knowingly assisting in a fraudulent or dishonest transaction on the part of the trustee/fiduciary'. This was the original basis on which the test of liability was presented by Lord Selborne in *Barnes v Addy* (1874) (see above) but in the leading case of *Royal Brunei Airlines v Tan* [1995] 2 AC 378, Lord Nicholls reviewed the law concerning 'accessory liability'. He opined that the liability of a third party who assisted a trustee to commit a breach of trust is dependent on the state of mind of the third party and is fault based. Dishonesty on the part of the third party is an essential ingredient of liability, irrespective of the state of mind of the trustee who committed the breach of trust. The trustee will be liable in any event for breach of trust, even if he acted innocently, unless he is relieved by the court or is protected by an exclusion clause in the trust instrument. Dishonesty on the part of the trustee is, however, not a prerequisite in order to attach liability to the dishonest third party.

8.8.6 *Royal Brunei v Tan* analysis

The leading authority under this head is now *Royal Brunei v Tan* (1995). In this case the Privy Council reviewed the authorities and concluded that the test of liability is dishonesty. In addition, there is no precondition for the liability of the defendant to establish that the trustee was fraudulent.

CASE EXAMPLE

Royal Brunei Airlines v Tan [1995] 2 AC 378

The claimant appointed a travel agent, Borneo Leisure Travel (BLT), to act as its general travel agent for the sale of passenger and cargo transportation. BLT was required to account to the claimant for all amounts received from such sales. In breach of trust, sums received were not paid into a separate account, but were paid into BLT's current account and used for its own purposes. The defendant was BLT's managing director and principal shareholder. BLT's payments fell into arrears and the claimant terminated the agreement. The company later became insolvent. The claimant commenced an action against the defendant claiming an account in respect of the unpaid money. This claim was based on the second limb of Lord Selborne's dictum in *Barnes v Addy* (1874): 'strangers are not to be made constructive trustees merely because they act as the agents of trustees in transactions … unless they assist with knowledge in a dishonest and fraudulent design on the part of the trustees'. The question in issue was whether the breach of trust, which was a prerequisite to liability, had to be a dishonest and fraudulent breach of trust by the trustee. The Privy Council allowed the claim on the ground that a stranger to a trust is liable to make good resulting loss if he dishonestly procured or assisted in a breach of trust or fiduciary obligation. It was not a prerequisite of that liability that, in addition, the trustee or fiduciary acted dishonestly.

JUDGMENT

'What matters is the state of mind of the third party sought to be made liable, not the state of mind of the trustee. The trustee will be liable in any event for the breach of trust, even if he acted innocently, unless excused by an exemption clause in the trust instrument or relieved by the court. But his state of mind is essentially irrelevant to the question whether the third party should be made liable to the beneficiaries for the breach of trust. If the liability of the third party is fault-based, what matters is the nature of his fault, not that of the trustee. In this regard dishonesty on the part of the third party would seem to be a sufficient basis for his liability, irrespective of the state of mind of the trustee who is in breach of trust. *The next step is to seek to identify the touchstone of liability. By common accord, dishonesty fulfils this role* … their Lordships' overall conclusion is that dishonesty is a necessary ingredient of accessory liability. It is also a sufficient ingredient. A liability in equity to make good resulting loss attaches to a person who dishonestly procures or assists in a breach of trust or fiduciary obligation. Knowingly is better avoided as a defining ingredient of the principle, and in the context of this principle the *Baden* … scale of knowledge is best forgotten.'

Lord Nicholls of Birkenhead

It may be concluded that the decision in *Tan* altered the conditions that must be satisfied before accessory liability can be established, but did not alter the nature of the liability. The nature of the liability is that a dishonest assistant (like a knowing recipient) has the responsibility of an express trustee and that responsibility includes the liability to account.

The elements of liability, in order to successfully pursue a dishonest assistance claim, have been identified by Mance LJ in *Grupo Torras v Al Sabah* [1999] CLC 1469, as involving the following ingredients:

1. a breach of trust or fiduciary duty by someone other than the defendant;
2. assistance by the defendant;
3. the existence of a dishonest or fraudulent design of a third party concerning the trust property;
4. dishonesty on the part of the defendant;
5. resulting loss suffered by the claimant.

Breach of trust

In relation to the first element, the trust need not be a formal express trust. The trust may be resulting or constructive. What is required is the existence of a fiduciary relationship that is linked to the claimant's property. A fiduciary is one who is aware that his confidence and judgment is relied on (and this is, in fact, relied on) by another. Thus, bankers, directors and agents may stand in a fiduciary relationship to their customers, companies or principals.

Assistance

In connection with the second requirement, the defendant is required to assist a third party without acquiring control of the property. It may well be that the third party has control over the trust property, but the issue here is whether the defendant has rendered assistance to the third party that materially assists in the commission of the fraud. The expression 'assistance' assumes any act (including an omission when there is a duty to act) effected by the stranger which enables the trustee to commit a fraudulent breach of trust. Whether this element is satisfied or not is a question of fact. To render assistance as an accessory to a dishonest breach of trust transaction, the defendant is required to lend assistance in the knowledge of, or belief in, the existence of the trust, and the knowledge that his or her assistance will facilitate the breach of trust. In *Brinks v Abu-Saleh* (1995) the claim against Mrs Elcombe failed on this ground.

CASE EXAMPLE

Brinks Ltd v Abu-Saleh and Others (No 3), The Times, 23 October 1995, HC

Brinks Ltd suffered a bullion robbery in 1983 when gold and other valuables worth some £26 million were stolen from its warehouse at Heathrow. In order to recover the proceeds, it brought civil proceedings against 57 defendants who were allegedly involved in the robbery and subsequent laundering operations. One of the defendants was Mrs Elcombe. It was alleged that, between August 1984 and February 1985, she assisted her husband, the twelfth defendant, in the part he played in laundering part of the proceeds of the stolen gold by carrying approximately £3 million in cash to Mr Parry, one of the convicted robbers, from England to Zurich by car.

In dismissing the claim, Rimer J decided that:

(i) Mrs Elcombe went on the trips in the capacity of Mr Elcombe's wife. Her presence on such trips did not constitute 'assistance' in furtherance of a breach of trust.
(ii) The claim based on accessory liability could only be brought against someone who knew of the existence of the trust, or at least of the facts giving rise to the trust, and dishonestly rendered assistance in pursuance of a design intended to defeat the trust. It was not proved that Mrs Elcombe was aware that the funds in question were the proceeds of the robbery, as distinct from a tax evasion exercise.

Fraudulent or dishonest venture

With regard to the third element, no distinction is drawn between the words 'fraudulent' and 'dishonest'. They mean the same thing. But the words are to be construed in accordance with principles of equitable relief. Thus, conduct which is morally reprehensible can be said to be dishonest and fraudulent. Accordingly, not every breach of trust will satisfy this requirement, for a breach of trust falling short of dishonesty or fraud would be insufficient to create liability under this head. Fraud, in this context, involves the taking of a risk which the stranger honestly knows that he has no right to take and which is prejudicial to another's right.

Lord Nicholls, in *Royal Brunei Airlines v Tan* (1995) (see below), declared that, in order to decide whether a person is dishonest, the court is required to look at all the circumstances known to the defendant. This would require the court to have regard to the personal attributes of the defendant, such as his experience, intelligence and possible explanations for his actions. The court decided that a dishonest third party who assisted a trustee, or procured him to commit a breach of trust, was liable to the beneficiaries for the resulting loss. It was not necessary to prove, in addition, that the trustee's conduct was dishonest or fraudulent.

In *Heinl v Jayske Bank (Gibraltar)*, *The Times*, 28 September 1999, the Court of Appeal decided that the standard of proof for dishonestly assisting in breaches of fiduciary duties exceeds a balance of probabilities, but is not as high as beyond a reasonable doubt. It is submitted that this test as to the standard of proof is excessive, unnecessary and lacks authority.

Resulting loss suffered by the claimant

The requirement here is the need for a causal connection between the wrong committed by the accessory (dishonest assistance) and the loss suffered by the claimant. Unlike the breach of fiduciary duties, the test here is a sufficient direct causal connection between the assistance and the profit. This is not the simple 'but for' test that is applicable to breaches of fiduciary duties. Instead, the courts apply the common law rules of causation and remoteness of damage by analogy with breaches of trustees' duties of care and skill.

On the other hand, in the case of a fiduciary who has committed a breach of fiduciary duties, such as the receipt of secret profits, the broader 'but for' test of causation is applicable to the transaction. The reason is that the core duty imposed on the fiduciary is the single minded loyalty to his beneficiary or principal. Thus, the breach of duty does not consist in the making of a profit by the fiduciary, but in the retention of such profit for his benefit. In short, an abuse of the trust and confidence reposed in him by the settlor or principal. The response of equity was to enforce the duty rather than to award equitable compensation or damages.

Thus, the question as to whether a narrower, 'direct cause' test, or the broader 'but for' test is applicable to breaches of duties is dependent on whether the breach was committed by a non-fiduciary or fiduciary. In *Novoship (UK) Ltd v Nikitin and Others* [2014] EWCA 908, the Court of Appeal decided that in respect of accessory liability, a direct substantive, causal link between the breach and profit was required to be established.

CASE EXAMPLE

Novoship (UK) Ltd v Nikitin and Others [2014] EWCA 908

Mr Mikhaylyuk (M) was employed as a general manager in Novoship (UK) (NOUK). M's duties included negotiating the charter of vessels owned by NOUK Group. In a series of schemes M acted in a corrupt and dishonest manner in defrauding the claimants and enriching himself and others. These schemes involved bribes to Mr Nikitin (N) and his company in order to charter vessels. The issues in this case were *inter alia*, whether the remedy of account of profits was available against a dishonest assistant (N) as opposed to a fiduciary and, if so, whether there was a requirement of a causal connection between the dishonest assistance and the profit made by N. The trial judge decided both questions in favour of the claimant. On appeal the court decided that the remedy of account was available against a dishonest accessory, subject to the remedy not being disproportionate, but there was an insufficient link between the bribe and the profits generated by N's efforts.

JUDGMENT

'We conclude that the remedy of an account of profits is available against one who dishonestly assists a fiduciary to breach his fiduciary obligations, even if that breach does not involve a misapplication of trust property.

Where a claim based on equitable wrongdoing is made against one who is not a fiduciary, we consider that … there is no reason why the common law rules of causation, remoteness and measure of damages should not be applied by analogy. We recognize that these rules do not apply to the case of a fiduciary sued for breach of a fiduciary duty.

We would therefore hold that there was an insufficient direct causal connection between entry into the Henriot charters and the resulting profits. We must stress, however, that had Mr Nikitin been a true fiduciary, and had entry into the Henriot charters been a breach of fiduciary duty, then the causation test we have adopted would not have applied.'

Longmore LJ

8.8.7 Dishonesty

In *Royal Brunei Airlines v Tan* (1995), Lord Nicholls considered that in place of the morally neutral and vague concept of knowledge, dishonesty was to be the touchstone of liability for dishonest assistance claims. His view is that dishonesty, or lack of probity, which is synonymous, meant not acting as an honest person would in the circumstances, judged on an objective basis.

JUDGMENT

'[A]cting dishonestly … means simply not acting as an honest person would in the circumstances. This is an objective standard … *Honesty has a connotation of subjectivity, as distinct from the objectivity of negligence … Honesty is a description of a type of conduct assessed in the light of what a person actually knew at the time, as distinct from what a reasonable person would have known or appreciated.* Further, honesty and its counterpart dishonesty are mostly concerned with advertent conduct, not inadvertent conduct. Carelessness is not dishonesty. Thus for the most part dishonesty is to be equated with conscious impropriety.

However, these subjective characteristics of honesty do not mean that individuals are free to set their own standards of honesty in particular circumstances. The standard of what constitutes honest conduct is not subjective. Honesty is not an optional scale, with higher or lower values according to the moral standards of each individual. If a person knowingly appropriates another's property, he will not escape a finding of dishonesty simply because he sees nothing wrong in such behaviour … to decide whether a person was acting honestly a court will look at all the circumstances known to the third party at the time. The court will also have regard to personal attributes of the third party such as his experience and intelligence and the reason why he acted as he did.' [Emphasis added]

Lord Nicholls

In 2002, the House of Lords in *Twinsectra Ltd v Yardley* considered the standards that are required to be adopted in order to determine whether the defendant has acted dishonestly. The Law Lords treated the opinion of Lord Nicholls in *Royal Brunei Airlines v Tan* (1995) as definitive and subjected his speech to detailed analysis. The Law Lords considered that there were three possible standards by which a person's dishonesty may be judged – purely subjectively, purely objectively, and a combination of objectivity and subjectivity. The majority of the Law Lords (Lord Millett dissenting) rejected the first two standards and decided in favour of the combined standard. The purely subjective standard was rejected for it would have been impractical for the defendant to set his own standards of honesty. The purely objective standard (which appealed to Lord Millett) was rejected by the majority of the Law Lords on the basis that dishonesty involves an element of subjectivity. The personal attributes of the defendant ought to be taken into account. The majority of the Law Lords adopted the criminal law test for dishonesty (as laid down by Lord Lane CJ in *R v Ghosh* [1982] QB 1053), namely the defendant's conduct is dishonest by reference to the ordinary standards of reasonable and honest people and that he himself realised that his conduct was dishonest by those standards.

CASE EXAMPLE

Twinsectra Ltd v Yardley [2002] UKHL 12, HL

Mr Leach (L), the second defendant, was a solicitor. He acted for an entrepreneur, Mr Yardley (Y), in a transaction involving a loan of £1 million from Twinsectra Ltd. L did not deal directly with Twinsectra. Another firm of solicitors, Sims (S), acted on behalf of Y. S received the money in return for an undertaking to the effect that the fund would be applied solely in the acquisition of a specified property. Contrary to the undertaking, S did not retain the money, but paid it over to L. The latter in turn took no steps to ensure that it was utilised for the stated purpose but simply paid it out upon Y's instructions. The result was that £357,700 was used by Y for purposes other than the acquisition of property. Twinsectra suffered loss and sued all the parties involved, including L. The claim against him was based on dishonestly assisting S in a breach of trust. The trial judge made a significant finding to the effect that L did not act dishonestly (but was misguided) in receiving the money and paying it to Y without concerning himself about its application. The issue before the House of Lords was whether L was liable for dishonestly assisting S in a fraudulent breach of trust. The court decided that the claim did not succeed, on the following grounds:

(a) (Lord Millett dissenting) In determining whether a defendant acted dishonestly under accessorial liability a combined objective/subjective test was applicable. The test requires the claimant to prove that the defendant was (i) dishonest by the ordinary standards of reasonable and honest people (objective) and (ii) that he himself realised that his conduct was dishonest by those standards (subjective).

(b) A reversal of the decision of the trial judge on a question of fact may only be done in exceptional circumstances. On the facts there was sufficient evidence to indicate that the trial judge had not misdirected himself as to the appropriate test for dishonesty.

JUDGMENT

'Whatever may be the position in some criminal or other contexts (see, for instance, *R v Ghosh* [1982] QB 1053), in the context of the accessory liability principle acting dishonestly, or with a lack of probity, which is synonymous, means simply not acting as an honest person would in the circumstances. This is an objective standard. Further, Lord Nicholls in *Tan* said: Ultimately, in most cases, an honest person should have little difficulty in knowing whether a proposed transaction, or his participation in it, would offend the normally accepted standards of honest conduct.

The use of the word "knowing" in the first sentence would be superfluous if the defendant did not have to be aware that what he was doing would offend the normally accepted standards of honest conduct, and the need to look at the experience and intelligence of the defendant would also appear superfluous if all that was required was a purely objective standard of dishonesty. Therefore I do not think that Lord Nicholls was stating that in this sphere of equity a man can be dishonest even if he does not know that what he is doing would be regarded as dishonest by honest people.'

Lord Hutton

In the same case (*Twinsectra*) Lord Millett dissented in respect of the standard applicable to dishonesty. His interpretation of the standard laid down by Lord Nicholls in *Tan* concerned an objective test with an element of subjectivity in that the expertise of the defendant will be taken into consideration in order to increase the standard.

JUDGMENT

'In my opinion Lord Nicholls [in *Tan*] was adopting an objective standard of dishonesty by which the defendant is expected to attain the standard which would be observed by an honest person placed in similar circumstances. Account must be taken of subjective considerations such as the defendant's experience and intelligence and his actual state of knowledge at the relevant time. But it is not necessary that he should actually have appreciated that he was acting dishonestly; it is sufficient that he was.'

Lord Millett

In *Satnam v Heywood* [1999] 3 All ER 652, the Court of Appeal decided that in order to make a third party liable as a constructive trustee, a link has to be established between a profit made by the third party and confidential information obtained from a fiduciary.

CASE EXAMPLE

Satnam v Heywood [1999] 3 All ER 652

Satnam Investments (S Ltd), a property development company, acquired an option to purchase a site with development potential. The site owners were entitled to terminate the option if S Ltd went into receivership. S Ltd was placed into receivership by its banks. Shortly afterwards Dunlop Heywood Ltd (H Ltd), a company of surveyors which had acted for S Ltd in respect of the site, made unauthorised disclosures of confidential information to Morbaine Ltd (M Ltd), a rival development company. After receiving the information M Ltd sought to acquire an interest in the site. The owners of the site terminated S Ltd's option and sold the site to M Ltd. After the discharge of the receivers, S Ltd brought proceedings against H Ltd and M Ltd contending that H Ltd had breached its fiduciary obligations by disclosing the information to M Ltd and that M Ltd had been aware of the breach and became a constructive trustee of the site for S Ltd. The trial judge upheld the claim even though he made no finding that M Ltd had acted dishonestly or participated in H Ltd's breach of fiduciary duty. M Ltd appealed.

The Court of Appeal allowed the appeal on the following grounds:

1. H Ltd was a fiduciary and acted in breach of its duties to S Ltd in disclosing confidential information to M Ltd without S Ltd's authority.
2. Some of the information disclosed to M Ltd was either available to M Ltd or would have been available on reasonable enquiry, once the news of S Ltd's receivership had become known.
3. If the information could be treated as trust property, there was insufficient nexus between the information and the acquisition of the site in order to make M Ltd liable as a constructive trustee for knowingly receiving trust property.
4. Since the judge made no finding that M Ltd acted dishonestly, M Ltd could not be liable as an accessory to a dishonest breach of trust by H Ltd.

In *Barlow Clowes International Ltd v Eurotrust International Ltd,* the Privy Council acknowledged that there was an element of ambiguity in the remarks of Lord Hutton in *Twinsectra.* This was sufficient to encourage some academics to suggest that the *Twinsectra* case had changed the law by inviting an inquiry not merely into the defendant's mental state about the nature of the transaction, but also into his views about generally acceptable standards of honesty. However, their Lordships in the Privy Council did not consider that was what Lord Hutton meant. Their view of Lord Hutton's statement as to the test of dishonesty meant only that *the defendant's knowledge of the transaction had to be such as to render his participation contrary to normally acceptable standards of honest conduct. It did not require that he should have had reflections about what those normally acceptable standards were.*

CASE EXAMPLE

Barlow Clowes International Ltd (in liquidation) v Eurotrust International Ltd and others [2006] 1 All ER 333, Privy Council

The claimant, a Gibraltar company in liquidation, had previously operated a fraudulent off-shore investment scheme purporting to offer high returns from investments in gilt-edged securities. It claimed that the first defendant, an Isle of Man company and its principal directors, had dishonestly assisted in the misappropriation of investors' funds. The claimant brought proceedings in the High Court of the Isle of Man. The trial judge found that the second defendant, Mr Henwood, was dishonest. On appeal, the Privy Council found in favour of the claimant. The Privy Council decided that an inquiry into the defendant's view about standards of honesty was not required. *Consciousness of dishonesty required consciousness of those elements of the transaction which made participation transgress ordinary standards of honest behaviour. It did not also require the defendant to have thought about what those standards were.* There was sufficient evidence to justify the trial judge's findings. She found that Mr Henwood had solid grounds for suspicion, which he consciously ignored, that the disposals in which Mr Henwood participated involved dealings with misappropriated funds.

JUDGMENT

'[After referring to Lord Hutton's speech in *Twinsectra*] The reference to what he knows would offend normally accepted standards of honest conduct meant only that (i) his knowledge of the transaction had to be such as to render his participation contrary to normally acceptable standards of honest conduct. (ii) Such a state of mind may involve knowledge that the transaction is one in which he cannot honestly participate (e.g. a misappropriation of other people's money), or it may involve suspicions combined with a conscious decision not to make inquiries which might result in knowledge. (iii) It is not necessary for the claimants to show that the person assisting knew of the existence of a trust or fiduciary relationship between the claimants and defendants … It was sufficient that he should have entertained a clear suspicion that this was the case. It did not require that he should have had reflections about what those normally acceptable standards were. Although a dishonest state of mind is a subjective mental state, the standard by which the law determines whether it is dishonest is objective. If by ordinary standards a defendant's mental state would be characterized as dishonest, it is irrelevant that the defendant judges the transaction by a different standard.'

Lord Hoffmann

In *Abou-Rahmah v Abacha,* the court observed that this was the first opportunity since the *Barlow Clowes* case for the Court of Appeal to consider the element of dishonesty for accessory liability. The court decided that the test of dishonesty is predominantly objective but with a subjective element and the *Barlow Clowes* decision did not involve a departure from the *Twinsectra* case. Rather the *Barlow Clowes* case gives guidance as to the proper interpretation of *Twinsectra* and demonstrates how *Royal Brunei* and *Twinsectra* could be read together to form a consistent corpus of law.

CASE EXAMPLE

Abou-Rahmah v Abacha [2006] All ER (D) 80, Court of Appeal

The claimants were a lawyer practising in Kuwait, and a Kuwaiti trading company. They were the victims of a fraud practised by three of the defendants. The fraudsters contacted the claimants seeking the latter's assistance in investing a substantial amount in an Arab country on behalf of a trust. The claim concerned the payment of £625,000 paid by the claimants into the account of a Nigerian bank, City Express Bank, held at HSBC in London for onward transfer to a client described as Trusty International. The bank transferred the sum to its customer's account held at its branch in Nigeria. No trust money ever materialised; the sums paid into the account were withdrawn shortly after payment in, and the fraudsters disappeared. The claimants commenced proceedings against the bank for knowing assistance, and restitution of money had and received. The bank raised the defence of change of position. The trial judge dismissed the claims on the ground that there was no dishonesty on the part of the defendant bank and accepted the defendant's defence that there had been a change of position in that the bank was not conscious that the fraudulent transaction amounted to a money-laundering scheme. The claimants appealed to the Court of Appeal.

The Court dismissed the appeal and ruled as follows:

- Since the trial judge decided that the bank did not act dishonestly it would be inappropriate to reverse this finding. The bank's general suspicion that the fraudsters (clients) were involved in money laundering at the instance of corrupt politicians was not sufficient to attribute dishonesty to the bank. The bank had no particular suspicions about the transactions in question. There were no grounds for the bank to raise additional inquiries of any person or to decline to act.
- The bank acted *bona fide* in changing its position to such an extent that it would be inequitable to require it to make restitution to the claimants: see later. In reliance on the trial judge's findings the court (Rix LJ expressed some doubt without dissenting) decided that the bank had no particular suspicions that the transactions constituted money laundering. The bank had done all that it had to do by complying with the requirements of Nigerian law on money laundering and satisfied itself that there were no doubts about the transactions.

JUDGMENT

'It is unnecessary to show subjective dishonesty in the sense of consciousness that the transaction is dishonest. It is sufficient if the defendant knows of the elements of the transaction which make it dishonest according to normally accepted standards of behaviour.

The *Barlow Clowes* decision does not involve a departure from, or refusal to follow, the *Twinsectra* case. Rather, the *Barlow Clowes* case gives guidance as to the proper interpretation to be placed on it as a matter of English law. It shows how the *Royal Brunei* case and the *Twinsectra* case can be read together to form a consistent corpus of law.

There is no overriding reason why in respect of dishonesty in the context of civil liability (as opposed to criminal responsibility) the law should take account of the defendant's views as to the morality of his actions.'

Arden LJ

Rix LJ in *Abou-Ramah* analysed the elements of the cause of action from the point of view of the defendant's knowledge. But the standard of evaluating his knowledge is objective:

JUDGMENT

'A claimant in this area needs to show three things: first, that a defendant has the requisite knowledge; secondly, that, given that knowledge, the defendant acts in a way which is contrary to normally acceptable standards of honest conduct (the objective test of honesty or dishonesty); and thirdly, possibly, that the defendant must in some sense be dishonest himself (a subjective test of dishonesty which might, on analysis, add little or nothing to knowledge of the facts which, objectively, would make his conduct dishonest).'

Rix LJ

Lord Clarke MR, in an article entitled, 'Claims against professionals: negligence, dishonesty and fraud' (2006) 22 Professional Negligence 70, tracks the development of the law in this area. He suggests that the test of dishonesty is clearly an objective question but the breach involves a subjective assessment of the defendant in the light of what he knew at the time of the breach, as distinct from what a reasonable person would have known and appreciated. Carelessness is not dishonesty and dishonesty is to be equated with conscious impropriety. It is a jury question.

In *AG of Zambia v Meer Care & Desai* [2007] EWHC 952 (Ch), Smith J in the High Court reviewed the leading cases that considered the issue of dishonesty, and expressed his opinion thus:

JUDGMENT

'In my view when the cases are analysed the question of subjective/objective test is an over elaboration. All of the cases when analysed in my view actually determine that the test for dishonesty is essentially a question of fact whereby the state of mind of the defendant had to be judged in the light of his subjective knowledge but by reference to an objective standard of honesty.

The test is clearly an objective test but the breach involves a subjective assessment of the person in question in the light of what he knew at the time as distinct from what a reasonable person would have known or appreciated. Carelessness is not dishonesty and dishonesty is to be equated with conscious impropriety. However self-evidently a person is not allowed to set his own standard of honesty in particular circumstances.'

Smith J

This is a rather peculiar way of expressing the test of dishonesty. Admittedly, the judge was attempting to steer away from the purely subjective test whereby the defendant would be inclined to set his own standards of dishonesty (the Robin Hood standard of defence). At the same time the judge was prepared to distinguish carelessness or incompetence from dishonesty. This involves an element of subjectivity. Likewise the experience and skill of the defendant are factors to be taken into consideration in determining this question of fact. The Court of Appeal in *AG of Zambia v Meer Care & Desai* [2008] EWCA Civ 1007, without evaluating the validity of the test for dishonesty laid down by Smith J, decided that the judge had inaccurately applied it to the facts of the case because the judge had mistakenly assumed that the defendant was competent, by comparing his conduct with that of a hypothetical competent individual and deciding that an honest solicitor would not have acted the way that the defendant did. Lloyd LJ, who gave the leading judgment in the Court of Appeal, said:

JUDGMENT

'At some point the judge used the benchmark of the honest and competent solicitor … That hypothetical comparator is not appropriate, because it assumes that Mr Meer was competent. Of course Mr Meer would have wished to be thought competent, but there were many indications to the judge that, in relevant respects, he was not. It seems to us that the judge failed to give adequate consideration to the possibility that Mr Meer was honest but not competent, and was not in truth knowledgeable or experienced in relation to the sort of transaction with which he was faced, and in particular did not really understand what was involved in money-laundering.'

In *Dolley v Ogunseitan* [2009] All ER (D) 66 (Jul), the High Court decided that a claim for dishonestly assisting failed on the grounds that a payment of a fund by the claimant did not constitute trust property, but was the working capital of a partnership. Further, there was no evidence that the defendants were aware that the moneys paid might have been obtained in a dishonest manner.

CASE EXAMPLE

Dolley v Ogunseitan [2009] All ER (D) 66 (Jul)

In this case the parties signed a joint partnership agreement for the purpose of operating commercial flights along various routes. The claimants and defendants each contributed a sum of £200,000 to the partnership. The money contributed by the claimants was used to finance flights between Ghana and the UK. The claimants contended that their contribution was intended to fund flights between Ghana and the USA. Proceedings were commenced by the claimants to recover the sum they contributed on the grounds that the sum constituted trust money and *inter alia* that the first defendant knowingly assisted in a fraudulent scheme. The court dismissed the claim on the grounds that the fund did not constitute trust money and there was no evidence that the first defendant was aware that there were suspicious circumstances surrounding the payment and that he had deliberately refrained from making inquiries for fear that those inquiries would reveal to him the true position.

In *Starglade v Nash* (2011) the Court of Appeal reviewed the leading cases that considered the test of dishonesty, and decided that the standard by which the defendant is to be judged is objective, and that it is for the court to determine that standard and apply it to the facts of the case. The subjective understanding of the defendant as to whether his conduct is dishonest is irrelevant. Likewise, it is irrelevant that there may be a body of opinion which regards the ordinary standard of honest behaviour as being set too high. The court is required to decide whether the standard had been satisfied on the facts of each case.

CASE EXAMPLE

Starglade Properties Ltd v Nash [2011] Lloyd's Report FC 102, CA

In November 1998 the claimant, Starglade Properties Ltd, instructed Technograde Ltd to produce a site investigation report as to the suitability of a plot of land in Kent for development of a sloping site. In its report dated 14 December 1998 Technograde indicated that the site was suitable for development of a number of two-storey houses. On 21 June 1999 Starglade sold the site to Larkstore Ltd, which duly commenced its development. On 13 October 2001 there was a landslip, causing substantial damage to properties uphill from the site. In March 2003 the owners of those properties commenced proceedings against Larkstore.

On 6 October 2004 Larkstore commenced proceedings against Technograde. These proceedings were settled on 26 January 2007, whereunder the sum of £365,000 was paid to the solicitors for Larkstore. After deducting further costs, £154,577 was held by Larkstore in trust for Starglade. Larkstore at this time was insolvent, but instead of accounting to Starglade and taking steps to put Larkstore into liquidation, Mr Nash, the sole director of Larkstore, distributed the entire net amount received from Technograde to its creditors. Proceedings were commenced against Nash for restitution of £154,577 on the basis that he dishonestly assisted in the breach of trust by Larkstore. The trial judge dismissed the claim and applied a test of dishonesty based on 'all normal people'. The Court of Appeal allowed the appeal and decided that the trial judge had incorrectly applied the test for dishonesty to the facts of the case. There was no sliding scale of honesty as the judge inferred. Accordingly, the court decided that there was sufficient evidence of dishonesty to reverse the trial judge's decision.

JUDGMENT

'I consider the deputy judge's comments are apt to mislead. The relevant standard ... is the ordinary standard of honest behaviour. Just as the subjective understanding of the person concerned as to whether his conduct is dishonest is irrelevant, so also is it irrelevant that there may be a body of opinion which regards the ordinary standard of honest behaviour as being set too high. Ultimately, in civil proceedings, it is for the court to determine what that standard is and to apply it to the facts of the case. The deliberate removal of the assets of an insolvent company so as entirely to defeat the just claim of a creditor is, in my view, not in accordance with the ordinary standards of honest commercial behaviour, however much it may occur.'

Morritt LJ

Disciplinary proceedings and Twinsectra

In *Bryant v Law Society* [2007] All ER (D) 379 (Dec), the court decided that there were strong reasons why the *Ghosh* test for dishonesty (laid down by Lord Lane CJ in the criminal case *R v Ghosh* [1982] 1 QB 1053) was appropriate in respect of disciplinary proceedings against professional persons. The *Ghosh* test was adopted by the House of Lords in *Twinsectra v Yardley* as a standard which combines an objective test with a subjective test (combined test). This test requires the claimant to establish that the defendant's conduct was dishonest by the ordinary standards of reasonable and honest people, *and* that the defendant himself realised that, by those standards, his conduct was dishonest.

The court considered that the position has become complicated by the way in which *Twinsectra* has been interpreted by the Privy Council's decision in *Barlow Clowes Int v Eurotrust Int Ltd* [2005] UKPC 37. In particular the Privy Council found that there was an element of ambiguity in the *Twinsectra* approach and may have encouraged a belief that *Twinsectra* had departed from the law that was previously understood (see the discussion above).

In *Bryant* the court decided that the practice of the tribunal was to apply the *Twinsectra* test for dishonesty and it would be wrong to depart from this practice. It was accepted by the Divisional Court in *D v Law Society* [2003] EWHC 408 (Admin) that the test for dishonesty involved a subjective element in accordance with the speech of Lord Hutton in *Twinsectra*. The court also felt bound by the Court of Appeal's decision in *Bultitude v Law Society* [2004] EWCA Civ 1853, which decided that the *Twinsectra* test for dishonesty was the appropriate test for the solicitor's disciplinary tribunal to apply. Such disciplinary proceedings are not criminal in character, but may involve issues of dishonesty that could give rise to criminal charges. In any event a tribunal's finding of dishonesty against a solicitor is likely to have extremely serious consequences for him, both professionally and personally, sufficient to justify the type of state of mind required in the criminal context.

CASE EXAMPLE

Bryant v Law Society [2007] All ER (D) 379 (Dec) (Divisional Court)

The appellant, Mr Bryant (B) was found guilty by the solicitor's disciplinary tribunal on seven charges of professional misconduct involving dishonesty and was ordered to be struck off the roll of solicitors. The allegations involved B acting for clients who were involved in dubious or fraudulent investment schemes. The tribunal was guided by the test of dishonesty as laid down in *Twinsectra Ltd v Yardley* [2002] 2 All ER 377, but did not doubt B's strong belief in his honesty in implementing the transactions. It did not suggest that B believed that his conduct was dishonest by the ordinary standards of his profession. On appeal, B claimed that the tribunal had erred in applying a purely objective test in finding him guilty of dishonesty. The Divisional Court allowed the appeal and decided that the 'combined' objective and subjective tests laid down in *Twinsectra* concerning dishonesty were not applied by the tribunal. In particular the court decided that the tribunal had applied the purely objective test of dishonesty by reference to the standards of an honest and competent solicitor, but made no finding that B was aware that by those standards he was acting dishonestly. The court accepted that B was guilty of serious professional misconduct and imposed a penalty of suspension for two years.

JUDGMENT

'[T]here are strong reasons for adopting such a test in the disciplinary context and for declining to follow in that context the approach in *Barlow Clowes*. As we have observed earlier, the test corresponds closely to that laid down in the criminal context by *R v Ghosh*; and in our view it is more appropriate that the test for dishonesty in the context of solicitors' disciplinary proceedings should be aligned with the criminal test than with the test for determining civil liability for assisting in a breach of a trust. The tribunal's finding of dishonesty against a solicitor is likely to have extremely serious consequences for him both professionally (it will normally lead to an order striking him off) and personally. It is just as appropriate to require a finding that the Defendant had a subjectively dishonest state of mind in this context as the court in *R v Ghosh* considered it to be in the criminal context.

Accordingly, the tribunal in the present case should, in our judgment, have asked itself two questions when deciding the issue of dishonesty: first, whether Mr Bryant acted dishonestly by the ordinary standards of reasonable and honest people; and, second, whether he was aware that by those standards he was acting dishonestly.

Most pertinently, although the tribunal found that Mr Bryant acted dishonestly by the standards of an honest and competent solicitor, it did not make any finding or even any suggestion that Mr Bryant was aware that by those standards he was acting dishonestly.

It follows that in our judgment the tribunal's finding of dishonesty is vitiated by a serious legal error.'

Richards LJ

Strangers as constructive trustees

General rule	
Third parties, strangers to a trust or agents of the trustees do not become constructive trustees simply because of a breach of trust committed by the trustees or even a neglect of duties by the agent	*Mara v Browne* (1896); *Barnes v Addy* (1874)

Intermeddlars/constructive trustees	
A trustee *de son tort* (of his own wrongdoing)	*Taylor v Davies* (1920); *Boardman v Phipps* (1967)
Categories of knowledge	*Re Baden Delvaux* (1983)
Knowingly receiving or dealing with trust property for his own use	*Nelson v Larholt* (1948); *Karak v Burden (No 2)* (1972); *El Ajou v Dollar Land* (1994); *Belmont Finance Corporation v Williams Furniture & Others (No 2)* (1980); *International Sales and Agencies Ltd v Marcus* (1982); *Carl Zeiss Stiftung v Herbert Smith & Co (No 2)* (1969); *Re Montagu's Settlement* (1987); *Cowan de Groot Properties Ltd v Eagle Trust plc* (1992); *Polly Peck International plc v Nadir and Others (No 2)* (1992); *Barclays Bank v Quincecare Ltd* (1992); *Lipkin Gorman v Karpnale* (1992); *Satnam v Heywood* (1999)
Alternative rationale – unconscionability, dishonesty	*BCCI v Akindele* (2000); *Charter v City Index* (2008); *Armstrong v Winnington* (2012)
Dishonest assistance or accessory liability	*Re Baden Delvaux* (1983); *Royal Brunei Airlines v Tan* (1995); *Grupo Torras v Al Sabah* (1999)
Is dishonest assistance a genuine category of constructive trust?	*Paragon Finance Ltd v Thakerar* (1999); *Dubai Aluminium v Salaam* (2003)
The standard of proof	*Heinl v Jayske Bank (Gibraltar)* (1999)
Test for dishonesty	*Royal Brunei Airlines v Tan* (1995); *Twinsectra Ltd v Yardley* (2002); *Barlow Clowes v Eurotrust* (2006); *Abou-Ramah v Abacha* (2006); *Starglade v Nash* (2011)

ACTIVITY

Self-test questions

1. In what circumstances will an agent or stranger to a trust be liable to account for 'knowingly receiving and dealing' with trust property and 'knowingly assisting in a fraudulent design'?

2. During negotiations for the purchase of Blackacre, Paul, the purchaser, purporting to act on behalf of the vendors, sought and obtained planning permission for the land, thereby

greatly increasing its value. Victor, the vendor, was unaware of this, but had he known, would have demanded a higher price for Blackacre. Paul has recently sold the property to Thomas for a handsome profit.

Victor seeks your advice as to whether he may force Paul to account for the profit resulting from the grant of planning permission.

3. 'The principles of law laid down in the House of Lords decision in *Stack v Dowden* (2007) create such a degree of uncertainty that is tantamount to the retrograde, unpredictable and unjust step taken by the Court of Appeal in the 1970s.'

Do you agree?

4. John and Smith are the trustees of a settlement created in 1993. At the time the trust was set up, the trust assets included a savings account at the Royal Bank of Scotland, 40,000 shares in Prospects Co Ltd and a terrace of flats in Bristol. The entire shareholding in Prospects Ltd is 100,000 carrying equal voting rights. At the time of John's appointment as trustee he already held 40,000 shares in the company in his own right. The remaining 20,000 shares were owned by various other individuals.

The beneficiaries under the settlement are two minors, Ken and Ron.

Since the creation of the settlement, the following events have occurred:

(i) at a shareholders' meeting of Prospects Ltd, John was elected as a director of the company and has been receiving remuneration as director each year;

(ii) Smith has bought Ron's beneficial interest in the property in Bristol for £250,000; and

(iii) Ben, who is solicitor to the trust, has been deeply unhappy with the management of the company affairs of Prospects Ltd for some time. He has advised the trustees to acquire a majority shareholding in order to reorganise the company. The trustees have, however, refused to take his advice. Ben has subsequently acquired a majority shareholding in Prospects Ltd by dishonestly using money from the trust's savings account, with the assistance of Andrew, a clerk at Royal Bank of Scotland.

Analyse whether any of the events above raise liability to account as constructive trustees.

SUMMARY

■ A constructive trust is declared by the courts, irrespective of the express or presumed intentions of the parties, in order to grant relief to a claimant in respect of unconscionable conduct or fraud committed by the defendant, in his fiduciary capacity. Over the centuries the courts have justified the existence of the constructive trust in a variety of ways.

● The expression, 'constructive trusts' has been used as a synonym to denote the personal liability of the fiduciary to account for unauthorised profits where he allows his duties to conflict with his interests.

● Equally, the term has been used to impose liability on the defendant who acts unconscionably in denying the claimant an interest in property, see Millett LJ in *Paragon Finance v Thakerar* [1999] 1 All ER 400.

■ The traditional view of the constructive trust is that it is a property-based institution that is called into play whenever the defendant conducts himself in an unconscionable manner. The interest of the claimant does not arise for the first time when the court declares it to exist, see *Halifax Building Society v Thomas* [1996] 2 WLR 63, *Re Polly Peck International plc (No 4)* [1998] 3 All ER 812. This is the 'institutional' constructive trust. The effect is that the court does not create the trust as such, but recognises the circumstances which give rise to the trust and, in appropriate cases, makes a declaration that the trust exists. On the other hand, the 'remedial' constructive trust has been used as a means of articulating a remedy created by the courts to rectify inequitable conduct, see Lord Browne-Wilkinson in *Westdeutsche Landesbank v Islington BC* [1996] AC 669.

- The rule in *Keech v Sandford* is that any benefit a trustee or fiduciary receives, or becomes entitled to receive, by virtue of his position as a trustee or fiduciary is held on constructive trust for the beneficiary or claimant. The rule is applied strictly and it is irrelevant that the trustee acted honestly and the beneficiary would be entitled to profit from the breach of trust, see *Boardman v Phipps* [1967] 2 AC 46; *Williams v Barton* [1927] 2 Ch 9; *Brudenell-Bruce v Moore* [2014] EWHC 3679; *Breitenfeld v Harrison* [2015] EWHC 399; *Re Macadam* [1946] Ch 73; *Regal (Hastings) v Gulliver* [1942] 1 All ER 378.

- The occasions when a trustee may be remunerated for his services are:
    - authority in trust instrument;
    - statutory authority, see ss 28, 29 and 31 of the Trustee Act 2000;
    - authority of the court;
    - agreement with all the beneficiaries;
    - rule in *Cradock v Piper* (1850);
    - rule in *Re Northcote* (1949).

- Where two or more parties (A and B) make an arrangement to the effect that, prior to the acquisition of specific property by one party (A), the other party (B) will acquire an interest in the property. Provided that B relies on the agreement and refrains from acquiring the property, a constructive trust may arise in favour of B, see *Pallant v Morgan* [1953] Ch 43; *Banner Homes v Luff* [2000] 2 WLR 772; *Kilcarne v Targetfollow* [2005] All ER (D) 203; *Generator Development v Lidl* [2016] EWHC 814.

- A bribe or secret commission received by a fiduciary in breach of his fiduciary duties creates a constructive trust in respect of the bribe, as distinct from merely a debtor/creditor relationship. This has been the solution adopted by the Privy Council in *AG for Hong Kong v Reid* [1994] 1 All ER 1; the High Court in *Daraydan Holdings v Solland* [2004] EWHC 622; and the Supreme Court in *FHR European Ventures v Cedar Partners* [2014] UKSC 45.

- On public policy grounds equity intervenes and prevents a person who kills another from inheriting the deceased's property, see *Re Crippen* [1911] P 108. The Forfeiture Act 1982 empowers the court to modify the forfeiture rule where the justice of the case so requires, except in cases of murder. The approach of the courts as to the exercise of its discretion was considered in *Dunbar v Plant* [1997] 4 All ER 289; *Chadwick v Collinson* [2014] EWHC 3055; *Henderson v Wilcox* [2015] EWHC 3469.

- Where a contract for the sale of land has been formed but not completed, the vendor holds the property on constructive trust for the purchaser, see *Lysaght v Edwards* [1876] 2 Ch D 499.

- Where it would be unconscionable to allow a party to commit a fraud on another party by insisting on compliance with a formal statutory provision, the court may suspend the operation of the provision and impose a constructive trust on the defendant, see *Rochefoucauld v Boustead* [1897] 1 Ch 196.

- A stranger to a trust may become a constructive trustee or be accountable for any benefits received where:
    - he is a trustee *de son tort*; or
    - he knowingly receives trust property for his own benefit, see *Polly Peck International plc v Nadir (No 2)* (1992); *Re Montagu* [1987] Ch 264; *BCCI v Akindele* [2000] 3 WLR 1423; *Armstrong v Winnington* [2012] EWHC 10; or

he dishonestly assists another in a fraudulent transaction, see *Royal Brunei Airlines v Tan* (1995); *Brinks v Abu-Saleh, The Times*, 23 October 1995; *Twinsectra v Yardley* [2002] UKHL 12; *Barlow Clowes v Eurotrust* [2006] 1 All ER 333; *Abou-Rahmah v Abacha* [2006] All ER (D) 80; *Starglade v Nash* [2011] 1 Lloyd's Report 102.

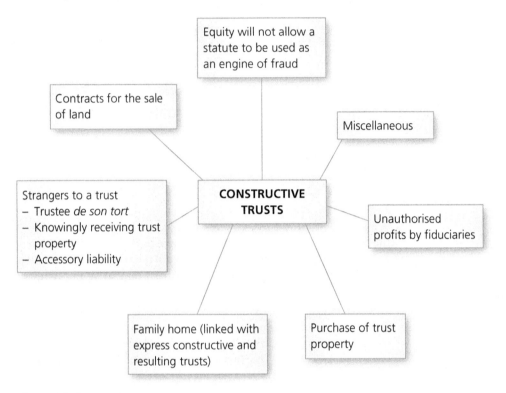

Figure 8.1 Constructive trusts

SAMPLE ESSAY QUESTION

Consider the following essay question:

Consider the nature of a trustee's liability when he obtains a bribe by virtue of his position as a trustee.

Answer plan

State the general principles regarding fiduciaries and the definition of fiduciaries, e.g. see Millett LJ in *Bristol and West BS v Mothew* [1996] 4 All ER 698.

A trustee is evidently a fiduciary.

Consider the distinction between the duty to account and constructive trusts, e.g. see *Paragon Finance v Thakerar* (1999).

A trustee is subject to an obligation to account for unauthorised profits, see *Regal (Hastings Ltd) v Gulliver* (1942), see also *Halifax BS v Thomas* (1996) and *Crown Dilmun v Sutton* (2004) where this approach was adopted.

Consider whether the courts have kept the above distinction clear:

- In the House of Lords decision, *Boardman v Phipps* [1967] 2 AC 46, the rationale for the decision was unclear. It would appear that either theory would suffice.
- With regard to bribes, for many years the solution involved the creditor/debtor relationship requiring the defendant to repay the same amount that was received as bribes, see *Lister v Stubbs* (1890).
- More recently, the Privy Council in *AG for Hong Kong v Reid* (1994) refused to follow the *Lister* solution and decided that on receipt of the bribe, the defendant held the same on constructive trust for the claimant (innocent party and person to whom the fiduciary owes duties). If the property representing the bribe increases in value the defendant is deprived of the surplus because a fiduciary is not entitled to profit from his position as a fiduciary, without authority. The fiduciary is thus required to hold the bribe and any consequential profit for the benefit of the defendant. This is based on a constructive trust and may be subject to the rules of tracing. This principle was followed in the recent High Court decision *Daraydan Holdings Ltd v Solland Interiors Ltd* (2004).

In *FHR European Ventures v Cedar Partners* [2014] UKSC 45, the Supreme Court affirmed *Reid and Daraydan* and conclusively decided that the receipt of such a bribe creates a proprietary interest by way of a constructive trust in favour of the claimant. *Lister v Stubbs*; *Sinclair v Versailles* (2011) and cases that followed this line of reasoning were overruled.

CONCLUSION

Further reading

Andrews, G, 'The redundancy of dishonest assistance' (2003) Conv 398.

Baughen, S, '*Quistclose* trusts and knowing receipt' (2000) Conv 351.

Beatson, J and Prentice, D, 'Restitutionary claims by company directors' (1990) 106 LQR 365.

Chong, A, 'The common law choice of law rules for resulting and constructive trusts' (2005) 54(4) ICLQ 855.

Clark, Lord, 'Claims against professionals: negligence, dishonesty and fraud' (2006) 22 Professional Negligence 70.

Conte, C, 'No proprietary relief for breach of fiduciary duty' (2012) LQR 184.

Elliott, S and Mitchell, C, 'Remedies for dishonest assistance' (2004) 64 MLR 16.

Etherton, T, 'Constructive trusts: a new model for equity and unjust enrichment' (2008) 67(2) Cambridge Law Journal 265.

Ferris, G, 'The advice of the Privy Council in *Royal Brunei Airlines v Tan*' (1996) 30 Law Teacher 111.

Gardner, S, 'Two maxims of equity: casenote on *AG for Hong Kong v Reid*' (1995) 54 CLJ 60.

Gardner, S, 'Knowing assistance and knowing receipt: taking stock' (1996) 112 LQR 56.

Halliwell, M and Prochaska, E, 'Assistance and dishonesty: ring-a-ring o' roses' (2006) Conv 465.

Hibbert, T, 'Dishonesty and knowledge of accessories and recipients' (2000) JIBL 138.

Hicks, A, 'Constructive trusts of fiduciary gain: *Lister* revived' (2011) Conv PL 62.

Hodgkinson, K, 'Casenote on *Re Duke of Norfolk Settlement Trust*' (1982) Conv 231.

Jones, A, 'Bribing the DPP: should he profit from abusing his position? *AG for Hong Kong v Reid*' (1994) Conv 156.

Low, K, 'Nonfeasance in equity' (2012) LQR 63.

McGrath, P, 'Clawing back fraudulent profits: the narrowed ambit of proprietary claims' (2010) 11 JIBFL 654.

Millett, P, 'Restitution and constructive trusts' (1998) 114 LQR 399.

Millett, P, 'Bribes and secret commissions again' (2012) CLJ 583.

Mitchell, C, 'Dishonest assistance, knowing receipt, and the law of limitation' (2008) Conv 226.

Panesar, S, 'A loan subject to a trust and dishonest assistance by a third party' (2003) 18 JIBL 9.

Parry, N, 'Remuneration of trustees' (1984) Conv 275.

Pawlowski, M, 'Forfeiture relief' (2007) 157 NLJ 318.

Ridge, P, 'Justifying the remedies for dishonest assistance' (2008) 124 LQR 445.

Ryan, D, 'Royal Brunei dishonesty: a clear welcome for *Barlow Clowes*' (2007) Conv 168.

Shine, P, 'Dishonesty in civil commercial claims: a state of mind or course of conduct?' (2012) JBL 29.

Watts, P, 'Bribes and constructive trusts' (1994) 110 LQR 178.

Watts, P, 'Tests of knowledge in the receipt of misapplied funds' (2015) LQR 511.

Webb, C, 'What is unjust enrichment?' (2009) OJLS 29.

Worthington, S, 'Fiduciary duties and proprietary remedies: addressing the failure of equitable formulae' (2013) CLJ 720.

Yeo, T, 'Dishonest assistance: a restatement from the Privy Council' (2006) 122 LQR 171.

9

Constructive trusts II – the family home

AIMS AND OBJECTIVES

By the end of this chapter you should be able to:

- appreciate the inadequacy of the presumptions of resulting trusts and advancements in order to ascertain the interests of parties in the family home
- understand the relevant principles that are applicable in determining proprietary interests in the family home
- comprehend the methods that are available to quantify the interest of a party in shared homes
- understand the status of 'nuptial agreements' freely entered into between parties to a marriage or civil partnership

9.1 Introduction

Parties (whether married or unmarried) may contribute to the purchase of a home for themselves, but subsequent events may give rise to a dispute as to the ownership of the property. In these circumstances the courts may step in to settle the matter by (i) giving effect to the express intentions of the parties, (ii) imposing a common intention constructive trust, (iii) creating a resulting trust in exceptional cases, such as investment properties, or (iv) applying statutory principles under the Matrimonial Causes Act 1973 in the event of a divorce, decree of nullity or judicial separation. The property dispute may stem from a breakdown in the relationship between the parties. In this event, the matter will be resolved by the court by reference to the circumstances related to the purchase of the property. But if the dispute arises on the bankruptcy or death of one of the parties this may involve the rights of third parties. As a final introductory point, the status of ante-nuptial and post-nuptial agreements, freely entered into between parties to a marriage or civil partnership, has been resolved by the Supreme Court in favour of validity.

9.2 Proprietary rights in the family home

The presumptions of resulting trusts and advancements in the context of the family home and other family assets were regarded by the middle of the twentieth century as outmoded and best suited for a different society: see Lord Diplock's judgment in *Pettitt v Pettitt* (below). In their place the courts have substituted settled principles of property law – the resulting and constructive trusts, although the modern view is that common intention constructive trusts are better suited to reflect the intentions of the parties.

JUDGMENT

'The consensus of opinion which gave rise to the presumptions of advancement and resulting trusts in transactions between husbands and wives is to be found in cases relating to the propertied class of the nineteenth century and the first quarter of the twentieth century among whom marriage settlements were common and it was unusual for the wife to contribute by her earnings to the family income. It was not until after World War II that the courts were required to consider the proprietary rights in family assets of a different social class … It would be an abuse of the legal technique for ascertaining or imputing intention to apply to transactions between the post-war generation of married couples, "presumptions" which are based upon inferences of fact which an entire generation of judges drew as to the most likely intentions of an earlier generation of spouses belonging to the propertied classes of a different social era.'

Lord Diplock in *Pettitt v Pettitt* [1970] AC 777

The Civil Partnership Act 2004 came into force on 5 December 2005 and enables same-sex couples to obtain legal recognition of their relationship by forming a civil partnership. 'Partners' include a civil partnership registered under the Civil Partnership Act 2004. A civil partnership is required to be registered in England and Wales at a registered office or approved premise. Civil partners have equal treatment with married couples in a wide range of matters including property rights, taxation including inheritance tax, inheritance of tenancy agreements and recognition under intestacy rules. Consequently, a registered civil partnership, to all intents and purposes, is treated as a marriage.

9.2.1 Legal title in the joint names of the parties

The starting point for ascertaining the existence of a beneficial interest in the family home is the conveyance, or the transfer, of the legal title to the property. The principle is that 'equity follows the law' and the equitable interest reflects the nature of the legal ownership. Thus, whether we are dealing with joint or sole legal ownership, the beneficial interest will *prima facie* be enjoyed by the party(ies) with the legal title. This principle is applicable until the contrary is proved and such evidence may be established by way of an express declaration of trust and, failing this, by way of the implied trust.

If the legal title to property has been conveyed in the joint names of the partners, subject to an express trust of the land for themselves as equitable joint tenants or tenants in common registered in the Land Registry, the express declaration of trust will be conclusive of the equitable interests of the parties, in the absence of fraud, mistake, undue influence or evidence varying the original declaration of trust.

CASE EXAMPLE

Goodman v Gallant [1986] 2 WLR 236

The claimant and defendant purchased a house which was conveyed in their joint names 'upon trust to sell … and until sale upon trust for themselves as joint tenants'. The defendant left the house following a dispute between the parties. The claimant gave written notice of severance of the joint tenancy and claimed a declaration to the effect that she was entitled to a three-quarters share in the house. The court decided that in the absence of any claim for rectification or rescission, the express declaration in the conveyance was conclusive as to the intentions of the parties. The notice of severance had the effect of terminating the joint tenancy and substituting a tenancy in common in respect of the beneficial interest.

JUDGMENT

'If ... the relevant conveyance contains an express declaration of trust which comprehensively declares the beneficial interests in the property or its proceeds of sale, there is no room for the application of the doctrine of resulting implied or constructive trusts unless and until the conveyance is set aside or rectified; until that event the declaration contained in the document speaks for itself.'

Slade LJ

The paramount nature of the express declaration of trust, as compared with the implied trust, may be illustrated by the Court of Appeal decision in *Pankhania v Chandegra* [2012] EWCA Civ 1438.

CASE EXAMPLE

Pankhania v Chandegra [2012] EWCA Civ 1438 (Court of Appeal)

The appellant (P) appealed against the decision of a High Court judge who dismissed his claim for an order of sale of a residential property in Leicester. The property was purchased in July 1987 for £18,500 in the joint names of the appellant and respondent (C) as joint tenants for themselves as tenants in common in equal shares. The transfer contained an express declaration of trust to that effect. C had insufficient income to obtain a mortgage so P agreed to become a joint mortgagor so that his salary would be taken into account. P had alleged that the property was bought as a home for his uncle to live in and after his death as an investment for P and C (his aunt). C claimed that, notwithstanding the express declaration of trust, there was an understanding between the parties at the time of the purchase that she was to have sole beneficial ownership of the property. Over the years the mortgage had been paid solely by C but between 2005 and 2008 he made mortgage payments to the building society amounting to £2,600. P applied to the court for an order of sale of the property.

The trial judge referred to the constructive trust principles laid down in the definitive cases, *Stack v Dowden* [2007] UKHL 17 (see later) and *Jones v Kernott* [2011] UKSC 53, and decided that a contrary intention to joint beneficial ownership could be inferred from the evidence of the parties' common intention. The effect was a declaration of sole beneficial ownership in favour of C. P appealed to the Court of Appeal. The court allowed the appeal and decided that the judge had erred in applying the implied trust principles in substitution for an express declaration of trust.

JUDGMENT

'The parties (both of them of full age) had executed an express declaration of trust over the property in favour of themselves as tenants in common in equal shares and had therefore set out their respective beneficial entitlement as part of the purchase itself. In these circumstances, there was no need for the imposition of a constructive or common intention trust of the kind discussed in *Stack v Dowden* nor any possibility of inferring one because as Baroness Hale recognised, such a declaration of trust is regarded as conclusive unless varied by subsequent agreement or affected by proprietary estoppel.'

Patten LJ

But the mere fact that the legal title to property is vested in the joint names of the parties does not, on its own, entitle the surviving legal owner to an equitable interest in the property, if this does not accord with the intention of the parties.

CASE EXAMPLE

Goodman v Carlton [2002] All ER (D) 284 (Apr)

The claimant was the son and next of kin of Mr Goodman (G), who died intestate. The defendant, Anita (A), was the surviving legal owner of real property. The legal title to the house was acquired by G and A in 1994. G accepted an offer to purchase the house at a discount. His original intention was to purchase the house alone and register it in his sole name. As G did not have sufficient income to finance a mortgage he arranged to purchase the property with A as co-mortgagee. In 1997 G tentatively instructed his solicitors to transfer the house into his sole name but this was not followed up. Shortly afterwards G died. As surviving joint tenant, A acquired the legal title to the house and G's son commenced proceedings, claiming that A held the house on trust for G's estate absolutely. The trial judge decided in favour of the claimant. A appealed to the Court of Appeal. The court dismissed the appeal and decided that the property was held on resulting trust for the claimant, as administrator of G's estate. A failed to contribute to the purchase of the property and there was no evidence of any agreement, understanding or common intention to share the beneficial ownership with A, who therefore acquired no interest.

JUDGMENT

'Mr Goodman was the person at whose expense the house was provided. He paid all the deposit. The discount in the price was solely referable to him as sitting tenant. He was to pay (and did in fact pay) all the mortgage payments and all the premiums on the endowment policy. There was no intention that the transfer of the house into joint names should confer a beneficial interest on Anita. It was part of the arrangements undertaken to acquire the house for his sole use, occupation and benefit. Anita's participation was intended only to be a temporary involvement on the basis of the limited understanding between them. A resulting trust arose by operation of law for the sole benefit of Mr Goodman.'

Mummery LJ

Alternatively, the parties may declare the terms of the trust outside the conveyance. Provided that s 53(1)(b) of the Law of Property Act 1925 has been complied with (evidenced in writing), the declaration of trust will be conclusive as to the beneficial interests of the parties, in the absence of fraud, mistake or undue influence held out by one party.

The difficulty arises where there is no written evidence of an express declaration of trust but the claimant alleges that the equitable interest is enjoyed in equal shares. In *Stack v Dowden* the House of Lords restated the principles concerning the occasion when a conveyance of the legal title to property is taken in the joint names of the parties, but without an express declaration of trust as to their respective beneficial interests. As a starting point, the maxims 'Equity follows the law' and 'Equality is equity' are applicable in order to identify the existence of the equitable interest, subject to evidence to the contrary. Thus, whether we are dealing with joint legal ownership (as in *Stack v Dowden*) or sole legal ownership (see later), the beneficial interest will *prima facie* be enjoyed by the party(ies) with the legal title. Until the contrary is proved, the extent of the beneficial interest will also follow the legal title. Thus, where the transfer of the legal title is in joint names then *prima facie* the beneficial interest will be enjoyed in equal shares until the contrary is proved. The onus of proof is therefore on the party seeking to establish that the beneficial interest is different from the legal title, such as the defendant in the present case.

The contrary may be established where the legal owner(s) expressly declares a trust. Such a declaration is conclusive of the interests of the parties in the absence of fraud, mistake or variation by subsequent agreement: see *Goodman v Gallant* (above). In *Stack v Dowden* the court decided that a declaration that the survivor of the two legal owners can give a valid receipt for capital moneys arising on a disposition of the land did not amount to an express declaration of a beneficial joint tenancy. In this respect the court followed *Huntingford v Hobbs* [1993] 1 FLR 736.

Likewise, on the issue of evidence to the contrary, Baroness Hale in *Stack v Dowden* raised the question whether the starting point ought to be the presumption or inference of a resulting trust (purchase money resulting trust), i.e. the beneficial ownership being held in the same proportions as the contributions to the purchase price, or by looking at all the relevant circumstances in order to discern the parties' common intention, reliance and detriment (constructive trust). In Baroness Hale's view the emphasis in the domestic context has moved away from crude factors of money contributions (resulting trusts) towards more subtle factors of intentional bargain (constructive trusts). Accordingly, strict mathematical calculations as to who paid what at the time of the acquisition of the property may be less significant today. The common intention constructive trust has the consequence of giving effect to the common intentions of the parties. The quantification or valuation of the interests of the parties will reflect a more realistic approach as to the intentions of the parties and achieve fairness, as opposed to the narrower purchase moneys resulting trust. The common intention constructive trust was advocated in the 1970s by Lord Diplock in *Gissing v Gissing* and endorsed by Baroness Hale.

JUDGMENT

'A resulting, implied or constructive trust – and it is unnecessary for present purposes to distinguish between these three classes of trust – is created by a transaction between the trustee and the cestui que trust in connection with the acquisition by the trustee of a legal estate in land, *whenever the trustee has so conducted himself that it would be inequitable to allow him to deny to the cestui que trust a beneficial interest in the land acquired. And he will be held so to have conducted himself if by his words or conduct he has induced the cestui que trust to act to his own detriment in the reasonable belief that by so acting he was acquiring a beneficial interest in the land.'* [Emphasis added]

Lord Diplock in *Gissing v Gissing* [1971] AC 886

Where the legal title is taken in the joint names of the parties the presumption is that equity follows the law and the equitable interest is acquired by both parties as joint tenants. The joint tenancy is capable of severance and may be converted into an equitable tenancy in common with the parties becoming entitled to equal shares in equity. If a party wishes to contest this solution and claim a greater interest, he or she has a burden of proving the existence of such interest by way of a common intention constructive trust. The elements of such a constructive trust require evidence that is related to the acquisition of the property, or exceptionally subsequent to such acquisition, of an express or implied intention to share the property, relied on by the claimant to his or her detriment.

CASE EXAMPLE

Stack v Dowden [2007] UKHL 17, HL

The family home (Chatsworth Road) was transferred in 1993 in the joint names of Ms Dowden (defendant) and Mr Stack (claimant). The purchase of the property was for £190,000. This was funded by a mortgage advance of £65,000 for which both parties were liable, the proceeds of sale of £67,000 from the first property (Purves Road, which was registered in the sole name of the defendant) and savings of £58,000 from a building society account in the defendant's name. The transfer contained no words of trust but included a declaration by the purchasers that the survivor of them was entitled to give a valid receipt for capital moneys. There was no discussion between the parties, at the time of the purchase, as to their respective share in the property. In 2002, owing to the deterioration of the relationship between the parties, the defendant served a notice of severance which had the effect of converting the joint tenancy into a tenancy in common. In April 2003 the parties agreed to a time-limited order in the Family Proceedings Court which excluded Mr Stack from the house and required Ms Dowden to pay him £900 per month which reflected the cost of alternative accommodation. After that order expired Mr Stack effectively accepted Ms Dowden's decision to exclude him. The result was that Ms Dowden remained in exclusive occupation and Mr Stack continued to pay for alternative accommodation. The claimant petitioned the court for a declaration that the property was held upon trust for the parties as tenants in common in equal shares. The trial judge ruled that the claimant had an interest in the first property and the savings and made an order to the effect that the claimant had an equal share in the property. In addition the court ordered that the defendant pay the claimant £900 per month as occupation rent. The defendant appealed against the order on the ground that the judge had misdirected himself.

The Court of Appeal allowed the appeal and decided that the beneficial interests in the house were held in the proportion of 65 per cent/35 per cent in her favour. Further there was no basis for assessing the compensation to the claimant at £900 per month. The claimant appealed to the House of Lords contending that the trial judge's original order be restored.

The House of Lords unanimously dismissed Mr Stack's appeal on the ground that there was no basis for varying the split of beneficial ownership (65 per cent/35 per cent) in favour of the defendant, which arose in 1993 on the acquisition of the Chatsworth Road house.

A declaration as to the receipt for capital moneys in the transfer document could not be construed as an express declaration of trust, following *Huntingford v Hobbs* [1993] 1 FLR 736.

Having regard to all the circumstances and wishes of the beneficiaries, as the court is obliged to do under s 15 of the Trusts of Land and Appointment of Trustees Act 1996, the court would not award rent to the defendant (Lord Neuberger dissenting).

JUDGMENT

'In the domestic consumer context, a conveyance into joint names indicates both legal and beneficial joint tenancy, unless and until the contrary is proved.

The starting point is that it is for Ms Dowden to show that the common intention, when taking a conveyance of the house into their joint names or thereafter, was that they should hold the property otherwise than as beneficial joint tenants.

There are many factors to which Ms Dowden can point to indicate that these parties did have a different common intention. The first, of course, is that on any view she contributed far more to the acquisition of Chatsworth Road than did Mr Stack. There are many different ways of calculating this ... The Court of Appeal rejected the judge's view ... and held that the whole of the purchase price, other than the mortgage loan, had been contributed by Ms Dowden. She had also contributed more to the capital repayment of that loan, although Mr Stack had made all the payments necessary to keep it going. It is not surprising that the Court of Appeal reached the conclusion that Ms Dowden was entitled to at least the 65 per cent she claimed.'

Baroness Hale

student
mentor tip

'Stack v Dowden is pertinent, so read the case in full.'
Pelena, University of Surrey

In *Stack v Dowden* Lord Neuberger arrived at the same conclusion but by a different route. He adopted the same starting point by regarding the equitable interest(s) as following the legal title(s), subject to evidence to the contrary. However, with regard to rebutting evidence he followed the traditional approach by having regard to the resulting and constructive trusts. Where the parties contributed to the purchase price of the property (including mortgage repayments) the beneficial ownership will be held in the same proportions as the contributions to the purchase price. This is the purchase money resulting trust solution. It must be emphasised that the position today is that Lord Neuberger's resulting trust solution no longer represents the law concerning beneficial interests in family homes.

To summarise, in *Stack v Dowden* two different approaches as to the interests of the parties were advocated by the Law Lords as manifested by Baroness Hale and Lord Neuberger. Both approaches led to the same result. However, the view expressed by Baroness Hale is firmly established as a correct statement of the current principles governing the interests in the family home namely, the common intention constructive trust. The Law Commission (2001, Law Com No 274) in its review of the law relating to the property rights of those who share homes commented that: 'It is widely accepted that the present law is unduly complex, arbitrary and uncertain in its application. It is ill-suited to determining the property rights of those who, because of the informal nature of their relationship, may not have considered their respective entitlements.' In 2002, the Commission published 'Sharing homes, a discussion paper' (2002, Law Com No 278) but failed to recommend any proposals for reform. The Commission declared: 'It is simply not possible to devise a statutory scheme for the ascertainment and quantification of beneficial interests in the shared home which can operate fairly and evenly across the diversity of domestic circumstances which are now to be encountered.'

In *Fowler v Barron* [2008] All ER (D) 318 (Apr), the Court of Appeal had the opportunity to consider the scope of the principles laid down in *Stack v Dowden*. In *Fowler v Barron*, the Court of Appeal decided that the trial judge had incorrectly concentrated on the parties' financial contributions and gave disproportionate weight to such a factor. But the crucial factor identified in *Stack* is not necessarily the amount of the parties' contributions to the property, but consideration of *all the circumstances which may throw light on the parties' common intentions in relation to ownership of the property.*

CASE EXAMPLE

Fowler v Barron [2008] All ER (D) 318 (Apr)

In this case, the parties were in an unmarried relationship for some 23 years from 1983 to 2005. In 1998 they bought the property in issue in Bognor Regis for £64,950 to provide a home for themselves and two children. The parties made a conscious decision to put the property in their joint names but did not take legal advice as to the consequences for doing so. Mr Barron (B), a retired fireman, paid the deposit on the house and arranged a mortgage for £35,000 in the joint names of the parties. B also paid the balance of the purchase price out of the proceeds of sale of his flat. There was no express declaration of trust, although the transfer stated that either surviving party was entitled to give a valid receipt for capital money. B alone paid the mortgage instalments and direct fixed costs of the property, such as council tax and utility bills, out of his pension. Miss Fowler (F) was employed and the judge found that she spent her income on herself and children. There was no joint bank account but the parties executed mutual wills, each leaving their interest in the property to the other.

The relationship between the parties deteriorated and the issue arose as the extent of the parties' beneficial interest in the property. The trial judge concentrated on the financial contributions of the parties and decided that F did not have a beneficial share in the property. F appealed and the Court of Appeal allowed the appeal, and decided that F had a 50 per cent share in the property, on the ground that the judge had erred in concentrating exclusively on the parties' financial contributions to the property. The facts as found by the judge were inconsistent with a common intention to exclude F from a beneficial interest.

The judge found that F used her income to spend as she chose, on the other hand, B paid the expenses of acquiring and maintaining the house.

The Court of Appeal decided that, having regard to all the circumstances, the parties' intentions were that it made no difference to their interests in the house who incurred what expense. On the question of the quantification of the appropriate share of each of the parties in the property the Court of Appeal decided that each case is determined on its own facts. The primary objective of the court is to ascertain the common intention of the parties by reference to the entire course of conduct regarding the house. Where the parties have made unequal contributions to the cost of acquiring their home, there is a thin dividing line between the case where the parties' shared intention is properly inferred to be ownership in equal shares, and the case where the parties' common intention is properly inferred to be that the party who contributed less should have a smaller share. In the present case, there was no evidence that the parties had any substantial assets apart from their income and their interests in the property. Thus, the Court of Appeal decided that there was no evidence that the parties intended F to have no share in the house if the relationship broke down. Indeed, by reference to the circumstances of the case the parties' objective intention was that F was entitled to a half share in the property.

The Supreme Court in *Jones v Kernott* (2011) had the first opportunity to review the state of the common intention constructive trust principles. The court considered the rules regarding the determination and quantification of interests in the family home in the context of joint legal ownership of the property. Undoubtedly the same principles, with appropriate adjustments, will apply to cases of sole legal ownership. One controversial principle that was laid down in an *obiter* pronouncement by the Supreme Court concerned the remedial constructive trust. The principle is that in joint legal ownership cases where it is clear either that the parties had not intended a joint tenancy at the outset or had changed their original intention, but their actual real intentions cannot be positively discerned by reference to the evidence, the courts will strive to construct (or impute) an intention that is fair and just. This question of fairness is determined by reference to the entire course of dealing between the parties and is applied in order to quantify the interests of the parties. However, this principle is not applicable to decide the first question as to whether the parties had a common intention to share their interests, but is strictly only relevant to value the interest.

CASE EXAMPLE

Jones v Kernott [2011] UHSC 53

In 1985 the claimant and the defendant bought a property in their joint names. The claimant paid the deposit, and the balance was raised by way of an endowment mortgage in their joint names. The parties paid the mortgage and other household expenses out of their joint resources.

In 1993 the defendant moved out of the property. The claimant continued living there with their two children and took sole responsibility for outgoings. The defendant made no further contribution towards the acquisition of the property. In 1995 the property was put on the market but failed to sell.

The parties cashed in a separate joint life insurance policy and divided the proceeds between them. This enabled the defendant to put down a deposit on a home of his own, which he bought with a mortgage in 1996. The claimant commenced proceedings for a declaration as to the value of her interest in the house. The High Court decided that in the interests of fairness, the claimant had acquired a 90 per cent interest and the defendant a 10 per cent interest in the property. The Court of Appeal allowed the appeal by a majority and decided that the parties acquired an equal share in the property on the ground that there was no evidence to infer that the parties has changed their intentions after the separation. On appeal, the Supreme Court allowed the appeal, restored the trial judge's decision and divided the property as to 90 per cent to the claimant and 10 per cent the defendant. The ground for this division was that the intentions of the parties had changed after the separation, as determined by the trial judge. Considering the evidence of conduct between the parties on an objective basis, an inference could be drawn that their intentions had changed significantly and in 1996 the claimant's interest in the property had crystallised. In these circumstances a rough calculation produced a result so close to the trial judge's rulings that it was wrong for the Court of Appeal to interfere.

Lord Collins in *Jones v Kernott* summarised the principles that were laid down in *Stack v Dowden* thus:

JUDGMENT

'(1) When property is held in joint names, and without any express declaration of trust, the starting point is that the beneficial interest is held equally and there is a heavy burden on the party asserting otherwise.

(2) That is because it will almost always have been a conscious decision to put the property into joint names, and committing oneself to spend large sums of money on a place to live is not normally done by accident or without giving it thought.

(3) Consequently it is to be expected that joint transferees would have spelled out their beneficial interests when they intended them to be different from their legal interests and cases in which the burden will be discharged will be very unusual.

(4) The contrary can be proved by looking at all the relevant circumstances in order to discern the parties' common intention.

(5) There is no presumption that the parties intended that the beneficial interest be shared in proportion to their financial contributions to the acquisition of the property (thereby rejecting the approach of the resulting trust analysis as a starting point favoured by Lord Neuberger in *Stack v Dowden*, dissenting, but not as to the result).

(6) The search is to ascertain the parties' shared intentions, actual, inferred or imputed, with respect to the property in the light of their whole course of conduct in relation to it.

(7) The search was for the result which reflected what the parties must, in the light of their conduct, be taken to have intended, and it did not enable the court to abandon that search in favour of the result which the court itself considered fair.

(8) The matters to be taken into account are discussed in detail at paras 33–34 and 68–70, and it is not necessary to rehearse them here.'

Lord Collins

Analysis of the principles in *Stack v Dowden* and *Jones v Kernott*

In these two definitive cases the House of Lords and Supreme Court laid down a framework of principles to determine beneficial interests in family homes and the assessment of the quantum of such interests.

1. If the parties have declared their interest in the Land Registry this statement will be conclusive in the absence of fraud, mistake, undue influence or a variation of the original declaration.

2. However, as frequently happens, where the parties have failed to expressly declare the trust the courts will need to construe the circumstances to determine whether an implied trust had been created between the parties. In the domestic context the constructive trust concept, rather than the resulting trust, will be adopted by the courts.

3. The same principles of common intention constructive trusts are applicable to interests in shared family homes, whether the legal title is in the joint names of the parties or in sole ownership. The starting point is that equity follows the law. The effect is that, subject to evidence to the contrary, in joint names ownership the beneficial interest is *prima facie* enjoyed jointly. In the case of legal ownership in the sole name of one party the starting point is that that person is the sole beneficial owner. Accordingly, a party wishing to claim a beneficial interest different from the starting point will bear the burden of proof, see Baroness Hale in *Stack v Dowden*.

JUDGMENT

'Just as the starting point where there is sole legal ownership is sole beneficial ownership, the starting point where there is joint legal ownership is joint beneficial ownership. The onus is upon the person seeking to show that the beneficial ownership is different from the legal ownership. So in sole ownership cases it is upon the non-owner to show that he has any interest at all. In joint ownership cases, it is upon the joint owner who claims to have other than a joint beneficial interest.'

Baroness Hale

4. There is two-stage process in determining and quantifying the interests of the parties in the family home. The first stage is to decide whether the parties had a common intention to share the interest in the property. The evidence that may support this is determined objectively and may amount to a common intention between the parties either *express or by inference*. Thus, it is not possible for the court to *impute* an intention to the parties (where none exists) in order to create a constructive trust. The courts are required to find that the parties had subjectively intended to share their beneficial interests. The second stage involves the evaluation of the interest of each party. This is based on the intentions of the parties, actual, inferred or imputed. Accordingly, an intention may be imputed as to the quantification of the interest but only after the courts have decided that the parties had a shared interest, see the joint judgment of Lord Walker and Baroness Hale in *Jones v Kernott*.

JUDGMENT

'The search is primarily to ascertain the parties' actual shared intentions, whether expressed or to be inferred from their conduct. However, there are at least two exceptions. The first is where the classic resulting trust presumption applies. Indeed, this would be rare in a domestic context, but might perhaps arise where domestic partners were also business partners.

The second is where it is clear that the beneficial interests are to be shared, but it is impossible to divine a common intention as to the proportions in which they are to be shared. In those two situations, the court is driven to impute an intention to the parties which they may never have had.

Lord Diplock, in *Gissing v Gissing* [1971] AC 886, 909, pointed out that, once the court was satisfied that it was the parties' common intention that the beneficial interest was to be shared in some proportion or other, the court might have to give effect to that common intention by determining what in all the circumstances was a fair share.'

Lord Walker and Baroness Hale

An 'inferred' intention is one which the parties subjectively entertained but this is decided objectively by the courts. Whereas an 'imputed' intention is one which, on construction of the facts, the parties did not have, but which the courts attribute to the parties on the principle of what the parties would have intended based on the circumstances of each case. The yardstick here is fairness between the parties, see Lord Neuberger in *Stack v Dowden*.

5. The courts will consider the whole course of dealing by the parties in relation to the property, including circumstances that may have changed during the course of the relationship. The factors to be taken into consideration by the courts in determining and quantifying beneficial interests are included the following list, laid down by Baroness Hale in *Stack v Dowden*.

JUDGMENT

'In law, "context is everything" and the domestic context is very different from the commercial world. Each case will turn on its own facts. Many more factors than financial contributions may be relevant to divining the parties' true intentions. These include: any advice or discussions at the time of the transfer which cast light upon their intentions then; the reasons why the home was acquired in their joint names; the reasons why (if it be the case) the survivor was authorised to give a receipt for the capital moneys; the purpose for which the home was acquired; the nature of the parties' relationship; whether they had children for whom they both had responsibility to provide a home; how the purchase was financed, both initially and subsequently; how the parties arranged their finances, whether separately or together or a bit of both; how they discharged the outgoings on the property and their other household expenses. When a couple are joint owners of the home and jointly liable for the mortgage, the inferences to be drawn from who pays for what may be very different from the inferences to be drawn when only one is owner of the home. The arithmetical calculation of how much was paid by each is also likely to be less important. It will be easier to draw the inference that they intended that each should contribute as much to the household as they reasonably could and that they would share the eventual benefit or burden equally. The parties' individual characters and personalities may also be a factor in deciding where their true intentions lay. In the cohabitation context, mercenary considerations may be more to the fore than they would be in marriage, but it should not be assumed that they always take pride of place over natural love and affection. At the end of the day, having taken all this into account, cases in which the joint legal owners are to be taken to have intended that their beneficial interests should be different from their legal interests will be very unusual.

This is not, of course, an exhaustive list. There may also be reason to conclude that, whatever the parties' intentions at the outset, these have now changed. An example might be where one party has financed (or constructed himself) an extension or substantial improvement to the property, so that what they have now is significantly different from what they had then.'

Baroness Hale

6. The parties' common intention may change over the course of their relationship owing to changed circumstances. In such a case the courts have the discretion to impute an intention to the parties and determine what is *fair in the circumstances at stage two* in the analysis, see Lord Walker and Baroness Hale in *Jones v Kernott*.

JUDGMENT

'It was also accepted that the parties' common intentions might change over time, producing what Lord Hoffmann referred to in the course of argument as an " 'ambulatory' constructive trust": Lady Hale, at para 62. An example, given in para 70, was where one party had financed or constructed an extension or major improvement to the property, so that what they had now was different from what they had first acquired. But of course there are other examples.'

Lord Walker and Baroness Hale

In *Barnes v Phillips* (2015) the Court of Appeal was required to decide whether the *Stack/ Kernott* principles were correctly applied by the trial judge. The issue was whether the judge had correctly imputed an intention between the parties as to their respective shares of ownership of a family home at the second stage of the analysis, after inferring that the parties had a common intention to share the beneficial interest. In the present case the judge was entitled to impute an intention to vary the beneficial interests in the property in order to reflect the changed circumstances of the parties.

CASE EXAMPLE

Barnes v Phillips [2015] EWCA Civ 1056 (Court of Appeal)

The parties lived together, had two children and subsequently bought the family home in 1996. The property was taken in the joint names of the parties. The respondent worked full time except for a short period when her children were very small. The appellant was a self-employed businessman. He paid the mortgage and some of the household bills. The respondent paid the remainder of the bills. The appellant subsequently bought three investment properties all in his name with the aid of mortgages. In 2005 he became financially insecure and had to remortgage the family home to pay off some of his personal debts. A few weeks later the relationship broke down and the parties separated. In 2008 the respondent assumed the responsibility for paying the mortgage on the family home and taking care of the children. The respondent commenced proceedings for a declaration as to her beneficial interest in the home. The judge awarded an interest in the property in the ratio of 85–15 per cent in favour of the respondent after deciding that the parties had a common intention to share the property. On appeal, the Court of Appeal dismissed the appeal and decided that the trial judge had accurately applied the *Stack/Kernott* principles. The imputed intention concerning the relevant ratio was based on adjustments to reflect the repayment of the appellant's debt following the remortgage of the property, the sole responsibility by the respondent to pay the mortgage from 2008 and undertaking the financial responsibility for the children.

JUDGMENT

'To my mind his use of "impute" in paragraph 38 of his judgment was both intentional and appropriate. As I read this paragraph, the judge is here addressing the second stage of the analysis, namely that which seeks to determine the shares in which the parties are to own the property following a change in the basis on which their beneficial interests are held. The use of "impute" in this context is entirely appropriate.

[On the issue of the variation of circumstances and consequent intention regarding the remortgage:] In the present case the weight of the evidence supports an inference that the parties intended to alter their shares in the property. Throughout the relationship the appellant was carrying on business activities. The remortgage of the property in May 2005 was entered into for the sole benefit of the appellant, in order to pay off debts which he had incurred in his personal capacity.

I consider that the judge did not infer that the parties had formed a common intention to hold the property in shares of 85% to the respondent and 15% to the appellant. On the contrary, having inferred a common intention to vary their interests in the property he imputed an intention to them as to their respective shares.

[On the issue of financial support for the children:] In view of the very wide terms in which the House of Lords in *Stack v Dowden* and the Supreme Court in *Jones v Kernott* described the relevant context, I consider that, in principle, it should be open to a court to take account of financial contributions to the maintenance of children (or lack of them) as part of the financial history of the parties save in circumstances where it is clear that to do so would result in double liability. However, there seems to be no danger of that in the present case.'

Lloyd Jones LJ

9.2.2 Investment properties

In *Laskar v Laskar* [2008] All ER (D) 104 (Feb), the Court of Appeal decided that the *Stack v Dowden* principles were not applicable to the acquisition of investment properties, i.e. properties bought for rental income and capital appreciation. In such cases the traditional resulting trust principles with their focus on mathematical computations of the contributions made by the individuals were *prima facie* applicable to ascertain the interests of the parties to the dispute.

CASE EXAMPLE

Laskar v Laskar [2008] All ER (D) 104 (Feb)

In this case, the defendant and her husband had been secure tenants of a council house for such a period of time entitling them to purchase the property at a discount under the Housing Act 1985. The defendant's husband had left her. The defendant made several unsuccessful attempts to purchase the property on her own. Finally, in 1998 the defendant made a joint application with the claimant (her daughter) to purchase the property. This application was successful and the property was vested in the joint names of the claimant and defendant. The purchase price was £50,085, which included a discount of £29,415 representing the defendant's occupation. The purchase price was funded by a deposit of £7,000, of which the claimant contributed £3,400 and the defendant raised £3,600. The balance of the purchase price was funded by a mortgage of £43,000 taken out in the joint names of the parties. The claimant did not live in the property and her room was let out to a lodger. As was contemplated, within a short period after the purchase another of the defendant's daughters purchased a house and the defendant went to live with this daughter. The original property was then fully let out. In 2003, the claimant and the defendant had a serious falling-out and the claimant sought to realise her interest in the property. The judge found that there were no discussions between the parties as to the beneficial ownership of the property. In addition, whilst the claimant and defendant were jointly liable on the mortgage the judge found that this liability was not one the claimant was ever 'likely to be asked to meet' because the rental income would be applied to service the mortgage. The judge ruled that the claimant was entitled to 4.28 per cent of the property based on a contribution of £3,400 towards the undiscounted value of the property at the time of the purchase (£79,500).

The claimant appealed and the Court of Appeal allowed the appeal and decided that the claimant was entitled to 33 per cent interest in the property. In the case of an arm's length commercial transaction, such as the present, the presumption of a resulting trust, based on the parties' monetary contributions, is appropriate to determine the beneficial interests of the parties. The *Stack v Dowden* principles were not applicable to occasions where the intentions of the parties were to acquire an investment property as distinct from a dwelling house for their use.

JUDGMENT

'The presumption of joint ownership

… It was argued that this case was midway between the cohabitation cases of co-ownership where property is bought for living in, such as *Stack*, and arm's-length commercial cases of co-ownership, where property is bought for development or letting. In the latter sort of case, the reasoning in *Stack* would not be appropriate and the resulting trust presumption still appears to apply. In this case, the primary purpose of the purchase of the property was as an investment, not as a home. In other words this was a purchase which, at least primarily, was not in "the domestic consumer context" but in a commercial context. To my mind it would not be right to apply the reasoning in *Stack* to such a case as this, where the parties primarily purchased the property as an investment for rental income and capital appreciation, even where their relationship is a familial one …

The discount

When it comes to assessing the contributions to the purchase price the appellant argues either that no account should be taken of the discount of £29,415 or that it should be attributable equally to both parties. I do not agree. In the absence of authority the position seems to me to be this. The reason the property could be bought at a discount – indeed, the reason the property could be bought at all – was that the respondent had been the secure tenant of the property and had resided there in that capacity for a substantial period … It was therefore the respondent, and solely the respondent, to whom the discount of £29,415 could be attributed …

The effect of taking the mortgage in joint names

There is obvious force in the appellant's contention that, as she and the respondent took out a mortgage in joint names for £43,000, for which they were jointly and separately liable, in respect of a property which they jointly owned, this should be treated in effect as representing equal contributions of £21,500 by each party to the acquisition of the property. It is right to mention that I pointed out in *Stack* that, although simple and clear, such a treatment of a mortgage liability might be questionable in terms of principle and authority.

However, it appears to me that in this case it would be right to treat the mortgage loan of £43,000 as representing a contribution of £21,500 by each of the parties as the two joint purchasers of the property.

There was no agreement or understanding between the parties that one or other of them was to be responsible for the repayments. The repayments had effectively been met out of the income from the property, which, so far as one can gather, was intended from the inception, and the property was, as I have mentioned, primarily purchased and has been retained as an investment. In those circumstances I would have thought that there was a very strong case for apportioning the mortgage equally between the parties when it comes to assessing their respective contributions to the purchase price …

Conclusions on the beneficial interest

In light of these conclusions on these three points, I am of the view that it would be right to substitute for the judge's decision that the appellant has 4.28 per cent of the beneficial interest in order that she has a 33 per cent interest in the property. I arrive at that conclusion on the basis that the respondent's contribution was the aggregate of £21,500 (half of the mortgage) £29,500 (the discount) and £3,600 (her share of the balance), and that the appellant's contribution was £21,500 (half the mortgage) and £3,400 (her share of the balance). That produces share of 33%.'

Lord Neuberger

In *Erlam v Rahman* (2016) the High Court adopted the principle laid down in *Laskar* and decided that the purchase of property for letting was subject to the resulting trusts principles based on actual contributions to the purchase price. Accordingly, where the investment property has been acquired in the name of one party to a marriage, the other party who claims an interest in the property is required to prove the existence of a valid declaration of trust in writing (which complies with s 53(1)(b) of the Law of Property Act 1925) or that he or she has made substantial contributions to the purchase price of the property.

CASE EXAMPLE

Erlam v Rahman [2016] EWHC 111 (High Court)

The claimants, a group of private individuals, successfully challenged the election of the first defendant (R) as the Mayor of the Borough of Tower Hamlets. An application had been issued in respect of a charging order concerning three investment properties acquired by R before he became bankrupt. The present case was in respect of one such property, 3 Grace Street. R's wife, Farid (F), was added as a second defendant and alleged that a declaration of trust had been executed by R concerning the property in which he held the property as to 74 per cent for her and 26 per cent for himself. The declaration was not construed as a gift of the interest to her but as contributions to the purchase price in the respective proportions. The issues before the court were: the effect of the declaration of trust; the relevance of the *Stack/Kernott* principles in this context; alternatively, whether the resulting trust is applicable; and whether the declaration of trust constituted a sham. The court allowed the application and decided that the declaration of trust was not evidence of a 74 per cent interest in the property in favour of F. The *Stack/Kernott* approach was restricted to disputes between cohabiting couples in family property. The appropriate principles in a commercial context involve the resulting trust solution, see *Laskar v Laskar*. There was no satisfactory basis for accepting the evidence of F that she, with the assistance of others, had contributed 74 per cent of the purchase monies. It was not necessary to decide whether the declaration of trust was a sham, but had that been necessary, there was sufficient evidence to conclude that it was a sham. Consequently, R owned 100 per cent of the property.

JUDGMENT

'The *Stack v Dowden* approach has no application to a property bought by a married couple for investment rather than as a home. It was not a purchase in the "domestic consumer context". It follows that the proper approach is to follow the "classic resulting trust doctrine" by looking at the actual contributions to the purchase.

Mrs Farid is not able to show that on the balance of probabilities she made any contribution to the purchase price of 3 Grace Street. It follows that she cannot establish a resulting trust.

The declaration of trust is based on the premise that she made a contribution of 74% to the purchase price; however, that does not reflect the reality. The declaration of trust does not amount to a gift of a beneficial interest to Mrs Farid and its purported effect to declare that she has a 74% interest based on a contribution of that proportion is a fiction.'

Chief Master Marsh

It is now well established that with respect to investment properties the *Stack/Kernott* principles are not applicable in order to determine the respective interests of the parties. Instead, *Laskar/Erlam* illustrate that the narrower resulting trusts principles are applicable and the interests of the parties will be determined on the basis of contributions made by the parties at the time of the purchase of the property or, exceptionally, thereafter. However, it is arguable that in addition to the resulting trust principles, a traditional form of common intention constructive trust or proprietary estoppel may be relevant in this context. This type of constructive trust may be established in accordance with the *Rosset* principles (see later).

In *Williams v Parris* [2008] EWCA Civ 1147, the Court of Appeal decided, in accordance with the principles laid down in *Lloyds Bank v Rosset*, that once the claimant had established a common intention or agreement to share a beneficial interest in property, a constructive trust will arise if the claimant had acted to his detriment or significantly altered his position in reliance on the agreement or understanding. It was not necessary for the claimant to proceed further and establish that the arrangement or agreement had involved the making of a bargain between the parties, and that the claimant had performed his part of that bargain.

CASE EXAMPLE

Williams v Parris [2008] EWCA Civ 1147

In *Williams* the claimant ran into financial problems and entered into an individual voluntary arrangement with his creditors. The defendant was offered an opportunity to purchase two flats (flats 1 and 6) and discussed this with the claimant. The claimant was unable to contribute, partly as a result of the IVA. Despite that, the claimant's case was that they agreed to proceed with the purchase of the flats as a joint venture. The defendant would buy them, but on the basis that flat 6 would belong beneficially to him (the claimant). The defendant bought both flats in his own name. The claimant issued proceedings seeking a declaration that the defendant held flat 6 on trust for him absolutely. On the evidence the judge found that an informal agreement had been reached between the parties that the flats would be purchased by the defendant on the basis that they would have an equal interest. That would take the form of each one having one flat in due course. The claimant had supplied what he could, namely, labour to begin with, later on some money and undoubtedly maintenance charges. The defendant appealed on the ground that the party claiming the benefit of the trust should be able to show not merely that there was an agreement between him (claimant) and the legal owner that he should have a beneficial interest, but also that he had acted under that agreement in the manner provided for in the agreement.

The Court of Appeal dismissed the appeal and decided that once a finding of express arrangement or agreement had been made, all that the claimant needed to show in support of a beneficial share under a constructive trust was that he had acted to his detriment or had significantly altered his position in reliance on the agreement.

JUDGMENT

'[Referring to Lord Bridge's remarks in *Rosset*:] What he said was advanced by way of express guidance to trial judges. The first type of case he identified was a case such as this one; and he made it plain that, once a finding of an express arrangement or agreement has been made, all that the claimant to a beneficial share under a constructive trust needs to show is that he or she has acted to his or her detriment or significantly altered his or her position in reliance on the agreement. ... That amounts to solid support for the approach reflected in *Grant* (1986) and for the way in which the Recorder directed himself in the present case. It implicitly rejects any suggestion that might be derived from Lord Diplock's remarks in *Gissing* (1971) ... that it is necessary to show that the arrangement or agreement involved the making of something in the nature of a bargain between the parties, and that the claimant has performed his part of that bargain.'

Rimer LJ

In accordance with the principles concerning investment properties it follows that the starting point is the ownership of the legal title. If the legal title is vested in joint parties the equitable interest will mirror this interest. If the legal title is vested in the name of one party the starting point is that the equitable interest will follow the legal title. A claimant who alleges to the contrary will be put to proof to establish that a different proportion of interest has been acquired by him. If there is no evidence in writing, such as a declaration of trust, the claimant will be required to establish an implied trust in his favour, resulting or constructive. If the purchase moneys were provided solely by the party without the legal title it may be necessary to establish a common intention constructive trust, i.e. the common intention of the parties is that the claimant acquires the equitable interest and he relied on this intention to his detriment, see *Agarwala v Agarwala* (2013).

CASE EXAMPLE

Agarwala v Agarwala [2013] Unreported (CA)

The appellant (J) was the sister-in-law of the respondent (S). S identified an investment property which he proposed to purchase in the name of his friend, Andy Prior, a builder, subject to a trust deed. This arrangement fell through and S approached J about the investment potential of the property stating that it was a good deal but he did not have the credit rating to purchase it. She agreed and in April 2007 the property was purchased. The property was to be used as a 'bed and breakfast' (B&B) business. The purchase, subject to a mortgage, was made in J's name (legal title) and it was agreed that S would pay the mortgage instalments and operate and manage the B&B. The parties fell out in July 2008 and J's husband (H) took over the day-to-day running of the business and changed the locks to exclude S from the premises. S forged J's signature on the lease and trust deed to benefit himself and backdated the documents to 2007. S's deceit was detected, and although he was arrested, he was not prosecuted.

S issued proceedings claiming the beneficial ownership. The parties agreed that there was a clear, oral agreement or understanding between them as to the terms on which they bought, held and used the property but the details of that agreement was disputed by the parties. J's case was that the property and business were hers beneficially and that S had agreed to manage the conversion and operate the business at no charge. The benefit to S was that he would have been entitled to accommodate surplus guests from his other B&B business. S's case was that J had agreed to help him to purchase the property because of his bad credit rating and that since he had provided the money for the conversion and mortgage payments, the property and business were his beneficially. Thus, S alleged that J held the property as bare trustee for him as absolute beneficial owner.

The judge ruled that S's account of the terms of the agreement was more credible and that J held the property on constructive trust for S, based on a common understanding, reliance and detriment in accordance with the principles laid down in the *Stack v Dowden* [2007] UKHL 17. J appealed to the Court of Appeal against this ruling. The court dismissed the appeal and decided that the trial judge had correctly directed himself on the appropriate weight to be attached to each party's version of the agreement. No weight was attached to the forged documents executed by S in deciding on S's credibility. The money and work put in by S in converting, setting up and running the business was to his detriment and supported his contention. Accordingly, J held the property on constructive trust for S.

JUDGMENT

'It was common ground that this was a business venture in which there was an agreement as to the terms on which the property was to be bought, held and used. The fact that the mortgage was in [J's] name and that she paid the instalments was of little help in deciding the issue of beneficial ownership if [J] was, in effect, a conduit for the payment of the instalments out of the profits of the business venture.'

Sullivan LJ

9.2.3 Legal title in the name of one party only

Where the legal title to property has been conveyed in the name of one party only, and his or her partner wishes to claim a beneficial interest, the claimant is required to establish the existence of a common intention constructive trust. The presumptions of resulting trust and advancement will not be readily adopted in order to quantify the interests of the parties because such presumptions have outlived their usefulness in this context. It was not until after the Second World War that the courts were required to consider the proprietary rights in family assets of a different social class. It was considered to be an abuse of legal principles for ascertaining or imputing intention, to apply to transactions between the post-war generation of married couples artificial 'presumptions' as to the most likely intentions of a culturally different generation of spouses in the nineteenth century, *per* Lord Diplock (above). These sentiments were expressed by the House of Lords in two definitive decisions: *Pettitt v Pettitt* [1970] AC 777 and *Gissing v Gissing* [1971] AC 886.

Having dispelled notions of the presumed resulting trust and advancement the House of Lords replaced the presumptions with common intention constructive trusts. The effect is that where the legal title is vested in the name of one party the inference is that equity follows the law and the party with the legal title is *prima facie* solely entitled to the equitable interest. If the party without the legal title wishes to claim an interest in the property, he or she bears the legal burden of proving that both parties had an intention to give the claimant an interest in the property which was relied on to his or her detriment. This solution, with the appropriate adaptation, is similar to the principles that are applicable to transfers of the property in joint names mentioned earlier.

CASE EXAMPLE

Pettitt v Pettitt [1970] AC 777

Mrs Pettitt purchased a cottage with her own money and had the legal title conveyed in her name. Mr Pettitt from time to time redecorated the property, expending a total of £725. On a breakdown of the marriage he claimed a proportionate interest in the house (£1,000 *pro rata* value). The court decided that Mr Pettitt's expenditure was not related to the acquisition of the house. In the absence of an agreement or understanding, his expenditure was to be treated as a gift. The court decided that settled principles of property law were applicable in this context.

JUDGMENT

'Where the acquisition or improvement is made as a result of contributions in money or money's worth by both spouses acting in concert the proprietary interests in the family asset resulting from their respective contributions depend upon their common intention as to what those interests should be.

In the present case we are concerned not with the acquisition of a matrimonial home on mortgage, but with improvements to a previously acquired matrimonial home.

It is common enough nowadays for husbands and wives to decorate and to make improvements in the family home themselves, with no other intention than to indulge in what is now a popular hobby, and to make the home pleasanter for their common use and enjoyment. If the husband likes to occupy his leisure by laying a new lawn in the garden or building a fitted wardrobe in the bedroom while the wife does the shopping, cooks the family dinner or bathes the children, I, for my part, find it quite impossible to impute to them as reasonable husband and wife any common intention that these domestic activities or any of them are to have any effect upon the existing proprietary rights in the family home on which they have undertaken. It is only in the bitterness engendered by the break-up of the marriage that so bizarre a notion would enter their heads.'

Lord Diplock

CASE EXAMPLE

Gissing v Gissing [1971] AC 886

Mr Gissing purchased the matrimonial home in his name out of his own resources. Mrs Gissing paid £220 for furnishings and laying a lawn. There was no common understanding as to the beneficial interest in the house. On a breakdown of the marriage, the question arose as to the beneficial ownership of the house. The court decided that Mrs Gissing was not entitled to an interest in the house, for she had made no contributions to the purchase price.

JUDGMENT

'Any claim to a beneficial interest in land by a person, whether spouse or stranger, in whom the legal estate in the land is not vested must be based upon the proposition that the person in whom the legal estate is vested holds it as a trustee upon trust to give effect to the beneficial interest of the claimant as *cestui que trust*. The legal principles applicable to the claim are those of the English law of trusts.

Where the wife has made no initial contribution to the cash deposit and legal charges and no direct contribution to the mortgage instalments nor any adjustment to her contribution to other expenses of the household which it can be inferred was referable to the acquisition of the house, there is in the absence of evidence of an express agreement between the parties no material to justify the court in inferring that it was the common intention of the parties that she should have any beneficial interest in a matrimonial home conveyed into the sole name of the husband, merely because she continued to contribute out of her own earnings or private income to other expenses of the household. For such conduct is no less consistent with a common intention to share the day to day expenses of the household, while each spouse retains a separate interest in capital assets acquired with their own moneys or obtained here to rebut the *prima facie* inference that a purchaser of land who pays the purchase price and takes a conveyance and grants a mortgage in his own name intends to acquire the sole beneficial interest as well as the legal estate: and the difficult question of the quantum of the wife's share does not arise.'

Lord Diplock

Likewise, Lord Walker in *Stack v Dowden* disapproved of the purchase money resulting trust principles in the context of ownership of the family home in favour of the broader constructive trust rules. Contributions to the purchase price in money or money's worth may be relevant in determining the existence of a common intention.

JUDGMENT

'In a case about beneficial ownership of a matrimonial or quasi-matrimonial home (whether registered in the name of one or two legal owners) the resulting trust should not in my opinion operate as a legal presumption, although it may (in an updated form which takes account of all significant contributions, direct or indirect, in cash or in kind) happen to be reflected in the parties' common intention.'

Lord Walker

In the *Estate of York* (2015) (see later) the Court of Appeal decided that in the case of property purchased in the name of one party there was no presumed starting point of equality of interests. This is the position even if the party without the legal title made a substantial contribution to the acquisition of the property. The burden of proof in establishing a share and the quantification of the share lies on the party against whom the presumption operates. Further, the appeal court will not interfere with the trial judge's decision unless he misdirects himself on the appropriate principles of law. It was irrelevant that the claimant to an interest in the property had endured years of physical abuse at the hands of the party with the sole legal interest in the property. The reason is that in imputing an intention concerning the relevant shares in the property, the court is not concerned with redistributive justice.

It is clear that if, on a review of the material circumstances, the trial judge objectively decides that the claimant made no contribution (financial or otherwise) to the acquisition or retention of the property, there will be no ground to infer a common intention to share the beneficial interest in the property. Accordingly, in a sole ownership case, the claimant may fail to discharge the burden of proof. Equally, where the legal owner makes an excuse for not transferring the legal title in the parties' joint names it does not follow that this may constitute an agreement to share the beneficial interest, see *Curran v Collins* (2015).

CASE EXAMPLE

Curran v Collins [2015] EWCA Civ 404 (Court of Appeal)

Mr Collins was the sole owner of a house in Feltham bought in 1986. He met Ms Curran in 1977 and formed a relationship with her but they did not live together until 2002. In 2007 Mr Collins sold the Feltham house and bought another with the aid of a mortgage, 'The Haven', which was taken in his sole name. The relationship deteriorated and Ms Curran was asked to leave The Haven. Ms Curran brought a claim alleging an equitable interest in The Haven. In addition she claimed that she had an interest in the Feltham house which 'rolled over' to The Haven. She supported her claim by testifying that Mr Collins provided an excuse for her not acquiring a joint interest in the legal title to the Feltham house. The excuse was the extra costs of insurance. The judge decided against her on the ground that there was no evidence of a common intention to share the property because she had failed to make a contribution to The Haven. On appeal, the Court of Appeal dismissed her appeal on the grounds that there was no evidence of an agreement to share the equitable interest in the property. The excuse provided by Mr Collins did not amount to an agreement to share the interest in the Feltham house that preceded the purchase of The Haven.

JUDGMENT

'Given that the parties were not living together and the absence of significant contribution by Ms Curran, it is clear that the judge in my judgment applied the objective test in her interpretation of the Excuse.

I would therefore dismiss this ground of appeal.'

Arden LJ

'The starting point is the assumption that beneficial ownership of real property follows the legal title. In a "single name" case, of which this is one, that means that the sole legal owner is assumed to be the sole beneficial owner unless the contrary is shown.

[On the issue of the excuse given by Mr Collins:] 'It cannot be right that the giving of a reason why someone is not on the title deeds inevitably leads to the inference that it must have been agreed that they would have an interest in the property. If one who is not versed in the difference between legal and beneficial ownership asks to be on the deeds and is told "No", the more usual inference would be that they would have understood that they were not to become owners or part owners of the property. I cannot see that the result is very different if the reason given is that it is too expensive. Ms Curran had no intention of moving into the Feltham house at the time it was acquired.'

Levison LJ

In *Capehorn v Harris* (2015), in a sole legal ownership case, the trial judge made a fundamental error in confusing the two stage analysis by *imputing* an intention to the parties in order to establish the existence of an agreement to share the relevant properties. This was done at stage one of the analysis, despite finding that objectively there was no actual agreement between the parties. Accordingly, the Court of Appeal allowed the appeal and reversed the decision of the trial judge.

CASE EXAMPLE

Capehorn v Harris [2015] EWCA Civ 955 (Court of Appeal)

Mr Harris (H) ran a frozen food business in which Mrs Capehorn (C) was employed. The parties formed a relationship and from 1983 they were living together. In 1991 H was declared bankrupt and C took over the business as a sole trader. In 1993 C bought a property in her name, called 'Sunnyside Farm', with the aid of a mortgage. The parties lived in this property. In 2004 H set up his own business in which he owned all the shares. The business was run from Sunnyside Farm. Eventually relations between the parties deteriorated and C moved out of the house. She commenced proceedings against him for a declaration as to her rights in the house and H's company. The trial judge concluded that there was no agreement between the parties as to a shared interest in the house and company but nevertheless imputed an intention to share the house as to 25 per cent in favour of H and 75 per cent in favour of C. The company was shared 65 per cent to H and 35 per cent to C. On appeal, the Court of Appeal allowed the appeal on the ground that the judge had erred in imputing an agreement between the parties as to a shared interest. This was at stage one of the analysis. Since there was no agreement (express or inferred) between the parties there was no basis of establishing a common intention.

JUDGMENT

'In my judgment, the judge erred in this paragraph of the judgment. She imputed an intention to the parties for the first stage of the two-stage analysis rather than identifying an actual agreement made by them that Mr Harris should have any beneficial interest in Sunnyside Farm. No actual agreement to that effect was ever made by Mrs Capehorn and Mr Harris, as the judge's findings elsewhere in the judgment made clear.'

Sales LJ

9.3 Nature of the trust

In the domestic context, the notion of the 'purchase money' resulting trust has been finally castigated in favour of the common intention constructive trust in a long line of decisions culminating with *Stack v Dowden* and *Jones v Kernott*. The constructive trust regime is regarded as an appropriate vehicle that reflects the genuine intentions of the parties at the time of the acquisition of the property, or exceptionally at a later date.

The constructive trust will be created whenever the trustee has so conducted himself that it would be inequitable to allow him to deny to the beneficiary an equitable interest in the land acquired. He will be treated as having conducted himself inequitably if, by his words or conduct, he had induced the beneficiary to act to his own detriment in the reasonable belief that by so acting he will acquire a beneficial interest in the land. In other words, the court gives effect to the implied trust that reflects the common intention of the parties that if each acts in the manner provided for in the agreement the beneficial interests in the matrimonial home will be held as they have agreed; for example, if both the husband and wife contributed to the purchase of the house but the legal title to the property was placed solely in the name of the husband, the wife will need to establish that it would be inequitable for the husband to deny her a share in the property. This would be the case if the court is satisfied that it was the common intention of both spouses that the contributing wife should have a share in the beneficial interest and that her contributions were made upon this understanding. The court, in the exercise of its equitable jurisdiction, would not permit the husband in whom the legal estate was vested and who had accepted the benefit of the contributions to take the whole beneficial interest merely because, at the time the wife made her contributions, there had been no express agreement as to how her share in it was to be quantified. The same principles apply where the legal title is conveyed in the joint names of the parties. The presumption is in favour of a legal and equitable joint tenancy until the contrary is proved.

The intentions of the parties are determined objectively, by reference to their statements and conduct in respect of the property. The court is required to draw inferences from such evidence and make value judgments as to their intentions. This is the position even though a party did not consciously formulate that intention in his own mind or may have acted with some different intention which he did not communicate to the other party. The subjective intentions of the parties are not decisive: more so, if such intention has not been communicated to the other party. Lord Diplock in *Gissing v Gissing* [1971] AC 886, explained the process adopted by the courts for identifying the intentions of the parties.

JUDGMENT

'[T]he relevant intention of each party is the intention which was reasonably understood by the other party to be manifested by that party's words and conduct notwithstanding that he did not consciously formulate that intention in his own mind or even acted with some different intention which he did not communicate to the other party.'

Lord Diplock

The time for drawing an inference as to what the parties said and did which led up to the acquisition of a matrimonial home is on a different footing from what they said and did after the acquisition was completed. The material time for the court to draw inferences from the conduct of the parties is up to and including the time of the acquisition of the property. In exceptional circumstances, subsequent evidence may be relevant only if it is alleged that there was some subsequent fresh agreement, acted upon by the parties, to vary the original beneficial interests created when the matrimonial home was acquired. In other words, what the parties said and did after the acquisition was completed will be relevant if it is explicable only upon the basis of their having manifested to one another at the time of the acquisition some particular common intention as to how the beneficial interests should be held.

CASE EXAMPLE

James v Thomas [2008] 1 FLR 1598

The claimant, who did not have the legal title to the property, failed to discharge the burden of proof cast on her to demonstrate, based on evidence related to the entire course of dealing, that she acquired an interest in the property. In this case, Miss James entered into a relationship with the defendant and subsequently moved into the house owned by the defendant. Miss James worked as a partner without remuneration with Mr Thomas in his business as an agricultural building and drainage contractor. Over the years the couple carried out extensive works of renovation at the property, funded by income generated by the business. Some years later the relationship broke down, Miss James moved out, and the partnership was dissolved by notice served by Miss James. The latter claimed an interest in the property on the ground of a constructive trust or alternatively proprietary estoppel. The judge dismissed her claim and she appealed. The Court of Appeal dismissed her appeal but observed that the common intention necessary to found a constructive trust could be formed at any time before, during or after the acquisition of a property; a constructive trust could therefore arise some years after the property had been acquired by, and registered in the sole name of, one party. However, in the absence of an express post-acquisition agreement, the court would be slow to infer from conduct alone that the parties intended to vary existing beneficial interests established at the time of acquisition

JUDGMENT

'He (the judge) referred, in terms to the absence of an allegation by Miss James, that there were any discussions between the parties *either at the time of the acquisition or subsequently* to the effect that they had an agreement or an understanding that the property would be shared. To my mind, the better view (when the judgment is read as a whole) is that the judge did recognise that there was a need to consider (in relation to constructive trust as well as in relation to proprietary estoppel) whether the parties formed a common intention, in or after 1989, that Miss James should have a beneficial share in the property. Accordingly – although not without hesitation – I reject the submission that the judge erred in law.' [Emphasis added]

Chadwick LJ

In *O'Kelly v Davies* (2014) the Court of Appeal declared that where a claimant secured the transfer of the family home in her sole name in order to facilitate a fraud, no distinction ought to be drawn between a possible unenforceable constructive trust of the property on the one hand, and an enforceable resulting trust on the other hand. In either case the focus is on whether the claimant is required to rely on the unlawful transaction in order to establish an interest in the property. If this is not the case the claimant will be entitled to establish an equitable interest in the property.

CASE EXAMPLE

O'Kelly v Davies [2014] EWCA Civ 1606 (Court of Appeal)

The appellant (O) and respondent (D) were cohabiting partners. O purchased Lon Olchfa, which was used as the family home. The legal title was taken in O's name, which assisted in her fraudulent benefits claim. The parties separated in 2011 and D brought a claim for a declaration as to his interest in Lon Olchfa. He alleged that he had an equal interest in the property. The court held that the parties had an equal share in Lon Olchfa in accordance with an inferred common intention constructive trust. On appeal, the Court of Appeal dismissed the appeal. The judge was entitled to consider whether the conduct of the parties had objectively demonstrated a common intention to share the property. The issue was whether public policy in accordance with the *Tinsley v Milligan* (1994) principle ought to intervene to prevent him from enforcing his interest (see 7.4.5). No reliance on the unlawful conduct was required in order to establish an intention to share an interest in the property.

JUDGMENT

'While the reason for purchase in the defendant's sole name was unlawful, *the acquisition of a beneficial interest in the property arose not from the illegal purpose but from the parties' common intention*, inferred from their continuing course of dealing, that the claimant should have such an interest. The unlawful purpose may have explained their conduct but it was the conduct itself that gave rise to the constructive trust.' [Emphasis added]

Pitchford LJ

Lady Justice Gloster summarised the issue thus:

JUDGMENT

'I also agree that this appeal should be dismissed. Whether the analysis depends on constructive or resulting trust, or merely the ascertainment of the parties' common intention, there was no need for the claimant to rely on the illegality relating to the reason for the legal title to 74 Lon Olchfa being in the defendant's name in order to establish his beneficial interest in the property. The decision in *Tinsley v Milligan [1994] 1 AC 340* was clearly applicable.'

Gloster LJ

9.3.1 Common intention

The key concept that underpins the establishment of an interest in the family home today is the single regime of the common intention constructive trust. The purchase money resulting trust principles will not be adopted to identify and quantify the interests of the parties. The time for deciding on the existence of the parties' intention is at the time of the purchase of the property or exceptionally at some later date. This is the position whether the legal title to the property is placed in the joint names of the parties or in the sole name of one party. In both cases the rule is that equity follows the law. The effect is that in the case of joint names legal ownership the inference is that the parties are joint tenants and in cases of sole legal ownership the *prima facie* rule is that the party with the legal title is the equitable owner. If a party wishes to claim an interest different from the *prima facie* rule he or she bears the legal burden of proving the existence of a common intention of the parties that he or she has an equitable interest, or a greater interest, than is reflected by reference to the legal title, relied on by such party to his or her detriment. This intention is determined objectively by reference to the conduct of the parties, see the joint speech by Lord Walker and Baroness Hale in *Jones v Kernott* (2011).

JUDGMENT

'The time has come to make it clear, in line with *Stack v Dowden* (see also *Abbott v Abbott* [2007] UKPC 53, [2007] 2 All ER 432, [2008] 1 FLR 1451), that in the case of the purchase of a house or flat in joint names for joint occupation by a married or unmarried couple, *where both are responsible for any mortgage*, there is no presumption of a resulting trust arising from their having contributed to the deposit (or indeed the rest of the purchase) in unequal shares. The presumption is that the parties intended a joint tenancy both in law and in equity. But that presumption can of course be rebutted by evidence of a contrary intention, which may more readily be shown where the parties did not share their financial resources.' [Emphasis added]

Lord Walker and Baroness Hale in *Jones v Kernott* [2011] UKSC 53.

The italicised words in the above judgment in *Jones v Kernott* are somewhat puzzling. It is ludicrous to suggest that the *Stack v Dowden* and *Jones v Kernott* principles are only applicable where there is a joint mortgage between the parties. Equally, it is irrational to suggest that the common intention constructive trust principles are not applicable where the property had been bought without a mortgage. The reality may well be that Lord Walker and Baroness Hale were in this sentence focusing on rules regarding the acquisition of the property in joint names rather than only occasions when the mortgage is taken in the parties' joint names.

The existence of a common intention may be express or implied by reference to the circumstances of each case. The court is required to interpret the surrounding facts with a view to ascertaining the intentions of the parties in respect of a share in the home. In *Lloyds Bank v Rosset* (1990), Lord Bridge opined that evidence of express intention is based on *express discussion between the parties,* even though the terms of the discussion may not be precisely recalled. In this respect the discussions need not be as to the precise interest to be acquired by the parties, provided that they are centred on the existence of an interest. With regard to implied or inferential common intention, Lord Bridge advocated the test of looking at the conduct of the parties and decided that substantial direct financial contributions to the purchase price, by paying the deposit or mortgage instalments on the house, may be sufficient.

CASE EXAMPLE

Lloyds Bank v Rosset [1990] 1 All ER 1111, HL

A semi-derelict farmhouse was conveyed in the name of the husband but the wife spent a great deal of time in the house supervising the work done by builders. She also did some decorating to the house. Unknown to the wife, her husband had taken out an overdraft with the bank. The couple later separated but the wife remained in the house. The husband was unable to repay the overdraft, with the result that the bank started proceedings for the sale of the property. The wife resisted the claim on the ground that she was entitled to a beneficial interest in the house under a constructive trust. The trial judge and the Court of Appeal decided that the husband held the property as constructive trustee for his wife and himself. The bank appealed. The House of Lords held in favour of the bank on the ground that the wife had no beneficial interest in the property. There was no understanding between the parties that the property was to be shared beneficially, coupled with detrimental action by the claimant, nor had there been direct contributions to the purchase price. In any event, the court decided that the monetary value of the wife's work was trifling compared with the cost of acquiring the house.

JUDGMENT

'The first and fundamental question which must always be resolved is whether, independently of any inference to be drawn from the conduct of the parties in the course of sharing the house as their home and managing their joint affairs, *there has at any time prior to acquisition, or exceptionally at some later date, been any agreement, arrangement or understanding reached between them that the property is to be shared beneficially. The finding of an agreement or arrangement to share in this sense can only, I think, be based on evidence of express discussions between the partners,* however imperfectly remembered and however imprecise their terms may have been. Once a finding to this effect is made it will only be necessary for the partner asserting a claim to a beneficial interest against the partner entitled to the legal estate to show that he or she has acted to his or her detriment or significantly altered his or her position in reliance on the agreement in order to give rise to a constructive trust or a proprietary estoppel.

In sharp contrast with this situation is the very different one where there is no evidence to support a finding of an agreement or arrangement to share, however reasonable it might have been for the parties to reach such an arrangement if they had applied their minds to the question, and *where the court must rely entirely on the conduct of the parties both as the basis from which to infer a common intention to share the property beneficially and as the conduct relied on to give rise to a constructive trust. In this situation direct contributions to the purchase price by the partner who is not the legal owner, whether initially or by payment of mortgage instalments, will readily justify the inference necessary to the creation of a constructive trust. But, as I read the authorities, it is at least extremely doubtful whether anything less will do.'* [Emphasis added]

Lord Bridge

It has been recognised that Lord Bridge's view of the evidence of implied common intention by reference solely to direct financial contributions to the purchase price may have been too restrictive and narrow. Instead the courts tend to adopt a more holistic approach to evidence of common intention by considering circumstances other than financial contributions. In *Stack v Dowden*, Baroness Hale identified a number of non-financial factors that may be considered by the courts. These include the purpose of the acquisition of the home, whether there were any children of the relationship, the obligations undertaken towards the children, how the parties arranged their finances etc.

JUDGMENT

'In law, context is everything and the domestic context is very different from the commercial world. Each case will turn on its own facts. Many more factors than financial contributions may be relevant to divining the parties' true intentions. These include: any advice or discussions at the time of the transfer which cast light upon their intentions then; the reasons why the home was acquired in their joint names; the reasons why (if it be the case) the survivor was authorised to give a receipt for the capital moneys; the purpose for which the home was acquired; the nature of the parties' relationship; whether they had children for whom they both had responsibility to provide a home; how the purchase was financed, both initially and subsequently; how the parties arranged their finances, whether separately or together or a bit of both; how they discharged the outgoings on the property and their other household expenses. When a couple are joint owners of the home and jointly liable for the mortgage, the inferences to be drawn from who pays for what may be very different from the inferences to be drawn when only one is the owner of the home. The arithmetical calculation of how much was paid by each is also likely to be less important. It will be easier to draw the inference that they intended that each should contribute as much to the household as they reasonably could and that they would share the eventual benefit or burden equally. The parties' individual characters and personalities may also be a factor in deciding where their true intentions lay ... At the end of the day, having taken all this into account, cases in which the joint legal owners are to be taken to have intended that their beneficial interests should be different from their legal interests will be very unusual.'

Baroness Hale in *Stack v Dowden*

Although *Rosset* has not been overruled by *Stack v Dowden* or *Jones v Kernott*, there has been some unease as to Lord Bridge's narrow interpretation of the conduct of the parties that may give rise to a constructive trust. Lord Walker in *Stack v Dowden* [2007] UKHL 17, said:

JUDGMENT

'Lord Bridge's extreme doubt whether anything less will do was certainly consistent with many first instance and Court of Appeal decisions, but I respectfully doubt whether it took full account of the views (conflicting though they were) expressed in *Gissing v Gissing* (especially Lord Reid [1971] AC 886 ... and Lord Diplock...). It has attracted some trenchant criticism from scholars as potentially productive of injustice. Whether or not Lord Bridge's observation was justified in 1990, in my opinion the law has moved on, and your Lordships should move it a little more in the same direction.'

Lord Walker

It follows that not all applications of money towards the purchase price of the home would entitle the payor to an interest in the house. The provision of the money may constitute a gift or loan to the purchaser divorced from an arrangement or requirement connected with the purchase of the property. In these circumstances the donor or lender may be unable to establish the existence of an agreement linked to the purchase of the property.

In *Arif v Anwar* [2015] EWHC 124, the High Court decided that in the context of a father–son relationship, where the property is owned by the father but the son contributed 50 per cent of the estimated value of the property for refurbishment works, he (son) was not entitled to a beneficial interest by way of a constructive trust. This was because of a finding by the judge that there was no evidence of an agreement between the parties to share an interest in the property. However, he was entitled to succeed to a 25 per cent share of the property on the basis of a proprietary estoppel. The court found that there was an understanding between father and son that the use of the son's money to renovate the property will earn him an interest. Reliance and detriment were also established and the minimum equity to do justice between the parties represented a 25 per cent share in the property. It may seem odd that the court decided that a substantial contribution to the renovation of the property was insufficient to amount to a *Stack/Kernott* inferred common agreement to share but the same evidence was sufficient to amount to a proprietary estoppel understanding or agreement. Once an actual agreement was found, despite the precise details being unclear, the court could have imputed an intention in respect of the relevant proportions.

JUDGMENT

'I reject the argument that a constructive trust arises as to 50% of the Property by virtue of an agreement to that effect made between the Husband (father) and Raziz (son) in July 2006. This gives rise to the third main issue: if Raziz does not obtain an interest under a constructive trust, is the pleaded alternative of an entitlement by operation of a proprietary estoppel available? Was some representation made or some understanding reached that as a result of use of monies held in his name he would acquire some interest in the Property, such that if he relied upon that (to his detriment by permitting use of the monies) then equity would award him the minimum interest necessary to do justice?

I answer that in the affirmative.'

Norris J

9.3.2 Domestic duties

It follows that domestic duties undertaken by a party (such as caring for and bringing up the children), unconnected with a common intention to share the property in reliance on such duties, are insufficient to create an interest in the property.

CASE EXAMPLE

Burns v Burns [1984] 1 All ER 244

The defendant bought a house in his sole name with the assistance of a mortgage. The claimant made no financial contributions to the purchase of the house but gave up paid employment in order to perform the duties of bringing up their children. The defendant gave her a generous housekeeping allowance and did not ask her to contribute to household expenses. Subsequently, the claimant became employed and used her earnings for household expenses and to purchase fixtures and fittings. Ultimately, the claimant left the defendant and claimed a beneficial interest in the house. The court rejected the claim and held that the claimant had failed to prove that she had made a contribution, directly or indirectly, to the acquisition of the property, and therefore did not have an interest in the property. A common intention that the claimant had acquired an interest in the property cannot be imputed to the parties on the basis that the claimant lived with the defendant for 19 years, brought up the children and did a fair share of domestic duties.

JUDGMENT

'So far as housekeeping expenses are concerned, I do not doubt that (the house being bought in the man's name) if the woman goes out to work in order to provide money for the family expenses, as a result of which she spends her earnings on the housekeeping and the man is thus able to pay the mortgage instalments and other expenses out of his earnings, it can be inferred that there was a common intention that the woman should have an interest in the house – since she will have made an indirect financial contribution to the mortgage instalments. But that is not this case.

But, one asks, can the fact that the plaintiff performed domestic duties in the house and looked after the children be taken into account? The mere fact that parties live together and do the ordinary domestic tasks is, in my view, no indication at all that they thereby intended to alter the existing property rights of either of them.'

Fox LJ

9.3.3 Indirect contributions

Lord Bridge in *Rosset* made no reference to the significance of indirect contributions to the purchase of the property. It is arguable that this was an oversight on the part of Lord Bridge and not an abolition of such contributions. Indirect contributions to the purchase price of the house (like direct contributions) would equally give the party contributing to the purchase an interest in the property. The claimant may acquire an interest in the property by making a substantial indirect contribution to the acquisition of the property (including mortgage repayments) if he succeeds in proving that such contributions were by arrangement between the parties. This arrangement may be achieved by an undertaking between the parties to the effect that the claimant agrees to pay the household expenses on condition that the legal owner pays the mortgage instalments. In short, a link between the mortgage payments and the expenses undertaken by the claimant is required to be established and the claimant's expenses are required to be of a substantial nature (per Lord Pearson in *Gissing v Gissing* (1971)):

JUDGMENT

'Contributions are not limited to those made directly in part payment of the price of the property or to those made at the time when the property is conveyed into the name of one of the spouses. For instance there can be a contribution if by arrangement between the spouses one of them by payment of the household expenses enables the other to pay the mortgage instalments.'

Lord Pearson

The concept of indirect contributions by undertaking substantial housekeeping expenses in order to facilitate the legal owner to keep up with the mortgage instalments may be illustrated by the Court of Appeal decision in *Grant v Edwards* (1986).

CASE EXAMPLE

Grant v Edwards [1986] Ch 638

The claimant, a woman who lived with the defendant, was given a false reason for not having the house put in their joint names. The woman made substantial contributions to the family expenses in the hope of acquiring an interest in the house. The expenses undertaken by the woman enabled the man to keep up the mortgage instalments. The claimant applied to the court for a declaration concerning an interest in the house. The court decided that the claimant was entitled to a half-share in the property. She would not have made the substantial contributions to the housekeeping expenses, which indirectly related to the mortgage instalments, unless she had an interest in the house. This was the inevitable inference of the claimant's conduct which established a common intention and reliance to her detriment. The court reviewed the earlier case of *Eves v Eves* [1975] 1 WLR 1338 and declared that that case involved indirect contributions in kind made in reliance on a promise by the legal owner to grant her an equitable interest in the property.

In *Grant v Edwards* (1986) two Lords Justices of Appeal disagreed as to the type of conduct that may constitute indirect contributions. Nourse LJ adopted a narrow interpretation of such conduct. In his view it is conduct in respect of which the actor could not have been reasonably expected to embark unless he or she had an interest in the house. On the other hand, Browne-Wilkinson LJ was prepared to adopt a wider interpretation of conduct that may give rise to indirect contributions. In his view, once a common intention is established, 'any act done by her to her detriment relating to the joint lives of the parties is ... sufficient to qualify. The acts do not have to be referable to the house.'

In *Burns v Burns* [1984] 1 All ER 244, Fox LJ identified payments which may be referable to the acquisition of the house. This is the case if 'the payer (a) pays part of the purchase price or (b) contributes regularly to the mortgage instalments or (c) pays off part of the mortgage or (d) makes substantial financial contributions to the family expenses so as to enable the mortgage to be paid'.

The disputed intention of the parties may be established by direct evidence of an express agreement in writing between the parties, or may be an inferred common intention from the conduct of the parties. Direct or indirect substantial financial contributions to the acquisition of the house (including the mortgage instalments) will have this effect. Indeed, contributions may be relevant for four different purposes:

(a) in the absence of direct evidence of intention, as evidence from which the parties' intentions can be inferred;

(b) as corroboration evidence of the intention of the parties;

(c) to show that the claimant has acted to his detriment in reliance on the common intention;

(d) to quantify the extent of the beneficial interest.

During the 1970s and early 1980s the Court of Appeal, in a series of decisions, advocated its own peculiar solution to disputes involving the family home. Its approach was based on a liberal interpretation of justice and good conscience. The court attempted to do justice between the parties on a case-by-case basis, by declaring property rights based on fairness. This system of 'palm tree' justice, called the 'new model constructive trust', had the counterproductive effect of creating unpredictable property rights which might affect third parties. *Eves v Eves* is an illustration of this approach.

CASE EXAMPLE

Eves v Eves [1975] 1 WLR 1338, CA

An unmarried couple bought a house which was conveyed in the name of the man (defend-ant) instead of both parties, on the ground that the plaintiff (as suggested by the defendant) was under 21. She bore him two children and did a lot of heavy work in the house and garden before he left her for another woman. The plaintiff applied to ascertain her share of the house.

The court found in favour of the plaintiff and awarded her a quarter-share of the house on the ground that the property was acquired and maintained by both parties for their joint benefit.

In *Grant v Edwards*, the Court of Appeal reviewed *Eves v Eves* and considered the case as an illustration of conduct manifesting a common intention between the parties which was relied on by the claimant. Nourse LJ in *Grant v Edwards* made the following observations con-cerning *Eves v Eves*.

JUDGMENT

'It would be possible to take the view that the mere moving into the house by the woman amounted to an acting upon the common intention. But that was evidently not the view of the majority in *Eves v Eves* [1975] 1 WLR 1338. And the reason for that may be that, in the absence of evidence, the law is not so cynical as to infer that a woman will only go to live with a man to whom she is not married if she understands that she is to have an interest in their home. So what sort of conduct is required? In my judgment it must be conduct on which the woman could not reasonably have been expected to embark unless she was to have an interest in the house. If she was not to have such an interest, she could reasonably be expected to go and live with her lover, but not, for example, to wield a 14 lb sledge hammer in the front garden. In adopting the latter kind of conduct she is seen to act to her detriment on the faith of the common intention.'

Nourse LJ

In *Curran v Collins* [2015] EWCA Civ 404 (see earlier), on the issue of a 'specious excuse' for not transferring a house into joint names, the Court of Appeal distinguished *Eves v Eves* (1975) on the ground that in the latter case the parties were living with each other in the relevant property. Whereas, in *Curran* the claimant had no intention of moving into the defendant's house at the time it was acquired. *Grant v Edwards* was distinguished on the grounds that in that case, unlike *Curran*, the house that was being acquired was intended as a family home and there was a positive representation that Mrs Grant would have been a joint owner but for her matrimonial dispute.

In the post-*Rosset* decision of *Le Foe v Le Foe* [2001] All ER (D) 325 (Jun), the High Court analysed Lord Bridge's judgment and decided that he did not intend to exclude indirect contributions.

CASE EXAMPLE

Le Foe v Le Foe [2001] All ER (D) 325 (Jun)

The parties were married and the family home was put in the husband's sole name with the assistance of a mortgage. The wife was in paid employment and assisted the husband in the repayment of the mortgage. On a breakdown of the marriage the issue arose as to the extent of the wife's interest in the house. The court decided that by virtue of the wife's indirect contributions to the mortgage repayments the court was entitled to infer that the parties had a common intention that the wife would acquire an interest in the property. This was quantified at 50 per cent.

JUDGMENT

'In my view what Lord Bridge is saying is that in the second class of case to which he is adverting, namely where there is no positive evidence of an express agreement between the parties as to how the equity is to be shared, and where the court has fallen back on inferring their common intention from the course of their conduct, it will only be exceptionally that conduct other than direct contributions to the purchase price, either in cash to the deposit, or by contribution to the mortgage instalments, will suffice to draw the necessary inference of a common intention to share the equity.'

Nicholas Mostyn QC

9.3.4 The unwarranted requirement for express discussions between the parties

Lord Bridge's insistence in *Rosset* that an express agreement between the parties as to an interest in the home may be gained only by means of express discussion appears to be over-simplistic, for an agreement or understanding may be inferred from conduct. Generally, in order to establish an agreement between two parties the courts do not insist on evidence of oral discussions between the parties. Oral discussion ordinarily is a significant factor to be taken into consideration but ought not to be the only consideration.

In *Hammond v Mitchell* [1991] 1 WLR 1127 the High Court adopted the narrow approach of express discussion as evidence of the intention of the parties as laid down by Lord Bridge in *Rosset* (1990).

CASE EXAMPLE

Hammond v Mitchell [1991] 1 WLR 1127

The parties, Mr Hammond (H) and Miss Mitchell (M), lived together from 1977 to 1988. In 1979, the couple moved into a bungalow in Essex, which was bought in H's name with the assistance of a mortgage. H assured M that as he was going through a divorce it would be in their best interests if the house was put in his name. He then told her: 'Don't worry about the future because when we are married it will be half yours anyway...'. In 1980, surrounding land was bought and the bungalow was extended. M assisted H in his business ventures. H purchased a house in Spain and for a short while they lived there, but never gave up possession of the Essex house. In 1988, the relationship was terminated and M brought an action claiming a beneficial interest in the properties and other assets. The court held that in relation to the bungalow, there was evidence of an express understanding that M should have a beneficial interest, quantified as one-half. But in relation to the Spanish house there was no evidence to justify an intention to share the beneficial interest.

JUDGMENT

'In relation to the bungalow there was express discussion which, although not directed with any precision as to proprietary interests, was sufficient to amount to an understanding at least that the bungalow was to be shared beneficially.'

Waite J

Similarly, in *Springette v Defoe* [1992] 2 FLR 388, the court adhered rigidly to the *Rosset* (1990) principles.

CASE EXAMPLE

Springette v Defoe [1992] 2 FLR 388

The parties lived as man and wife in a council house. In 1982, they made a formal offer to purchase the house for £14,445, which represented a discount of 41 per cent because the claimant, Miss Springette (S), had been a council tenant for 11 years or more. They bought the house jointly with the aid of a mortgage of £12,000. By agreement, they each contributed 50 per cent of the mortgage instalments. The balance of the purchase price was provided by S. The legal title was registered in their joint names but no quantification of their interests was registered in the Land Registry. During 1985, the relationship between the parties became strained and the defendant (D) left the home. S claimed that she was entitled to a 75 per cent share of the proceeds of sale of the house, as represented by her contribution to the purchase. The learned Recorder decided that the beneficial interests were shared equally, despite the lack of evidence of any discussion concerning this issue. S appealed to the Court of Appeal. The interests of the parties were determined by reference to the contributions made. There was no evidence which had the effect of varying the interest acquired by way of a resulting trust because there was no discussion between the parties to that effect. Accordingly, the interests were shared in a 75: 25 ratio.

JUDGMENT

'It is not enough to establish a common intention which is sufficient to found an implied or constructive trust of land that each of them happened at the same time to have been thinking on the same lines in his or her uncommunicated thoughts, while neither had any knowledge of the thinking of the other.'

Dillon LJ

9.3.5 Reliance and detriment

In addition to a common intention in respect of a beneficial interest in the family home, the claimant is required to show that he or she has relied on the understanding to his or her detriment or adjusted his or her position. This requires evidence of some action undertaken by the claimant, in reliance on the agreement, to be shown by the claimant. In other words, the claimant is required to show that he or she has acted on a common intention to such an extent that it would be inequitable or unconscionable to deny him or her an interest or enlarged interest in the property. In *Burns v Burns* we have seen that the claim failed where there was no express discussion between the parties as to the existence of a beneficial interest in the house and the claimant could not prove the existence of an implied intention as to a shared ownership. Lord Bridge affirmed this principle in *Rosset*:

JUDGMENT

'[I]t will only be necessary for the partner asserting a claim to a beneficial interest against the party entitled to the legal estate to show that he or she has acted to his or her detriment or significantly altered his or her position in reliance on the agreement in order to give rise to a trust.'

Lord Bridge

9.3.6 Date and method of valuation of the interest

If the claimant has discharged the burden of proving a common intention as to a beneficial interest and that he or she has relied on that intention to his or her detriment, the next stage is to quantify the beneficial interest. If the parties have made an express declaration as to the size of the interest, the courts will give effect to this agreement except in cases of fraud or mistake. In the absence of such agreement the courts' task will be to consider the entire course of dealings between the parties that is relevant to their ownership of the property in order to determine the extent of the beneficial interests. Financial contributions to the purchase price as well as a range of other factors (stated earlier) will be taken into account by the courts. The evidence that is considered by the courts concerning a variation of beneficial interest will be the same for joint and sole legal ownership cases, see Baroness Hale in *Stack v Dowden*:

JUDGMENT

'The approach to quantification in cases where the home is conveyed into joint names should certainly be no stricter than the approach to quantification in cases where it has been conveyed into the name of one only. The questions in a joint names case are not simply what is the extent of the parties' beneficial interests, but did the parties intend their beneficial interests to be different from their legal interests and if they did, in what way and to what extent? There are differences between sole and joint names cases when trying to divine the common intentions or understanding between the parties.

The burden will therefore be on the person seeking to show that the parties intend their beneficial interests to be different from their legal interests, and in what way. This is not a task to be lightly embarked upon. In family disputes, strong feelings are aroused when couples split up. These often lead the parties, honestly, but mistakenly, to reinterpret the past in self-exculpatory or vengeful terms.'

Baroness Hale

In the post-*Rosset* decision in *Midland Bank v Cooke* [1995] 4 All ER 562, the Court of Appeal took the bold decision to move away from the rigid principle laid down in *Rosset* and adopted a modified approach to the quantification issue. The approach was to the effect that where a party acquired an equitable interest in property by way of direct contributions to the purchase price of the property the court may take into consideration a broader view of the conduct of the parties in order to quantify their shares. The court was not bound to deal with the matter on the strict basis of the trust resulting from the cash contribution to the purchase price, and was free to attribute to the parties an intention to share the beneficial interest in some different proportions.

CASE EXAMPLE

Midland Bank v Cooke [1995] 4 All ER 562

H and W married and moved into a house which was purchased with the assistance of a mortgage in H's sole name. The deposit was raised through H's savings and a wedding gift. This mortgage was replaced by a general mortgage in favour of the Midland Bank in order to secure H's business overdraft. The property was subsequently transferred into the joint names of H and W. There was no discussion between the parties as to their beneficial interests. In proceedings brought by the bank against H and W for arrears of payments and possession of the property, W claimed a declaration that she was entitled to a 50 per cent share in the house. The judge held that W was entitled to a beneficial interest of 6.74 per cent in the property, equivalent to a half-share of the wedding gift. W appealed to the Court of Appeal. The court allowed the appeal and awarded W a 50 per cent share in the value of the house, in accordance with the principles in *Pettitt v Pettitt* (1970), *Gissing v Gissing* (1971) and *Grant v Edwards* (1986). Since W had established an interest in the house through direct contributions, the court was entitled to look at all the circumstances in order to give effect to the true intentions of the parties. Accordingly, the court might attribute to the parties an interest in the property which was different from the resulting trust contributions to the purchase price.

JUDGMENT

'The general principle to be derived from *Gissing v Gissing* [1971] AC 886 and *Grant v Edwards* [1986] Ch 638 can, in my judgment, be summarised in this way. When the court is proceeding, in cases like the present, where the partner without legal title has successfully asserted an equitable interest through direct contribution, to determine (in the absence of express evidence of intention) what proportions the parties must be assumed to have intended for their beneficial ownership, the duty of the judge is to undertake a survey of the whole course of dealing between the parties relevant to their ownership and occupation of the property and their sharing of its burdens and advantages.

… Equity has traditionally been a system which matches established principle to the demands of social change. The mass diffusion of home ownership has been one of the most striking social changes of our own time. There will inevitably be numerous couples, married or unmarried, who have no discussion about ownership and who, perhaps advisedly, make no agreement about it. It would be anomalous, against that background, to create a range of home buyers who were beyond the pale of equity's assistance in formulating a fair presumed basis for the sharing of beneficial title, simply because they had been honest enough to admit that they never gave ownership a thought or reached any agreement about it.'

Waite LJ

Similarly, in *Drake v Whipp* [1996] 1 FLR 826, the court gave a broad interpretation of the intention of the parties. This intention is not measured solely by the direct contributions of the parties, in the absence of evidence to the contrary. The court is entitled to look at all the circumstances of the case to identify the scope of the common intention of the parties. Direct contributions are only one factor to be taken into account. The court also classified the types of trusts involved into constructive and resulting trusts.

CASE EXAMPLE

Drake v Whipp [1996] 1 FLR 826

The claimant and the defendant purchased a barn with the intention of converting it into a residence. The property was conveyed into the sole name of the defendant. Both parties contributed to the purchase price and the cost of the conversion work. The claimant made a direct contribution of one-fifth. It was found that the parties had a common intention that the claimant would acquire a beneficial interest. The court decided that it was entitled to adopt a 'broad brush' approach in determining the parties' respective shares under the constructive trust. It was entitled to look at the parties' entire course of conduct in evaluating their respective shares. This might involve direct and indirect contributions in money or money's worth and any other evidence of intention of the parties. Accordingly the claimant acquired a one-third interest in the property.

JUDGMENT

'I would approach the matter more broadly, looking at the parties' entire course of conduct together. I would take into account not only those direct contributions, but also the fact that Mr Whipp and Mrs Drake together purchased the property with the intention that it should be their home, that they both contributed their labour in 70:30 per cent proportions, that they had a joint account out of which the costs of conversion were met, but that that account was largely fed by his earnings, and that she paid for the food and some other household expenses and took care of the housekeeping for them both. I note that, whilst it was open to Mrs Drake to argue at the trial for a constructive trust and for a 50 per cent share, she opted to rely solely on a resulting trust and a 40.1 per cent share. In all the circumstances I would hold that her fair share should be one-third.'

Peter Gibson LJ

Commentary

Martin Dixon in an article entitled 'A case too far' [1997] Conv 66, took the view that the approach of Waite LJ in *Midland Bank v Cooke* allows quantification on the basis of a presumed, fictitious intention. The parties claiming an interest in the matrimonial home through payments may trigger an interest larger than the actual payments.

The Law Commission in its discussion paper on 'Sharing homes' (2002) endorses the holistic approach towards quantification of the beneficial interest in the domestic context:

QUOTATION

'If the question really is one of the parties' "common intention", we believe that there is much to be said for adopting what has been called a "holistic approach" to quantification, undertaking a survey of the whole course of dealing between the parties and taking account of all conduct which throws light on the question what shares were intended.'

The value of the interest is ascertained at the time the property is sold. Accordingly, any increases or decreases in the value of the property are taken into consideration. If a party remains in occupation paying the mortgage, rates and other outgoings, he is credited with these expenses. Conversely, the party in occupation is debited with occupation rent for using the premises partly owned by the other. In *Oxley v Hiscock* [2004] EWCA Civ 546, the Court of Appeal declared that decided cases had created three methods of valuation. These are:

- The approach adopted by Lord Diplock in *Gissing v Gissing* (1971) and by Nourse LJ in *Stokes v Anderson* [1991] 1 FLR 391: the respective shares of the parties are not to be determined at the time of the acquisition of the property but are left to be determined when their relationship comes to an end or the property sold. Thus, a complete picture of the whole course of dealing is available to the court in order to determine what is fair.

- The approach suggested by Waite LJ in *Midland Bank v Cooke* (1995): the court undertakes a survey of the whole course of dealing between the parties in order to determine what proportions the parties must be assumed to have intended from the outset for their beneficial ownership. Thus evidence of what the parties intended at the time of the acquisition may be inferred from the conduct of the parties while they were living together.

The suggestion put forward by Browne-Wilkinson VC in *Grant v Edwards* (1986) and approved by Walker LJ in *Yaxley v Gotts* [2000] Ch 162: the court in its discretion makes such an order as the circumstances require in order to give effect to the beneficial interest in the property of the one party, the existence of which the party with the legal title is estopped from denying.

In *Oxley* (2004) the Court of Appeal expressed a preference for the third approach. The second approach was capable of leading to an artificial or fictional intention of the parties. Likewise, the same point could be made of the first approach, i.e. at the time of the acquisition the parties' intention was that their shares should be left for later determination. The analysis of Chadwick LJ in *Oxley* as to the quantification of the parties' interests was endorsed by the House of Lords in *Stack v Dowden* (2007).

CASE EXAMPLE

Oxley v Hiscock [2004] EWCA Civ 546, (CA)

The claimant and defendant had lived together as an unmarried couple. In April 1991, 35 Dickens Close was purchased as a home for the claimant, defendant and the claimant's children by a former marriage. The property was purchased in the name of the defendant for £127,000. The purchase price was funded by (i) a building society advance of £30,000, (ii) the net proceeds of the claimant's former house amounting to £61,000 (of which £36,600 was provided by the claimant and £25,200 was contributed by the defendant) and (iii) the balance of £35,500 (approximately) by the defendant from his own savings. The relationship came to an end in 2001. At this time the mortgage had been paid off and the property was sold by the defendant for £232,000. The claimant brought proceedings against the defendant pursuant to s 14 of the Trusts of Land and Appointment of Trustees Act 1996 for a declaration that the proceeds of sale were held by the defendant upon trust for the claimant and defendant in equal shares. The judge found that there was no express discussion between the parties as to their respective share in the property, but decided that there was in effect a pooling of resources (although there was no joint bank account) to such an extent that the court may infer that the parties intended to share the asset equally. Accordingly the judge ordered an equal division of the proceeds of sale. The defendant appealed to the Court of Appeal.

The Court of Appeal allowed the appeal on the ground that the judge had misdirected herself by failing to follow established law and had given insufficient weight to the contribution by the defendant. He had directly contributed £60,700 to the purchase price of the house which was substantially greater than the claimant's contribution of £36,300. Accordingly, a fair division of the proceeds of sale would be 40 per cent to the claimant and 60 per cent to the defendant.

JUDGMENT

'Three strands of reasoning can be identified. (1) That suggested by Lord Diplock in *Gissing v Gissing* [1970] 2 All ER 780 at 793, [1971] AC 886 at 909 and adopted by Nourse LJ in *Stokes v Anderson* [1991] FCR 539 at 543. The parties are taken to have agreed at the time of the acquisition of the property that their respective shares are not to be quantified then, but are left to be determined when their relationship comes to an end or the property is sold on the basis of what is then fair having regard to the whole course of dealing between them. The court steps in to determine what is fair because, when the time came for that determination, the parties were unable to agree. (2) That suggested by Waite LJ in *Midland Bank plc v Cooke* [1995] 4 All ER 562 at 574. The court undertakes a survey of the whole course of dealing between the parties relevant to their ownership and occupation of the property and their sharing of its burdens and advantages in order to determine what proportions the parties must be assumed to have intended [from the outset] for their beneficial ownership. On that basis the court treats what has taken place while the parties have been living together in the property as evidence of what they intended at the time of the acquisition. (3) That suggested by Browne-Wilkinson V-C, in *Grant v Edwards* [1986] 2 All ER 426 at 439, [1986] Ch 638 at 656, 657 and approved by Robert Walker LJ in *Yaxley v Gotts* [2000] 1 All ER 711 at 722, [2000] Ch 162 at 177. The court makes such order as the circumstances require in order to give effect to the beneficial interest in the property of the one party, the existence of which the other party (having the legal title) is estopped from denying. That, I think, is the analysis which underlies the decision of this court in *Drake v Whipp* (see [1996] 2 FCR 296 at 302).

For my part, I find the reasoning adopted by this court in *Cooke's* case to be the least satisfactory of the three strands. It seems to me artificial – and an unnecessary fiction – to attribute to the parties a common intention that the extent of their respective beneficial interests in the property should be fixed as from the time of the acquisition, in circumstances in which all the evidence points to the conclusion that, at the time of the acquisition, they had given no thought to the matter. The same point can be made – although with less force – in relation to the reasoning that, at the time of the acquisition, their common intention was that the amount of the respective shares should be left for later determination. But it can be said that, if it were their common intention that each should have some beneficial interest in the property – which is the hypothesis upon which it becomes necessary to answer the second question – then, in the absence of evidence that they gave any thought to the amount of their respective shares, the necessary inference is that they must have intended that question would be answered later on the basis of what was then seen to be fair. But, as I have said, I think that the time has come to accept that there is no difference in outcome, in cases of this nature, whether the true analysis lies in constructive trust or in proprietary estoppel.'

Chadwick LJ

In *Abbott v Abbott* the Privy Council comprising three Law Lords who decided the *Stack v Dowden* case reiterated the holistic approach towards quantification of interests. This case involved common law principles concerning the ownership of the family home on a breakdown of a marriage.

CASE EXAMPLE

Abbott v Abbott [2008] 1 FLR 1451 (PC)

The parties contracted a valid marriage at a time when the husband was a medical student. His mother donated a plot of land to the couple, but in the name of her son, in order to build their matrimonial home. The building works were financed through a mortgage from the Barbados Mutual Life Assurance Society. The legal title to the property was taken in the name of the husband but the wife made herself jointly and severally liable for the repayment of the loan. The couple's income was paid into a joint bank account from which the mortgage was paid. There were two children from the marriage. The parties' relationship became strained and eventually they were divorced. The issue involved the ownership of the former matrimonial home. The trial judge divided the property equally between the parties. On appeal the Court of Appeal reversed this decision and decided that the wife's share reflected her financial contributions which was valued at 8.31 per cent in accordance with the *Rosset* principles. On appeal, the Privy Council allowed the appeal and upheld the trial judge's decision of equal shares based on the whole course of conduct between the parties.

JUDGMENT

'Not only did they (the parties) organise their finances entirely jointly, having only a joint bank account into which everything was paid and from which everything was paid. They also undertook joint liability for the repayment of the mortgage loan and interest. This has always been regarded as a significant factor: see *Hyett v Stanley* [2003] EWCA Civ 942.

The Court of Appeal appears to have attached undue significance to the dictum of Lord Bridge in *Lloyds Bank plc v Rosset*, in particular as to what conduct is to be taken into account in quantifying an acknowledged beneficial interest. The law has indeed moved on since then. The parties' whole course of conduct in relation to the property must be taken into account in determining their shared intentions as to its ownership.'

Baroness Hale

9.3.7 Imputed intention

In *Pettitt v Pettitt* (1970) Lord Diplock in the House of Lords considered that it was possible to impute the existence of an agreement between the parties in the interests of justice, in cases where there was no evidence that the parties embraced the existence of such an agreement. The imputation of an intention requires the court to conclude what the parties would have intended had they given any thought to the situation. It is, in effect, a deemed intention constructed by the courts and attributed to the parties. This is distinct from inferred intention, which is based on the actual intentions of the parties, objectively considered by reference to their conduct throughout their dealings with the property.

JUDGMENT

'[T]he court imputes to the parties a common intention which in fact they never formed and it does so by forming its own opinion as to what would have been the common intention of reasonable men as to the effect of that event upon their contractual rights and obligations if the possibility of the event happening had been present to their minds at the time of entering into the contract.'

Lord Diplock

Lord Reid's observations on this issue in *Gissing v Gissing* (1971) was expressed in a more guarded manner:

JUDGMENT

'Returning to the crucial question there is a wide gulf between inferring from the whole conduct of the parties that there probably was an agreement, and imputing to the parties an intention to agree to share even where the evidence gives no ground for such an inference. If the evidence shows that there was no agreement in fact then that excludes any inference that there was an agreement. But it does not exclude an imputation of a deemed intention if the law permits such an imputation. If the law is to be that the court has power to impute such an intention in proper cases then I am content, although I would prefer to reach the same result in a rather different way. But if it were to be held to be the law that it must at least be possible to infer a contemporary agreement in the sense of holding that it is more probable than not there was in fact some such agreement then I could not contemplate the future results of such a decision with equanimity.'

Lord Reid

In *Jones v Kernott* the Supreme Court in an *obiter* pronouncement decided that the proper place for the court to impute an intention is at the second stage when deciding on the proportions of interests to be divided between the parties. The guiding principle for such imputed intention is fairness and justice. An intention will not be imputed to ascertain whether the parties have an interest in the property in the first place. This is the province of express, implied or inferential intention based on the conduct of the parties. It is only after the courts have decided that there is such an intention to share the property, as manifested by the conduct of the parties, that the courts may impute an intention to quantify their interests, in the absence of any evidence of the intentions of the parties as to their respective shares.

JUDGMENT

'[W]e accept that the search is primarily to ascertain the parties' actual shared intentions, whether expressed or to be inferred from their conduct. However, there are at least two exceptions. The first, which is not this case, is where the classic resulting trust presumption applies. Indeed, this would be rare in a domestic context, but might perhaps arise where domestic partners were also business partners: see *Stack v Dowden*, para 32. The second ... is where it is clear that the beneficial interests are to be shared, but it is impossible to divine a common intention as to the proportions in which they are to be shared. In those two situations, the court is driven to impute an intention to the parties which they may never have had.

[The learned Supreme Court judges concluded thus:] In those cases where it is clear either (a) that the parties did not intend joint tenancy at the outset, or (b) had changed their original intention, but it is not possible to ascertain by direct evidence or by inference what their actual intention was as to the shares in which they would own the property, the answer is that each is entitled to that share which the court considers fair having regard to the whole course of dealing between them in relation to the property: Chadwick LJ in *Oxley v Hiscock* [2005] Fam 211, para 69. In our judgment, the whole course of dealing ... in relation to the property should be given a broad meaning, enabling a similar range of factors to be taken into account as may be relevant to ascertaining the parties' actual intentions.'

Lord Walker and Lady Hale

In *Barnes v Phillips* [2015] EWCA Civ 1056 (see earlier), the Court of Appeal affirmed the decision of the trial judge. In a joint ownership case an intention may be imputed to the parties to reflect the consequences of adverse financial circumstances of her partner and her undertaking financial responsibility to care for the children.

In the *Estate of York* (2015), the Court of Appeal declared that judicial evaluation of what is a fair share is not subject to precision and the trial judge's decision may only be interfered with if it is clear that he has misdirected himself on the correct principles to apply. But the court is not concerned with some form of redistributive justice. Accordingly, a claimant who had endured years of abusive conduct by her partner was not entitled to be awarded a greater interest in the property. This is not a factor to be taken into account in considering 'the whole course of dealing between the parties in relation to the property'. Likewise, the length of cohabitation per se is not a factor to be taken into account. Instead, the court seemingly focused on the contributions (both financial and non-financial) to the property.

CASE EXAMPLE

Estate of York [2015] EWCA Civ 72 (Court of Appeal)

The appellant, Kamarah (K), cohabited with her partner, Norton (N), for 33 years until his death. The relationship was described as dysfunctional and K was subjected to years of abuse by N. The couple had one child. N purchased a house in his sole name with the assistance of a mortgage. K used her modest income as a singer to pay for the household expenses and made a small contribution to the mortgage debt. After N's death she continued to live in the property but was unable to keep up with the mortgage payments. The building society sought possession of the property and K counter-claimed for a declaration concerning her equitable interest. The trial judge awarded K 25 per cent share in the property. On appeal, the Court of Appeal dismissed her appeal and decided that the judge had directed herself as to the correct criteria to be taken into account in imputing an intention as to a fair share. The length of abusive relationship was irrelevant in quantifying her share as well as the length of co-habitation between the parties. The focus here was on financial and non-financial contributions to the property.

JUDGMENT

'It is essential, in my judgment, to bear in mind that in deciding what shares are fair, the court is not concerned with some form of redistributive justice. Thus it is irrelevant that it may be thought a "fair" outcome for a woman who has endured years of abusive conduct by her partner to be allotted a substantial interest in his property on his death. Miss Graham-York is "entitled to that share which the court considers fair having regard to the whole course of dealing between them in relation to the property". It is these last words, which I have emphasised, which supply the confines of the enquiry as to fairness.

The judge in the present case, with the advantage of having heard argument and evidence over five days, regarded her evaluation of a 25% interest as "generous". The judge directed herself properly as to the approach which she should take to the evaluative exercise. She fell into no legal or analytical error. I can discern no principled basis upon which this court can regard her evaluation as falling outside the ambit of reasonable decision-making. I would dismiss the appeal.'

Tomlinson LJ

9.4 Section 37 of the Matrimonial Proceedings and Property Act 1970

Section 37 of the Matrimonial Proceedings and Property Act 1970 provides as follows:

SECTION

'It is hereby declared that where a husband and wife [or registered civil partners] contribute in money or money's worth to the improvement of real or personal property in which or in the proceeds of sale of which either or both of them has or have a beneficial interest, the husband or wife [or registered civil partner] so contributing shall, if the contribution is of a substantial nature and subject to any agreement between them to the contrary express or implied, be treated as having then acquired ... a share or an enlarged share ... in that beneficial interest of such an extent as may have been agreed or, in default of such agreement, as may seem in all the circumstances just to any court.'

Section 37 is only applicable to married couples and registered civil partners under the Civil Partnership Act 2004. Unmarried spouses who make contributions in similar circumstances may only rely on the common law rules. The court decides in its discretion whether a contribution is substantial or not.

9.5 Order of sale

Section 14 of the Trusts of Land and Appointment of Trustees Act 1996 repeals and replaces s 30 of the Law of Property Act 1925. The section declares that any person interested in the trust property (including the trustees of land) may apply to the court for an order relating to the exercise of the trustees' functions or declaring the extent of the beneficial interests.

The court is directed in s 15 of the 1996 Act to have regard to a number of factors when deciding an application under s 14. These are:

(a) the intentions of the settlor;

(b) the purposes for which the property subject to the trust is held;

(c) the welfare of any minor who occupies or might reasonably be expected to occupy any land subject to the trust as his home;

(d) the interests of the mortgagee of any beneficiary;

(e) in the case of an application relating to the beneficiary's right to occupy under s 13, the circumstances and wishes of each of the beneficiaries entitled to occupy;

(f) in all other cases, except conveying the land to beneficiaries absolutely entitled, the circumstances and wishes of the adult beneficiaries entitled to possession.

The underlying purposes of the trust, including the rights of children, are required to be taken into account before any decision is reached by the court. The approach of the courts was declared in *Mortgage Corporation v Silkin* [2000] 2 FCR 222, concerning an application by a mortgagee for an order of sale:

JUDGMENT

'[I]t does not seem to me unlikely that the legislature intended to relax the fetters on the way in which the court exercised its jurisdiction … so as to tip the balance somewhat more in favour of families and against banks and other chargees … As a result of s 15, the court has greater flexibility than heretofore, as to how it exercises its jurisdiction on an application for an order of sale … Once the relevant factors to be taken into account have been identified, it is a matter for the court as to what weight to give to each factor in a particular case.'

Neuberger J

9.6 Status of ante-nuptial and post-nuptial agreements

The Privy Council in *Macleod v Macleod, The Times*, 29 December 2008, decided that it was for the legislature, rather than the courts, to decide whether ante-nuptial agreements (or pre-nuptial agreements) ought to be regarded as binding under English law. The Privy Council decided that at common law such agreements are contrary to public policy and thus not valid or binding in the contractual sense. The court considered a pre-nuptial agreement as an agreement made before the parties had committed themselves to the rights and responsibilities of their marital status (or registered civil partnership status) and purporting to govern what may happen in an uncertain future. This approach has now been overruled by the Supreme Court in *Radmacher v Granatino* (see below), and no longer represents the view of English law.

In 2008 the Law Commission for England and Wales announced their intention to examine the status and enforceability of agreements made between spouses and civil partners, or those contemplating marriage or civil partnership, concerning their property and finances. The view of the Privy Council was that the difficult issue of the validity and effect of ante-nuptial agreements was more appropriate to legislative, rather than judicial, development.

Post-nuptial agreements, however, were very different from pre-nuptial agreements, which was the view of the Privy Council in *Macleod v Macleod*. In post-nuptial agreements the couple would have been married or the civil partnership registered before the parties had entered into the formal agreement and thus would not have appeared to be the price of a wedding. The parties would have undertaken towards each another the obligations and responsibilities appertaining to marriage or a registered civil partnership. There was nothing, within reason, to stop a couple from entering into contractual financial arrangements governing their lives together, as in the present case. These agreements were capable of being varied by the parties if there had been a change of circumstances or where the agreement did not contain proper financial arrangements with respect to any child of the family.

In *Macleod v Macleod* (2008), the parties were married in Florida in 1994 and then moved to the Isle of Man a year later. They were married for 10 years. Both had previously been married and had children from those relationships. They went on to have a further five children from their marriage with each other. They had signed their pre-nuptial agreement on the day of their wedding, even arranging for the signing to be videotaped. But they then agreed to vary the pre-nuptial agreement one year before the divorce application was filed, when the marriage was already 'on the rocks' and the wife was having an affair. The Privy Council found for Mr Macleod, and upheld an amended version of the agreement that was signed after the marriage, but before the couple had split up, i.e. a post-nuptial agreement.

The current status of the law on ante-nuptial and post-nuptial agreements has now been definitively laid down by the Supreme Court. In *Radmacher v Granatino* (2010), the Supreme Court had an opportunity to review the law relating to ante-nuptial agreements and decided that *prima facie* such agreements are binding on the parties, in the absence of evidence of an unconscionable bargain. The same principles apply to post-nuptial agreements. An unconscionable bargain may manifest itself in a variety of ways, such as entering into the agreement under duress or undue influence, or under a mistake, or without full knowledge of the material facts. Each case will be decided on its own facts. The effect is that on a breakdown of the marriage, English courts today are more likely to give weight to ante- and post-nuptial agreements when exercising its discretion (to adjust the interests of the parties to a marriage in the family home) under s 25(1) of the Matrimonial Causes Act 1973.

CASE EXAMPLE

Radmacher v Granatino [2010] UKSC 42

G, a French national and R, a German national, had married in the United Kingdom. R had considerable family wealth and the parties had signed an ante-nuptial agreement in Germany, for a significant payment from R's family was dependent upon this. Under the agreement, which had a German-law clause, neither party was entitled to benefit from the property of the other either during the marriage or on its termination. G did not take independent advice. At that time he had been a banker, they had two children and separated after eight years. When the marriage had broken down he had left banking to become a student. He applied for ancillary relief and was awarded a substantial sum, the judge attaching limited weight to the agreement because of the circumstances in which it had been signed. The Court of Appeal, however, held that the agreement should have been given decisive weight. There was an appeal to the Supreme Court. The issues were (i) whether the circumstances attending the making of the agreement detracted from the weight that should be accorded to it; (ii) whether the foreign element enhanced that weight; (iii) whether the circumstances prevailing at the time of the court's order made it fair or just to depart from the agreement.

Held: The Supreme Court (Baroness Hale dissenting) dismissed the appeal on the following grounds:

1. Although the court has the final say as to whether or not an agreement between the parties would determine the arrangements for ancillary relief between the parties when a marriage comes to an end, the rule that agreements providing for future separation of the parties to a marriage was contrary to public policy was obsolete and no longer applied.
2. The court was entitled to give effect to an agreement made between the parties to a marriage as to the manner in which their financial affairs should be regulated in the event of a separation, where it was fair to do so. This is the position despite the fact that the courts would have reached a different solution in the absence of an agreement.
3. There was no inherent difference, in policy terms, between an ante-nuptial and post-nuptial agreement. The same principles apply to both types of agreement. The principles in *Macleod v Macleod* were no longer applicable.
4. A nuptial agreement would be given full weight only if the parties entered it of their own free will, with knowledge of all the material facts, and intending that it should govern the financial arrangements in the event of the marriage coming to an end. The court may only intervene when it would be unfair to hold the parties to the agreement. In particular where such agreement will prejudice the reasonable requirements of minor children of the family, or one partner will be left in a predicament of real need while the other enjoyed sufficient resources, the court may interfere with the agreement.
5. In the circumstances, the needs of the husband did not warrant the exercise of the court's discretion in the interests of fairness.

JUDGMENT

'The reason why the court should give weight to a nuptial agreement is that there should be respect for individual autonomy. The court should accord respect to the decision of a married couple as to the manner in which their financial affairs should be regulated. It would be paternalistic and patronising to override their agreement simply on the basis that the court knows best. This is particularly true where the parties' agreement addresses existing circumstances and not merely the contingencies of an uncertain future.'

Lord Phillips

The Law Commission in its Report, 'Matrimonial Property, Needs and Agreements', published in 2014, considered *inter alia* the efficacy of pre-nuptial and post-nuptial agreements (collectively referred to as 'marital property agreements' or 'nuptial agreements'), made recommendations in order to achieve an element of legal certainty in this field and introduced a draft bill ('Nuptial Agreements Bill') to be put to Parliament.

The Law Commission made recommendations that legislation be enacted to introduce 'qualifying nuptial agreements'. The effect would be to create enforceable contracts about the financial consequences of divorce or dissolution that will restrict the court from making financial orders inconsistent with the agreement, save in so far as the financial needs of a party or the interests of a child of the family justify the court in intervening. Thus, the scope of a qualifying nuptial agreement is not to remove the court's jurisdiction in areas covered by the agreement. Rather, it prevents the court from making financial orders that are inconsistent with the qualifying nuptial agreement. This approach empowers the court to make orders dealing with an extensive range of financial remedies that might be needed in any particular case.

'Qualifying nuptial agreements' are required to satisfy six prerequisites in order to satisfy the test of fairness. These are as follows:

(a) The agreement must be a valid and enforceable contract (for example, be able to withstand a challenge on the basis of undue influence or misrepresentation) – the 'validity' requirement. Any presumption of undue influence is to be disregarded. This is the case where such presumption will normally arise from the facts of the parties' relationship as a couple or another relationship that they have together. Undue influence may still be proved, rather than presumed, on the facts of the particular case.

(b) The agreement must have been made by deed and must contain a statement signed by both parties that he or she understands that the agreement is a qualifying nuptial agreement that will partially remove the court's discretion to make financial orders – the 'formation' requirement.

(c) The agreement must not have been made within the 28 days immediately before the wedding or the celebration of civil partnership – the 'timing' requirement.

(d) Both parties to the agreement must have received, at the time of the making of the agreement, disclosure of material information about the other party's financial situation – the 'disclosure' requirement.

(e) Both parties must have received legal advice from a qualified lawyer at the time that the agreement was formed – the 'advice' requirement.

(f) If the parties to a qualifying nuptial agreement vary the terms of that agreement, the validity, formation, timing, disclosure and advice requirements must be met in respect of the varied agreement for it to remain a qualifying nuptial agreement – the 'variation' requirement. If the agreement is altered by the court, the variation requirement does not have to be met.

The merits of such agreements entered into before or during a marriage or civil partnership will enable couples to regulate their own financial affairs on divorce or dissolution and enhance clearer protection of family property, inheritance and businesses. There may be increased confidence in the legal system and financial savings on divorce or dissolution where couples comply with their agreement rather than take court action.

The review and recommendations by the Law Commission on the law relating to nuptial agreements, as well as the draft Bill to be introduced in Parliament, are welcome suggested improvements in the law. However, there are a number of issues which are still unclear. First, the scope of qualifying nuptial agreements. The issue here is whether qualifying nuptial agreements ought to embrace any property owned by the parties, whether acquired before or during the relationship, or should such agreements incorporate only matrimonial property? Second, under a qualifying nuptial agreement it is not possible to contract out of the 'financial needs' requirement of the family. Should financial needs be defined in statute? The Commission was content not to change the law and to leave the application of this requirement to the discretion of the court. Needs are not limited to income needs, but includes property/housing needs for spouses or civil partners and children.

KEY FACTS

Proprietary rights in the family home

The legal title to property may be conveyed in the joint names of the partners, subject to an express trust for land for themselves as equitable joint tenants or tenants in common. Alternatively, the parties may declare the terms of the trust outside the conveyance. Provided that s 53(1)(b) of the Law of Property Act 1925 has been complied with, the declaration of trust will be conclusive as to the beneficial interests of the parties, in the absence of fraud or mistake	*Goodman v Gallant* (1986); *Goodman v Carlton* (2002); *Stack v Dowden* (2007)
Where the legal title to property is conveyed in the name of one party only, and his or her partner wishes to claim a beneficial interest, the claimant is required to establish the existence of a trust – resulting or constructive	s 53(2) of the LPA 1925
The presumptions of resulting trust or advancement will not be readily adopted in order to quantify the interests of the parties	*Pettitt v Pettitt* (1970); *Gissing v Gissing* (1971)
Instead a presumption that the equitable interest follows the legal title will arise. This is the position whether the legal title is in joint names or in the sole name of one party	*Stack v Dowden* (2007); *Jones v Kernott* (2011)
The burden of proof is on the party alleging the contrary	*Stack v Dowden* (2007); *Jones v Kernott* (2011)
Where the legal title to property is taken in the joint names of the parties, the presumption is in favour of a legal and beneficial joint tenancy. The party alleging the contrary bears the legal burden of proof	
In the domestic context, the court will consider all the circumstances to ascertain the intentions of the parties, including but not restricting itself to financial contributions. A number of factors were identified by Baroness Hale in *Stack v Dowden*	*Fowler v Barron* (2008); *Barnes v Phillips* (2015)
Investment properties acquired by one or more of the parties are subject to the resulting trust	*Laskar v Laskar* (2008); *Erlam v Rahman* (2016);
Where the legal title is taken in the name of one party the starting point is that the equitable interest follows the legal title, subject to evidence to the contrary	*Pettitt v Pettitt* (1970); *Gissing v Gissing* (1971); *Abbott v Abbott* (2008); *O'Kelly v Davies* (2014); *Estate of York* (2015); *Curran v Collins* (2015); *Capehorn v Harris* (2015); *Arif v Anwar* (2015)
Domestic duties undertaken by a party, without more, are insufficient to create an interest in the property	*Burns v Burns* (1984)
The two guidelines laid down by Lord Bridge in *Lloyds Bank v Rosset* were regarded as too narrow:	*Lloyds Bank v Rosset* (1990)
(i) **Evidence of agreement**: 'Any agreement, arrangement or understanding reached between the parties that the property is to be shared beneficially … this can only be based on evidence of express discussion between the partners. The [claimant is then required to show] that he or she acted to his or her detriment or significantly altered his or her position.'	*Eves v Eves* (1975); *Grant v Edwards* (1986)
(ii) **Evidence of conduct**: 'Where the court must rely entirely on the conduct of the parties … to infer a common intention to share the property beneficially and … to give rise to a constructive trust. In this situation direct contributions to the purchase price by the [claimant], whether initially or by payment of mortgage instalments, will readily justify the inference necessary to the creation of a constructive trust. But … it is extremely doubtful whether anything less will do.' (Lord Bridge)	*Pettitt v Pettitt* (1970); *Gissing v Gissing* (1971); *Re Rogers' Question* (1948)

Difficulties created by this dichotomy of evidence

Constructive or resulting trust? The second category of evidence seems consistent with a resulting trust, but Lord Bridge categorises this as evidence of a constructive trust based on the common intention of the parties	
Indirect financial contributions are relevant to ascertain an intention to share the beneficial interest in the property	*Gissing v Gissing* (1971); *Burns v Burns* (1984); *Grant v Edwards* (1986); *Le Foe v Le Foe* (2001)
Lord Bridge's unwarranted requirement for express discussions between the parties appears to be over-simplistic for an agreement or understanding may be inferred from conduct	*Hammond v Mitchell* (1991); *Springette v Defoe* (1992); *Midland Bank v Cooke* (1995); *Drake v Whipp* (1996)
Equation of constructive trust (first category) with proprietary estoppel?	
Date and method of valuation. The courts will take into consideration the express, inferred and imputed intentions between the parties in order to value their interests	*Midland Bank v Cooke* (1995); *Drake v Whipp* (1996); *Oxley v Hiscock* (2004); *Jones v Kernott* (2011)
s 37 of the Matrimonial Proceedings and Property Act 1970	Applicable to married spouses or those contracting civil partnerships
ss 14 and 15 of the Trusts of Land and Appointment of Trustees Act 1996	Declaration as to an interest and order for sale
Pre-nuptial and post-nuptial agreements are *prima facie* binding on the parties in the absence of evidence of unconscionable bargains	*Radmacher v Granatino* (2010)

ACTIVITY

Applying the law

Harold and Winifred have been living together as man and wife for several years (although not married). Consider the extent of their beneficial interests in the family home (bought for £200,000), which is now worth £600,000, in each of the following alternative sets of circumstances:

(i) The purchase price was entirely provided by Harold and the title to the property vested in his sole name. Harold repeatedly told Winifred that the beneficial interest belonged to both of them in equal shares.

(ii) The entire purchase price was provided by Winifred but the house was conveyed into the sole name of Harold in the hope of preventing the house falling into the hands of her creditors should her business fail. As things turned out, her fears regarding her business proved unfounded and her business flourished.

(iii) Winifred provided £50,000 of the purchase price of £200,000 and the remainder of the purchase price was obtained by way of a mortgage of the house. The mortgage was taken in Harold's name as the legal title was vested in the sole name of Harold. Winifred provided housekeeping money and extensively redecorated the house.

(iv) Assume the facts as in (iii) above, but Harold and Winifred were legally married.

SUMMARY

The rules concerning proprietary rights in the family home are the following:

- Where the transfer of property is subject to an express agreement or understanding between the parties as to their proprietary rights this would be conclusive as to their intentions, in the absence of duress, fraud or mistake, see *Goodman v Gallant* (1986); *Goodman v Carlton* (2002).

- Such express agreements are required to be evidenced in writing in accordance with the provisions of s 53(1)(b) of the Law of Property Act 1925.

- In the absence of an enforceable, express intention the court may enforce an implied intention between the parties as to their beneficial interests.

- The starting point is that beneficial ownership in the property follows the legal title. If the property is put in the joint names of the parties, the presumption is in favour of joint beneficial ownership, *Stack v Dowden* (2007); *Jones v Kernott* (2011).

- The onus of proof lies on the person seeking to show that the beneficial ownership is different from legal ownership.

- The contrary could be shown by ascertaining the parties' shared intentions, actual or inferred, with respect to the property. According to *Stack v Dowden* (2007), this involves the constructive trust rather than the resulting trust.

  - Thus, in a domestic context, where the legal title to property is conveyed in the joint names of the parties, the starting point is that the parties intend to create a legal and beneficial joint tenancy, subject to evidence to the contrary, see *Stack v Dowden* (2007); *Jones v Kernott* (2011); *Fowler v Barron* (2008); *Barnes v Phillips* (2015).

  - Likewise, in a domestic context, where the legal title to property is taken in the name of one party, the starting point is that the equitable interest follows the legal title. The party against whom the presumption operates bears the legal burden of proving to the contrary, see *Pettitt v Pettitt* (1970); *Gissing v Gissing* (1971); *Abbott v Abbott* (2008); *O'Kelly v Davies* (2014); *Estate of York* (2015); *Curran v Collins* (2015); *Capehorn v Harris* (2015); *Arif v Anwar* (2015).

- The process of ascertaining the parties' intention is conducted by reference to the entire course of dealing in the property between the parties. This requires a holistic view of the parties' conduct, according to *Stack v Dowden*; *Jones v Kernott*; *Abbott v Abbott*.

- In the domestic context, financial contributions (direct and indirect) will amount to one factor, amongst many others, in ascertaining the parties' shared intentions. This was the position in *Stack* as distinct from the *Pettitt v Pettitt* (1970), *Gissing v Gissing* (1971) and *Rosset* (1990) principles. The focus is on evidence of the common intention of the parties.

  - Domestic duties and the endurance of long periods of domestic abuse are irrelevant factors in determining the relevant interests of the parties, see *Burns v Burns* (1984); *Estate of York* (2015).

  - The restricted view of the need for express discussions between the parties concerning their common intention advocated by Lord Bridge in *Lloyds Bank v Rosset* (1990) has been criticised in *Midland Bank v Cooke* (1995) and *Stack v Dowden*.

- In quantifying the shares of the parties the court ought to resist the temptation of deciding what is fair, as was advocated by the Court of Appeal in *Oxley v Hiscock* (2005). Instead, the courts ought to be guided exclusively by the parties' intentions, express, inferred or imputed at stage two, after deciding that the parties manifested a common intention to share an interest in the property, see *Barnes v Phillips* (2015).

⊙ In respect of commercial properties acquired by one or more of the parties, the approach of the courts as to the extent of the beneficial interests is by way of a purchase money resulting trust, see *Laskar v Laskar* (2008); *Erlam v Rahman* (2016).

▨ Section 37 of the Matrimonial Proceedings and Property Act 1970 and ss 23–25 of the Matrimonial Causes Act 1973 have all enhanced the position of spouses and civil partners.

⊙ After some hesitation by the courts, it has now been decided that pre-nuptial and post-nuptial agreements between married couples and civil partners are *prima facie* binding on the parties, in the absence of evidence of unconscionable bargains between them, see *Radmacher v Granatino* (2010).

SAMPLE ESSAY QUESTION

'The introduction of the constructive trust as a means of resolving disputes between parties as to their proprietary rights in shared homes may lead to an unjustified degree of inconsistency and uncertainty in this important area of the law.' **Discuss**

Answer plan

- The decline of the presumptions of resulting trusts and advancements in the mid-twentieth century as a means of resolving property owning disputes between parties represents a practical improvement in the law.
- The primary evidence of the parties' intention is based on an express agreement or understanding as to their interests. Such express agreements will be conclusive as to their interests, in the absence of duress, fraud or mistake, see *Goodman v Gallant* (1986); *Goodman v Carlton* (2002).
- The principles that initially replaced the presumptions were regarded as settled principles of property law, namely the 'purchase price' resulting trusts and 'common intention' constructive trusts, see *Pettitt v Pettitt* (1970) and *Gissing v Gissing* (1971).
- The rationale behind the property law principles was to give effect to the intentions (express or implied) of the parties.
- An express agreement or understanding between the parties as to their interests will be conclusive in the absence of duress, fraud or mistake, see *Goodman v Gallant*.
- To be enforceable, such express agreement is required to be evidenced in writing, see s 53(1)(b) of the Law of Property Act 1925.
- Implied intention may be manifested by the purchase money resulting trust or common intention constructive trust.
- The purchase money resulting trust requires a party to make a substantial direct or indirect contribution to the purchase of the property in order to obtain an equivalent interest in the property.

- In *Eves v Eves* (1975) the court adopted an open ended (new model) constructive trust.
- A common intention constructive trust arises whenever a party with the legal title has so conducted himself that it would be inequitable to allow him to deny the claimant an interest in the property. This requires the claimant to establish a common intention between the parties as to shared ownership, reliance on the intention and some detriment, see *Grant v Edwards* (1986) and *Lloyds Bank v Rosset* (1990). In *Rosset* the court laid down two categories of evidence of common intention.
- The evidence necessary to support the resulting or constructive trust, as laid down in *Rosset*, was criticised in *Stack v Dowden* (2007) as being too restrictive.
- In *Rosset*, the possible exclusion of indirect contributions to the acquisition of the property was not applied in *Le Foe v Le Foe* (2001)
- In *Midland Bank v Cooke* (1995) and *Drake v Whipp* (1996) the courts adopted a modified form of the *Rosset* principles.
- However, in two definitive cases, *Stack v Dowden* and *Jones v Kernott*, the House of Lords, and subsequently the Supreme Court, sought to clarify the governing principles in this field. The courts restated the appropriate principles that are applicable in this context. In addition to express declarations of trusts, the common intention constructive trust will be utilised to give effect to the intentions of the parties. The effect is that in the domestic context, there is no longer room for the purchase price resulting trust as a means of reflecting the intentions of the parties.
- Accordingly, in the context of the family home, the presumption is that the equitable interest follows the legal title. This is the position whether the legal title is taken in either the joint names of the parties or the sole name of one of the parties.
- The effect of the respective presumption is that the party wishing to establish the contrary bears the legal burden of proof of establishing a common intention constructive trust. The resulting trust institution in the context of the family home has been castigated in favour of the remedial constructive trust.
- The courts will look at all the circumstances of the case (including financial contributions, the purpose for which the home was acquired, whether the parties had dependent children, how the parties arranged their finances etc.) in order to ascertain the parties' intentions.
- Domestic duties conducted by one or more of the parties is regarded as irrelevant in ascertaining the common intention of the parties, see *Burns v Burns* (1984).
- In *Arif v Anwar* (2015) the court drew a distinction between a common intention constructive trust and proprietary estoppel.
- However, with regard to investment properties acquired by one or more of the parties, the purchase money resulting trust has been retained as the institution for ascertaining the equitable interests of the parties, see *Laskar v Laskar* (2008) and *Erlam v Rahman* (2016).

- In quantifying the interests of the parties the court is entitled to 'infer' or 'impute' an intention to the parties by reference to all the circumstances of the case, see *Oxley v Hiscock* (2004); *Barnes v Phillips* (2015). An intention may be imputed to the parties in the interests of fairness, see *Midland Bank v Cooke*.

- Where the parties are married, additional statutory principles may be applicable, see s 37 of the Matrimonial Proceedings and Property Act 1970 and ss 23–25 of the Matrimonial Causes Act 1973.

CONCLUSION

Further reading

Battersby, G, 'Ownership of the family home: *Stack v Dowden* in the House of Lords' (2008) CFLQ 255.

Chandler, A, 'Express declarations of trust, rectification and rescission: *Goodman v Gallant* revisited' (2008) Fam Law 1210.

Clark, P, 'The family home: intention and agreement' (1992) Fam Law 73.

Dixon, M, 'The never-ending story: co-ownership after *Stack v Dowden*' (2007) Conv 456.

Dymond, A, 'Inference and imputation: cases after Jones v Kernott' (2016) JHL 57.

Etherton, T, 'Constructive trusts and proprietary estoppel: the search for clarity and principle' (2009) 73 Conv 104.

Gardner, S and Davidson, K, 'The Supreme Court on family homes' (2012) LQR 178.

Hayton, D, 'Constructive trusts of homes: a bold approach' (1993) 109 LQR 485.

Hayward, A, 'Family values in the home: *Fowler v Barron*' (2009) CFLQ 242.

Hess, E, 'The rights of cohabitants: when and how will the law be reformed?' (2009) Fam Law 405.

Lee, R, '*Stack v Dowden*: a sequel' (2008) LQR 124.

Mee, J, '*Jones v Kernott*: inferring and imputing in Essex' (2012) Conv PL 167.

Millett, Lord, 'The husband the wife and the bank' (2001) PCB 238.

Ockelton, C, 'Keeping it in the family' (1981) CLJ 243.

Panesar, S and Gompertz, K, '*Jones v Kernott*: non-marital cohabitation: joint ownership – constructive trusts and beneficial interests' (2011) Cov LJ 48.

Pawlowski, M, 'Beneficial ownership and detriment' (2008) 152 SJ 16.

Pawlowski, M, 'Resulting trusts, joint borrowers and beneficial shares' (2008) Fam Law 654.

Pawlowski, M, 'Imputed intention and joint ownership: a return to common sense: *Jones v Kernott*' (2012) Conv PL 149.

Roche, J, '*Kernott, Stack* and *Oxley* made simple: a practitioner's view' (2011) Conv PL 123.

Tattersall, M, '*Stack v Dowden*: imputing an intention' (2008) Fam Law 424.

Yip, M, 'The rules applying to unmarried cohabitants' family home: *Jones v Kernott*' (2012) Conv PL 159.

10

Secret trusts and mutual wills

AIMS AND OBJECTIVES

By the end of this chapter you should be able to:

- identify and distinguish between the two types of secret trust
- understand the theoretical justification for enforcing secret trusts
- comprehend the requirements for the creation of fully and half-secret trusts
- follow the arguments regarding unresolved issues relating to secret trusts
- appreciate the requirements for the creation of trusts of mutual wills

10.1 Introduction

testator
A person who dies having made a valid will.

A secret trust is an equitable obligation communicated to an intended trustee during the **testator**'s lifetime, but which is intended to attach to a gift arising under the testator's will.

A testator who wishes to create a trust over his property upon his death is required to express this intention as well as the terms of the trust in his will. The formalities necessary to create a valid will are required to be complied with. These formalities are enacted in s 9 of the Wills Act 1837 (as amended). The basic requirement is the need for writing signed by the testator and witnessed by two or more witnesses. The secret trust is an exception to this rule because in limited circumstances where a testator has not fully complied with the necessary formalities, equity will nevertheless impose a duty upon the party acquiring the property under the will (legatee or devisee) to carry out the wishes of the testator. This will require the legatee or devisee to hold the property upon trust for the secret beneficiaries.

On a testator's death his will becomes a public document and wills are consequently open to public scrutiny. But the testator may wish to make provision, after his death, for what he considers to be some embarrassing object, such as a mistress or an illegitimate child or any object that he does not wish to be disclosed to the public. To avoid adverse publicity, he may make an apparent gift by will to an intended trustee, subject to an understanding to hold the property for the benefit of the secret beneficiary. In construing the will the courts adopt an approach which is similar to construction of the terms of a contract, save when s 21 of the Administration of Justice

Act 1982 is applicable in respect of meaningless or ambiguous terms (in this case extrinsic evidence may be admitted). In other words, despite the will being a unilateral document and contracts being bilateral agreements, the approach of the courts in the context of interpretation is the same. This was stated by Lord Neuberger MR in *Royal Society for the Prevention of Cruelty to Animals v Sharp* [2010] EWCA 1474.

JUDGMENT

'The court's approach to the interpretation of wills is, in practice, very similar to its approach to the interpretation of contracts. Of course, in the case of a contract, there are at least two parties involved in negotiating its terms, whereas a will is a unilateral document. However, it is clear ... that the approach to interpretation of unilateral documents ... is effectively the same as the court's approach to the interpretation of a bilateral or multilateral document such as a contract.'

Lord Neuberger MR

In interpreting a contract or a will the objective of the court is to ascertain the intention of the parties or the testator. It gives effect to the meaning of relevant words in the light of the natural and ordinary meaning of those words, the context of any other provisions of the document, the facts known to the parties or the testator at the time that the document was executed but ignoring subjective evidence of the parties' or testator's intention, see *Marley v Rawlins* [2014] UKSC 2, in the context of proceedings to rectify a will which, by an oversight, was signed by the wrong party.

10.2 Two types of secret trust

There are two types of secret trust:

- fully secret trusts;
- half-secret trusts.

legatee
A person who inherits personal property under a valid will, as opposed to a 'devisee' who takes real property under a will.

a fortiori
More conclusively.

A fully secret trust is an obligation which is fully concealed on the face of the will. The obligation is communicated to the **legatee** during the lifetime of the testator and the will transfers the property to the legatee without mention of the existence of a trust, i.e. both the existence and *a fortiori* terms of the trust are fully concealed on the face of the instrument creating the trust, namely the will, for example a disposition by will 'to A absolutely'.

A half-secret trust is intended when the will indicates or acknowledges the existence of the trust but the terms are concealed on the face of the will. The trustee will then take the property on trust subject to a valid communication of the terms effected *inter vivos*, for example a disposition by will 'to A on trust for purposes communicated to him'.

Thus, assuming there has been a valid communication of the terms of the trust with the appropriate intention to create a trust, the category of secret trust involved depends on whether the trust has been acknowledged on the face of the will or not. This is important, for the two types of secret trust are subject to different rules.

In enforcing secret trusts, equity does not contradict s9 of the Wills Act 1837, as amended, because the trust operates outside (*dehors*) the Wills Act. Indeed, the secret trust complements the will in that a valid will is assumed, but it is recognised that the will on its own does not reflect the true intention of the testator. The bare minimum requirements are a validly executed will which transfers property to the trustees, whether named as such under the will or not; and the acceptance by the trustees *inter vivos* of an equitable obligation. Section 15 of the Wills Act 1837 is not applicable in this context. Section 15 of the 1837 Act enacts that an **attesting witness** (including his spouse) loses his interest under the will. It will be recalled that one of the formalities under the Wills Act 1837 involves two or more attesting witnesses. The Wills Act 1968 amended this requirement to allow additional attesting witnesses (and their spouses) exceeding two to acquire property under the testator's will. Accordingly, if there are three attesting witnesses under a will and one of these has been bequeathed property under the will, that witness's interest will not lapse. In *Re Young* [1951] Ch 344, the court decided that the secret trust operated outside the will in the sense that it was immaterial that one of the intended beneficiaries under the *trust*, as distinct from the *will*, witnessed the will.

attesting witness

Witness who signs a document verifying the signature of a person who executes the document.

CASE EXAMPLE

Re Young [1951] Ch 344

A testator made a bequest to his wife subject to a direction made outside the will to the effect that on her death she would leave the property for the purpose which he had communicated to her. One of the purposes was that she would leave a legacy of £2,000 to the testator's chauffeur, who witnessed the will. The question in issue was whether the chauffeur had forfeited his interest. The court held that the trust in favour of the chauffeur was not contained in the will but was created separately outside the will. Section 15 of the Wills Act 1837 was not applicable.

JUDGMENT

'The whole theory of the formation of a secret trust is that the Wills Act 1837 has nothing to do with the matter because the forms required by the Wills Act are entirely disregarded, since the persons do not take by virtue of the gift in the will, but by virtue of the secret trusts imposed upon the beneficiary who does in fact take under the will.'

Danckwerts J

A variation of the *dehors* theory is to the effect that the trust is created *inter vivos* and outside or independently of the will. The notion here is that the trust is created by reason of the personal obligation accepted by the legatee. Thus, the argument proceeds on the assumption that the date of the creation of the trust is during the lifetime of the settlor: see *Re Gardner (No 2)* [1923] 2 Ch 230. This theory is fundamentally flawed in both trusts and probate law. On the date of the communication of the terms of the trust to the legatee (trustee) the trustee has not acquired the intended property. Thus, there cannot be a valid trust. In probate law a will speaks from the date of the death of the testator. Before this date the legatee has merely a hope of acquiring a benefit under the will.

Traditionally, the trust property is transferred by will on condition that the trustee (who takes under the will as legatee or devisee) holds the property subject to an agreement entered into between the testator and himself. Likewise, the secret trust principles will extend to intestacies. These are occasions (as illustrated by *Sellack v Harris* (1708)) where the settlor decides not to make a will on the faith of a promise by his next of kin to dispose of the property in accordance with the settlor's wishes as disclosed to him during the lifetime of the settlor.

CASE EXAMPLE

Sellack v Harris [1708] 5 Vin Ab 521

A father was induced by his heir presumptive (entitled to realty on an intestacy before 1925) not to make a will on the ground that the heir himself would make provision for his mother. After the death of his father, the heir refused to make provision as promised. The court held that the heir was obliged to make the relevant provision, for he had induced his father to refrain from making a will.

10.3 Basis for enforcing secret trusts

The theoretical justification for enforcing secret trusts is said to be the need to prevent fraud. The court originally applied the maxim 'Equity will not allow a statute to be used as an engine for fraud'. The statute in this respect is the Wills Act 1837. The jurisdiction adopted by the courts in order to enforce secret trusts was to prevent the legatee or devisee fraudulently denying the binding nature of his promise and attempting to set up s9 of the Wills Act 1837 as a defence, for example if, during his lifetime, a testator (T) made an agreement with A (a legatee) to the effect that on T's death, £50,000 would be transferred to him to hold on trust for B and T made a will to that effect. Following T's death, it would be a fraud on the estate of T and B for A to deny the agreement, or non-compliance with s9 of the 1837 Act, and claim the property beneficially. The persons who may be the victims of the fraud by the legatee are the testator and the beneficiaries under the intended secret trust. Consequently the court will step in and compel A to honour his agreement. This theory was enunciated by Lord Westbury in *McCormick v Grogan* (1869) LR 4 HL 82:

JUDGMENT

'My Lords, the jurisdiction which is invoked here by the appellant is founded altogether on personal fraud. It is a jurisdiction by which a Court of Equity, proceeding on the ground of fraud, converts the party who has committed it into a trustee for the party who is injured by that fraud ... It is incumbent on the Court to see that a fraud ... is proved by the clearest and most indisputable evidence. ... The Court of Equity has, from a very early period, decided that even an Act of Parliament shall not be used as an instrument of fraud; and if in the machinery of perpetrating a fraud an Act of Parliament intervenes, the Court of Equity, it is true, does not set aside the Act of Parliament but fastens on the individual who gets a title under the Act, and imposes on him a personal obligation, because he applies the Act as an instrument for accomplishing a fraud.'

A similar view was stated by Lord Hardwicke in the earlier case of *Drakeford v Wilkes* (1747) 3 Atk 539:

JUDGMENT

'[I]f a testatrix has a conversation with a legatee, and the legatee promises that, in consideration of the disposition in favour of her, she will do an act in favour of a third person, and the testator lets the will stand, it is very proper that the person who undertook to do the act should perform, because, as I must take it, if (the secret trustee) has not so promised, the testatrix would have altered her will.'

Lord Hardwicke

The justification for enforcing secret trusts put forward by Lord Hardwicke (above) appears to support both fully and half-secret trusts. Enforcement of the trust does not depend upon the actual fraudulent enrichment of the secret trustee. Support for this view may be found in the following authorities: *Reech v Kennigate* (1748) Amb 67, *Stickland v Turner* (1804) 9 Ves Jun 517, *Chamberlain v Agar* (1813) 2 V & B 257, *Wallgrave v Tebbs* (1855) 2 K & J 313, *Re Fleetwood* (1880) 15 Ch D 594, *Barrow v Greenough* (1796) 3 Ves Jun 152, *Jones v Badley* (1868) LR 3 Ch App 362, *Re Cooper* [1939] Ch 811, *Re Boyes* (1884) 26 Ch D 531, *Russell v Jackson* (1852) 10 Hare 204, *Podmore v Gunning* (1836) 8 Sim 644.

Lord Buckmaster, in *Blackwell v Blackwell* [1929] AC 318, identified the victim as the beneficiary under the intended secret trust. He said:

QUOTATION

'A testator having been induced to make a gift on trust in his will in favour of certain named persons, the trustee is not at liberty to suppress the evidence of the trust and thus destroy the whole object of its creation, in fraud of the beneficiaries.'

Lord Buckmaster

However, in *McCormick v Grogan*, Lord Hatherley put forward a different interpretation of the notion of fraud. His view of the fraud focused on an inducement by the intended legatee (trustee) to assure the testator that the transfer of property to the legatee will be held upon trust in accordance with his wishes, and the legatee subsequently attempts to deny the promise. In the above example the court proceeded on the basis of frustrating A's course of action if he induced T to transfer property to him in order to carry out T's wishes, and after T's death A attempts to claim the property beneficially by relying on the statute. Half-secret trusts cannot be justified on this basis, for the will transfers the property to persons named as trustees and such persons are not allowed to take property beneficially. Thus, the trustee may not profit from his fraud. If the intended half-secret trust fails, a resulting trust will be set up.

JUDGMENT

'This doctrine [secret trusts] evidently requires to be carefully restricted within proper limits. It is in itself a doctrine which involves a wide departure from the policy which induced the Legislature to pass the Statute of Frauds, and it is only in clear cases of fraud that this doctrine has been applied – cases in which the Court has been persuaded that there has been a fraudulent inducement held out on the part of the apparent beneficiary in order to lead the testator to confide to him the duty which he so undertook to perform.'

Lord Hatherley in *McCormick v Grogan* (1869)

But half-secret trusts cannot be justified on this basis, for the will transfers the property to persons named as trustees and such persons are not allowed to take property beneficially. The trustee may not profit from his fraud. If the intended half-secret trust fails, a resulting trust will be set up. The effect is that this notion of the fraud theory cannot justify the existence of half-secret trusts.

An alternative basis for enforcing secret trusts is the transfer and declaration theory. The approach here is that the will transfers the property to the trustee, subject to an express, conditional declaration of trust executed by the testator outside the will. The conditional declaration of trust will be activated when the trustee acquires the relevant property under the testator's will. The secret trust becomes effective when the trustee acquires the property under the testator's will, subject to the valid declaration. The court steps in and compels the trustee to carry out the wishes of the testator as indicated in the declaration. The conditional *inter vivos* declaration becomes effective on the death of the testator and specifically when the legatee acquires the property. The trust is not created *inter vivos*, but on death, and subject to an *inter vivos* declaration or communication of the testator's wishes. This approach was advocated by Lord Sumner in *Blackwell v Blackwell* [1929] AC 318:

JUDGMENT

'The court of equity finds a man in the position of an absolute legal owner of a sum of money, which has been bequeathed to him under a valid will and it declares that, on proof of certain facts relating to the motives of the testator, it will not allow the legal owner to exercise his legal right to do what he wishes with the property. In other words it lets him take what the will gives him and then makes him apply it as the Court of Conscience directs, and it does so in order to give effect to the wishes of the testator, which would not otherwise be effectual.'

Lord Sumner

A variation on this theory is the *dehors* the Wills Act 1837 analysis, as outlined above.

10.4 Requirements for the creation of fully secret trusts

The primary requirement is proof that the testator intended to create a trust and, in particular, a secret trust by making the legatee a trustee for the secret beneficiaries. This is the position with regard to both fully and half-secret trusts. The type of intention that is contemplated here is legal, as distinct from merely a moral obligation. In the event of a dispute, the court will construe the evidence on an objective basis and form an opinion as to whether the test is satisfied. In *McCormick v Grogan* (1869), the issue was whether a fully secret trust was created where a testator transferred his estate absolutely to his friend, subject to inconclusive instructions in a letter.

CASE EXAMPLE

McCormick v Grogan (1869) LR 4 HL 82 (House of Lords)

A testator, in 1851, left all his property by a three line will to his friend Mr Grogan. In 1854, the testator was struck down by cholera and had only a few hours to live. He sent for Mr Grogan and told him in effect that his will and a letter would be found in his desk. The letter named various intended beneficiaries and the intended gifts to them. The letter concluded with the words: 'I do not wish you to act strictly to the foregoing instructions, but leave it entirely to your own good judgment to do as you think I would if living, and as the parties are deserving.'

The issue was whether a fully secret trust was intended by the testator. The court decided that on an objective analysis of the facts no trust was created, because the testator did not intend to impose a trust on the executor.

Likewise, in *Re Snowden* (1979) the intended fully secret trust failed for lack of evidence of an intention to create a trust.

CASE EXAMPLE

Re Snowden [1979] Ch 528

A testatrix, aged 86, made her will six days before she died. She had no children and her nearest relatives apart from her brother were five nephews and nieces, 13 great-nephews and great-nieces. She left her residuary estate to her brother, Bert (B), absolutely. B died six days after the testatrix, leaving all of his property to his son. Evidence was given by members of a firm of solicitors who had prepared and witnessed the will that the testatrix wished to be fair to everyone, including her nephews and nieces, and wanted B to look after the division for her. The question in issue was whether a fully secret trust was created.

The court decided that, on an objective construction of the facts, no secret trust had been created and B's son took beneficially. B was subject only to a moral obligation to respect the wishes of the testatrix. In the absence of fraud or other special circumstances, the standard of proof that was required to establish a secret trust was merely the ordinary civil standard of proof required to establish an ordinary trust.

In similar vein the Court of Appeal in *Kasperbauer v Griffith* (2000) decided that the evidence adduced before the court was insufficient to establish that the testator had intended to impose a fully secret trust on his wife at a family meeting to discuss his will. The claimant is required to convince the court that testator's wishes were consistent with the three certainties test (see Chapter 3).

CASE EXAMPLE

Kasperbauer v Griffith [2000] WTLR 333 (Court of Appeal)

The testator's solicitors prepared his will and he called a family meeting with his wife and his two children by a former marriage. He indicated that he will devise his house and a pension lump sum to his wife and that she should use the lump sum to pay off the mortgage on the house. The children were also entitled to receive a cash sum equivalent to the nil rate band for inheritance tax. He indicated that the house was to be sold within one year of his death and the proceeds divided equally between the children. The testator said that his wife 'knew what she had to do'. No part of this conversation was committed to writing. The wife remained silent throughout the meeting. The testator subsequently made a will in a different form leaving his entire estate to his wife. The children claimed that a fully secret trust had been created. The court decided that the evidence as to the existence of a secret trust was inconclusive and, at best, only a moral obligation was imposed on the wife.

JUDGMENT

'The authorities make plain that what is needed is (i) an intention by the testator to create a trust, satisfying the traditional requirement of three certainties (that is to say certain language in imperative form, certain subject-matter and certain objects or beneficiaries); (ii) the communication of the trust to the legatee, and (iii) acceptance of the trust by the legatee, which acceptance can take the form of silent acquiescence. The crucial question in the present case is whether there was that intention and, as Mr Justice Brightman said in *Ottaway v Norman* [1972] Ch. 698 at 711, it is an essential element that the testator must intend to subject the legatee to an obligation in favour of the intended beneficiary. That will be evidenced by appropriately imperative, as distinct from precatory, language. Within a family many dispositions are made in the declared hope and expectation that the recipient will pass on what is received to others but without any intention that enforceable rights will by that declaration be created in those others.

To my mind the phrase which the testator repeated, that the widow knew what she had to do, is equivocal and is at least consistent with the belief and intention on the part of the testator that his expressed intentions imposed only a moral obligation on her.

I would add too that the very fact that the testator changed his mind in a number of important respects is again consistent with the view that the expression of his intentions at the meeting … was not intended to be a definitive instruction to the widow, presumptively intended to impose a legally enforceable obligation on her.'

Peter Gibson LJ

....

execution of a will
The signature of a testator in the presence of two or more attesting witnesses.
....

- The claimant is required to prove that the testator, during his lifetime, communicated the terms of the trust to the legatee. It is immaterial whether the communication was made before or after the **execution of the will** provided that it was made before the death of the testator. Communication may take place directly by means of an oral statement or in writing outside the will. In addition, communication may take place constructively, i.e. by delivery of a sealed envelope containing the terms of the trust to the trustee during the lifetime of the testator, but headed 'Not to be opened before my death'. Provided that the trustee is aware that the contents of the envelope are connected with the testator's will, communication is deemed to be effective on the date of the delivery of the envelope. This is illustrated by *Re Keen* [1937] Ch 236 (below).

- The trustee is required to accept the trust obligation during the testator's lifetime. This may be manifested by means of an acknowledgement by the legatee (trustee) to be bound by the terms of the trust. Alternatively, acceptance may exist through acquiescence or silence on the part of the legatee. Once the legatee is aware of the intention of the testator and this intention is complete in the sense that all the terms have been communicated to the legatee, he is bound to hold on trust for those purposes. The legatee is not required to do anything positive to demonstrate acceptance, he is deemed to accept the terms of the trust once he is aware of the testator's wishes during his lifetime.

Brightman J, in *Ottaway v Norman* [1972] Ch 698, identified the basic requirements for a fully secret trust thus:

JUDGMENT

'It will be convenient to call the person upon whom such a trust is imposed the primary donee and the beneficiary under the trust the secondary donee. The essential elements which must be proved to exist are:

(i) the intention of the testator to subject the primary donee to an obligation in favour of the secondary donee;

(ii) communication of that intention to the primary donee; and

(iii) the acceptance of that obligation by the primary donee either expressly or by acquiescence. It is immaterial whether these elements precede or succeed the will of the donor.'

Brightman J

As a corollary to the communication principle, where the legatee does not wish to be bound by the terms of the trust communicated to him he is under an obligation to notify the testator of his refusal during the testator's lifetime. Failure to accomplish this means that the legatee is bound by the terms communicated to him. In *Moss v Cooper* (1861) 1

J & H 352, it was decided that a legatee's failure to communicate his intention to the testator during the latter's lifetime did not absolve him from the liability to hold on trust for purposes known to him.

10.4.1 No agreement for transferee to hold as trustee

If there is no agreement between the testator and the legatee whereby the transferee is intended to hold as trustee, the transferee takes beneficially and may set up s9 of the Wills Act 1837 as a defence. The distinction here is between a legacy *simpliciter* and a legacy upon trust.

CASE EXAMPLE

Wallgrave v Tebbs [1855] 2 K & J 313

A testator, by will, transferred personal and real property to two individuals absolutely. The testator was contemplating the identities of the ultimate beneficiaries under the trust but failed, during his lifetime, to notify the two individuals of his selection. The court decided that the two individuals were entitled to the properties beneficially. They had not acted unconscionably by claiming the properties beneficially because they did not make an agreement to hold on trust.

JUDGMENT

'I am satisfied that I ought not overstep the clear line which separates mere trusts from devises and bequests … Where a person, knowing that a testator in making a disposition in his favour intends it to be applied for purposes other than for his own benefit either expressly promises, or by silence implies, that he will carry out the testator's intention into effect, and the property is left to him upon the faith of an undertaking, it is in effect a case of trust and the court will not allow the devisee to set up the Statute of Frauds – or rather the Statute of Wills as a defence. But the question here is totally different. Here there has been no promise or undertaking on the part of the legatee. The latter knew nothing of the testator's intention until after his death. Upon the face of the will, the parties take indisputably for their own benefit.'

Wood VC

10.4.2 Terms of trust not communicated

If the transferee agreed to hold the property on trust, but the terms of the trust have not been communicated during the testator's lifetime, the transferee will hold the property on resulting trust for the testator's heirs. The intended secret trust fails because there has been a failure to communicate the terms of the trust to the legatee during the lifetime of the testator. But, since the legatee is aware that he is required to hold on trust and acquires the property on the basis of this understanding, he holds the same on resulting trust for the testator. This principle was applied in *Re Boyes* (1884) 26 Ch D 531.

CASE EXAMPLE

Re Boyes; Boyes v Carritt [1884] 26 Ch D 531

A testator, by will, transferred property to a legatee, having secured an agreement from the legatee to hold on trust. The testator died before he communicated the terms to the legatee. The court decided that the intended secret trust failed but a resulting trust was created for the testator's heirs.

JUDGMENT

'If the trust was not declared when the will was made, it is essential, in order to make it binding, that it should be communicated to the devisee or legatee in the testator's lifetime and that he should accept that particular trust.'

Kay J

The fully secret trust obligation normally takes the form of the legatee (trustee) holding the property on trust for the secret beneficiary. Alternatively, the obligation may involve the legatee executing a will in favour of the secret beneficiary. In this event, the legatee may enjoy the property beneficially during his lifetime, but the obligation undertaken requires him to transfer the relevant property by his will to the named beneficiary. Accordingly, there are two beneficiaries involved in the transaction – the 'primary beneficiary' who acquires an interest for life and the 'secondary beneficiary' who is entitled to acquire the property under the will of the primary beneficiary.

CASE EXAMPLE

Ottaway v Norman [1972] Ch 698

A testator, Harry Ottaway, by his will devised his bungalow (with fixtures, fittings and furniture) to his housekeeper, Miss Hodges, in fee simple and gave her a legacy of £1,500. It was alleged that Miss Hodges had verbally agreed with the testator to leave by her will the bungalow and fittings etc., and whatever 'money' was left over at the time of her death to the claimants, Mr and Mrs William Ottaway (the testator's son and daughter-in-law). By her will, Miss Hodges left all her property to someone else. The claimants sued Mr Norman (Miss Hodges' executor) for a declaration that the relevant parts of Miss Hodges' estate were held upon trust for the claimants. The court decided that there was clear evidence that a fully secret trust was created only in respect of the bungalow and fittings etc., but not in respect of the 'money'. The intended trust of the money was uncertain and void. Mr Norman as her executor therefore held the bungalow on trust for Mr and Mrs William Ottaway.

JUDGMENT

'I am content to assume for present purposes but without so deciding that if property is given to the primary donee on the understanding that the primary donee will dispose by his will of such assets, if any, as he may have at his command at his death in favour of the secondary donee, a valid trust is created in favour of the secondary donee which is in suspense during the lifetime of the primary donee, but attaches to the estate of the primary donee at the moment of the latter's death. There would seem to be at least some support for this proposition in an Australian case *Birmingham v Renfrew* (1937) 57 CLR 666.'

Brightman J

10.4.3 Two or more legatees

Where a testator leaves property to two or more legatees but informs one or some of them (but not all of them) of the terms of the trust, the issue arises as to whether the uninformed legatees are bound by the communication to the informed legatees. The solution here depends on the timing of the communication and the status of the legatees. If (a) the communication was made to the legatees before or at the time of the execution of the will and (b) they take as joint tenants, the uninformed legatees are bound to hold for the purposes communicated to the informed legatees. The reason commonly ascribed to this principle is that no one is allowed to take property beneficially under a fraud committed by another. But if any of the above conditions is not satisfied, the uninformed legatees are entitled to take the property beneficially; the reason stated for this aspect of the rule is that the gift is not tainted with any fraud in procuring the execution of the will. Thus, if some of the legatees were told of the terms of the trust after the execution of the will but during the lifetime of the testator, the uninformed legatees will take part of the property beneficially. The informed legatees, of course, will hold on trust. In *Re Stead* [1900] 1 Ch 237, Farwell J reviewed the authorities and the justification for the rule, and confessed that he was unable to see any difference between a gift made on the faith of an antecedent promise and a gift left unrevoked on the faith of a subsequent promise to carry out the testator's wishes. He added, however, that he was bound by the principle.

This rule, by its nature, may not be extended to half-secret trusts for the trustee on the face of the will is not entitled to the property beneficially.

10.5 Requirements for the creation of half-secret trusts

This classification arises where the legatee or devisee takes as trustee on the face of the will but the terms of the trust are not specified in the will: for instance T, a testator, transfers property to L, a legatee, to 'hold upon trust for purposes that have been communicated to him'. The will acknowledges the existence of the trust but the terms have been concealed.

The following points are relevant in order to establish a half-secret trust.

The will is irrevocable and sacrosanct on the death of the testator
Accordingly, evidence is not admissible to contradict the terms of the will. To adduce such evidence would have the potential to perpetrate a fraud: for instance, if the will points to a past communication (i.e. a communication of the terms of the trust before the will was made), evidence is not admissible to prove a future communication. Similarly, since the will names the legatee as trustee, evidence is not admissible to prove that he is a beneficiary, even of part of the property. This is the position even though the testator may wish the legatee to receive part of the property beneficially. If the testator wishes to benefit the legatee (trustee) he is required to express his intention in a separate disposition under the will.

CASE EXAMPLE

Re Rees [1950] Ch 204

A testator, by his will, appointed his friend H and his solicitor W to be executors and trustees and he devised and bequeathed all his property to 'my trustees absolutely, they well knowing my wishes concerning the same'. The testator told the executors and trustees at the time of making the will that he wished them to make certain payments out of the estate and retain the remainder for their own use. After the payments were made, there was a substantial surplus remaining. The executors claimed that they were entitled to keep the surplus in that there was no secret trust but a conditional gift in their favour. The court held that the surplus could not be taken by the executors and trustees beneficially. The relevant clause in the will created a half-secret trust and the trustees were not entitled to adduce evidence to show that they were entitled beneficially. The surplus funds passed on intestacy to the next of kin.

JUDGMENT

'I agree with the judge that to admit evidence to the effect that the testator informed of the executors – or I will assume both of the executors – that he intended them to take beneficial interests, would be to conflict with the terms of the will as I have construed them; for the inevitable result of admitting that evidence and giving effect to it would be that the will would be regarded not as conferring a trust estate only upon the two trustees, but as giving them a conditional gift which on construction is the thing which, if I am right, it does not do.'

Evershed MR

Communication before or at the time of execution of the will

It is imperative that the testator communicate the terms of the trust before or at the time of the execution of the will and the intended trustees are required to accept (expressly or by acquiescence) the obligation to hold on trust before or at the time of the execution of the will. Thus, an agreement between the parties is required to be made at the time of the execution of the will. On this basis the terms of the trust may be proved and the equitable obligation will be effective.

CASE EXAMPLE

Blackwell v Blackwell [1929] AC 318

A testator, by a codicil (an alteration of a will executed in accordance with the Wills Act 1837), bequeathed a legacy of £12,000 to five persons 'to apply for the purposes indicated by me to them'. Before the execution of the codicil, the terms of the trust were communicated to the legatees and the trust was accepted by them all. The beneficiaries were the testator's mistress and her illegitimate son. The claimant asked the court for a declaration that no valid trust in favour of the objects had been created, on the ground that parol evidence (oral evidence) was inadmissible to establish the trust. The court held that the trust was valid. Parol evidence was admissible to establish the terms of a half-secret trust in order to prevent the testator's intention being fraudulently avoided. The evidence did not vary the will; it merely gave effect to the intention of the testator.

JUDGMENT

'Why should equity forbid an honest trustee to give effect to his promise, made to a deceased testator, and compel him to pay another legatee, about whom it is quite certain that the testator did not mean to make him the object of his bounty? ... the testator's wishes are incompletely expressed in his will.'

Lord Sumner

Communication after the execution of the will

If the agreement between the testator and the trustees is made *after* the execution of the will, even if this is made in accordance with the will and during the lifetime of the testator, it is settled law that such evidence may not be adduced to prove the terms of the trust. The reason given for this controversial principle was stated by Viscount Sumner in *Blackwell v Blackwell* [1929] AC 318:

JUDGMENT

'A testator cannot reserve to himself a power of making future unwitnessed dispositions by merely naming a trustee and leaving the purposes of the trust to be supplied afterwards, nor can a legatee give testamentary validity to an unexecuted codicil by accepting an indefinite trust, never communicated to him in the testator's lifetime … To hold otherwise would indeed be to enable the testator to give the go-by to the requirements of the Wills Act, because he did not choose to comply with them. It is communication of the purpose to the legatee coupled with acquiescence or promise on his part, that removes the matter from the provision of the Wills Act and brings it within the law of trusts.'

Viscount Sumner

CASE EXAMPLE

Re Keen [1937] Ch 236

A testator bequeathed a legacy to two legatees, A and B, 'to be held upon trust and disposed of by them among such persons or charities as may be notified by me to them or either of them during my lifetime'. Prior to the execution of the will, A had been given a sealed envelope subject to the direction, 'Not to be opened before my death'. A considered himself bound to hold the legacy subject to the terms declared in the envelope. The envelope contained the name of the beneficiary under the intended trust. Subsequently, the testator revoked the original will and executed a new will which contained an identical bequest. No fresh directions were issued to A, who was still prepared to carry out the testator's wishes. After the testator's death, an application was made to the court to determine whether the executors were required to distribute the property to A and B as trustees for the specified beneficiary or, alternatively, for the residuary estate. The Court of Appeal held that the trust failed and the property fell into residue on the grounds that:

(a) The delivery of the envelope constituted communication of the terms of the trust at the time of delivery. Since this was made prior to the execution of the will and was inconsistent with the terms of the will (which referred to a future communication), the letter was not admissible.
(b) The provision in the will contained a power to declare trusts in the future. This power was not enforceable and the terms of the intended trust were not admissible.

JUDGMENT

'In the present case, while clause 5 refers solely to a future definition, or to future definitions, of the trust, subsequent to the date of the will, the sealed letter relied on as notifying the trust was communicated before the date of the will. That it was communicated to one trustee only, and not to both, would not, I think, be an objection. But the objection remains that the notification sought to be put in evidence was anterior to the will, and hence not within the language of clause 5, and inadmissible simply on that ground, as being inconsistent with what the will prescribes.'

Lord Wright MR

But the theory underlying a secret trust (even a half-secret trust) is that it operates outside the will. The will merely transfers the property to the trustees who then hold subject to the obligation undertaken during the lifetime of the testator. The agreement between the testator and the trustees does not contradict the will but merely complements it, in that the will acknowledges a trust and the agreement supplies evidence of the trust. It is highly probable that the prohibition of post-will communications amounts to a confused or corrupt version of the probate doctrine of 'incorporation by reference'. In accordance with this doctrine an unattested document (e.g. a letter) may be joined and read with an attested document (e.g. a will). The conditions are that the former document is executed before, or at the time of, and is specifically referred to in, the attested document. In these circumstances, in probate law, the unattested document becomes public in much the same way as the will. In half-secret trusts there is no general requirement that the communication of the terms of the trust to the trustees be made in writing as is required under the probate doctrine.

In the context of fully secret trusts, it will be recalled, there is no equivalent to this rule. The terms of the fully secret trust may be agreed either before or after the execution of the will, provided that it was done during the lifetime of the testator.

In *Rawstron v Freud* [2014] EWHC 2477, the High Court was asked to construe the will of the famous painter, Lucian Freud, to determine whether an absolute gift or, alternatively, a transfer on trust of the residuary estate was made to his executrices. This involved a question of construction of the terms of the residuary clause under the testator's will. The testator executed his will on 10 May 2006, having revoked his earlier will made on 25 June 2004. In his 2006 will he transferred the residue of his estate to the two claimants jointly, his solicitor and his daughter. The residuary estate was valued at £42 million. The claimants contended that the gift of the residue was subject to a secret trust (fully secret trust) under which the first claimant (solicitor) was not entitled to benefit. The defendant, the deceased's son, contended that the gift of the residue was made to the claimants as trustees (half-secret trust) and the 2006 will was to be construed subject to the earlier revoked will executed in 2004 which purported to create a half-secret trust. The court decided in favour of the claimants. The 2006 will was worded differently from the 2004 will and there was no evidence that the deceased had intended to create a half-secret trust. Instead, the residuary estate was expressed as a simple gift to the claimants.

tutor tip

'Secret trusts and the mutual wills doctrine, although not of regular occurrence in modern society, have a great deal of significance in equity.'

JUDGMENT

'In summary, in the light of (a) the natural and ordinary meaning of the words used in clause 6 of the will, (b) the overall purpose of the will, (c) the other provisions of the will, (d) the material factual matrix when the will was made and (e) common sense, I consider that the claimants' interpretation of clause 6 of the will is to be preferred to that suggested by the defendant.'

Richard Spearman QC (Deputy Judge)

Trustees not entitled to take property beneficially

The persons named as trustees on the face of the will are not entitled to take any part of the property beneficially. The reason is that to admit such evidence would have the effect of contradicting the will. Accordingly, it is immaterial that the testator made such an arrangement with the trustees before the execution of the will, see *Re Rees* (1950) (above). Likewise, on a failure, wholly or partly, of the secret trust, the trustee holds the property on resulting trust for the testator's estate or next of kin.

It should be noted that this principle does not apply to fully secret trusts. In such cases there is no objection to the intended trustees leading evidence to prove that they were intended to benefit in accordance with the intention of the testator, for the will does not name them as trustees but as apparent beneficiaries. There will be no contradiction of the will.

Testator adding further property

If the testator wishes to add further property he is required to make an agreement with the trustees to that effect. This may involve the testator executing a new will or codicil. If the testator fails to take the trustees into his confidence regarding the additional amount the trust of this amount will fail and a resulting trust will arise.

CASE EXAMPLE

Re Colin Cooper [1939] Ch 811

A testator bequeathed the sum of £5,000 to two trustees upon trust for purposes 'already communicated to them'. Shortly before his death he executed a codicil giving the same trustees the sum of £10,000, declaring that 'they [know] my wishes regarding that sum'. The testator failed to inform the trustees of this new bequest. On the question of the validity of the trust of the additional bequest, the Court of Appeal held that the gift failed and a resulting trust of the additional £5,000 was created. In respect of the £5,000 which the trustees had agreed to hold upon trust, a valid secret trust was created.

JUDGMENT

'I cannot myself see that the arrangement between the testator and the trustees can be construed as though it had meant £5,000 or whatever sum I may hereafter choose to bequeath. That is not what was said and it was not with regard to any sum other than the £5,000 that the consciences of the trustees were burdened.'

Lord Greene MR

Although *Re Colin Cooper* (1939) involved a half-secret trust there is no reason, in principle, why this rule should not be extended to fully secret trusts. The consequence of failure, however, may be different. When a fully secret trust fails, the legatee takes the property beneficially. Thus, if there has been no agreement between the testator and the legatee (intended trustee) concerning the additional amount, the legatee may be entitled to take this sum beneficially. The conscience of the legatee may not be affected.

KEY FACTS

Requirements for the creation of secret trusts

Fully secret trusts	
The transfer of property to the legatee (by will or on intestacy)	
Creation of a clear agreement or understanding (including) the terms) between the testator (or transferor) and the intended trustee *inter vivos* (legatee/devisee/next of kin)	*Ottaway v Norman* (1972)
Proof of intention to create a trust	*McCormick v Grogan* (1869); *Kasperbauer v Griffith* (2000)

Note the contrasting position and effect where a broad agreement has been made between the transferor and transferee whereby the latter has agreed to become a trustee but the material terms have not been settled *inter vivos* (*Re Boyes* (1884)), and the occasion where no agreement was made between the parties (*Wallgrave v Tebbs* (1855))

Half-secret trusts	
▪ The transfer of property to the legatee (by will or on intestacy)	S 9 of the Wills Act 1837
▪ Communication of the terms before or at the time of the execution of the will	*Blackwell v Blackwell* (1929)
▪ Evidence not admissible to contradict the terms of the will	*Re Rees* (1950); *Re Keen* (1937)
▪ Trustee not entitled to take property beneficially	*Re Rees* (1950)

10.6 Unresolved issues connected with secret trusts

10.6.1 Standard of proof

The traditional rule regarding the standard of proof applicable to fully and half-secret trusts is 'clear evidence', i.e. the quality of evidence that is required to rectify an instrument. In other words, the standard of proof to establish a secret trust exceeds the ordinary civil standard of a balance of probabilities but it is not as high as the criminal standard of proof.

JUDGMENT

'[I]f a will contains a gift which is in terms absolute, clear evidence is needed before the court will assume that the testator did not mean what he said. It is perhaps analogous to the standard of proof which this court requires before it will rectify a written instrument, for there again a party is saying that neither meant what they have written.'

Brightman J in *Ottaway v Norman* [1972] Ch 698

More recently, Megarry VC in *Re Snowden* [1979] Ch 528 introduced a more flexible standard of proof which is dependent on whether an allegation of fraud exists or not. In cases involving an allegation of fraud the standard of proof is higher. This exceeds a balance of probabilities. In other cases the ordinary civil standard of proof on a balance of probabilities is required:

JUDGMENT

'I am not sure that it is right to assume that there is a single, uniform standard of proof for all secret trusts ... If a secret trust can be held to exist in a particular case only by holding the legatee guilty of fraud, then no secret trust should be found unless the standard of proof suffices for fraud. On the other hand, if there is no question of fraud, why should so high a standard apply? In accordance with the general rule of evidence the standard of proof should vary with the nature of the issue and its gravity, see *Hornal v Neuberger* [1956] 3 All ER 970. I therefore hold that in order to establish a secret trust where no question of fraud arises, the standard of proof is the ordinary civil standard of proof that is required to establish an ordinary trust.'

Megarry VC

On the question of what constitutes an allegation of fraud, which will import a higher standard of proof? Megarry VC in *Re Snowden* (1979) decided that these are cases when the legatee denies the existence of a trust, with the effect that he may be entitled to the property beneficially under the will:

'It seems to me that fraud comes into the matter in two ways. First, it provides an historical explanation of the doctrine of secret trusts: the doctrine was evolved as a means of preventing fraud. That, however, does not mean that fraud is an essential ingredient for the application of the doctrine: the reason for the rule is not part of the rule itself. Second, there are some cases within the doctrine where fraud is indeed involved. *There are cases where for the legatee to assert that he is a beneficial owner, free from any trust, would be a fraud on his part.*' [Emphasis added]

Megarry VC

The effect of this description of fraud is that it is restricted to allegations of fully secret trusts when the legatee denies the existence of an agreement with the testator to hold on trust. If the legatee acknowledges the existence of a trust but disputes a term of the trust, such as the identity of the beneficiary, the higher standard of proof may not be applicable. On the other hand, if the allegation concerns the existence of a half-secret trust, the lower standard of proof is applicable because the named trustee cannot adduce evidence that he is entitled beneficially.

10.6.2 Death of a secret beneficiary

If an intended secret beneficiary dies during the lifetime of the testator without a variation of the agreement, in principle his interest under the intended trust ought to lapse. The reason is that the trust is created after the death of the testator or the latest moment in time when the trustees acquire the property. This can only happen after the death of the testator. However, in *Re Gardner (No 2) (1923)*, Romer J came to the absurd conclusion that the secret beneficiary's interest did not lapse and his heirs were entitled to the property. It is generally recognised that this view cannot be supported in both trusts law and probate law. In the law of trusts, as explained above, the trust may be created at the earliest moment on the death of the testator. During the testator's lifetime a trust cannot exist because the trustees do not acquire the trust property and the intended beneficiaries obtain merely a *spes* or hope of enjoying the property. It is trite law that a *spes* cannot become the subject-matter of a trust. In any event, in probate law a disposition by will takes effect only on the death of the testator.

It is unlikely that the *Re Gardner (No 2) (1923)* solution will be extended to half-secret trusts where the intended secret beneficiary predeceases the testator. In principle, the trust will fail and a resulting trust for the testator's estate may arise.

10.6.3 Death of a secret trustee

The effect of an intended secret trustee predeceasing the testator varies with the type of secret trust intended by the testator. If a fully secret trust was intended by the testator but the trustee dies before the testator without a new agreement being reached with a different trustee, the intended trust will fail, the reason being that in probate law a legatee's interest in these circumstances will lapse. The effect is that the property will revert to the testator's estate. Cozens-Hardy MR in *Re Maddock* [1902] 2 Ch 220, in an *obiter* pronouncement, enunciated this view:

'[T]he so-called trust does not affect property except by reason of a personal obligation binding the individual devisee or legatee. If he renounces and disclaims, or dies in the lifetime of the testator, the persons claiming under memorandum can take nothing against the heir at law or next of kin or residuary devisee or legatee.'

Cozens-Hardy MR

In the context of a half-secret trust, if the terms can be ascertained, the trust may remain valid. The court may appoint new trustees, for the maxim is 'Equity will not allow a trust to fail for want of a trustee'. The will names the legatee as a trustee and the probate rule involving lapse may not be relevant.

10.6.4 Classification of secret trusts

It is not clear whether fully secret trusts are 'express' or 'constructive'. The issue was left open in *Ottaway v Norman* (1972). The importance of the classification concerns the extent to which the formalities are applicable to the agreement between the testator and the trustee. In *Re Baillie* (1886) 2 TLR 660, it was decided that half-secret trusts are express, for the trust is apparent on the face of the will, and furthermore that s 53(1) (b) of the Law of Property Act 1925 (or its equivalent) was required to be complied with. Thus, an oral agreement between the testator and the intended trustee concerning land was unenforceable.

With regard to intended fully secret trusts, the original basis for enforcement was to prevent fraud and this was consistent with the constructive trust theory. The fraud that the trustee was prevented from perpetrating was to allege that the agreement did not comply with s 9 of the Wills Act 1837: see earlier. Section 53(2) of the Law of Property Act 1925 exempts constructive trusts from the requirements of writing under s 53(1)(b). Thus, fully secret trusts of land may be enforced despite not being evidenced in writing.

KEY FACTS

Secret trusts

General
The idea is to create a trust without revealing the identity of the beneficiaries on the face of a will – possibly because of moral obligations to the beneficiary
Courts accept them if: (i) there is an intention to create a trust and the 'three certainties' are satisfied (ii) the trust is communicated to the legatee (iii) *Ottaway v Norman* (1972) the trust is accepted by the legatee
Fully secret trusts are an apparent gift to the ostensible beneficiary Half-secret trusts are apparent as trusts on the face of the will

Theoretical basis of secret trusts	Case
▨ Both secret and half-secret trusts fail to comply fully with Wills Act requirements ▨ So the testator is 'opting out' ▨ The fraud argument cannot apply to half-secret trusts ▨ So an 'independent trust' theory has been applied to both ▨ But has caused anomalies ▨ Uncertainty whether they are express or constructive	*McCormick v Grogan* (1869); *Blackwell v Blackwell* (1929); *Re Young* (1951) *Re Snowden* (1979); *Re Gardner* (1923); *Ottaway v Norman* (1972); *Re Baillie* (1886)
Fully secret trusts	**Case**
▨ Ostensible beneficiary must be told of trust and agree to be bound before testator's death – or ostensible beneficiary takes absolutely ▨ Acquiescence is sufficient for acceptance ▨ They cannot be changed so are clearly inconsistent with the Wills Act ▨ Traditional reason they are enforced is to prevent fraud on the beneficiary	*Wallgrave v Tebbs* (1855); *Moss v Cooper* (1861) *Ottaway v Norman* (1972)
Half-secret trusts	**Case**
▨ Traditionally not enforced – because fraud on beneficiary not possible ▨ But were accepted in: ▨ But, to be valid, must be communicated before making of will – not before death of testator as in fully secret	*McCormick v Grogan* (1869); *Blackwell v Blackwell* (1929) *Re Keen* (1937)

ACTIVITY

Applying the law

By his will made in 2001, Albert devised all his realty to Bertha 'in the sure and certain hope that she will carry out my wishes relating thereto'. In 2002, Albert informed Bertha verbally that she was to hold any property left to her by his will upon trust for Charles, David and herself in equal shares. Bertha remained silent. David died in January 2003. Albert has just died and his realty is worth £600,000.

Advise Bertha, Charles and David's executors on the distribution of the estate. Would your advice differ if:

(i) the communication of the terms of the trust to Bertha had been by unattested, but signed, writing handed to her in 2001, just prior to the execution of the will?

(ii) Charles had witnessed Albert's will?

10.7 Mutual wills

The Law Reform Committee in its twenty-second report (1980) noted particular problems with the mutual wills doctrine. Nevertheless, it recommended that the difficulties would 'be better clarified by judicial development than by legislation'. The effect is that there is no legislative guidance in this area and the law was developed exclusively by the courts.

Where two or more testators wish to pool their resources together for the benefit of the ultimate beneficiary and to give the survivor an interest, such as a life interest in the property of the first testator to die, the 'mutual will' doctrine may be adopted by the parties. Mutual wills arise out of an agreement between two or more persons that they will make substantially similar testamentary dispositions in favour of a particular beneficiary. It must be clearly proved that the agreement between the parties constitutes a contract between them (i) to make such wills and (ii) not to revoke them without the consent of the other. For example, A and B decide that after their death their joint property will be transferred to Cancer Research. They may each make separate wills transferring their property to the named charity. This does not involve mutual wills. Assume, further, that the parties agree that the survivor ought to enjoy a life interest in the deceased's estate and then transfer their joint resources to the specified charity. Each testator makes a will in substantially identical terms, transferring his estate to the survivor, on the understanding that the *inter vivos* agreement is binding. Each testator's will may spell out the terms of the trust, that is, to the survivor for life with remainder to Cancer Research. Alternatively, each testator may transfer his entire estate to the survivor. When the first testator dies (say, A) his will is required to be probated, a trust will be created and B will enjoy a life interest in accordance with the agreement. When B dies his entire estate (including the property taken under A's will) will be held upon trust for Cancer Research in accordance with the *inter vivos* agreement.

10.7.1 The agreement

The agreement may be express or implied, written or oral, but it is essential that it is intended to be binding on the survivor of the first to die. In other words, the intention of the parties must be sufficient to amount to a contract. The parties to the agreement need not be married, although, in practice, this is usually the case. This also makes proof of a contractual intention difficult. The basis of the agreement and the consideration for the promise is that each party will make specific testamentary dispositions in return for the other party doing the same. The nature and extent of the property subject to the agreement varies with each case. The parties may limit the agreement to a specific fund or item of property (e.g. '50,000 Marks and Spencer plc shares') so that the survivor acquires a life interest in the property with remainder to another. But it is common for the agreement to cover the entirety of the parties' estates.

The agreement is required to be proved by clear and satisfactory evidence that, on a balance of probabilities, there had been an irrevocable agreement between the parties to dispose of their property by mutual wills. The mere fact that the wills were in identical terms and executed on the same date is not sufficient, by itself, to establish the agreement, although it will be a relevant factor to be taken into account along with the other evidence.

CASE EXAMPLE

Re Oldham [1925] Ch 75

A married couple made substantially similar wills. There was no direct evidence of an agreement that the wills were irrevocable. The husband was the first to die, leaving his estate to his widow. She later remarried and made a new will that was substantially different from the original will. On her death the claimant sought to make the widow's executor a trustee for the original purpose. The court rejected this claim and decided that there was no evidence of an irrevocable agreement between the original married couple.

JUDGMENT

'[T]he fact that two wills were made in identical terms does not necessarily connote any agreement beyond that of so making them. There is no evidence that there was an agreement that the trust should in all circumstances be irrevocable. In order to enforce the trust I must be satisfied that its terms are certain and unequivocal and such as in the circumstances I am bound to give effect.'

Astbury J

A similar result was reached in *Re Goodchild (Decd)* [1997] 3 All ER 63, where identical wills between a husband and wife did not import the existence of an irrevocable agreement not to revoke the will.

JUDGMENT

'Two wills may be in the same form as each other. Each testator may leave his or her estate to the other with a view to the survivor leaving both estates to their heir. But there is no presumption that a present plan will be immutable in future. A key feature of the concept of mutual wills is the irrevocability of the mutual intentions. Not only must they be binding when made, but the testators must have undertaken, and so must be bound, not to change their intentions after the death of the first testator. The test must always be: suppose that during the lifetime of the surviving testator the intended beneficiary did something which the survivor regarded as unpardonable, would he or she be free not to leave the combined estate to him? The answer must be that the survivor is so entitled unless the testators agreed otherwise when they executed their wills. Hence the need for a clear agreement.'

Leggatt J

However, in the exceptional circumstances that existed in *Charles v Fraser* (2010), the court decided that identical wills, made at the same time by two elderly sisters, satisfied the test of an irrevocable agreement between the parties to dispose of their property by mutual wills. The terms of the wills in carefully dividing up the estate in equal shares between Mabel and Ethel's (the testatrices') chosen beneficiaries, the surrounding circumstances and the close relationship of the sisters, amounted to clear evidence of an irrevocable agreement between the two sisters to transfer their joint estates to the named beneficiaries.

CASE EXAMPLE

Charles v Fraser [2010] EWHC 2154

In 1991, two elderly sisters, Mabel Cook and Ethel Wilson, aged 78 and 76 respectively, made identical wills with the intention of benefiting named persons. Each will devised and bequeathed the residue of the estate to her trustees upon trust to divide the proceeds into 40 shares to be divided between 15 named beneficiaries in specified shares. Mrs Thompson, a relative of the deceased, was the claimant and one of the beneficiaries. Mabel died in 1995. In 2003, Ethel altered her will to add two individuals, including Mrs Fraser, as beneficiaries and altering the allocation of the other shares. In 2006, when aged 92, Ethel made a new will under which she appointed Mrs Fraser as her sole executrix, and bequeathed virtually the whole of her estate to Mrs Fraser. Ethel died in November 2006 and Mrs Fraser acquired over £300,000 under the terms of the 2006 will. She used some of the proceeds to purchase a property.

Mrs Thompson subsequently informed Mrs Fraser that Mabel and Ethel had made mutual wills and that Ethel's estate fell to be distributed in accordance with her 1991 will. Further, Mrs Fraser was requested to refund the net estate for distribution in accordance with the 1991 will. Mrs Fraser declined to do so. Mrs Thompson brought a claim on behalf of the beneficiaries under the 1991 will. The question in issue was whether the persons who would have been beneficiaries under Ethel's original will in 1991 could claim that her estate should be held on the trusts of that will and not subject to the trusts of her final will.

Held: In favour of the claimant based on the principle that the doctrine of mutual wills had been satisfied on the facts. The effect was that under Ethel's 2006 will, Mrs Fraser acquired and held the proceeds of Ethel's estate on constructive trust to give effect to the provisions of Ethel's 1991 will.

10.7.2 The effect of the agreement

An analysis of the operation of the agreement may be conducted in two stages: during the lifetime of both parties and on the death of the first to die.

During the lifetime of both parties

The agreement between the parties making mutual wills not to revoke the wills amounts to a contract and is binding on both parties from the date of the agreement. If one party, in breach of the agreement, revokes his will, the other party is entitled to sue for damages for breach of contract. The amount of loss may be nominal, for it would be difficult to quantify the loss suffered by a claimant who is aware that the other party has changed his will. The same will be the case if the ultimate beneficiary brings the claim under the Contracts (Rights of Third Parties) Act 1999. In addition, the breach of the contract by one party has the effect of releasing the other party from the agreement: see *Re Hobley, The Times,* 16 June 1997.

CASE EXAMPLE

Re Hobley, The Times, 16 June 1997

On 4 December 1975, Mr and Mrs Hobley executed mutual wills in favour of each other, whosoever might survive, with substitutionary gifts to common beneficiaries. The house at No 65 Russel Terrace was devised to Mr Blyth and there were 11 pecuniary legatees, eight of whom were entitled to the residue. Some time later, Mr Hobley executed a codicil revoking the devise of No 65 Russel Terrace to Mr Blyth and left it as part of the residuary estate. There was no evidence as to the reason for the change or whether Mrs Hobley knew of or consented to it. Mr Hobley died on 13 January 1980 and Mrs Hobley inherited his entire estate, including No 65 Russel Terrace. On 13 March 1992, Mrs Hobley executed a will which was substantially different from the 1975 will. She died on 23 May 1993. The National Westminster Bank plc was appointed executor of Mrs Hobley's will and commenced the application to the court. The question in issue concerned the effect on the mutual will arrangement of the alteration of Mr Hobley's will. Counsel for the original beneficiaries, relying on *Hong Kong Fir Shipping Co v Kawasaki Kisen Kaisha Ltd* [1962] 2 QB 26, argued that Mr Hobley's codicil did not amount to a fundamental breach of the 1975 agreement so as to discharge Mrs Hobley from the agreement.

The High Court decided that the principles on which the court acted in order to impose a constructive trust, so as to give effect to an agreement to make and not revoke mutual wills, were not precisely the same as applied in the law of contract. The court could neither evaluate the significance to the parties of any alteration in the terms of the will of the first testator, nor their subjective intentions. Moreover, it is irrelevant that the alteration did not personally disadvantage the survivor. Accordingly, the unilateral alteration of Mr Hobley's will had the effect of discharging Mrs Hobley from the agreement in 1975. She was, therefore, free to dispose of her estate as she wished.

A revocation of the agreement for these purposes is required to be intentional in the sense that it involves a positive act on the part of the party in breach. Section 18 of the Wills Act 1837 enacts that remarriage has the effect of revoking a will. This is the effect by operation of law. However, the better view is that this section is not applicable in the mutual wills context.

CASE EXAMPLE

Re Marsland [1939] Ch 820

A husband executed a deed of separation and covenanted in the same deed not to revoke a will previously made. The husband later obtained a divorce and expressed his wishes to remarry. The wife brought an action against him claiming damages for breach of covenant. The court held that remarriage does not have the effect of revoking the contract. To be actionable, a revocation of the agreement is required to be intentional.

On the death of the first testator

On the first death of one of the parties to the irrevocable agreement a trust is created by the courts in favour of the beneficiaries and is imposed on the survivor. If the survivor alters or executes another will, as he is entitled to do in accordance with probate rules, this adjusted or new will will be admitted to probate but his personal representatives will hold his property upon trust to perform the agreement.

CASE EXAMPLE

Re Hagger [1930] 2 Ch 190

A married couple made an irrevocable agreement not to revoke a joint will that transferred property to the surviving partner for life and in remainder to specified beneficiaries. The husband survived his wife and changed his will. The heirs of one of the beneficiaries, who died after the wife but before the husband, brought a successful claim to a share of the estate.

JUDGMENT

'[O]n the death of the first testator the position as regards that part of the property which belongs to the survivor is that the survivor will be treated in this court as holding the property on trust to apply it so as to carry out the effect of the joint will.'

Clauson J

In *Thomas and Agnes Carvel Foundation v Carvel* [2007] EWHC 1314 (Ch), Lewison J identified the time when the trust arises as follows:

JUDGMENT

'The essential point, to my mind, is that the trust does not arise under the will of the surviving testator. Nor does it arise under any previous will of the surviving testator. It arises out of the agreement between the two testators not to revoke their wills, and the trust arises when the first of the two dies without having revoked his will. In so far as there is an operative will, it seems to me that it is the will of the first testator (and his death with that will unrevoked) which brings the trust into effect. That being so, I do not consider that a person who claims under the doctrine of mutual wills is a person beneficially interested in the estate under the will of the deceased.'

Lewison J

A similar view was expressed by Mummery LJ in *Olins v Walters* [2008] EWCA Civ 782.

CASE EXAMPLE

Olins v Walters [2008] EWCA Civ 782

The claimant was a solicitor and grandson of the defendant. The defendant's principal assets were a substantial house and shares in the family property company. In 1988 the defendant and his wife (deceased) executed wills in almost identical terms. The will of the deceased appointed the defendant and the claimant (her grandson and newly qualified solicitor) as executors. Clause 6 of the deceased's will provided that the residue of her estate was to be left to the defendant if he survived her, with remainder to the grandchildren in equal shares. In 1998 a codicil was apparently executed by the deceased. Clause 2 of the codicil provided: 'This codicil is made pursuant to an agreement made between my husband and me for the disposal of our property in a similar way by mutual testamentary disposition.' The codicil revoked clause 6 of the 1988 will and introduced a new clause 6 providing the entirety of the residuary estate to the defendant, with life interests to their two daughters, and remainder to their grandchildren absolutely. A mirror codicil was apparently executed by the defendant. The papers relating to the codicil were prepared by the claimant and sent to the deceased and defendant with a covering letter explaining the effect of clause 2 and confirming that the codicils were drafted to reflect their instructions. A dispute arose between the parties as to the testamentary instruments. In 2006, the defendant's wife (deceased) died. She was survived by the defendant, their two daughters and five grandchildren.

The claimant commenced proceedings seeking a declaration that the codicil took effect as a valid and effective mutual will. The defendant alleged *inter alia* that there was no contract between himself and the deceased to the effect that the codicil became irrevocable after the death of the first to die. In the alternative, if there was an agreement between the parties that agreement would not have been valid for failure to comply with the requirements under s 2 of the Law of Property (Miscellaneous Provisions) Act 1989. The High Court allowed the claim on the grounds that the wills of 1988 and the codicils of 1998 created mutual wills in accordance with the intentions of the parties. The claimant was not attempting to enforce a contract but instead a constructive trust to which s 2 has no application. The defendant appealed to the Court of Appeal on the ground that Norris J granted the declaration on insufficient evidence because the agreement between the defendant and the deceased was too vague to amount to a binding contract to attract the mutual wills doctrine.

The Court of Appeal dismissed the appeal and affirmed the decision of the High Court. The intentions of the defendant and the deceased were sufficiently expressed in the contract to lay the foundations for the equitable obligations that bound the conscience of the defendant, as the survivor, in relation to the deceased's estate. The trial judge had correctly directed himself on the law and there was sufficient evidence to support his decision.

JUDGMENT

'The obligation on the surviving testator is equitable. It is in the nature of a trust of the property affected, so the constructive trust label is attached to it. The equitable obligation is imposed for the benefit of third parties, who were intended by the parties to benefit from it. It arises by operation of law on the death of the first testator to die so as to bind the conscience of the surviving testator in relation to the property affected.'

Mummery LJ

The constructive trust created by the courts is imposed on the survivor, irrespective of whether or not he takes an interest in accordance with the agreement made between the two testators. The reason for this rule is to prevent the survivor committing a fraud on the beneficiaries by attempting to withdraw from the agreement.

JUDGMENT

'I see no reason why the doctrine [of mutual wills] should be confined to cases where the second testator benefits when the aim of the principle is to prevent the first testator from being defrauded. A fraud on the first testator will include cases where the second testator benefits, but I see no reason why the principle should be confined to such cases.'

Morritt J in *Re Dale* [1993] 3 WLR 652

10.7.3 The scope of the agreement

It is a question of construction to determine the scope and extent of the property subject to the agreement and thus the trust. If the agreement is expressed to bind the whole of the interest owned by each party, the trust will bind the entire property owned by each party and the surviving testator may be unable to deal with his own property during his lifetime. Each case is determined on its own facts. In *Re Green* [1951] Ch 148, the constructive trust attached to half of the estate of the surviving testator in accordance with the agreement.

Norris J at first instance in *Olins v Walters* summarised the principles that are applicable to the mutual wills doctrine thus:

JUDGMENT

'In my judgment its irreducible core [doctrine of mutual wills] is that there must be a contract between T1 and T2 that in return for T1 agreeing to make a will in form X and not to revoke it without notice to T2, then T2 will make a will in form Y and agree not to revoke it without notice to T1. If such facts are established then upon the death of T1 equity will impose upon T2 a form of constructive trust (shaped by the exact terms of the contract that T1 and T2 have made). The constructive trust is imposed because T1 has made a disposition of property on the faith of T2's promise to make a will in form Y, and with the object of preventing T1 from being defrauded. So much is established in *Re Dale* [1994] Ch 31. There is no need to refer to decisions that precede *Re Dale*, but I should refer to *Re Goodchild* [1997] 1 WLR 1216 for its confirmation of the need (a) for an underlying contract and (b) for agreement on the irrevocability of the intended disposition after the death of the first to die.'

Norris J

Mutual wills

Test	Qualifier	Case
Similar wills made by two or more testators or joint wills on the death of the first to die	Insufficient on their own to create trusts	*Re Oldham* (1925)
Plus agreement intended to bind the survivor of the first to die	During the lifetime of both testators (law of contract)	*Re Hobley* (1997)
	Death of the first testator (creation of constructive trust)	*Re Hagger* (1930)
	Scope of trust (construction of the agreement to ascertain the extent of the trust)	*Re Green* (1951)

ACTIVITY

Applying the law

Two years ago, John and his sister Jane (both unmarried) decided that they would like to leave all their property by way of absolute gift to whoever survived the other, but with a view to the survivor leaving everything to their two nieces, Anna and Barbara. They consulted solicitors and, pursuant to their advice, John and Jane executed wills in similar terms under which each left his or her property to the other absolutely if she or he should be the survivor and in the event of her or his predeceasing the testator or testatrix then to Anna and Barbara absolutely.

John died last year, leaving a net estate worth £200,000, which passed under his will and in consequence Jane's total assets are now worth £500,000.

Jane has recently been befriended by Jasper and she is proposing:

(i) to provide the purchase price of a house of £150,000 to be vested in the joint names of herself and Jasper; and

(ii) to make a fresh will leaving all her property to Jasper.

Advise Anna and Barbara as to their positions in regard to each of these proposals.

SUMMARY

- A fully secret trust arises where a will makes an absolute gift to a legatee or devisee but during the testator's lifetime he agrees with the legatee or devisee that the property will be held as trustee. A half-secret trust is created when the will acknowledges the existence of a trust but the terms are concealed on the face of the will. In the case of a half-secret trust the communication of the terms must take place before or at the time of the execution of the will.

- The theoretical justification for the creation of the trust is to prevent a fraud being committed on the beneficiaries. There are many permutations of fraud that vindicate the existence of secret trusts. But this theory explains why the intended trustee should not take the property beneficially. It does not, on its own, explain why the secret trust ought to be enforced in favour of beneficiaries. A different approach involves the *dehors* theory to the effect that the trust is created *inter vivos* and outside the Wills Act 1837. But it is questionable whether the trust is created during the lifetime of the testator. Alternatively, the transfer and conditional declaration theory may explain that the secret trust becomes effective when the trustee acquires the property under the testator's will subject to a valid declaration of trust.

The requirements for the creation of a fully secret trust involve a communication to the intended trustee and acceptance by the latter of the terms of the trust during the lifetime of the testator provided that a will transfers the property as an absolute gift to the intended trustee. A half-secret trust is created where a testator acknowledges that the legatee acquires the property as trustee, but before or at the time of the execution of the will the testator agrees the material terms of the trust with the trustee.

Unresolved issues connected with secret trusts concern:

- The standard of proof of the terms of the trust. The standard of proof varies with the extent to which fraud is alleged.
- On principle where a secret beneficiary dies before the testator the trust for that person will fail, but this principle was not followed in *Re Gardner No 2*.
- Where a secret trustee predeceases the testator the fully secret trust will fail but the half-secret trust will remain valid and new trustees will be appointed.
- Half-secret trusts have been classified as express trusts requiring compliance with s 53(1)(b) of the Law of Property Act 1925. The classification of fully secret trusts is yet to be resolved but may be treated as constructive trusts that are exempt from s 53(1)(b) by virtue of s 53(2) of the LPA 1925.

The doctrine of mutual wills involves the law of trusts where two or more testators execute wills as a result of a contract to create irrevocable interests in favour of ascertainable beneficiaries.

- The agreement is required to be proved by satisfactory evidence on a balance of probabilities.
- The creation of identical wills by two or more parties may not satisfy this test.
- During the lifetime of both parties to a mutual will arrangement their rights are crystallised in the law of contract.
- On the death of the first testator a constructive trust is created in favour of the named beneficiaries.
- The extent of the trust varies with the scope of the agreement created during the lifetime of the parties.

SAMPLE ESSAY QUESTION

Consider the following essay question:

On what theoretical basis may secret trusts be enforced?

Answer plan

Define and distinguish between fully and half-secret trusts.

The 'fraud' theory:

- to prevent a fraudulent denial of the trust obligations in order to acquire property for the intended trustee's benefit;
- to prevent a fraudulent inducement of the testator to transfer property to trustee;
- to prevent the trustees from defeating the interests of the intended beneficiaries.

The difficulties associated with the 'fraud' theory as a justification for enforcing secret trusts:

- the unwarranted consequence for enforcing half-secret trusts;
- to avoid inconsistencies between fully and half-secret trusts;
- half-secret trusts are classified as express trusts;
- different requirements for the creation of half-secret trusts;
- inconsistencies with fully and half-secret trusts in respect of one or more trustees who have not been informed of the terms of the trust.

The standard of proof of the terms of the secret trust varies with the existence or non-existence of an allegation of fraud.

The *dehors* theory – secret trusts operate outside the Wills Act 1837. They are *inter vivos* declarations of trust by the testator.

The unrealistic nature of the *dehors* theory:

- conflict with probate law;
- attempt to create a trust of a *spes*;
- no transfer of property to the intended trustees during the lifetime of the testator.

No consistent theory but simple a pragmatic attempt to enforce the trust according to the needs of the parties.

CONCLUSION

Further reading

Allan, G, 'The secret is out there: searching for the legal justification for the doctrine of secret trusts through analysis of the case law' (2011) 40(4) CLWR 311.

Ambrose, M, 'The feeling's mutual' (2003) 153 NLJ 979.

Andrews, J, 'Creating secret trusts' (1963) 27 Conv 92.

Brierly, A, 'Mutual wills: Blackpool illuminations' (1995) 58 MLR 95.

Critchley, P, 'Instruments of fraud, testamentary dispositions and the doctrine of secret trusts' (1999) 115 LQR 631.

Davis, C, 'Mutual wills; formalities; constructive trusts' (2003) Conv 238.

Gratton, S, 'Mutual wills and remarriage' (1997) Conv 153.

Kincaid, D, 'The tangled web: the relationship between a secret trust and the will' (2000) 64 Conv 421.

Luxton, P, '*Walters v Olin*: uncertainty of subject matter – an insoluble problem in mutual wills?' (2009) Conv 498.

Mathews, P, 'The true basis of the half-secret trust' (1979) Conv 360.

Pawlowski, M, 'Till death us do part' (2002) 146 Sol J 700.

Perrins, B, 'Can you keep half a secret?' (1972) 88 LQR 225.

Richardson, N, 'Floating trusts and mutual wills' (1996) 10 Tru LI 88.

Sunnocks, F, 'Close relations of the secret trust' (1988) 138 NLJ 35.

Wilde, D, 'Secret and semi-secret trusts: justifying distinctions between the two' (1995) Conv 366.

11

Private purpose trusts

AIMS AND OBJECTIVES

By the end of this chapter you should be able to:

- understand the rationale behind the general rule of non-enforceability of private purpose trusts
- comprehend the rule against perpetuities
- recognise the exceptions to the *Astor* principle
- define the *Denley* principle
- define an unincorporated association and appreciate the difficulties created in respect of gifts to such associations

11.1 Introduction

Attorney General

The legal adviser to the government; in addition, the legal representative of objects under a charitable trust.

An additional requirement concerning express private trusts is the need to identify beneficiaries who are capable of enforcing the trust. A purpose, as expressed by the settlor, is incapable of enforcing a trust. Alternatively, a public purpose trust, or charitable trust, is capable of being enforced by the **Attorney General**. One of the duties of the Attorney General is to act as a representative of the Crown on behalf of charitable bodies. In this context a charitable trust is a trust that promotes a public benefit and advances one or more of the 13 purposes laid down in the Charities Act 2006. Many of these purposes coincide with the law on charitable purposes that preceded the 2006 Act.

An intended private purpose trust is void. A purpose trust is designed to promote a purpose as an end in itself, for instance the discovery of an alphabet of 40 letters, to provide a cup for a yacht race, or the boarding up of certain rooms in a house. Such intended trusts are void, for the court would be incapable of supervising their proper administration. As there is no beneficiary with a *locus standi* capable of enforcing such a trust, there is a real risk that improper behaviour by the trustees could go unnoticed. In consequence, a resulting trust arises in favour of the donor or settlor, on the failure of a non-charitable purpose trust.

CASE EXAMPLE

Morice v Bishop of Durham [1804] 9 Ves 399

A bequest was made to the Bishop of Durham on trust for 'such objects of benevolence and liberality as the Bishop of Durham shall in his own discretion most approve of'. The court decided that this bequest failed as a charity because the objects were not exclusively charitable, and was invalid as a private trust, for there were no ascertainable beneficiaries.

JUDGMENT

'[I]t is a maxim, that the execution of a trust shall be under the control of the court, it must be of such a nature, that it can be under that control; so that the administration of it can be reviewed by the court; or, if the trustee dies, the court itself can execute the trust; a trust therefore, which, in case of maladministration could be reformed; and a due administration directed; and then, unless the subject and objects can be ascertained, upon principles, familiar in other cases, it must be decided, that the court can neither reform maladministration, nor direct a due administration.'

Lord Eldon

The court came to a similar conclusion in *Re Astor's Settlement Trust* [1952] Ch 534.

CASE EXAMPLE

Re Astor's Settlement Trust [1952] Ch 534

Lord Astor purported to create a trust for 'the maintenance of good understanding between nations and the preservation of the independence and integrity of newspapers'. The court held that the trust was void for uncertainty on the grounds that the means by which the trustees were to attain the stated aims were unspecified and the person who was entitled, as of right, to enforce the trust was unnamed. In other words, a trust creates rights in favour of beneficiaries and imposes correlative duties on the trustees. If there are no persons with the power to enforce such rights, then equally there can be no duties imposed on trustees.

JUDGMENT

'[T]he only beneficiaries are purposes and at present unascertainable persons, it is difficult to see who could initiate proceedings. If the purposes are valid trusts, the settlors have retained no beneficial interest and could not initiate them. It was suggested that the trustees might proceed **ex parte** to enforce the trusts against themselves. I doubt that, but at any rate nobody could enforce the trusts against them.'

Roxburgh J

ex parte
An interested person who is not a party; or, by one party in the absence of the other.

11.2 Reasons for failure of a private purpose trust

There are a number of common reasons why private purpose trusts fail. The list is not exhaustive, but pitfalls which a settlor should avoid are:

- the lack of a beneficiary principle;
- uncertainty of objects; and
- the infringement of the perpetuity rule.

11.2.1 Lack of beneficiaries

A trust is mandatory in nature and imposes enforceable obligations on the trustees. Those capable of enforcing such obligations are the beneficiaries. These persons are granted rights *in rem* in the subject-matter of the trust. The courts have always jealously guarded the rights and interests of the beneficiaries under trusts. But such rights may be protected only if the beneficiary has a *locus standi* to enforce the same. Purposes cannot initiate proceedings against the trustees. Accordingly, a purported trust for private purposes is void because it lacks a beneficiary. In effect, in trusts law the courts regard two features of primary importance, namely ownership of property and the fiduciary office of trusteeship. The beneficiary, as an equitable owner, has the capacity of ensuring that the trustees carry out their duties in a responsible manner.

In other jurisdictions, such as the Cayman Islands, an alternative philosophy has been adopted whereby a settlor may expressly nominate a person to be obliged to enforce a private purpose trust against the trustees. In this context the focus of attention is not ownership but enforcement. The 'enforcer' has a public duty to enforce the trust, which is followed up with severe penalties for breaches. On analogy, the English equivalent of such a third person is the Attorney General, but only in respect of charities.

11.2.2 Uncertainty

As a corollary to the above-mentioned rule, it is obvious that the rights of the beneficiaries will be illusory unless the court is capable of ascertaining to whom those rights belong. Thus, as a second ground for the decision in *Re Astor* (1952), the trust failed for uncertainty:

JUDGMENT

'If an enumeration of purposes outside the realm of charities can take the place of an enumeration of beneficiaries, the purposes must be stated in phrases which embody definite concepts and the means by which the trustees are to try to attain them must also be prescribed with a sufficient degree of certainty.'

Roxburgh J

A case which illustrates this principle is *Re Endacott* [1960] Ch 232.

CASE EXAMPLE

Re Endacott [1960] Ch 232

A testator transferred his residuary estate to the Devon Parish Council 'for the purpose of providing some useful memorial to myself'. Lord Evershed MR held that no out-and-out gift to the Council was created, but the testator intended to impose an obligation in the nature of a trust on the Council, which failed for uncertainty of objects.

JUDGMENT

'[N]o principle has greater sanctity of authority behind it than the general proposition that a trust by English law, not being a charitable trust, in order to be effective must have ascertained or ascertainable beneficiaries.'

Lord Evershed MR

Charitable trusts, on the other hand, are subject to a special test for certainty of objects, namely whether the objects are exclusively charitable: see later.

11.2.3 Perpetuity rule

The perpetuity rule is a common law principle (as modified by statute) of general application in property law which restricts the maximum period in which the vesting of property, real or personal, may be postponed (the rule against remote vesting). In addition, if the property has vested in the beneficiary the rule specifies the maximum period in which the property is required to be retained (the rule against excessive duration).

The Law Commission in its 1998 report on the 'Rules against Perpetuities and Accumulations' concluded that the principle is unnecessarily complex, out of date and disproportionate in its extension to commercial transactions. The report recommended a fundamental reform of measuring the perpetuity period.

QUOTATION

'The application of the rule against perpetuities has developed over time and is now too wide. It applies to many commercial dealings (such as future easements, options and rights of pre-emption) which have nothing to do with the family settlements that the rule was designed to control. The application of the rule to pension schemes is not consistent with the policy of the rule.

The existence of multiple methods for calculating the perpetuity period (which includes the use of lives in being at common law, as well as periods of up to 80 years under the 1964 Act) is unnecessarily complex and confusing. In addition, the use of lives in being gives rise to practical difficulties. For example, where a "royal lives clause" has been used, it may be impossible for the trustees to identify who the last remaining descendants of a monarch are, or indeed whether they are still alive.'

The Law Commission recommendations were endorsed in the Perpetuities and Accumulations Act 2009 (which came into force on 6 April 2010). Section 5 of the Act abolishes the general common law period and substitutes a precise, standard period that does not exceed 125 years. This period is applicable to both aspects of the perpetuity rule, namely the rule against remote vesting and the rule against excessive duration. The 125-year period is an overriding provision that is written into all instruments taking effect on or after 6 April 2010. The effect is that a gift is required to vest in the donee within 125 years from the date of the execution of the instrument creating the gift, and provided that the gift has vested, may not be inalienable for a period exceeding 125 years. The Act is not retrospective, and does not affect gifts in instruments taking effect before the date when the Act came into force. However, s 18 of the 2009 Act excludes non-charitable purpose from the 125-year perpetuity period. The effect is that the common law periods of 'a life or lives in being and/or 21 years' continue to apply to private purpose trusts. This is outlined below.

At common law, the perpetuity period was measured in terms of a life or lives in being, plus 21 years. Time begins to run from the date that the instrument creating the gift takes effect (a will takes effect on the date of the death of the testator or testatrix; a deed takes effect on the date of execution). Only human lives may be chosen and not the lives of animals, some of which are noted for their longevity (such as tortoises and elephants). An embryonic child (*en ventre sa mère*) constitutes a life in being if this is relevant in measuring the period. A life or lives in being, whether connected with the gift or not, may be chosen expressly by the donor or settlor in order to extend the perpetuity period. Any number of lives may be selected. The test is whether the group of lives selected is certain and identifiable to such an extent that it is practicable to ascertain the date of death of the last survivor. This test was clearly incapable of being satisfied in *Re Moore* [1901] 1 Ch 936, where a testator defined the period as '21 years from the death of the last survivor of all persons who shall be living at my death'. The gift was considered void for uncertainty.

Indeed, the settlor may even select lives which have no connection with the trust. It became the practice to select royal lives, such as 'the lineal descendants of Queen Elizabeth II living at my death', with the objective of ascertaining the date of death of the last survivor.

Alternatively, a life or lives in being may be implied in the circumstances if the life or lives is or are so related to the gift or settlement that it is or they are capable of being used to measure the date of the vesting of the interest. If no lives are selected or are implied, the perpetuity period at common law is 21 years from the date of the creation of the gift.

ab initio
From the beginning.

The common law approach to the perpetuity rule was based on the assumption that if there was a mere possibility, however slight, that a future interest may vest outside the perpetuity period, the grant of the interest is void *ab initio*. This was the approach of the courts before 1964. For example, if S, a settlor, during his lifetime transfers a portfolio of shares to T1 and T2 as trustees, on trust contingently for his first child to marry and S has unmarried children, this gift, before the Perpetuities and Accumulations Act 1964, would be void. S would be treated impliedly as the life in being and it was possible that none of his children would marry within 21 years after his death. Thus, there was a possibility that the gift might not vest within the perpetuity period.

The Perpetuities and Accumulations Act 1964 introduced three major reforms to the law. Under the Act, a future interest is no longer void on the ground that it 'might' vest outside the perpetuity period. It is void if, in the circumstances, the interest does not vest within the perpetuity period. In the meantime, the court will 'wait and see' whether or not the gift vests. Moreover, the Act introduced a certain and fixed period not exceeding 80 years which the grantor may expressly nominate as the perpetuity period. In addition, s 3(5) of the Act introduced a variety of persons who may be treated as a 'statutory life'. These are: the grantor, the beneficiary or potential beneficiary, the donee of a power, option or other right, parents and grandparents of the grantor and any person entitled in default. Where there are no lives within any of these categories, the 'wait and see' period is 21 years from the date the instrument takes effect.

Closely related to the perpetuity rule is the rule against excessive duration. This rule renders void any obligation to retain property for longer than the perpetuity period. The issue here is not whether the property or interest is, in fact, tied up forever but whether the owner is capable of disposing of the same within the perpetuity period. The question concerns merely the power to dispose of the capital. Thus, property may be owned perpetually by persons, companies or unincorporated associations if these bodies are entitled to dispose of the same at any time.

CASE EXAMPLE

Re Chardon [1928] Ch 464

A testator gave a fund to a cemetery company subject to the income being required to be used for the maintenance of two specified graves, with a gift over. The court held that the gift was valid, for the company was capable of alienating the property.

Charitable trusts, because of their public nature, are exempt from this principle.

11.3 Exceptions to the *Astor* principle

There are a number of private purpose trusts which are exceptionally considered to be valid. Despite the objections to the validity of purpose trusts as stated above, a number of anomalous exceptions exist. These trusts are created as concessions to human weakness. But it must be emphasised that the only concession granted by the courts is that it is unnecessary for the beneficiaries (purposes) to enforce the trust. The other rules applicable to express trusts are equally applied to these anomalous trusts (see *Re Endacott* (1960), above). Accordingly, such gifts are required to satisfy the test for certainty of objects and the perpetuity rule. These exceptionally valid trusts are not mandatory in effect but are merely 'directory' in the sense that the trustees are entitled to refuse to carry out the wishes of the settlor and the courts will not force them to do otherwise. At the same time, the courts will not forbid the trustees from carrying out the terms of the trust, if they express an intention to do so. In the latter event the traditional fiduciary duties attach to the trustees. These anomalous trusts are called 'hybrid trusts' or 'trusts for imperfect obligations'.

11.3.1 Trusts for the maintenance of animals

Gifts for the maintenance of animals generally are charitable, but trusts for the maintenance of specific animals, such as pets, are treated as valid private purpose trusts.

CASE EXAMPLE

Pettingall v Pettingall [1842] 11 LJ Ch 176

The testator's executor was given a fund in order to spend £50 per annum for the benefit of the testator's black mare. On her death, any surplus funds were to be taken by the executor. The court held that in view of the willingness of the executor to carry out the testator's wishes, a valid trust in favour of the animal was created. The residuary legatees were entitled to supervise the performance of the trust but they were not the primary beneficiaries. They were interested not in the validity of the gift but in its failure.

In *Re Dean* (1889) 41 Ch D 552, the testator directed his trustees to use £750 per annum for the maintenance of his horses and hounds should they live so long. It was held that the trust was valid. The difficulty with this case is the possible infringement of the perpetuity rule. The court treated the horses and hounds as the lives in being for the purpose of the perpetuity rule. It was stated earlier that for the purpose of the perpetuity rule a 'life' is treated as a human life. In any event, it was unclear who was entitled to enforce the trust against the trustees. In *Re Kelly* [1932] IR 255, the court took the view that lives in being were required to be human lives. In any event the court is entitled to take judicial notice of the lifetime of animals. In *Re Haines*, *The Times*, 7 November 1952, the court took notice that a cat could not live for longer than 21 years.

In *Re Thompson* [1934] Ch 342, the *Pettingall* principle was unjustifiably extended to uphold a trust for the promotion and furtherance of fox hunting.

11.3.2 Monument cases

A trust for the building of a memorial or monument in memory of an individual is not charitable, but may exist as a valid purpose trust if the trustees express a desire to perform the task.

In *Mussett v Bingle* [1876] WN 170, a testator bequeathed £300 to his executors to be used to erect a monument to the testator's wife's first husband. The court held that the gift was valid. Similarly, a gift for the maintenance of a specific grave or particular graves may be valid as private purpose trusts but additionally, the donor is required to restrict the gift within the perpetuity period, otherwise the gift may be invalidated. In *Re Hooper* [1932] 1 Ch 38, a bequest to trustees on trust to provide 'so far as they can legally do so' for the care and upkeep of specified graves in a churchyard was upheld as a private trust. The perpetuity period was satisfied by the phrase 'so far as they can legally do so'.

On the other hand, a gift for the maintenance of all the graves in a churchyard may be charitable.

11.3.3 Saying of masses

In *Bourne v Keane* [1919] AC 815, the House of Lords decided that the saying of masses was valid. Prior to this decision the courts had adopted the view that such trusts were void, not because of the lack of a human beneficiary, but because they were superstitious activities. It should be noted that the *Bourne* (1919) principle is now restricted to masses to be said in private, for public masses may be treated as charitable events (see later). In *Khoo Cheng Teow* [1932] Straits Settlement Reports 226, a trust for the performance of non-Christian ceremonies was upheld as a valid private purpose trust.

11.4 The *Denley* approach

The approach adopted by the courts is to ascertain whether a gift or trust is for the promotion of a purpose *simpliciter* (within the *Astor* principle) which is void, or alternatively whether the trust is for the benefit of persons who are capable of enforcing the trust. This is a question for the courts to decide, on construction of the relevant trust instrument. The promotion of virtually any purpose will affect persons. The settlor may, in form, create what appears to be a purpose trust but, in substance, the trust may be considered to be for the benefit of human beneficiaries.

In this respect, there is a distinction between a form of gift remotely in favour of individuals, to such an extent that those individuals do not have a *locus standi* to enforce the trust. On the other hand, a gift may appear to propagate a purpose which is directly or indirectly for the benefit of individuals. In this event, if the beneficiaries satisfy the test for certainty of objects, the gift may be valid. The courts are required to consider each gift prior to classification.

CASE EXAMPLE

Re Bowes [1896] 1 Ch 507

A testator bequeathed a fund for the planting of a clump of trees on land settled for the benefit of A and B. A and B did not want the money to be used for the planting of the trees but instead claimed the money for their benefit. North J held in favour of A and B on the ground that, on construction of the will, the money was intended for the benefit of the individuals and not for the benefit of the estate. The expressed purpose of planting trees was not intended to be imperative, but merely indicated the testator's motive for creating a trust for the benefit of A and B.

A similar approach was adopted in *Re Denley's Trust Deed* [1969] 1 Ch 373:

CASE EXAMPLE

Re Denley's Trust Deed [1969] 1 Ch 373

A plot of land was conveyed to trustees for use, subject to the perpetuity rule, as a sports ground primarily for the benefit of employees of a company and secondarily for the benefit of such other person or persons as the trustees may allow to use the same. The question in issue was whether the trust was void as a purpose trust. Goff J held that the trust was valid in favour of human beneficiaries. The test for certainty of objects and the perpetuity rule were satisfied. The court stated that the objection to purpose trusts was not that they sought to achieve a purpose but that they lacked any human beneficiary to enforce them. Thus, the 'lack of beneficiary principle' applied only where the trust was abstract or impersonal as opposed to where the trust, though expressed as a purpose, was directly or indirectly for ascertainable beneficiaries, within the perpetuity rule and was not otherwise uncertain.

JUDGMENT

'I think there may be a purpose or object trust, the carrying out of which would benefit an individual or individuals, where that benefit is so indirect or intangible or which is otherwise so framed as not to give those persons any *locus standi* to apply to the court to enforce the trust, in which case the beneficiary principle would, as it seems to me, apply to invalidate the trust, quite apart from any question of uncertainty or perpetuity. Such cases can be considered if and when they arise. The present is not, in my judgment, of that character, and it will be seen that clause 2(d) of the trust deed expressly states that, subject to any rules and regulations made by the trustees, the employers of the company shall be entitled to the use and enjoyment of the land.

Where the trust, though expressed as a purpose, is directly or indirectly for the benefit of an individual or individuals, it seems to me that it is in general outside the mischief of the beneficiary principle … In my judgment, however, it would not be right to hold the trust void on this ground [lack of beneficiary]. The court can, as it seems to me, execute the trust both negatively by restraining any improper disposition or use of the land, and positively by ordering the trustees to allow the employees and such other persons (if any) as they may admit to use the land for the purpose of a recreation or sports ground.'

Goff J

The issue in *Denley* concerned the classification of the nature of the trust. Was it a private purpose trust (void), or a traditional private trust for ascertainable human beneficiaries (valid)? The court decided that the trust was valid for an ascertainable group of beneficiaries. The focus of attention, in the court's view, was the issue of enforceability, i.e. whether the trust was capable of being enforced by beneficiaries who satisfied the test for certainty of objects. The problem with this approach is that it is questionable whether the gift corresponded with a traditional private trust. In a traditional private trust the beneficiaries acquire 'in rem' interests in the property and may be capable of terminating the trust under the *Saunders v Vautier* principle. It is arguable that these features were absent in *Denley*, for the beneficiaries amounted to a fluctuating class of objects, namely the employees of the company and others permitted to benefit at the instance of the trustees. Further, the intended beneficiaries were entitled to the use of the sports ground rather than acquiring a proprietary interest therein. The *Denley* principle was applied or extended by Oliver J in *Re Lipinski* (1977) (see later), to a gift on trust for the subsisting members of an unincorporated association. Oliver J explained *Denley* as a private trust, although expressed as a purpose, but was directly or indirectly for the benefit of individuals who were ascertainable. In *Re Grant's Will Trust* (1980) (see later), Vinelott J endorsed the approach in *Denley*, but regarded the decision as a discretionary trust for the use of the sports ground by the stated objects, analogous to a discretionary trust to distribute income amongst a class of objects.

■ *Enforcement theory* – A few Commonwealth tax haven jurisdictions (such as the Cayman Islands and Bermuda) have introduced legislation to overcome the difficulties posed by the beneficiary principle in respect of non-charitable purpose trusts. The solution here is that the court has the power to appoint an enforcer/protector to ensure that the private purpose trust is achieved. This person is appointed independently of the trustees and beneficiaries under the trust, but is accountable to the court. Such an innovation in the UK would require legislation.

A separate alternative to overcome the beneficiary problem involves the creation of a gift to a person, coupled with a power to distribute property in favour of stated non-charitable purposes (see Chapter 3). This power may be subject to an express gift over in default of appointment. If the donee of the power fails to exercise his discretion, the gift over will take effect. On the other hand, the donee of the power is entitled to exercise his discretion to distribute the property in favour of the non-charitable purposes. But it is crucial that the power is drafted carefully so as not to impose an obligation on the donee of the power to distribute the property. Otherwise the gift to the donee of the power will be construed as a trust and may fail.

KEY FACTS

Private purpose trusts

Trusts to promote private purpose trusts	Void	Lack of a beneficiary with a *locus standi* to enforce	*Morice v Bishop of Durham* (1804); *Leahy v AG for NS Wales* (1959) (see below); *Re Astor* (1952)
Exceptions ■ Maintenance of animals	Valid	Subject to the tests of certainty and perpetuity	*Pettingall v Pettingall* (1842); *Re Haines* (1952)
■ Erection of monuments	Valid	Subject to the tests of certainty and perpetuity	*Musset v Bingle* (1876)
■ Maintenance of monuments	Valid	Subject to the tests of certainty and perpetuity	*Re Hooper* (1932)
■ Saying of masses (N.B. could be charitable)	Valid	Subject to the test of perpetuity	*Bourne v Keane* (1919)
■ Alternatively, on construction (subject to the tests of certainty and perpetuity) the court may decide that a gift for a purpose may be treated as a gift for persons ■ Enforcer	Valid Valid	Enforcement by beneficiaries Appointment and enforcement by the courts	*Re Bowes* (1896); *Re Denley* (1969)

ACTIVITY

Applying the law

John, who has recently died, by his will bequeathed the following legacies:

(1) £5,000 to use the income each year to provide a trophy for the winner of the Utopia Yacht Racing Competition, an annual event organised by the Utopia Yacht Club.
(2) £600 to my executors to maintain my pet cat, Tiddles, for the rest of her life.
(3) £15,000 to erect and maintain a tombstone, for a period not exceeding 21 years, in memory of my late wife, Ophelia.
(4) £500 to the vicar of my parish church in Utopia for the saying of private masses for my soul.

Consider the validity of these bequests.

11.5 Gifts to unincorporated associations

There is some difficulty in deciding whether a gift to an unincorporated association creates a trust for a purpose which fails for want of a beneficiary to enforce the trust (under the *Astor* (1952) principle), or whether the gift will be construed in favour of human beneficiaries, the members of the association. This involves a question of construction of the circumstances surrounding the gift and the rules of the association.

For instance, a gift to the National Anti-Vivisection Society (an unincorporated non-charitable body) may be construed as a gift on trust for the work or purpose of such association and not for the benefit of its members. Accordingly, the gift may be considered void under the *Astor* (1952) principle.

JUDGMENT

'A gift can be made to persons (including a corporation) but it cannot be made to a purpose or to an object. So also, a trust may be created for the benefit of persons as *cestuis que trust* but not for a purpose or object unless the purpose or object be charitable. For a purpose or object cannot sue, but if it be charitable, the Attorney General can sue to enforce it.'

Viscount Simonds in *Leahy v AG for New South Wales* [1959] AC 457

An unincorporated association (as distinct from an incorporated association) is not a legal person but may take the form of a group of individuals joined together with common aims, usually laid down in its constitution. The association was defined by Lawton LJ in *Conservative and Unionist Central Office v Burrell* [1982] 1 WLR 522. In this case the Court of Appeal decided that the Conservative Party was not an unincorporated association but an amorphous combination of various elements. The legal rights created in favour of donors and contributors exist on the basis of a mandate or agency.

JUDGMENT

'[An unincorporated association means] ... two or more persons bound together for one or more common purposes, not being business purposes, by mutual undertakings each having mutual duties and obligations, in an organisation which has rules which identify in whom control of it and its funds rests and on what terms and which can be joined or left at will.'

Lawton LJ

In *Neville Estates Ltd v Madden* [1962] Ch 832, Cross J, in an *obiter* pronouncement, outlined various constructions concerning gifts or trusts in favour of unincorporated associations:

JUDGMENT

'The position, as I understand it, is as follows. Such a gift may take effect in one or other of three quite different ways. In the first place, it may, on its true construction, be a gift to the members of the association at the relevant date as joint tenants, so that any member can sever his share and claim it whether or not he continues to be a member of the association. Secondly, it may be a gift to the existing members not as joint tenants, but subject to their respective contractual rights and liabilities towards one another as members of the association. In such a case a member cannot sever his share. It would accrue to the other members on his death or resignation, even though such members include persons who become members after the gift took effect. If this is the effect of the gift, it will not be open to objection on the score of perpetuity or uncertainty unless there is something in its terms or circumstances or in the rules of the association which precludes the members at any given time from dividing the subject of the gift between them on the footing that they are solely entitled to it in equity. Thirdly, the terms or circumstances of the gift or the rules of the association may show that the property in question is not to be at the disposal of the members for the time being, but is to be held in trust for or applied for the purposes of the association as a quasi-corporate entity. In this case the gift will fail unless the association is a charitable body. If the gift is of the second class, i.e. one which the members of the association for the time being are entitled to divide among themselves, then, even if the objects of the association are in themselves charitable, the gift would not, I think, be a charitable gift.'

Cross J

The following solutions have been adopted from time to time by the courts in respect of gifts to unincorporated associations. Although the courts have a wide discretion in construing the intention of the donor or settlor and the function and purpose of the association, the adoption of any of these solutions will vary with the facts of each case.

Gift to members as joint tenants

A settlor may make a gift to an unincorporated association which, on a true construction, is a gift to the members of that association who take as joint tenants free from any contractual fetter. Any member is entitled to sever his share and may claim it beneficially. In these circumstances, the association is used as a label or definition of the class which is intended to take. For instance, a testator may give a legacy to a dining or social club of which he is a member, with the intention of giving a joint interest, which is capable of being severed, to the members. Such cases are extremely uncommon.

CASE EXAMPLE

Cocks v Manners [1871] LR 12 Eq 574

The testatrix left part of her estate to the Dominican Convent at Carisbrooke, 'payable to the supervisor for the time being'. The institution consisted of a group of Roman Catholic nuns, under the supervision of a common superior, living in a commune in a state of celibacy and who devoted themselves to prayer and pious contemplation. The court held that the gift was not charitable but was valid in favour of the individual members of the stated community as joint tenants.

JUDGMENT

'The gift is ordered to be paid to the superior for the time being; and the superior, when she receives it, will be bound to account for it to the convent – to put it, so to speak, into a common chest; but when there it will be subject to no trust which will prevent the existing members of the convent from spending it as they please. It would, I conceive, be an extreme stretch of the rule against perpetuity to hold that it applies to a gift of this sort. Therefore I hold the gift to the Dominican convent to be simply good.'

Wickens VC

It may be noted that in *Cocks v Manners*, the donees or nuns acquired beneficial interests as joints tenants which could be severed and converted into tenancies in common. The effect is that, in theory, a member of the convent who wished to leave may sever the joint tenancy and take her share beneficially, or alternatively assign her interest to another. In the latter case, the assignment would be required to be executed in writing in order to comply with s 53(1)(c) of the Law of Property Act 1925 (see Chapter 5).

Gift to members (subsisting) as an accretion to the funds (contract holding theory)

More frequently, the gift to the association may be construed as a gift to the members of the association on the date of the gift, not beneficially, but as an accretion to the funds of the society which is regulated by the contract (evidenced by the rules of the association) made by the members *inter se*. Thus, a subsisting member on the date of the gift is not entitled *qua* member to claim an interest in the property but takes the property by reference to the rules of the society. A member who leaves the association by death or resignation will have no claim to the property, in the absence of any rules to the contrary. This approach was supported in an *obiter* pronouncement by Brightman J in *Re Recher's Will Trusts* [1972] Ch 526:

inter se
Between
themselves.

CASE EXAMPLE

Re Recher's Will Trusts [1972] Ch 526

A testatrix gave her residuary estate to the 'Anti-Vivisection Society, 76 Victoria Street, London SW1'. The London and Provincial Anti-Vivisection Society had carried on its activities at this address but, shortly before the will was made, the society ceased to exist (it was amalgamated with other societies) and it gave up its premises in Victoria Street. The question in issue was whether the gift could be taken by the amalgamated society, or failed and was subject to a resulting trust. The court held that, on construction of the will, the testator intended to benefit the Society at Victoria Street and not the larger body. Accordingly, the gift failed and a resulting trust was set up.

JUDGMENT

'[I]t appears to me that the life members, the ordinary members and the associate members of the London Provincial Society were bound together by a contract *inter se*, with the result that the society represented an organisation of individuals bound together by a contract. Now just as two parties to a bi-partite bargain can vary or terminate their contract by mutual assent, so it must follow that the members of the society could, at any moment of time by agreement, authorised by its constitution, vary or terminate their multi-partite contract. There is no private trust or trust for charitable purposes or other trust to hinder the process. The funds of such an association may, of course, be derived not only from the subscriptions of contracting parties but also from donations from non-contracting parties and legacies from persons who have died. In the case of a donation which is not accompanied by any words which purport to impose a trust, it seems that the gift takes effect in favour of the existing members of the association not as joint tenants or tenants-in-common so as to entitle each member to an immediate share, but as an accretion to the funds of the organisation.'

Brightman J

tutor tip

'The law on private purpose trusts demonstrates how creative the courts can be at times.'

The effect of the approach in *Re Recher* (1972) is that if a donor transfers property to the association for its general purposes, the gift may be construed as intended for the benefit of the members of the association to be enjoyed collectively.

The High Court in *Re Horley Town Football Club* endorsed the *Recher* approach and decided on the facts that the trust deed would be construed as a gift to the Club as a 'contract-holding' gift to the Club and its members. In addition, the beneficial ownership of the assets of the Club was vested in the current full members of the Club on a bare trust. Moreover, a clause would be implied into the rules of the Club to the effect that the surplus funds of the club on a dissolution will be divided amongst its members at the time of dissolution on a *per capita* basis, irrespective of the length of membership or subscriptions paid.

CASE EXAMPLE

Re Horley Town Football Club; Hunt v McLaren [2006] All ER (D) 34 (Oct), High Court

In 1948 Major Jennings, the president of Horley Town Football Club (the Club) settled land by deed on trust to secure a permanent sports ground for the Club. In May 2002 the land was sold to a developer for almost £4 million. The trustees used the proceeds to purchase another site for £850,000 and to construct a club house and ancillary facilities amounting to approximately £2.2 million. This new sports complex was subject to certain restrictive covenants which limited its use to sports and leisure. As a consequence the land was worth less than the amount spent on it. The rules of the Club made provisions for several varieties of membership, ranging from the current full members to temporary and associate members. The claimants (trustees) applied to the court for directions concerning the basis on which they held the assets of the Club and the proper construction of the rules of the Club.

The High Court decided as follows:

- A gift to or in trust for an unincorporated association might take effect as a gift to the existing members, not as joint tenants, but subject to their respective contractual rights and liabilities towards each other as members of the association. In this event the member could not sever his share and it would accrue to the other members on his death or resignation. Such members include persons who became members after the gift took effect.
- The deed of 1948 was construed as a gift to the members of the Club as a contract-holding gift to the Club and its members including subsequent members.
- The beneficial ownership of the assets of the Club was in the subsisting full members, but not the temporary and associate members. The trustees of the Club held the assets on bare trust for the full members.
- The members acquired the assets of the Club subject to the current rules and could unanimously or by a general meeting call for the assets to be transferred.

JUDGMENT

'In the absence of any rule to the contrary, there is to be implied into the rules of the Club a rule to the effect that the surplus funds of the Club should be divided on a dissolution amongst the members of the Club, and this distribution will normally be per capita among the members (irrespective of length of membership or the amount of subscriptions paid) but may reflect different classes of membership: *Re Sick and Funeral Society of St John's Sunday School, Golcar* [1973] Ch 51, at 60; *Re Bucks Constabulary Widows' and Orphans' Fund Friendly Society (No 2)* [1979] 1 WLR 936, at 952; *Re GKN Bolts & Nuts Ltd etc. Sports & Social Club* [1982] 1 WLR 774, at 778.'

Collins J

Gift to subsisting members beneficially

Moreover, a gift to an association for a particular purpose may be construed as a gift to the members of the association for the time being for their own use. Where the association exists solely for the benefit of its members the gift will be valid. In this respect, the members of the association would be both trustees and beneficiaries. The purpose stated by the settlor may be construed as not imposing an obligation on the officers of the society to carry out such stated purpose but merely a manifestation of the motive of the settlor concerning a suggested use to which the property may be put.

CASE EXAMPLE

Re Turkington [1937] 4 All ER 501

A gift was made in favour of a masonic lodge 'as a fund to build a suitable temple in Stafford'. The members of the lodge were both the trustees and the beneficiaries. The court held that the gift was absolute in favour of the members of the lodge for the time being. The purpose stipulated was construed by Luxmoore J as 'simply an indication by the testator of the purpose for which he would like the money to be expended, without imposing any trust on the beneficiaries'.

JUDGMENT

'The decision of Farwell J, as he then was, in *Re Selous, Thomson v Selous* [1901] 1 Ch 921, seems to me to lay down the governing principle which is applicable to this case. I therefore hold that this gift is a gift to the masonic lodge for the purpose of the lodge, and that the members of the lodge for the time being are at liberty to deal with it in accordance with their constitution in the ordinary way, in the way they think fit; in other words, they have complete domination over the fund.'

Luxmoore J

Gift to present and future members

Alternatively, the court may construe a gift to an association as a gift for the benefit of the members of the association, both present and future. In coming to this conclusion, the courts are required to consider the rules of the association, its function, in addition to the intention of the donor. Moreover, if the members of the society (in accordance with its constitution) are incapable of disposing of the assets of the society or are incapable of altering the rules of the association, the gift will fail for infringing the perpetuity rule.

CASE EXAMPLE

Re Drummond [1914] 2 Ch 90

A testator transferred his residuary estate to the 'Old Bradfordians Club to be utilised as the Committee of the Club should think best in the interests of the Club'. On the issue of the validity of the gift, the court held that the gift was valid since the committee was free to spend the capital in any manner it might consider fit.

However, in *Re Grant's Will Trusts* [1980] 1 WLR 360, the gift failed for infringing the perpetuity rule.

CASE EXAMPLE

Re Grant's Will Trusts [1980] 1 WLR 360

A gift for the purposes of the Chertsey Labour Party Headquarters (non-charitable unincorporated association) failed for infringing the perpetuity rule because the members of the local association did not control the society's property nor could they change the rules and obtain control, for the rules were subject to the approval of the National Executive Committee. Accordingly, the members of the local Labour Party did not have the power to liquidate the association and distribute its assets among themselves.

JUDGMENT

'It is, in my judgment, impossible, in particular having regard to the gift over to the National Labour Party, to read the gift as a gift to the members of the National Labour Party at the testator's death, with a direction not amounting to a trust, for the National Party to permit it to be used by the Chertsey and Walton CLP for headquarters purposes.'

Vinelott J

Gift on trust to promote the purpose of the association

If a settlor transfers property on trust for an association, it is possible for the court to decide that on construction, the transfer is made on trust for the function or operation of the society and not for its members. If this construction is adopted the court may decide that the trust fails under the *Astor* (1952) principle, because of the intention to promote a purpose. Such a construction would be exceptional. In addition, if the intention of the settlor is to set up an endowment in favour of the beneficiary, the gift may fail on the separate ground of the infringement of the perpetuity rule.

CASE EXAMPLE

Leahy v Attorney General for New South Wales [1959] AC 457

A testator devised a plot of land of 730 acres on trust for 'such order of nuns of the Catholic church or the Christian brothers as my trustees shall select'. This transfer was not wholly charitable, as it permitted the trustees to select cloistered nuns. Under Australian law the trust was capable of being saved as a charitable donation by confining the gift to non-cloistered orders. The trustees, however, wanted to retain the freedom to give to cloistered nuns if possible. The question in issue was whether the trust in its existing form was valid as a non-charitable trust. The court held that, as a non-charitable gift, the trust failed as the testator's intention was clearly to create an endowment for the order of nuns (both present and future) and not for the benefit of individuals.

JUDGMENT

'[I]t seems reasonably clear that the testator's intention was to create a trust, not merely for the benefit of the existing members of the selected Order, but for its benefit as a continuing society and for the furtherance of its work.'

Viscount Simonds

Gift on trust for the subsisting members of the association

A transfer of property or trust for an association may be construed as a transfer of property on trust for the current members of the association, and not on trust for purposes. In this event, provided that the rules of the association empower the members to liquidate and distribute the assets of the association, the perpetuity rule will not be infringed and the trust will be valid. The position remains the same even though the settlor may specify a purpose for which the fund may be used. Such stipulation may not be sufficient to prevent the members (beneficiaries) disposing of the property in any way they consider appropriate within the rules of the society.

CASE EXAMPLE

Re Lipinski's Will Trust [1977] 1 All ER 33

A testator transferred one-half of his residuary estate to the Hull Judeans (Maccabi) Association, an unincorporated, non-charitable association, 'in memory of my late wife to be used *solely* in the work of constructing new buildings for the association and/or improvements to the said buildings'. The question in issue was whether the trust was valid. The court held that the trust was for the benefit of ascertainable beneficiaries (the members at the date of the gift). On construction, the expression 'in memory of my late wife' was not intended as a permanent endowment but merely a tribute which the testator paid to his wife. The stipulation concerning the use of the funds ('solely') was not intended to reduce the power of the members to dispose of the assets of the association in accordance with the rules of the association. For the same reason, the perpetuity rule was not infringed.

JUDGMENT

'The beneficiaries, the members of the association for the time being, are the persons who could enforce the purpose and they must, as it seems to me, be entitled not to enforce it or, indeed, to vary it … Thus, it seems to me that whether one treats the gift as a purpose trust or as an absolute gift with a superadded direction or, on the analogy of *Re Turkington* [1937] 4 All ER 501, as a gift where the trustees and the beneficiaries are the same persons, all roads lead to the same conclusion. The gift is a valid gift.'

Oliver J

It should be noted that in *Re Lipinski* (1977) the court adopted a benevolent construction of the terms of the will. Oliver J stated that, as a matter of common sense, a clear distinction ought to be drawn between cases where a purpose is prescribed clearly for the benefit of ascertainable beneficiaries, particularly where those beneficiaries have the power to make the capital their own, and cases where no beneficiary is intended or where the beneficiaries are unascertainable. He went on to say that if a valid gift may be made to an unincorporated association as a simple accretion to the funds that are the subject-matter of the contract which the members have made *inter se*, then there is no reason why such a gift, which specifies a purpose that is within the powers of the association and of which the members of the association are the beneficiaries, should fail. He then decided that there were three alternative bases for holding the transfer by will valid. First, the will could be construed as creating a valid gift to the present members of the association. Second, a trust for the present and future members could be spelt out (which did not infringe the perpetuity rule) on construction of the will. Third, a trust for the present members of the association could be ascertained.

It should be noted that in Chapter 7 we considered the distribution of funds on a liquidation of an unincorporated association. Those rules should be read in conjunction with this chapter.

ACTIVITY

Essay writing

'The objection [to non-charitable purpose trusts] is not that the trust is for a purpose or an object per se, but that there is no beneficiary or *cestui que trust*', Goff J in *Re Denley's Trust Deed* (1969).

Discuss.

ACTIVITY

Applying the law

Consider the validity of the following testamentary dispositions:

(i) 50,000 to the Dealing Bowls Club (an unincorporated association) for the purpose of constructing a new clubhouse.

(ii) Blackacre (a five-acre plot of land) to my trustees for the purpose of maintaining and using the same as a recreation ground for the benefit of the employees of Monkey Business plc.

Void	Valid
Lack of beneficiary	Specific
Uncertainty	Animals
Perpetuity	Monuments
	Masses
	Denley
	A gift to an unincorporated association is valid if it is: ▪ in trust for present members, or ▪ a gift to present members, or ▪ a gift to present members as accretion funds, or ▪ a gift to present and future members

Figure 11.1 Private purpose trusts

SUMMARY

▪ The rationale behind the general rule of non-enforceability of private purpose trusts involves the requirement that a valid private trust must be capable of being enforced by a person in whose favour the court may grant a decree. This is known as the 'beneficiary' principle or the rule in *Re Astor*. In the absence of the beneficiary principle the intended trust will fail and the property may be held on resulting trust. This general rule is subject to a number of exceptions.

- The rule against perpetuities is by origin a common law rule directed against attempts to make property inalienable. The approach of the courts was based on the possibility that where a future interest might vest outside the perpetuity period the transfer of the interest was void. The common law perpetuity period was a 'life or lives in being and/or twenty one years'. The Perpetuities and Accumulations Act 1964 has created a period not exceeding 80 years which must be expressly chosen, and substituted the principle of 'mere possibilities' with the 'wait and see' principle.

- The exceptions to the *Astor* principle are:
    - charitable trusts which are enforceable by the Attorney General;
    - trusts for the erection and maintenance of monuments;
    - trusts for the maintenance of particular animals;
    - trusts for the saying of private masses.

- The *Denley* principle involves a question of construction of the instrument creating the gift to ascertain whether the gift is void as a purpose trust or, alternatively, whether there is a valid gift on trust for ascertainable beneficiaries.

- An unincorporated association has been defined by Lawton LJ in *Conservative and Unionists Central Office v Burrell* (1982) as: 'Two or more persons bound together for one or more common purposes, not being business purposes, by mutual undertakings each having mutual duties and obligations, in an organisation which has rules which identify in whom control of it and its funds rests and on what terms.' The association is not a legal person and if its purposes are non-charitable a gift to the association may be construed as void. Two important problems are created in respect of such gifts.
    - How may gifts to such associations be construed? There have been many solutions adopted by the courts over the years. Most of these are designed to validate the gift.
    - To whom may surplus funds be distributed when the association is wound up? The modern rule is that the resulting trust is inappropriate and the destination of the surplus funds is governed by the law of contract.

SAMPLE ESSAY QUESTION

Consider the following essay question:

To what extent are gifts to unincorporated associations valid?

Answer plan

Highlight the principle that such an association is not a legal person and the difficulties created in respect of gifts to such associations.

Consider the approach by the courts to the effect that, as a trust for the purpose of the association, the gift will fail.

Alternatively, the courts may construe the trust as existing for the benefit of its subsisting members in accordance with the *Denley* principle.

The gift may be acquired by the subsisting members of the association on the date of the gift as joint tenants.

The gift may be acquired by the subsisting members of the association on the date of the gift, not individually, but as an accretion to the funds of the society.

The gift may be acquired by present and future members of the association.

The gift to the association may be construed as a private purpose trust for the association.

CONCLUSION

Further reading

Emery, C, 'Do we need a rule against perpetuities?' (1994) 57 MLR 602.

Gardner, S, 'A detail in the construction of gifts to unincorporated associations' (1998) Conv 8.

Gravells, N, 'Gifts to unincorporated associations: where there is a will there is a way' (1977) 40 MLR 231.

Lovell, P, 'Non-charitable purpose trusts: further reflection' (1970) Conv 77.

Luxton, P, 'Gifts to clubs: contract-holding is trumps' (2007) Conv 274.

McKay, L, 'Trusts for purposes: another view' (1973) Conv 420.

Matthews, P, 'A problem in the construction of gifts to unincorporated associations' (1995) Conv 302.

Pawlowski, M and Summers, J, 'Private purpose trusts: a reform proposal' (2007) Conv 440.

Rickett, C, 'Unincorporated associations and their dissolution' (1980) CLJ 88.

Warburton, J, 'The holding of property by unincorporated associations' (1985) Conv 318.

12

Charitable trusts

AIMS AND OBJECTIVES

By the end of this chapter you should be able to:

- appreciate the privileges enjoyed by charitable trusts
- define a charity within the new Charities Act 2011
- recognise a charitable purpose within the Charities Act 2011
- understand the *cy-près* doctrine

12.1 Introduction

A charitable trust is a type of purpose trust in that it promotes a purpose and does not primarily benefit specific individuals. However, in furthering a purpose the performance of the trust may result in individuals or members of the public deriving direct benefits. Even so, the trust remains one for a purpose and not for the benefit of those individuals. The purpose of the trust is to benefit society as a whole or a sufficiently large section of the community so that it may be considered public. Thus, a charitable trust is a public purpose trust and is enforceable by the Attorney General on behalf of the Crown.

Private trusts, on the other hand, seek to benefit defined persons or narrower sections of society than charitable trusts and, as we saw, a private purpose trust is void for lack of a person to enforce the trust.

Generally, charitable trusts are subject to the same rules as private trusts but, as a result of the public nature of such bodies, they enjoy a number of advantages over private trusts in respect of:

(a) certainty of objects;

(b) the **perpetuity** rule;

(c) the *cy-près* rule; and

(d) fiscal privileges.

The Charities Act 2006 introduced five main statutory modifications to the law of charities. These are:

perpetuity
Endless years. There is a rule against perpetuities which, if infringed, will make a gift void.

cy-près
Nearest alternative gift.

1. the restatement of charitable purposes in a modern statutory form;
2. the public benefit obligation;
3. changes in the function of the Charity Commission;
4. the establishment of a Charity Tribunal;
5. the improvement of the range of legal entities that are available to charities.

The principles that were enacted in the 2006 Act have since been repealed and replaced by equivalent provisions in the Charities Act 2011. This Act was brought into force on 14 March 2012. The Charities Act 2011 is divided into 19 Parts, contains 358 sections and 11 Schedules.

Section 1(1) of the Charities Act 2011 adopts a two-tier definition of a charity. It is an institution which:

(a) is established for charitable purposes only; and

(b) falls to be subject to the control of the High Court in the exercise of its jurisdiction with respect to charities.

The definition in s 1(1)(a) of the 2011 Act is related to the test for certainty of charitable objects (see below). In addition, the institution is required to be subject to the control of the High Court. This is the jurisdictional aspect of the definition.

A number of British registered charities carry on their activities abroad. There is little judicial authority on the attitude of the courts to such overseas activities. In 1963, the Charity Commissioners issued guidelines on the way they would approach this problem. Their view is that activities of trusts within the first three heads of Lord Macnaghten's classification (trusts for the relief of poverty, for the advancement of education and for religion) are charitable wherever such operations are conducted. In respect of the fourth head, such purposes would be charitable only if carried on for the benefit (direct or reasonably direct) of the UK community, such as medical research. The Commissioners added that it may be easier to establish this benefit in relation to the Commonwealth (although this link has become weaker since the statement was made).

The limited number of authorities in this field seem to make no distinction between activities conducted abroad as opposed to UK activities.

CASE EXAMPLE

Keren Kayemeth Le Jisroel Ltd v IRC [1932] AC 650

A company was formed with the main object of purchasing land in Palestine, Syria and parts of Turkey for the purpose of settling Jews in such lands. It was argued that the company was established for charitable purposes, namely the advancement of religion, the relief of poverty and other purposes beneficial to the community. The court held that the company was not charitable, because of the lack of evidence of religion and poverty. In addition, the company was not charitable under the fourth head because of the uncertainty of identifying the community.

In *Re Jacobs* (1970) 114 SJ 515, a trust for the planting of a clump of trees in Israel was held to be charitable because soil conservation in arid parts of Israel is of essential importance to the Israeli community. The court relied on *IRC v Yorkshire Agricultural Society* [1928] 1 KB 611: the promotion of agriculture is a charitable purpose.

However, if the organisation is not registered in the United Kingdom but abroad, and carries on its activities substantially abroad, the connection with the UK could be so insignificant that the English courts may reject jurisdiction. The justification for this rule is that the activities of the charity as well as the trustees will be outside the court's control. In *Gaudiya Mission v Brahmachary* (1997), the Court of Appeal refused jurisdiction on the ground that the statutory and practical controls could not have been extended to such institutions.

CASE EXAMPLE

Gaudiya Mission v Brahmachary [1997] 4 All ER 957, CA

The claimant, an Indian charity (the Mission), maintained preaching centres and temples in order to advance the doctrines of the Vaishnava faith throughout India and also Cricklewood, north-west London. The Mission was not registered in England. Rival factions within the Mission set up a trust under the name 'Gaudiya Mission Society Trust' (the Society), which was a registered English charity. The defendants were the priest in charge of the charity's London temple and the trustees of the English registered Society. The claimant contended that the assets held by the Society belonged to it and that the Society was passing itself off as the Mission. The question in issue was whether the Mission was an institution established for charitable purposes, and thereby subject to the control of the High Court under its supervisory jurisdiction. The judge decided that the Mission was within the control of the High Court and, consequently, that the Attorney General ought to be added as a party to the proceedings. The Attorney General appealed to the Court of Appeal.

Held: The Court of Appeal allowed the appeal on the ground that the English law of charities was not applicable to institutions other than those established for charitable purposes in England and Wales. Charitable institutions within England and Wales are required to register with the Charity Commission. The legal and practical considerations of enforceability are decisive factors, which indicate that the law was never intended to extend to an institution registered abroad. Thus, the Mission was not a charity within English law and the Attorney General was not a proper party to be joined.

JUDGMENT

'Under English law charity has always received special treatment. It often takes the form of a trust; but it is a public trust for the promotion of purposes beneficial to the community, not a trust for private individuals. It is therefore subject to special rules governing registration, administration, taxation and duration. Although not a state institution, a charity is subject to the constitutional protection of the Crown as *parens patriae*, acting through the Attorney General, to the state supervision of the Charity Commissioners and to the judicial supervision of the High Court. This regime applies whether the charity takes the form of a trust or of an incorporated body. The English courts have never sought to subject to this regime institutions or undertakings established for public purposes under other legal systems. [The authorities] show that the courts of this country accept that they do not have the means of controlling an institution established in another country, and administered by trustees there.'

Mummery LJ

12.2 Certainty of objects

In s 1(1)(a) of the Charities Act 2011, the expression, 'charity' has been partially defined by reference to the exclusivity of charitable purposes promoted by the institution. This is a reference to the test for certainty of the charitable objects and amounts to a statutory recognition of the common law approach that preceded the passing of the Act. At common law a charitable trust is subject to a unique test for certainty of objects, namely whether the funds of the institution are applicable for charitable purposes. In other words, if the trust funds may be used solely for charitable purposes, the test will be satisfied. Indeed, it is unnecessary for the settlor or testator to specify the charitable objects which are intended to take the trust property: provided that the trust instrument manifests a clear intention to devote the funds for 'charitable purposes', the test will be satisfied. Thus, a gift 'on trust for charitable purposes' will satisfy this test. The Charity Commission and the courts have jurisdiction to establish a scheme for the application of the funds for charitable purposes (i.e. the court will make an order indicating the specific charitable objects which will benefit).

But if the trust funds are capable of being applied in a substantial manner to promote charitable and non-charitable purposes the trust will fail to satisfy the test for certainty of charitable objects and a resulting trust may arise in favour of the settlor or his estate, if he is dead. In *Morice v Bishop of Durham*, the gift failed as a charity on this ground.

CASE EXAMPLE

Morice v Bishop of Durham [1804] 9 Ves 399

A fund was given upon trust for such objects of benevolence and liberality as the Bishop of Durham should approve. The question in issue was whether the fund was charitable.

Held: The gift was not valid as a charity because the objects were not exclusively charitable. A resulting trust was created.

JUDGMENT

'[I]t is now settled, upon authority, which it is too late to controvert, that, where a charitable purpose is expressed, however general, the bequest shall not fail on account of the uncertainty of the object: but the particular mode of application will be directed by the King in some cases, in others by this court. I am not aware of any case, in which the bequest has been held to be charitable, where the testator has not either used that word, to denote his general purpose or specified some particular purpose, which this court has determined to be charitable in its nature.'

Grant MR

In *Moggridge v Thackwell* (1807) 13 Ves 416, a bequest to 'such charities as the trustee sees fit' was valid as a gift for charitable purposes. The court approved a scheme for the disposition of the residuary estate.

On the other hand, where the settlor in the trust instrument identifies two sets of purposes, one set of charitable objects and another set of non-charitable objects, the court will construe the objects to determine the scope of the disposition. If the trust funds are capable of being devoted to both charitable and non-charitable purposes the gift will be invalid as a charity for uncertainty of objects.

CASE EXAMPLE

IRC v City of Glasgow Police Athletic Association [1953] 1 All ER 747

The association promoted both a charitable purpose (efficiency of the police force) and a non-charitable purpose (promotion of sport). The court decided that the association was not charitable.

JUDGMENT

'The private advantage of members is a purpose for which the association is established and it therefore cannot be said that this is an association established for a public charitable purpose only. In principle, therefore, if an association has two purposes, one charitable and the other not, and if the two purposes are such and so related that the non-charitable purpose cannot be regarded as incidental to the other, the association is not a body established for charitable purpose only.'

Lord Normand

The courts have created a distinction between, on the one hand, the broad notion of a trust for benevolent purposes and, on the other hand, a charitable trust for the benefit of the community. On construction, the court may decide that benevolent purposes involve objectives that are much wider than charitable purposes and accordingly the gift may fail as a charity. Thus, where the draftsman of the objects clause uses words such as 'charitable or benevolent purposes', the court may, on construction of the clause, decide that the word 'or' ought to be interpreted disjunctively, with the effect that benevolent purposes which are not charitable are capable of taking, thereby invalidating the charitable gift. In *Chichester Diocesan Fund v Simpson* (1944), the gift failed as a charity on construction of the objects clause.

CASE EXAMPLE

Chichester Diocesan Fund v Simpson [1944] 2 All ER 60, HL

A testator directed his executors to apply the residue of his estate 'for such charitable or benevolent objects' as they might select. The executors assumed that the clause created a valid charitable gift and distributed most of the funds to charitable bodies. The House of Lords decided that the clause did not create charitable gifts and therefore the gifts were void. A resulting trust was set up for the testator's estate.

JUDGMENT

'It is not disputed that the words charitable and benevolent do not ordinarily mean the same thing; they overlap in the sense that each of them, as a matter of legal interpretation, covers some common ground, but also something which is not covered by the other. It appears to me that it inevitably follows that the phrase charitable or benevolent occurring in a will must, in its ordinary context, be regarded as too vague to give the certainty necessary before such a provision can be supported or enforced.

The conjunction or may be sometimes used to join two words whose meaning is the same, but, as the conjunction appears in this will, it seems to me to indicate a variation rather than an identity between the coupled conceptions.

I regret that we have to arrive at such a conclusion, but we have no right to set at nought an established principle such as this in the construction of wills, and I, therefore, move the House to dismiss the appeal.'

Viscount Simon LC

Prima facie, the conjunction 'and' is construed conjunctively but may exceptionally be construed disjunctively in a way similar to the word 'or'. The construction of the expression will depend ultimately in the context in which the words were used in the trust instrument or will. In *Re Best* [1904] 2 Ch 354, a testator transferred property by his will for 'such charitable and benevolent institutions in the city of Birmingham as the Lord Mayor should choose'. The court decided, on construction, that the will created a valid charitable trust.

JUDGMENT

'I think the testator here intended that the institutions should be both charitable and benevolent; and I see no reason for reading the conjunction and as or.'

Farwell J

But in *AG of the Bahamas v Royal Trust Co* [1986] 1 WLR 1001, a bequest to provide education 'and' welfare for Bahamian children failed as a charitable bequest. The expression 'welfare' was a word of wide import and, taken in the context of the expression 'education and welfare', was not restricted to the educational prosperity of the objects. The gift was therefore void for charitable purposes.

JUDGMENT

'[I]t is not easy to imagine a purpose connected with the education of a child which is not also a purpose for the child's welfare. Thus, if welfare is to be given any separate meaning at all it must be something different from and wider than mere education, for otherwise the word becomes otiose ... the phrase education and welfare in this will inevitably fall to be construed disjunctively. It follows that, for the reasons which were fully explored in the judgments in the courts below, and as is now conceded on the footing of a disjunctive construction, the trusts in paragraph (t) do not constitute valid charitable trusts.'

Lord Oliver

In *Helena Partnerships Ltd v Revenue and Customs* [2012] EWCA Civ 569, the Court of Appeal decided that a registered company formed to provide housing for persons other than those in need was not a charitable organisation and that corporation tax was payable on its profits.

JUDGMENT

'I conclude that the provision of housing without regard to a relevant charitable need is not in itself charitable.'

Lloyd LJ

In two circumstances, an objects clause which seeks to benefit both charitable and non-charitable purposes will not fail as a charity if:

(i) The non-charitable purpose is construed as being incidental to the main charitable purpose. This involves a question of construction for the courts to evaluate the importance of each class of objects. In *Re Coxen* [1948] Ch 747, a bequest of £200,000 provided for the income to be paid to orthopaedic hospitals, subject to £100 per annum for dinners for trustees when they met on trust business. The issue was whether the objects were charitable. The court decided that, on construction of the relevant clause, a valid charitable gift was created. The provision for the trustees' dinners was purely incidental to the main charitable purpose of benefiting orthopaedic hospitals.

(ii) The court is able to apportion the fund and devote the charitable portion of the fund for charitable purposes. An apportionment will be ordered where part only of the fund is payable for charitable purposes and the other part for non-charitable purposes. In the absence of circumstances requiring a different division, the court will apply the maxim 'Equality is equity' and order an equal division of the fund. In *Salusbury v Denton* (1857) 3 K & J 529, severance was permitted where an unspecified part of a fund was made for charitable purposes (the relief of poverty) and the remainder for a private purpose (the testator's relatives).

JUDGMENT

'It is one thing to direct a trustee to give a part of a fund to one set of objects, and the remainder to another, and it is a distinct thing to direct him to give either to one set of objects or to another ... This is a case of the former description. Here the trustee was bound to give a part to each.'

Page Wood VC

12.3 Perpetuity

Charities are not subject to the rule against excessive duration. Indeed, many charities (schools and universities) continue indefinitely and rely heavily on donations. But charitable gifts, like private gifts, are subject to the rule against remote vesting, i.e. the subject-matter of the gift is required to vest in the charity within the perpetuity period. But even in this respect the courts have introduced a concession for charities, namely charitable unity. Once a gift has vested in a specific charity, then, subject to any express declarations to the contrary, it vests forever for charitable purposes. Accordingly, a gift which vests in one charity (A) with a gift over in favour of another charity (B) on the occurrence of an event will be valid even if the event occurs outside the perpetuity period. This concessionary rule does not apply to a gift over to a charity after a gift in favour of a non-charity. The normal rules as to vesting apply. Similarly, a gift over from a charity to a non-charity is caught by the rules as to remote vesting.

12.4 The *cy-près* doctrine

The advantage over private trusts is that when a gift vests in a charity then, subject to express provisions to the contrary, the gift vests for charitable purposes. Accordingly, the settlor (and his estate) is excluded from any implied reversionary interests by way of a resulting trust in the event of a failure of the charitable trust. Thus, the *cy-près* doctrine is an alternative to the resulting trust principle. This principle will be dealt with in more detail later in this chapter.

12.5 Fiscal advantages

A variety of tax reliefs are enjoyed both by charitable bodies and by members of the public (including companies) who donate funds for charitable purposes. A detailed analysis of such concessions is outside the scope of this book.

12.6 Registration

Section 30 of the Charities Act 2011 lays down the requirement that all charitable bodies must be registered with the Charity Commission, subject to exemptions, exceptions and small charities. Section 29 of the Charities Act 2011 deals with the register of charities, including its contents, which the Charity Commission will continue to maintain. Section

34 of the 2011 Act deals with the circumstances when the Commission may remove charities or institutions that are no longer considered to be charities.

The effect of registration is governed by s37 of the 2011 Act. This provision declares that, except for the purposes of rectification, the organisation 'shall be conclusively presumed to be or to have been a charity' while it remains on the register.

12.7 Status of charitable organisations

Charitable bodies may exist in a variety of forms. The choice of charitable medium is determined by the founders of the charity.

Express trusts

An individual may promote a charitable purpose by donating funds *inter vivos* or by will to trustees on trust to fulfil a charitable objective. The purpose need not be specified by the donor, for the test here is whether all the purposes are charitable; for example, a trust will be charitable if the donor disposes of property on trust for 'charitable and benevolent purposes'. It may be necessary for the trustees to draw up a scheme with the Charity Commission or with the approval of the court in order to identify the specific charitable purposes which will benefit. It was pointed out earlier that charitable trusts are exempt from the test for certainty of objects applicable to private trusts. Alternatively, the donor may identify the charitable objectives which he or she had in mind and, if these objectives are contested, the courts will decide whether the purposes are indeed charitable.

Corporations

A great deal of charitable activity is conducted through corporations. Such bodies may be incorporated by royal charter, such as the 'old' universities, or by special statute under which many public institutions, such as hospitals and 'new' universities, have been created. In addition, many charitable bodies have been created under the Companies Act 2006, usually as private companies limited by guarantee. In these circumstances, there is no need for separate trustees; since the corporations are independent persons, the property may vest directly in such bodies.

Charitable incorporated organisations

Part 11 (ss204–250) of the Charities Act 2011 introduces provisions creating a new legal form known as a 'charitable incorporated organisation' (CIO). The CIO is the first legal form to be created specifically to meet the needs of charities. A CIO is a body corporate with a constitution with at least one member. The purpose of a CIO is to avoid the need for charities that wish to benefit from incorporation to register as companies and be liable to comply with regulations from Companies House and the Charity Commission. Any one or more persons may apply to the Charity Commission for a CIO to be registered as a charity. The effect of registration is that all the property of the applicant's organisation shall become vested in the CIO. The Minister may make provisions for the winding up, insolvency, dissolution and revival of CIOs. The regulations may provide for the transfer of the property and rights of a CIO to the official custodian or another person or body or *cy-près*.

Unincorporated associations

A group of persons may join together in order to promote a charitable purpose. Such an association, unlike a corporation, has no separate existence. The funds are usually held by a committee in order to benefit the charitable purpose. In the absence of such a committee, the funds may be vested in the members of the association on trust for the charitable activity.

12.8 Charitable purposes

Pre-Charities Act 2011

The purpose of this section is to introduce the reader to the approach of the courts over four centuries in clarifying the law as to charitable purposes. Most of the case law is still relevant today in deciding whether a purpose is charitable or not.

Prior to the passing of the Charities Act 2011 (consolidating the provisions laid down in the Charities Act 2006), there was no statutory or judicial definition of charitable purposes. It was at one time believed that a statutory definition of charitable purposes would have created the undesirable effect of restricting the flexibility which existed in allowing the law to keep abreast with the changing needs of society.

Ever since the passing of the Charitable Uses Act 1601 (sometimes referred to as the Statute of Elizabeth I), the courts developed the practice of referring to the preamble for guidance as to charitable purposes. The preamble contained a catalogue of purposes which at that time were regarded as charitable. It was not intended to constitute a definition of charities. The purposes included in the preamble to the 1601 Act are:

SECTION

Preamble to the Statute of Elizabeth I

'The relief of aged, impotent and poor people; the maintenance of sick and maimed soldiers and mariners, schools of learning, free schools and scholars of universities; the repair of bridges, ports, havens, causeways, churches, sea banks and highways; the education and preferment of orphans; the relief, stock or maintenance of houses of correction; the marriages of poor maids; the supportation, aid and help of young tradesmen, handicapped men and persons decayed; the relief or redemption of prisoners or captives; and the aid or care of any poor inhabitants concerning the payments of fifteens, setting out of soldiers and other taxes.'

Admittedly, the above-mentioned purposes were of limited effect, but Lord Macnaghten in *IRC v Pemsel* [1891] AC 531 classified charitable purposes within four categories, thus:

JUDGMENT

'[C]harity in its legal sense comprises four principal divisions:

- trusts for relief of poverty;
- trusts for the advancement of education;
- trusts for the advancement of religion;
- trusts for other purposes beneficial to the community.'

Lord Macnaghten

The approach of the courts treated the examples stated in the preamble as a means of guidance in deciding on the validity of the relevant purpose. Two approaches have been adopted by the courts, namely:

- *Reasoning by analogy*: the approach here is to ascertain whether a purpose has some resemblance to an example as stated in the preamble or to an earlier decided case which was considered charitable, for example the provision of a crematorium was considered charitable by analogy with the repair of churches as stated in the preamble in the following case:

JUDGMENT

'What must be regarded is not the wording of the preamble, but the effect of decisions given by the Courts as to its scope, decisions which have endeavoured to keep the law as to charities moving according as new social needs arise or old ones become obsolete or satisfied.'

Lord Wilberforce in *Scottish Burial Reform and Cremation Society v City of Glasgow Corporation* [1968] AC 138

The spirit and intendment of the preamble: this approach is much wider than the previous approach. The courts decide whether the purpose of the organisation is 'within the spirit and intendment' or 'within the equity' of the statute, unhindered by the specific purposes as stated in the preamble. In other words, the examples enumerated in the preamble are treated as the context or 'flavour' against which the purpose under scrutiny may be determined. In this respect it has been suggested that purposes beneficial to the community are *prima facie* charitable, unless they could not have been intended by the draftsman of the Statute of Elizabeth I, assuming that he was aware of the changes in society.

JUDGMENT

'[I]f a purpose is shown to be so beneficial or of such utility it is *prima facie* charitable in law, but the courts have left open a line of retreat based on the equity of the statute in case they are faced with a purpose (e.g. a political purpose) which could not have been within the contemplation of the statute even if the then legislators had been endowed with the gift of foresight into the circumstances of later centuries.'

Russell LJ in *Incorporated Council of Law Reporting v AG* [1972] Ch 73

CASE EXAMPLE

Incorporated Council of Law Reporting v AG [1972] Ch 73

The court decided that the Incorporated Council of Law Reporting was a charitable body, on the grounds that it advanced education and other purposes beneficial to society. The fact that the reports may be used by members of the legal profession for their 'personal gain' was incidental to the main charitable purposes.

JUDGMENT

'In a case such as the present in which the object cannot be thought otherwise than beneficial to the community and of general public utility, I believe the proper question to ask is whether there are any grounds for holding it to be outside the equity of the statute; and I think the answer to that is here in the negative.'

Russell LJ

A second requirement for a trust to gain charitable status is that the entity exists for the public benefit, i.e. that it confers some tangible benefit to the public at large or a sufficiently wide section of the community. This feature distinguishes a charitable trust (public trust) from a private trust. In practice, the conferment of some tangible benefit was presumed to exist when the trust purpose fell within the first three categories of the *Pemsel* classification. With regard to the fourth category laid down in *Pemsel* the trustees were required to prove the existence of a benefit. The Charities Act 2011 has changed this practice.

From this brief outline of the pre-2011 law of charities three conclusions may be drawn:

- There was no statutory definition of a charity.
- A formidable body of case law on charitable purposes was built up over the centuries. This wealth of case law is still relevant in deciding charitable purposes today.
- It was perceived that a presumption existed in favour of public benefit concerning the first three heads of Lord Macnaghten's classification in *Pemsel*.

12.9 Public benefit or element

Section 2(1) of the Charities Act 2011 defines a 'charitable purpose' as a purpose that:

(a) falls within s 3(1) of the Act (see later); and

(b) also satisfies the definition of 'public benefit' as laid down in s 4 of the Act.

The effect is that a two-tier definition of charitable purposes has been adopted by the Act. We will first examine the concept of public benefit before embarking on a discussion of the 13 specific charitable purposes.

It must not be assumed that all public trusts will be treated as charitable: *Chichester Diocesan Fund v Simpson* [1944] AC 341 (see earlier) where a gift for 'charitable or benevolent purposes' failed as a charity because benevolent purposes, which were not charitable, were capable of deriving substantial benefits.

In order to qualify for charitable status the entity is required to promote a benefit to society within one or more of the purposes enacted within s 3 of the Charities Act 2011 (the benefit aspect) and the beneficiaries who are capable of enjoying the facility comprises the public or an appreciable section of the society (the public aspect), i.e. the public benefit test. In *Verge v Sommerville* [1924] AC 650, Lord Wrenbury commented on the public benefit requirement in the following manner:

JUDGMENT

'To ascertain whether a gift constitutes a valid charitable trust so as to escape being void on the ground of perpetuity, a first inquiry must be whether it is public – whether it is for the benefit of the community or of an appreciably important class of the community. The inhabitants of a parish or town, or any particular class of such inhabitants, may for instance, be the objects of such a gift, but private individuals, or a fluctuating body of private individuals, cannot.'

Lord Wrenbury

12.9.1 Public benefit

The 'public benefit' test is used as a means of distinguishing a public trust from a private trust. A public or charitable trust is required to exist for the benefit of the public (the community) or an appreciable section of society, with the exception of trusts for the relief of poverty. Section 4(3) of the 2011 Act consolidates the case law interpretation of the public benefit test that existed before the introduction of the Charities Act. Thus, the wealth of case law that existed over four centuries may still be relevant. Section 4(3) declares that 'any reference to the public benefit is a reference to the public benefit as that term is understood for the purposes of the law relating to charities in England and Wales'. This test incorporates two limbs.

The first requirement involves the usefulness of the activity to society ('the benefit or merit aspect'). Prior to the Charities Act 2011 a practical approach was adopted that *prima facie* assumed that public benefit to the community existed if the purpose was within the first three heads of the *Pemsel* classification (trusts for the relief of poverty and advancement of education and religion). This *prima facie* approach was assumed (incorrectly) to create a presumption which had, in any event, been abolished by s 4(2) of the Charities Act 2011. The effect is that all charitable purposes are put on an equal footing with the trustees being required to prove that the activity satisfies the test of usefulness to society within one or more of the stated purposes listed in the statute. In *Independent Schools Council v Charity Commission* [2011] UHUT 421, in judicial review proceedings, the Upper Tribunal decided that on a review of the cases there was no evidence that the courts had adopted a legal presumption with regard to public benefit. Instead, the approach of the courts, on a practical level, was to have regard to the purpose of the organisation in order to determine whether there was a correlation between the alleged charitable purpose and the public benefit aspect. The public benefit test would be satisfied if there was no cause for concern. But if there was any credible argument that this was not the case the court would require evidence to establish the public benefit test.

JUDGMENT

'[The judge] would start with a predisposition that an educational gift was for the benefit of the community; but he would look at the terms of the trust critically and if it appeared to him that the trust might not have the requisite element, his predisposition would be displaced so that evidence would be needed to establish public benefit. But if there was nothing to cause the judge to doubt his predisposition, he would be satisfied that the public element was present. This would not, however, be because of a presumption as that word is ordinarily understood; rather, it would be because the terms of the trust would speak for themselves, enabling the judge to conclude, as a matter of fact, that the purpose was for the public benefit.'

Warren J

In deciding whether the 'benefit aspect' is satisfied, the approach of the courts is to weigh up the benefits to society as against the adverse consequences to the public and determine whether the net balance of benefits is in favour of the public. In *Independent Schools Council v Charity Commission* (2011), Warren J expressed the point in the following manner:

JUDGMENT

'The court … has to balance the benefit and disadvantage in all cases where detriment is alleged and is supported by evidence. But great weight is to be given to a purpose which would, ordinarily, be charitable; before the alleged disadvantages can be given much weight, they need to be clearly demonstrated.'

Warren J

This principle may be illustrated by the House of Lords decision in *National Anti-Vivisection Society v IRC* [1948] AC 31. The court decided that a society whose main object was the abolition of vivisection was not charitable for its purpose was detrimental to medical science and was political in the sense that it involved a change in the law.

JUDGMENT

'There is not, so far as I can see, any difficulty in weighing the relative value of what it called the material benefits of vivisection against the moral benefit which is alleged or assumed as possibly following from the success of the appellant's project. In any case the position must be judged as a whole. It is arbitrary and unreal to attempt to dissect the problem into what is said to be direct and what is said to be merely consequential. The whole complex of resulting circumstances of whatever kind must be foreseen or imagined in order to estimate whether the change advocated would or would not be beneficial to the community.'

Lord Wright

The second requirement concerns the identification of the class of beneficiaries to be regarded as the public (the community) or an appreciable section of society. The satisfaction of the test is a question of law for the judge to decide on the evidence submitted to him. Further, the courts have decided this question in a flexible manner by reference to the description of the purposes of the entity within s 3(1) of the Charities Act 2011. In short, the public benefit test may be approached differently where the trust promotes education, relieves poverty or advances religion. In *Gilmour v Coats* [1949] AC 426, Lord Simonds expressed the point in the following manner:

JUDGMENT

'It is a trite saying that the law is life, not logic. But it is, I think, conspicuously true of the law of charity that it has been built up not logically but empirically. It would not, therefore, be surprising to find that, while in every category of legal charity some element of public benefit must be present, the court had not adopted the same measure in regard to different categories, but had accepted one standard in regard to those gifts which are alleged to be for the advancement of education and another for those which are alleged to be for the advancement of religion, and it may be yet another in regard to the relief of poverty. To argue by a method of syllogism or analogy from the category of education to that of religion ignores the historical process of the law.'

Lord Simonds

In *IRC v Baddeley* [1955] AC 572 (see below), a gift to promote recreation for a group of persons forming a class within a class did not satisfy the public benefit test. Lord Somervell expressed the flexible approach to the public benefit test, thus:

> I cannot accept the principle submitted by the respondents that a section of the public sufficient to support a valid trust in one category must as a matter of law be sufficient to support a trust in any other category. I think that difficulties are apt to arise if one seeks to consider the class apart from the particular nature of the charitable purpose. They are, in my opinion, interdependent. There might well be a valid trust for the promotion of religion benefiting a very small class. It would not at all follow that a recreation ground for the exclusive use of the same class would be a valid charity.

> Lord Somervell in *IRC v Baddeley* [1955] AC 572

In essence, this test will be satisfied if the potential beneficiaries of the trust are not numerically negligible and there is no personal bond or link between the donor and the intended beneficiaries, subject to the exception regarding trusts for the relief of poverty.

The policy that underpins the second limb of the public benefit test was laid down by Lord Simonds in *IRC v Baddeley* [1955] AC 572. The policy distinguishes between gifts that are limited for the benefit of a defined class of individuals on the one hand, and gifts that are available to the community as a whole, but may be enjoyed by those beneficiaries who are willing to avail themselves of the benefit. In this case, a trust in favour of Methodists in West Ham and Leyton failed the public element test because the beneficiaries were composed of a class within a class:

JUDGMENT

'[There is a] distinction between a form of relief accorded to the whole community yet by its very nature advantageous only to a few and a form of relief accorded to a selected few out of a larger number equally willing and able to take advantage of it … for example, a bridge which is available for all the public may undoubtedly be a charity and it is indifferent how many people use it. But confine its use to a selected number of persons, however numerous and important; it is then clearly not a charity. It is not of general public utility; for it does not serve the public purpose which its nature qualifies it to serve.'

Lord Simonds in *IRC v Baddeley*

In the provision of education, the public benefit test will not be satisfied if there is a personal nexus between the donor and the beneficiaries or between the beneficiaries themselves. The personal nexus may take the form of a 'blood' relationship. In *Re Compton* [1945] 1 All ER 198, the Court of Appeal decided that the test was not satisfied where the gift was on trust for the education of the children of three named relatives:

JUDGMENT

'I come to the conclusion, therefore, that on principle a gift under which the beneficiaries are defined by reference to a purely personal relationship to a named propositus cannot on principle be a valid charitable gift. And this, I think, must be the case whether the relationship be near or distant, whether it is limited to one generation or is extended to two or three or in perpetuity.'

Lord Greene MR

This test was approved and extended to a personal nexus by way of contract in *Oppenheim v Tobacco Securities Trust Co Ltd* [1951] AC 297, HL.

CASE EXAMPLE

Oppenheim v Tobacco Securities Trust Co Ltd [1951] AC 297, HL

Trustees were directed to apply moneys in providing for the education of employees or ex-employees of British American Tobacco or any of its subsidiary companies. The employees numbered 110,000. The court held that in view of the personal *nexus* between the employees themselves (being employed by the same employer), the public element test was not satisfied.

JUDGMENT

'[The] words section of the community have no special sanctity, but they conveniently indicate first, that the possible (I emphasise the word possible) beneficiaries must not be numerically negligible, and secondly, that the quality which distinguishes them from other members of the community, so that they form by themselves a section of it, must be a quality which does not depend on their relationship to a particular individual.'

Lord Simonds

Lord MacDermott dissented and expressed the view that although the 'common link' test was of some value, it ought not to be an overriding consideration, as the majority believed:

JUDGMENT

'If the bond between those employed by a particular railway is purely personal, why should the bond between those who are employed as railwaymen be essentially different? ... Are miners in the service of the National Coal Board now in one category and miners in a particular pit or of a particular district in another? Is the relationship between those in the service of the Crown to be distinguished from that obtaining between those of some other employer?'

Lord MacDermott

More recently, in *Dingle v Turner* [1972] AC 601, Lord Cross of Chelsea gave his support to this view.

There is some support for the view, albeit weak, that if the donor sets up a trust for the benefit of the public or a large section of the public, but expresses a preference (not amounting to an obligation) in favour of specified individuals, the gift is capable of satisfying the public element test.

CASE EXAMPLE

Re Koettgen's Will Trust [1954] Ch 252

A trust was created for the promotion and furtherance of the commercial education of British-born subjects, subject to a direction that preference be given to the employees of a company. The court decided that, on construction, the preference was intended as permitting, without obliging, the trustees to consider distributing the property in favour of the employees.

This decision had been criticised by the Privy Council in *Caffoor v Commissioners of Income Tax, Colombo* [1961] AC 584 as being in essence an 'employee trust' and 'had edged very near to being inconsistent with *Oppenheim*'s case'.

In *IRC v Educational-Grants Association Ltd* [1967] 3 WLR 341, the Court of Appeal refused to follow *Re Koettgen's Will Trust* (1954).

CASE EXAMPLE

IRC v Educational-Grants Association Ltd [1967] 3 WLR 341

An association was established for the advancement of education by, *inter alia*, making grants to individuals. Its principal source of income consisted of annual sums paid to it by Metal Box Ltd. About 85 per cent of the association's income during the relevant years was applied to the children of employees of Metal Box Ltd. The question in issue was whether the association was a charitable body. The Court of Appeal affirmed the decision of Pennycuick J and decided that the application of the high proportion of the income for the benefit of children connected with Metal Box Ltd was inconsistent with an application for charitable purposes.

JUDGMENT

'I find considerable difficulty in the *Re Koettgen* decision. I should have thought that a trust for the public with reference for a private class comprised in the public might be regarded as a trust for the application of income at the discretion of the trustees between charitable and non-charitable objects.'

Pennycuick J

In essence, the public element test will be satisfied if:

(i) the beneficiaries are not numerically negligible; and

(ii) the beneficiaries have no 'link' in contract or in blood between themselves or with a narrow group of individuals.

JUDGMENT

'To constitute a section of the public, the possible beneficiaries must not be numerically negligible and secondly, the quality which distinguishes them from other members of the community so that they form by themselves a section of it must be a quality which does not depend on their relationship to a particular individual … A group of persons may be numerous but, if the *nexus* between them is their personal relationship to a single proposition or to several propositus they are neither the community nor a section of the community for charitable purposes.'

Lord Simonds in *Oppenheim v Tobacco Securities Trust Co* (1951)

The 'numerical negligibility' test was applied in *Re Duffy* [2013] EWHC 2395, in the context of a gift to staff and residents of a residential home. The potential beneficiaries numbered 73. On construction, the court decided that the public benefit test was not satisfied and the gift failed as a charity.

Subject to the absence of a personal nexus between the beneficiaries and/or a limited class of individuals, the issue of whether or not the beneficiaries constitute a section of the public in order to satisfy the public element test is a question of degree. There are many decisions which appear to be inconsistent with each other. In *Gilmour v Coats* [1949] 1 All ER 848, HL, the court decided that a gift to a community of 20 cloistered nuns who devoted themselves to prayer and contemplation did not satisfy the public element test:

JUDGMENT

'The community [order of nuns] does not engage in – indeed, it is by its rules debarred from – any exterior work, such as teaching, nursing, or tending the poor, which distinguishes the active branches of the same order.'

Lord Simonds

On the other hand, in *Neville Estates Ltd v Madden* [1962] 1 Ch 832, the members of the Catford Synagogue were treated as an appreciable section of the public and satisfied the public element test because they integrated with the rest of society.

JUDGMENT

'The two cases [*Gilmour v Coats* and *Neville Estates v Madden*], however, differ from one another in that the members of the Catford Synagogue spend their lives in the world, whereas the members of a Carmelite Priory live secluded from the world.'

Cross J

In *Re Lewis* [1954] 3 All ER 257, a gift to 10 blind boys and 10 blind girls in Tottenham was charitable. But in *Williams' Trustees v IRC* [1947] AC 447, HL, a gift in order to create an institute in London for the promotion of Welsh culture failed as a charity:

JUDGMENT

'I doubt whether the public benefit test could be satisfied if the beneficiaries are a class of persons not only confined to a particular area but selected from within the area by reference to a particular creed … the persons to be benefited must be the whole community, or all the inhabitants of a particular area. Not a class within a class.'

Lord Simonds

The same principle was applied in *IRC v Baddeley* (1955) (see above).

In 2008, the Charity Commission published guidelines on the public benefit requirement and declared that the test will not be satisfied, as stated in paras 2(b) and (c) of the guide, if the provision of the benefit is determined by the ability to pay fees charged and excludes people in poverty. In *Independent Schools Council v Charity Commission* [2011] UKUT 421, the Upper Tribunal, in judicial review proceedings, decided that the Charity Commission guidelines were defective and ought to be quashed in respect of paras 2(b) and (c) as stated above. The issue in the proceedings concerned the accuracy of the Charity Commission's published guidelines on the public benefit requirement and its application to fee-paying independent schools. Charitable independent schools would fail to act for the public benefit if they failed to provide some benefit for its potential beneficiaries, other than its fee-paying students. The Upper Tribunal decided that it was a matter for the trustees to decide how their obligations might be fulfilled. Benefits for potential beneficiaries who may not have the capacity to pay the full fees for their education may be provided in a variety of ways including, for example, the remission of all or partial fees to 'poor' students and the sharing of educational facilities with the maintained sector.

As a result of the judgment in the *Independent Schools Council* case, the Charity Commission modified its guidelines on public benefit. The salient points in the guidelines include the following:

- There are two aspects of public benefit – the 'benefit' and 'public' aspects.
- The 'benefit aspect' involves an inquiry as to whether the trust purposes comply with one or more of the 13 purposes laid down in s 2 of the Charities Act 2011, and any detriment or harm that results from the purpose does not outweigh the benefit. The benefit is required to be identifiable and capable of being proved, where necessary. In some cases the purpose may be so clearly beneficial that there may be little need for trustees to provide evidence of this.
- The 'public aspect' concerns those who may benefit from the funds of the trust and is required to be the public in general, or a sufficient section of the public. There is no set minimum number of persons who may comprise a sufficient section of the public. This issue is decided on a case-by-case basis and the approach is not the same for every purpose. With the exception of trusts for the relief or prevention of poverty, the test will not be satisfied if the beneficiaries are identified by reference to their family relationship, employment by an employer or membership of an unincorporated association.

12.9.2 Public benefit and poverty exception

Before the introduction of the Charities Act 2011 (or the Charities Act 2006, which was consolidated in the 2011 Act) the courts adhered to the view that trusts for the relief of poverty were exempt from the public benefit test. Trusts for the relief of poverty are charitable even though the beneficiaries are linked *inter se* or with an individual or small group of individuals. In short, it is arguable that trusts for the relief of poverty are not subject to the strict public benefit test. The practice of the courts has always been to exclude such trusts from the public benefit test.

The justification for this exception or exemption is that the creation of such trusts is prompted by motives of altruism with inherently public benefit characteristics, see Lord Greene's judgment in *Re Compton* [1945] Ch 123:

JUDGMENT

'There may perhaps be some special quality in gifts for the relief of poverty which places them in a class by themselves. It may, for instance, be that the relief of poverty is to be regarded as in itself so beneficial to the community that the fact that the gift is confined to a specified family can be disregarded.'

Lord Greene

Accordingly, in *Gibson v South American Stores Ltd* [1950] Ch 177 and *Dingle v Turner* [1972] AC 601, the courts decided that gifts in order to relieve the poverty of employees of a company were charitable.

JUDGMENT

'[C]ounsel for the appellant hardly ventured to suggest that we overrule the poor relations cases. His submission was that which was accepted by the Court of Appeal for Ontario in *In Re Cox* [1951] OR 205 – namely that while the poor relations cases might have to be left as long-standing anomalies there was no good reason for sparing the poor employees cases which only date from *In Re Gosling* [1900] 48 WR 300, and which have been under suspicion ever since the decision in *In Re Compton*. But the poor members and the poor employees decisions were a natural development of the poor relations decisions and to draw a distinction between different sorts of poverty trusts would be quite illogical and could certainly not be said to be introducing greater harmony into the law of charity. Moreover, though not as old as the poor relations trusts poor employees trusts have been recognised as charities for many years; there are now a large number of such trusts in existence; and assuming, as one must, that they are properly administered in the sense that benefits under them are only given to people who can fairly be said to be, according to current standards, poor persons, to treat such trusts as charities is not open to any practical objection. So it seems to me it must be accepted that wherever else it may hold sway the *Compton* rule has no application in the field of trusts for the relief of poverty.'

Lord Cross

At the same time, the courts have drawn a subtle distinction between private trusts for the relief of poverty and public trusts for the same purpose. The distinction has been expressed as a private trust for identifiable individuals with the motive of relieving poverty, and a charitable trust in order to relieve poverty amongst a class of persons; for example a gift for the settlor's poor relations, A, B and C, may not be charitable but may exist as a private trust, whereas a gift for the benefit of the settlor's poor relations without identifying them may be charitable. It appears that the distinction between the two types of trust lies in the degree of precision in which the objects have been identified. The more precise the language used by the settlor in identifying the poor relations, the stronger the risk of failure as a charitable trust. This is a question of degree.

CASE EXAMPLE

Re Scarisbrick [1951] Ch 622, CA

A bequest was made on trust 'for such relations of my said son and daughters as in the opinion of the survivor shall be in needy circumstances'. The court held that the gift was charitable.

JUDGMENT

'[T]he true question in each case [is] whether the gift was for the relief of poverty amongst a class of persons, or rather … a particular description of poor, or was merely a gift to individuals, albeit with relief of poverty amongst those individuals as the motive of the gift … It should be added that the class of beneficiaries falls to be ascertained at the death of the survivor of the three children, not at the testatrix's death. Thus, the class of beneficiaries is so extensive as to be incapable of being exhaustively ascertained and includes persons who the testatrix may never have seen or heard of.'

Jenkins LJ

The court came to a similar conclusion in *Re Segelman* [1996] 2 WLR 173. Chadwick J was influenced by the fact that the class of 'poor and needy' relatives was not closed on the date of the testator's death. The list of beneficiaries included six named members of the testator's family and the issue (unnamed) of five of them who were 'poor and needy', provided that they were born within 21 years following the death of the testator. There were 26 persons within the class. The court decided that the gift was charitable for the relief of poverty.

JUDGMENT

'*Prima facie*, a gift for the benefit of poor and needy persons is a gift for the relief of poverty … [and] is no less charitable because those whose poverty is to be relieved are confined to a particular class limited by ties of blood or employment: see *In Re Scarisbrick* [1951] Ch 622; and *Dingle v Turner* [1972] AC 601. The gift with which I am concerned has, in common with the gift which the Court of Appeal had to consider in *Re Scarisbrick*, the feature that the class of those eligible to benefit was not closed upon the testator's death. It remained open for a further period of 21 years. During that period issue of the named individuals born after the death of the testator will become members of the class. It is, in my view, impossible to attribute to the testator an intention to make a gift to those after-born issue as such. His intention must be taken to have been the relief of poverty amongst the class of which they would become members.'

Chadwick J

The position today is that there is an element of ambiguity as to whether trusts for the relief of poverty are subject to a different test of public benefit since the introduction of the Charities Act 2011 (or its predecessor, the Charities Act 2006). On the one hand, no such concession has been enacted in s 4 of the 2011 Act and any presumptions regarding public benefit have been abolished. On the other hand, s 4(3) consolidates the common law meaning of public benefit and declares that 'any reference to the public benefit is a reference to the public benefit as that term is understood'. The Charity Commission and the Attorney General's office are concerned that the law on public benefit may have been modified by statute, but recognise that it is only a question of time before the courts consider the issue. The possible outcomes are:

(a) The law has been changed and trusts for the relief of poverty are subject to the rigorous public benefit test.

(b) The law has not been modified and a special approach to the public benefit test in the context of trusts for the relief of poverty remains.

(c) A third approach is that the law in this context has been changed, not retrospectively, but only from the date that the Charities Act 2006 came into force, namely 1 April 2008. The provisions of the Charities Act 2006 were consolidated in the Charities Act 2011. The effect may be that the funds of charitable trusts for the relief of poverty that existed before 1 April 2008 which contain a 'personal nexus' may be applied *cy-près*.

However, in *Attorney General v Charity Commission* [2012] WTLR 977, the Upper Tribunal allayed fears that the public benefit test applicable to trusts for the relief of poverty has been modified by the Charities Act. The Upper Tribunal clarified this area of the law on the test of public benefit. The Upper Tribunal ruled that the pre-2008 approach of the courts is still relevant and applicable today to determine whether the public benefit test for the relief of poverty is satisfied.

The *Attorney General v Charity Commission* case involved a non-adversarial reference by the Attorney General. The Upper Tribunal published its opinion on the public benefit requirement that is applicable to charitable trusts for the relief of poverty. The Tribunal decided:

(i) Where a trust for the relief of poverty is limited, owing to a personal nexus, by reference to a class of individuals, their employment by a commercial company, or their membership of an unincorporated association, the trust was nevertheless capable of satisfying the public benefit test.

(ii) Such trusts are not automatically treated as charitable but the approach is based on whether the evidence satisfies the dual nature test for public benefit.

(iii) The abolition of the presumption of public benefit by statute will have no impact on whether a trust for the relief of poverty is charitable or not.

(iv) In deciding whether a trust satisfied the public benefit test in the pre-Charities Act era, the courts had proceeded not by way of presumption, but on the evidence that existed on the facts of each case.

(v) There was no real distinction between the expressions 'prevention' and 'relief' of poverty, as used in the Charities Act 2011.

In 2013 the Charity Commission published its guidelines on the public benefit requirement and affirmed that trusts for the relief of poverty were subject to a broader set of rules. The public benefit requirement may be met by satisfying the 'benefit' aspect only. Accordingly, trusts for the relief of poverty may satisfy the public benefit test where the beneficiaries are defined by reference to their family relationship, employment by an employer or membership of an unincorporated association. But the test will not be satisfied if the beneficiaries comprise a group of named individuals.

12.9.3 Classification of charitable purposes

Prior to the introduction of the Charities Act 2006 (consolidated in the Charities Act 2011), a useful classification of the charitable purposes, laid down in the preamble to the Charitable Uses Act 1601 (see earlier), was adopted by Lord Macnaghten in *IRC v Pemsel* (1891), as follows:

(a) the relief of poverty;

(b) the advancement of education;

(c) the advancement of religion; and

(d) other purposes beneficial to the community.

It must be emphasised that Lord Macnaghten's statement did not constitute a definition of charitable purposes but merely a classification of the purposes within the preamble. In short, prior to the Charities Act 2006, there was no comprehensive definition of charitable purposes. The purposes stated in the preamble (albeit obsolete) were the closest to a definition of charitable purposes. It became the practice of the courts to refer back to the preamble or precedents decided in accordance with the purposes within the preamble or indeed the 'spirit' (or flavour) of the preamble.

There is no doubt that the classification of charitable purposes and approaches of the courts have provided a degree of flexibility that has allowed the meaning of charity to adapt to the changing needs and expectations of society. However, the four heads of charity provide little effective guidance to the public about what is a charitable purpose. The classification of charitable purposes by Lord Macnaghten is a vague indication of some charitable activities. Charitable purposes extend beyond education, religion and relief of the poor. Indeed, but for the creative approach of the courts, as evidenced by the multitude of judicial decisions, the law of charities would have been in a state of disarray. This state of affairs prompted Lord Sterndale MR in *Re Tetley* [1923] 1 Ch 258 to express his dissatisfaction at being unable to find any guidance as to what constitutes a charitable purpose:

JUDGMENT

'I am unable to find any principle which will guide one easily and safely through the tangle of cases as to what is and what is not a charitable gift. If it is possible I hope sincerely that at some time or other a principle will be laid down.'

Lord Sterndale MR

Section 3 of the Charities Act 2011 addresses some of these limitations by adopting a statutory definition of 'charitable purposes'. This is achieved by reference to a two-step approach – the listing or identification of a variety of charitable purposes, and the public benefit test. This is the first-ever statutory definition of a charity. Section 3(1) contains a list of some 13 charitable purposes – 12 specific descriptions of charitable purposes and a general provision designed to maintain flexibility in the law of charities. The charitable purposes enacted are intended to be a comprehensive list of charitable activities. Most of these purposes, in any event, were charitable before the Act was introduced. These purposes are:

(a) the prevention or relief of poverty;

(b) the advancement of education;

(c) the advancement of religion;

(d) the advancement of health (including the prevention or relief of sickness, disease or human suffering);

(e) the advancement of citizenship or community development;

(f) the advancement of the arts, heritage or science;

(g) the advancement of amateur sport (games which promote health by involving physical or mental skill or exertion);

(h) the advancement of human rights, conflict resolution or reconciliation;

(i) the advancement of environmental protection or improvement;

(j) the relief of those in need, by reason of youth, age, ill-health, disability, financial hardship or other disadvantage (including the provision of accommodation and care to the beneficiaries mentioned within this clause);

(k) the advancement of animal welfare;

(l) the promotion of the efficiency of the armed forces of the Crown, or of the efficiency of the police, fire and rescue services or ambulance services;

(m) any other purposes (the residual category).

With the exception of amateur sport, arguably, all of these purposes were charitable under the law that existed before the 2011 Act, as illustrated by the wealth of case law.

Section 3(3) endorses the common law approach to charitable objects by reference to the purposes declared in paragraphs (a) to (l) above. This is done by determining whether a purpose has some resemblance to an example as stated in the preamble, or to an earlier decided case that was considered charitable. In these cases the same meaning will be attributable to the term. Section 3(3) of the 2011 Act states that 'where any of the terms used in any of the paragraphs (a) to (l) ... has a particular meaning under the law relating to charities in England and Wales, the term is to be taken as having the same meaning where it appears in that provision'.

Section 3(1)(m)(i)–(iii) consolidates the common law approach to the residual category of charitable purposes.

SECTION

'Other purposes –

(i) that are not within paragraphs (a) to (l) but are recognised as charitable purposes by virtue of section 5 (recreational and similar trusts, etc.) or under the old law;

(ii) that may reasonably be regarded as analogous to, or within the spirit of, any purposes falling within any of the paragraphs (a) to (l) ...;

(iii) that may reasonably be regarded as analogous to, or within the spirit of, any purposes which have been recognised, under the law relating to charities in England and Wales, as falling within sub-paragraph (ii) or this paragraph.'

This subsection affirms the pre-2008 (the date that the Charities Act 2006 came into force) broad approach to purposes within the fourth heading of the *Pemsel* classification as summarised by Lord Wilberforce in *Scottish Burial Reform and Cremation Society v City of Glasgow Corporation* [1968] AC 138, including the 'spirit' of charitable purposes, thus:

JUDGMENT

'The purposes in question, to be charitable, must be shown to be for the benefit of the public, or the community, in a sense or manner within the intendment of the preamble to the [Charitable Uses Act 1601]. The latter requirement does not mean quite what it says; for it is now accepted that what must be regarded is not the wording of the preamble itself, but the effect of decisions given by the court as to its scope, decisions which have endeavoured to keep the law as to charities moving according as new social needs arise or old ones become obsolete or satisfied.'

Lord Wilberforce

12.9.4 Consideration of the charitable purposes

Category 1: the prevention or relief of poverty

Section 3(1)(a) of the Charities Act 2011 enacts that the 'prevention or relief of poverty' is capable of being a charitable purpose. As stated earlier, this description consolidates the common law approach. Very little turns on the distinction between 'prevention' and 'relief'. Lord Macnaghten in *Pemsel*, in classifying charitable purposes, referred to trusts for the 'relief' of poverty but case law and the Charity Commission drew no distinction between 'prevention' and 'relief'. Accordingly, trusts for the provision of the basic essentials of life, agriculture, irrigation and shelter in order to prevent an impending natural disaster are as much charitable as dealing with the consequences of such disasters.

'Poverty' includes destitution but is not interpreted so narrowly as to mean destitution. It connotes that the beneficiaries are in straitened circumstances and unable to maintain a modest standard of living (determined objectively).

The Charity Commission in its report in December 2008 explained the concept of poverty:

QUOTATION

'The expression, "people in poverty" does not just include people who are destitute, but also those who cannot satisfy a basic need without assistance. The courts have avoided setting an absolute criteria to be met in order for poverty to be said to exist, although they have been prepared to state in specific cases whether or not a particular level of income or assets meant that a person was "poor". In essence, "people in poverty" generally refers to people who lack something in the nature of necessity or quasi-necessity, which the majority of the population would regard as necessary for a modest, but adequate standard of living.'

CASE EXAMPLE

Re Coulthurst [1951] Ch 661, CA

A bequest of £20,000 to trustees was subject to the direction that the income be paid to the widows and orphans of deceased officers and ex-officers of Coutts & Co, as the trustees may decide the most deserving of such assistance, having regard to their financial circumstances. The court decided that, on construction of the terms of the gift, the gift was charitable for the relief of poverty.

JUDGMENT

'Poverty does not mean destitution; it is a word of wide and somewhat indefinite import; it may not unfairly be paraphrased for present purposes as meaning persons who have to go short in the ordinary acceptation of that term, due regard being had to their status in life and so forth.'

Evershed MR

In addition, the gift is required to relieve the misery of poverty by providing the basic necessities of human existence – food, shelter and clothing. The expression 'relief' signifies that the beneficiaries have a need attributable to their condition which requires alleviating and which the beneficiaries may find difficulty in alleviating from their own resources.

In *Biscoe v Jackson* (1887) 25 Ch D 460, a gift to establish a soup kitchen in Shoreditch was construed as a valid charitable trust for the relief of poverty. Likewise, in *Shaw v Halifax Corporation* [1915] 2 KB 170 it was decided that a home for ladies in reduced circumstances was charitable. Similarly, in *Re Clarke* [1923] 2 Ch 407 a gift to provide a nursing home for persons of moderate means was charitable. But a gift for the 'working classes' does not necessarily connote poverty: see *Re Saunders' Will Trust* [1954] Ch 265, although a gift for the construction of a 'working men's hostel' was construed as charitable under this head: see *Re Niyazi's Will Trust* [1978] 1 WLR 910.

JUDGMENT

'The word hostel has to my mind a strong flavour of a building which provides somewhat modest accommodation for those who have some temporary need for it and are willing to accept accommodation of that standard in order to meet the need. When hostel is prefixed by the expression working men's, then the further restriction is introduced of this hostel being intended for those with a relatively low income who work for their living, especially as manual workers.'

Megarry VC in *Re Niyazi*

Under this head of poverty, it is essential that all the objects fall within the designation 'poor'. If someone who is not poor is able to benefit significantly from the funds, the gift will fail as not being one for the relief of poverty. In *Re Gwyon* [1930] 1 Ch 225, a trust to provide free trousers for boys resident in Farnham was not charitable because there was no restriction to the effect that the boys were required to be poor.

Relief of poverty may be provided directly for the intended beneficiaries, and includes: apprenticing poor children, see *AG v Minshull* (1798) 4 Ves 11; the provision of allotments or buying land to be let to the poor at a low rent, see *Crafton v Firth* (1851) 4 De G & Sm 237; the provision of cheap flats to be let to aged persons of small means at rents that they can afford to pay, see *Re Cottam* [1955] 1 WLR 1299; gifts for the establishment or support of institutions for the benefit of particular classes of poor persons such as railway servants, see *Hull v Derby Sanitary Authority* (1885) 16 QBD 163; and policemen, see *Re Douglas* (1887) 35 Ch D 472. Relief may be provided indirectly, such as providing accommodation for relatives coming from a distance to visit patients critically ill in hospital, see *Re Dean's Will Trust* [1950] 1 All ER 882; a home of rest for nurses at a particular hospital, see *Re White's Will Trust* [1951] 1 All ER 528.

As stated earlier, the approach of the courts to the public benefit test has been fairly relaxed in this context.

Category 2: the advancement of education

Section 3(1)(b) of the Charities Act 2011 identifies the advancement of education as a charitable purpose. This classification originates from the preamble to the 1601 Act, which refers to 'the maintenance of schools of learning, free schools and scholars in universities'.

The Charity Commission in its Guide for Consultation, published in March 2008, identified many forms of education.

QUOTATION

'Education today includes:

- formal education;
- community education;
- physical education and development of young people;
- training (including vocational training) and life-long learning;
- research and adding to collective knowledge and understanding of specific areas of study and expertise;
- the development of individual capabilities, competencies, skills and understanding.'

Charity Commission 2008

'Education' has been interpreted generously and is not restricted to the classroom mode of disseminating knowledge, but requires some element of instruction or supervision. Thus, research is capable of being construed as the provision of education.

CASE EXAMPLE

Re Hopkins' Will Trust [1964] 3 All ER 46

Money was bequeathed to the Francis Bacon Society, to be used to search for the manuscripts of plays commonly ascribed to Shakespeare but believed by the Society to have been written by Bacon. The court decided that the gift was for the advancement of education. The discovery of such manuscripts would be of the highest value to history and literature.

JUDGMENT

'The word education must be used in a wide sense, certainly extending beyond teaching, and the requirement is that, in order to be charitable, research must either be of educational value to the researcher or must be so directed as to lead to something which will pass into the store of educational material, or so as to improve the sum of communicable knowledge in an area which education may cover – education in this last context extending to the formation of literary taste and appreciation.'

Wilberforce J

More recently, Slade J in *McGovern v AG* [1981] 3 All ER 493 summarised the principles governing research:

JUDGMENT

'(i) A trust will ordinarily qualify as a charitable trust if, but only if, (a) the subject matter of the proposed research is a useful object of study; and (b) it is contemplated that the knowledge acquired as a result of the research will be disseminated to others; and (c) the trust is for the benefit of the public, or a sufficiently important section of the public.

(ii) In the absence of a contrary context, however, the court will be readily inclined to construe a trust for research as importing subsequent dissemination of the results thereof.

(iii) Furthermore, if a trust for research is to constitute a valid trust for the advancement of education, it is not necessary either (a) that the teacher/pupil relationship should be in contemplation, or (b) that the persons to benefit from the knowledge to be acquired should be persons who are already in the course of receiving "education" in the conventional sense.'

Slade J

On the other hand, the mere acquisition of knowledge without dissemination or advancement will not be charitable. The emphasis here is on the publication or sharing of the information or knowledge.

CASE EXAMPLE

Re Shaw; Public Trustee v Day [1957] 1 All ER 745

The testator, George Bernard Shaw, bequeathed money to be used to develop a 40-letter alphabet and translate his play *Androcles and the Lion* into this alphabet. The court held that the gift was not charitable, as it was aimed merely at the increase of knowledge.

JUDGMENT

'The research and propaganda enjoined by the testator seem to me merely to tend to the increase of public knowledge in a certain respect, namely, the saving of time and money by the use of the proposed alphabet. There is no element of teaching or education combined with this, nor does the propaganda element in the trusts tend to more than to persuade the public that the adoption of the new script would be a good thing, and that, in my view, is not education.'

Harman J

Gifts which have been upheld as charitable under this head have included: trusts for choral singing in London (*Royal Choral Society v IRC* [1943] 2 All ER 101); the diffusion of knowledge of Egyptology and the training of students in Egyptology (*Re British School of Egyptian Archaeology* [1954] 1 All ER 887); the encouragement of chess playing by boys or young men resident in the city of Portsmouth (*Re Dupree's Trusts* [1944] 2 All ER 443); the furtherance of the Boy Scout movement by helping to purchase sites for camping (*Re Webber* [1954] 3 All ER 712); the promotion of the education of the Irish by teaching self-control, elocution, oratory, deportment and the arts of personal contact and social intercourse (*Re Shaw's Will Trust* [1952] 1 All ER 712); the publication of law reports which record the development of judge-made law (*Incorporated Council of Law Reporting for England and Wales v AG* [1971] 3 All ER 1029); the promotion of the works of a famous composer (*Re Delius' Will Trust* [1957] 1 All ER 854) or celebrated writer (*Re Shakespeare Memorial Trust* [1923] 2 Ch 389); the students' union of a university (*Baldry v Feintuck* [1972] 2 All ER 81); the furtherance of the Wilton Park project, i.e. a conference centre for discussion of matters of international importance (*Re Koeppler's Will Trust* [1986] Ch 423); the provision of facilities at schools and universities to play association football or other games (*IRC v McMullen* [1981] AC 1); and professional bodies which exist for the promotion of the arts or sciences (*Royal College of Surgeons of England v National Provincial Bank Ltd* [1952] 1 All ER 984). Many of these purposes will now overlap with other specified purposes laid down in the Charities Act 2006.

Before deciding whether the gifts are charitable or not, the courts are required to take into account the usefulness of the gifts to the public. This may be effected by judicial notice of the value of the gift to society. In the event of doubt, the courts may take into account the opinions of experts. The opinions of the donors are inconclusive. In *Re Pinion* [1965] Ch 85, a gift to the National Trust of a studio and contents to be maintained as a collection failed as a charity. The collection as a whole lacked any artistic merit. The judge could conceive of no useful purpose in foisting on the public this 'mass of junk'.

'The law on
charitable trusts
involves a vast
array of cases and
literature, with a
good starting
point being the
Preamble to the
Statute of
Elizabeth 1601
and culminating in
the Charities Act
2006.'

The promotion of education of a political nature will be subject to the process of construction by the courts to ascertain the primary purpose of the gift. If the main object is political the gift will fail as a charity. But if the political element is subsidiary to the main political objective the gift will be valid.

In *Buxton v Public Trustee* (1962) TC 235, the trust was designed to promote and aid the improvement of international relations and intercourse by various prescribed methods. The court held that the trust was not charitable because its objects were 'public utility or political'. Whereas, in *Re Koeppler's Will Trust* [1986] Ch 423 the gift created a valid charitable trust. In this case the gift was to create 'Wilton Park', i.e. a conference centre for participants who were capable of influencing opinion in Member States of the Organisation for Economic Co-operation and Development. The court decided that, on construction of the objects of the centre, there was no question of the conferences being intended to further the interests of political parties, or to procure changes in the law or government policy of any country. Even when the conferences touched on political issues they constituted no more than genuine attempts to ascertain and disseminate the truth, see the judgment of Slade LJ.

JUDGMENT

'In the present case, the activities of Wilton Park are not of a party political nature. Nor, so far as the evidence shows, are they designed to procure changes in the laws or government policy of this or any other country: even when they touch on political matter, they constitute, so far as I can see, no more than genuine attempts in an objective manner to ascertain and disseminate the truth. In these circumstances I think that no objections to the trust arise on a political score. The trust is, in my opinion, entitled to what is sometimes called a "benignant construction", in the sense that the court is entitled to presume that the trustees will only act in a lawful and proper manner appropriate to the trustees of a charity and not, for example, by the propagation of tendentious political opinions.'

Slade LJ

The advancement of amateur sport is now a charitable head in its own right under s 3(1)(g) of the Charities Act 2011. Before this classification of charitable purpose was introduced, it was recognised that the provision of sport *simpliciter* was not a charitable purpose (see *Re Nottage* [1895] 2 Ch 649, yacht racing), but the provision of sport within schools was an essential part of the educational curriculum. Accordingly, in *Re Mariette* [1915] 2 Ch 284, the court decided that the provision of five squash courts within a school was charitable. Likewise, in *IRC v McMullen* [1981], the provision of football within schools and universities was considered to be charitable for the advancement of education.

Public benefit

The public benefit test was considered earlier. It may be recalled that in the context of the advancement of education, the requirement is that the facilities are provided for the benefit of members of the public as a whole, or a sufficiently large section of society. A personal nexus in contract, provided by an employer, or in blood, by a relative, will be detrimental to the public benefit test. This is still the position today.

The Charity Commission published its guidance in 2008 on the public benefit test and fee paying schools, but was considered by the Upper Tribunal in *Independent Schools Council v Charity Commission* (2011) to be defective and a modified form of the guidance was published in 2013. However, the Upper Tribunal in the *Independent Schools Council* case decided the following matters:

- Public benefit is composed of two aspects – a purpose beneficial to the community and the public aspect, i.e. benefits being available to the public or a sufficient section of the public.

- The abolition of the presumption of public benefit in respect of some purposes, as laid down in s 4(2) of the 2011 Act, is otiose because there was no evidence that the courts proceeded by way of presumptions.

- Neither the court nor the Charity Commission may determine whether the public benefit in the first sense provided by independent schools was outweighed by the dis-benefits arising from charging fees. This is a matter to be determined by the trustees.

- A trust whose purposes exclude the poor cannot be charitable. Thus, a school with the sole purpose of educating children whose parents may afford to pay the fees is not charitable.

- To be classified as a charity a fee charging school must provide education that does not exclude the poor.

- The benefits that are provided for the poor must exceed the *de minimis* limit or merely token advantages.

- The provision of scholarships and bursaries to students who may not be able to pay the full fees will satisfy the test of public benefit.

Category 3: the advancement of religion

This purpose has been endorsed in s 3(1)(c) of the Charities Act 2011 and clarifies the common law with regard to polytheistic religions and religions that do not involve belief in God.

The preamble to the 1601 Statute refers to 'the repair of churches'. English law steers a neutral course between all forms of religions. 'Religion' is defined in the *Oxford Dictionary* as a 'recognition on the part of man of some higher unseen power as having control of his destiny and as being entitled to obedience, reverence and worship' or 'a particular system of faith and worship'. There is not a great deal of case law recognising non-Christian religions (although Judaism has been recognised in *Strauss v Goldsmith* (1837) 8 Sim 614 and *Neville Estates v Madden* [1962] Ch 832), but regulations made under the Charities Act 1993 (and its predecessor) assume that non-Christian religions are charitable. The Goodman Report (1976) declared that account must be taken of all religions, whether monotheistic or not.

However, in *Re South Place Ethical Society* [1980] 1 WLR 1565, it was decided that the study and dissemination of ethical principles, but which did not involve faith in a deity, did not fall within the definition of religion. But the society was charitable on the ground of advancement of education. The court limited its approach to theistic religions only. In theory this could have had an adverse effect on religions, such as Buddhism, which does not involve belief in God:

JUDGMENT

'Religion, as I see it, is concerned with man's relations with God and ethics is concerned with man's relation with man. The two are not the same and are not made the same by sincere inquiry into the question: What is God? If reason leads people not to accept Christianity or any known religion, but they do believe in the excellence of qualities such as truth, beauty and love, their beliefs may be to them the equivalent of a religion but viewed objectively they are not religion.'

Dillon J

In a multi-cultural society with a diverse set of beliefs it was expedient to embrace an 'all inclusive' description of religion so as not to alienate sections of society. This was achieved by statute. Section 3(2)(a) of the Charities Act 2011 partially defines religion as including 'a religion which involves belief in more than one god and a religion which does not involve belief in god'. This would include a polytheistic religion such as Hinduism. Buddhism, which does not involve a belief in God, is universally regarded as a religion and will be treated as a religion under the English law of charities. In *R v Registrar General of Births, Deaths and Marriages* [2014] AC 610, the Supreme Court decided that the Church of Scientology was a place for religious worship and that Scientology was properly to be regarded as a religion. The tenets of Scientology involve belief in and worship of a Supreme Being or Creator. Understanding of the Creator was attainable only through spiritual enlightenment and the goal of Scientology was to help its members to obtain such enlightenment. The justification for broadening the scope of religion was stated by Lord Toulson JSC, thus:

JUDGMENT

'[R]eligion should not be confined to religions which recognise a supreme deity. First and foremost, to do so would be a form of religious discrimination unacceptable in today's society. It would exclude Buddhism, along with other faiths such as Jainism, Taoism, Theosophy and part of Hinduism. The evidence in the present case shows that, among others, Jains, Theosophists and Buddhists have registered places of worship in England. Further, to confine religion which involves belief in a supreme deity leads into difficult theological territory … Scientologists do believe in a supreme deity of a kind, but of an abstract and impersonal nature. Ideas about the nature of God are the stuff of theological debate.'

Lord Toulson JSC

In *R v Registrar General of Births, Deaths and Marriages* the Supreme Court recognised how difficult it was to attempt a definition of religion. Instead, the court offered a description of the concept that is consistent with the modern view of religion:

JUDGMENT

'I would describe religion in summary as a spiritual or non-secular belief system, held by a group of adherents, which claims to explain mankind's place in the universe and relationship with the infinite, and to teach its adherents how they are to live their lives in conformity with the spiritual understanding associated with the belief system. By spiritual or non-secular I mean a belief system which goes beyond that which can be perceived by the senses or ascertained by the application of science. Such a belief system may or may not involve belief in a supreme being, but it does involve a belief that there is more to be understood about mankind's nature and relationship to the universe than can be gained from the senses or from science. I emphasise that this is intended to be a description and not a definitive formula.'

Lord Toulson JSC

In any event, a body such as the Freemasons Society, whose rules demand the highest personal and social standards, does not constitute a religion: see *United Grand Lodge of Freemasons in England and Wales v Holborn Borough Council* [1957] 1 WLR 1090. The objects of the lodge did not seek to organise religious instruction, or hold religious services or be engaged in pastoral or missionary work of any kind. Likewise, in principle, a trust to demonstrate that religious belief is erroneous will not be charitable under this head.

Unlike trusts for the advancement of education, the courts do not evaluate the merit of one religion as opposed to another or indeed the benefit to the public of religious instruction. Provided that the religious gift is not subversive of all morality, the gift will be charitable.

CASE EXAMPLE

Thornton v Howe [1862] 31 Beav 14

A trust was created for the publication of the writings of Joanna Southcote who believed that she would miraculously conceive and give birth, at an advanced age, to the second Messiah. Although the judge thought that she was foolish, deluded and confused, he held that the gift was charitable.

Similarly, in *Re Watson* [1973] 3 All ER 678, the court decided that a gift to publish the religious works of Hobbs (which had no intrinsic value) was charitable:

JUDGMENT

'[P]rovided that the purposes are not immoral, then, even though the courts might consider the relevant opinions as foolish and devoid of foundation, or not capable of leading to moral improvement, the gift remains charitable as being for the advancement of religion.'

Plowman

Moreover, the institution or association is required to promote or advance religion. This was considered by Donovan J in *United Grand Lodge of Freemasons in England and Wales v Holborn Borough Council* (1957):

JUDGMENT

'To advance religion means to promote it, to spread its message ever wider among mankind; to take some positive steps to sustain and increase religious belief; and these things are done in a variety of ways which may be comprehensively described as pastoral and missionary. It should include religious instruction, a programme for the persuasion of unbelievers, religious supervision to see that its members remain active and constant in the various religions they may profess.'

Donovan J

Religion may be advanced in a variety of ways, such as the maintenance of places of worship including the upkeep of churchyards, gifts for the clergy, the provision of an organ or maintenance of a choir and the active spread of religion at home and abroad, although a gift for 'parish work' will be void as including many objects within the parish which are not charitable (*Farley v Westminster Bank* [1939] 3 All ER 491). Whereas, a gift to an officer of the church in his official capacity (the vicar), to be applied in his absolute discretion, may be construed as imposing an implied limitation for ecclesiastical purposes (*Re Garrard* [1907] 1 Ch 382). A gift for the saying of masses in public is charitable because *inter alia* the gift increases the stipend of priests (*Re Caus* [1934] Ch 162). Moreover, a gift for the saying of masses *simpliciter* is presumed to require masses to be said in public and therefore charitable (*Re Hetherington* [1989] 2 All ER 129). In addition, in *Funnell v Stewart* [1996] 1 WLR 288, the promotion of faith healing, within limits, was considered to be a charitable activity.

Public benefit

It was stated earlier that the public benefit test is applicable to all charitable purposes. In the context of advancement of religion both aspects of the public benefit test are applicable, i.e. the benefit aspect and the public aspect. The benefit aspect is approached by reference to conformity with the classic tenets of a religion, such as faith (although this need not be in a supreme being but extends beyond the sciences), worship, tolerance, peace and respect. The public aspect concerns the extent to which the faith is embraced within the community. In *Gilmour v Coats* [1949] 1 All ER 848, the House of Lords decided that a gift to a Carmelite convent which consisted of 20 cloistered nuns, who devoted themselves to prayers and contemplation and engaged in no religious activity outside the convent, did not satisfy the public benefit test. Whereas, in *Neville Estates v Madden* [1962] 1 Ch 832, the members of the Catford synagogue were treated as an appreciable section of the community because the objects were not numerically negligible and integrated with the rest of society. In *IRC v Baddeley* [1955] AC 572, the provision of recreational activities in favour of Methodists resident in West Ham and Leyton failed the public benefit test on the ground that the beneficiaries formed a class within a class.

Category 4: the advancement of health etc.

Section 3(1)(d) of the Charities Act 2011 enacts that the advancement of health or the saving of lives is a charitable purpose. Section 3(2)(b) of the 2011 Act declares that the 'advancement of health includes the prevention or relief of sickness, disease or human suffering'.

The promotion of health has always been treated as a charitable purpose, and includes the establishment and maintenance of hospitals, see *Re Resch's Will Trust* [1969] 1 AC 514; the supply of contraceptives, *Family Planning Association* [1969] Ch Comm Rep 111; the provision of a 'home of rest' for nurses in a hospital, *Re White's Will Trust* [1951] 1 All ER 528; and the provision of emergency services, *Re Wokingham Fire Brigade Trusts* [1951] Ch 373.

The Charity Commission in August 2009 declared that this head of charitable activity includes:

QUOTATION

'[C]onventional methods as well as complementary, alternative or holistic methods which are concerned with healing the mind, body and spirit in the alleviation of symptoms and the cure of illness.'

The charging of fees for the services is not a ground per se for disqualification under this or any other head of charitable purposes. The public benefit test may be satisfied provided that the less well-off members of society are not excluded by the level of the fee. This is a question of degree.

Category 5: the advancement of citizenship etc.

Section 3(1)(e) of the Charities Act 2011 specifies that 'the advancement of citizenship or community development' is a charitable purpose. Section 3(2)(c) adopts an inclusive definition of these purposes. Citizenship and community development includes '(i) rural or urban re-generation, and (ii) the promotion of civic responsibility, ... the voluntary sector or the ... efficiency of charities'.

Under this head the Charity Commission refers to 'the improvement of the social and economic infrastructure and by assisting people who are at a disadvantage because of their social and economic circumstances'. Thus, voluntary organisations that are responsible for giving free or discounted legal advice or advice on business or employment opportunities may satisfy this test.

Category 6: the advancement of arts, culture, heritage etc.

Section 3(1)(f) of the Charities Act 2011 enacts that the advancement of the arts, culture, heritage or science is regarded as a charitable purpose. Obviously, the purposes are construed disjunctively. Such purposes have always been regarded as charitable, even before the introduction of the Charities Act. The promotion of the arts and sciences generally was treated as charitable at common law under the heading of advancement of education, and/or the residual category of the *Pemsel* classification. Accordingly, the National Trust, the provision of museums, art galleries, arts festivals, craft fairs, the preservation of historic monuments and the promotion of centres for the performing arts will be classified as charitable under this head. Examples include the promotion of the works of a famous composer or a celebrated author, see *Re Delius' Will Trust* [1957] 1 All ER 854; see also *Re Shakespeare Memorial Trust* [1923] 2 Ch 389; and professional bodies that promote the arts and sciences, see *Royal College of Surgeons of England v National Provincial Bank Ltd* [1952] 1 All ER 984.

The Charity Commission published its guidelines in August 2002:

QUOTATION

'Museums and art galleries will need to demonstrate that their collections or exhibits –

(i) are set up for the benefit of the public, that is:
  - they provide sufficient public access;
  - any private benefit gained by individuals is incidental and properly regulated;
  - they are not used for non-charitable purposes, such as trading;
(ii) they satisfy the criterion of merit, that is:
  - there is sufficient evidence that the collections and exhibits either will educate the minds of the public, or at least will be capable of doing so;
  - what is conveyed to the public is an idea, emotion or experience which is enlightening and which is, or is capable of being, of value to them.'

In determining whether a collection of artefacts or assets ought to be available for public viewing, the courts are required to take into account the usefulness of the gifts to the public. This may be effected by judicial notice of the value of the gift to society. In the event of doubt, the courts may take into account the opinions of experts. The opinions of the donors are inconclusive: see *Re Pinion*.

CASE EXAMPLE

Re Pinion [1965] 1 Ch 85, CA

Gifts of a studio and contents, to be maintained as a collection, were made to the National Trust. The National Trust refused to accept the donation as a collection, although it was willing to accept selected items as valuable for display. The question in issue was whether the gifts were valuable as a collection.

Held: After due consideration of the expert evidence, the court decided that the donation failed as a charity. The collection as a whole lacked any artistic merit. Harman LJ could conceive of no useful purpose in 'foisting upon the public this mass of junk':

JUDGMENT

'Where a museum is concerned and the utility of the gift is brought in question it is, in my opinion, and herein I agree with the judge, essential to know at least something of the quality of the proposed exhibits in order to judge whether they will be conducive to the education of the public. There is a strong body of evidence here that as a means of education this collection is worthless. The testator's own paintings, of which there are over 50, are said by competent persons to be in an academic style and atrociously bad and the other pictures without exception worthless. Even the so-called Lely turns out to be a 20th century copy.

The most that skilful cross-examination extracted from the expert witnesses was that there were a dozen chairs which might perhaps be acceptable to a minor provincial museum and perhaps another dozen not altogether worthless, but two dozen chairs do not make a museum and they must, to accord with the will, be exhibited stifled by a large number of absolutely worthless pictures and objects.

I can conceive of no useful object to be served in foisting upon the public this mass of junk. It has neither public utility nor educative value. I would hold that the testator's project ought not to be carried into effect and that his next of kin is entitled to the residue of his estate.'

Harman LJ

Category 7: the advancement of amateur sport

Section 3(1)(g) of the Charities Act 2011 enacts that the 'advancement of amateur sport' is a charitable purpose. Thus, the charitable status of such activity is dependent on the way the facility is organised.

Section 3(2)(d) defines 'sport' as sport and games which promote health by involving physical or mental skill or exertion. Thus the focus here is on health, and those sporting activities that do not promote health, e.g. tiddlywinks, will not be treated as charitable. Likewise, some dangerous sports, e.g. bungee jumping, may be outside this category of charitable purposes. It is arguable that this provision has modified the common law treatment of sport. The promotion of sport *simpliciter*, prior to the introduction of the Charities Act 2011 (and the earlier Charities Act 2006), was not regarded as a charitable purpose because such activity was not within the spirit and intendment of the preamble: see *IRC v City of Glasgow Police Athletic Association* (1953). But in appropriate cases such gifts may be included under the heading advancement of education or under the Recreational Charities Act 1958 (now s 5 of the Charities Act 2011).

The promotion of sport may, in appropriate cases, be included under the heading 'advancement of education'. To achieve this status, the sport is required to be provided within a school or as part of the educational curriculum. It is well recognised that adequate recreational activities (physical and mental development) are an integral part of the educational process – see *Re Mariette* [1915] 2 Ch 284 (the provision of prizes for sport in a school). Similarly, in *Inland Revenue Commissioners v McMullen*, the promotion of football within schools and universities was considered to be charitable for the advancement of education.

CASE EXAMPLE

IRC v McMullen [1981] AC 1

The Football Association Youth Trust was established to promote football and other sports within schools and universities. The object was to provide physical education and develop the minds of pupils. The House of Lords decided that the trust was charitable for the advancement of education.

JUDGMENT

'I regard the limitation to the pupils of schools and universities in the instant case as a sufficient association with the provision of formal education to prevent any danger of vagueness in the object of the trust or irresponsibility or capriciousness in application by the trustees.'

Lord Hailsham

Equally, the provision of recreational facilities has been regarded as a charitable purpose, and many village and town halls are used partly for recreational purposes. The decision of the House of Lords in *IRC v Baddeley* (1955) created doubts as to whether a number of bodies created for recreational purposes were charitable, and the Recreational Charities Act 1958 was passed in order to clarify the law. This Act has been repealed and replaced by s 5 of the Charities Act 2011. Section 5(1) of the 2011 Act stipulates that the provision of recreational facilities shall be charitable if the facilities are provided in the interests of social welfare. Social welfare is provided if the basic conditions are met. These basic conditions are laid down in s 5(3)(a) and (b) of the 2011 Act. Section 5(3)(a) declares:

SECTION

'The facilities are provided with the object of improving the conditions of life for the persons for whom the facilities are primarily intended, and

(b) either –
    (i) those persons have need for such facilities by reason of their youth, age, infirmity or disablement, poverty or social and economic circumstances; or
    (ii) the facilities are available to the members of the public at large or to male or to female members of the public at large.'

Under the 2011 Act, the social welfare test will be complied with if two conditions are satisfied as enacted in s 5(3). The first requirement is continuous, as stipulated in s 5(3)(a). The second requirement may be satisfied in alternative ways: either by proving that the facilities are available to a limited class of objects who have a need for such facilities by virtue of one or more of the factors enumerated within s 5(3)(b)(i) (such as a youth club or an organised outing for orphaned children) or the facilities are available to the entire public (such as a public swimming pool or a public park) or male or female members of the public (Women's Institutes etc.).

The House of Lords in *Guild v IRC* [1992] 2 All ER 10, HL construed the requirements under the predecessor to s 5(3)(a) liberally and rejected the view that it is necessary to prove that the beneficiaries were deprived of the relevant facilities. The test today is whether the facilities are provided with the purpose of improving the conditions of life of the beneficiaries, irrespective of whether the participating members of society are disadvantaged or not. In short, the material issue concerns the nature of the facilities, rather than the status of the participants.

CASE EXAMPLE

Guild v IRC [1992] 2 All ER 10, HL

A testator by his will disposed of the residue of his estate to the Town Council of North Berwick '(i) for the use in connection with the Sports Centre in North Berwick and (ii) some similar purpose in connection with sport'. The court held that the gift was charitable under the Recreational Charities Act 1958 (the predecessor to s 5 of the Charities Act 2011).

JUDGMENT

> 'Hyde Park improves the conditions of life for residents in Mayfair and Belgravia as much as those in Pimlico or the Portobello Road, and the village hall may improve the conditions of life for residents for the squire and his family as well as the cottagers.'
>
> Bridge LJ, cited by Lord Keith in *Guild v IRC*

Subsequent to this decision the Charity Commission has expressed the view that, consistently with other legislation involving 'social welfare', two elements are required to be established. These are 'ethical' and 'altruistic' elements. The ethical element involves a moral justification for the facilities that ought to be met by society. The altruistic element concerns the availability of the facilities to other members of society rather than an insular group of individuals. In this respect, organisations that promote a single sport or one that assumes a certain level of skill may be put in jeopardy. In any event the sporting body needs to establish that the public benefit test is satisfied.

Category 8: the advancement of human rights etc.

Section 3(1)(h) of the Charities Act 2011 enacts that 'the advancement of human rights, conflict resolution or reconciliation or the promotion of religious or racial harmony or equality and diversity' are charitable purposes. Section 3(1)(h) provides a statutory basis for the promotion and preservation of human rights. This may be achieved in a variety of ways such as education and providing a redress for victims of human rights abuses. In addition, mediation services for conflict resolution are included as charitable activities. Equally, the provision of harmony amongst diverse groups based on race, religion, gender or sexual orientation has always been treated as a charitable activity.

The difficulty here is the thin line that divides, on the one hand, political activities which are not charitable, and on the other, the variety of beneficial activities stipulated in s3(1)(h). Activities or organisations whose main purpose is to campaign for changes in the law, domestic or foreign, may be regarded as political by nature and not charitable. In *McGovern v Attorney General* (1981), the High Court decided that the objects clause of Amnesty International was primarily political and failed as a charity.

CASE EXAMPLE

McGovern v AG [1981] 3 All ER 493, HC

Amnesty International, an unincorporated, non-profit-making association, established a trust and sought registration with the Charity Commissioners. This was refused and the trustees appealed to the court.

Held: The organisation was not a charitable body because some of its purposes (for example, procuring the abolition of torture, or inhuman or degrading treatment) were political and did not comply with the definition of charitable purposes. Admittedly, some of its purposes were charitable, such as the promotion of research into the maintenance and observance of human rights. On construction, its main purposes were not exclusively charitable.

JUDGMENT

> 'The point with which I am at present concerned is whether a trust of which the direct and main object is to secure a change in the laws of a foreign country can ever be regarded as charitable under English law. Though I do not think that any authority cited to me precisely covers the point, I have come to the clear conclusion that it cannot.

Furthermore, before ascribing charitable status to an English trust of which a main object was to secure the alteration of a foreign law, the court would also, I conceive, be bound to consider the consequences for this country as a matter of public policy. In a number of such cases there would arise a substantial *prima facie* risk that such a trust, if enforced, could prejudice the relations of this country with the foreign country concerned: compare *Habershon v Vardon* (1851) 4 De G & Sm 467. The court would have no satisfactory means of assessing the extent of such risk, which would not be capable of being readily dealt with by evidence and would be a matter more for political than for legal judgment.'

Slade J

The Charity Commission in 2005 published guidance as to the distinction between the advancement of human rights and political activities. The purposes and activities of the organisation will be construed by the courts to ascertain whether its dominant purpose is charitable or not:

QUOTATION

'Charity law draws a distinction between political purposes and political activities. An organisation which has purposes which include the promotion of human rights by seeking a change in the law, or a shift in government policy, or a reversal of a government decision has (at least in part) political purposes and cannot be a charity. However, the trustees of a charity may nonetheless use political means without jeopardising charitable status. What is important for charitable status is that political means should not be the dominant method by which the organisation will pursue its apparently charitable objects.'

Section 3(1)(h) of the 2011 Act refers specifically to the 'promotion of religious or racial harmony or equality and diversity' as instances of charitable purposes. Little needs to be said as to the obvious benefit to society in promoting such purposes. Clearly, organisations that investigate and confront such objectionable conduct, as well as educate the public of the divisive nature of such conduct, are engaged in activities for the public benefit.

Category 9: the advancement of environmental protection etc.
Section 3(1)(i) of the Charities Act 2011 enacts as a charitable purpose 'the advancement of environmental protection or improvement'. This fundamental principle of conservation of the environment includes areas of natural beauty, as well as particular species of flora and fauna. Independent expert evidence that is authoritative and objective may be required to show that a particular species, land or habitat to be conserved is worthy of conservation. There is very little case law under this head.

Category 10: the relief of those in need because of youth, age etc.
Section 3(1)(j) of the Charities Act 2011 enacts that 'the relief of those in need because of youth, age, ill-health, disability, financial hardship or other disadvantage' are charitable purposes. There is an obvious overlap with category 1, the prevention and relief of poverty, and many organisations may provide facilities that fall under both heads. Section 3(2)(e) declares that the subsection includes 'relief given by the provision of accommodation or care to the persons mentioned in the sub-section'. The two material issues here are first, the fact that the beneficiaries are deprived in the way described in the subsection, and second, the promotion of facilities designed to address those needs.

The common law regarded the stated purposes as charitable and interpreted the expression 'relief' as requiring individuals to establish a need for such facilities in the first place. In *Joseph Rowntree Memorial Trust Housing Association v AG* [1983] Ch 159, the court decided that the provision of housing for the elderly was a charitable activity. Peter Gibson J defined the expression 'relief' in the following manner:

JUDGMENT

'[T]he word, "relief" implies that the persons in question have a need attributable to their condition as aged, impotent or poor persons which require alleviating, and which those persons could not alleviate, or would find difficulty in alleviating themselves from their own resources. The word "relief" is not synonymous with "benefit". Thus a gift of money to aged millionaires of Mayfair would not relieve a need of theirs as aged persons.'

Peter Gibson J

The approach of the courts may be summarised by Vaisey J in *Re Hillier* [1944] 1 All ER 480. In deciding that a trust for the sick and wounded was charitable, he said:

JUDGMENT

'The charitable element in a purpose is to be found ... in the notion of rendering assistance to those persons who are in dire want of it, or to meet some form of human need – need which would appeal to the benevolent feelings of mankind and not necessarily that which has its origin in the lack of money.'

Vaisey J

Accordingly, the provision of medical care including rehabilitation programmes for addicts, accommodation, meals and advice and guidance for the vulnerable members of society may satisfy the requirement.

Category 11: the advancement of animal welfare

Section 3(1)(k) of the Charities Act 2011 enacts as a charitable purpose, 'the advancement of animal welfare'.

The common law that existed prior to the 2011 Act treated such activities as charitable, under Lord Macnaghten's fourth heading in *Pemsel*. It is submitted that the common law approach to animal welfare will be endorsed under the Act. This view is enacted in s 3(1) and (3) of the Charities Act 2006.

A trust which promotes the welfare of animals generally, or even a species of animals (as opposed to benefiting specific animals) is a valid charitable trust because it is calculated to promote public morality by checking an inborn tendency in humans towards cruelty. In *Re Wedgwood* [1915] 1 Ch 113, CA, a trust for the protection and benefit of animals was charitable. Similarly, in *University of London v Yarrow* (1857) 1 De G & J 72, a hospital for sick animals was charitable. In *Re Moss* [1949] 1 All ER 495, a home for unwanted or stray cats was charitable.

It is essential to establish that the welfare of the animals provides some benefit to mankind, albeit indirect. Failure to establish such benefit was fatal in *Re Grove-Grady* [1929] 1 Ch 557. An animal sanctuary (a game reserve) where all animals were allowed to live free from 'molestation or destruction by man' was not charitable because there were no safeguards against the destruction of the weaker animals by the stronger:

JUDGMENT

'It is not a trust directed to ensure absence or diminution of pain or cruelty in the destruction of animal life. If this trust is carried out according to its tenor, no animal within the area may be destroyed by man no matter how necessary that destruction may be in the interests of mankind or in the interests of the other denizens of the area or in the interests of the animal itself; and no matter how painlessly such destruction may be brought about. It seems to be impossible to say that the carrying out of such a trust necessarily involves benefit to the public. Consistently with the trust the public could be excluded from entering the area or even looking into it. All that the public need know about the matter would be that one or more areas existed in which all animals were allowed to live free from any risk of being molested or killed by man, though liable to be molested and killed by other denizens of the area.'

Russell LJ

Moreover, where the welfare of animals (anti-vivisection) conflicts with the interests of mankind (scientific research) the latter prevails and the animal welfare association will not be charitable: see *National Anti-Vivisection Society v IRC* [1948] AC 31, per Lord Simonds:

JUDGMENT

'Where on the evidence before it the court concludes that, however well intentioned the donor, the achievement of his object will be greatly to the public disadvantage, there can be no justification for saying that it is a charitable object.'

Lord Simonds

Category 12: the promotion of the efficiency of the armed forces etc.

Section 3(1)(l) of the Charities Act 2011 provides that 'the promotion of the efficiency of the armed forces of the Crown or of the efficiency of the police, fire and rescue services or ambulance services' are charitable purposes.

This subsection reflects the undisputed policy that the efficiency of the emergency services has always been treated as a charitable purpose. Examples include: the training of officers of the Royal Navy, *Re Corbyn* [1941] Ch 400; the protection of the UK from hostile attack, *Re Driffill* [1950] Ch 92; the promotion of the defence of the UK, *Re Good* [1950] 2 All ER 653; the provision of a local fire brigade, *Re Wokingham Fire Brigade Trusts* [1951] 1 All ER 454.

Category 13: any other purposes

Section 3(1)(m) of the Charities Act 2011 creates a general residual class of charitable purposes similar to the miscellaneous charitable purposes recognised by the courts before the Act. In addition, the court has the power to identify new charitable purposes as the need arises, i.e. purposes not listed specifically in s 3(1)(a) to (l).

Section 3(1)(m)(i)–(iii) of the Charities Act 2011 provides:

SECTION

'The purposes within this subsection are –

(i) any purposes not within paragraphs (a) to (l) of subsection (1) but recognised as charitable purposes under existing charity law or by virtue of section 5 (recreational and similar trusts, etc) or under the old law;

(ii) any purposes that may reasonably be regarded as analogous to, or within the spirit of, any purposes falling within any of the paragraphs (a) to (l) or sub-paragraph (i); or

(iii) any purposes that may reasonably be regarded as analogous to, or within the spirit of, any purposes which have been recognised under charity law as falling within sub-paragraph (ii) or this paragraph.'

By virtue of s 3(4), the 'old law' means the law relating to charities in England and Wales immediately before 1 April 2008 (the date that the Charities Act 2006 came into force).

The process of reasoning by analogy was explained by Lord Reid in *Scottish Burial Reform and Cremation Society v Glasgow City Corporation* [1968] AC 138, in the following manner:

JUDGMENT

'The courts appear to have proceeded first by seeking some analogy between an object mentioned in the preamble and the object with regard to which they had to reach a decision. And then they appear to have gone further and to have been satisfied if they could find an analogy between an object already held to be charitable and the new object claimed to be charitable. And this gradual extension has proceeded so far that there are few modern reported cases where a bequest or donation was made or an institution was being carried on for a clearly specified object which was for the benefit of the public at large and not of individuals, and yet the object was held not to be within the spirit and intendment of the Statute of Elizabeth 1.'

Lord Reid

The effect of this provision is that the wealth of case law that existed before the passing of the 2006 Act (the predecessor to the current 2011 Act) will be relevant in identifying miscellaneous charitable purposes.

This is a residual category of charitable purposes that not only consolidates the diverse multitude of charitable purposes that exist, but allows the law to be maintained as new purposes arise. Illustrations include: the general improvement of agriculture, *IRC v Yorkshire Agricultural Society* [1928] 1 KB 611; the promotion of inexpensive and sanitary methods of disposal of the dead, *Scottish Burial Reform and Cremation Society v Glasgow City Corporation* [1968] AC 138; the study and dissemination of ethical principles, *Re South Place Ethical Society* [1980] 1 WLR 1565; a gift to the inhabitants of a town or village, *Goodman v Saltash Corporation* (1882) 7 App Cas 633; a gift 'unto my country, England', *Re Smith* [1932] 1 Ch 153; a bequest to the Chancellor of the Exchequer for the benefit of Great Britain, *Nightingale v Goulbourn* (1849) 5 Hare 484; a gift to benefit the black community, *Re Harding* [2007] EWHC 3; a gift to the schoolchildren of Turton, *Re Mellody* [1918] 1 Ch 228; a gift for the relief of the national debt, *Newland v AG* (1809) 3 Mer 684; and many more.

Section 3(1)(m) of the 2011 Act authorises the courts to approach a novel purpose by drawing an analogy with, or the spirit of, one or more of the 12 purposes declared in s 3(1)(a) to (l). In addition, the courts may draw an analogy with any other purposes. Outside this statutory guidance is an approach that was adopted under the 'old law', namely, the approach that was advocated by Russell LJ in *ICLR v AG* [1972] Ch 73 of deciding that a beneficial purpose is charitable until the contrary is shown.

JUDGMENT

'If a purpose is shown to be so beneficial, or of such utility, it is *prima facie* charitable in law, but the courts have left open a line of retreat based on the equity of the statute in case they are faced with a purpose (for example, a political purpose) which could not have been within the contemplation of the statute even if the then legislators had been endowed with the gift of foresight into the circumstances of later centuries.'

Russell LJ

For example, in *Nightingale v Goulbourn* (1849) 5 Hare 484, a bequest made 'to the Queen's Chancellor of the Exchequer for the time being, ... to the benefit and advantage of Great Britain' was charitable. In *Goodman v Mayor of Saltash* (1882) 7 App Cas 633, Lord Selborne decided that a gift subject to a condition or trust for the benefit of the inhabitants of a parish or town, or of any particular class of such inhabitants, was a charitable trust. *Scottish Burial Reform and Cremation Society Ltd v Glasgow City Corporation* [1968] AC 138 concerned the promotion of inexpensive and sanitary methods of disposal of the dead, in particular, cremation, and similarly was held to be charitable. Likewise, a gift for a patriotic purpose, as was decided in *Re Smith* [1932] 1 Ch 153, 'unto my country, England'.

JUDGMENT

'I come to the conclusion that there is a definitive purpose – namely, that the bequest is to be for England. That is good in the same sense that, although general, when the sum bequeathed comes to be used it is to be applied to charitable purposes, as in *AG v Webster* (1875) LR 20 Eq 483. There is no area or purpose of distribution suggested which is not charitable. Why not then give effect to the plain meaning that it is for the advantage, within the meaning of the rule as to the interpretation of the word charitable, of the inhabitants of England?'

Lord Hanworth MR

In *Re Harding* [2007] EWHC 3, the High Court considered the consequence of the gift being in terms expressly limited to benefit the black community. The court took into account that the law permitted a charitable trust to be made for the benefit of a particular section of the community. The phrase 'the black community' was not uncertain and is taken to mean, in modern usage, black people and a reference to 'the community' does not negative a charitable intention. In this case the testatrix in her will disposed of 'everything I possess be taken over by the Roman Catholic Diocese of Westminster to hold in trust for the black community of Hackney, Haringey and Tower Hamlet'. The court decided that the gift was charitable and the details would be subject to a scheme.

JUDGMENT

'[T]he phrase the Black community is no more than another way of saying, in modern usage, black people. Second, judicial usage does not suggest that a reference to the community negatives a charitable intention. In *Re Mellody* [1918] 1 Ch 228, Eve J, in upholding the gift to the schoolchildren of Turton, described the gift as a gift for purposes beneficial to a section of the community; and described the schoolchildren themselves as a very important section of the community. He did not appear to regard the use of this word as being incompatible with a charitable gift.'

Lewison J

The Equality Act 2010 repeals and replaces a number of anti-discrimination legislative provisions and enacts that it is unlawful to discriminate (directly or indirectly) against an individual on the grounds of at least one of a number of 'protected characteristics'. Section 4 of the Act lists these characteristics as age, disability, gender reassignment, marriage and civil partnership, pregnancy and maternity, race, religion or belief, sex and sexual orientation. Charities, like individuals and organisations, are subject to the provisions in the Act. However, charities may not contravene the provisions of the Act, provided that their activities are restricted to a number of defined single-sex organisations, for example, the YMCA, YWCA, Boys Scouts, Girl Guides etc. (see s 193(7)). In addition, charities may limit their benefits to individuals who share a 'protected characteristic' provided that this amounts to a 'proportionate means of achieving a legitimate aim' (see s 193(2)). In *Catholic Care (Diocese of Leeds) v Charity Commission for England and Wales* [2012] UKUT 395, the issue was whether a Roman Catholic charity, involved in screening and identifying potential adoptive parents willing to adopt children, was entitled to restrict its activities to heterosexual parents only who may constitute a family of mother, father and child. Did the charity adduce sufficient evidence to establish a proportionate means of achieving a legitimate aim in excluding homosexual potential parents? The Charity Commission and First Tier Tribunal were not convinced that the continued voluntary funding of the charity's work, under the auspices of the Roman Catholic Church, would inevitably lead to the prospect of an increased number of adoptions. On appeal, the Upper Tribunal dismissed the appeal and decided that there was an inherent conflict between the general interests of homosexuals willing to adopt children, the interests of the children to be placed with good adoptive parents and the restrictive purposes of the charity. Accordingly, there was insufficient evidence that the legitimate aim identified by the charity may be achieved by the restriction to heterosexual adoptive parents.

JUDGMENT

'In my judgment the First-tier Tribunal was right to conclude that the Charity had failed to show that there were sufficiently weighty reasons to justify the discrimination it proposed to engage in. The fact that same sex couples could seek to have access to adoption services offered elsewhere tended to reduce somewhat the immediate detrimental effect on them, but it did not remove the harm that would be caused to them through feeling that discrimination on grounds of sexual orientation was practised at some point in the adoption system nor would it remove the harm to the general social value of promotion of equality of treatment for heterosexuals and homosexuals – a value endorsed by Parliament in assessing and responding to the needs of society by legislating general rules to promote equality of treatment for homosexuals. It did not have the effect that the Charity could be permitted to proceed on the basis of some less demanding standard than that declared in the relevant judgments of the European Court of Human Rights, which require that particularly weighty and convincing reasons be shown in order to provide objective justification for discrimination on grounds of sexual orientation.'

Sales J

12.10 Political purposes

Political purposes include attempts to change the law and gifts to further the objects of political parties. A trust for political purposes is incapable of subsisting as a charity. Common justifications for the general principle include the lack of sufficient evidence to equip the court to decide on the validity of the political activity, the impartiality of the judiciary, the usurpation of the function of Government, the inappropriate use of public funds to support such activities and the failure to satisfy the public benefit test. In *National Anti-Vivisection Society v IRC* [1948] AC 31 the general rule was stated by Lord Parker:

JUDGMENT

'A trust for the attainment of political objects has always been held invalid, not because it is illegal, for everyone is at liberty to advocate or promote by any lawful means a change in the law, but because the court has no means of judging whether a proposed change in the law will or will not be for the public benefit, and therefore cannot say that a gift to secure the change is a charitable gift.'

Lord Parker

Accordingly, an educational trust along the lines of the Labour Party failed in *Re Hopkinson* [1949] 1 All ER 346. Similarly, prior to the Charities Act 2006, a gift to Amnesty International failed in *McGovern v AG* [1981] 3 All ER 493, Slade J said: 'The court will ordinarily have no sufficient means of determining whether the desired reversal would be beneficial to the public, and in any event could not properly encroach on the functions of the executive, acting intra vires, by holding that it should be acting in some other manner.'

Section 2(2)(h) of the Charities Act 2006 has enacted that 'the advancement of human rights, conflict resolution or reconciliation or the promotion of religious or racial harmony or equality and diversity' are charitable purposes. It is arguable that the decision in *McGovern v AG* has been overruled as a result of this modification of the law.

Alternatively, a trust may be treated as charitable if its political purpose, on construction, is purely incidental to its main charitable purpose. This is a question of degree and will involve construction of the objects of the organisation, including its activities. A borderline case is *Re Scowcroft* [1898] 2 Ch 638, where the gift for the maintenance of a village club and reading room was construed as charitable, for the advancement of education, even though the reading room was 'to be used for the furtherance of conservative principles'.

In *Southwood v AG* [2000] WTLR 1199, the High Court decided that, on construction, the purposes of a trust designed to challenge the current policies of Western governments to promote military disarmament were not charitable. The purposes were considered political.

JUDGMENT

'There are differing views as to how best to secure peace and avoid war. To give two obvious examples: on the one hand, it can be contended that war is best avoided by 'bargaining through strength'; on the other hand, it can be argued, with equal passion, that peace is best secured by disarmament – if necessary, by unilateral disarmament. The court is in no position to determine that promotion of the one view rather than the other is for the public benefit. Not only does the court have no material on which to make that choice; to attempt to do so would be to usurp the role of government.'

Chadwick LJ

A fine line is to be drawn between the activities of a charity in campaigning, lobbying or highlighting deficiencies in the law in furtherance of its charitable objectives on the one hand, and being involved in political activity on the other hand. If such activities are purely incidental to its main charitable purposes the organisation will not cease to be charitable. In this context the court adopts a 'benignant construction' of the objectives of the association, as indicated by Slade LJ in *Re Koeppler* [1986] Ch 423 (see earlier). The possible sanctions for a charity overstepping the mark and being actively engaged in promoting political purposes are breach of trust, loss of tax and other privileges and ultimately being struck off the register of charities. No doubt the Charity Commission will monitor the activities of the charity and in appropriate cases may give the trustees a warning. It is crucial that the trustees are aware of the limits to which they may subject the charitable funds in an attempt to promote its charitable purposes. In 2008 the Charity Commission published guidelines in its paper, 'Speaking Out: Guidance on Campaigning and Political Activity by Charities'. General guidelines include the entitlement of charities to comment publicly on social, economic and political issues, express their opinion on proposed changes in the law and provide information to its supporters, provided that such activities do not form the main purpose of the association. These guidelines go some way in clarifying the quality of charitable activities in the modern world.

12.11 The *cy-près* doctrine

The expression *'cy-près'* originates from Norman French, meaning 'near this'. Over the centuries the expression has been taken to mean 'as near as possible'. The *cy-près* doctrine is a principle applicable to gifts for charitable purposes which fail (initially or subsequently) because of the impossibility or impracticality of giving effect to the donor's intention. Schemes may be approved by the Charity Commission and the courts for the application of the funds as nearly as possible to the original purposes as stated by the settlor. When the *cy-près* doctrine is adopted the donor or his estate is excluded from benefiting by way of a resulting trust.

Figure 12.1 Charitable purposes

Charitable trusts

Advantages enjoyed by charitable trusts:	
• Certainty of objects – private trusts are subject to strict tests for certainty of objects. The test for certainty of charitable objects is whether the objects are exclusively charitable • Enforcement – a private trust is ultimately required to be enforced by the beneficiaries, but charitable trusts are enforced by the Attorney General on behalf of the Crown • Perpetuities – the perpetuities rule has a modified application to charitable trusts • Tax privileges – charities enjoy a number of tax privileges not enjoyed by private trusts • *Cy-près* – on a failure of a private trust, a resulting trust may arise, but when a charitable trust fails the property may be applied *cy-près* (to the nearest alternative) In private trusts, trustees are required to act unanimously, but in administering charitable trusts, trustees act by a majority	

Requirements of a charitable trust:	
In order for a trust to be considered to be charitable, the following three requirements must be satisfied: • the purposes are required to be, in law, charitable • the trust is required to promote a public benefit and • the objects of the trust must be exclusively charitable	

Definition of a charity:	
• Statutory definition of 'charitable purposes' in s 3 of the Charities Act 2011 • Section 1(1) of the Charities Act 2011: 'charity' is described as any institution, corporate or not (including a trust), which is established for charitable purposes • What is a charity is a question of law • In novel cases, prior to the Charities Act 2011, the approach adopted by the courts has been:	
1. to treat as charitable any purpose which clearly falls within the preamble and	s 38(4) Charities Act 1960
2. to include, by analogy, any purpose which has been treated as charitable in the past	*Scottish Burial Reform and Cremation Society v City of Glasgow Corporation* (1968)
3. to declare that a purpose which falls within the spirit and intendment of the preamble is charitable	*ICLR v AG* (1972)
By virtue of s 3(1) of the Charities Act 2011, 13 purposes are specified as charitable, including s 3(1)(m) which creates a general description. The common law is still relevant in order to interpret these statutory provisions	

The purposes laid down in the preamble have been classified by Lord Macnaghten in *IRC v Pemsel* (1891) into the following four categories: • trusts for the relief of poverty • trusts for the advancement of education • trusts for the advancement of religion and • trusts for other purposes beneficial to the community This is now regarded as a restrictive classification and the current classification is in s 3(1) of the 2011 Act • The public benefit test is twofold, see s 4 of the Charities Act 2011: • the purposes are required to provide some useful benefit to members of the community in accordance with the preamble or spirit of the preamble	*IRC v Pemsel* (1891)
the class of persons who are entitled to enjoy the property must not be numerically negligible and connected in blood or contract to the donor. This condition does not apply to trusts for the relief of poverty	*Re Compton* (1945); *IRC v Baddeley* (1955); *Williams' Trustees v IRC* (1947); *Gilmour v Coats* (1949); *Re Lewis* (1954)
Trusts for the relief of poverty	*Re Saunders* (1954); *Re Niyazi* (1978); *Re Scarisbrick* (1951); *Dingle v Turner* (1972)
Trusts for the advancement of education	*Re Shaw* (1957); *Re Hopkins* (1964); *Re British School of Egyptian Archaeology* (1954); *Royal Choral Society v IRC* (1943); *Re Delius* (1957); *Re Pinion* (1965)
The encouragement of sport is charitable if carried out as part of the activities of a school or university	*IRC v McMullen* (1981); *Re Dupree* (1944)
Section 5 of the Charities Act 2011, previously the Recreational Charities Act 1958	*Guild v IRC* (1992)
Trusts for the advancement of religion	*Bowman v Secular Society* (1917); *Neville Estates v Madden* (1962); *Re South Place Ethical Society* (1980); *United Grand Lodge of Freemasons v Holborn BC* (1957); *Gilmour v Coats* (1949); *Re Garrard* (1907); *Re Simson* (1946); *Farley v Westminster Bank* (1939); *Thornton v Howe* (1862); *Re Watson* (1973); *Re Hetherington* (1989)
Advancement of health	*Re White* (1951); *Re Wokingham Fire Brigade Trust* (1951); *Re Resch* (1969)
Advancement of citizenship Advancement of arts, culture and heritage	*Re Delius* (1957); *Re Shakespeare Memorial Trust* (1923)
Advancement of amateur sport	*Re Mariette* (1915); *IRC v McMullen* (1981); *Guild v IRC* (1992)
Advancement of human rights Advancement of environmental protection	Reversal of *McGovern v AG* (1981)

The relief of those in need	*Re Hillier* (1944); *Joseph Rowntree Memorial Trust* (1983)
Advancement of animal welfare	*Re Wedgwood* (1915)
The promotion of the efficiency of the armed forces	*Re Corbyn* (1941)
Other purposes beneficial to the community	*ICLR v AG* (1972); *National Anti-Vivisection Society v IRC* (1948); *Re Wedgwood* (1915); *Re Grove-Grady* (1929); *IRC v City of Glasgow Police Athletic Association* (1953); *IRC v Baddeley* (1955)
Political purposes are not charitable	*Re Shaw* (1957); *McGovern v AG* (1981); *Re Koeppler* (1986)
Charitable activities overseas	*Keren Kayemeth Le Jisroel v IRC* (1932); *Re Jacobs* (1970); *Gaudiya Mission v Brahmachary* (1997)

There are only two conditions to be satisfied for a *cy-près* application, namely:

1. the impossibility or impracticality of carrying out the original charitable purpose or the existence of a surplus of funds after the charitable purpose has been fulfilled; and

2. the manifestation of a general charitable intention by the donor as opposed to a specific charitable intention.

12.11.1 Impossibility

Prior to the introduction of the Charities Act 1960, the courts approached this question by considering whether the purposes, as stated by the settlor, were capable of being achieved as distinct from merely being undesirable.

CASE EXAMPLE

Attorney General v City of London [1790] 3 Bro CC 171

Trust funds to be used for the advancement and propagation of the Christian religion among the infidels in Virginia were applied *cy-près* when it became clear that there were no longer any infidels in Virginia.

Similarly, in *AG v Ironmongers Company* (1834) 2 My & K 567, funds devoted to the redemption of British slaves in Turkey and Barbary were applied *cy-près* when the purpose subsequently became impossible to achieve.

The test of 'impossibility' was construed broadly in *Re Dominion Students' Hall Trust* [1947] 1 Ch 183, where a limited company was formed for charitable purposes.

CASE EXAMPLE

Re Dominion Students' Hall Trust [1947] 1 Ch 183

The memorandum of association declared its object as being to maintain a hostel for students 'of European origin' from the overseas dominions of the British Empire. The company proposed a scheme, for approval of the court, whereby the offensive words 'of European origin' would be deleted so that the company would be better equipped to administer the funds for the benefit of all students from the dominions, regardless of racial origin. The court approved the scheme because the retention of the colour bar had the effect of defeating the main object of the charity.

JUDGMENT

'It is true that the word impossible should be given a wide significance. It is not necessary to go to the length of saying that the original scheme is absolutely impracticable … it is said that to retain the condition, so far from furthering the charity's main object might defeat it and would be liable to antagonise those students, both white and coloured, whose support and goodwill it is the purpose of the charity to sustain. The case, therefore, can be said to fall within the broad description of impossibility.'

Evershed

On the other hand, the test of impossibility was not satisfied in *Re Weir Hospital* [1910] 2 Ch 124.

CASE EXAMPLE

Re Weir Hospital [1910] 2 Ch 124

The testator devised property to be used as the site for a hospital. Expert evidence was admitted to the effect that the site was not suitable for a hospital, and a scheme was proposed for the building of a nurses' home instead. The court refused to approve the scheme on the ground that it was not impossible to carry out the testator's wishes but simply inadvisable.

12.11.2 Section 62 of the Charities Act 2011

This consolidates to some extent and substantially extends the powers of the Charity Commission and the courts to apply property *cy-près*. The circumstances when the purposes of the charity will become impractical or impossible were enacted in s 13(1)(a)–(e) of the Charities Act 1993. This provision has been repealed and replaced by s 62 of the Charities Act 2011.

Section 62(1)(a) of the 2011 Act, replacing s 13(1)(a) of the Charities Act 1993, states that:

SECTION

'where the original purposes wholly or partly have been as far as may be fulfilled, or cannot be carried out according to the directions given and to the spirit of the gift.'

This paragraph gives the court the jurisdiction to decide that the original purposes of the gift have been fulfilled or have become impractical. The only restriction on the discretion of the court is in regard to the construction of 'the spirit of the gift'. This phrase has been interpreted by Pennycuick VC in *Re Lepton's Charity* [1972] Ch 276 as meaning 'the basic intention underlying the gift, as ascertained from its terms in the light of admissible evidence'.

CASE EXAMPLE

Re Lepton's Charity [1972] Ch 276

A testator who died in 1716 devised specific property to trustees on trust to pay an annual sum of £3 to the Protestant Minister in Pudsey, and the surplus income to the poor and aged people of Pudsey. In 1716, the total income was £5. On the date of the application to the court that income was £790 per annum. Two questions arose for the determination of the court, namely:

(i) whether, on a true construction of the will, the minister ought to be paid a fixed sum of £3 or three-fifths of the annual income and

(ii) whether the court would approve a *cy-près* scheme increasing the minister's entitlement to £100 per annum.

The court held that on a construction of the will the minister was not entitled to three-fifths of the annual income but only a fixed sum of £3 per annum, but having regard to the spirit of the gift a *cy-près* scheme would be approved entitling the minister to £100 per annum.

CASE EXAMPLE

Oldham Borough Council v AG, The Times, 20 August 1992

The Court of Appeal was required to consider the original purpose of a devise of land to Oldham Borough Council 'on trust to preserve and manage the same as playing fields known as the "Clayton Playing Fields" for the benefit of inhabitants of Oldham, Chatterton and Royton'. The Court of Appeal, reversing the decision of the High Court, held that, on construction, the original purpose of the devise was not intended to impose an obligation on the council to retain the site in perpetuity, for use only as playing fields for the local community, but to make provision for playing fields for the benefit of the local community. Accordingly, the council was entitled to sell the site to developers and use the proceeds to acquire a new site for playing fields for the local community.

In *Re Laing Trust* [1984] Ch 143, the court drew a distinction between the 'original purposes' of the trust under s 13 of the Charities Act 1960 (the predecessor to s 13 of the Charities Act 1993) which may be reviewed by the court on a *cy-près* application, and a direction to distribute within a specific period of time, which is treated as an administrative provision outside s 13. Under the inherent jurisdiction of the court a scheme may be approved even though the court has no jurisdiction within s 13.

CASE EXAMPLE

Re Laing Trust [1984] Ch 143

In 1922, a settlor transferred shares to the plaintiff company as trustee to hold for charitable purposes. Both capital and income were to be wholly distributed during the lifetime of the settlor or within 10 years of his death. The settlor died in 1978. By 1982 the capital which was undistributed was worth £24 million. The plaintiff company applied to the court to sanction a scheme dispensing with the obligation to distribute the capital within 10 years of the settlor's death. The court decided that it had no jurisdiction under s 13, as the 'original purposes' of the charitable gift did not include an administrative provision concerning the date of distribution, but in the exercise of its inherent jurisdiction the court would approve the proposed scheme.

JUDGMENT

'I would regard it as an abuse of language to describe the requirement as to distribution as a purpose of the gift … I remain unpersuaded that such a gift is capable of being applied *cy-près* and, in particular, I am not persuaded that the requirement as to distribution is a purpose within the meaning of section 13. Rather, it seems to me to fall on the administrative side of the line, going, as it does, to the mechanics of how the property devoted to charitable purposes is to be distributed. Accordingly, I must refuse the application so far as it is based on section 13 … I have no hesitation in reaching the conclusion that the court should, in the exercise of its inherent jurisdiction, approve a scheme under which the trustees for the time being of the charity will be discharged from the obligation to distribute the capital within 10 years of the death of the settlor.'

Peter Gibson J

Section 62(1)(b) of the Charities Act 2011 repeals and replaces s 13(1)(b) of the Charities Act 1993. The subsection provides that:

SECTION

'where the original purposes provide a use for part only of the property available by virtue of the gift.'

The approval of the court may be granted under this paragraph where a surplus of funds are left over after the original charitable purposes have been carried out.

CASE EXAMPLE

Re North Devon and West Somerset Relief Fund [1953] 2 All ER 1032

A public appeal was launched following extensive flooding in North Devon and West Somerset. There was an overwhelming response and the question arose whether the surplus ought to be applied *cy-près* or be repayable to the donors. The court decided that the surplus funds would be applied *cy-près*.

Section 62(1)(c) of the 2011 Act repeals and replaces s 13(1)(c) of the Charities Act 1993 and declares that:

SECTION

'where the property available by virtue of the gift and other property applicable for similar purposes can be more effectively used in conjunction, and to that end can suitably, regard being had to the appropriate considerations, be made applicable to common purposes.'

This provision enables a number of small charities with common purposes to be amalgamated in order to create larger funds.

CASE EXAMPLE

Re Faraker [1912] 2 Ch 488

A testatrix, who died in 1911, left a legacy to 'Mrs Bailey's Charity, Rotherhithe'. A charity was founded by Mrs Hannah Bayly in 1756 for poor widows in Rotherhithe. In 1905 the charity was consolidated with a number of local charities under a scheme, approved by the Charity Commissioners, for the benefit of the poor in Rotherhithe. The court decided that the legacy was taken by the consolidated charities.

Section 62(1)(d) of the 2011 Act repeals and replaces s 13(1)(d) of the 1993 Act, and declares that:

SECTION

'where the original purposes were laid down by reference to –

(i) an area which then was but has since ceased to be a unit for some other purpose, or

(ii) a class of persons or an area which has for any reason since ceased to be suitable, regard being had to the appropriate considerations or to be practical in administering the gift.'

Under this paragraph, the court is entitled to consider that, because of local government boundary changes, the original class of beneficiaries has become difficult to identify, or the class of beneficiaries has dwindled over the years. See *AG v City of London* (1790) and *Ironmongers Co v AG* (1844).

CASE EXAMPLE

Peggs and Others v Lamb, The Times, 19 March 1993

The court considered a *cy-près* scheme under s 13(1)(d) of the Charities Act 1960. Freemen and their widows in the Ancient Borough of Huntingdon were entitled to the income from specific plots of land. In 1992 the number of beneficiaries had dwindled to 15 and the income available for distribution had risen to £550,000. The court decided, under s 13(1)(d), that the original purpose of the gift was to benefit the freemen and widows in the Huntingdon Borough but the class of beneficiaries had dwindled to such an extent that they ceased to be a suitable class for the deployment of the funds (due consideration being paid to the spirit of the gift). Accordingly, a scheme would be approved whereby the class of beneficiaries would be enlarged to include the inhabitants of the borough as a whole.

Section 62(1)(e) of the 2011 Act repeals and replaces s 13(1)(e) of the Charities Act 1993 and declares as follows:

SECTION

'where the original purposes, in whole or in part, have since they were laid down:

(i) been adequately provided for by other reasons; or

(ii) ceased, as being useless or harmful to the community, or, for other reasons, to be in law charitable; or

(iii) ceased in any other way to provide a suitable and effective method of using the property given, regard being had to the [appropriate considerations].' (Amended by the Charities Act 2006)

Section 62(2) of the 2011 Act repeals and replaces s 13(1)(A) of the Charities Act 1993, and provides that:

SECTION

'the appropriate considerations mean –

(a) (on the one hand) the spirit of the gift concerned, and

(b) (on the other) the social and economic circumstances prevailing at the time of the proposed alteration of the original purposes.'

Section 62(2) of the Charities Act 2011 amended s 13(1)(c), (d) and (e)(iii) of the Charities Act 1993 by substituting the expression 'the appropriate considerations' for 'the spirit of the gift' in that section. Section 62(2) of the 2011 Act defines the expression 'appropriate considerations' to include the spirit of the gift and the social and economic circumstances prevailing at the time of the proposed alteration in the purpose. Thus, the Charity Commission is required to take these circumstances into consideration when making a scheme.

Subsection 62(1)(e)(i) empowers the court to modify the original purposes as stated by the donor, in view of the charitable purposes being provided for by other bodies such as central and local government; for example the repair of roads and bridges may not be an appropriate mode of utilising charitable resources.

Subsection 62(1)(e)(ii) will rarely be used. It assumes that a purpose was once charitable but because of changed circumstances the purpose ceases to be charitable; for example anti-vivisection in the early nineteenth century was considered a charitable purpose (see *Re Fouveaux* [1895] 2 Ch 501), but with the advance of medical research, anti-vivisection is no longer treated as a charitable purpose. At the time when the Anti-Vivisection Society was removed from the Charities Register its funds could have been applied *cy-près*. Subsection 13(1)(e)(ii) merely confirms this approach.

Subsection 62(1)(e)(iii) enacts a wide-ranging provision giving the courts the power to consider whether the original purposes selected by the donor represent an effective method of using the property. In *Re Lepton's Charity* (1972) the court assumed jurisdiction *inter alia*, under s 13(1)(e)(iii) (the predecessor to s 62(1)(e)(iii)), to sanction the scheme.

CASE EXAMPLE

Varsani v Jesani [1983] 3 All ER 273

A charitable trust had been established for the purpose of promoting the faith of a particular Hindu sect. The sect split into two groups. The majority brought proceedings seeking a scheme for the administration of the property of the charity. The court decided that it had jurisdiction under s 13(1)(e)(iii) of the 1993 Act. The original purpose had ceased to be a suitable and effective method of using the available property. The scheme involved dividing the property between the two groups.

In a recent case, *White v Williams* [2010] EWHC 940, the High Court decided that it had jurisdiction to make a *cy-près* scheme of a church and its assets under s 13(1)(e)(iii) of the 1993 Act. The consequence was that a place of worship belonging to one charity was transferred to another charity whose role was directed to the fulfilment of purposes specific to the congregation or locality.

12.11.3 General charitable intention

This is the second condition which is required to be fulfilled before the charitable funds may be applied *cy-près*.

Subsequent failure

But there is one type of event where the courts have dispensed with the need to prove a general charitable intention. These are cases of 'subsequent failure', i.e. occasions when the charitable bodies exist at the appropriate date of vesting but cease to exist subsequently. The appropriate date of vesting varies with the nature of the instrument creating the gift. An *inter vivos* transfer by deed takes effect on the date of the execution of the deed and a transfer by will takes effect on the date of death of the donor. Once the gift vests in the charity the donor and his heirs are excluded from benefiting on a subsequent liquidation of the charity, irrespective of whether the gift was made subject to a general or specific charitable intention.

CASE EXAMPLE

Re Wright [1954] Ch 347

A testatrix, who died in 1933, gave her residuary estate to trustees on trust for a tenant for life, Mr Webb (who died in 1942), with the remainder to found and maintain a convalescent home for 'impecunious gentlewomen'. On the date of the testatrix's death the residuary estate was sufficient to implement her wishes, but at the time of Webb's death, the fund was insufficient to carry out the charitable purpose. It was argued that the appropriate date for deciding whether the charitable purpose was practical or not was on the date of Webb's death. The court rejected this argument and decided that the date for deciding whether the funds were applicable *cy-près* was on the date of vesting, namely the date of death of the testatrix.

JUDGMENT

'Once money is effectually dedicated to charity, whether in pursuance of a general or a particular charitable intent, the testator's next of kin or residuary legatees are forever excluded and no question of subsequent lapse, or of anything analogous to lapse, between the date of the testator's death and the time when the money becomes available for actual application to the testator's purpose can affect the matter so far as they are concerned.'

Romer LJ

The same principle applies where the charity existed at the testator's death but was liquidated before the gift took effect. A charitable unincorporated association does not have a separate entity and exists to promote the purposes of the association. Accordingly, where the association ceases to exist after the date of vesting, the gift may be transferred to other associations to promote similar purposes. This arose in *Re Slevin* [1891] 2 Ch 236; the testator left money to St Dominic's orphanage in Newcastle. The orphanage existed at the date of the death but closed down soon afterwards, before it received the legacy. The court held that the fund was applied *cy-près*.

JUDGMENT

'Properly speaking, a lapse can only occur by failure of the object in the lifetime to the testator … The orphanage did come to an end before the legacy was paid over. In the case of a legacy to an individual, if he survived the testator it could not be argued that the legacy would fall into the residue. Even if the legatee died intestate and without next of kin, still the money was his, and the residuary legatee would have no right whatever against the Crown.

Obviously it can make no difference that the legatee ceases to exist immediately after the death of the testator. The same law must be applicable whether it was a day, or month, or year, or, as might well happen, 10 years after; the legacy not having been paid either from delay occasioned by the administration of the estate or owing to part of the estate not having been got in. The legacy became the property of the legatee upon the death of the testator, though he might not, for some reason, obtain the receipt of it till long after. When once it became the absolute property of the legatee, that is equivalent to saying that it must be provided for; and the residue is only what remains after making such provision. It does not for all purpose cease to be part of the testator's estate until the executors admit assets and appropriate and pay it over; but that is merely for their convenience and that of the estate. The rights as between the particular legatee and the residue are fixed at the testator's death.'

Kay LJ

A similar result was achieved in *Phillips v Royal Society for the Protection of Birds* [2012] EWHC 618. The High Court decided that a charitable bequest will be applied *cy-près* where the association had ceased trading three years before the testatrix's death but was dissolved shortly after her death.

In *Re ARMS* (1997), the High Court decided that bequests made to a charitable company (a separate legal entity), which was in existence on the dates of death of the testators but subsequently went into liquidation, took effect *prima facie* as gifts beneficially to the company. Unless there was some indication that the gifts took effect as trusts, the testators' estates were excluded from benefiting from a return of the properties. While it is possible that, had the testators known of the company's insolvent liquidation, they might not have wished to donate their properties to it, the court was reluctant to speculate about the testators' intentions in the face of the plain words of the wills. Accordingly, the gifts were taken by the company beneficially and were available for distribution amongst the company's creditors.

CASE EXAMPLE

Re ARMS (Multiple Sclerosis Research Ltd) [1997] 1 WLR 877, HC

Several testators made testamentary gifts to a named company which had been incorporated to carry out charitable purposes. The principal objects of the company, as stated in its memorandum of association, were the promotion of research into the cause, cure and prevention of multiple sclerosis and the assistance of its victims. Various gifts by wills were made by deceased testators to the company before it was formally liquidated. The liquidator applied to the court for directions as to how the bequests should be dealt with.

Held: The bequests formed part of the company's assets and were available for distribution among its creditors.

JUDGMENT

'This gift raises the issue which was of concern to Millett J, namely, whether a gift to a charitable company takes effect according to its terms if the testator dies after the company has gone into compulsory liquidation, but before it has been formally dissolved.

In the present case, at the date of Mr Dove's death, the company was still in existence: indeed, even now it has not been dissolved. Accordingly, Mr Alleyne and the trust contend that Mr Dove has effected a simple bequest to a corporate body, namely, the company, which takes effect simply as a gift to that body beneficially. The fact that the body is in liquidation does not alter the fact that it still exists. Furthermore, they contend that there are no circumstances to suggest that the company was intended to take the gift as a trustee.

If, as a matter of construction of the will, the gift is expressed to be for a company then unless there are circumstances which show that the recipient is to take the gift as a trustee (*per* Buckley J in *In re Vernon's Will Trusts (Note)* [1972] Ch 300, p. 303) it takes effect so long as the company is in existence at the date of the testator's death.'

Neuberger J

However, it is essential that an absolute and perpetual gift be made to the charity at the time of vesting. If, alternatively, a limited gift (for a number of years) is made to the charity which existed on the date of vesting, but it ceases to exist at the time the gift purported to take effect, on construction, the court may decide that a resulting trust in favour of the settlor's estate may take effect. This was decided in *Re Cooper's Conveyance Trusts* [1956] 3 All ER 28.

Initial failure

In the event of an initial failure of the charitable institution, it is essential to prove a general charitable intention before the funds are applied *cy-près*. In other words, if, at the time of the vesting of the gift, the charitable body, specified by the donor, did not exist, the fund may only be applied *cy-près* on proof of a general charitable intention as opposed to a specific charitable intention. This crucial issue was recently considered by the High Court in *Kings v Bultitude* (2010).

CASE EXAMPLE

Kings v Bultitude [2010] EWHC 1795, HC

The claimant was the executor and trustee of the will of the deceased, Mrs Pamela Schroder who died on 2 January 2008. Her residuary estate was transferred to 'the Trustees of the Ancient Catholic Church known as the Church of the Good Shepherd at present meeting at Rookwood Road, London N16 ... for the general purposes of the said Church'. The defendants were representatives of the beneficiaries of the estate, who were entitled on a partial intestacy, and the Attorney General.

In 1968 Mr Schroder (the husband of the deceased) was elected as Primate of this Church. In the 1970s the Church community continued to occupy the building at Rookwood Road under a licence from Mr and Mrs Schroder. In 1985 Mr Schroder died. After Mr Schroder's death Mrs Schroder continued to pay some form of rent and the arrangement continued until her death. Mrs Schroder assumed the title of 'Reverend' and began to conduct services. From about 1995 until her death, she conducted all the services as the only minister and priest of the Church. Mrs Schroder ran the church, conducted services and paid its rent. When she went on holidays the building was closed and there were no services. After her death the church was closed and its building was taken over by another institution.

It was common ground that in principle the testamentary gift was charitable. The issue was whether these events involved the principle of 'initial' or 'subsequent' failure of charitable purposes. The former involved the *cy-près* doctrine only where there is proof of a general charitable intention, whereas in the latter case, the *cy-près* doctrine will be applied without proof of the intention of the testatrix.

Mrs Schroder also operated bank accounts at Barclays Bank in the name of the church. At the time of her death these accounts had credit balances of £6,063 in the current account and £12,215 in the deposit account.

Held: The court decided that:

1. The gift in Mrs Schroder's will constituted a valid charitable trust for the advancement of religion.
2. The purposes of the institution were legally discontinued in 1985 when Mr Schroder died, but were continued de facto by Mrs Schroder until her death in 2008.
3. After this event the congregation no longer met but went their separate ways. There was therefore an initial failure of the charitable purposes.
4. The evidence pointed to a gift in favour of a specific charitable purpose, namely the continued existence of the church as an institution. The residuary gift failed and passed to the beneficiaries of the estate on a partial intestacy.
5. The funds in the bank accounts were kept separate from Mrs Schroder's finances and were devoted for charitable purposes generally and were therefore applicable *cy-près*.

JUDGMENT

'[T]here is a distinction between the *de jure* (strict legal) position and the de facto (factual) position. Although the Church had departed from its constitution, it continued as an institution under Mrs Schroder's ministry in accordance with the tenets and beliefs that she prescribed and which she plainly believed fundamentally conformed to those of … Mr Schroder. In her mind and for her purposes the Church continued … It seems to me that Mrs Schroder was essential to the activities of the Church and without her it simply ceased to exist. I accept … that the Church became constitutionally defunct on the death of Mr Schroder. I would add that it, and, importantly, its purposes, went on to become defunct in practical terms on the death of his wife.'

Proudman J

General/specific charitable intention

The intention of the donor is essentially a question of fact. The courts are required to consider all the circumstances in order to determine whether the donor intended to benefit a charitable 'purpose' *simpliciter* identified by reference to a charitable institution (paramount charitable intention), or whether the settlor's intention was to benefit a specific charitable body identified by him.

The court adopted a broad approach to this question in *Re Lysaght* [1966] Ch 191.

CASE EXAMPLE

Re Lysaght [1966] Ch 191

A testatrix bequeathed £5,000 to the Royal College of Surgeons (trustees) on trust to apply the income in establishing studentships, with disqualifications in respect of Jews and Roman Catholics. The College declined to accept the gift but declared that if the religious bar was excised it would be willing to accept the gift. The court decided that in accordance with the paramount charitable intention of the testatrix the religious bar would be deleted. On construction, the court decided that the paramount charitable intention of the testatrix was to make the College a trustee of the fund and since this paramount intention was capable of being defeated if the religious bar was upheld, the court was entitled to delete the offending clause in order to give effect to the paramount intention of the settlor.

Buckley J distinguished a general charitable intention from a specific charitable intention:

JUDGMENT

'A general charitable intention may be said to be a paramount intention on the part of the donor to effect some charitable purpose which the court can find a method of putting into operation, notwithstanding that it is impracticable to give effect to some direction by the donor which is not an essential part of his true intention – not, that is to say, part of his paramount intention. In contrast, a particular charitable intention exists where the donor means his charitable disposition to take effect if, but only if, it can be carried into effect in a particular specified way.'

Buckley J

The court came to a similar conclusion in *Re Woodhams* [1981] 1 All ER 202.

CASE EXAMPLE

Re Woodhams [1981] 1 All ER 202

A limitation attached to scholarships to two music colleges, restricting applicants to boys from Dr Barnardo's Homes and the Church of England Children's Society Homes, was deleted because the colleges would otherwise have declined the gifts on the ground that the limitation was impractical.

Form/substance

The classic statement of the distinction between a general charitable intention and a specific charitable intention was issued by Parker J in *Re Wilson* [1913] 1 Ch 314:

JUDGMENT

'The authorities must be divided into two classes. First of all we have a class of cases where, in form, the gift is given for a particular charitable purpose, but it is possible, taking the gift as a whole, to say that, notwithstanding the form of the gift, the paramount intention is to give property in the first instance for a general charitable purpose rather than a particular charitable purpose, and to graft into the general gift a direction as to the desires or intentions of the donor as to the manner in which the general gift is to be carried into effect. Then there is the second class of cases where, on the true construction of the gift, no such paramount general intention can be inferred, and where the gift being in form a particular gift – a gift for a particular purpose, and it being impossible to carry out that particular purpose, the whole gift is held to fail.'

Parker J

Examples of cases within the first class are *Re Lysaght* (1966) and *Re Woodhams* (1981). In *Biscoe v Jackson* (1887) 35 Ch D 460, a legacy for the establishment of a soup kitchen and a cottage hospital in the parish of Shoreditch disclosed, on construction of the will, a general charitable intention to benefit the poor in Shoreditch.

Within the second category of cases, the courts are entitled to draw the inference that the donor has manifested a specific charitable intention if he has described the charitable purpose with precision. Indeed, the clearer the description of the charitable objective which the donor has in mind, the stronger the inference that the intention is specific.

CASE EXAMPLE

Re Wilson [1913] 1 Ch 314

A testator gave property upon trust to pay the salary of a schoolmaster (whose duties were specified) who was expected to teach in a school which he expected would be built with funds raised from the public. Detailed directions were given as to the expected location of the school and the running of the school. There was no possibility of carrying out these instructions and on construction the court decided that the testator manifested a specific charitable intention.

CASE EXAMPLE

Re Good [1950] 2 All ER 653

A legacy to provide rest homes in Hull was subject to a detailed scheme as to the types of homes to be provided, the types of inmates to be admitted and the management powers of the trustees. When the scheme proved impracticable because the funds were insufficient the court decided that the testator did not manifest a general charitable intention. Accordingly, the funds resulted to the residuary legatees.

A factor which may influence the judge in deciding the question of the intention of the donor is the fact that the charitable body selected by the donor has never been in existence. The approach here is that the specification by the donor of a named charitable institution which never existed may be construed as a reference to the purpose to which the donor intended to devote his funds and is evidence of a general charitable intention.

CASE EXAMPLE

Re Harwood [1936] Ch 285

A testatrix bequeathed legacies to (a) the 'Wisbech Peace Society, Cambridge' (a society which had existed at one time but had ceased to exist before the testatrix's death) and (b) the 'Peace Society of Belfast' (which had never existed). The court held that the gift to the Wisbech Peace Society manifested a specific charitable intention for the object of the testatrix's bounty was carefully selected and identified and that portion of the estate was held on resulting trust. But the legacy to the Belfast Society was applicable *cy-près* because her intention must have been to benefit any charitable society which promoted peace in Belfast.

JUDGMENT

'[W]here the testator selects as the object of his bounty a particular charity and shows in the will itself some care to identify the particular society which he desires to benefit, the difficulty of finding any general charitable intent in such case if the named society once existed, but ceased to exist before the death of the testator, is very great. Here the testatrix has gone out of her way to identify the object of her bounty. In this particular case she has identified it as being the Wisbech Peace Society Cambridge (which is a branch of the London Peace Society). Under those circumstances, I do not think it is open to me to hold that there is in this case any such general charitable intent as to allow the application of the *cy-près* doctrine.'

Farwell J

A similar approach was adopted by the Court of Appeal in the following case:

CASE EXAMPLE

Re Satterthwaite's Will Trust [1966] 1 WLR 277

A testatrix who announced to a bank official that she hated the whole human race and wished to leave her estate to animal charities made her will in December 1952 and died in 1962 leaving her residuary estate equally to nine animal-welfare organisations selected from a telephone directory. Seven of these bodies were animal charities but the remaining two were an anti-vivisection society and the London Animal Hospital. The question in issue concerned the one-ninth share bequeathed in favour of the London Animal Hospital. This share was claimed *inter alia* by a veterinary surgeon who had carried on his profession under that name from 1943 to July 1952 when, following the Veterinary Surgeons Act 1948, the name was withdrawn from the Register of Animal Hospitals. At all material times this hospital was private and not charitable. There was no evidence that the testatrix had any knowledge of the surgeon's establishment or that she knew that it was a private hospital. The court decided that the one-ninth share was applicable *cy-près*. The evidence suggested that the testatrix meant to benefit a purpose and not an individual. The other bequests taken as a whole (despite the one-ninth share to the anti-vivisection society) showed a general charitable intention to benefit animals

JUDGMENT

'I have already indicated that the testatrix is to be taken as intending to benefit a charitable activity. But the organisation picked by name was not such … any assumption is that the testatrix was pointing to a particular charitable application of this one-ninth of residue. If a particular mode of charitable application is incapable of being performed as such, but it can be discerned from her will that the testatrix has a charitable intention (commonly referred to as a general charitable intention) which transcends the particular mode of application indicated, the court has jurisdiction to direct application of the bequest to charitable purposes *cy-près*. Here I have no doubt from the nature of the other dispositions by this testatrix of her residuary estate that a general intention can be discerned in favour of charity through the medium of kindness to animals. I am not in any way deterred from this conclusion by the fact that one-ninth was given to an anti-vivisection society which in law – unknown to the average testator – is not charitable.'

Russell LJ

Incorporated and unincorporated associations

Another factor which has found favour with the courts in deciding the intention of the settlor concerns the distinction between charitable corporations and unincorporated associations. An incorporated association, as distinct from an unincorporated association, has an independent legal existence distinct from its members. In *Re Vernon's Will Trust* [1972] Ch 300, Buckley J expressed the view that a gift to a corporate charity is *prima facie* intended to take effect as a beneficial gift to the named body and will lapse if the charity ceases to exist before the testator's death. It will only be possible to apply the funds *cy-près* if the court, on construction, finds a general charitable intention. On the other hand, where the gift is to an unincorporated association, the gift *prima facie* takes effect for the purposes of the association. The named unincorporated association is treated as the trustee to carry out the charitable purpose. Accordingly, if the association ceases to exist the court is entitled to use its inherent jurisdiction to ensure that the trust will not fail for want of a trustee and may appoint new trustees to continue the charitable purposes. (This *prima facie* rule may be rebutted by evidence which shows that the gift was dependent upon the continued existence of the particular trustees.) This approach appealed to Goff J in the following case.

CASE EXAMPLE

Re Finger's Will Trust [1972] Ch 286

A testatrix who died in 1965, by her will made in 1930, transferred her residuary estate on trust in favour of 11 charitable institutions equally. One share was given to the 'National Radium Commission'. No institution by that name existed, although an unincorporated body called the 'Radium Commission' had existed since 1929 but was liquidated in 1947 when the National Health Service was set up. The work previously undertaken by the Commission was carried on by the Minister of Health. The court construed the bequest as intended for the Radium Commission. Another share of the bequest was given to the National Council for Maternity and Child Welfare. This was a corporate body which was in existence at the time of the execution of the will but was wound up in 1948. The bulk of its assets were transferred to the National Association for Maternity and Child Welfare, an association similar to the Council and which continued the Council's activities. The question in issue was whether both shares might be applied *cy-près*.

The court held that the testatrix exhibited a general charitable intention in respect of both gifts. The gift to the unincorporated association (the Radium Commission) was construed as intended for the purposes of the Commission which was not dependent on the continued existence of the Commission. The gift to the incorporated association which ceased to exist on the date of vesting was treated *prima facie* as a gift to the body (see *Re Harwood* (1936)) but was still capable of being construed as a general charitable gift since virtually the whole estate was devoted for charitable purposes, the testatrix regarded herself as having no relatives and the Council had merely a co-ordinating function.

JUDGMENT

'[Distinguishing *Re Harwood* (1936)] In the present case the circumstances are very special … First, virtually the whole estate is devoted to charity and again the nature of the Council was mainly, if not exclusively, a co-ordinating body. I cannot believe that this testatrix meant to benefit that organisation and that alone. Finally, I am entitled to place myself in the armchair of the testatrix and I have evidence that she regarded herself as having no relatives. Taking all these matters into account, in my judgment I can and ought to distinguish *Re Harwood* and find, as I do, a general charitable intent.'

Goff J

This basis of distinguishing *Re Harwood* (1936) was doubted by Megarry VC in the following case.

CASE EXAMPLE

Re Spence [1979] Ch 483

A testatrix who died in 1972, by her will dated 4 December 1968, bequeathed part of her estate to the 'Old Folks Home at Hillworth Lodge, Keighley, for the benefit of the patients'. Hillworth Lodge was built as a workhouse in 1858 and was closed in 1939. In 1948, it became an aged persons' home under the National Assistance Act 1948 but was closed down in 1971. Since then the building had been used as government offices. The question in issue was whether the testatrix had manifested a general or specific charitable intention.

The court held (applying *Re Harwood* (1936) and refusing to follow *Re Finger's Will Trust* (1972)) that the testatrix had manifested a specific charitable intention by identifying a particular charitable purpose which on the date of the will was capable of being carried out but was incapable of being fulfilled at the time of death.

JUDGMENT

'This is a fairly plain case of a will which made a gift for a particular purpose in fairly specific terms. The gift was for the benefit of the patients at a particular home. At the date of the will there were several patients at that home, but when the testatrix died, there was no longer any home there, but offices instead; and so there were no longer any patients there, or any possibility of them … if a particular purpose is specified, then it is that purpose and no other, that is the object of the benefaction. The specific displaces the general. I am not sure that I have been able to appreciate to the full the cogency of the special circumstances that appealed to Goff J in *Re Finger*.'

Megarry J

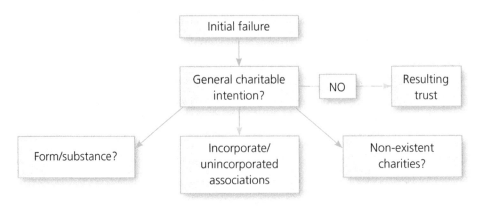

Figure 12.2 The *cy-près* doctrine

12.11.4 Sections 63–66 of the Charities Act 2011

The general rule, as detailed above, is that property given for a specific charitable purpose which fails from the outset cannot be applied *cy-près* if no general charitable intention can be imputed to the donor. Such property will be held on resulting trust for the donor.

By way of exception to the general rule, s 63 of the Charities Act 2011 (repealing and replacing s 14 of the Charities Act 1993) enacts that property given for specific charitable purposes which fail shall be applicable *cy-près* as if given for charitable purposes generally where the property belongs to a donor who cannot be identified or found after reasonable enquiries and advertisements have been made or who disclaims his right to the property in writing. In *Re Henry Wood National Memorial Trusts* (1965) 109 SJ 876, in the case of a nationwide appeal, notices in *The Times*, *Telegraph* and *Scotsman* newspapers and letters to addresses of donors noted in the appeal records constituted reasonable advertisements and enquiries.

Section 64 of the Charities Act 2011 (replacing s 14(3) of the Charities Act 1993) enacts to the effect that in the case of cash collections by use of collecting boxes or where it is not possible to distinguish one gift from another or in the case of money raised by lotteries, entertainment and similar money-raising activities, the property will be conclusively presumed to belong to unidentifiable donors without a need for advertisement and enquiry.

Moreover, s 64(2) (replacing s 14(4) of the 1993 Act) enacts that, in any other cases, the court may order that property may be treated as belonging to donors who cannot be identified (without an advertisement or enquiry) if the amounts are so small that it would be unreasonable to incur the expense of returning the property to the donors, or it would otherwise be unreasonable to do so, having regard to the nature and circumstances of the gift or the lapse of time since the gifts were made.

Section 65 of the Charities Act 2011 introduces a provision intending to enlarge the jurisdiction of the court or the Commission to make schemes for the application of the property *cy-près*.

Section 65 of the 2011 Act is applicable where funds are given for specific charitable purposes in response to a solicitation, but accompanied by a statement permitting an ⸳application of the funds *cy-près* in appropriate cases.

The purpose of s 67 of the 2011 Act is designed to clarify the operation of the powers of the court or the Commission when applying property *cy-près*. The court or the Commission is required to have regard to the matters set out in s 67(3), including the spirit of the original gift, when making a scheme changing the charitable purposes for which the property was donated. This applies either when the scheme involves the transfer of property from one charity to another or when there is no transfer and the scheme changes the purposes of the charity as the court or the Commission considers appropriate.

KEY FACTS

 The *cy-près* doctrine

Introduction	
The *cy-près* doctrine enables the court (and the Charity Commission) to make a scheme for the application of the property for other charitable purposes, as closely as possible to those intended by the donor. There are two conditions to be satisfied before a *cy-près* scheme is made. These are impossibility or impracticality in carrying out the charitable purpose and the manifestation of a general charitable intention by the settlor	
Impossibility	
Prior to the Charities Act 1960 (predecessor to the Charities Act 1993 and 2011) this question was approached as to whether the charitable purposes were capable of being achieved as opposed to merely being undesirable	*AG v City of London* (1790); *AG v Ironmongers Co* (1834); *Re Dominion Students' Hall* (1947)
Section 62 of the Charities Act 2011 (successor to s13 Charities Act 1993)	*Re Lepton* (1972); *Oldham BC v AG* (1992); *North Devon and West Somerset Relief Fund* (1953); *Re Faraker* (1912); *Peggs v Lamb* (1993); *Re Fouveaux* (1895); *Varsani v Jesani* (1983)
General charitable intention	
Subsequent failure:	
Where a gift made to a charity ceases to exist after the gift has taken effect, there is no need to demonstrate a general charitable intention in order to apply the gift *cy-près*	*Re Wright* (1954); *Re Wokingham Fire Brigade Trusts* (1951)
Initial failure:	
A general charitable intention may not be inferred if the gift was for a particular, specified charity which once existed but no longer does at the date of vesting of the gift	*Re Spence* (1979)
Where the institution has never existed it is easier to find a general charitable intention	*Re Harwood* (1936)
If the institution subsequently fails to exist in its original form (merger with other bodies) a general charitable intention may be inferred if the original purposes of the institution are promoted by the new body	*Re Faraker* (1912); *Re Vernon* (1972)

A gift to an unincorporated charity by name *prima facie* takes effect as a gift for charitable purposes (as a trust). If the charitable body has ceased to exist, the gift may be applied *cy-près* if the purposes of the association are carried out by the new entity	*Re Finger* (1972); *Re Harwood* (1936)
A gift to an incorporated charity takes effect simply as a gift to that body beneficially. If the charity has ceased to exist *prima facie* the gift will fail unless, exceptionally, a general charitable intention is found	*Re Finger* (1972); *Re Spence* (1979)
A gift to a non-charitable institution is not made charitable by being included in a list of charitable gifts, even if the purposes are similar	*Re Jenkins* (1966); *Re Satterthwaite* (1966)
Sections 63–66 of the Charities Act 2011 (successors to s 14 Charities Act 1993)	

12.12 The Charity Commission

The office of the Charity Commissioners was established in 1853 by the Charitable Trusts Act of that year to provide a simple and inexpensive means of dealing with difficulties encountered by charities. The office had no legal existence as a body but carried out a number of important functions on behalf of the Crown. Section 13 of the Charities Act 2011 abolishes the office of the Charity Commissioners and sets up a new body corporate in its place, called the Charity Commission. This new body has inherited the functions, property, rights and liabilities of its predecessor. The Commission will be a non-ministerial government department and will have a significant degree of independence from ministers and other government departments. The Commission will consist of a chairman and at least four, but not more than eight, other members: see Sched 1 of the 2011 Act. The Commission is subject to the jurisdiction of the High Court in the exercise of their quasi-judicial powers, and appeals from their decisions may be made to the High Court.

Section 14 of the 2011 Act provides the Commission with five objectives. Section 15 declares six general functions and ss 16 and 20 six general duties and incidental powers of the Commission.

12.13 Charity Tribunal (First Tier Tribunal)

Part 17 of the Charities Act 2011 introduces new provisions creating a new tribunal called the Charity Tribunal to act as 'the court of first instance' for appeals and applications in respect of certain decisions of the new Charity Commission. It also enables the Tribunal to consider matters referred to it by the Attorney General or, with the Attorney General's consent, by the Charity Commission. The provisions cover the practice, procedure, membership and appointments to the Tribunal. Appeals from the Tribunal are made to the High Court only on points of law.

12.14 The Attorney General

The role of the Attorney General is to represent the beneficial interests or objects of the charity. His duty is to protect the interests of charity generally, and in so doing he contributes to a framework of supervision and control over charities in which the Charity Commission plays a significant role. The Attorney General is generally a necessary party to all claims relating to charities.

12.15 Litigation by charities

Section 114 of the Charities Act 2011 (successor to s 32(1) of the Charities Act 1993) confers on the Commission the same powers with respect to the taking of legal proceedings or the compromise of claims as are exercisable by the Attorney General acting *ex officio*.

Section 115 of the 2011 Act (successor to s 33(1) of the 1993 Act) authorises 'charity proceedings' (as defined) to be taken with reference to a charity either by the charity, or by any of the charity trustees, or by any person interested in the charity, or by two or more inhabitants of the area if it is a local charity, but not by any other person.

In *Gunning v Buckfast*, *The Times*, 9 June 1994, the High Court decided that parents of children at a school possessed a sufficient standing to bring proceedings opposing the closure of the school.

Section 115(2) of the 2011 Act provides that no charity proceedings shall be entertained or proceeded with in any court unless the taking of the proceedings is authorised by order of the Commission. If the Commission refuses to authorise the taking of proceedings, leave can be obtained from a High Court judge. Section 115(8) defines 'charity proceedings' as proceedings in any court in England and Wales brought under the court's jurisdiction with respect to charities.

ACTIVITY

Essay writing

'There is a distinction between a form of relief accorded to the whole community yet, by its very nature, advantageous only to a few and a form of relief accorded to a selected few out of a larger number equally willing and able to take advantage of it … for example a bridge which is available for all the public may undoubtedly be a charity and it is indifferent how many people use it. But confine its use to a selected number of persons … it is then clearly not a charity.'

Explain and discuss.

ACTIVITY

Applying the law

1. By his will, a testator, who died last year, made the following gifts:
    (a) £10,000 to A upon trust to distribute it among such persons or charitable objects as he shall select;
    (b) £200,000 to B upon trust to purchase a suitable site near Birmingham for a football field for use of all inhabitants of Birmingham;
    (c) £50,000 to C to hold upon trust to promote such activities as will further the spread of socialist principles in Great Britain;
    (d) £100,000 to the University of London upon trust to establish and maintain in perpetuity a School for Law Reform.
    Consider the validity of these gifts as charitable trusts.

2. By his will made in 2003 John bequeaths £150,000 to his trustees, Sarah and Susan, directing them to invest the same and to apply the income arising therefrom for the following purposes:

   (a) one-third to be used to further the education of the children of employees and ex-employees of AB Co Ltd;

   (b) one-third to be used to relieve poverty among ex-employees of YZ Co Ltd; and

   (c) one-third to be given to the vicar of Littleacre for him to use for such benevolent purposes as to him seem suitable.

   John has recently died and Sarah and Susan seek your advice as to whether all or any of these purposes are of a charitable nature.

3. In 2001 a public appeal for funds to establish a community centre for young persons of the Baptist faith living in Greater London was launched.

   (a) £50,000 was raised by street collections;

   (b) £80,000 was donated anonymously;

   (c) £90,000 was bequeathed by the late Mrs Tremble;

   (d) £70,000 was realised from various entertainments held in aid of the appeal.

   It is impossible to obtain a suitable site for the community centre and the trustees seek your advice as to what is to be done with the funds raised.

4. A testator bequeathed the following legacies:

   (a) 'I leave £200,000 for the Methodist Church at [X address].'

   (b) 'I leave £50,000 to such charitable institutions or public purposes as my trustees may select.'

   (c) 'I leave £100,000 to the Central Hospital at [Y address], provided that if at any time it ceases to be a free hospital the legacy shall pass to John Smith.'

   There has never been a Methodist Church at X address.

   Consider what will happen to these gifts.

SUMMARY

- The privileges enjoyed by charities are in respect of taxation, certainty of objects, the rule against perpetuities and the *cy-près* doctrine.

- A charity is defined in s1(1) of the Charities Act 2011 in terms of the exclusivity of charitable purposes and being subject to the control of the High Court. Charitable purposes are required to satisfy the 'public benefit' test and fall within at least one of the purposes listed in s3(1) of the 2011 Act.

  - The public benefit test is a principle to distinguish a charitable trust from a private trust. Section 4(3) of the Charities Act 2011 consolidates the case law that existed before the passing of the Charities Act.

  - There is a two-tier test for public benefit. The 'public' test requires the court to determine whether the class of beneficiaries is sufficiently large to constitute an appreciable section of society. The second aspect of the test involves the 'utility' or 'benefit' test that concerns the usefulness of the activity to society.

- Trusts for the relief of poverty were accorded special treatment by the courts when considering the public benefit test.

- Almost all of the purposes listed in s3(1) of the 2011 Act were treated as charitable at common law. The first 12 purposes listed in the 2011 Act (a)–(l) are specific purposes and the final purpose in paragraph (m) is a general category sufficient to keep the law of charities abreast with the changing needs of society. The purposes enacted in s3(1)(a)–(c) are similar to Lord Macnaghten's classification in *Pemsel's* case. Section

3(1)(d)–(l) comprise specific purposes that were generally regarded as charitable before the enactment. The advancement of amateur sport is clearly a charitable purpose today. The pervasive public benefit test is interpreted in the same way as before the passing of the Act, except that the presumption in favour of a public benefit has been abolished by s 4(2) of the Charities Act 2011. It is questionable whether, prior to the passing of the Charities Act, the courts interpreted the public benefit test by way of presumptions.

- The residual category of purposes within s 3(1)(m) of the 2011 Act empowers the court to draw an analogy with, or the spirit of, one or more of the 12 purposes laid down in s 3(1)(a)–(l).
- Political purposes are not treated as charitable purposes.

The *cy-près* doctrine is unique to charitable trusts and applies where a charitable purpose cannot be carried out because it is impossible or impractical to do so. In these circumstances, provided that a general charitable intention may be established (as modified by ss 63–66 of the Charities Act 2011) the funds may be devoted *cy-près*. Whether or not a general charitable intention exists is a question of construction of the document and surrounding circumstances purporting to create the trust.

- Proof of a general charitable intention is unnecessary in cases of subsequent failure of charitable purposes.
- Section 62(1)(a) to (e) of the Charities Act 2011 enacts the circumstances when charitable purposes become impractical or impossible to achieve.

SAMPLE ESSAY QUESTION

Consider the following essay question:

Explain the public benefit test.

Answer plan

> The significance of the public benefit test. Section 2 of the Charities Act 2011 enacts that a charitable purpose must include the public benefit test.

> The Charity Commission is required to publish guidance on the public benefit requirement in order to promote public awareness.

> Section 4(2) of the 2011 Act abolishes the presumption in favour of public benefit, although it is questionable whether such a presumption ever existed at common law, see *Independent Schools Council v Charity Commission* (2011). However, the common law meaning of the term has been retained.

Public benefit in respect of the purpose:

- At common law the significance of this test in respect of purposes (a)–(c) was purely evidential in the sense that in appropriate cases evidence was needed to establish that the gifts in fact satisfied the tests of those purposes. The same would apply to those purposes listed in s 3(1)(d)–(l) of the 2011 Act.
- The effect is that s 4(2) of the 2011 Act may have made little impact on the common law since almost all of the purposes that were held to be charitable under the common law have been held to be of public benefit.

Public benefit in respect of the community:

- the prohibition of a nexus in contract;
- the prohibition of a nexus in blood;
- the requirement that the beneficiaries are not numerically negligible: this is question of degree;
- does not benefit a class within a class.

- The 'benefit' aspect of the public benefit test will be satisfied where the purpose falls within any of the categories of charitable purposes laid down in s 3(1) of the Charities Act 2011.
- Prior to the passing of the Charities Act the approach of the courts was based on the assumption that the benefit element was satisfied if the purpose was within the first three categories of Lord Macnaghten's classification in *Pemsel*. This approach was wrongly assumed to create presumptions in respect of the public benefit test. In *ISC v Charity Commission* (2011) the Upper Tribunal decided that, on a review of the case law, there was no evidence that the courts proceeded by way of presumptions. Instead they proceeded by way of evidence.
- It was unclear whether the exemption from the public benefit test that was applied in respect of trusts in relief of poverty had survived the 2011 Act, but *AG v Charity Commission* (2012) has clarified the law on this issue.
- Section 4(3) of the 2011 Act consolidates the wealth of common law decisions on the public benefit test that existed before the passing of the Act.

CONCLUSION

Further reading

Atiyah, P, 'Public benefit in charities' (1958) 21 MLR 138.

Baxter, C, 'Trustees' personal liability and the role of liability insurance' (1996) Conv 12.

Biehler, H, 'Trusts for the relief of poverty and public benefit: time for a reappraisal?' (2014) Tru. L.I. 145.

Biehler, H, 'The political purposes exception – is there a future for a doctrine built on the foundations of sand?' (2015) Tru. L.I. 97.

Bowles, V and King, M, 'Sweet charity' (2009) TELTJ 8.

Chesterman, M, 'Foundations of charity law in the new welfare state' (1999) 62 MLR 333.

Claus, S, 'The public benefit test' (2008) 158 NLJ 286.

Cotterell, R, 'Gifts to charitable institutions: a note on recent developments' (1972) 36 Conv 198.

Cross, G, 'Some recent developments on the law of charity' (1956) 72 LQR 187.

Cross, S, 'New legal forms for charities in the United Kingdom' (2008) JBL 662.

Duncan, G, 'Re Broadbent: the ultimate destination of a testamentary gift to a non-existent charity' (2002) PCB 243.

Dunn, A, 'The governance of philanthropy and the burden of regulating charitable foundations' (2012) Conv PL 114.

Edwardes, J, 'Twelve heads are better than four' (2004) 154 NLJ 1076.

Gillard, C, 'Charitable incorporated organisations' (2008) 32 CSR 126.

Gravells, N, 'Public purpose trusts' (1970) 40 MLR 397.

Hackney, J, 'Charities and public benefit' (2008) LQR 34.

Harding, M, 'Trusts for religious purposes and the question of public benefit' (2008) MLR 159.

Harpum, C, 'Is civilisation a public benefit?' (2008) TELTJ 12.

Histed, E, 'Rectification of wills: charitable trusts for poor relations – broadening the boundaries: Re Segelman' (1996) Conv 379.

Hopkins, J, 'Trusts for the advancement of sport: Recreational Charities Act 1958' (1992) CLJ 429.

Langdon-Down, G, 'Charities: cause and effect' (2009) LS Gaz, 25 June.

Lawson, D, 'The Charities Act 2006 and independent schools' (2009) Ed Law 10.

Luxton, P, 'In pursuit of purpose through s 13 of the Charities Act 1960' (1985) Conv 313.

McCarthy, R, 'Charities and campaigning' (2008) PCB 235.

Morris, D, 'Broadcast advertising by charities' (1990) Conv 106.

Mullender, R, 'Charity law, education and public benefit: an Oakeshottian analysis (2012) LQR 188.

Norman, H, 'Sporting charities: social welfare defined: Guild v IRC' (1992) Conv 361.

Parry, N, 'Imperfect charitable trust instruments: AG of Bahamas v Royal Trust Co' (1987) 131 SJ 1537.

Rahmatian, A, 'The continued relevance of the poor relations and the poor employees cases under the Charities Act 2006' (2009) Conv 12.

Sloan, B, 'Public schools for public benefit?' (2012) CLJ 45.

Synge, M, 'Poverty: an essential element in charity after all?' (2011) CLJ 649.

Synge, M, 'Charitable status: not negligible matter' (2016) LQR 303.

Warburton, J, 'Casenote on Re JW Laing Trust' (1984) Conv 319.

Watkin, T, 'Casenote: – Re Koeppler' (1985) Conv 412.

White, S, 'The protection of legacies and gifts upon merger under the Charities Act 2006' (2007) PCB 375.

13

Appointment, retirement and removal of trustees

AIMS AND OBJECTIVES

By the end of this chapter you should be able to:

- identify when and how an appointment of trustees may be made
- understand the circumstances as to when a trustee may retire from the trust
- appreciate the occasions when a trustee may be removed from office

13.1 Introduction

The settlor has the freedom to select eligible persons to be the first trustees. He may appoint the trustees *inter vivos* or by his will. In the case of an *inter vivos* trust the settlor is required to transfer the property to the trustees for failure to achieve this result will make the trust imperfect. In the case of a trust created on the settlor's death, the trust can never be imperfect for the settlor has managed to part with the trust property. If he does not name the trustees in his will or those named are unable or unwilling to act, the trust will still be valid for it is completely constituted and the maxim is 'Equity will not allow a trust to fail for want of a trustee'.

A replacement trustee will be appointed under express or statutory power or by the court. Similarly, the retirement or removal of a trustee may be effected under express or statutory power or by the order of the court.

13.2 Appointment

There are only two occasions when it may be necessary to appoint trustees:

- on the creation of a new trust – whether *inter vivos* or by will; and
- during the continuance of an existing trust, either in replacement of a trustee or as an additional trustee.

13.2.1 Creation of a new trust

The settlor or testator who creates a trust usually appoints the first trustees. If, in purported creation of a trust *inter vivos*, the settlor fails to nominate trustees, the intended trust will be imperfect. This principle, however, does not extend to trusts created by wills because, on the death of the testator, the trust becomes completely constituted. The deceased would have managed to part with the trust property. On the assumption that the trust is completely constituted, but the testator does not name trustees in his will or the trustees named are unwilling or unable to act, a replacement trustee will be appointed as on a continuance of the trust (see below). The principle applied here is that 'Equity will not allow a trust to fail for want of a trustee.'

13.2.2 Continuance of the trust

When a trust is created (whether *inter vivos* or by will) the trust property (real or personal) vests in all the trustees as joint tenants. The effect is that on the death of a trustee the property devolves on the survivors. This is the effect of s 18(1) of the Trustee Act 1925.

On the death of the sole or surviving trustee, the property vests in his personal representatives, subject to the trust, until replacement trustees are appointed. This principle is enacted in s 18(2) of the Trustee Act 1925.

The authority to appoint replacement trustees is derived from three sources, namely:

- an express power;
- a statutory power;
- the court.

This hierarchical order of authority to appoint trustees is required to be followed strictly. It is only when there is no person in one group willing to make an appointment that the power can be exercised by a person in a different group: see *Re Higginbottom* [1892] 3 Ch 132, where the majority of the beneficiaries under a trust were not able to prevent the sole executrix of the sole surviving trustee from appointing new trustees.

Express power

The trust instrument may confer the authority to appoint a trustee. This is exceptional because the statutory power to appoint is generally regarded as adequate. The express authority may be 'general' or 'special'. A general authority is one which confers an authority to appoint trustees in any circumstances. If the person named in the instrument is willing to exercise the power, this will be decisive as to the authority to appoint trustees provided that the power is exercised in good faith. If the authority is special (i.e. exercisable in limited circumstances) it would be strictly construed by the courts.

CASE EXAMPLE

Re Wheeler and De Rochow [1896] 1 Ch 315

A nominee was entitled to appoint trustees in specified circumstances, including the occasion when a trustee became 'incapable' of acting. One of the trustees became bankrupt. The court decided that this made him 'unfit' but not incapable of acting as a trustee. Thus, the nominee did not have the authority to appoint.

Similarly, where two or more persons have the power to appoint new trustees, they are required to exercise the authority jointly, unless there are express provisions to the contrary. It follows that such a joint power cannot be exercised where one of the appointors dies or cannot agree on the candidate to be appointed as trustee. This was decided in *Re Harding* [1923] 1 Ch 182.

Statutory power (s 36 of the Trustee Act 1925)

The statutory power to appoint trustees is contained in s 36 of the Trustee Act 1925 (replacing the Trustee Act 1893). The occasions giving rise to the need to appoint trustees are enacted in s 36(1) (replacement trustees) and s 36(6) (additional trustees).

Replacement trustees (s 36(1))

There are seven circumstances listed in s 36(1) when a replacement trustee may be appointed. These are:

1. When a trustee is *dead*. Under s 36(8), this includes a person nominated as trustee under a will but predeceasing the testator.

2. Where a trustee remains *outside the United Kingdom* for a continuous period of 12 months or more. The United Kingdom includes England, Wales, Scotland and Northern Ireland but does not include the Channel Islands or the Isle of Man. The motive for remaining outside the UK is irrelevant; this condition will be satisfied even if the trustee remains outside the UK against his will.

3. Where a trustee desires to be *discharged* from all or any of the trusts or powers reposed in or conferred on him. Thus, a trustee may retire from part only of the trust.

4. Where a trustee *refuses* to act. This includes the occasion when the trustee disclaims his office. It is advisable that the disclaimer be executed by deed.

5. Where a trustee is *unfit* to act. Unfitness refers to some defect in the character of the trustee which suggests an element of risk in leaving the property in the hands of the individual, for example a conviction for an offence involving dishonesty or bankruptcy (see *Re Wheeler and De Rochow* (1896)).

6. Where a trustee is *incapable* of acting. Incapacity refers to some physical or mental inability to administer the trust adequately, but does not include bankruptcy (see *Re Wheeler and De Rochow* (1896)). Under s 36(3), a corporation becomes incapable of acting on the date of the dissolution.

7. Where the trustee is an *infant*, i.e. a person under the age of 18. Such a person may become a trustee under an implied trust (resulting or constructive). An infant is incapable of becoming an express trustee.

Section 36(1) lists, in chronological order, the persons who are entitled to exercise the statutory power of appointing replacement trustees. These are:

- The person or persons *nominated* in the trust instrument for the purpose of appointing new trustees (see the discussion earlier).

- The *surviving or continuing trustee,* if willing to act. This subsection was enacted to empower a sole retiring trustee to appoint his successor. It enables a 'retiring' or 'refusing' trustee to participate with the surviving trustees in appointing a successor (s 36(8) of the Trustee Act 1925). But there is no obligation on such a 'retiring' trustee to concur in making the appointment. An appointment by the remaining trustees would be valid if the retiring trustee did not participate in the appointment: see *Re Coates* (1886) 34 Ch D 370.

  A trustee who is legitimately removed as a trustee is not a 'continuing' or 'refusing' or 'retiring' trustee for the purposes of s 36(8). He is a removed trustee. This was decided in *Re Stoneham's Settlement Trust* [1953] Ch 59.

- The *personal representatives of the last surviving or continuing trustee.* In order to become a surviving or continuing trustee, the property is required to vest in the individual.

Accordingly, if all the persons entitled as trustees under a will predecease the testator, the personal representative of the last to die would not be empowered to appoint new trustees. The personal representative of the testator will become the trustee and, subject to provisions to the contrary, will be entitled to appoint new trustees.

Section 36(4) provides that the personal representative of the last surviving or continuing trustee includes those who have proved the will of the testator or the administrator of a person dying intestate.

Section 36(5) provides that a sole or last surviving executor intending to renounce probate shall have the power of appointment of trustees at any time before renouncing probate.

Additional trustees (s 36(6) of the Trustee Act 1925)

Section 36(6) authorises the appointment of additional trustees although no trustee needs to be replaced:

SECTION

'36(6) Where a sole trustee, other than a trust corporation, is or has been originally appointed to act in a trust, or where, in the case of any trust, there are not more than three trustees (none of them being a trust corporation) either original or substituted and whether appointed by the court or otherwise, then and in any such case –

(a) the person or persons nominated for the purpose of appointing new trustees by the instrument, if any, creating the trust; or

(b) if there is no such person, or no such person able and willing to act, then the trustee or trustees for the time being may, by writing, appoint another person or other persons to be an additional trustee or additional trustees, but it shall not be obligatory to appoint any additional trustee, unless the instrument, if any, creating the trust, or any statutory enactment provides to the contrary, nor shall the number of trustees be increased beyond four by virtue of any appointment.'

The subsection is self-explanatory but it may be observed that a trust corporation (corporate professional trustee, such as a bank or an insurance company) has the power of two or more individual trustees. No power exists under s 36(6) to increase the number of trustees beyond four.

Direction of the beneficiaries

Sections 19–21 of the Trusts of Land and Appointment of Trustees Act 1996 (TOLATA 1996) invested new powers in the beneficiaries to direct a retirement of trustees and/or appointment of trustees. These provisions relate to trusts of all types of property (whether land or personalty). But the provisions may be excluded in whole or in part by the trust.

Section 19 of TOLATA 1996 applies where there is no person nominated under the trust instrument to appoint new trustees, and all the beneficiaries are of full age and capacity and collectively are absolutely entitled to the trust property. The beneficiaries have either one or both of the following rights. A right to direct in writing that one or more of the trustees shall retire from the trust, and/or that a named person or persons be appointed, in writing, as new trustee or trustees. The direction may be by way of substitution for a trustee or trustees directed to retire or as an additional trustee or trustees.

tutor tip

'The mechanics of the appointment, retirement and removal of trustees are of practical significance and integral for express trusts.'

If a direction to retire is given, the trustee concerned *shall* execute a deed effecting his retirement if:

(a) reasonable arrangements have been made to protect his rights under the trust;

(b) after retirement, there will be either a trust corporation or at least two persons to act as trustees; and

(c) either a replacement trustee is to be appointed on his retirement or the continuing trustees, by deed, consent to his retirement.

The section contains no provision compelling the trustees (or the personal representative of the last surviving trustee) to act on a direction to appoint a person as a new trustee. On a practical level, the trustee is unlikely to refuse to make the appointment without good reason.

Section 20 of TOLATA 1996 applies where:

(a) a trustee becomes mentally incapable of exercising his functions as trustee; and

(b) no person entitled to appoint new trustees is willing and able to do so; and

(c) the beneficiaries are of full age and capacity and are collectively entitled to the trust property.

In these circumstances the beneficiaries may give a written direction to the trustee's receiver or his attorney under a registered enduring power or to a person authorised under the Mental Health Act 1983 to appoint a particular person to be a new trustee. The Act is silent on the consequences of a failure to act on the direction.

Section 21(1) of TOLATA 1996 declares that a direction for the purposes of s 19 or s 20 may take one of two forms:

either a single direction collectively executed by all the beneficiaries; or

a number of directions, whether solely or jointly with one or more, but not all, of the beneficiaries, identifying the same person or persons for retirement or appointment.

Section 21(3) of TOLATA 1996 enacts that the effect of an appointment of a new trustee under s 19 or s 20 is the same as if he were appointed under s 36(7) of the Trustee Act 1925, i.e. he shall have the same powers and discretions as if he was appointed under the trust.

Section 36(7) of the 1925 Act (as amended by TOLATA 1996) enacts that the effect of an appointment under s 36 or s 19 or s 20 of TOLATA 1996 shall have the same consequences 'as if he had been originally appointed a trustee by the instrument, if any, creating the trust'.

The number of trustees

Realty: s 34 of the Trustee Act 1925 (as amended by TOLATA 1996) provides that where land is held on trust there may not be more than four trustees. If the instrument purports to appoint more than four trustees, only the first four named as trustees will take the property.

On the other hand, while a sole trusteeship is not forbidden, s 14(2) of the Trustee Act 1925 enacts that a sole trustee (other than a trust corporation) may not give a valid receipt for the proceeds of sale arising under a disposition of a trust of land or capital money arising under the Settled Land Act 1925.

Personalty: in theory, there is no restriction on the number of persons who may be appointed trustees of personalty.

In practice, it may be inconvenient and cumbersome to have too many trustees. The office of trusteeship requires unanimous approval of all the trustees (charities are treated as an exception). The law does not recognise a 'sleeping' or inactive trustee. A breach may be committed by a 'sleeping' trustee in failing to oppose a decision taken by his colleagues. This was decided in *Bahin v Hughes* (1886) 31 Ch D 390.

There are rarely more than four trustees and if the appointment is made under s 36 of the Trustee Act 1925 there will be not more than four trustees.

Alternatively, a sole trustee is most unsatisfactory because of the danger or risks of fraud or misconduct in administering the trust.

Vesting of trust property in trustees

On an appointment of replacement or additional trustees, the trust property is required to be vested in the new trustee or trustees to enable him or them to carry out his or their duties. Trustees hold the property as joint tenants so that the right of survivorship applies.

The vesting of the property in new trustees may be effected in one of two ways, namely:

1. By a *conveyance* or *transfer* effective to vest the property in the transferee. The relevant formalities that are required to be complied with vary with the nature of the property involved. The legal title to unregistered land requires a conveyance, whereas registered land requires a deed to be executed in order to register the new owner. Shares require registration in the share register of the company.

2. Section 40(1) and (2) of the Trustee Act 1925 create short-form and inexpensive methods of vesting the trust property in the new trustee or trustees. By virtue of s 40(1)(a) if the deed merely declares that the property vests in the new trustee this would be sufficient without a conveyance etc. Section 40(1)(b) enacts that if the deed of appointment omits to include a vesting declaration, it will be treated as if it had contained the same.

Exceptions: s 40(4) of the Trustee Act 1925 excludes certain types of property from the general provisions in s 40(1) and (2). These include:

- land held by trustees on a mortgage as security for a loan of trust money;
- leases containing a condition prohibiting dispositions without consent unless the consent has already been obtained;
- stocks and shares.

In these circumstances the property is required to be transferred in accordance with the appropriate formalities for that type of property.

Appointment by the court

Section 41 of the Trustee Act 1925 enacts the sweeping power of the court to appoint new trustees either as replacement or as additional trustees. Section 41(1) enacts:

SECTION

'The court may, whenever it is expedient to appoint a new trustee or new trustees, and it is found inexpedient, difficult or impracticable so to do without the assistance of the court, make an order appointing a new trustee or new trustees either in substitution for or in addition to any existing trustee or trustees, or although there is no existing trustee.'

The most popular occasions when the court's discretion may be exercised are where a sole surviving trustee dies intestate, or where an appointor is incapable of making an appointment because of infancy, or where all the trustees of a testamentary trust predecease the testator or where there is friction between the trustees.

The court will only exercise its power to appoint trustees when all other avenues have been exhausted. Thus, the court will not exercise its power where an express or statutory power can be exercised.

In exercising its discretion under s 41, the court will have regard to the wishes of the settlor (if expressed in the trust instrument), the promotion of the interests of all the beneficiaries and the efficient administration of the trust. This was decided in *Re Tempest* (1866) 1 Ch App 485, where the court decided that a nominated person was unsuitable to be appointed as trustee in order to avoid family dissension:

JUDGMENT

'The following rules and principles may, I think, safely be laid down as applying to all cases of appointments by the court of new trustees. First, the court will have regard to the wishes of the persons by whom the trust has been created, if expressed in the instrument creating the trust, or clearly to be collected from it ... Another rule which may safely be laid down is this – that the court will not appoint a person to be trustee in opposition to the interests of the beneficiaries ... it is of the essence of the duty of every trustee to hold an even hand between the parties interested under the trust ... A third rule is that the court in appointing a trustee will have regard to the question, whether his appointment will promote or impede the execution of the trust, for the very purpose of the appointment is that the trust may be better carried into execution.'

Turner LJ

Section 43 of the Trustee Act 1925 enacts that the effect of an appointment by the court will be treated 'as if the appointee had been originally appointed a trustee by the instrument, if any, creating the trust'.

In addition the court has an inherent jurisdiction to appoint new trustees where the restrictions imposed by s 41 – 'inexpedient, difficult or impracticable' – are not established. This jurisdiction is based on the maxim, 'Equity will not allow a trust to fail for want of a trustee'. Accordingly, where trustees' power of appointment had been subject to a time restriction which has expired, so that the trustees are no longer capable of exercising such

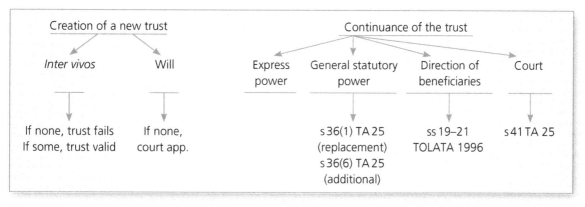

Figure 13.1 Appointment of trustees

a power, the court may exercise its inherent jurisdiction and appoint new trustees. The court so decided in *Barclay v Smith* [2016] EWHC 210. Under a cricket foundation trust the trustees had a power to appoint trustees for a period of five years. On the expiry of this power an application was made to the court to reappoint the original trustees. The court decided that the finances of the club were in order, there was no evidence of maladministration and the trustees were not unfit or unsuitable to be reappointed, so the best course under its inherent jurisdiction was to reappoint the trustees who were willing to act. Further, had it been necessary to decide it the court may have exercised its jurisdiction under s 41 of the Trustee Act 1925 as being both inexpedient and impracticable.

13.3 Retirement

A trustee may retire from the trust in one of five ways:

- by taking advantage of a power in the trust instrument; or
- by taking advantage of a statutory power under:
  (a) s 36(1) of the Trustee Act 1925 when a new trustee is appointed; or
  (b) s 39 of the Trustee Act 1925 where no new trustee is appointed; or
- by obtaining the consent of all the beneficiaries who are *sui juris* and absolutely entitled to the trust property under the principle in *Saunders v Vautier* (1841); or
- by direction from the relevant beneficiaries under s 19 of TOLATA 1996; or
- by obtaining the authority of the court.

13.3.1 Retirement procedure under s 39

Unlike a retirement under s 36(1), a trustee is not allowed to retire from part of a trust under s 39 of the Trustee Act 1925. He is required to retire from the trust as a whole or not at all. The procedure for retirement under s 39 is as follows:

1. at least two individuals will continue to act as trustees or a trust corporation; and

2. the remaining trustees (or trustee) and other persons empowered to appoint trustees consent to the retirement by deed; and

3. the retiring trustee makes such a declaration by deed.

It should be noted that a retiring trustee remains liable for breaches of trust committed while he was a trustee. He is absolved from liability in respect of subsequent breaches, unless he retired in order to facilitate a breach of trust. This was decided in *Head v Gould* [1898] 1 Ch 250.

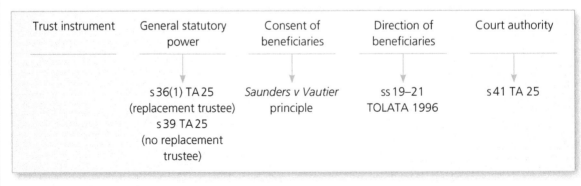

Figure 13.2 Retirement of trustees

13.3.2 Retirement under a court order

Generally speaking, the court will not discharge a trustee under its statutory jurisdiction under s 41 of the 1925 Act unless it appoints a replacement trustee. However, the court has an inherent jurisdiction to discharge a trustee without replacement, in accordance with its responsibility to administer the trust. This will be the position when s 39 is not applicable because the appropriate consent cannot be obtained.

13.4 Removal

A trustee may be removed from office in one of the following four ways:

- By virtue of a *power* contained in the trust instrument: this is highly unusual, but if such power exists the court is required to construe the instrument to ascertain whether the circumstances have arisen which give rise to the exercise of the power.

- Under s 36 of the Trustee Act 1925: this involves the removal of the existing trustee and appointment of a replacement trustee in circumstances laid down in s 36(1).

- In the circumstances specified in ss 19 and 20 of TOLATA 1996.

- Under a court order under s 41 of the Trustee Act 1925 or the inherent jurisdiction of the court.

13.4.1 Court order

Under s 41 of the Trustee Act 1925 (see earlier), the court has the jurisdiction to remove an existing trustee and appoint a replacement trustee when, in the limited circumstances, it is inexpedient, difficult or impracticable to do so without the assistance of the court.

However, under its inherent jurisdiction the court has a broad discretion to remove a trustee from his position. Under this jurisdiction, in an effort to secure the proper administration of the trust, the court has the power to remove a trustee without appointing a replacement trustee.

CASE EXAMPLE

Letterstedt v Broers [1884] 9 AC 371

The Privy Council declared that the court had a general duty to ensure that trusts were properly executed and their main guide was the welfare of the beneficiaries. Accordingly, friction and hostility between the trustees and the beneficiaries which is likely to prejudice the proper administration of the trust may be a ground for the removal of trustees. In this case, a beneficiary made allegations of misconduct against a trustee concerning the administration of the trust. The court decided that, notwithstanding the allegations were not substantiated, it would exercise its jurisdiction to remove the trustees.

JUDGMENT

'[I]f it appears clear that the continuance of the trustee would be detrimental to the execution of the trusts, even if for no other reason than that human infirmity would prevent those beneficially interested, or those who act for them, from working in harmony with the trustee … the trustee is always advised by his own counsel to resign, and does so. If, without any reasonable ground, he refused to do so, it seems that the court might think it proper to remove him.'

Lord Blackburn

The primary concern of the court in exercising its power of removal of a trustee is the protection and enhancement of the interests of the beneficiaries. In *Brudenell-Bruce v Moore* [2014] EWHC 3679, the High Court decided that trustees who committed numerous breaches of trust in failing to repair and re-let trust property and allowing a beneficiary to occupy one of the premises subject to trust, rent-free, were liable to compensate the trust for the loss. In addition, where there had been a breakdown in relations between one of the trustees and a beneficiary to such an extent that the welfare of the beneficiaries was put at risk, that trustee was required to be removed. The test is whether the acts or omissions of the trustee are such as to endanger the trust property or manifest a want of honesty or proper capacity to execute his duties. This will depend on the facts of each case.

JUDGMENT

'In the end, I have concluded that the right course is to order Mr Moore's [one of the trustees] removal as a trustee immediately after the sale of Tottenham House has been completed. Even if it is then decided that the Trust should be brought to an end, important decisions will remain to be taken, and I do not think it would be in the interests of the beneficiaries as a whole for Mr Moore to be involved in them. He might well struggle to approach them impartially, with a mind uncoloured by his personal feelings about Lord Cardigan [beneficiary]. At any rate, there would not, as it seems to me, be a sufficient appearance of fairness.'

Newey J

There many contexts in which trustees are required to make judgments that involve striking a balance between different competing interests and which may adversely affect some beneficiaries. It is to be expected that in such cases there will often be an element of friction between the trustee and a disappointed beneficiary. This, on its own, is insufficient reason for the court to exercise its jurisdiction to remove the trustee. The governing principle in exercising its jurisdiction to remove a trustee is whether the court is satisfied that the continuance of the trustee will prevent the trusts being properly executed. Evidence that demonstrates that the trustee is not fit to be in charge of other people's property will be sufficient to remove him from office. There does not appear to be much by way of authority that explains the extent to which the inherent jurisdiction may be exercised. Indeed, the absence of any guidelines in the exercise of the court's inherent jurisdiction has been attributed to the fact that each case must depend on its facts.

In *Alkin v Raymond* (2010), the court decided that friction and hostility with a beneficiary under a discretionary trust may be relevant factors to determine whether the trustees may give proper consideration to the merits of that beneficiary as well as others under the trust.

CASE EXAMPLE

Alkin v Raymond [2010] All ER (D) 48, HC

The testator died in October 2008 and by his will appointed the two defendants executors and trustees of the estate. The two claimants were the testator's widow (Mrs Alkin) and daughter (Mrs Price). The testator directed that his estate be divided into two parts. The first part comprised a legacy of the threshold for inheritance tax (nil rate band) to be held by the trustees on discretionary trust for a class of beneficiaries consisting of Mrs Alkin, Mrs Price, Mrs Price's children, remoter issue, any spouse, widow or widower of Mrs Price, and a registered charity.

The second part of the estate was held by the trustees on trust for Mrs Alkin for life and on her death for the same class of beneficiaries on discretionary trust. The two executors and trustees were Messrs Raymond and Whelan. They were close friends of the testator. Mr Whelan, a builder by occupation, had assisted the testator on various property development ventures. The claimants applied to the court for an order for the removal and replacement of the trustees, because they were unhappy with the way the defendants administered the trust and were concerned that the purposes of the trust would not be achieved. The grounds for removal were:

(i) circumstances surrounding the payment of an invoice from Mr Whelan's company, dated 29 September 2008 for £163,000;
(ii) the making of an offer of a loan from the estate to Mr Price, the divorced husband of Mrs Price, to enable him to fund the children's school fees. This offer was rejected by Mr Price;
(iii) a variety of miscellaneous allegations of a personal nature in respect of Mr Whelan's conduct towards Mrs Price.

Held: The court decided that although the testator's selection of executors and trustees should not lightly be set aside, in the circumstances, the presence of the two trustees impeded the proper administration of the trust and was detrimental to the welfare of the beneficiaries. The first ground of complaint was sufficient to justify the removal and appointment of new trustees. The other grounds of complaint were insufficient to justify the order that the claimants had requested.

JUDGMENT

'There are a variety of issues relating to [the invoice]. There is the question, of course, whether the invoice was in respect of a genuine debt of the estate. There is a question whether the invoice was one which called for scrutiny or investigation and, if so, whether there ever was any. And finally there is a question whether the way the matter was dealt with by the defendants and was presented to Mrs Price and her solicitors demonstrated that the defendants or either of them should not appropriately continue in office. It is not necessary for me to decide precisely what, if anything, was due to Hill & Whelan Ltd from Mr Alkin's estate for building or other work on the properties. But invoice no. 3453 was altogether unsatisfactory; and I do not think that anything approaching £163,000 was properly to be paid for Hill & Whelan's work on the development over and above what had already been paid by Mr Alkin.'

Bompas QC sitting as a Deputy Judge of the High Court

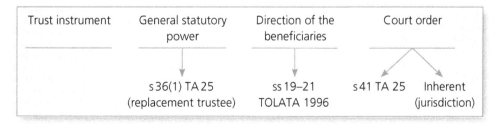

Trust instrument	General statutory power	Direction of the beneficiaries	Court order	
	↓	↓	↙	↘
	s 36(1) TA 25 (replacement trustee)	ss 19–21 TOLATA 1996	s 41 TA 25	Inherent (jurisdiction)

Figure 13.3 Removal of trustees

Self-test questions

1. In what circumstances and by whom may a trustee of a personalty settlement be removed from his trusteeship?
2. Is it necessary or useful for a new trustee to be appointed by deed rather than by writing under hand?
3. Can a trustee who retires ever be made liable for breaches of trust which take place after his retirement and, if so, in what circumstances?
4. Does the notion of a 'sleeping' trustee have any legal significance?

SUMMARY

Trustees may be appointed on the creation of a new trust or during the continuance of an existing trust. The appointment of trustees may be done under express authority in the trust instrument, or by virtue of statutory authority, namely s 36(1) of the Trustee Act 1925 or by the court under its inherent power or s 41 of the Trustee Act 1925.

- Additional trustees may be appointed under the default provision of s 36(6) of the Trustee Act 1925.
- The number of trustees who may be appointed varies with the nature of the trust property. For realty, the maximum number of trustees is four, see s 34 of the Trustee Act 1925. In respect of personalty there is no maximum number of trustees, but for practical purposes the number ought not to exceed four.

A trustee may retire from the trust under express authority, or by taking advantage of a statutory authority (ss 36 or 39 of the Trustee Act 1925) or by virtue of the rule in *Saunders v Vautier* (1841) where the beneficiaries are *sui juris* and of full age and consent to his retirement or by the direction of the beneficiaries under ss 19–21 of TOLATA 1996 or where the court orders his discharge under s 41 of the Trustee Act 1925 or under its inherent jurisdiction.

The occasions when a trustee may be removed from office are by virtue of an express power in the trust instrument, or by virtue of statutory authority (see s 36 of the Trustee Act 1925 and ss 19–21 of TOLATA 1996) or by court order under s 41 of the Trustee Act 1925 or under its inherent jurisdiction.

SAMPLE ESSAY QUESTION

Consider the following essay question:

In what circumstances may trustees be appointed to act on behalf of a trust?

Answer plan

Distinguish between the appointment of trustees on the date of creation of the trust and the appointment of replacement trustees.

Consider whether the nominated person has the capacity to become a trustee.

Initial trustees – 'Equity will not allow a trust to fail for want of a trustee' – the court as a last resort will appoint the trustees.

Replacement trustees may be appointed under express power, statutory power or by order of the court.

Consider whether there are any limits on the number of trustees.

Additional trustees may be appointed by a person or persons under express power in the trust instrument or the subsisting trustees, or by statute or by the court.

Consider whether the trustee has accepted his office as trustee and the procedure for vesting the property in the trustees.

CONCLUSION

Further reading

Bell, C, 'Some reflections on choosing trustees' (1988) TL&P 86.
Hopkins, N, 'The Trusts of Land and Appointment of Trustees Act 1996' (1996) Conv 411.

14

Duties and powers of trustees

AIMS AND OBJECTIVES

By the end of this chapter you should be able to:

- identify the trustees' fiduciary duties including the duty to avoid making profits from the trust
- define the standard of care imposed on trustees in the execution of their office
- understand the scope of the trustees' powers of delegation of duties
- comprehend the limits regarding exclusion clauses designed to protect trustees
- appreciate the changes made by the Trustee Act 2000 concerning the trustees' power of investment of trust funds
- understand the trustees' powers of maintenance and advancement under ss 31 and 32 of the Trustee Act 1925

14.1 Introduction

The office of trustee is subject to a wide-ranging group of duties. A trustee has control of the trust property and is regarded as a fiduciary and, on that basis, owes a collection of special duties to the beneficiaries. The overriding obligation of the trustee is to act in the best interests of all the beneficiaries and not to allow his interests to conflict with his duties; see Chapter 8. The list of duties discussed in this chapter is not intended to be exhaustive. The trustees' primary duties are to obey the terms of the trust and, subject thereto, to act for the benefit of the beneficiaries. It will become apparent that not only does the trustee owe a duty to all of the beneficiaries, but that he is under a duty to act fairly and impartially between them.

It will readily become apparent that the rules relating to the duties of the trustees are inextricably interwoven with other areas of trusts law, such as the powers of trustees, the liability of trustees for breach of trust and the remedies of the beneficiaries (see Chapter 16).

Trustees are endowed with a variety of powers in order to equip them with the discretion to respond to unforeseen or changed circumstances since the creation of the trust. It is imperative that the trustee identify and act in accordance with the source and scope of a power. Where a particular power does not exist and the trustee acts on the erroneous belief that it does, he may be in breach of trust.

The duties and powers of trustees have been laid down by the common law as modified by the trust instrument and statute.

14.2 Duties of trustees

The duties of a trustee are varied and extremely onerous. They are required to be executed with the utmost diligence and good faith. Otherwise he will be liable for breach of trust. The primary duty of the trustee is to comply with the terms of the trust and, subject thereto, to act in the best interests of the beneficiaries. In order to carry out these duties, the trustee is invested with a variety of powers and discretions which are required to be exercised for the benefit of the beneficiaries.

14.2.1 Duty and standard of care at common law

Throughout the administration of the trust the trustee is required to exhibit an objective standard of skill as would be expected from an ordinary prudent man of business. In the case of a power of investment the duty would be exercised so as to yield the best return for all the beneficiaries, judged in relation to the risks inherent in the investments and the prospects of the yield of income and capital appreciation. The classical statement of the rule was laid down by Lord Watson in *Learoyd v Whiteley* (1887) 12 AC 727:

JUDGMENT

'As a general rule the law requires of a trustee no higher degree of diligence in the execution of his office than a man of ordinary prudence would exercise in the management of his own private affairs.'

Lord Watson

The courts will have regard to all the circumstances of each case in order to ascertain whether the trustees' conduct fell below the standard imposed on such persons.

In considering the investment policy of the trust, the trustees are required to put on one side their own personal interests and views. They may have strongly held social or political views. They may be firmly opposed to any investments in companies connected with alcohol, tobacco, armaments or many other things. In the conduct of their own affairs, trustees are free to abstain from making any such investments. However, in performance of their fiduciary duties, if investments of the morally reprehensible type would be more beneficial to the beneficiaries than other investments, the trustees must not refrain from making the investments by reason of the views that they hold. Trustees may even act dishonourably (though not illegally), such as accepting a subsequent higher offer for the sale of trust property, if the interests of their beneficiaries require it.

CASE EXAMPLE

Buttle v Saunders [1950] 2 All ER 193

Trustees struck a bargain for the sale of trust property. This was not legally binding, but the court held that they were under a duty to consider and explore a better offer received by them.

CASE EXAMPLE

Cowan v Scargill and others [1984] 3 WLR 501

The defendants were trustees of the Mineworkers' Pension Scheme, who raised an objection to a new investment plan of trust funds in competing forms of energy. The court decided that the plan would yield the best return for the beneficiaries and refused the application for objection.

JUDGMENT

'Trustees must do the best they can for the benefit of their beneficiaries, and not merely avoid harming them. I find it impossible to see how it will assist trustees to do the best they can for their beneficiaries by prohibiting a wide range of investments that are authorised by the terms of the trust. Whatever the position today, nobody can say that conditions tomorrow cannot possibly make it advantageous to invest in one of the prohibited investments. It is the duty of trustees, in the interests of their beneficiaries, to take advantage of the full range of investments authorised by the terms of the trust, instead of resolving to narrow that range.'

Megarry VC

In an action for breach of trust the claimant is required to establish that the trust has suffered a loss which is attributable to the conduct or omission of the trustees. If the trustee's conduct or omission fell below the required standard imposed on trustees, he becomes personally liable whether he acted in good faith or not.

CASE EXAMPLE

Re Lucking's Will Trust [1968] 1 WLR 866

A trustee-director of a company was liable to the trust when he allowed the managing director and (a friend) to appropriate £15,000 of the company funds through the delivery of blank cheques to the managing director which were signed by the trustee.

With regard to professional trustees such as banks and insurance companies, the standard of care imposed on such bodies is higher than the degree of diligence expected from a non-professional trustee. The professional trustee is required to administer the trust with such a degree of expertise as would be expected from a specialist in trust administration. This objective standard is applied by the courts after due consideration of the facts of each case.

CASE EXAMPLE

Bartlett v Barclays Bank [1980] Ch 515

The trust estate was the majority shareholder in a property company and the trustee was a professional trust company. The board of directors, for good commercial reasons, decided to restructure the investment portfolio and invest in land development. The trustee did not actively participate in the company's deliberations, nor was he provided with regular information concerning the company's activities, but was content to rely on the annual balance sheet and profit and loss account. One of the schemes pursued by the company proved to be disastrous. In an action brought against the trustee the court held that the trustee was liable because it (the trust corporation) had not acted reasonably in the administration of the trust.

On the other hand, the claimant failed in her action in *Nestlé v National Westminster Bank* [1993] 1 WLR 1260 on the ground that she failed to prove positively that the defendant's action or inaction resulted in a loss to the trust.

But while the duties imposed on trustees are onerous, there is no liability for an error of judgment.

JUDGMENT

'A trustee who is honest and reasonably competent is not to be held responsible for a mere error in judgement when the question he has to consider is whether a security of a class authorised, but depreciated in value should be retained or realised, provided he acts with reasonable care, prudence and circumspection.'

Lopes J in *Re Chapman* [1896] 2 Ch 763

In *Lloyds TSB Bank plc v Markandan & Uddin* (2012), the Court of Appeal affirmed the decision of the trial judge and decided that where the defendants, a firm of solicitors, had acted honestly and conscientiously, but were deceived by a fraudulent third party, the defendants might nevertheless be in breach of trust by failing to act with due care and attention.

CASE EXAMPLE

Lloyds TSB Bank plc v Markandan & Uddin [2012] EWCA Civ 65, CA

The claimant bank was the successor in title to a mortgage lender, namely the Cheltenham and Gloucester Building Society (C&G). C&G offered a mortgage of £742,500 to a person calling himself Mr Victor Davies in order to purchase a residential property. The defendant firm of solicitors, Markandan & Uddin (MU), was instructed to act on behalf of the claimant in respect of the mortgage transaction. Mr Davies also instructed the defendants to act on his behalf in the purchase of the property.

In the event, C&G and the defendants were the victims of a fraud. The owners of the property (Gary and Monique Green) had not agreed to sell their property to Victor Davies or to anyone, and were ignorant of the fraud that was carried out. On 24 August 2007 a firm of solicitors called Deen Solicitors (Deen HP), with offices in Holland Park in west London, held themselves out as acting on behalf of the vendors. No such firm existed in Holland Park, although there was a firm called Deen Solicitors in Luton. The Luton firm was not involved in this transaction, and knew nothing of the circumstances of this arrangement. The Holland Park firm fraudulently passed itself off as a branch of the Luton firm. The defendants were sent the building society's standard form of certificate of title to complete. The certificate of title was completed by the defendants on 29 August 2007. On 31 August the claimant remitted an advance of £742,500 to the defendants. On the same day, Deen HP wrote to the defendants, saying that they had been instructed to pay the purchaser's legal costs to the defendants. This information ought to have put the defendants on notice as to the suspicious nature of the transaction. Deen HP confirmed that they wished to complete by post and listed the documents to be handed over on completion as the transfer, the certificate of discharge of the current mortgage, the charge certificate and the vendors' part of the contract. The defendants remitted the sum of £707,613.25 to the account nominated by Deen HP on 4 September. That sum was the advance from the building society less the defendants' legal fees, costs, stamp duty, land registry fees and disbursements. Although the amount was remitted to Deen HP, no signed contract was obtained from the vendor on that date. On 11 September 2007 the defendants wrote to Deen HP requesting the signed contract, transfer and discharge certificates. On 25 September 2007 Deen HP returned the sum they had received on 4 September, less £5,000, and requested the defendants to send the money back to a different account. On 28 September Deen HP wrote apologising for their conduct in not sending the documents and requesting the funds. On the same day the defendants complied with the request and remitted the funds to Deen HP, despite not having received the documents. Deen HP then disappeared, and the fraud was discovered.

The claimant sued for damages for breach of trust. The defendants denied a breach of trust and, in the alternative, claimed relief under s 61 of the Trustee Act 1925 and alleged contributory negligence on the part of the claimant. The High Court decided in favour of the claimant and awarded damages against the defendants. The defendants appealed to the Court of Appeal.

Held: The Court of Appeal dismissed the appeal and decided that:

1. The purported contract of sale was a nullity since the owners had not agreed to sell their property to Mr Victor Davies or anyone else.
2. There was no exchange of money for documents or a solicitor's undertaking.
3. In the circumstances, the defendants had had no authority to release the loan moneys. Thus, the remission of the moneys to Deen HP was a breach of trust for which the defendants were accountable.
4. Relief under s 61 of the Trustee Act 1925 was dependent on the defendants discharging a burden of proof to show that they acted honestly and reasonably and ought fairly to be excused. In the circumstances, the defendants had failed to discharge this burden in that they had not acted reasonably.

JUDGMENT

'In this case there was, however, no exchange of money for documents. There was instead a parting of the loan money in exchange for what [the defendants] believed to be the undertakings of Deen, a firm of solicitors. In fact, [the defendants'] belief was wrong and they received no such undertakings ... The result was that [the defendants] parted with the loan money in exchange for undertakings that were not of the nature they thought they were. They were themselves direct victims of the fraud and the relevant events of 4 September were in law a nullity ... It follows in my view that, as the events of 4 September did not amount to completion, [the defendants] had no authority from C&G to release the loan money to [Deen HP]. They paid it away in breach of trust for which ... they were accountable ... The careful, conscientious and thorough solicitor, who conducts the transaction by the book and acts honestly and reasonably in relation to it in all respects but still does not discover the fraud, may still be held to have been in breach of trust for innocently parting with the loan money to a fraudster.'

Rimer LJ

Section 61 of the Trustee Act 1925 may also apply to relieve a trustee from liability (see Chapter 16). This section applies where a trustee has acted honestly and reasonably, and ought fairly to be excused for the breach of trust. In these circumstances the court may relieve him either wholly or partly from personal liability.

14.2.2 Duty and standard of care under the Trustee Act 2000

The Trustee Act 2000 describes the duty of care which is applicable to trustees. Section 1(1) provides that whenever the duty under the subsection applies to a trustee, he must exercise such care and skill as is reasonable in the circumstances, having regard in particular:

(a) to any special knowledge or experience he has or holds himself out as having; and

(b) if he acts as a trustee in the course of a business or profession, to any special knowledge or experience that it is reasonable to expect of a person acting in the course of that kind of business or profession.

Thus, a solicitor who is a trustee will be under a more stringent duty of care and skill, as opposed to a lay trustee.

Schedule 1 of the 2000 Act specifies when the statutory duty of care applies to trustees. These are in the *exercise* of the statutory and express powers of investment, including the duty to have regard to the standard investment criteria and the duty to obtain and consider proper advice. In addition, the duty applies to the trustees' power to acquire land. Moreover, the duty of care applies when trustees enter into arrangements in order to delegate functions to agents, nominees and custodians as well as the review of their actions. The duty of care also applies to trustees when exercising their power under s 19 of the Trustee Act 1925 to insure property. However, para 7 of the Schedule enacts that the duty of care does not apply if, or in so far as, it appears from the trust instrument that the duty is not meant to apply. Thus, a settlor may expressly restrict the application of the statutory duty (or the common law duty of care).

14.3 Duty to act unanimously

Trustees are required to act unanimously, subject to any provision in the trust instrument to the contrary. The settlor has given all of his trustees the responsibility to act on behalf of the trust. Subject to provisions to the contrary in the trust instrument, the acts and decisions of some of the trustees (even a majority of trustees) are not binding on others. Thus, once a trust decision is made, the trustees become jointly and severally liable to the beneficiaries in the event of a breach of trust. In practice, it may be that one trustee is active or dominant, but nevertheless all the trustees must agree on a particular course of action concerning the trust. In *Bahin v Hughes* (1886) 31 Ch D 390, 'passive' trustees were liable to the beneficiaries for breach of trust along with an 'active' trustee.

JUDGMENT

'Miss Hughes was the active trustee and Mr Edwards did nothing, and in my opinion it would be laying down a wrong rule to hold that where one trustee acts honestly, though erroneously, the other trustee is to be held entitled to indemnity who by doing nothing neglects his duty more than the acting trustee … In my opinion the money was lost just as much by the default of Mr Edwards as by the innocent though erroneous action of his co-trustee, Miss Hughes. All the trustees were in the wrong, and everyone is equally liable to indemnify the beneficiaries.'

Cotton LJ

A claim by one trustee against his co-trustee is now subject to the Civil Liability (Contribution) Act 1978. Briefly, a trustee who is sued for breach of trust may claim a contribution from his co-trustee. The court has a discretion to make a contribution order, if such 'is just and equitable having regard to the extent of the [co-trustee's] responsibility for the damage in question'.

14.4 Duty to act impartially

In performing their duties, the trustees are required to act honestly, diligently and in the best interests of the beneficiaries. Thus, the trustees are not entitled to show favour to a beneficiary or group of beneficiaries, but are required to act impartially and in the best interests of all the beneficiaries.

CASE EXAMPLE

Lloyds Bank v Duker [1987] 3 All ER 193

The court refused an application requiring the trustees to transfer to a beneficiary his share of a trust fund, namely 574 shares out of a total of 999 shares (or 46/80 of the trust fund). The transfer would have entitled the beneficiary to a majority holding in the company, which would have exceeded the value of the remaining shares subject to the trust.

JUDGMENT

'I can … get some help from another general principle. I mean the principle that trustees are bound to hold an even hand among their beneficiaries, and not favour one as against another, stated for instance in *Snell's Principles of Equity, op cit*, p. 225. Of course Mr Duker must have a larger part than the other beneficiaries. But if he takes 46/80ths of the shares he will be favoured beyond what Mr Smith intended, because his shares will each be worth more than the others. The trustees' duty to hold an even hand seems to indicate that they should sell all 999 shares instead.'

Mowbray QC

The duty on the trustees to act impartially or with even-handedness is of paramount importance with regard to the exercise of the trustees' discretion. The claimant will undoubtedly bear the legal burden to prove that the trustee has acted in breach of his duty of impartiality, but it is not an easy task to challenge the exercise by a trustee of a discretion. One basis on which the trustee's decision might be challenged would be to establish that it was perverse, in the sense that no reasonable trustee could properly have taken it. Another would be to show that the trustee had proceeded on the basis of some mistake of fact or law which vitiates the decision. That is the principle often referred to as the rule in *Re Hastings Bass* [1975] Ch 25. It was established that in the case of a discretion which the trustee is not under a duty to exercise, a party seeking to challenge the trustee's decision has to show that the trustee would (and not merely might) have taken a different decision had he not made the mistake (see *Sieff v Fox* [2005] 1 WLR 3811 and *Betafence v Veys* [2006] EWHC 999 (Ch)). But in *Pitt v Holt; Futter v Futter* [2013] 2 AC 108 (see earlier), in a conjoined appeal, the Supreme Court decided that to lay down a rigid rule of proving that the trustees either 'would not' or 'might not' have made a different decision, would inhibit the court in seeking the best practical solution in the application of the *Hastings-Bass* rule in a variety of different factual situations. As a matter of principle there must be a high degree of flexibility in the range of the court's possible responses. A third basis would be to show that the trustee exercised his discretion to achieve an unlawful purpose, that is to say, a purpose other than that for which the power was given. In *Chirkinian v Arnfield* [2006] EWHC 1917 (Ch), the court decided that although a beneficial unsecured loan potentially puts the assets of the trust in jeopardy, the risks are taken for the benefit of the beneficiary. Such a loan should not be recalled unless the trustee considered it to be in the interests of the debtor beneficiary, or other beneficiaries to do so. The judge ruled that, on the facts of this case, a decision to call in a beneficial loan and pursue the beneficiary debtor to the point of bankruptcy could not be treated as an instance of the trustee acting neutrally. From the evidence no consideration was given to the interests of the beneficiary and the judgment of the trustee was seriously flawed. In reality the trustee appeared to prefer the interests of the liquidator as opposed to the interests of the beneficiary.

The effect of this even-handedness rule is that the trustees are required to take positive steps to avoid placing themselves in a position where their duties may conflict with their personal interests. If there is a conflict of the trustees' duties and interest, the trustees are required to hand over any unauthorised benefit to the beneficiaries. Thus, it is imperative that the trustees do not deviate from the terms of the trust without the authority of the beneficiaries or the court.

An additional feature of the duty imposed on the trustees to act impartially is to ensure that the trust property is properly balanced to accommodate the interests of present and future beneficiaries. Thus, the trustees are obliged to ensure that the trust property produces both a reasonable income for the benefit of those beneficiaries entitled to income, such as the life tenant, and to create capital growth for beneficiaries entitled to capital, such as the remainderman. Where the trust assets are likely to deteriorate, such as machinery, and the assets are held on trust for A for life with remainder to B absolutely, the trustees may be in breach of the duties to the remainderman if they do not consider reinvesting the trust property.

A duty to convert trust assets may arise from the express terms of the trust instrument, by statute or by rules of equity. Under s 3 of the Trusts of Land and Appointment of Trustees Act 1996, the doctrine of conversion has been abolished in respect of a trust of land. In short, where land is held by trustees subject to a trust for sale, the land is not treated in equity as personal property.

Prior to the Trusts (Capital and Income) Act 2013, the equitable rules of apportionment were created by the rule in *Howe v Earl of Dartmouth* (1802) 7 Ves 137, the rule in *Re Earl of Chesterfield's Trusts* (1833) 24 Ch D 643, the rule in *Allhusen v Whittell* (1867) LR 4 EQ 295 and s 2 of the Apportionment Act 1870. The first branch of the rule in *Howe v Earl of Dartmouth* created an implied trust for sale in respect of a residuary personal estate held on trust for beneficiaries in succession that are of a wasting, hazardous and unauthorised character. The second branch of this rule compensated the capital beneficiary for loss pending the conversion of the trust assets. The rule in *Re Earl of Chesterfield's Trusts* is to the effect that where the trust property, created by will, included a non-income producing asset, such as a reversion or a life policy, the proceeds of the non-income producing asset are apportioned between the life tenant and the remainderman. The remainderman will receive a sum which, if invested at compound interest at the date of death at 4 per cent per annum (less income tax), would produce the proceeds of sale. The balance is paid over to the life tenant. The rule in *Allhusen v Whittell* apportions debts, liabilities, legacies and other charges payable out of the residuary estate between capital and income beneficiaries. The effect of the rule is to charge the life tenant with interest on the sums used to pay debts and other liabilities in order to maintain equality between the beneficiaries. Section 2 of the Apportionment Act 1870 created a rule of time apportionment. The effect of the section is that income beneficiaries are entitled only to the proportion of income that is deemed to have accrued during their period of entitlement. The nature of these rules was summarised by the Law Commission in its Report, 'Capital and Income in Trusts: Classification and Apportionment', in 2009, thus:

QUOTATION

'These rules are all based on the principle that no beneficiary should take a disproportionate benefit at the expense of another. They are logical developments of the classification rules and of the duty to balance the interests of beneficiaries interested in capital and income. The difficulty is that they were formulated many decades ago and in circumstances much less likely to arise today. They are prescriptive, unclear in places and generally require complicated calculations relating to disproportionately small sums of money. Well drafted trust instruments exclude these rules. In most trusts where they have not been excluded (particularly those that arise by implication) they are either ignored or cause considerable inconvenience.'

The Law Commission concluded that the rules of apportionment were archaic and inconvenient and recommended their abolition for future trusts, subject to any contrary intention in the trust instrument. These recommendations were adopted by Parliament in enacting the Trusts (Capital and Income) Act 2013.

Section 1 of the Trusts (Capital and Income) Act 2013 provides:

SECTION

'1 Disapplication of apportionment etc rules

(1) Any entitlement to income under a new trust is to income as it arises (and accordingly section 2 of the Apportionment Act 1870, which provides for income to accrue from day to day, does not apply in relation to the trust).

(2) The following do not apply in relation to a new trust –

　(a) the first part of the rule known as the rule in *Howe v Earl of Dartmouth* (which requires certain residuary personal estates to be sold);

　(b) the second part of that rule (which withholds from a life tenant income arising from certain investments and compensates the life tenant with payments of interest);

　(c) the rule known as the rule in *Re Earl of Chesterfield's Trusts* (which requires the proceeds of the conversion of certain investments to be apportioned between capital and income);

　(d) the rule known as the rule in *Allhusen v Whittell* (which requires a contribution to be made from income for the purpose of paying a deceased person's debts, legacies and annuities).

(3) Trustees have power to sell any property which (but for subsection (2)(a)) they would have been under a duty to sell.

(4) Subsections (1) to (3) have effect subject to any contrary intention that appears –

　(a) in any trust instrument of the trust, and

　(b) in any power under which the trust is created or arises.

(5) In this section "new trust" means a trust created or arising on or after the day on which this section comes into force.'

The effect of s 1 of the Trusts (Capital and Income) Act 2013 is that in respect of future trusts ('new trusts'), namely trusts created on or after 1 October 2013 (the appointed date), the archaic and complex apportionment rules will not be implied into trust instruments. The apportionment rules are required to be expressly incorporated in the trust instrument if they are to operate. Instead, the possible sale and reinvestment of trust property will become part of the trustees' general duties of investment under the Trustee Act 2000.

14.5 Duty to act personally

delegatus non potest delegare

A delegate cannot delegate his duties.

Generally speaking, a trustee is appointed by a settlor because of his personal qualities. It is expected that the trustee will act personally in the execution of his duties. The general rule is ***delegatus non potest delegare***.

However, in the contemporary commercial climate the functions and needs for the proper administration of a trust have become increasingly complex, requiring specialised skill and knowledge. Accordingly, it is unrealistic to expect trustees to act personally in all matters relating to the trust. Trustees are entitled to appoint agents to perform acts in respect of the trust.

Part IV of the Trustee Act 2000 has reformed the law as to the trustees' powers of delegation. It repeals ss 23 and 30 of the Trustee Act 1925 (which created some confusion regarding the duties of trustees) and introduces provisions with a clearer framework for delegation. Generally, the new provisions deal with the appointment of agents, nominees and custodians and the liability of the trustees for such persons.

Sections 11–20 of the Trustee Act 2000 deal with the appointment of agents, nominees and custodians. Sections 21–23 deal with the review of acts of the agents, nominees and custodians and the question of liability for their acts.

Section 11(1) enacts that the trustees of a trust 'may authorise any person to exercise any or all of their *delegable functions* as their agent'. Section 11(2) defines 'delegable functions' as *any function* of the trustee, subject to four exceptions. These are:

(a) functions relating to the distribution of assets in favour of beneficiaries, i.e. dispositive functions;

(b) any power to allocate fees and other payments to capital or income;

(c) any power to appoint trustees; and

(d) any power conferred by the trust instrument or any enactment which allows trustees to delegate their administrative functions to another person.

Thus, the trustees cannot delegate their discretion under a discretionary trust to distribute the funds or to select beneficiaries from a group of objects. But they may delegate their investment decision-making power and thereby obtain skilled professional advice from an investment manager.

In the case of charitable trusts, the trustees' *delegable functions* are set out in s 11(3) as follows:

SECTION

'(a) any function consisting of carrying out a decision that the trustees have taken;

(b) any function concerning investment of assets subject to the trust;

(c) any function relating to the raising of funds for the trust otherwise than by means of profits of a trade which is an integral part of carrying out the trust's charitable purpose;

(d) any other function prescribed by order of the Secretary of State.'

Section 12 provides who may or may not be appointed an agent of the trustees. The trustees may appoint one of their number to act as an agent, but cannot appoint a beneficiary to carry out that function. If more than one person is appointed to exercise the same function, they are required to act jointly.

Section 14 authorises the trustees to appoint agents on such terms as to remuneration and other matters as they may determine. But certain terms of the agency contract are subject to a test of reasonableness. These are terms permitting the agent to sub-delegate to another agent, or to restrict his liability to the trustees or the beneficiaries, or to allow the agent to carry out functions that are capable of giving rise to a conflict of interest. Thus, sub-delegation to another trustee or the insertion of an exclusion clause in the contract appointing the agent is subject to a test of reasonableness.

Section 15 imposes special restrictions within certain types of agency contracts. With regard to asset-management functions the agreement is required to be evidenced in writing. In addition, the trustees are required to include a 'policy statement' in the agreement, giving the agent guidance as to how the functions ought to be exercised, and should seek an undertaking from the agent that he will secure compliance with the policy statement. In the ordinary course of events, the policy statement will refer to the 'standard investment criteria' and, in the case of beneficiaries entitled in succession, require the agent to provide investments with a balance between income and capital.

Section 24 provides that a failure to observe these limits does not invalidate the authorisation or appointment.

14.5.1 Power to appoint nominees

Section 16 of the Act of 2000 authorises trustees to appoint nominees in relation to such of the trust assets as they may determine (other than settled land). In addition, the trustees may take steps to ensure the vesting of those assets in the nominee. Such appointment is required to be evidenced in writing.

14.5.2 Power to appoint custodians

Section 17 of the Trustee Act 2000 authorises the trustees to appoint a person to act as custodian in relation to specified assets. A custodian is a person who undertakes the safe custody of the assets or any documents or records concerning the assets. The appointment is required to be evidenced in writing.

14.5.3 Persons who may be appointed as nominees or custodians

Section 19 of the Trustee Act 2000 provides that a person may not be appointed as a nominee or custodian unless he carries on a business which consists of or includes acting as a nominee or custodian, or is a body corporate controlled by the trustees. The trustees may appoint as a nominee or custodian one of their number if that is a trust corporation, or two (or more) of their number if they act jointly.

14.5.4 Review of acts of agents, nominees and custodians

Provided that the agent, nominee or custodian continues to act for the trust, the trustees are required to:

- keep under review the arrangements under which they act, and how those arrangements are put into effect;
- *consider* whether to exercise any powers of intervention, if the circumstances are appropriate;
- intervene if they consider that a need has arisen for such action.

14.5.5 Liability for the acts of agents, nominees and custodians

Section 23 of the Trustee Act 2000 provides that a trustee will not be liable for the acts of agents, nominees and custodians provided that he complies with the general duty of care laid down in s 1 and Sched 1, both in respect of the initial appointment of the agent etc., and when carrying out his duties under s 22 (review of acts of agents etc.). The effect of this provision is that it lays to rest the eccentric principles that were applied under the 1925 Act, and introduces one standard objective test concerning the trustees' duty of care.

14.6 Other statutory provisions permitting delegation of discretions

Trustees may delegate their discretions under the following statutory provisions:

- Part IV of the Trustee Act 2000 (see above);
- s 25 of the Trustee Act 1925 (as amended by the Trustee Delegation Act 1999); or
- s 9 of the Trusts of Land and Appointment of Trustees Act 1996 (see below).

Individual delegation

Section 25 of the Trustee Act 1925 (as re-enacted by s 5 of the Trustee Delegation Act 1999) enables a trustee to delegate, by a power of attorney, 'the execution or exercise of all or any of the trusts, powers and discretions vested in him either alone or jointly with any other person or persons'. The delegation of the powers commences on the date of execution or such time as stated in the instrument, and continues for a period of 12 months or such shorter period as mentioned in the instrument. Written notice is required to be given by the donor of the power to each nominee under the trust instrument who is entitled to appoint trustees, and each other trustee within seven days after its creation. The donor of the power remains liable for the acts or defaults of the donee.

14.6.1 Delegation under the Trusts of Land and Appointment of Trustees Act 1996

Section 9 of the 1996 Act enacts that trustees of land may delegate any of their powers in relation to the land by a power of attorney to adult beneficiaries who are currently entitled to interests in possession. In exercising their powers, the trustees are required to have regard to the rights of the beneficiaries and are obliged to observe any rules of law and equity. Thus, the trustees may not favour or prejudice the interest of any beneficiary when exercising their powers. It should be noted that the powers included in s 6 relate only to a trust of land and not to any personal property. In addition, the s 6 powers may be amended or excluded by the settlement, or made subject to obtaining the consent of any person (s 8). Thus, the settlor may prevent any dealing with the land (although this could be challenged under s 14: see above). In the case of charitable trusts, the trustees' powers may not be amended or excluded, but they may be made subject to obtaining consent.

Protection of purchasers from delegate

In respect of land, where a person deals with the delegate in good faith in the belief that the trustees were entitled to delegate to that person, it is presumed that the trustees were entitled to delegate to that person, unless the purchaser had knowledge at the time of the transaction that the trustees were not entitled to delegate to that person (s 9(2)). 'Knowledge' for these purposes has not been defined in the legislation, but it is submitted that since we are concerned here with a proprietary interest, any type of cognisance will suffice for these purposes, even constructive knowledge.

14.7 Exclusion clauses

Exclusion clauses which are validly inserted in trust instruments may have the effect of limiting the liability of trustees. Such clauses are not, without more, void on public policy grounds. Of course, in order for the trustee to secure protection from claims for breach of trust, the exclusion clause is required to exempt or exclude liability for the particular fault which is the subject-matter of the complaint. Moreover, provided that the clause does not purport to exclude the basic minimum duties ordinarily imposed on trustees, it may be valid. Some of the minimum duties which cannot be excluded are the duties of honesty, good faith and acting for the benefit of the beneficiaries: see *Armitage v Nurse* [1997] 3 WLR 1046. In this case, Millett LJ made the following observations:

JUDGMENT

'I accept the submission … that there is an irreducible core of obligations owed by the trustees to the beneficiaries and enforceable by them which is fundamental to the concept of a trust. If the beneficiaries have no rights enforceable against the trustees there are no trusts. But I do not accept the further submission that these core obligations include the duties of skill and care, prudence and diligence. The duty of the trustees to perform the trusts honestly and in good faith for the benefit of the beneficiaries is the minimum necessary to give substance to the trusts, but in my opinion it is sufficient. It is, of course, far too late to suggest that the exclusion in a contract of liability for ordinary negligence or want of care is contrary to public policy. What is true of a contract must be equally true of a settlement.'

Millett LJ

In *Armitage*, the claimant, under an accumulation and maintenance settlement, sued the trustees for breach of trust. The trust settlement contained an exclusion clause to the effect that the trustees were not liable to the trust for any loss or damage to the income or capital, 'unless such loss or damage shall be caused by their own actual fraud'. The court decided that the clause validly protected the trustees from liability. 'Actual fraud' involved an intention on the part of the trustee to pursue a course of action, either knowing that it is contrary to the interests of the beneficiaries or being recklessly indifferent whether it is contrary to their interests or not. The trustees were not guilty of actual fraud and could enlist the protection of the exemption clause.

tutor tip

'Note the distinction between the trustees' fiduciary and non-fiduciary duties.'

In *Armitage*, liability for negligence may be excluded, even liability for gross negligence. But Millett LJ declared that the trustees' duty to act 'honestly and in good faith for the benefit of the beneficiaries is the minimum necessary to give substance to the trust'. The question arises as to how far an exclusion clause may protect the trustees from liability for breach of trust. It is clear that dishonest conduct on the part of the trustees that causes a breach of trust will not protect them from liability for breach of trust. What is meant by 'dishonesty'? In Chapter 8 we considered the *Royal Brunei* test for dishonesty. In the context of exclusion clauses, it is arguable that a different test is envisaged, namely the subjective test. In *Armitage*, Millett LJ said that dishonesty requires 'at the minimum an intention on the part of the trustee to pursue a particular course of action, either knowing that it is contrary to the interests of the beneficiaries or being recklessly indifferent whether it is contrary to their interests or not'. This appears to be a subjective approach based on the defendant's knowledge of the circumstances. On the other hand, in *Walker v Stones* [2001] QB 902, the Court of Appeal was asked to determine whether a solicitor was dishonest if he did not subjectively appreciate that he was being dishonest because he believed that he was acting in the best interests of the beneficiaries. The court decided that there was sufficient evidence of dishonesty because no reasonable solicitor acting as a trustee would have considered it to be honest to act in this way. This is an objective test. Would recklessness on the part of the trustees entitle them to protection? In *Barraclough v Mell* [2005] EWHC B17 (Ch), an exclusion clause was inserted into a will trust. The trustee made unauthorised payments from the trust fund but was unaware of the wrongfulness of his actions. But when this was brought to his attention he immediately set out to recover the funds. The court decided that he was entitled to rely on the exclusion clause. The approach here was to consider the recklessness of the trustee as not equivalent to dishonesty.

The burden of proof lies on the party seeking to rely on the exclusion clause to establish that the clause was properly inserted into the trust instrument and it covers the breach that has taken place. Much depends on the wording of such clauses. The words used in the exclusion will be given their natural meaning. *Prima facie* any ambiguities are construed against the trustees.

CASE EXAMPLE

Wight v Olswang, *The Times*, 18 May 1999

A trust settlement incorporated two conflicting exemption clauses, one protecting all trustees from liability for breach of trust (a general exemption clause) and the other which applied only to unpaid trustees. The court decided that the paid trustees could not rely on the general exemption clause.

In substance, it would appear that there are two types of exclusion clause:

(a) a clause which excludes the trustees' *liability* for breach of trust; and

(b) a clause which not only excludes the trustees' liability, but also excludes the *duties*, or some of the duties, of the trustees from a claim for a breach of trust.

In respect of the first type of clause, Millett LJ in *Armitage v Nurse* (above) took the view that the trustees may only exclude their liability for negligence, but they remain liable for dishonest breaches of trust. Regarding the second type of clause, Millett LJ in the same case expressed his opinion that the 'core duties' of trustees cannot be effectively excluded for this may lead to repugnancy with the trust. He stated, 'the duty of the trustees to perform the trusts honestly and in good faith for the benefit of the beneficiaries is the minimum necessary to give substance to the trusts'.

The difficulties in pursuing a claim for breach of trust in seeking to restrict an exclusion clause in the trust deed by reference to the Unfair Contract Terms Act 1977 (UCTA 1977) (included in Tuckey LJ's judgment below) were considered by the Court of Appeal in *Baker v JE Clark & Co* [2006] All ER (D) 337 (Mar). The court decided that the notice requirement under the 1977 Act was impractical and the clause did not exclude liability under a 'contract'.

CASE EXAMPLE

Baker v JE Clark & Co [2006] All ER (D) 337 (Mar)

The claimant was the wife of the deceased who was employed by the defendant company. The company sponsored a personal pension plan which included provision for death-in-service benefits. The rules of the scheme were set out in a supplementary trust deed containing an exemption clause excluding liability unless there was bad faith. The deceased joined the scheme but subsequently the underwriters of the scheme refused to renew coverage under the scheme. The deceased later passed away from a brain tumour in the service of the company and no death benefits were payable. The claimant brought an action against the administrator of the scheme alleging breach of his duty of care at common law or equity and under UCTA 1977 was not entitled to rely on the exclusion clause in the trust deed. The court decided that there was no requirement of notice of the exemption clause to be given in advance. Indeed, such a requirement would be impractical. Trustees undertook unilateral obligations and their terms of service were not dependent on the consent of the beneficiary. Further, there were insuperable difficulties in applying UCTA 1977 to trustee exemption clauses. Such clauses did not necessarily arise under contracts with the trustees because trust deeds were not contracts.

JUDGMENT

'It seems to me that there are insuperable difficulties in seeking to apply the 1977 Act to an exemption clause of the kind with which this case is concerned. Assuming that there is a common law duty of care, the question is whether Cl 13.3 (of the scheme) is a notice of the kind referred to in s 2. I do not think it is.

This point was considered by the Law Commission in their consultation paper 171 published in 2003 on the subject of trustee exemption clauses. After having concluded that a trustee exemption clause is not a contract they say at para 2.62:

> While there may be a stronger argument that a trustee exemption clause is a form of "notice", this may also be somewhat speculative in that it would seem that "notice" within the 1977 Act is primarily intended to cover attempts to exclude liability by reference to a sign outside the confines of a formal legal document.'

Tuckey LJ

Law Commission proposals

On 19 July 2006 the Law Commission published its report on 'Trustee Exemption Clauses' and listed a number of recommendations. Prior to this, a consultation paper on 'Trustee exemption clauses', published in 2003, identified a number of responses. Some of these are:

1. There was a general distaste for wide exclusion clauses especially where the settlor is unaware of their existence or meaning.

2. A distinction ought to be drawn between professional and lay trustees but it was recognised that this may be difficult to apply and liable to cause unfairness (especially in relation to professionals acting *pro bono*).

3. The practicality of the proposal that all trustees should have the power to purchase indemnity insurance using trust funds was questioned on the grounds of cost and availability.

4. There was widespread concern about the likely adverse impact of statutory regulation restricting reliance on trustee exemption clauses. This may result in increased indem-

nity insurance premiums and the possible unavailability of insurance, a decrease in the flexibility of the management of trust property and the increase in speculative litigation for breach of trust and a possible reluctance to accept trusteeship.

The 2006 Report recommends that the trust industry adopt a non-statutory rule of practice and this should be enforced by the regulatory and professional bodies which govern trustees and drafters of trusts. The rule will be enforced by professional bodies who may discipline its members who fail to comply. The recommended rule of practice requires paid trustees and drafters of trust instruments to take reasonable steps to ensure that settlors understand the meaning and effect of exemption clauses to be included in trusts instruments, before the creation of such trusts. This rule will not apply to pension trusts or trusts already subject to statutory regulation.

14.8 Duty to provide accounts and information

Because of the nature of the fiduciary relationship of trustees, a duty is imposed on them to keep proper accounts for the trust. In pursuance of this objective, the trustees may employ an agent (an accountant) to draw up the trust accounts. The beneficiaries are entitled to inspect the accounts but if they need copies they are required to pay for these from their own resources.

In *O'Rourke v Darbishire* [1920] AC 581, Lord Wrenbury declared that the beneficiary's right to disclosure of trust documents is proprietary because they belong to him. He also drew a distinction between disclosure and discoveries:

JUDGMENT

'The beneficiary is entitled to see all trust documents because they are trust documents and because he is a beneficiary. They are in this sense his own. Action or no action, he is entitled to access to them. This has nothing to do with discovery. The right to discovery is a right to see someone else's documents. The proprietary right is a right to access to documents which are your own.'

Lord Wrenbury

In *Re Londonderry's Settlement* [1964] 3 All ER 855, Salmon LJ adopted the principle laid down by Lord Wrenbury and decided that the beneficiaries are entitled to inspect documents created in the course of the administration of the trust. These are trust documents and are *prima facie* the property of the beneficiaries. Indeed, 'trust documents' were described by Salmon LJ in *Re Marquess of Londonderry's Settlement* [1965] Ch 918 as possessing the following characteristics:

JUDGMENT

'(i) they are documents in the possession of the trustees as trustees;
(ii) they contain information about the trust, which the beneficiaries are entitled to know;
(iii) the beneficiaries have a proprietary interest in the documents, and, accordingly, are entitled to see them.'

Salmon LJ

However, in *Schmidt v Rosewood Trust Ltd* [2003] 3 All ER 76, the Privy Council rejected the statement of the principle in *O'Rourke v Darbishire* (1920), and decided that the more principled approach to the issue is to regard the right to seek disclosure of trust documents as one aspect of the court's inherent jurisdiction to supervise, and if necessary to intervene in, the administration of trusts. Accordingly, the beneficiary's right to inspect trust documents is founded not on an equitable proprietary right in respect of those documents, but upon the trustee's fiduciary duty to inform the beneficiary and to render accounts. This right to seek the court's intervention is not restricted to beneficiaries with fixed interests in the trust, but also extends to objects under a discretionary trust. The power to seek disclosure may be restricted by the court in the exercise of its discretion. The court is required to balance the competing interests of the different beneficiaries, the trustees and third parties.

CASE EXAMPLE

Schmidt v Rosewood Trust Ltd [2003] 3 All ER 76

The settlor executed two Isle of Man trust settlements which created a discretionary trust in favour of a group of objects, including the claimant. The defendant company became the sole trustee of the two settlements. The settlor died intestate. The claimant alleged that he devoted considerable time and resources to trace his father's assets and believed that his efforts had been frustrated by some of his father's co-directors. He applied in his personal capacity as a member of a class of objects, and as administrator for disclosure of trust accounts and information about the trust assets. The defendant contended that a beneficiary's right of disclosure of trust documents is treated as a proprietary right, and that an object of a discretionary power does not have such a right, but merely a hope of acquiring a benefit. The Isle of Man court held in favour of the defendant and the claimant appealed to the Privy Council.

The Court allowed the appeal and decided that:

(a) The right to seek the court's intervention does not depend on entitlement to an interest under the trust. An object of a discretionary trust (including a mere power of appointment) may also be entitled to protection from a court, although the circumstances concerning protection and the nature of the protection would depend on the court's discretion.

(b) No beneficiary has an entitlement, as of right, to disclosure of trust documents. Where there are issues of personal and commercial confidentiality, the court will have to balance the competing interests of the beneficiaries, the trustees and third parties and limitations or safeguards may be imposed.

JUDGMENT

'[T]he more principled and correct approach is to regard the right to seek disclosure of trust documents as one aspect of the court's inherent jurisdiction to supervise, and if necessary to intervene in, the administration of trusts. The right to seek the court's intervention does not depend on entitlement to a fixed and transmissible beneficial interest.'

Lord Walker

14.9 Duty to distribute to the correct beneficiaries

It is an elementary principle of trusts law that the trustees are required to distribute the trust property (income and/or capital) to the beneficiaries properly entitled to receive the same. Failure to distribute to the correct beneficiary subjects the trustees to liability for breach of trust, although in appropriate cases they may apply to the court for relief under s 61 of the Trustee Act 1925 (see Chapter 16). Thus, in *Eaves v Hickson* (1861) 30 Beav 136, trustees were liable to make good sums wrongly paid to a beneficiary in reliance on a forged marriage certificate. Likewise, in *Re Hulkes* (1886) 33 Ch D 552, the trustees were liable for sums paid to the wrong beneficiaries based on an honest, but incorrect, construction of the trust instrument.

Where the trustee makes an overpayment of income or instalment of capital, he may recover the amount of the overpayment by adjusting the payments subsequently made to the same beneficiary. Where the payment is made to a person who is not entitled to receive the sum, the trustee has the right to recover the amount based on a quasi-contractual claim of money paid under a mistake of fact. Such claim will not succeed if the mistake is one of law. This was illustrated in *Re Diplock* [1947] Ch 716 (see below).

CASE EXAMPLE

Woolwich Building Society v IRC (No 2) [1992] 3 All ER 737

The House of Lords decided that money paid by a member of the public to a public authority in the form of taxes paid, pursuant to an *ultra vires* demand by the authority, is *prima facie* recoverable by the member of the public as of right. An aggrieved beneficiary may, in addition to his right to sue the trustee, trace his property in the hands of the wrongly paid person.

Where the trustees have a reasonable doubt as to the validity of claims of the beneficiaries, they may apply to the court for directions, and will be protected, provided that they act in accordance with those directions. The court has the power to make a *Benjamin* order (derived from the case *Re Benjamin* [1902] 1 Ch 723), authorising the distribution of the trust property without identifying all the beneficiaries and creditors.

In addition, where the trustees cannot identify all the beneficiaries, they are entitled to pay the trust funds into court as a last resort: see *Re Gillingham Bus Disaster Fund* [1959] Ch 62. Where there is no good reason for a payment into court, the trustees may personally have to pay the costs of such an application.

By virtue of s 27 of the Trustee Act 1925, a simplified form of distribution is allowed and, at the same time, the trustees or personal representatives are given protection from claims for breach of trust. The section permits the trustees (or personal representatives) to advertise for beneficiaries in an appropriate newspaper or gazette, and after the expiration of a period of time, not being less than two months, they are entitled to distribute the property to the beneficiaries of whom the trustees are aware. If the trustees comply with the requirements of s 27, they will not be liable for breach of trust at the instance of beneficiaries, of whom the trustees were unaware. However, the ignored beneficiaries are entitled to trace their property in the hands of the recipient. Finally, the section is incapable of being excluded or modified by the trust instrument.

14.10 Duty not to make profits from the trust

This duty was dealt with earlier, in Chapter 8 to which reference ought to be made. A trustee is undoubtedly a fiduciary and accordingly his position attracts a number of fiduciary duties. The justification for this rule is the notion that the trustee has control over the trust property which he is required to use solely for the benefit of the beneficiaries. In addition, the confidential nature of the relationship imposes on the trustee an overriding duty of loyalty to the beneficiaries. It was stated earlier that a fiduciary is one whose judgment and confidence is relied on by the beneficiaries or the principal. In *Bristol and West Building Society v Mothew* [1996] 4 All ER 698, Millett LJ outlined the nature of the fiduciary relationship as follows:

JUDGMENT

'A fiduciary is someone who has undertaken to act for or on behalf of another in a particular matter in circumstances which give rise to a relationship of trust and confidence. The distinguishing obligation of a fiduciary is the obligation of loyalty. The principal is entitled to the single-minded loyalty of his fiduciary. This core liability has several facets. A fiduciary must act in good faith; he must not make a profit of his trust; he must not place himself in a position where his duty and interest may conflict; he may not act for his own benefit or the benefit of a third person without the informed consent of his principal. This is not intended to be an exhaustive list but it is sufficient to indicate the nature of fiduciary obligations. They are defining characteristics of the fiduciary.'

Millett LJ

The primary duty is to act in the best interests of the beneficiaries and not to allow his interest to conflict with his duties. The effect is that, in equity, there are two overlapping duties imposed on the fiduciary namely, the trustee is not allowed to make a profit from his fiduciary position (referred to as the 'no profit' rule) and a fiduciary may not be allowed to place himself in a position of conflict of duty and personal interest (referred to as the 'no conflict' rule). It is arguable that the first principle is part and parcel of the second rule. The better view, however, is that although the principles overlap they are distinct principles. The rationale for the harsh rule in *Keech v Sandford* (1726) 2 Eq Cas Abr 7419 was stated by Lord Herschell in *Bray v Ford* [1896] AC 44, as not based on principles of morality but as a deterrent to curb the excesses of human nature. Accordingly the 'no conflict' 'no profit' rule will be strenuously pursued by the courts.

JUDGMENT

'It is an inflexible rule of a court of equity that a person in a fiduciary position … is not, unless otherwise expressly provided, entitled to make a profit; he is not allowed to put himself in a position where his interest and his duty conflict. It does not appear to me that this rule is … founded upon principles of morality. I regard it rather as based on the consideration that human nature being what it is, there is a danger, in such circumstances, of the person holding a fiduciary interest being swayed by interest rather than duty, and thus prejudicing those he is bound to protect. It has, therefore, been deemed expedient to lay down this positive rule.'

Lord Herschell

The principles are of wide application, strictly adhered to, and it is irrelevant that the beneficiaries suffer no loss and that the trustee acts in good faith. The duty is sometimes referred to as the rule in *Keech v Sandford* (see Chapter 8). The court decided that the trustee held the renewed lease on trust for the infant beneficiary. The obligation attaches to any property added to the trust: see *Boardman v Phipps* [1967] 2 AC 46 (see Chapter 8), and also the interests of the beneficiaries. In the latter case, the purchase is voidable at the instance of the beneficiary, even if the market price was paid for the property.

14.10.1 The rule against self-dealing

A trustee, without specific authority to the contrary, is not entitled to purchase trust property for his own benefit: see *Keech v Sandford*, above. The position remains the same even if the purchase appears to be fair. Perhaps the purchase price might significantly exceed the market value of the property. In such a case, the transaction is treated as voidable, i.e. valid until avoided. In *Tito v Waddell (No 2)* [1977] Ch 106, Megarry VC said that 'if a trustee purchases trust property from himself, any beneficiary may have the sale set aside ... however fair the transaction'. This is the rule against self-dealing and involves a conflict of duty and interest. The objections to such transactions were laid down in *Ex parte Lacey* (1802) 6 Ves 265 and *Ex parte James* (1803) 8 Ves 337. They are that the trustee would be both vendor and purchaser and it would be difficult to ascertain whether an unfair advantage had been obtained by the trustee. In addition, the property may become virtually unmarketable since the title may indicate that the property was at one time trust property. Third parties may have notice of this fact and any disputes concerning the trust property may affect their interest.

The courts will consider all the circumstances to determine whether there is any attempt to avoid this strict rule. Thus, in *Wright v Morgan* [1926] AC 788, the trustee retired from the trust in order to purchase the trust property at a price which was fixed by an independent valuer. The Privy Council decided that there was a conflict of duty and interest and the sale was set aside at the instance of the beneficiaries. Equally, the rule extends to purchases by the spouses of trustees and to purchases by companies in which the trustee has an interest. The rule will also apply to a sale to a third party if there is an understanding that the trustee will then purchase the property.

In exceptional circumstances the rule may be relaxed, but these are occasions which are peculiar to the facts of each case. In *Holder v Holder* [1968] Ch 353, an executor purchased a farm which was part of the deceased estate at a fair price at an auction. The Court of Appeal refused to set aside the sale on the grounds that he performed minimal duties as executor before renouncing his duties long before the sale, he made no secret of his intention to purchase the farm, the beneficiaries entitled to share in the estate did not rely on the purchaser's confidence and judgment to protect their interests and in any event they had acquiesced in the purchase.

There are various exceptions to this rule. The burden of proof is on the trustee/ purchaser to establish clearly that there was no hint of impropriety on the part of the trustee after full disclosure was made to the beneficiaries. The following occasions exist when authority may be obtained to purchase the trust property. First, the settlement or will may expressly permit a trustee to purchase the trust property. Second, if all the beneficiaries are of full age and sound mind and absolutely entitled to the property they may agree to the sale. The underlying issues here would be whether the trustees had made full disclosure of all the material facts to the beneficiaries and whether the beneficiaries were capable of exercising an independent judgment. In this event, the beneficiaries may need separate legal advice.

14.10.2 The fair-dealing rule

The fair-dealing rule is applicable where the trustee purchases the beneficial interests of his beneficiaries. It is less stringent than the self-dealing rule. In a sense the trustee is not both vendor and purchaser. The issue here is whether the trustee can discharge the onus of proving that he has made full disclosure of the material facts to the beneficiary, and that the beneficiary exercised an independent judgment when selling his interest to the trustee. The duty of disclosure is required to be of such a degree that the beneficiary is able to exercise an independent judgment as to the nature and extent of the sale. If this burden is discharged so that the transaction is at arm's length the sale may not be set aside. In *Coles v Trescothick* (1804) 9 Ves 234, Lord Eldon explained the rule in the following manner:

JUDGMENT

'A trustee may buy from the *cestui que* trust, provided there is a distinct and clear contract, ascertained to be such after a jealous and scrupulous examination of all the circumstances, proving that the *cestui que* trust intended the trustee should buy; and there is no fraud, no concealment, no advantage taken, by the trustee of information, acquired by him in the character of trustee.'

Lord Eldon

In *Tito v Waddell (No 2)* [1977] Ch 106, Megarry VC summarised the rule in the following manner:

JUDGMENT

'The fair dealing rule is that if a trustee purchases the beneficial interest of any of his beneficiaries, the transaction is not voidable *ex debito justitiae*, but can be set aside by the beneficiary unless the trustee can show that he has taken no advantage of his position and has made full disclosure to the beneficiary, and that the transaction is fair and honest.'

Megarry VC

Whether the trustee can discharge the burden cast on him is a question of fact. The courts will scrupulously examine the facts to determine whether there has been an unfair advantage acquired by the trustee. In *Dougan v Macpherson* [1902] AC 197, a purchase of a beneficial interest by a trustee/beneficiary was set aside by the House of Lords after it transpired that the purchaser/trustee had withheld information from the beneficiary that affected the value of the property.

14.10.3 Remuneration and other financial benefits

As stated earlier in Chapter 8, the general rule is that the trustee is prohibited from receiving remuneration or other benefits (financial or otherwise) by virtue of his capacity as a fiduciary. Thus, in the absence of authority, the trustee may not be paid a salary or commission. He is accountable to the beneficiaries for any unauthorised benefits received in his capacity as a trustee because of a conflict of duty and interest. The occasions when a trustee may be authorised to receive remuneration were considered in Chapter 8, to which reference ought to be made.

The same principles apply to other fiduciaries such as agents and directors. In *Imageview Management Ltd v Jack* (2009), the Court of Appeal decided that an agent was accountable for remuneration and other benefits received in breach of his fiduciary duties owing to his failure to both disclose and obtain the consent of his principal. The effect was that the agent was liable to return to his principal the profits or benefits received and forfeited his right to all further remuneration from his principal.

CASE EXAMPLE

Imageview Management Ltd v Jack [2009] EWCA Civ 63

The defendant was a Trinidad and Tobago goalkeeper and wanted to play professional football in the UK. He had contact with Dundee United and asked Mr Berry (whose company was Imageview Management Ltd) to negotiate with the club as his agent. An agency contract was concluded between the defendant on the one hand and Mr Berry and Imageview on the other hand. The agency contract was of two years' duration and Mr Jack was required to pay the claimant 10 per cent of his monthly salary as consideration for effecting a football contract between Mr Jack and Dundee United. Mr Berry successfully negotiated a contract for Mr Jack to play with the club for two years.

At the same time Mr Berry made a secret agreement with Dundee United that the latter would pay Imageview a fee of £3,000 for getting Mr Jack a work permit. Mr Berry did not tell Mr Jack about the work permit receipt, which cost £750 to obtain. About a year later when Mr Jack asked about it, he was told that 'it was none of his business'. The work permit was obtained and the fee paid by Dundee United.

Mr Jack began paying 10 per cent of his salary to Imageview. When Mr Jack found out about the work permit payment he discontinued paying the claimant the commission. The claimant commenced proceedings claiming the agency fees from Mr Jack. The latter defended the claim on the grounds that he was entitled to recover the agency fees that were already paid and was entitled to recover the full £3,000 received by the claimant as a secret profit.

The main issue was the effect of the 'side deal', i.e. the fee for the work permit. The judge at first instance held in favour of the defendant. On appeal, the Court of Appeal dismissed the appeal and affirmed the decision of the trial judge. The grounds were that:

1. a secret profit obtained by a fiduciary or agent involved a breach of the agent's duty of good faith owed to his principal. Once a conflict of interest was shown to have existed the agent's right to remuneration was lost.
2. The right to grant the agent an allowance for work done was subject to the discretion of the court. The burden of proof was on the agent to discharge. This discretion is required to be exercised sparingly and in circumstances where it would be inequitable for the beneficiaries to take the profit. Where the agent has acted surreptitiously as in this case, no allowance ought to made in favour of the agent.

JUDGMENT

'The law imposes on agents high standards. Footballers' agents are not exempt from these. An agent's own personal interests come entirely second to the interest of his client. If you undertake to act for a man you must act 100%, body and soul, for him. You must act as if you were him. You must not allow your own interest to get in the way without telling him.

The present case is one of surreptitious dealing. I cannot see any reason for exercising the power [to grant an allowance for work done] – one to be exercised sparingly.'

Jacob LJ

The status of bribes and secret commissions received by fiduciaries was discussed fully in Chapter 8 to which reference ought to be made. In *Cobbetts v Hodge* (2009), the High Court decided that a senior employee who obtained secret profits in breach of his fiduciary duties was liable to account to his employers for those profits.

CASE EXAMPLE

Cobbetts v Hodge [2009] EWHC 786, HC

The defendant was a salaried partner with the claimant firm of solicitors. Envirotreat Ltd (EL) was a client of the claimants and had difficulty raising capital for its business. The defendant was instructed to act in relation to the restructuring of EL's business and the issue of further shares in EL. More than 20 per cent of the new shares were allocated to the defendant, who then retired from the claimants' firm. The claimants commenced proceedings against the defendant, seeking to claim the shares acquired by the defendant in breach of his fiduciary duties. The defendant denied the claim, and in the alternative argued that if he was required to return the shares he was nevertheless entitled to equitable allowance for the sum paid for the shares, and time and skill expended in enhancing the value of the shares.

Held: The High Court held in favour of the claimants.

1. Although the employment relationship did not per se create a fiduciary relationship, the nature of the employment might provide the context in which fiduciary duties might arise. The introduction of investors was within the scope of the defendant's employment. In carrying out these duties the defendant owed fiduciary duties to the claimants.
2. A feature of the fiduciary relationship is a duty on the part of the defendant not to place himself in a position of conflict of duty and interest. In particular, the defendant was prohibited from making a secret profit in carrying out his duties. The opportunity to acquire shares in EL had derived from his employment in the claimants' firm and amounted to a breach of his duties.
3. Despite the conflict of duty and interest, the court has a wide discretion to give the defendant an allowance for expenditure incurred and for his work and skill in benefiting the trust. But this discretion will not be exercised where the fiduciary has been guilty of dishonesty or bad faith. On the facts, the defendant had not simply omitted to disclose the material facts to the claimants, he had given them a misleading account of the basis of the acquisition of the shares. The result was that no allowance would be granted to the defendant, save for the costs of the shares acquired by the defendant.

JUDGMENT

'The opportunity to acquire the shares came to him by virtue of his employment, and by virtue of his involvement in the issue of the shares as part of his specific duties for LC [the claimants]. Mr Hodge did not simply omit to disclose the arrangement with EL ... he gave Mr Rimmer a misleading account of the basis of the acquisition of these shares. Moreover, to permit an allowance in these circumstances would be to encourage fiduciaries to place their own interests ahead of those whom they serve. For both those reasons I decline to order any allowance in the present case, beyond the cost of acquisition of the shares.'

Floyd

In *FHR European Ventures v Mankarious* (2011) the High Court decided that the effect of a breach of the agent's fiduciary duty in failing to disclose a secret commission is that he will be required to account to the principal for the sum. [N.B. in subsequent litigation the Supreme Court in *FHR European Ventures v Cedar Capital Partners* [2014] UKSC 45 (see Chapter 8) decided that on receipt of the secret commission the defendant became a constructive trustee for the claimant.] In addition, the principal is entitled to refuse to pay contractual commission in respect of the impugned transaction and is entitled to bring the agency contract to an end. It is immaterial that no damage was suffered by the principal or that the principal may obtain a benefit as a result of the breach of duty.

CASE EXAMPLE

FHR European Ventures and others v Mankarious and another [2011] EWHC 2308, HC

The defendant, M, established a business venture through the medium of a company called Cedar (Cedar). Cedar's clients included a number of claimants, such as the Bank of Scotland (BoS), 'Fairmont' and 'Kingdom'. BoS funded and invested in hotel businesses, Fairmont owned and managed a number of hotels and Kingdom represented the commercial interests of Prince Abdul Aziz al Saud, a well-known investor in luxury hotels around the world. The dispute concerned the sale of a long leasehold interest in the Monte Carlo Grand Hotel. The initial sale price was €215 million, negotiated on behalf of the claimants as purchasers, through Cedar. In 2004 an unforeseen liability for costs was discovered, and Cedar negotiated a reduction in the purchase price from €215 million to €211.5 million. The claimants contributed to the purchase price in agreed proportions. Following the successful acquisition of the hotel, Cedar continued to work on other projects, including the acquisition of three other hotels, and submitted invoices for the work it had done.

In 2005 Kingdom discovered that Cedar had been paid a fee by the vendor for the sale of the hotel. This fee was €10 million, and the claimants took an adverse view to this discovery, declining to pay Cedar's invoices and reserving the right to bring proceedings to recover the €10 million payment. The defendants contended that they were entitled to retain the commission for the payment was known to the claimants and counterclaimed for sums due in respect of other work done on behalf of the claimants.

Held:

1. Cedar, as agent for the claimants, had owed a fiduciary duty to its principals to refrain from entering into a transaction in which its personal interest may conflict with its duty, unless the principals, with full knowledge of the material circumstances, consented to the transaction.
2. The fiduciary duty was owed severally to each of the claimants.
3. The burden of proving full disclosure to the principals lay on the agent and Cedar failed to discharge this burden.
4. The effect of the breach by Cedar was that it was not entitled to claim contractual commission for services rendered in establishing the joint venture and the purchase of the hotel. The defendants were therefore accountable to the claimants for the commission received. [The Supreme Court in *FHR European Ventures v Cedar Capital Partners* decided that a constructive trust is imposed on the secret commission on the date of receipt.]
5. Further, Cedar was not in a position to assert that repayment of the commission was unjust or inappropriate.
6. However, in exceptional circumstances, the court in its discretion may make an equitable allowance in favour of the agent for expenditure incurred or work and skill applied for the benefit of the principal. Accordingly, the defendant will be entitled to be paid a proportionate amount for work it had done in securing a sale in respect of the three other hotels. This was assessed at £227,497 plus VAT.

In *Regal (Hastings) Ltd v Gulliver* [1942] 1 All ER 378 (see Chapter 8) the House of Lords decided that directors of a company were accountable for profits when they participated in an opportunity that was available to the company. It was immaterial that they acted in good faith. The duty to account arose from the mere fact that an unauthorised profit had been made.

A similar approach was adopted in *Boardman v Phipps* [1967] 2 AC 46, when a solicitor to a trust of a shareholding acquired information about the company, and the opportunity

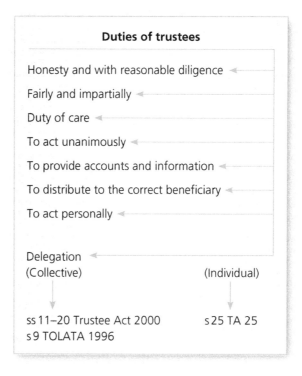

Figure 14.1 Duties of trustees

to re-organise the company, creating huge profits for himself and the trust. He was required to disgorge the profits, although the court awarded him generous remuneration for his effort. It was unclear whether the liability that arose involved a personal duty to account for the profits or was based on a constructive trust for the beneficiaries.

Likewise, where there is a causal connection between the trust share holding and an appointment as director of a company, the benefit acquired by the director in the form of salary is subject to a trust claim. In *Re Macadam* [1946] Ch 73, where the trustees were permitted to appoint directors and appointed themselves their salaries were payable to the beneficiaries. The test of liability here and causal connection with the trust is whether the trustees utilised their powers vested in them as trustees to secure their appointment as directors. This is a question of fact for the courts to decide. Accordingly, in *Re Dover Coalfield Extension Ltd* [1908] 1 Ch 65, the trustees/directors were allowed to retain their salaries because they were appointed directors at the request of the beneficiary.

14.10.4 Competition with the trust

In conformity with the 'no conflict' rule, where the trust property is included in a business activity, the trustee may be prohibited from carrying on a business for his benefit in competition with the trust. In appropriate cases the court may grant the beneficiaries an injunction to prevent the trustees carrying on the competing business. In *Re Thomson* [1930] 1 Ch 203, the trust asset consisted of a yacht broking business which was administered by the trustees. One of the trustees attempted to set up a similar business in the same town in competition with the trust. The court granted an injunction to restrain him from doing so. The yacht broking business was so specialised that it followed logically that setting up another business in the same town would have had an adverse effect on the trust. The position might have been different if the person appointed as trustee was already carrying on a similar business before his appointment. The issue then would be whether the person appointing the trustee was aware that he was carrying on a competing business and whether he was appointed because of his skill in running a similar business. In these circumstances the trustee may be allowed to continue running his business provided that his conduct does not adversely affect the trust business, e.g. by soliciting customers of the trust business.

14.11 Powers of investment

Trustees have an obligation to maintain the real value of trust funds and may need to consider investing the trust property. An 'investment' for these purposes refers to property which will produce an income yield. This was decided in *Re Wragg* [1918–19] All ER 233. The trustees are required to consider the investment policy of the trust with the standard of care expected from an ordinary prudent man of business (see above). The powers of investment may exist in the trust instrument or may be implied by statute or the court may enlarge the power of the trustees.

14.11.1 Express power

A prudent settlor will include a wide investment clause in the trust instrument in order to give the trustees the maximum flexibility in the selection of investments. The modern approach of the courts is to construe investment clauses liberally.

CASE EXAMPLE

Re Harari's Settlement [1949] 1 All ER 430

The issue concerned the effect of a clause in the trust instrument, to make 'such investments as the trustees may think fit'. The court decided that the words will be given their ordinary meaning without any restriction.

14.11.2 Statutory power under the Trustee Act 2000

The Trustee Act 2000 (which came into force on 1 February 2001) repeals and replaces the out-of-date Trustee Investment Act 1961. The new statutory power of investment is found in s 3(1) of the Trustee Act 2000, which enacts:

SECTION

'a trustee may make any kind of investment that he could make if he were absolutely entitled to the assets of the trust.'

The trustee must, of course, comply with the general duty of care as stated in s 1 of the 2000 Act (see above). This new power is required to be considered in the light of the new powers of delegation (see above). As will be seen, trustees will be able to delegate their discretion as well as their duty to invest.

The new power is treated as a *default provision* and will only operate in so far as there is no contrary provision in the trust instrument. It should be noted that restrictions imposed by the trust instrument prior to 3 August 1961 are treated as void (see s 7(2) of the Trustee Act 2000). This new power operates retrospectively in the sense that trusts existing before or after the commencement of the 2000 Act are subject to this default provision. However, the new regime does not apply to occupational pension schemes, authorised unit trusts and schemes under the Charities Act 1993.

Section 4 of the 2000 Act requires trustees to have regard to the 'standard investment criteria' when investing. This is defined in s 4(3) to mean the suitability of the investment to the trust and the need for diversification as is appropriate in the circumstances. Thus, trustees are no longer restricted as to the type of investments they make but are restricted by reference to the standard investment criteria. The standard investment criteria are important because the suitability of investments varies from trust to trust. Having exercised the power of investment the trustees are required to review the trust investments periodically by reference to the standard investment criteria (s 4(2)). The purpose of this provision is to require the trustees to determine whether the trust fund ought to be reinvested or not. In *Jeffrey v Gretton* [2011] WTLR 809, the High Court decided that trustees were in breach of their duty to regularly review the trust portfolio. The trustees acquired the deceased's house in 2001 in a dilapidated state. Without professional advice, they decided to retain and refurbish the property with a view to its eventual sale. There was a significant delay in renovating the house, and the property was eventually sold by auction in 2008. The court held that despite the breach of trust the claimant failed to establish that the breach created a loss.

By virtue of s 5 of the Trustee Act 2000, trustees are required to obtain and consider proper advice before investing, unless in the circumstances they reasonably conclude that it is unnecessary to do so; for example if funds are paid into an interest-bearing account pending investment by the trustees, it may be unnecessary to take advice regarding the interim account, or one or more of the trustees may be suitably qualified to give proper advice.

Section 5(4) defines 'proper advice' as follows:

SECTION

'advice of a person who is *reasonably believed* by the trustee to be qualified to give it by his ability in and practical experience of financial and other matters relating to the proposed investment.'

This is an objective issue and the test is not restricted to individuals with paper qualifications but includes those with practical experience. Although the provision does not require the advice to be in writing a prudent trustee will require advice to be in such form.

Mortgages

Prior to the Trustee Act 2000, the trustees' powers to invest in mortgages were laid down in the Trustee Investment Act 1961 and s 8 of the Trustee Act 1925. The effect of these provisions was that trustees were authorised to invest in mortgages of freehold or leasehold property, provided that in the latter case the lease had at least 60 years to run. Section 8 of the Trustee Act 1925 provided that a trustee was not impeachable for breach of trust if the amount of the loan did not exceed two-thirds of the value of the property, and he acted on the written advice of a suitable and independent valuer.

The Trustee Act 2000 repeals and replaces these provisions. Section 3 of the Act of 2000 authorises the trustees to invest by way of a loan secured on land. Although the point is far from clear, it is generally advisable for the trustees to invest in a legal estate by way of a legal mortgage as under the previous law. In addition, the security is restricted to land in the UK.

Acquisition of land

Before the passing of the Trustee Act 2000, trustees had no general power to purchase land as an investment. There were two exceptions to this rule. First, the trust instrument may authorise trustees to purchase land as an investment. For these purposes and subject to any contrary provision, the land was required to be bought in order to generate an income. Second, s 6(4) of the Trusts of Land and Appointment of Trustees Act 1996 empowered trustees of land to purchase land as an investment, or for the occupation by a beneficiary or for other purposes. The trustees may sell all of the land subject to the trust and purchase further land with the proceeds of sale (s 17 of the 1996 Act). The trustees of land have wide powers to mortgage or lease the land, though not to make a gift of the property, or sale at an undervalue (for such action will involve a loss to the trust, but may be lawful if all the beneficiaries, being of full age and capacity, consent to such action). The trustees under s 6 are subject to the statutory duty of care under s 1 of the Trustee Act 2000 and will be in breach of trust if they enter into a transaction for less than the full market value of the land. In exercising their powers under s 6, the trustees are required to have regard to the rights of the beneficiaries and any rule of law or equity or statute. The trustees are required to consult the beneficiaries entitled to possession and give effect to the wishes of the majority, measured by reference to the value of their interest (if consistent with the general interests of the trust). Moreover, the trust deed may impose an obligation on the trustees to obtain the consent of any person prior to the transaction. Failure to consult such a person may not necessarily invalidate the transaction, but will give rise to liability for breach of trust, unless the court dispenses with the need to obtain consent by an order under s 14 of the 1996 Act.

By virtue of s 8 of the Trustee Act 2000, trustees are now entitled to purchase freehold or leasehold land in the UK:

- as an investment; or
- for the occupation by a beneficiary; or
- for any other purpose.

Thus, the new power mirrors the power of trustees under s 6(4) of the Trusts of Land and Appointment of Trustees Act 1996, which has been repealed and replaced by s 8 of the 2000 Act. Once trustees have acquired the relevant land they will be vested with the same powers as an absolute owner of land. Accordingly, the trustees will be able to sell, lease and mortgage the land. This new power is a default provision which may be excluded by a contrary intention in the trust instrument.

Duty of care

Section 1 of the Trustee Act 2000 reformulates the duty of care applicable to powers exercisable by trustees under the Act. This provision replaces the common law standard of care as indicated above. The section enacts that the trustees are required to exercise such care and skill as is reasonable in the circumstances:

(a) having regard to any special knowledge or experience he has or holds himself out as having; and

(b) if he acts as a trustee in the course of a business or profession, to any special knowledge or experience that it is reasonable to expect of a person acting in the course of that kind of business or profession.

Thus, the section has created a combined objective and subjective test of the standard of care required from the trustees. The minimum degree of care and skill expected from a trustee is to be determined objectively by the court. But this standard of care may be increased by reference to the trustees' special knowledge or experience acquired personally or held out by him. This provision echoes the view of Brightman J in *Bartlett v Barclays Bank* [1980] Ch 515.

Schedule 1 to the Trustee Act 2000 lists the occasions when the duty of care arises. These are in the exercise of the statutory and express powers of investment, including the duty to have regard to the standard investment criteria and the duty to obtain and consider proper advice. In addition, the duty applies to the trustees' power to acquire land. Moreover, the duty of care applies when trustees enter into arrangements in order to delegate functions to agents, nominees, custodians as well as the review of their actions.

14.11.3 Enlargement of investment powers

Trustees are entitled to apply to the court under s 57 of the Trustee Act 1925 or under the Variation of Trusts Act 1958 in order to widen these investment powers. The approach of the courts has been encouraging in granting its approval in order to update the investment policy of trusts beyond the scope of the Trustee Investments Act 1961. In *Mason v Farbrother* [1983] 2 All ER 1078, the court approved a scheme to widen the investment powers of trustees of the employees of the Co-operative Society's pension fund, because of the effects of inflation and the size of the funds (some £127 million).

14.12 The right of beneficiaries to occupy land

Section 12 of the Trusts of Land and Appointment of Trustees Act 1996 confers on a beneficiary entitled to an interest in possession under a trust of land the right to occupy the land. But this right does not apply where the land is not available or is unsuitable for occupation by the beneficiary.

Where a number of beneficiaries are entitled under s 12, the trustees are entitled under s 13 to exclude or restrict, on reasonable grounds, the right of some of the beneficiaries to occupy. Moreover, the trustees are entitled to impose reasonable conditions on an occupying beneficiary and, if appropriate, to compensate a beneficiary whose right of occupation has been excluded or restricted.

14.13 Powers of maintenance and advancement

14.13.1 Power of maintenance

A power of maintenance is a discretion granted to the trustees to pay or apply income for the benefit of an infant beneficiary at a time prior to the beneficiary acquiring a right to the income or capital of the trust. Maintenance payments are expenditure incurred out of the income of a fund for routine recurring purposes such as food, clothing, rent and education.

The issues that are required to be considered by the trustees are:

1. whether they have a power to maintain an infant beneficiary;
2. whether there is any income available for maintenance;
3. whether the trustees are prepared to exercise their discretion to maintain the beneficiary.

Power to maintain

Express power

A settlor may expressly include a power of maintenance in the trust instrument. Most professionally drafted settlements will include this power. If this is the case the trustees' duties will be encapsulated in the clause.

Inherent power

The court has an inherent power to authorise the trustees to maintain beneficiaries. The underlying unexpressed intention of the settlor must have been consistent with the maintenance payments in favour of infant beneficiary or beneficiaries.

Statutory power

Section 31 of the Trustee Act 1925 authorises the trustees in their discretion, to pay the whole or part of the income from the trust to the parent or guardian of an infant beneficiary, or otherwise apply the relevant amount towards the maintenance, education or benefit of the infant beneficiary, during his infancy or until his interest fails.

But this statutory power may be modified or excluded by the settlor in the trust instrument (see s 69(2) of the 1925 Act).

An exclusion of the power may be express or implied in the settlement. Section 31 was intended to be implied into every settlement subject to any contrary intention expressed by the terms of the instrument. A contrary intention will be established if the settlor has specifically disposed of the income, for example a payment of the income to another, or has directed an accumulation of income.

Availability of income

The issue here is whether the income of the trust is available to maintain the infant beneficiary. The effect of complex rules of case law, s 175 of the Law of Property Act 1925 and s 31(3) of the Trustee Act 1925, is that a vested interest carries the intermediate income, unless someone else is entitled to it or the income is required to be accumulated. **Contingent interests** created *inter vivos* or by will carry the intermediate income (save in so far as the settlor or testator has otherwise disposed of the income). A contingent pecuniary legacy does not carry the income, except where the gift was made by the infant's father or a person standing *in loco parentis*, and the contingency is attaining the age of majority and no other fund is set aside for the maintenance of the legatee.

contingent interest

An estate or interest transferred but subject to the satisfaction of a precondition.

Exercise of power during infancy

The trustees have a discretion to maintain infant beneficiaries. This discretion is required to be exercised responsibly and objectively, as ordinary prudent men of business. Thus, in *Wilson v Turner* (1883) 22 Ch 521, trustees who applied the income automatically to the infant's father without consciously exercising their discretion, were liable to the beneficiaries for breach of trust when the father used the sums for his own benefit. Prior to the enactment of the Inheritance and Trustees' Powers Act 2014, s 31(1)(i) of the Trustee Act 1925 enacted that the discretion of the trustees was required to be exercised 'reasonably in all the circumstances'. The Law Commission in its Report entitled 'Intestacy and Family Provision Claims on Death', published in December 2011, recommended the abolition of the test of reasonableness. It was content to rely on the general law that is applicable to the trustees' duties on decision making, i.e. the duty to act in good faith after taking into account all the relevant circumstances. This recommendation has been endorsed in s 8(a) of the Inheritance and Trustees' Powers Act 2014 in respect of trusts created after 1 October 2014. For example, if the trust property consists of shares held on trust for beneficiaries, A, B and C equally until they attain the age of 25, the trustees may exercise their discretion to pay each child, during his infancy, a maximum of one-third of the dividends on the shares for his maintenance, education or benefit.

Under the proviso to s 31(1) of the Trustee Act 1925, the trustees are required to take a number of factors into account such as the age and requirements of the infant and whether other income is applicable for the same purpose and generally all the surrounding circumstances. The exercise of the power will vary with the facts of each case. This was the position under the proviso before 1 October 2014. However, s 8(b) of the Inheritance and Trustees' Powers Act 2014 repeals the proviso to s 31(1) and therefore the specific factors identified in the proviso for trusts created on or after 1 October 2014. Thus, the trustees are now free to pay out as much of the income as they see fit, subject to the general legal requirement of taking relevant factors into consideration. The effect of the amendment is to broaden the scope of the trustees' discretion.

Accumulations

Alternatively, the trustees may accumulate the income instead of maintaining the infant with the fund. Such accumulations (or capitalised income) will produce further income if invested in authorised investments. The additional income as well as accumulations of income become available for maintenance of the infant beneficiary in the future, should the need arise (proviso to s 31(2)).

If, in accordance with the express terms of the trust instrument, the beneficiary attains a vested interest in the income on attaining the age of majority (18) or marries under that age, he becomes entitled to the accumulated income (s 31(2)(i)(a)).

Where the beneficiary acquires a vested interest in capital on attaining the age of majority or earlier marriage, he also becomes entitled to the accumulated income (s 31(2)(i)(b)), for example 'shares are held on trust for A provided that he attains the age of 18'. On attaining the age of majority A becomes entitled to the accumulated dividends from the shares in addition to the capital.

Attaining the age of majority

If the beneficiary attains the age of majority without attaining a vested interest under the terms of the trust, the trustees are required to pay the income to the beneficiary until he acquires a vested interest or dies or his interest fails (s 31(1)(ii)). The payment includes accumulated income. Accordingly, a beneficiary acquires a vested interest in the income of the trust by statute on attaining the age of majority even though under the trust he does not enjoy a vested interest in the capital, for example 'On trust for A provided he attains the age of 25.' On attaining the age of 18, the beneficiary becomes entitled to an interest in possession.

However, this provision is subject to any contrary intention stipulated by the settlor. In *Re Turner's Will Trust* [1937] Ch 15, it was decided that such contrary intention may be manifested by the settlor directing the income to be accumulated beyond the age of majority.

14.13.2 Power of advancement

An advancement is a payment from the capital funds of a trust to, or on behalf of, a beneficiary in respect of some long-term commitment, such as the purchase of a house or establishment of a business. A potential beneficiary may be in need of capital from the trust fund prior to becoming entitled, as of right, to the capital from the fund. In such a case the trustees may be entitled to accelerate the enjoyment of his interest by an advance payment of capital: for example S, a settlor, transfers £50,000 to T(1) and T(2) on trust for B contingently on attaining the age of 25. Assuming that while B is only 14 years old, a legitimate need for capital arises. But for special provisions to the contrary, the trustees would be prevented from making an advancement to B on the grounds that the contingency entitling B to the capital has not taken place and in any event B, as a minor, is incapable of giving a valid receipt for the payment of capital. If, on the other hand, the trustees validly exercise their power of advancement, capital may be released in favour of B before the satisfaction of the contingency and B will be prevented from claiming the capital a second time.

Authority to advance

The authority to exercise a power of advancement may originate from a variety of sources such as the trust instrument, the inherent jurisdiction of the courts or statutory power. Only the statutory power is considered below.

Statutory power

Section 32 of the Trustee Act 1925 creates a statutory power of advancement, which is not limited to minors. The section empowers the trustees with a discretion to distribute any money or apply any other property forming part of the capital of the trust property in favour of any beneficiary. The maximum amount that may be advanced may not exceed the beneficiary's presumptive share of the capital, who may become entitled to the whole or part of the capital in the future. In respect of trusts created before 1 October 2014, the maximum amount that could have been advanced was an amount not exceeding one-half of the beneficiary's presumptive share of the capital. Section 9(3)(b) of the Inheritance and Trustees' Powers Act 2014 has abolished the ceiling of half of the beneficiary's presumptive share of the capital in respect of trusts created on or after 1 October 2014.

However, this statutory power may be excluded expressly or impliedly by the settlor. An implied exclusion involves any power of advancement which is inconsistent with the statutory power. In *IRC v Bernstein* [1961] Ch 399, it was decided that an express power which exceeded the statutory maximum amount that may be used to advance to the beneficiaries amounted to an implied exclusion. The effect was to widen the discretion of the trustees. This was the approach taken in many professionally drafted trust instruments.

Advancement or benefit

Under s32, the trustees are entitled to pay or apply capital in their discretion for the 'advancement or benefit' of a beneficiary. The expression has been considered liberally by the courts and 'benefit' has been interpreted as extending the wide ambit of 'advancement':

JUDGMENT

'The word advancement itself meant ... the establishment in life of the beneficiary ... The expression [benefit] means any use of the money which will improve the material situation of the beneficiary.'

Viscount Radcliffe in *Pilkington v IRC* [1964] AC 612

Thus, the phrase includes the use of money not only for the immediate personal benefit of the beneficiary but also an indirect 'benefit'. In *Re Clore's Settlement* [1966] 2 All ER 272, the phrase included a moral obligation to donate funds to a charity. Similarly, in *Re Kershaw* (1868) LR 6 Eq 322, it was held that the power may be exercised by making a loan to the beneficiary's husband to facilitate him to set up a business in England in order to keep the family together.

The policy of the original s 32 was to invest trustees with a discretion to appoint up to one-half of the presumptive share of the capital of the beneficiary for his advancement or benefit. The value of the presumptive share of the beneficiary is measured on the date of the advancement. If the ceiling concerning the statutory power of advancement has been reached (i.e. half of the presumptive share of capital) the statutory power of advancement would be exhausted even if the value of the capital increases subsequently. This was the position in *Marquess of Abergavenny v Ram* [1981] 2 All ER 643. However, the settlor was entitled to increase the ceiling of sums which may be advanced, but this may only be done expressly.

In respect of trusts created on or after 1 October 2014, as was stated earlier, s 9(3)(b) of the Inheritance and Trustees' Powers Act 2014 removes the limit of one-half of the presumptive share of the capital. Thus, the trustees may, in the exercise of their discretion, advance or apply for his benefit the whole of the beneficiary's prospective share of the capital. The purpose of the change is to give the trustees greater flexibility in advancing capital sums to beneficiaries in accordance with the practice in professionally drafted trust instruments. The trustees retain their fiduciary duty to act in the best interests of the beneficiaries.

In addition, s 9(2) of the 2014 Act amends the statutory power of advancement under s 32 of the 1925 Act in order to clarify the extent of property subject to the trustees' discretion. The trustees are entitled to pay out not only cash, but also to transfer or apply any trust property for, or on behalf of, the beneficiary. If the trustees wish to create a sub-trust for the benefit of one or more of the beneficiaries, they may be entitled to transfer the property directly to the trustees of the sub-trust. This provision is read into all private trusts, whether created before or after 1 October 2014, but subject to any contrary intention expressed in the trust instrument, s 69(2) of the Trustee Act 1925.

The property advanced or sums paid to, or on behalf of, the beneficiary are credited to the prospective share of the beneficiary's (or beneficiaries') interest, so that if a beneficiary becomes absolutely entitled to a share as of right, the sum advanced is taken into account (s 32(1)(b), as amended). In this regard s 9(6) of the Inheritance and Trustees' Powers Act 2014 introduces a new s 32(1A) of the Trustee Act 1925. The money or other property advanced to the beneficiary may, at the choice of the trustees, be treated as a percentage of the overall value of the trust property when it is brought into account, as opposed to its monetary value. The trustees may exercise their choice expressly in writing, or impliedly through dividing up the trust fund amongst beneficiaries.

Powers of trustees	Express power	Statutory power
Investment	YES	YES Trustee Act 2000
Rights of beneficiaries to occupy land	YES	YES s 12 TOLATA 1996
Maintenance	YES	YES s 31 Trustee Act 1925
Advancement	YES	YES s 32 Trustee Act 1925
Sale of trust assets	YES	YES s 6 TOLATA 1996
Insure trust property	YES	YES s 19 TA 1925
Reimbursements	YES	YES s 31 Trustee Act 2000

Figure 14.2 Powers of trustees

Prior interests

If a beneficiary is entitled to a prior interest (life interest), whether vested or contingent, the consent in writing of such beneficiary is required to be obtained prior to the exercise of the power of advancement, provided that such person is in existence and of full age. The reason is that an advancement reduces the income available to other beneficiaries (s 32(1)(c), as amended).

Trustees' duties

The trustees are required to exercise their power of advancement in a fiduciary manner. In *Molyneux v Fletcher* [1898] 1 QB 648, the court decided that the exercise will not be *bona fide* and will be void if the trustees advance funds to a beneficiary on condition that the sum is used to repay a loan made by one of the trustees. Moreover, the trustees may transfer the capital to the beneficiary directly if they reasonably believe that he may be trusted with the money. If the trustees specify a particular purpose which they reasonably believe the beneficiary is capable of fulfilling, they (trustees) may pay the fund over to him. But in *Re Pauling's Settlement Trust* [1964] Ch 303, the court decided that the trustees are under an obligation to ensure that the beneficiary, recipient of the fund, expends the sum for the specific purpose.

14.14 Power of trustees to give receipts

Section 14(1) of the Trustee Act 1925 provides that the receipt in writing of a trustee for any money, securities, investments or other personal property or effects payable, transferable or deliverable to him under any trust or power shall be a sufficient discharge to the person paying, transferring or delivering the same and shall effectually exonerate him.

Section 14(2) provides that the section does not, except where the trustee is a trust corporation, enable a sole trustee to give a valid receipt for:

(a) the proceeds of sale or other capital money arising under a trust of land;

(b) capital money arising under the Settled Land Act 1925.

14.15 Power to partition land under a trust of land

Section 7 of the Trusts of Land and Appointment of Trustees Act 1996, which repeals s 28 of the Law of Property Act 1925, confers on trustees of land the power to partition the land, or part of it, among adult beneficiaries who are absolutely entitled in undivided shares, subject to their consent. If an infant is absolutely entitled to a share, partition may still take place, but the trustees will hold his share on trust for him. This may end the co-ownership of the whole or part of the land subject to the trust. This section may be excluded or varied by the settlement, except in the case of trusts for ecclesiastical, public or charitable trusts.

The trust settlement may require the trustees to obtain the consent of any person before exercising any of their powers as trustees of land. If the consent of more than two persons is required, and has not been obtained, the purchaser is protected if at least two consents are obtained (s 10). But, this is without prejudice to the liability of the trustees for breach of trust. In the case of land held on ecclesiastical, charitable or public purposes, the purchaser is required to ensure that all necessary consents have been obtained. The consent of an infant is not required, but in such a case the trustees are duty bound to obtain the consent of the person with parental responsibility for the infant or his guardian.

ACTIVITY

Applying the law

1. Under the trusts of a settlement, a personalty fund worth £150,000 is held by the trustees upon trust for such of the settlor's grandchildren, Tom, Dick and Harriet, as attain the age of 25 and in equal shares absolutely. Tom is now 25, Dick is 18 and Harriet is 13. Advise the trustees:

   (i)   whether they may now distribute one-third of the capital of the trust fund to Tom;
   (ii) whether they should distribute any, and if so what, trust income and to whom;
   (iii) whether they may advance the sum of £25,000 out of capital to enable Dick to train for a commercial pilot's licence;
   (iv) whether they may pay out of trust moneys the school fees of Harriet who is about to go to a boarding school.

2. David is a solicitor to a trust. The trustees are Margaret and Norman and the beneficiaries Edward and Francis. The assets of the trust included a painting which David wished to buy. David informed the trustees of his wish and, upon David's suggestion, the trustees approached a valuer, Tony, from whom they sought a valuation of the painting. David was aware that Tony had previously been convicted of an offence involving fraud but did not reveal that fact to the trustees. The trustees themselves made no enquiry as to Tony's character and merely accepted David's nomination of him.

   Having been told by David of his wish to buy the painting, Tony put its value at £100,000, approximately one-half of its true market value, and David bought it from the trustees at that price. He has just sold it for £210,000.
   Discuss the possible liabilities of Margaret, Norman, David and Tony to the beneficiaries.

SUMMARY

The trustees' fiduciary duties stem from the position of confidence which the trustees enjoy. Hence, trustees should ensure that their interests do not conflict with their duties as trustees.

- Trustees should ensure that they do not receive any unauthorised profits, including unauthorised remuneration for his services as trustee. Any such profits are held on trust for the beneficiaries.
- Likewise, trustees who purchase the trust property may run the risk that the sale will be considered to be voidable and be set aside at the instance of the beneficiaries. This is a strict rule and the sale may be set aside even though the trustee acts in good faith and pays the market price for the property. This is known as the self-dealing rule.
- Allied to the self-dealing rule is the fair-dealing rule where the trustee purchases the beneficiary's interest in the trust property. The burden of proof is on the trustee to show that he had made full disclosure of the material facts to the beneficiary and has not taken advantage of his position and that the transaction was fair and honest.
- Trustees are under a duty to act unanimously. Accordingly, trustees are jointly and severally liable for their conduct in managing the affairs of the trust.
- Trustees are required to act impartially, with even-handedness and in the best interests of all the beneficiaries. As a corollary to this principle the trustees are required to ensure that the trust property is properly balanced in order to accommodate the interests of the beneficiaries.

- Trustees are duty bound to keep proper accounts of the affairs of the trust and to disclose this information to the beneficiaries, on request.

- The standard of care imposed on trustees in the execution of their office is laid down in s 1 of the Trustee Act 2000. The care and skill to be exercised by the trustee is required to be reasonable and, in particular, the courts will have regard to any special knowledge or expertise that the trustee holds himself out as possessing and any expertise or skill acquired in the course of his business or profession. This is an objective question which varies with the facts of each case.

- The trustees' powers of delegation of duties have been considerably updated by the Trustee Act 2000. Trustees are entitled to delegate to their agent any of their 'delegable functions'. Section 11(2) of the Trustee Act 2000 defines this term. The effect is that, subject to s 25 of the Trustee Act 2000, trustees may not delegate their discretions.

- If the trustees appoint agents or custodians on behalf of the trust they are required to review the latter's acts with the appropriate standard of care and intervene in appropriate cases.

- Exclusion clauses are designed to protect trustees from being sued for breaches of trust. Provided that the clause has been validly inserted in the trust instrument and covers the type of breach committed, even liability for gross negligence, the trustees may be protected from breach of trust claims. This is the position for all types of trustees, including professional trustees. However, there are limits to exclusion clauses, despite the width of such clauses. A clause cannot exclude or limit the liability of trustees for breaches involving fraud or dishonesty. The reason is that the duty to act in good faith is an irreducible core obligation of trusteeship.

- The Law Commission in its 2006 report recommended that professional bodies adopt self-regulatory rules governing the use of exclusion clauses by trustees.

- The new broad powers of investment under the Trustee Act 2000 are treated as default provisions and will be adopted to the extent that there are no contrary provisions. Section 3 of the 2000 Act creates the power of investment.

- Trustees are required to have regard to the 'standard investment criteria', i.e. the suitability of the proposed investments and the need for diversification. In addition the trustees are required to consider 'proper advice' from a person whom he reasonably believes is qualified to give it by virtue of his experience. Moreover, the trustees are required to review the investments periodically.

- As default provisions, ss 31 and 32 of the Trustee Act 1925 create the powers of maintenance and advancement for the benefit of the beneficiaries.

- Section 31 of the Trustee Act 1925 authorises trustees to use their discretion to pay the income from the trust to maintain infant beneficiaries who have an interest in the trust property and are entitled to the intermediate income from the trust. The trustees are directed to have regard to the beneficiary's age, his requirements, the availability of other income to maintain the infant and any other relevant circumstances. The court has statutory power under s 53 of the Trustee Act 1925 to order maintenance of the beneficiary out of capital.

- When the beneficiary attains the age of 18 the trustees are required to pay the income from the trust property over to him, subject to prior rights.

- The statutory power of advancement under s 32 of the Trustee Act 1925 is exercisable in favour of a beneficiary with an interest in trust capital. The sum advanced must not exceed one-half of the vested or presumptive share of the beneficiary in the property, although this ceiling has been abolished for trusts created on or after 1 October 2014. The sum advanced is required to be taken into consideration as part of his share when the beneficiary becomes entitled to receive his share of the trust property.

SAMPLE ESSAY QUESTION

Consider the following essay question:

To what extent has the Trustee Act 2000 satisfactorily reformed the investment powers of trustees?

Answer plan

Give a brief outline of the old law on trustees' investment powers:
- express powers of investment – general or limited;
- Trustee Investment Act 1961 – default provision, narrow range investments Parts I and II, Part III wider range investments, splitting of the trust property, additions to the fund and withdrawals from the fund, investments in mortgages, s 8 of the Trustee Act 1925.

Identify the problems with the old law:
- the statutory power of investment was extremely limited;
- obsolete;
- subject to many expensive applications to the court under s 57 of the Trustee Act 1925 to increase the power of investment.

Law Commission Report No 260 (1999) 'Trustees' powers and duties' for a commentary on the limitations of the law.

Outline the changes made by the Trustee Act 2000:
- s 3 of the 2000 Act creates the new power of investment as a default mechanism;
- the duty of care under s 1(1);
- standard investment criteria;
- periodic review of investments;
- mortgage investments, s 3 of the 2000 Act;
- acquisitions of land, s 8 of the 2000 Act and s 6 of TOLATA 1996.

Evaluate the changes made in the 2000 Act.

CONCLUSION

Further reading

Clements, L, 'The changing face of trusts: the Trusts of Land and Appointment of Trustees Act 1996' (1998) 61 MLR 56.

Duckworth, A, 'Legal aspects of trustee investment: is the prudent man still alive and well?' (1997) PCB 22.

Gilbert & Sullivan, 'Trustee exemption clauses: a call for caution' (2015) Tru LI 114.

Goodhart, W, 'Trustee exemption clauses and the Unfair Contract Terms Act 1977' (1980) Conv 333.

Hochberg, D and Norris, W, 'The rights of beneficiaries to information concerning a trust' (1999) PCB 292.

Hunter, R, 'The Trustee Act 2000 and the Human Rights Act' (2001) PCB 101.

Luxton, P, 'Ethical investments in hard times' (1992) 55 MLR 587.

McCormack, G, 'The liability of trustees for gross negligence' (1998) Conv 100.

Megarry, R, 'The ambit of a trustee's duty of disclosure' (1965) 81 LQR 192.

Nicholls of Birkenhead, Lord, 'Trustees and their broader community: where duty, morality and ethics converge' (1995) 9 Tru LI 71.

O'Hagan, P, 'Trustees' duty to disclose' (1995) 145 NLJ 1414.

Panesar, S, 'The Trustee Act' (2001) ICCLR 151.

Samuels, A, 'Disclosure of trust documents' (1965) 28 MLR 220.

Watt, G, 'Escaping s 8(1) provisions in new style trusts of land' (1997) Conv 263.

15

Variation of trusts

AIMS AND OBJECTIVES

By the end of this chapter you should be able to:

- appreciate the rule in *Saunders v Vautier*
- understand the various methods of varying the management powers of trustees
- list the various methods of varying beneficial interests prior to the passing of the Variation of Trusts Act 1958
- comprehend the relevant conditions to be satisfied under the Variation of Trusts Act 1958
- distinguish between a variation of trusts and re-settlements

15.1 Introduction

Trustees are required to administer the trust in accordance with its terms. They have a primary duty to obey the instructions as detailed by the settlor or implied by law. Any deviation from the terms of the trust is a breach making them personally liable, irrespective of how well intentioned the trustees may have been. But circumstances may arise, since the setting up of the trust, which indicate that the trust might be more advantageously administered if the terms were altered.

For example, authority may be needed to use funds from the trust to maintain an infant beneficiary; an investment or the impact of a potential liability to taxation may have the effect of depreciating the trust assets if no action is taken. A partitioning of the trust property between the life tenant and remainderman may have the effect of avoiding inheritance tax if the life tenant survives for seven years or more, whereas, if no action is taken, the entire capital may suffer inheritance tax on the death of the life tenant and a second time on the death of the remainder.

In these circumstances the trustees are in need of some mechanism whereby authority may be conferred on them to depart from or vary the terms of the trust. Such authority may be conferred in a variety of ways.

15.2 The rule in *Saunders v Vautier*

Where the beneficiaries are of full age and of sound mind and are absolutely entitled to the trust property, they may deal with the equitable interest in any way they wish. They may sell, exchange or gift away their interest. As a corollary to this rule, such beneficiaries acting in unison are entitled to terminate the trust. Equally, such beneficiaries acting in concert are entitled to empower the trustees to perform such acts as they (the beneficiaries) consider appropriate. In short, the beneficiaries, collectively, are entitled to rewrite the terms of the trust.

CASE EXAMPLE

Saunders v Vautier [1841] 4 Beav 115

Stock was bequeathed upon trust to accumulate the dividends until Vautier (V) attained the age of 25. At this age, the trustees were required to transfer the capital and accumulated income to V. V attained the age of majority (21) and claimed the fund at this age. The question in issue was whether the trustees were required to transfer the fund to V. Lord Langdale MR decided that since the fund had vested in V, the sole beneficiary, subject to the enjoyment being postponed, and he was of full age, he was entitled to claim the entire fund. The beneficiary had a vested interest in the income, and the accumulations were for his sole benefit, which he was entitled to waive:

JUDGMENT

'I think that principle has been repeatedly acted upon; and where a legacy is directed to accumulate for a certain period, or where the payment is postponed the legatee, if he has an absolute indefeasible interest in the legacy, is not bound to wait until the expiration of that period, but may require payment the moment he is competent to give a valid discharge.'

Lord Langdale MR

But where minors or persons under a disability or persons unborn are beneficiaries (or potential beneficiaries) there cannot be a departure from the terms of the trust without the court's approval.

The courts drew a distinction between:

- a variation concerning the management and administration of trusts; and
- a variation of the beneficial interests under the trusts.

We shall now consider the first of these.

15.3 Variation of the management powers of trustees

15.3.1 Inherent jurisdiction of the court

The court has an inherent jurisdiction to depart from the terms of a trust in the case of an 'emergency', i.e. an occasion when no provision was made in the trust instrument and the event could not have been foreseen by the settlor. This power is very narrow and arises in order to 'salvage' the trust property, such as effecting essential repairs to buildings.

The power was exercised in *Re New* [1901] 2 Ch 534, which was described as the 'high water mark' of the emergency jurisdiction.

CASE EXAMPLE

Re New [1901] 2 Ch 534

The trust property consisted of shares in a company divided into £100 units. The court approved a scheme of capital reconstruction on behalf of minors and unborn persons by splitting the shares into smaller units so that they could be more easily realised.

JUDGMENT

'In a case of this kind, which may reasonably be supposed to be one not foreseen or anticipated by the author of the trust, where the trustees are embarrassed by the emergency that has arisen and the duty cast on them to do what is best for the estate, and the consent of all the beneficiaries cannot be obtained by reason of some of them not being *sui juris* or in existence, then it may be right for the court to sanction on behalf of all concerned such acts on behalf of the trustees.'

Romer LJ

In *Re Tollemache* [1903] 1 Ch 955, the court refused to sanction a scheme authorising the mortgage of the life tenant's beneficial interest in order to increase her income. There was no emergency.

15.3.2 Section 57 of the Trustee Act 1925

The section is drafted in fairly wide terms and empowers the court to confer the authority on the trustees to perform functions whenever it is expedient to do so.

Section 57(1) provides:

SECTION

'57(1) Where in the management or administration of any property, ... any sale, lease, mortgage, surrender, release or other disposition or any purchase, investment, acquisition, expenditure or other transaction is in the opinion of the court expedient, but the same cannot be effected by reason of the absence of any power ... the court may by order confer on the trustees, either generally or in any particular instance the necessary power.'

The purpose of s 57 is to secure that the trust property is managed as advantageously as possible in the interests of the beneficiaries and to authorise specific dealings with the trust property outside the scope of the inherent jurisdiction of the court. It may not be possible to establish an emergency or that the settlor could not reasonably have foreseen the circumstances which have arisen. In these circumstances the court may sanction the scheme presented for its approval.

However, there are a number of limitations within s 57. First, the scheme proposed by the trustees is required to be for the benefit of the trust as a whole and not only for an individual beneficiary. In *Re Craven's Estate (No 2)* [1937] Ch 431, the court refused to sanction a scheme authorising an advancement to a beneficiary for the purpose of becoming a Lloyd's underwriter. The scheme would not have been expedient for the trust as a whole. Second, additional powers may only be conferred on the trustees with regard to the 'management or administration' of the trust. No power exists under s 57 to alter the beneficial interest or to rewrite the trust administration clause as opposed to merely authorising specific dispositions or transactions. This distinction is one of degree.

In *Re Coates' Trusts* [1959] 1 WLR 375 and *Re Byng's Will Trusts* [1959] 1 WLR 375, orders were made approving arrangements to confer wider powers of investment on the trustees. Orders approving such arrangements were frequently made between the passing of the Variation of Trusts Act in 1958 and the passing of the Trustee Investment Act 1961.

Under s 57 the courts have sanctioned schemes for the partition of land (*Re Thomas* [1939] 1 Ch 194); a sale of land where the necessary consent could not be obtained (*Re Beale's Settlement Trust* [1932] 2 Ch 15); the sale of a reversionary interest which the trustees had no power to sell until it fell into possession (*Re Heyworth's Contingent Reversionary Interest* [1956] Ch 364); blended two charitable trusts into one (*Re Shipwrecked Fishermen's and Mariners' Benevolent Fund* [1959] Ch 220); and extended investment powers of pension fund trustees (*Mason v Farbrother* [1983] 2 All ER 1078).

On a variation of beneficial interests, the court has the jurisdiction to approve schemes which go beyond an alteration of the management powers of trustees and to effect arrangements which vary the beneficial interests under a trust.

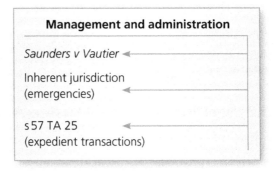

Figure 15.1 Variation of trusts – management and administration

15.4 Variation of beneficial interests

15.4.1 Section 53 of the Trustee Act 1925

Where an infant is beneficially entitled to real or personal property and the property does not produce income which may be used for the infant's maintenance and education or benefit, the court may adopt a proposal authorising a 'conveyance' of the infant's interest with a view to the application of the capital or income for his maintenance, education or benefit.

The section may not be used simply to terminate a settlement without making some new trust provision for the infant.

CASE EXAMPLE

Re Meux [1958] Ch 154

The claimant was a life tenant of a trust fund and his infant son was entitled to a contingent reversionary interest. The court sanctioned a scheme on behalf of the infant whereby a person was appointed to convey the infant's interest to the claimant in consideration of a purchase price which was paid to the trustees for the benefit of the infant.

15.4.2 Section 64 of the Settled Land Act 1925

This section applies where land is settled. The court has the power to sanction 'any transaction … which in the opinion of the court would be for the benefit of the settled land or the persons interested under the settlement'.

This section has a wider application than s 57 of the Trustee Act 1925, because it is not limited to managerial or administrative matters but allows alterations to be made to the beneficial interests. Moreover, it extends to both settled land and land held under a trust for sale. In *Raikes v Lygon* [1988] 1 All ER 884, the court decided that s 64 was wide enough to permit the creation of a second settlement.

This statutory provision was recently considered in the following case:

CASE EXAMPLE

Hambro v Duke of Marlborough, The Times, 25 March 1994

The court decided that it had jurisdiction under s 64 of the Settled Land Act 1925 to authorise the tenant for life to vary the beneficial interest of a beneficiary under the 1706 parliamentary settlement of Blenheim Palace, without that beneficiary's consent. However, this is subject to the condition that the variation is either for the benefit of the settled land or all the beneficiaries under the settlement.

15.4.3 Sections 23 and 24 of the Matrimonial Causes Act 1973

These sections give the court power to make property adjustment orders between spouses on divorce, separation or nullity, and this includes a power to make orders extinguishing or reducing the interest of either of the parties to the marriage.

15.4.4 Section 96 of the Mental Health Act 1983

This section gives the Court of Protection wide powers to authorise the making and variation of settlements of the property of mental patients.

15.4.5 Compromise (inherent jurisdiction)

The court has an inherent jurisdiction to approve compromise arrangements governing the rights of beneficiaries including infants and unborn persons under trusts. Before the House of Lords' decision in *Chapman v Chapman* [1954] AC 429, there was some doubt as to whether the jurisdiction existed if there was not a genuine dispute between the beneficiaries. The House of Lords in that case clarified the meaning of the expression 'compromise', by deciding that its jurisdiction concerned cases of genuine disputes about the existence of rights.

CASE EXAMPLE

Chapman v Chapman [1954] AC 429

The trustees applied for leave to execute a scheme releasing certain properties from the trust in order to avoid estate duty. Some of the interests were enjoyed by infants and might be enjoyed by unborn persons, so that any rearrangement of interests required the consent of the court. The House of Lords held that the scheme would not be approved because the court had no jurisdiction to sanction a rearrangement of beneficial interests on behalf of infants and unborn persons where there was no real dispute.

JUDGMENT

'[T]he question which presents difficulty in this case … is whether … the compromise category should be extended to cover cases in which there is no real dispute as to rights and, therefore, no compromise, but it is sought by way of bargain between the beneficiaries to rearrange the beneficial interests under the trust instrument and to bind infants and unborn persons to the bargain by order of the court.

…in the present case it appears to me that to accept this extension in any degree is to concede exactly what has been denied. It is the function of the court to execute a trust, to see that the trustees do their duty and to protect them if they do it, to direct them if they are in doubt and, if they do wrong, to penalise them. It is not the function of the court to alter a trust because alteration is thought to be advantageous to an infant beneficiary.'

Lord Simonds LC

15.4.6 The Variation of Trusts Act 1958

The Variation of Trusts Act 1958 was passed in order to reverse the decision of the House of Lords in *Chapman v Chapman* (1954) and to introduce sweeping changes in the law. The jurisdiction of the courts was extended in order to approve variations of trusts (in respect of both administrative matters and beneficial interests) on behalf of infants, unborn persons and others who lacked the capacity to consent to an arrangement. The court is entitled to sanction 'any arrangement varying or revoking all or any trusts or enlarging the powers of the trustees of managing or administering any of the property subject to the trusts'.

The court in its discretion may make an order approving a scheme, provided that the following four conditions are satisfied:

1. property, whether real or personal, is held on trust; and
2. the trust was created by will or *inter vivos* settlement or other disposition; and
3. the four categories as enumerated in s 1(1) of the 1958 Act, namely:

SECTION

'1(1)(a) any person having directly or indirectly, an interest, whether vested or contingent under the trusts, who, by reason of infancy or other incapacity is incapable of assenting, or

(b) any person (whether ascertained or not) who may become entitled, directly or indirectly, to an interest at a future date or on the happening of a future event, a person of any specified description or a member of any specified class of persons, but not including any person who would be of that description or a member of that class if the said date had fallen or the said event had happened at the date of the application to the court, or

(c) any person unborn, or

(d) any person in respect of any discretionary interest of his under protective trusts where the interest of the principal beneficiary has not failed or determined.'

and:

4. provided that, with the exception of para (d) above, the arrangement was carried out for the benefit of that person.

The purpose of the 1958 Act is to permit the court to approve arrangements on behalf of beneficiaries who cannot give their consent by virtue of infancy or other incapacity or because their identity is unascertained, such as a future spouse. It follows, therefore, that the court has no jurisdiction to approve arrangements on behalf of beneficiaries who are *sui juris*, adult and ascertained. Thus, the consent of all adult, ascertained beneficiaries must be obtained before the court may grant its approval to a scheme.

ACTIVITY

T1 and T2 hold property on trust for A (adult) for life, with the remainder to B (an infant) for life, with the remainder to C (adult) absolutely. A scheme of equal division is proposed. The court may approve the scheme on behalf of B (the infant) but not in respect of A and C. Will their consent be required?

The only exception to the above rule is to be found in s 1(1)(d) of the 1958 Act, namely the court may consent on behalf of an adult 'beneficiary' who may become entitled to an interest on the failure of the principal beneficiary's interest under a protective trust.

ACTIVITY

Trustees hold property on protective trust for M for life. A scheme is submitted for the approval of the court to grant M's wife, W, a one-fifth share of the capital.

1. Will the court approve the arrangement on behalf of W?
2. Is M required to consent to the scheme?

In *Allen v Distillers Co (Biochemicals) Ltd* [1974] QB 384, the court decided that the Act was not applicable to an out-of-court settlement of litigation.

CASE EXAMPLE

Allen v Distillers Co (Biochemicals) Ltd [1974] QB 384

The trust funds were received pursuant to a negotiated settlement of the Thalidomide litigation. The desire of many of the parents of children affected was to ensure that the sums held for their children should not become their absolute property at the age of 18. Eveleigh J decided that he had the power to achieve the objective of the parents under the court's inherent jurisdiction, but he had no power under the 1958 Act because that Act did not apply to the payment out to trustees under an out-of-court settlement of litigation. This was not the type of trust contemplated in the 1958 Act:

JUDGMENT

'The Act contemplates a situation where a beneficial interest is created which did not previously exist and probably one which is related to *at least one other beneficial interest*. Moreover, the Act is designed to deal with a situation where the original disposition was intended to endure according to its terms but which in the light of changed attitudes and circumstances it is fair and reasonable to vary.'

Eveleigh J

In *D (a child) v O* [2004] 3 All ER 780, the High Court decided that it had the power to lift the statutory limitation that exists under s 32 of the Trustee Act 1925 (power of advancement). This power was exercisable under the Variation of Trusts Act 1958, whereas in *Allen v Distillers* (see above) the court ruled that it did not have jurisdiction to modify an interest under the VTA 1958. However, in the present case the court distinguished *Allen v Distillers* on the ground that Eveleigh J was not considering the sort of case of absolute entitlement that was before the court on this occasion. In *D v O*, what was proposed would have the effect of accelerating the benefit to the claimant by allowing the whole of the claimant's fund or capital to be used for her benefit while she was still under age. It could not have been for the claimant's benefit to divert any part of the fund from her.

Section 1(1)(b) of the 1958 Act

Generally, the court may consent on behalf of potential beneficiaries who have a contingent interest in the trust (see s 1(1)(b)), i.e. 'a person who may become entitled … to an interest', for example a future spouse of a beneficiary. But the proviso to s 1(1)(b) prevents the court from approving on behalf of adult beneficiaries who are ascertainable and stand *only one step removed from entitlement under the trust*. It was the intention of Parliament that such persons should be allowed to consent for themselves.

For example: trustees hold property on trust for A for life with an ultimate remainder for his next of kin. A is a widower with one son, B (adult). A scheme is proposed in order to divide the fund equally between A and B. In such a case B is required to consent to the arrangement under the proviso to s 1(1)(b), on the ground that B is only one step removed from acquiring a vested interest, namely the death of A. This principle may be illustrated by the following case.

CASE EXAMPLE

Re Suffert's Settlement [1961] Ch 1

Under a settlement, B was granted a protected life interest with a power to appoint the capital and income on trust for her children. The settlement provided that if B had no children the property was to be transferred to anyone in respect of whom B may appoint (i.e. a general power) with a gift over in default of appointment in favour of B's statutory next of kin. B was 61 years of age, unmarried and without issue. She had three first cousins (next of kin) all of whom had attained the age of majority. B and one of her cousins sought to vary the settlement. The other two cousins had not consented and were not joined as parties. The court was asked to approve the arrangement on behalf of any unborn or unascertained persons and the two adult cousins. The court held that it had jurisdiction to approve on behalf of unborn and unascertained persons, but could not approve on behalf of the two cousins. Their consent was required.

JUDGMENT

'What the subsection required was that the applicant should be treated as having died at the date of the issue of the summons, to find out who in that event would have been her statutory next of kin, and any persons who are within that class are persons whose interest the section provides that the court cannot bind. It is impossible to say who are the statutory next of kin of somebody who is alive, but it is not impossible to say who are the persons who would fill that description on the hypothesis that the propositus is already dead.'

Buckley J

In *Knocker v Youle* [1986] 1 WLR 934 the court decided that it could not grant its approval on behalf of beneficiaries with contingent interests in the trust property.

CASE EXAMPLE

Knocker v Youle [1986] 1 WLR 934

Under a settlement created in 1937 property was settled on trust for the settlor's daughter for life and on her death (her share including accumulated income) was to be held on trust for such persons as she might appoint by her will. In default of appointment, the property was to be acquired by the settlor's son upon a similar trust. It was provided in the trust instrument that in the event of the trusts failing, the property was to be held on trust for the settlor's wife for life, and subject thereto for the settlor's four married sisters or their children *per stirpes*. The settlor's wife and sisters were all dead. There were numerous children from the four sisters. The settlor's daughter and son sought a variation of the trust under s 1(1)(b) of the 1958 Act which would have affected the interests of the children of the settlor's four sisters.

The court decided that it had no jurisdiction in the circumstances. Section 1(1)(b) of the Act was not applicable to a person who had an interest under the trust. The children of the sett-lor's four sisters had a contingent interest under the trust, however remote, thus depriving the court of jurisdiction.

JUDGMENT

'It is not strictly accurate to describe the cousins as persons who may become entitled … to an interest under the trusts. There is no doubt of course that they are members of a specified class. Each of them is, however, entitled now to an interest under the trusts, albeit a contin-gent one (in the case of those who are under 21, a doubly contingent one) and albeit also that it is an interest that is defeasible on the exercise of the general testamentary powers of appoint-ment vested in Mrs Youle and Mr Knocker. Nonetheless, it is properly described in legal lan-guage as an interest, and the word interest is used in its technical, legal sense. Otherwise, the words whether vested or contingent in s 1(1)(a) would be out of place. It seems to me, however, that a person who has an actual interest directly conferred upon him or her by a settlement, albeit a remote interest, cannot properly be described as one who may become entitled to an interest.'

Warner J

Variation or re-settlement?

Although the 1958 Act gives the court a wide discretion to approve a scheme varying the terms of a trust, there appears to be a limitation on this discretion. The courts have adopted the policy of not 'rewriting' the trust. Accordingly, a distinction is drawn between a 'variation' and a 're-settlement'. A 'variation' retains the basic fundamental purpose of the trust but alters some important characteristic of the trust, whereas a 're-settlement' destroys the foundation or substance of the original design or purpose of the trust. Whether a scheme amounts to a variation or a re-settlement will vary with the facts of each case.

CASE EXAMPLE

Re Ball's Settlement [1968] 1 WLR 899

A settlement conferred a life interest on the settlor, with the remainder, subject to a power of appointment, in favour of his sons and grandchildren. In default of appointment the fund was to be divided between the two sons of the settlor or their issue *per stirpes* (i.e. to the son's issue if either predeceased the settlor). A scheme was proposed for approval by the court whereby the original settlement would be revoked and replaced by new provisions in which the fund would be split into two equal portions for each of the sons for life and subject thereto, equally for such of the son's children as were born before 1 October 1977. The court approved the scheme.

JUDGMENT

'The test is if the arrangement changes the whole substratum of the trust, then it may well be that it cannot be regarded merely as varying that trust. But if an arrangement, while leaving the substratum, effectuates the purpose of the original trusts by other means, it may still be possible to regard that arrangement as merely varying the original trusts, even though the means employed are wholly different and even though the form is completely changed ... In this case, it seems to me that the substratum of the original trust remains. True, the settlor's life interest disappears; but the remaining trusts are still in essence trusts of half the fund for each of the two named sons and their families ... The differences between the old and new provisions lie in detail rather than substance.'

Megarry J

In *Re T's Settlement Trusts* [1964] Ch 158, a mother sought to restrict her financially immature daughter from acquiring a large capital fund when she attained the age of 21 years, the age of majority at this time. She applied to the court for the approval of a scheme whereby the daughter's share of the fund will be transferred to new trustees to be held on protective trusts for the daughter's life with remainder to her issue. Wilberforce J declined jurisdiction to approve such a scheme on the ground that it amounted to a re-settlement and not a variation.

JUDGMENT

'[The scheme went too far] because it was not confined to dealing in a beneficial way with the special requirements of this infant [beneficiary], but seeks authorisation for a complete resettlement which can only be justified if the court accepted (as, in my view, it should not) that such resettlement is for her benefit within the meaning of the Act. Though presented as a 'variation' it is in truth a completely new resettlement. The former trust funds were to be got in from former trustees and held upon wholly new trusts such as might be made by an absolute owner of the funds. I do not think the court can approve this.'

Wilberforce J

In *Re T*, it is arguable that the absence of jurisdiction was one of the grounds for refusing the scheme. The statutory test of 'benefit' was not satisfied (see later) for the scheme involved the replacement of an absolute interest with a life interest to the financial detriment of the infant. In any event, it would appear to be too late in the day for the court to reverse the self-imposed limitation on its jurisdiction in respect of schemes that vary, and not re-settle, the trust funds. To this end, the distinction between 'variation' and 're-settlement' has been firmly established under the Variation of Trusts Act 1958.

There is no single litmus test that may be applied by the courts to determine the issue definitively. Each case is determined on its own facts. Factors to be taken into consideration by the judge include whether the new trust would involve the segregation of assets, the appointment of new trustees, benefiting additional beneficiaries and administrative powers which make reference to the original settlement redundant.

A non-exhaustive list of indicia to be considered by the courts to determine whether there is one or two separate settlements was laid down by Lord Wilberforce in *Roome v Edwards* [1982] AC 279. This case involved liability to capital gains tax and the issue was whether the exercise of a power of appointment contained in a settlement gave rise to a settlement apart from the main settlement. If so, liability to capital gains tax would accrue, called an exit charge. The House of Lords decided that since the original settlement was still in existence and the second settlement was treated as being held on the trusts of the first, as varied by the first, the two settlements could be treated as one.

JUDGMENT

'There are a number of obvious indicia which may help to show whether a settlement, or a settlement separate from another settlement, exists. One might expect to find separate and defined property; separate trusts; and separate trustees. One might also expect to find a separate disposition bringing the separate settlement into existence. These indicia may be helpful, but they are not decisive ... There are so many possible combinations of fact that even where these indicia or some of them are present, the answer may be doubtful, and may depend upon an appreciation of them as a whole ... I think that the question whether a particular set of facts amounts to a settlement should be approached by asking what a person, with knowledge of the legal context of the word under established doctrine and applying this knowledge in a practical and common-sense manner to the facts under examination, would conclude.'

Lord Wilberforce

Although the test laid down by Lord Wilberforce in *Roome v Edwards* was applicable to determine whether an exit charge to capital gains tax was payable, the principle has been extended to distinguish cases of 'variation' from 're-settlement' under the Variation of Trusts Act 1958. In *Wyndham v Egremont* [2009] EWHC 2076, Blackburne J extended the indicia test to applications under the Variation of Trusts Act. In this case the proposed changes to the trust were to the remainder and the period of the trust. The court approved the arrangement as merely varying the original trust.

JUDGMENT

'The trustees remain the same, the subsisting trusts remain largely unaltered and the administrative provisions affecting them are wholly unchanged. The only significant changes are (1) to the trusts in the remainder, although the ultimate trust in favour of George and his personal representatives remains the same, and (2) the introduction of the new and extended period.'

Blackburne J

In *Allfrey v Allfrey (A Child)* (2015), the material issue in this application was in respect of the criteria for distinguishing arrangements that 'vary' a trust from those that might be regarded as 're-settlements' and on which side of the line did the arrangement fall in this case? The proposed arrangement ensured that the terms of the trust were maintained, save for the extension of the trust period. The purpose of the scheme was designed to further the interests of the settlement by avoiding the need to realise assets in order to meet inheritance tax charges. The beneficial interests under the settlement were not exhausted, the administrative powers remained the same and the same trustees continued in their post. In these circumstances the court decided that the scheme fell on the variation side of the line.

CASE EXAMPLE

Allfrey v Allfrey (A Child) [2015] EWHC 1717 (High Court)

An accumulation and maintenance settlement was created in 1986 for the benefit of the settlor's children, their spouses and issue, subject to an 80-year perpetuity period. At this initial stage the trust was exempt from Inheritance tax (IHT). However, since the mid-2000s the trust attracted IHT at 10-yearly intervals. The next charge was due in July 2016. In 2014 the trustees exercised their power of revocation and reappointment so that the entire trust fund was re-settled on discretionary trusts for the same beneficiaries. In order to avoid the necessity of selling the trust assets, the trustees expressed a preference to accumulate the income in order to meet the periodic charges. But this power was absent from the trust. In order to redress this omission, a scheme was proposed to vary the trust by enlarging the power of appointment to incorporate a power to accumulate the trust income, and to take advantage of the generous perpetuity period created by the Perpetuities and Accumulations Act 2009. Such a scheme required the approval of the court on behalf of minor and unborn children. The question in issue was whether this scheme constituted a variation of trusts or, alternatively, amounted to a re-settlement. The High Court approved the scheme and decided that, consistently with the authorities, this arrangement amounted to a variation and not a re-settlement.

JUDGMENT

'Applying Lord Wilberforce's approach in *Roome v Edwards*, it is easy to ascertain what were the intentions of the parties. The intention was to supplement the provisions of the existing settlement, thereby enhancing its operation. In my judgment, the arrangement quite clearly is to be described as a variation rather than a resettlement. The parties intended to continue the existing trusts, but with modifications.'

Jeremy Cousins QC (Deputy High Court judge)

Settlor's intention

The 1958 Act makes no mention of the settlor or testator. Rules of Court (RSC Ord 93 r 6(2)) have been made requiring the joinder of the settlor, if living, as a defendant to an application under the Act. In exercising its discretion whether to approve an arrangement or not, the function of the court is to determine, by reference to all the circumstances, whether the arrangement as a whole is beneficial to the stipulated class of beneficiaries. However, in the context of deciding whether to approve an arrangement or not, the intention of the settlor or testator is only a factor (if relevant) to be taken into consideration by the court. But the settlor's or testator's intention is certainly not an overriding factor, nor even a weighty consideration in determining how the discretion of the court is to be exercised. The role of the court is not to act as a representative of the settlor or testator in varying the trusts.

In *Re Steed's Will Trust* [1960] Ch 407, the court took into consideration the testator's intention and refused to approve the proposed arrangement.

In *Goulding v James* [1997] 2 All ER 239, Mummery LJ reviewed *Re Steed* (1960) and decided that the latter case did not lay down 'any rule, principle or guideline of general application on the importance of the intentions and wishes of the settlor or testator to applications to approve arrangements under the 1958 Act'. In other words, the settlor's wishes coincided with, but were not a cause for, the court's refusal to vary the trust.

tutor tip

'Variations of trust may affect the trustees' managerial powers and duties and also the interests of the beneficiaries.'

CASE EXAMPLE

Goulding v James [1997] 2 All ER 239

The court decided that, in the exercise of its discretion, it would approve a scheme of variation of a trust, despite the contradiction of the clear intention of a testatrix concerning adult, ascertained beneficiaries. In this case June and Marcus Goulding – the beneficiaries under will trusts – applied to the court for a variation under s 1(1)(c) of the 1958 Act. The proposed variation was partly in favour of a grandchildren's trust fund, and would benefit unborn great-grandchildren of the testatrix. However, the variation was contrary to the wishes of the testatrix. Despite the testatrix's wishes, the court approved the scheme. Mummery LJ summarised the court's approach.

JUDGMENT

'The fact that the rules of court require a living settlor to be joined as a party to proceedings under the 1958 Act does not mean that the court attaches any overbearing or special significance to the wishes of the settlor. The court has a discretion to approve an arrangement under the Act, even though the settlement or will may make it crystal clear that the settlor or testator does not want any departure from any of the strict terms of the trust.'

Mummery LJ

Benefit (proviso to s 1(1))

The scheme of variation is required to display some benefit for the persons as stated in s 1(1)(a)–(c) of the Variation of Trusts Act 1958. No such requirement exists for persons in category (d) of s 1(1) of the Act. The statute does not list the factors which the court is required to take into account in deciding the issue. It seems that all the circumstances are required to be considered and the court must weigh up the possible advantages against the disadvantages of adopting a scheme of variation of the trust and decide accordingly.

CASE EXAMPLE

D (a child) v O [2004] 3 All ER 780

An application to vary a settlement under the Variation of Trusts Act 1958 was made in writing, in chambers and without a hearing, but subject to written submissions. The application was made to increase the ceiling of 50 per cent of the presumptive share of an infant beneficiary's capital (imposed by s 32 of the Trustee Act 1925) in order to make an advancement for school fees. The court decided that it had the jurisdiction under the Variation of Trusts Act 1958 to modify the statutory power of advancement and that it was for the claimant's benefit that the limit imposed by s 32 of the Trustee Act 1925 be lifted.

A wide variety of factors have been prominent in either approving or rejecting schemes of variations. Some of these include tax avoidance, moral benefits and the avoidance of family dissension.

Tax avoidance

The majority of applications have been made with a view to reducing the tax which would otherwise have been payable if the variation was not made.

For example: property was settled on trust for A for life, with the remainder to B absolutely. Inheritance tax would be payable on the entire estate on A's death and a second time on B's death. If the settlement was varied so that the fund is divided between A and B equally, inheritance tax would be payable on only half of the trust fund on the death of each of the beneficiaries.

The courts are required to be satisfied that the scheme as a whole is advantageous to the objects. It follows that the court will not approve a scheme if the overall effect is detrimental to the objects, even though there may be financial rewards inherent in the scheme. Tax avoidance is merely one factor to be taken into account by the courts.

CASE EXAMPLE

Re Weston's Settlement [1969] 1 Ch 223

The settlor created two settlements in 1964 for the benefit of his two sons. A total of 500,000 shares were transferred to the trustees. In 1965 capital gains tax was introduced. The shares rose in value and at the time of hearing the tax due on a disposal of the shares was £163,000. The settlor lived in England until 1967. He made three short visits to Jersey in 1967 and then in August 1967 purchased a house there in which he intended to live. In November 1967 an application was made to the court under the Variation of Trusts Act 1958 to appoint two trustees in Jersey as trustees of the two English settlements. In addition, the plaintiff sought the court's sanction to 'export' the trust to Jersey on identical terms. The motive was to save capital gains tax and estate duty. The Court of Appeal decided that the scheme would not be approved because it would have been morally and socially detrimental to the beneficiaries despite being financially advantageous.

JUDGMENT

'The Court should not consider merely the financial benefit to the infants and unborn children but also their educational and social benefit. There are many things in life more worthwhile than money. One of these things is to be brought up in this our England, which is still the envy of less happier lands. I do not believe it is for the benefit of children to be uprooted from England and transported to another country simply to avoid tax. I should imagine that even if they had stayed in this country they would have had a very considerable fortune at their disposal even after paying tax. The only thing that Jersey can do for them is to give them a greater fortune. Many a child has been ruined by being given too much. The avoidance of tax may be lawful, but it is not yet a virtue. The children may well change their minds and come back to this country to enjoy their untaxed gains. Are they to be wanderers over the face of the earth, moving from this country to that according to where they can best avoid tax? Children are like trees, they grow stronger with firm roots.'

Lord Denning

On the other hand, where the applicants have a long-standing connection with the foreign country concerned in the proposed scheme, the court may grant its approval.

CASE EXAMPLE

Re Windeatt's Will Trust [1969] 1 WLR 692

The settlor was domiciled in England. He created a trust for the benefit of his children, who had lived in Jersey for 19 years prior to the application to transfer the trust to Jersey. The court approved the scheme because the beneficiaries were permanently resident in Jersey.

CASE EXAMPLE

Ridgwell v Ridgwell [2007] EWHC 2666 (Ch)

In this case, the High Court approved a variation of trusts scheme by postponing children's interest where this was demonstrated to be for their financial benefit as a tax-saving device. The court, in exercising its discretion for the benefit of the beneficiaries, is required to fulfil the objective of protecting those who cannot protect themselves. In so doing, the court may consent to a tax avoidance scheme. Nearly all variations of trusts schemes that have come before the court have tax avoidance as their principal object and this is not contrary to public policy. In this case the claimant was both trustee and life tenant of a settlement. On his death the trust funds were to be held for distribution to his children or remoter issue when such children reached the age of 30. The effect of this settlement was the loss of the nil rate band of inheritance tax that would otherwise have been available if the funds passed through the claimant's wife. The trustees applied to have the trust varied by interposing a life interest for the claimant's wife before the capital could be distributed to the children. The court approved the scheme and decided that the addition of the life interest did not fundamentally alter the settlement and constituted an 'arrangement' under the Variation of Trusts Act 1958. The potential savings of inheritance and capital gains taxes amounted to a 'benefit' to the children which outweighed the theoretical disadvantage of postponing their interest in remainder.

JUDGMENT

'I reserved judgment in this case because I was concerned that the postponement of the children's interests might not be for their benefit. However, [counsel for the trustees] have persuaded me that the greater flexibility that the variation gives to the trustees in the timing of making advances to effect inheritance tax savings, taken together with the potential savings in capital gains tax … amount to a benefit to the children which outweigh the theoretical disadvantage of the postponement of their interest in remainder. It follows that I am satisfied that there is jurisdiction to approve the variation. As a matter of discretion I agree that the variation is a sensible solution to a difficult problem.'

Judge Behrens QC

Moral benefit

The court may have regard to evidence which establishes the financial instability of infant beneficiaries and adopt a scheme which has the effect of postponing the vesting of such a beneficiary's interest in capital.

CASE EXAMPLE

Re T's Settlement [1964] Ch 158

An infant was entitled absolutely to one-quarter of a trust fund on attaining the age of 21 years (age of majority at this time) and a further one-quarter on the death of her mother. Eighteen days before she reached the age of majority her mother asked the court to approve a transfer to new trustees of the infant's share, to be held either:

(i) on protective trust for her life or

(ii) to postpone the vesting of capital until she reached the age of 25, but in the meantime the property would be held on protective trusts. It was conceded that the infant was alarmingly immature and irresponsible in respect of financial matters. The court held that:

(a) the protective trust for life would have amounted to a 're-settlement' of property which was outside the jurisdiction of the court and in any event would not be beneficial to the child; but

(b) the postponement of the capital until a later date and the interim protective trust were approved.

JUDGMENT

'[I]t appears to me to be a definite benefit for this infant for a period during which it is to be hoped that independence may bring her to maturity and responsibility to be protected against creditors … And this is the kind of benefit which seems to be within the spirit of the Act.'

Wilberforce J

In *Re Holt's Settlement* [1969] 1 Ch 100, the court approved the decision in *Re T's Settlement* (1964) but postponed the vesting of an infant's benefit without evidence of financial immaturity.

CASE EXAMPLE

Re Holt's Settlement [1969] 1 Ch 100

Personal property was settled on Mrs Wilson for life with remainder to such of her children as would reach the age of 21 years and, if more than one, in equal shares. She wanted to surrender her life interest in half of the income for the benefit of the children (in order to reduce the impact of income tax on her husband and her) and to rearrange the trusts so that the interest of the children would vest at the age of 30 years. The court sanctioned the scheme because, on the whole, it was for the benefit of the children.

JUDGMENT

'It seems to me that the arrangement proposed is for the benefit of each of the beneficiaries contemplated by s 1(1) of the 1958 Act. The financial detriment to the children is that the absolute vesting of their interests will be postponed from age 21 to 30. As against this, they will obtain very substantial financial benefits, both in the acceleration of their interests in a moiety [half] of the trust fund and in the savings of estate duty … it is also most important that young children should be reasonably advanced in a career and settled in life before they are in receipt of an income sufficient to make them independent of the need to work. The word benefit in the proviso to s 1(1) is plainly not confined to financial benefit, but may extend to moral and social benefit as is shown in *Re T's Settlement*.'

Megarry J

Avoidance of family dissension

The court may approve an arrangement if its effect would be to prevent real or potential conflict within a family. In this respect, although the intention of the settlor carries a great deal of weight, it is not conclusive.

CASE EXAMPLE

Re Remnant's Settlement Trust [1970] Ch 560

A trust gave contingent interests to the children of two sisters, Dawn and Merrial, and contained a forfeiture clause if they practised Roman Catholicism or married or lived with a Roman Catholic. The children of Dawn were Protestants, whereas the children of Merrial were Roman Catholics. The sisters sought the court's approval of a scheme which deleted the forfeiture clause. The court gave its approval in order to prevent a family conflict. Although Dawn's children did not benefit financially from the deletion of the clause, the court decided that on the whole they would be better off because the religious bar could have deterred them from selecting a spouse.

JUDGMENT

'Obviously a forfeiture provision of this kind might well cause very serious dissension between the families of two sisters … I am entitled to take a broad view of what is meant by benefit, and so taking it, I think this arrangement can fairly be said to be for their benefit…

It remains to be considered whether the arrangement is a fair and proper one. As far as I can see, there is no reason for saying otherwise, except that the arrangement defeats this testator's intention. That is a serious but by no means conclusive consideration. I have reached the clear conclusion that these forfeiture provisions are undesirable in the circumstances of this case and that an arrangement involving their deletion is a fair and proper one.'

Pennycuick J

Effect of variation

The variation takes effect as soon as the order is made by the court and without the necessity of any further instrument. As equitable interests are being dealt with, one would have thought that compliance with s 53(1)(c) of the Law of Property Act 1925 (requiring the written consent of adult beneficiaries) would be necessary. However, in *Re Holt's Settlement* (1969) Megarry J concluded that it is not necessary to satisfy this requirement, declaring that s 53(1)(c) had been impliedly excluded by the Variation of Trusts Act 1958. Alternatively, where the variation was made for consideration, the consenting adults could be compelled to perform the contract. They therefore held their original interests on constructive trusts, which did not require fulfilment of s 53(1)(c).

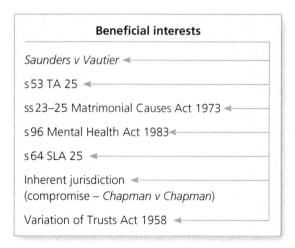

Figure 15.2 Variation of trusts – beneficial interests

ACTIVITY

Essay writing

What differences are apparent in the law's attitude to variations of administrative provisions and dispositive provisions?
  Discuss.

ACTIVITY

Applying the law

Under the trusts of a settlement of personalty, a trust fund currently worth £250,000 is held by the trustees upon trust to pay the income thereof to Amy during her life upon a s 33 Trustee Act 1925 protective trust for her life and, subject thereto, upon trust for such of Amy's children as she shall by deed appoint, and in default of appointment upon trust for such of Amy's children as shall attain the age of 21 and if more than one in equal shares.

  Amy is 56 years of age and has two children: Janet (aged 20) and John (aged 18). Amy, Janet and John would like to divide up the capital of the trust fund among themselves.

  Advise them as to whether this may be done and, if so, as to the legal steps that would need to be taken.

SUMMARY

▪ The rule in *Saunders v Vautier* (1841) is a doctrine of general application. It is to the effect that when the beneficiaries are of full age and sound mind and are absolutely entitled to the trust property, they (collectively) are entitled to terminate the trust by directing the trustees to transfer the property to them provided that they act in unison.

▪ Variation of the management powers of the trustees may be achieved in one of the following ways:

  ● under the inherent jurisdiction of the court to deal with 'emergencies';
  ● by virtue of s 57 of the Trustee Act 1925, where the court is of the opinion that it is 'expedient' to grant the application.

▪ Applications to vary the beneficial interests of the objects of the trust may be made under one of the following:

  ● s 53 of the Trustee Act 1925;
  ● s 64 of the Settled Land Act 1925;
  ● ss 23 and 24 of the Matrimonial Causes Act 1973;
  ● s 96 of the Mental Health Act 1983;
  ● s 1 of the Variation of Trusts Act 1958.

▪ The Variation of Trusts Act 1958 was passed to approve variations of trusts in respect of administrative matters and beneficial interests.

▪ The court is empowered to approve arrangements on behalf of beneficiaries who do not have the capacity to consent to the arrangement.

▪ The courts have drawn a limitation in its jurisdiction between a 'variation' on the one hand and a 're-settlement'.

▪ In approving a variation the intention of the settlor is a factor, but not a decisive factor, to be taken into account.

▪ The variation takes effect on the date of the court order.

SAMPLE ESSAY QUESTION

Consider the following essay question:

When may the court approve a variation of the terms of a trust under the Variation of Trusts Act 1958?

Answer plan

> Consider the rationale behind the passing of the Variation of Trusts Act 1958. Brief reference to the HL refusal to exercise its 'compromise' jurisdiction under *Chapman v Chapman* (1954). This prompted the enactment of the Variation of Trusts Act 1958.
>
> Outline the four categories of persons under the Variation of Trusts Act 1958 in whose favour the court may grant approval, see s(1)(1).

> The section applies to real and personal property and to trusts created inter vivos or by will.

> The Act empowers the court to approve arrangements for the 'benefit' of persons who do not have the capacity to consent to the arrangement.

> Define the expression 'benefit' within the Act by reference to case law.

> Variations of a fraudulent nature will not be sanctioned.

> Bring out the distinction between a 'variation' and a 're-settlement'.

> Consider the significance of the settlor's intention.

> State the effect of a variation of trust.

> **CONCLUSION**

Further reading

Cotterell, R, 'The requirement of benefit under the Variation of Trusts Act 1958' (1971) 34 MLR 96.

Evans, D, 'The Variation of Trusts Act in practice' (1963) 27 Conv 6.

Harris, J, 'Ten years of variation of trusts' (1969) 33 Conv 113 and 183.

Hayes, M, 'Breaking and varying trusts painlessly' (1998) 4 MLR 17.

Luxton, P, 'An unascertainable problem in variation of trusts' (1986) 136 NLJ 1057.

Luxton, P, 'Variations of trust: settlor's intention and the consent principle in *Saunders v Vautier*' (1997) MLR 719.

Marshall, O, 'Deviation from the terms of a trust' (1954) 17 MLR 420.

Riddall, J, 'Does it or doesn't it? Contingent interests and Variation of Trusts Act 1958' (1987) Conv 144.

VARIATION OF TRUSTS

16

Breach of trust

AIMS AND OBJECTIVES

By the end of this chapter you should be able to:

- recognise whether a breach of trust has been committed by the trustees
- apply the principles concerning the measure of the trustee's liability
- ascertain whether simple or compound interest is payable in addition to damages for breach of trust
- determine whether a contribution is obtainable by a trustee
- identify whether the trustees are entitled to relief
- understand the limitation periods
- apply the principles regarding proprietary remedies in tracing the claimant's assets generally and funds in bank accounts

16.1 Introduction

A trustee is liable for breach of trust if he fails to perform his duties, either by omitting to do any act which he ought to do, or by doing an act which he ought not to do. Such duties may be created by the settlor in the trust instrument (such as the duty to distribute both income and capital) or may be imposed generally in accordance with trust law (e.g. duties of care and impartiality). A breach of trust may range from a fraudulent disposal of trust property to an innocent dereliction of duties by investing trust moneys in unauthorised investments. The beneficiary is required to establish a causal connection between the breach of trust and the loss suffered either directly or indirectly by the trust. Indeed, even if the trust suffers no loss, the beneficiary is entitled to claim any profit occurring to the trustees as a result of a breach.

16.2 Measure of liability

Trustees' liability for breach of trust is based on the principle of restoring to the trust estate losses connected with trust assets and funds that the trustees wrongfully dealt with in breach of trust. The trust is required to be compensated fully for any loss caused by the trustee's breach. The extent of this liability is not restricted by common law principles governing remoteness of damage in actions in tort or breach of contract, such as reasonable foreseeability of the loss. Once a breach has been committed the trustees become liable to place the trust estate in the same position as it would have been in if no breach had been committed. Considerations of causation, foreseeability and remoteness do not readily feature in this question.

CASE EXAMPLE

Caffrey v Darby [1801] 6 Ves 488

Trustees, because of their negligence, failed to recover possession of part of the trust assets and later still the assets became lost. The trustees argued that the loss was not attributable to their neglect. The court rejected this argument and decided that once the trustees had committed a breach of trust, they were responsible for compensating the estate in respect of any loss, whether consequential on the breach or not.

JUDGMENT

'[I]f they have already been guilty of negligence they must be responsible for any loss in any way to that property, for whatever may be the immediate cause, the property would not have been in a situation to sustain that loss if it had not been for their negligence. If the loss had happened by fire, lightning, or any other accident, that would not be an excuse for them if guilty of previous negligence.'

Lord Eldon

The effect of this strict rule is that the liability of the trustees to account for losses suffered by the trust estate is absolute. Accordingly, it may be possible to obtain damages for breach of trust in cases where it is not possible to recover damages at common law in actions for breach of contract and tort.

JUDGMENT

'The obligation of a trustee who is held liable for breach of trust is fundamentally different from the obligation of a contractual or tortious wrongdoer. The trustee's obligation is to restore to the trust estate the assets of which he has deprived it.'

Brightman J in *Bartlett v Barclays Bank Trust Co Ltd (No 2)* [1980] 2 All ER 92

The same sentiments were expressed by Lord Browne-Wilkinson in the House of Lords' decision in *Target Holdings v Redferns* [1995] 3 All ER 785:

JUDGMENT

'[T]he basic rule is that a trustee in breach of trust must restore or pay to the trust estate either the assets which have been lost ... or compensation for such loss ... the common law rules of remoteness ... and causation do not apply.'

Lord Browne-Wilkinson

It appears that in equity, although the strict common law test of foreseeability is not applicable in assessing damages for breach of trust, it is essential that the compensation awarded is linked to the breach of trust. The House of Lords in *Target Holdings v Redferns* (1995) decided that in assessing compensation for loss arising from a breach of trust, the nature of the breach of duty and whether the trust is a traditional (family trust) or commercial trust is important.

Where the breach occurs in a traditional type of trust (e.g. a family trust for a number of beneficiaries in succession), equity acted *in personam* and may order the trustee to account for all the funds that have been lost by the trust. This requires the trustee to restore to the trust fund the assets that ought to have been held upon trust, but were wrongly paid away by him. In the absence of specific restitution, the trustee will be required to compensate the trust for the loss it has suffered.

In *Target Holdings v Redfern*, Lord Browne-Wilkinson laid down the following principle:

JUDGMENT

'The basic right of a beneficiary is to have the trust duly administered in accordance with the provisions of the trust instrument, if any, and the general law. Thus, in relation to a traditional trust, where the fund is held in trust for a number of beneficiaries having different, usually successive, equitable interests (for example, A for life with remainder to B), the right of each beneficiary is to have the whole fund vested in the trustees so as to be available to satisfy his equitable interest when, and if, it falls into possession. Accordingly, in the case of a breach of such a trust involving the wrongful paying away of trust assets, the liability of the trustee is to restore to the trust fund, often called the trust estate, what ought to have been there, see *Nocton v Ashburton (Lord)* [1914] AC 932, pp. 952, 958, *per* Viscount Haldane LC. Thus, the common law rules of remoteness of damage and causation do not apply.

However, there does have to be some causal connection between the breach of trust and the loss to the trust estate for which compensation is recoverable, viz, the fact that the loss would not have occurred but for the breach: see also *In re Miller's Deed Trusts* (1978) 75 LSG 454; *Nestlé v National Westminster Bank plc* [1993] 1 WLR 1260.'

Lord Browne-Wilkinson

But where the trustees hold the property on bare trust for the beneficiary and subsequently commit a breach of trust, the payment of compensation, as opposed to restitution, would be treated as appropriate for the benefit of the beneficiary, the reason being that in this event the trust comes to an end and the beneficiary becomes the sole owner of the property. Lord Browne-Wilkinson in *Target Holdings* explained the rule thus:

JUDGMENT

'What if at the time of the action claiming compensation for breach of trust those trusts have come to an end? There is no reason for compensating the breach of trust by way of an order for restitution and compensation to the trust fund *as opposed to the beneficiary himself*. The beneficiary's right is no longer simply to have the trust duly administered: he is, in equity, the sole owner of the trust estate. Nor is restitution to the trust fund necessary to protect other beneficiaries. In the ordinary case, where a beneficiary becomes absolutely entitled to the trust fund, the court orders, not restitution to the trust estate, but the payment of compensation directly to the beneficiary. The measure of such compensation is the same, that is, the difference between what the beneficiary has in fact received and the amount he would have received but for the breach of trust.' [Emphasis added]

Lord Browne-Wilkinson

But what is the position where the breach of trust is in respect of a commercial transaction, as distinct from traditional trusts? In commercial transactions it is unnecessary to reconstitute the trust. In *Target Holdings*, their Lordships declared that in the case of a breach arising out of a commercial transaction, the basis of compensation is similar to that applied in the case of common law damages, i.e. that the beneficiary is put into the position he would have been in had the breach not occurred. In such a case the common law rules of remoteness and causation would apply. In *Target Holdings* Lord Browne-Wilkinson explained the justification for the rule in the following manner:

JUDGMENT

'Even applying the strict rules so developed in relation to traditional trusts, it seems to me very doubtful whether Target is now entitled to have the trust fund reconstituted. But in my judgment it is in any event wrong to lift wholesale the detailed rules developed in the context of traditional trusts and then seek to apply them to trusts of quite a different kind [such as commercial and financial trusts].

The obligation to reconstitute the trust fund applicable in the case of traditional trusts reflects the fact that no one beneficiary is entitled to the trust property and the need to compensate all beneficiaries for the breach. That rationale has no application to a case such as the present. To impose such an obligation in order to enable the beneficiary solely entitled (that is, the client) to recover from the solicitor more than the client has in fact lost, flies in the face of common sense and is in direct conflict with the basic principles of equitable compensation. In my judgment, once a conveyancing transaction has been completed, the client has no right to have the solicitor's client account reconstituted as a trust fund.'

Lord Browne-Wilkinson

CASE EXAMPLE

Target Holdings v Redferns [1995] 3 All ER 785

The claimants, mortgagees, loaned a company £1.525 million, to be secured by way of a mortgage on property which was fraudulently made to appear to be worth £2 million, but in reality was worth only £775,000. The defendants, a firm of solicitors, were not parties to this fraud and acted for the purchasers and the mortgagees. The purchasers became insolvent and the claimants repossessed the property and sold it for £500,000. The claimants sued the firm of solicitors. The firm conceded that it acted in breach of trust by paying out the mortgage funds without authority, but argued that it was not liable to compensate the claimant for the loss suffered because its breach did not cause the loss sustained by the claimant. The firm of solicitors alleged that the claimants' loss was wholly caused by the fraud of the third parties. The House of Lords decided in favour of the firm of solicitors. The claimant company advanced the same amount of money, obtained the same security and received the same amount on the realisation of that security, with or without the breach of trust committed by the defendant.

JUDGMENT

'I reach the conclusion that, on the facts which must currently be assumed, Target has not demonstrated that it is entitled to any compensation for breach of trust. Target obtained exactly what it would have obtained had no breach occurred, that is, a valid security for the sum advanced. Therefore, on the assumption made, Target has suffered no compensatable loss.'

Lord Browne-Wilkinson

In *Templeton Insurance Ltd v Penningtons* [2006] All ER (D) 191 (Feb), the High Court decided that a firm of solicitors who received a fund subject to a *Quistclose* trust (i.e. for a specified purpose) but disposed of a part of the fund for an unauthorised purpose in breach of trust, was liable to compensate the claimant by way of damages. Similarly, in *Wise v Jimenez* [2013] Lexis citation 84 (considered in Chapter 7), the High Court decided that a claimant who made a *Quistclose* payment of £500,000 towards a scheme for the development of a golf course in France, but which failed to materialise in breach of trust, was entitled to equitable compensation by way of damages. Since the trust arose out of a commercial transaction the basis of compensation was similar to that applied in the case of common law damages, i.e. that the beneficiary will be put in the position he would have been had the breach not occurred. In such a case the common law rules of remoteness and causation would apply in quantifying the damages.

In *Nationwide Building Society v Various Solicitors (No 3)* [1999] PNLR 52, the High Court applied the principles laid down by Lord Browne-Wilkinson in the *Target* case (1995) in assessing damages for breach of fiduciary duties. The court decided that the correct approach in such a claim is to put the beneficiary in the position he would have been in if the fiduciary had performed his duty.

In the Supreme Court decision in *AIB Group (UK) plc v Redler & Co Solicitors* (2014), the issue was whether the principles governing equitable compensation for breach of trust laid down by Lord Browne-Wilkinson in *Target Holdings v Redferns* ought to be followed, qualified or reinterpreted. The Supreme Court decided that it would have been a backward step to depart from or reinterpret the equitable principles of compensation laid down in *Target* by Lord Browne-Wilkinson. In *Target* Lord Browne-Wilkinson had framed the question thus: 'Is the trustee liable to compensate the beneficiary not only for losses caused by the breach but also for losses which the beneficiary would, in any event, have suffered even if there had been no such breach?' The Supreme Court affirmed the principle that equitable compensation involved making good a loss in fact suffered by the beneficiaries and which, using hindsight and common sense, can be seen to have been caused by the breach.

CASE EXAMPLE

AIB Group (UK) plc v Redler & Co Solicitors [2014] UKSC 58 (Supreme Court)

The claimants ('AIB' or 'the bank') agreed to loan Mr and Mrs Sondhi (S) £3.3m to be secured by way of a first charge on their home, valued at £4.25m. At that time the property was subject to a first legal charge in favour of Barclays Bank plc ('Barclays'). The Barclays charge was secured on borrowings on two accounts totalling £1.5m (£1.2m was secured on one account and £0.3m on another account). AIB retained the defendants ('solicitors') to act for it and, as is customary, the borrowers appointed the same firm of solicitors to act for them. On request AIB transmitted the funds (£3.3m) to the solicitors as completion was imminent. AIB telephoned Barclays for a redemption figure. There was then a misunderstanding. The solicitors were given a redemption figure for *one of the two* Barclays accounts (£1.2m), which they mistakenly took to be the total figure. The solicitors remitted to Barclays £1.2m in order to redeem the mortgage and the balance of £2.1m to S. Barclays refused to release its charge until the outstanding debt of £0.3m was paid in full. At first, S promised to pay the outstanding sum to Barclays but failed to keep their word. The solicitors did not immediately tell AIB of their error because they hoped to resolve it. When they eventually informed AIB of their error Barclays consented to the registration of AIB's charge as a second charge. Subsequently S defaulted and the property was repossessed and sold by Barclays for £1.2m, of which AIB received £867,697.

AIB brought a claim against the solicitors for breaches of trust, contract and in negligence. In particular, AIB claimed (1) reconstitution of the fund paid away in breach of trust, (2) equitable compensation for breach of trust, and (3) damages for breach of contract and negligence. In short, AIB claimed to be entitled to the full amount of its loan less the amount recovered. The solicitors admitted that they were negligent and acted in breaches of trust and contract, but contended that they were liable to AIB for the loss occasioned on the assumption that they had done what they were required to do, i.e. a loss of £0.3m (the difference between £1.5m and £1.2m). The trial judge decided that the solicitors committed a breach of trust and the loss suffered by AIB was £0.3m and not the whole of the payment of £3.3m. This decision was affirmed by the Court of Appeal. On appeal, the Supreme Court dismissed the appeal on the following grounds:

(i) In the absence of fraud, it would not be right to create a rule that gave redress to a beneficiary for loss which would have been suffered even if the trustee had properly performed his duties. There needs to be a direct link between the trustee's breach of duties and the loss suffered by the beneficiaries. The claimants' argument that the party in breach is required to reconstitute the trust fund has the effect of penalising the defendants, for it is equivalent to a monetary award which reflected no loss caused by the trustee's breach of trust.

(ii) The equitable principles of compensation for breach of trust laid down by Lord Browne-Wilkinson in *Target Holdings v Redferns* were correct and it would be a backward step to depart from such principles.

(iii) The basic right of a beneficiary was to have the trust duly administered in accordance with trusts law. Where that duty had been breached the purpose of any remedy was to either put the beneficiary in the same position as if the breach had not occurred or to vest in the beneficiary any profit which the trustee might have made by reason of the breach.

(iv) The trustee's liability for breach of trust in the context of a commercial transaction was not generally the same as a liability in damages for breach of contract or in tort. Accordingly the common law rules of remoteness of damage and causation do not apply, for foreseeability of loss is not a concern in assessing equitable compensation. At the same time a nexus between the loss and the breach of trust is required to be established.

(v) In a commercial transaction where a party (solicitor) acts in breach of trust but completes the transaction the beneficiary is entitled to be compensated for any loss he suffered because of the breach. Prior to the completion of the transaction the defendant (solicitor) may be required to restore to the claimant the trust funds that were wrongly paid away. But once the transaction has been completed the beneficiary becomes entitled to compensation for the loss that has been occasioned only by virtue of the breach of trust.

JUDGMENT

'AIB argue that they are entitled to payment of the entire £3.3m less £867,697 which they received on the sale of the property, on the basis of Redler's liability for their breach of trust is unlimited by causation or remoteness. In my opinion that argument is based on three fallacies, each of which is fatal to AIB's claim. First, it assumes that Redler misapplied the entire £3.3m, whereas in my opinion all that was misapplied was the £309,000 which was paid to the Sondhis rather than Barclays. The second fallacy in AIB's argument is that it assumes that the measure of Redler's liability was fixed as at the date of the breach of trust. The third fallacy is that the argument assumes that liability does not depend on a causal link between the breach of trust and the loss: Redler is sought to be made liable for the consequences of the hopeless inadequacy of the security accepted by AIB before Redler's involvement.'

Lord Reed

The following examples illustrate the principles that have been applied by the courts.

Where the trustees make an unauthorised investment they are liable for any loss incurred on the sale of the assets. The position remains the same even if the sale is ordered by the courts and, but for the order of sale within a specified time, the investments would have produced a profit had they been retained for a longer period. The loss is measured by deducting the proceeds of sale of the unauthorised investment (accruing to the trust) from the amount improperly invested.

CASE EXAMPLE

Knott v Cottee [1852] 16 Beav 77

A testator, who died in 1844, directed his trustee to invest in government stocks and land in England and Wales. In 1845 and 1846 the executor-trustee invested part of the estate in Exchequer bills which in 1846 were ordered into court and sold at a loss. In 1848, the court declared that the investment was improper. If, however, the investment had been retained, its realisation at the time of the declaration in 1848 would have resulted in a profit. The court held that the trustee was liable to compensate the estate for the difference in value of the assets in 1848 and the sale proceeds in 1846.

JUDGMENT

'The case must either be treated as if these investments had not been made, or had been made for his own benefit out of his own monies, and that he had at the same time retained monies of the testator in his hands.'

Romilly MR

Where the trustees, in breach of their duties, fail to dispose of unauthorised investments and improperly retain the assets, they will be liable for the difference between the current value of the assets and the value at the time when they should have been sold.

CASE EXAMPLE

Fry v Fry [1859] 28 LJ Ch 591

A testator, who died March 1834, directed his trustees to sell a house 'as soon as convenient after [his death] … for the most money that could be normally obtained'. In April 1836 the trustees advertised the house for £1,000. In 1837 they refused an offer of £900. In 1843 a railway was built near the property which caused it to depreciate in value. The property remained unsold in 1856, by which time both the original trustees had died. The court held that their estates were liable for the difference between £900 and the sum receivable for the house when it was eventually sold.

Where the trustees retain an authorised investment they will not be liable for breach of trust unless their conduct falls short of the ordinary prudence required of trustees. This was decided in *Re Chapman* [1896] 2 Ch 763. Under s 6 of the Trustee Investment Act 1961 (now repealed), the trustees, from time to time, were required to obtain and consider advice on whether the retention of the investment was satisfactory, having regard to the need for diversification and suitability of the investment.

Where the trustees improperly sell authorised investments and reinvest the proceeds in unauthorised investments, they will be liable to replace the authorised investments if these have risen in value, or the proceeds of sale of the authorised investments.

CASE EXAMPLE

Re Massingberd's Settlement [1890] 63 LT 296

The trustees of a settlement had power to invest in government securities. In 1875 they sold Consols (authorised investments) and reinvested in unauthorised mortgages. The mortgages were called in and the whole of the money invested was recovered. At this time the Consols had risen in value. In an action for an account the court held that the trustees were required to replace the stock sold or its money equivalent.

Where the trustees are directed by the settlor to invest in an identified or specific investment (e.g. shares in British Telecom plc) and the trustees fail to acquire the stipulated investments, they will be required to purchase the same at the proper time. If the specified investments have fallen in value, the trustees may be ordered to pay compensation to the trust equivalent to the difference between the value of the investments at the time the investments should have been made, and the value of the investments at the time of the judgment.

On the other hand, where the trustees retain a discretion to invest in a specified range of investments and they fail to invest, they are chargeable with the trust fund itself and not with the amount of one or other of the investments which might have been purchased. In *Shepherd v Mouls* (1845) 4 Hare 500, it was decided that there is no one specific investment which may be used to measure the loss suffered by the trust. Where the trustees in breach of trust make a profit on one transaction and a loss on another they are not allowed to set off the loss against the profit, unless the profit and loss are treated as part of one transaction.

CASE EXAMPLE

Bartlett v Barclays Bank Trust Co (No 2) [1980] Ch 515

The trust estate consisted of a majority shareholding in a property company and the trustees were a professional trust company. For a number of years the property company maintained traditional investments and these were sufficient to maintain large dividends. As a result of inflation, the board resolved to restructure the investment portfolio into land developments. The new investments, known as the 'Old Bailey' project and the 'Guildford' project, were not completely successful and resulted in a loss to the trust. The court found that the new investments were in breach of trust and *inter alia* the trustees attempted to set off a loss made in the 'Old Bailey' project against a gain made in the 'Guildford' scheme. The court allowed the set-off as the mixed fortunes originated from the same transaction.

JUDGMENT

'The general rule as stated in all the textbooks, with some reservations, is that where a trustee is liable in respect of distinct breaches of trust, one of which has resulted in a loss and the other a gain, he is not entitled to set off the gain against the loss unless they arise in the same transaction. The relevant cases are not, however, altogether easy to reconcile. All are centenarians and none is quite like the present. The Guildford development stemmed from exactly the same policy and exemplified the same folly as the Old Bailey project. Part of the profit was in fact used to finance the Old Bailey disaster. By sheer luck the gamble paid off handsomely on capital account. I think it would be unjust to deprive the bank of this element of salvage in the course of assessing the cost of the shipwreck. My order will therefore reflect the bank's right to an appropriate set-off.'

Brightman J

The principles of restitution which govern the computation of the loss to the trust are concerned with the gross loss suffered by the estate. The tax position of the beneficiaries is irrelevant in the assessment of the loss to the estate. Accordingly, compensation to the trust will not be reduced by an equivalent amount of tax which the beneficiaries would have paid, had the trustees not committed a breach of trust (the principle in *British Tax Commission v Gourley* [1956] AC 185 is excluded).

JUDGMENT

'I have reached the conclusion that tax ought not to be taken into account … but I do not feel that the established principles on which equitable relief is granted enable me to apply the *Gourley* principles to this case.'

Brightman J in *Bartlett v Barclays Bank Trust Co Ltd (No 2)* (1980)

16.2.1 Interest

As a general rule, the court is entitled to award simple interest under s 35A of the Senior Courts Act 1981 (formerly the Supreme Court Act 1981) on monetary sums payable by the trustees. The rate of interest that may be charged is 1 per cent above the banks' base rate. The court has a discretion to award compound interest against the trustees. The purpose of such an order is not designed to punish the trustees, but to require them to disgorge the benefit of the use of the trust funds. The principle here stems from the policy of preventing the trustees from profiting from their breach. The Law Lords, in *Westdeutsche Landesbank Girozentrale v Islington Borough Council* [1996] 2 All ER 961, considered that the jurisdiction to award compound interest originated exclusively in equity. In the absence of fraud, this jurisdiction is exercised against a defendant who is a trustee or otherwise stands in a fiduciary position, and makes an unauthorised profit or is assumed to have made an unauthorised profit. The majority of the Law Lords decided that, since the defendant did not owe fiduciary duties to the bank in relation to the payments made, compound interest would not be awarded. To award compound interest in the circumstances of this case would be tantamount to the courts usurping the function of Parliament. However, simple interest would be awarded on the balance of the fund remaining outstanding, calculated from the date of the original payment by the bank to the local authority.

The two dissenting Law Lords in *Westdeutsche*, Lords Goff and Woolf, adopted a broader view concerning the award of compound interest. They took the view that since the council had the use of the bank's money, which it would otherwise have had to borrow at compound interest, it had, to that extent, profited from the use of the bank's money. Moreover, if the bank had not advanced the money to the council, it would have employed the money in its business. The award of compound interest should be based on the principle of promoting justice or to prevent unjust enrichment. If the defendant has wrongfully profited, or may be presumed to have so profited from having the use of the claimant's money, justice demands that the sum be repayable with compound interest. This would be the position irrespective of whether the claimant's action arises *in personam* or *in rem*.

CASE EXAMPLE

Westdeutsche Landesbank Girozentrale v Islington Borough Council [1996] 2 All ER 961

The council entered into an interest rate swap agreement with the claimant bank. The nature of this agreement involved an understanding between the two parties, whereby each agrees to pay the other on a specified date or dates, an amount calculated by reference to the interest which would have accrued over a given period, on a notional principal sum. The claimant made an 'upfront' payment of £2.5 million to the defendant. The council made four payments totalling £1.35 million to the defendant. The court decided that the arrangement was void. The claimant demanded the return of its funds along with compound interest. The defendant admitted its liability to repay the outstanding fund but resisted the claim for compound interest. The House of Lords, by a majority, decided that it had no jurisdiction to award compound interest for the defendant did not stand in a fiduciary relationship towards the claimant, but awarded simple interest on the principal sum.

JUDGMENT

'[After referring to the following authorities, *Burdick v Garrick* (1870) LR 5 Ch App 233, *Wallersteiner v Moir (No 2)* [1975] QB 373, *AG v Alford* (1855) De GM & G 843] These authorities establish that, in the absence of fraud, equity only awards compound (as opposed to simple) interest against a defendant who is a trustee or otherwise in a fiduciary position, by way of recouping from such a defendant an improper profit made by him. It is unnecessary to decide whether in such a case compound interest can only be paid where the defendant has used trust moneys in his own trade or (as I tend to think) extends to all cases where a fiduciary has improperly profited from his trust. Unless the local authority owed fiduciary duties to the bank in relation to the upfront payment, compound interest cannot be awarded.'

Lord Browne-Wilkinson

In *Sempra Metals Ltd v HM Commissioners of Inland Revenue*, the House of Lords considered the scope of the jurisdiction of the courts to award compound interest. The House of Lords decided that the courts have:

- a common law jurisdiction to award interest, simple and compound, as damages on claims for non-payment of debts as well as on other claims for breaches of contract and in tort;

- jurisdiction at common law to award compound interest where the claimant sought a restitutionary remedy for the time value of money paid under a mistake.

The award of interest originated from three sources – statute, equity and the common law.

Section 35A(1) of the Senior Courts Act 1981 enacts that 'in proceedings for the recovery of a debt or damages there may be included in any sum for which judgment is given, simple interest at such rate as the court thinks fit or as rules of court may provide on all or any part of the debt or damages'. There is no consistent view as to the rate of simple interest that is payable on the debt or damages. In recent years, some courts have taken the view that the rate of interest is 1 per cent above the minimum lending rate (see *Belmont Finance Corp v Williams Furniture Ltd (No 2)* [1980] 1 All ER 393). Other courts have suggested that the appropriate rate is that allowed from time to time on the court's short-term investment account (see *Bartlett v Barclays Bank (No 2)* [1980] 2 WLR 448).

In equity, the court has a discretion to award compound interest against trustees and other fiduciaries. The purpose of such an order is not designed to punish the trustees but to require them to 'disgorge' the benefit from the unauthorised use of the trust funds or other property. The principle stems from the policy of preventing the trustees (and other fiduciaries) from profiting from their breach.

CASE EXAMPLE

Sempra Metals Ltd v HM Commissioners of Inland Revenue [2007] UKHL 34

The claimant company paid advance corporation tax (ACT) on its dividends which were in turn paid to a member of a group of companies. ACT was a form of advance payment of mainstream corporation tax. The claimant company sought group relief on the ACT paid. Section 247 of the Income and Corporation Taxes Act 1988 enabled parent and subsidiary companies jointly to make an election, having the effect of excluding dividends paid by a subsidiary to its parent from the obligation to pay ACT. The Revenue refused its claim on the ground that group relief was available only when the parent company and its subsidiary were resident in the UK. A group income election was not available if the parent company was resident outside the UK. The European Court of Justice rejected the contention put forward by the Revenue on the ground that that provision contravened parent companies' freedom of establishment, contrary to Art 52 (now Art 43) of the EC Treaty. On a claim by the taxpayer company for compensation in respect of the UK's breach of Art 52, the judge held that the compensation should be calculated on a compound basis. The Revenue's appeal was dismissed by the Court of Appeal, which held that ordinary commercial rates of interest would be used. The Revenue appealed. The House of Lords dismissed the appeal (by a three to two majority) on the ground of unjust enrichment by the Revenue. The claimant was entitled to a restitutionary award for the time value of money in terms of compound interest.

JUDGMENT

'We live in a world where interest payments for the use of money are calculated on a compound basis. Money is not available commercially on simple interest terms. This is the daily experience of everyone, whether borrowing money on overdrafts or credit cards or mortgages or shopping around for the best rates when depositing savings with banks or building societies. If the law is to achieve a fair and just outcome when assessing financial loss it must recognise and give effect to this reality.'

Lord Nicholls

KEY FACTS

Measure of liability of trustees

In the context of traditional trusts the measure of the trustees' liability for breach of trust is restitution based, i.e. to reconstitute the trust fund	*Bartlett v Barclays Bank* (1980); *Target Holdings v Redferns* (1995); *Nationwide BS v Various Solicitors* (1999)
In respect of commercial transactions, the basis of compensation is to put the beneficiary into the position he would have been in had the breach not occurred	*Target Holdings v Redferns* (1995); *Templeton Insurance v Pennington* (2006); *Wise v Jimenez* (2013); *AIB v Redler* (2014)

Unauthorised investment	*Knott v Cottee* (1852)
Failure to dispose of unauthorised investments	*Fry v Fry* (1859)
Trustees improperly sell authorised investments and invest the proceeds in unauthorised investments	*Re Massingberd* (1890)
In breach of trust the trustees make a profit on one transaction and a loss on another ☐ Tax is not deductible from the damages payable by trustees under the *BTC v Gourley* (1956) rule	*Bartlett v Barclays Bank* (1980) *Bartlett v Barclays Bank* (1980)
Interest on damages	*Westdeutsche Landesbank v Islington BC* (1996); *Sempra Metals Ltd v HM Comm of Inland Revenue* (2007)

16.3 Contribution and indemnity between trustees

Trustees are under a duty to act jointly and unanimously. In principle, each trustee has an equal role and standing in the administration of the trust. Accordingly, if a breach of trust has occurred each trustee is equally liable or the trustees are collectively liable to the beneficiary. Thus, the liability of the trustees is joint and several. The innocent beneficiary may sue one or more or all of the trustees.

If a successful action is brought against one trustee he has a right of contribution against his co-trustees, with the effect that each trustee will contribute equally to the damages awarded in favour of the claimant, unless the court decides otherwise. The position today is that the right of contribution is governed by the Civil Liability (Contribution) Act 1978. The court has a discretion concerning the amount of the contribution which may be recoverable from any other person liable in respect of the same damage. The discretion is enacted in s 2 of the 1978 Act, thus:

SECTION

'2 …the amount of contribution shall be such as may be found by the court to be just and equitable having regard to the extent of that person's responsibility for the damage in question.'

Section 6(1) of the 1978 Act provides:

SECTION

'A person is liable in respect of any damage … if the person who suffered it … is entitled to recover compensation from him in respect of that *damage* (whatever the legal basis of his liability, whether tort, breach of contract, breach of trust or otherwise).'

In the recent decision, *Charter plc v City Index Ltd* [2006] EWHC 2508 (Ch), the High Court considered whether a knowing receipt claim is one to 'recover compensation or damage' within the 1978 Act. The court decided that the effect of the authorities concerning a knowing receipt claim involves a disposal of the assets of the claimant in breach of trust or fiduciary duty. In other words, a claim for knowing receipt is parasitic on a claim for breach of trust in the sense that it cannot exist in the absence of the breach of trust from which the receipt originated. Such an unauthorised disposal must give rise to a loss to the trust and a liability on the part of the trustee to make good that which he wrongly took or transferred. Accordingly, the legal basis of liability is a breach of trust within the express terms of s 6(1) of the 1978 Act. The loss to the trust constitutes 'damage' in the wide sense of the word. In these circumstances the right of the beneficiary is to recover, on behalf of the trust, compensation in respect of that loss within the 1978 Act. The court concluded that a disposition in breach of trust gives rise to damage, loss or harm to the trust and consequently a liability on the part of both the defaulting trustee and a knowing recipient based on that breach of trust. The effect is that they are required to compensate the trust for that damage, loss or harm by restoring to the trust the equivalent of that loss.

The Act does not apply to an indemnity which is governed entirely by case law. There are three circumstances when a trustee is required to indemnify his co-trustees in respect of their liability to the beneficiaries.

16.3.1 Fraudulent benefit from breach of trust

Where one trustee has fraudulently obtained a benefit from a breach of trust. Such a claim for indemnity failed in *Bahin v Hughes* (1886) 31 Ch D 390.

CASE EXAMPLE

Bahin v Hughes (1886) 31 Ch D 390

A testator bequeathed a legacy of £2,000 to his three daughters, Miss Hughes, Mrs Edwards and Mrs Burden, on specified trusts. Miss Hughes did all the administration of the trust. The trust money was invested in unauthorised investments, resulting in a loss. Miss Hughes and Mrs Burden (in whose name the money was entered) selected the investment and by letter told Mrs Edwards, who failed to give her consent. The trustees were liable to the beneficiaries for breach of trust. Mr Edwards (whose wife had died) claimed that Miss Hughes, as an active trustee, ought to indemnify him against his late wife's liability. The court decided that the defendants were jointly and severally liable to replace the £2,000 and Mr Edwards had no right of indemnity against Miss Hughes.

JUDGMENT

'[W]here one trustee has got the money into his own hands, and made use of it, he will be liable to his co-trustee to give him an indemnity ... relief has only been granted against a trustee who has himself got the benefit of the breach of trust, or between whom and his co-trustees there has existed a relation which will justify the court in treating him solely liable for the breach of trust ... Miss Hughes was the active trustee and Mrs Edwards did nothing, and in my opinion it would be laying down a wrong rule that where one trustee acts honestly, though erroneously, the other trustee is to be held entitled to an indemnity who by doing nothing neglects his duty more than the acting trustee ... In my opinion the money was lost just as much by the default of Mrs Edwards as by the innocent though erroneous action of her co-trustee, Miss Hughes.'

Cotton LJ

16.3.2 Breach committed on advice of a solicitor-trustee

The requirements here, in addition to a breach of trust, are:

1. a co-trustee is a solicitor; and
2. the breach of trust was committed in respect of his advice; and
3. the co-trustees had relied solely on his advice and did not exercise an independent judgment.

CASE EXAMPLE

Re Partington [1887] 57 LT 654

Mrs Partington and Mr Allen, a solicitor, were trustees who were liable for a breach of trust. The trust fund was invested in an improper mortgage which resulted in a loss. Mr Allen had assured Mrs Partington that he would find a good investment on behalf of the trust. He failed in his duties to verify statements by the borrower, he failed to give proper instructions to the valuers and he did not give sufficient information to Mrs Partington to enable her to exercise an independent judgment. The court held that Mrs Partington was entitled to claim an indemnity from Mr Allen.

CASE EXAMPLE

Head v Gould [1898] 2 Ch 250

The claim for an indemnity against a solicitor-trustee failed because the co-trustee actively encouraged the solicitor-trustee to commit the breach of trust. The mere fact that the co-trustee is a solicitor is insufficient to establish the claim.

JUDGMENT

'I do not think that a man is bound to indemnify his co-trustee against any loss merely because he was a solicitor, when that co-trustee was an active participator in the breach of trust complained of, and is not proved to have participated merely in consequence of the advice and control of the solicitor.'

Kekewich J

16.3.3 The rule in *Chillingworth v Chambers*

The rule in *Chillingworth v Chambers* [1896] 1 Ch 685 is to the effect that where a trustee is also a beneficiary (whether he receives a benefit or not is immaterial) and participates in the breach of trust, he is required to indemnify his co-trustee to the extent of his beneficial interest. Thus, the trustee/beneficiary's property is taken first to meet the claim against the trustees. If the loss exceeds the beneficial interest, the trustees will share the surplus loss equally in so far as it exceeds the beneficial interest.

Contribution and indemnity

Contribution	Civil Liability (Contribution) Act 1978
Indemnity Where a trustee has fraudulently obtained a benefit from a breach of trust	*Bahin v Hughes* (1886)
Where the breach of trust was committed on the advice of a solicitor/trustee ▪ Trustee/beneficiary who instigates a breach indemnifies co-trustee up to the amount of his beneficial interest	*Re Partington* (1887); *Head v Gould* (1898) *Chillingworth v Chambers* (1896)

16.4 Defences to an action for breach of trust

In pursuance of an action against trustees for breach of trust, there are a number of defences which the trustees are entitled to raise. These are as follows.

16.4.1 Knowledge and consent of the beneficiaries

A beneficiary who has freely consented to or concurred in a breach of trust is not entitled to renege on his promise and sue the trustees.

In order to be prevented from bringing an action against the trustees, the beneficiary is required to be of full age and sound mind, with full knowledge of all the relevant facts, and to exercise an independent judgment. The burden of proof of establishing these elements will be on the trustees.

CASE EXAMPLE

Nail v Punter [1832] 5 Sim 555

The husband of a life tenant under a trust encouraged the trustees to pay him money from the trust fund, in breach of trust. The life tenant commenced proceedings against the trustees but died shortly afterwards. The husband became a beneficiary and continued the action against the trustees for breach of trust. The court held that the action could not succeed because the husband was a party to the breach.

The trustees are required to prove that the consent was not obtained as a result of undue influence. In *Re Pauling's Settlement Trust* [1964] Ch 303 (see Chapter 14), the trustees claimed that the children were not entitled to bring an action because they had consented to the advancements. The court rejected this argument and decided that the consent was not freely obtained from the children because they were under the influence of their parents who benefited from the advancements. The statement of the principle by Wilberforce J (below) was approved by the Court of Appeal.

JUDGMENT

'The court has to consider all the circumstances in which the concurrence of the beneficiary was given with a view to seeing whether it is fair and equitable that, having given his concurrence, he should afterwards turn around and sue the trustees … subject to this, it is not necessary that he should know that what he is concurring in is a breach of trust, provided that he fully understands what he is concurring in, and … it is not necessary that he should himself have directly benefited by the breach of trust.'

Wilberforce J

16.4.2 Impounding the interest of a beneficiary

In the above section the beneficiary who concurs or acquiesces in a breach of trust will not be allowed to bring an action against the trustees. But this principle does not prevent other beneficiaries from bringing an action against the trustees. In these circumstances the court has a power to impound the interest of the beneficiary who instigated the breach.

Under the inherent jurisdiction of the court a beneficiary who instigated the breach of trust may be required to indemnify the trustees. The rule was extended in s 62 of the Trustee Act 1925, which declares:

SECTION

'62 Where a trustee commits a breach of trust at the instigation or request or with the consent in writing of a beneficiary, the court may if it thinks fit make such order as the court seems just for impounding all or any part of the interest of the beneficiary in the trust estate by way of indemnity to the trustee or persons claiming through him.'

It is clear from the section that the court has a discretion which it will not exercise if the beneficiary was not aware of the full facts. Section 62 is applicable irrespective of an intention, on the part of the beneficiary, to receive a personal benefit or not. The beneficiary's consent is required to be in writing.

16.4.3 Relief under s 61 of the Trustee Act 1925

Section 61 of the Trustee Act 1925 provides:

SECTION

'61 If it appears to the court that a trustee … is or may be personally liable for any breach of trust … but has acted honestly and reasonably, and ought fairly to be excused for the breach of trust and for omitting to obtain the directions of the court in the matter in which he committed such breach, then the court may relieve him either wholly or partly from personal liability for the same.'

This section re-enacted, with slight modifications, s 3 of the Judicial Trustees Act 1896.

The rationale behind the original provision was not to discourage lay persons from acting as trustees. The relieving provision is applicable to both lay and professional trustees. The predecessor to s 61 of the Trustee Act 1925 was described by one commentator as an exercise by the court of a 'dubious prerogative of mercy'. But this description of the provision has been castigated by the courts in favour of a more sombre balancing exercise of fairness to the trustees and the consequences to innocent beneficiaries, see Briggs LJ in *Santander (UK) plc v R.A. Legal (firm of solicitors)* [2014] EWCA Civ 183 (see later).

JUDGMENT

> 'Relief under section 61 is often described as an exercise of mercy by the court. In my judgment the requirement to balance fairness to the trustee with a proper appreciation of the consequences of the exercise of the discretion for the beneficiaries means that this old-fashioned description of the nature of the section 61 jurisdiction should be abandoned. In this context mercy lies not in the free gift of the court. It comes at a price.'
>
> Briggs LJ

The section provides three main ingredients for granting relief, namely:

(a) the trustee acted honestly; and

(b) the trustee acted reasonably; and

(c) the trustee ought fairly to be excused in respect of the breach and omitting to obtain directions of the court.

These ingredients are cumulative and the trustee bears the burden of proof. Once the claimant has established that the trustee has acted in breach of his duties with the consequence of creating a loss to the trust, the trustees are liable to make good that loss. In this respect the trustee's liability is strict, owing to equity's high expectations of a trustee discharging his fiduciary obligations. But if the trustee wishes to claim relief under s 61 he bears the burden of proving all three elements laid down in the provision. Stage one of the relief imposes an obligation on the trustee to prove that he acted both honestly and reasonably in respect of the breach of trust. On the assumption that he has discharged the burden at stage one, he may then proceed to stage two to convince the court that in its discretion he ought fairly to be excused.

The expression 'trustee' is defined in s 68(17) of the Trustee Act 1925 as referring to all types of trustees such as express, resulting and constructive trustees, including personal representatives. In the light of the decision of the Supreme Court in *Williams v Central Bank of Nigeria* [2014] UKSC 10 (see later), it would appear that this definition does not include a third party such as a knowing recipient or a dishonest assistant who are treated as 'false' trustees and are subject to a personal liability. The effect is that a knowing recipient or dishonest assistant may be unable to claim relief under s 61 of the Trustee Act 1925.

The expression 'honestly' assumes that the trustee has acted in good faith in the interests of the trust. This is a question of fact. The claimant beneficiary is not required to prove that the trustee acted dishonestly; rather the trustee is required to prove affirmatively that, despite the breach of trust, his conduct was *inter alia* not dishonest. This is a negative burden imposed on the trustee and is determined objectively by reference to the facts of each case.

The word 'reasonably' indicates that the trustee acted prudently in that the conduct of the defendant complied with the standard of care required from a reasonable trustee. Such conduct is not required to reach a standard of perfection.

The Court of Appeal in *Lloyds TSB Bank plc v Markandan & Uddin* (2012) (considered in Chapter 14) decided that relief under s 61 of the Trustee Act 1925 was dependent on the defendants discharging a burden of proof to show that they had acted honestly and reasonably and ought fairly to be excused. In the circumstances, the defendants failed to discharge this burden, in that they did not prove that they acted reasonably. Accordingly, the court refused relief under s 61, despite the trustees being the innocent victims of a fraud practised by a third party. The Court of Appeal affirmed the decision of the trial judge.

JUDGMENT

'I do not believe that the Defendant's conduct was reasonable in a number of respects. The Defendant paid the money to what Mr Markandan [a senior partner in the defendant's firm of solicitors] believed was the firm of solicitors acting on behalf of the vendors of the property although it had not received the signed contract, transfer and discharge certificates. The money, less £5,000, was paid back to the Defendant with a request to the Defendant to pay it to a different account. Even though the Defendant's requests for the necessary documentation had not been complied with, the Defendant paid the money again to the purported solicitors for the vendor. Combined with the failure to establish properly that the firm Deen actually had an office in Holland Park … this conduct cannot be said to be reasonable.'

Mr Roger Wyand QC (trial judge), affirmed by the Court of Appeal in *Lloyds TSB Bank plc v Markandan & Uddin* [2012] EWCA Civ 65

JUDGMENT

'If they [the firm of solicitors] had instead performed their role as solicitors with exemplary professional care and efficiency, but had still parted with the loan money in circumstances that were objectively reasonable, the decision on the s 61 application might have been different. It is, therefore, the discretionary power under section 61 that provides the key to the claimed unfairness of holding a solicitor liable for breach of trust in circumstances such as the present.'

Rimer LJ in *Lloyds TSB plc v Markandan & Uddin*

In *Nationwide Building Society v Davisons Solicitors* (2012), the Court of Appeal distinguished *Markandan* and, on similar facts, granted relief under s 61 of the Trustee Act 1925 to the solicitors who were in breach of their duties. In *Nationwide*, the court decided that although the standard of care expected from the trustee is high, owing to the discharge of fiduciary obligations, the test remains one of reasonableness, not perfection. In any event there must be a causal connection between the trustee's conduct and the loss suffered by the trust.

CASE EXAMPLE

Nationwide Building Society v Davisons Solicitors [2012] EWCA 1626, (CA)

The appellant firm of solicitors (D) appealed against the decision of the High Court to the effect that it was liable for breach of trust and was not entitled to relief under s 61 of the Trustee Act 1925. On 12 December 2008 the respondent, Nationwide Building Society (N), had offered a mortgage to a residential purchaser. D had been instructed by N and the purchaser to deal with the mortgage and conveyance. On 30 January 2009 Rothschild, a firm of solicitors based in Corporation Street, Birmingham, wrote to D from an office in Coventry Rd, Small Heath, declaring that they were acting for the vendors. As required by the CML Handbook, D checked the websites maintained by the Law Society and the Solicitors Regulation Authority to verify the credentials of the solicitor acting for Rothschild. All appeared to be in order. In response to requisitions, Rothschild confirmed that the existing mortgage on the property would be discharged. On 9 March 2009, N released the mortgage amount to D. On 12 March 2009 contracts were signed and exchanged by telephone, the charge in favour of N was executed and the purchase price was remitted by D to Rothschild and the purchaser was registered as the proprietor. However, the existing charge on the property was not discharged and N's charge was not registered. It transpired that an impostor had notified the Law Society and the Solicitors Regulation Authority of a false business address for an existing sole practitioner. The genuine practitioner had informed the Law Society and SRA that the information was false but they had failed to rectify their websites. The trial judge found against the appellants and ordered them to pay damages and costs. The solicitors' firm appealed. The Court of Appeal allowed the appeal and decided that, despite acting in breach of trust, the appellants were entitled to relief under s 61 of the Trustee Act 1925. The firm had acted 'honestly, reasonably and ought fairly to be excused'. The appellants had acted reasonably in obtaining an undertaking to discharge the existing mortgage from a person purporting to act as the vendor's solicitors, and reasonably believed to be so. The appellants had verified the branch office of Rothschild and the solicitor who was purporting to deal with the transaction from the websites of the Law Society and the SRA. Further, the respondent's loss was not directly linked to the appellants' conduct.

JUDGMENT

'The section [s 61 of the Trustee Act 1925] only requires Mr Wilkes to have acted reasonably. That does not, in my view, predicate that he has necessarily complied with best practice in all respects. *The relevant action must at least be connected with the loss* for which relief is sought and the requisite standard is that of reasonableness not perfection. It is seldom helpful to compare conduct found to be reasonable or not in one case with that of another; but the factual similarity of this appeal with that in *Lloyds TSB Bank plc v Markandan & Uddin* justifies pointing out that the conduct of the solicitors in that case was quite different from that relied on in this case.

[In this case] The lapse from best practice, if any, did not cause the loss to Nationwide. Given that the trustee acted both honestly and reasonably I can see no ground on which Davisons should be denied relief from all liability.'

Morritt LJ

In *Santander (UK) plc v R.A. Legal (firm of solicitors)* (2014), on the issue of whether the trustee acted reasonably in connection with the loss to the trust, the court is not entitled to consider each breach of trust separately, but is required to make a judgment as to the seriousness of the breaches as a whole. The extent of the breaches of trust is relevant to the exercise of the discretion of the court on whether to grant relief.

CASE EXAMPLE

Santander (UK) plc v R.A. Legal (firm of solicitors) [2014] EWCA Civ 183

The appellants (S) had agreed to lend £150,000 to an individual (V) for the purpose of purchasing a property. The respondents (R) conducted the conveyancing, acting for both V and S. A second firm of solicitors (X) fraudulently presented itself as acting for the vendor. But the vendor, who was not involved in the fraud, had never agreed to sell the property. Owing to the fraud, R released S's money to X on the day before completion was due in the belief that it was completing the sale. Completion did not take place, and S did not obtain a charge over the property. The money was not recovered. S brought a claim against R for breach of trust on the basis that it had released the advance without completion ever taking place. There was no suggestion that R acted otherwise than honestly. The High Court decided that the respondents acted in breach of fiduciary duties but granted relief under s 61 of the Trustee Act 1925. The Court of Appeal allowed S's appeal and decided that R's conduct was wholly unreasonable and sufficiently connected with S's loss. R's failings represented a significant departure from a sophisticated regime whereby risks of loss to lenders and clients were minimised, even if not wholly eradicated. R had not shown that it acted reasonably in all respects connected with S's loss, therefore discretionary relief did not strictly arise. Even if R had acted reasonably, the court would have been hard pressed to exercise its discretion to grant relief from liability.

JUDGMENT

'The question whether a trustee has acted reasonably in respect of matters connected with the beneficiary's loss is not in my judgment to be resolved purely by considering each specific complaint separately. The question is whether the trustee's relevant conduct was reasonable, taken as a whole. Looking at the matter in the round, I have been driven to the conclusion that the judge took an altogether too lenient view of the seriousness of R.A. Legal's numerous departures from best practice, during the whole of the period from its request for the funds from Abbey, until they were misappropriated from Sovereign's client account on 13th August.

In the present case I have come to the clear conclusion that the particular failures [on the part of R.A. Legal] beginning with the inadequate making of Requisitions on Title, transferring the completion money without the adoption of the Completion Code by Sovereign, and then failing to deal with the absence of a prior mortgage discharge on the pretended completion, were indeed unreasonable, and sufficiently connected with Abbey's loss. In any event, those failings of R.A. Legal formed part of a larger picture of the shoddy performance of a conveyancing transaction from start to finish, which leaves me in no doubt that it would not be fair to excuse the firm from liability, in whole or in part.'

Briggs LJ

Where a fraudster deceives both the purchaser's and vendor's solicitors and receives the purchase monies by impersonating the true owner of property so that the purchase was incapable of completion and the fraudster absconds with the funds, both firms of solicitors may be liable for breaches of trust. Although the vendor's solicitors do not owe a duty of care to the purchaser, the purchase monies received by them are held on trust for the purchaser pending completion of the purchase. Accordingly, where there has never been a completion of the transaction and the funds have been paid away, perhaps to a fraudster, the vendor's solicitors may be liable for breach of trust. The purchaser's solicitors clearly owe fiduciary duties to their client in trusts law and contractual duties. Once liability is established or admitted, it would then be incumbent on each firm of solicitors to convince the court that relief ought to be granted under s 61 of the Trustee Act 1925. On a failure to discharge this burden, the court has the power to allocate the responsibility between the parties for breach of trust under the Civil Liability (Contribution) Act 1978 (see earlier). The amount of contribution by each party that may be ordered by the court is left to the discretion of the judge. The test is the amount that is considered to be just and equitable having regard to the extent of each party's responsibility for the damage in question. These issues were considered by the High Court in *Purrunsing v A'Court & Co and another* (2016).

CASE EXAMPLE

Purrunsing v A'Court & Co (a Firm) and another [2016] EWHC 789 (High Court)

A fraudster (D) falsely claimed to be the owner of residential property and engaged the first defendant solicitors' firm (ACC) to act on his behalf in the sale of the property. The claimant sought to purchase the property and appointed the second defendant conveyancers' firm (HOC) to act on his behalf. Before the fraud was discovered the claimant made payments of the entire purchase price, totalling £470,000, to HOC, which in turn paid the amount to ACC and then from ACC to D's account. It was common ground that genuine completion of the transaction had not taken place and had ACC attempted to contact D at the property, they would have made contact with the real owner and the fraud would have been discovered. The claimant sued ACC and joined HOC as co-defendants in actions for breach of trust. There was no allegation of dishonesty on the part of the defendants. The defendants admitted liability for breach of trust but claimed relief under s 61 of the Trustee Act 1925. The court decided that the defendants did not act reasonably and refused to grant relief. Further, the court decided that, as between the defendants, the extent of each party's liability should be shared equally

JUDGMENT

'The obligation in relation to purchase money is an absolute obligation not to release the money before completion as that concept is to be understood in this context – see *Lloyds TSB* [2012] EWCA Civ 65, *per* Rimer LJ. The liability that arises from a breach of that obligation is strict because of equity's high expectations of a trustee discharging fiduciary obligations. Once it is found or admitted that a vendor's solicitor is a trustee of the purchase money and has parted with it in breach of trust, there is no obvious justification for interpreting s 61 more leniently in respect of such a breach of trust by a vendor's solicitor than would be the case in relation to such a breach by a purchaser's solicitor. Each are trustees. Each has breached the trust with which the purchase money was impressed and thus each has breached equity's high expectation of a trustee discharging fiduciary obligations. It follows therefore that for each the same standard of reasonableness applies though, of course, what each has to do in order to fulfil that standard may be different because of the different roles that each has in relation to the transaction.

[On the issue of the quantification of liability between the parties, Judge Pelling said] It is not in dispute in these proceedings that both defendants are liable in respect of the same damage. It is common ground between the parties that in assessing the level of contribution, the courts must have regard to considerations of relative causal potency as well as comparative blameworthiness. In my judgment, it is clear that HOC and ACC that must each bear equal liability for the loss.'

Judge Pelling

If these two criteria are satisfied at stage one (honesty and reasonableness) the court has a discretion to decide whether or not to excuse the trustee. The test in exercising the discretion is to have regard to the interests of both the trustees and the beneficiaries and to decide whether the breach of trust ought to be forgiven in whole or in part. It was stated in *Perrins v Bellamy* that, in the absence of special circumstances, a trustee who has acted honestly and reasonably ought to be relieved.

CASE EXAMPLE

Perrins v Bellamy [1899] 1 Ch 797

The trustees of a settlement were erroneously advised by their solicitor that they had a power of sale. They sold the leaseholds comprised in the settlement, thereby diminishing the income of the plaintiff, the tenant for life. The plaintiff brought an action against the trustees for breach of trust. The trustees claimed relief under the predecessor to s 61 of the Trustee Act 1925. The court, in its discretion, granted relief.

JUDGMENT

'I venture, however, to think that, in general and in the absence of special circumstances, a trustee who has acted reasonably ought to be relieved, and it is not incumbent on the court to consider whether he ought fairly to be excused, unless there is evidence of a special character showing that the provisions of the section ought not to be applied in his favour.'

Kekewich J

It may be added that *Perrins v Bellamy* involved exceptional circumstances that justified relief to the trustees. Each case is decided on its own facts. A factor which is capable of influencing the court is whether the trustee is an expert, professional trustee or not.

In *National Trustee Co of Australia Ltd v General Finance Co* [1905] AC 373, the court refused relief to professional trustees who had acted honestly and reasonably and on the advice of a solicitor in committing a breach of trust.

A similar view was echoed by Brightman J in *Bartlett v Barclays Bank* [1980] Ch 515 (see earlier): the professional trustee company was refused relief under s 61 of the Trustee Act 1925 because it acted unreasonably in failing to keep abreast or informed of the changes in the activities of the investment company:

JUDGMENT

'A trust corporation holds itself out in its advertising literature as being above ordinary mortals. With a specialist staff of trained trust officers and managers, with ready access to financial information and professional advice, dealing with and solving trust problems day after day, the trust corporation holds itself out, and rightly, as capable of providing an expertise which it would be unrealistic to expect and unjust to demand from the ordinary prudent man or woman who accepts, probably unpaid and sometimes reluctantly from a sense of family duty, the burden of trusteeship. Just as, under the law of contract, a professional person possessed of a particular skill is liable for breach of contract if he neglects to use the skill and experience which he professes, so I think that a professional corporate trustee is liable for breach of trust if loss is caused to the trust fund, because it neglects to exercise the special care and skill which it professes to have.'

Brightman J

In *Santander UK v R.A. Legal Solicitors* [2014] EWCA 183, Briggs LJ emphasised that in exercising its discretion, the court is required to consider the effect of the grant of relief not only to the trustee but on the beneficiary. Accordingly, the financial capability of absorbing the loss, including the availability of insurance to meet the loss, are relevant considerations.

JUDGMENT

'The second main stage of the section 61 analysis, usually described as discretionary, consists of deciding whether the trustee ought fairly to be excused for the breach of trust. This requires that regard be had to the effect of the grant of relief not only upon the trustee, but also upon the beneficiaries. Furthermore, section 61 makes it clear that even if the trustee ought fairly to be excused, the court still retains the discretionary power to grant relief from liability, in whole or in part, or to refuse it. In the context of relief sought by solicitor trustees from liability for breach of trust in connection with mortgage fraud, much may depend at this discretionary stage upon the consequences for the beneficiary. An institutional lender may well be insured (or effectively self-insured) for the consequences of third party fraud. But an innocent purchaser may have contributed his life's savings to the purchase and have no recourse at all other than against his insured solicitor, where for example the fraudster is a pure interloper, rather than a dishonest solicitor in respect of whose fraud the losers may have recourse against the Solicitors' Compensation Fund.'

Briggs LJ

Other factors that have been taken into account by the courts include the status of the adviser to the trust and the size of the trust estate. It has been suggested that nothing less than the advice of a Queen's Counsel should be taken by the trustees in respect of a large estate. The circumstances regarding the breach of trust will be considered by the courts, in particular, whether the breach of trust originated from a complicated rule of law and whether the trustees acted on the erroneous belief that the beneficiaries had consented.

16.4.4 Limitation and laches

The limitation periods concern the time limits during which a beneficiary is entitled to pursue a cause of action in respect of trust property. The remarks of Kekewich J in *Re Timmins* [1902] 1 Ch 176 refer to the rationale concerning an earlier limitation statute:

JUDGMENT

'The intention of the statute was to give a trustee the benefit of the lapse of time when, although he had done something legally or technically wrong, he had done nothing morally wrong or dishonest, but it was not intended to protect him where, if he pleaded the statute, he would come off with something he ought not to have, i.e. money of the trust received by him and converted to his own use.'

Kekewich J

Six-year limitation period

By virtue of s 21(3) of the Limitation Act 1980, the general rule concerning the limitation period for actions for breach of trust is six years from the date on which the cause of action accrued. A cause of action does not accrue in respect of future interests (remainders and reversions) until the interest falls into possession. Thus, a life tenant under a trust is required to bring an action within six years of the breach of trust but a remainderman has up to six years from the death of the life tenant before his cause of action becomes time-barred. In addition, time does not begin to run against a beneficiary suffering from a disability (infancy or mental incapacity) at the time of the breach until the disability ends:

JUDGMENT

'The rationale of s 21(3) of the Limitation Act 1980 appears to me to be not that a beneficiary with a future interest has not the means of discovery, but that he should not be compelled to litigate (at considerable personal expense) in respect of an injury to an interest which he may never live to enjoy.'

Millett LJ in *Armitage v Nurse* [1997] 3 WLR 1046

Section 21(3) of the Limitation Act 1980 is drafted by reference to claims brought by beneficiaries. If the trustees bring such a claim the courts will consider, in substance, who are the real litigants. In this respect the real litigants are required to be those who have a real interest in the outcome. Accordingly, trustees who do not have a personal interest may bring claims exclusively on behalf of beneficiaries with a personal interest, albeit in the future, outside the six-year limitation period, see *Cattley v Pollard*.

CASE EXAMPLE

Cattley v Pollard [2006] EWHC 3130 (Ch) (High Court)

A solicitor/trustee misappropriated a substantial amount of assets belonging to the estate of a deceased. New trustees were appointed and brought claims against the fraudulent former trustee. These proceedings were settled. Further proceedings were brought outside the six-year period against the former trustee's accomplices but on behalf of nine life beneficiaries and 17 residual beneficiaries whose interests were yet to fall into possession. The court decided that the claim was not statute-barred as regards the beneficiaries with future interests.

JUDGMENT

'I find that s 21(3) applies in the present case, at least by analogy to the present claim brought by the trustees. The claimants as trustees have no personal interest in the outcome. The real litigants – those with a real interest in the outcome – are the beneficiaries. I consider that when s 21(3) refers to an action by beneficiaries, it includes, at least by analogy, actions brought exclusively on their behalf by trustees who do not have any personal interest in the outcome. This approach echoes that followed in *St Mary Magdalen, Oxford (President, etc) v AG* (1857) 6 HL Cas 189 and the argument considered by Harman J in *AG v Cocke* [1988] 2 All ER 391, [1988] Ch 414. It follows that the last subparagraph of s 21(3) applies to the second proceedings. Time has not begun to run as regards the beneficiaries with a future interest in the estate and the second proceedings are therefore not time-barred.'

Richard Sheldon QC

A trustee, for these purposes, includes a personal representative and no distinction is drawn between express, implied or constructive trustees.

Section 23 of the Limitation Act 1980 enacts that in an action for an account, the same limitation period will apply as is applicable to the claim which is the basis for the account. The purpose of this provision is to restrict the period in which claims may be brought for an account by reference to the underlying nature and substance of the claim. Thus a claim for an account for breach of a simple contract is required to be brought within six years from the date of the breach of contract.

In *Paragon Finance Ltd v Thakerar* [1999] 1 All ER 400, the Court of Appeal refused to grant leave to amend a claim that was brought more than six years after the cause of action had accrued. In doing so, the court overruled *Nelson v Rye* [1996] 2 All ER 186.

An action for an account, in the absence of a trust, is based on legal, not equitable, rights. There is therefore no equitable content in such an action. Thus, an action for an account for breach of contract remains a contractual claim and the limitation period at common law applies. Accordingly, in *Coulthard v Disco Mix Club* [2000] 1 WLR 707, the High Court decided that the six-year limitation period was applicable to an action for an account arising out of a contractual claim.

Exceptions to the six-year rule

Under s 21(1) of the Limitation Act 1980, where a beneficiary brings a claim in respect of any fraud by the trustee or to recover trust property or the proceeds of sale from trust property (i.e. actions *in rem* (see below)), the fixed limitation periods shall not apply. A transferee from a trustee is in the same position as the trustee, unless he is a *bona fide* transferee of the legal estate for value without notice. Section 21(1) provides:

SECTION

'21(1)   No period of limitation prescribed by this Act shall apply to an action by the beneficiary under a trust, being an action –

(a) in respect of any fraud or fraudulent breach of trust to which the trustee was a party or privy; or

(b) to recover from the trustee trust property or the proceeds of trust property in the possession of the trustee, or previously received by the trustee and converted to his own use.'

The reason for this exception is that the possession of the property by a trustee is never by virtue of any right of his own, but is acquired initially for and on behalf of the beneficiaries. The trustee's ownership or possession is representative of the beneficiary's interest. The effect is that time does not run in the trustee's favour and against the beneficiary.

The concept of 'fraud' or 'fraudulent breach of trust' for the purposes of the Limitation Act 1980 involves dishonesty. The notion of dishonesty in this context is much broader than the common law definition of the term. Millett LJ in *Armitage v Nurse* [1998] Ch 241 (see earlier) posited that the term involves the defendant pursuing a course of conduct with a mindset which is equivalent to intentionally or recklessly committing a breach of trust.

JUDGMENT

'[The question in issue is] whether s 21(1)(a) is limited to cases of fraud or fraudulent breach of trust property so called, that is to say to cases involving dishonesty. The judge held that it is. In my judgment, he was plainly right. I have explained the meaning of the word "fraud" in a trustee exemption clause, and there is no reason to ascribe a different meaning to the word where it appears in s 21(1)(a) of the Limitation Act 1980.

[Dishonesty] connotes at the minimum an intention on the part of the trustee to pursue a particular course of action, either knowing that it is contrary to the interests of the company or being recklessly indifferent whether it is contrary to their interests or not … It is the duty of a trustee to manage the trust property and deal with it in the interests of the beneficiaries. If he acts in a way which he does not honestly believe is in the interests of the beneficiaries then he is acting dishonestly.'

Millett LJ

Section 32(1) of the Limitation Act 1980 enacts that the prescribed limitation period does not begin to run where an action is based on fraud, or any fact relevant to the claimant's cause of action has been deliberately concealed by the defendant, or the action is for relief from the consequences of a mistake. In these circumstances the limitation period begins to run from the time that the claimant discovered (or with reasonable diligence could have discovered) the fraud, concealed fact or mistake. In *Haysport Properties Ltd v Ackerman* (2016), the High Court considered the extent of breaches of the trustee's fiduciary duties in the context of the limitation period, in the absence of allegations of fraud or dishonesty.

CASE EXAMPLE

Haysport Properties Ltd v Ackerman [2016] EWHC 393 (High Court)

The defendant (A) was a former director of the two claimant companies. The claimants alleged that in 2005, A was instrumental in the grant of securities over various properties owned by them in order to support a facility in a different company in which A had an interest. This conduct by A was in breach of his fiduciary duties. The defendant resigned in 2011. The claim form was issued in 2014, which was outside the six-year limitation period. The claimants did not allege fraud or dishonesty on the part of the defendant but contended that he was in breach of his fiduciary duties, both past and continuing until his resignation in 2011. A defended on the ground that the claims were statute-barred. The court decided that although there were breaches of fiduciary duties, the limitation period was not extended by s 21(1)(a) of the 1980 Act. However, A owed a positive duty to the claimants to disclose breaches of his fiduciary duties. This duty of disclosure continued until A's resignation in 2011. Accordingly, the extension of the limitation period under s 32(1) of the Limitation Act 1980 was made out by the claimants.

JUDGMENT

'[Referring to the definition of dishonesty in *Armitage* above, the learned judge said:] I have come to the conclusion that Mr Ackerman was not dishonest. He clearly did not know that the matters were against the interests of the Claimants. Equally he, in my view, honestly believed that the transactions were in the interests of the Claimants and he was not recklessly indifferent. However he failed in his fiduciary duty because he failed to ensure the Claimants were properly advised and he failed properly to deal with the obvious conflict of interest that arose from his involvement on the other side of the transaction. Accordingly the Claimants' contention that the limitation period does not run because of section 21(1)(a) of the Limitation Act 1980 is in my view not made out.

It seems to me that the Claimants reliance on section 32 (1) (b) and (2) is made out.

Mr Ackerman whilst he was a director of the Claimants had owed a continuing duty to disclose his breaches of duty until he ceased to be a director. Accordingly that duty continued until his removal in April 2011. There is therefore in my judgment no limitation issue in relation to his breaches as established above.'

Smith J

Section 38 of the Limitation Act 1980 provides that the expressions 'trust' and 'trustee' have the same meanings respectively as in the Trustee Act 1925. This extends the meaning of those expressions to 'implied and constructive trusts': see s 68(17) of the Trustee Act 1925.

Thus, the relaxation of the limitation period laid down in s 21(1) of the 1980 Act is not restricted to express trustees but extends to those in an analogous position who have abused the trust and confidence reposed in them. In *James v Williams* [2000] Ch 1, the Court of Appeal decided that where a beneficiary acted as if he were the sole owner of trust property, he would be treated as a constructive trustee and a claim against him would be exempt from the limitation period.

In *Statek Corp v Alford* [2008] EWHC 32 (Ch), the High Court considered whether any of the exceptions enacted in s 21(1) of the Limitation Act 1980 was applicable, in a case where a de facto director dishonestly assisted in a fraudulent scheme. A material issue was whether a person who dishonestly assists another in breach of trust is to be treated as a trustee for the purposes of s 21(1) of the 1980 Act. On this issue, Millett LJ in *Paragon Finance v Thakerar* [1999] 1 All ER 400 (see Chapter 8) drew a distinction between two categories of fiduciaries, the first (traditionally called 'category 1' trustees) being trustees or fiduciaries established as such before the events complained of in the proceedings, and 'category 2' trustees being those whose status is created because of the transaction, the subject-matter of the claim. Millett LJ acknowledged that 'category 1' trustees are correctly to be classified as constructive trustees but 'category 2' 'trustees' are not in reality trustees but, owing to their fiduciary status, are required to account to the beneficiaries as if they are trustees. In Millett LJ's view, the expressions 'constructive trust' and 'constructive trustees' are misleading when referring to 'category 2' fiduciaries. The issue in *Statek* was whether the defendant (Mr A) was a 'category 1' trustee which would attract the exceptions in s 21(1) of the 1980 Act. It was significant that the defendant became a de facto director *before* he undertook the impugned transaction.

CASE EXAMPLE

Statek Corp v Alford [2008] EWHC 32 (Ch)

The claimant company (S Corp), a trading company incorporated in California, commenced proceedings against the defendant (Mr A) for damages for dishonest breaches of fiduciary duties owed to the claimant. Alternatively, the claimant sought an account for moneys received by the defendant as a constructive trustee. Mr Johnston (J), the president, and Sandra Spillane, the vice president, were the prime movers in a substantial fraud against S Corp. They treated Mr A as a director of S Corp and told him that he would be appointed as such. Although never formally appointed as director, Mr A regarded himself as a director and acted as such an officer so as to be constituted a de facto director of S Corp. J and Spillane procured a series of payments into and out of Mr A's personal bank accounts in the UK totalling in excess of $1.8 million. These sums were derived from the assets of S Corp. Mr A was told that the reason for paying S Corp's money into his accounts was to remove it from the 'normal banking system', i.e. to conceal the existence of the moneys. Mr A asked no questions when substantial amounts of the funds were paid to J and treated the transactions as normal.

S Corp's claims against Mr A were based on the premise that Mr A dishonestly assisted J and Spillane in their fraud by receiving S Corp's moneys into his personal bank accounts and paying out those sums in accordance with the directions of J and Spillane. Mr A contended that the claims were statute-barred as they fell within s 21(3) of the Limitation Act 1980. The court rejected this argument and held that the defendant (Mr A) was liable to the claimant as an accessory, in that he dishonestly assisted in a fraud perpetrated by J and Spillane. Mr A became a de facto director of the claimant company *before* the existence of the impugned transactions. Thus, Mr A owed fiduciary duties towards the claimant in respect of assets within his control and, in breach of those duties, became a constructive trustee within 'category 1'.

JUDGMENT

'In my judgment, s 21(1) of the Limitation Act 1980, is to be construed as applying to accessories to the fraudulent breaches of trust of others with the result that no period of limitation is applicable to claims against them. I do not read the decision of the House of Lords in the *Dubai Aluminium Ltd v Salaam* [2002] UKHL 48 as authority to the contrary.

For these reasons, if I had not already concluded that a defence of limitation was not available to Mr Alford because he was a category 1 fiduciary but was to be treated as an accessory to the fraudulent breaches of trust of Johnston and Spillane, with respect to him, I would not have followed Mr Sheldon's decision in *Cattley v Pollard* [2006] EWHC 3130, and would have concluded that no limitation period applied to Statek's claim against him as an accessory to that fraudulent breach of trust.'

Evans-Lombe J

On the other hand, a dishonest assistant or knowing recipient is not a 'trustee' for the purposes of s 21(1)(a) of the Limitation Act 1980. Such persons are accountable to the trust for the breach of their duties and the normal limitation period is applicable to claims against them. It would have been unreal to make them liable in the same way as trustees. In addition, on construction of s 21(1)(a), the exception to the limitation period with regard to trustees who were fraudulent did not include an action against a party who was not himself a trustee, but liable to account. In *Williams v Central Bank of Nigeria* [2014] UKSC 10, the Supreme Court reversed the decision of the Court of Appeal and decided that the limitation period was applicable to claims against a defendant who intermeddled with the trust property, i.e. the ancillary liability of strangers to a trust.

CASE EXAMPLE

Williams v Central Bank of Nigeria [2014] UKSC 10

The claimant, Dr Williams (W), a Nigerian national, was resident in the UK. W alleged that an English solicitor, Mr Gale (G), had defrauded him of a sum of over $6 million and the defendant, the Central Bank of Nigeria (CBN), was an active participant in the fraud. The claimant alleged that G held the sum of money in his client account on trust for him but had fraudulently paid the sum to CBN in an account in England. W sought to make CBN liable to account as a dishonest assistant. The claim was brought outside the limitation period. The issue in this case was whether s 21(1)(a) permits such a claim outside the limitation period against the fraudulent trustee only (i.e. category 1 constructive trustees in Millett LJ's classification in *Paragon Finance*, see Chapter 8) or whether the extension laid down in s 21(1)(a) is applicable to category 2 constructive trustees, i.e. fiduciaries who are liable to account. The Court of Appeal decided that the distinction between category 1 and category 2 constructive trustees had not been imported into the definitions of 'trusts' and 'trustees' within the 1980 Act or its predecessors. The wording of s 21(1)(a) of the 1980 Act could not justify an implication that the action may only be brought against the fraudulent trustee. On appeal, the Supreme Court allowed the appeal, reversed the decision of the Court of Appeal and decided that a stranger to a trust who knowingly received trust property for his own benefit (or a dishonest assistant) is accountable to the trust for the breach of duties, but is not a trustee for the purposes of the Limitation Act 1980. The Justices of the Supreme Court by a majority decided that s 21(1)(a) was concerned only with actions against trustees on account of their own fraud or fraudulent breach of trust. This conclusion was justified for five reasons:

(a) Section 21(3) was intended to relieve trustees without limitation in time, save in the two cases specified in s 21(1). The exceptions were required to apply to the same persons as the rule and the rule had never been applied to strangers who were subject to ancillary liability.

(b) Section 21(1)(a) was limited to cases of fraud or fraudulent breach of trust 'to which the trustee was a party or privy'. These words were enacted to relieve trustees who acted in good faith, including the honest co-trustees of a dishonest trustee. Such expressions would be unnecessary if the provision applied to actions against strangers to the trust.

(c) The ancillary liability of a stranger to the trust arises independently of any fraud on the part of the trustee. Liability on the footing of knowing receipt does not require proof of any dishonesty. Whereas liability based on dishonest assistance is based on fraud; but it is clear that such persons are liable on account of their own dishonesty, irrespective of the dishonesty of the trustees, see *Royal Brunei Airlines v Tan* [1995] 2 AC 378.

(d) There is no rational reason why the draftsman of s 21(1)(a) would have intended that the availability of limitation to a non-trustee should depend on a consideration which had no bearing on his liability, namely the honesty or dishonesty of the trustee.

(e) Section 21(1)(b) of the 1980 Act is limited to actions against the trustee. It does not apply to actions against third parties such as knowing recipients of trust property.

Accordingly the claim was struck out.

JUDGMENT

'[The second meaning of the phrase constructive trustee] comprises persons who never assumed and never intended to assume the status of a trustee, whether formally or informally, but have exposed themselves to equitable remedies by virtue of their participation in the unlawful misapplication of trust assets. Either they have dishonestly assisted in a misapplication of the funds by the trustee, or they have received assets knowing that the transfer to them was a breach of trust. In either case, they may be required by equity to account as if they were trustees or fiduciaries, although they are not. These can conveniently be called cases of ancillary liability. The intervention of equity in such cases … is purely remedial.'

Lord Sumption

In *Halton International Inc and another v Guernroy Ltd* [2006] EWCA Civ 801, the Court of Appeal decided that the exception enacted in s 21(1) of the Limitation Act 1980 was not applicable to a disputed transaction that did not involve proprietary rights. Carnwath LJ remarked that the exception is required to be clearly justified by reference to the statutory language and the policy behind it. The policy 'is not about culpability as such' but about 'deemed possession – the fiction that the possession of property by a trustee is treated from the outset as that of the beneficiary'.

Where the right of action is based on fraud or the material facts of the transaction have been deliberately concealed by the defendant or where the action is for relief from the consequences of a mistake, time does not begin to run until the claimant discovers the fraud or mistake or ought with reasonable diligence to have discovered it (s 32).

Besides fraud and mistake, there are two limbs to the extension of liability under s 32. The first requires 'deliberate concealment' by the defendant in the ordinary sense of these words (s 32(1)). The concealment may take place at any time during what would otherwise have been the running of the period of limitation. In such a case time does not begin to run until the concealment has been discovered or could have been discovered with reasonable diligence, see *Sheldon v RHM Outhwaite (Underwriting Agencies) Ltd* [1995] 2 All ER 558, per Lord Browne-Wilkinson. The second limb deals with deliberate breach of duty in 'circumstances in which it is unlikely to be discovered for some time' (s 32(2)). This has been the subject of authoritative consideration by the House of Lords in *Cave v Robinson Jarvis & Rolfe* [2002] 2 All ER 641. The House decided that s 32(2) applied to cases where the breach of duty was deliberately committed, in the sense that there was intentional wrongdoing: see Lord Millett. The other ingredient needed to bring s 32(2) into play is that the breach is committed in circumstances where it is unlikely to be discovered 'for some time'. Although the quoted phrase is imprecise, the better view is that the implicit contrast that it is setting up is one between a breach of duty that would be immediately discovered (e.g. the infliction of a physical injury) and one that would not. Section 32(1) then poses the question: when could the claimant have discovered the concealment with reasonable diligence? On this issue Millett LJ in *Paragon Finance* stated:

JUDGMENT

'The question is not whether the Plaintiffs should have discovered the fraud sooner; but whether they could with reasonable diligence have done so. The burden of proof is on them. They must establish that they could not have discovered the fraud without exceptional measures which they could not reasonably have been expected to take. In this context the length of the applicable period of limitation is irrelevant. In the course of argument May LJ observed that reasonable diligence must be measured against some standard, but that the six-year limitation period did not provide the relevant standard. He suggested that the test was how a person carrying on a business of the relevant kind would act if he had adequate but not unlimited staff and resources and were motivated by a reasonable but not excessive sense of urgency. I respectfully agree.'

Millett LJ

In *Page v Hewetts Solicitors* (2011), the High Court decided on the extent of knowledge within s 32(1) of the Limitation Act 1980 that is required for the extension of the limitation periods in respect of claims at common law and in equity. In respect of common law claims for damages for breach of contract or negligence, the knowledge required for limitation purposes is knowledge of the gist of the claim for damages. For claims in equity for breaches of fiduciary duties, time began to run when the claimants had the material facts necessary to allege a *prima facie* case against the defendant.

CASE EXAMPLE

Page v Hewetts Solicitors [2011] EWHC 2449

The claimants appealed against the decision of the master that their claim was statute-barred. The claimants were beneficiaries under their parents' will. The defendants were a firm of solicitors retained to advise and act for the claimants. A legal executive employed by the defendants recommended a sale of the estate property at an undervalue (£190,000) to a property development company. Unknown to the claimants, the true value of the property was £350,000 and the development company was connected to the legal executive employee. In November 2000 the claimants complained to the Office for the Supervision of Solicitors (OSS) about the conduct of the firm. The OSS replied in December 2002 detailing the employee's relationship with the property development company and confirming that the employee received a profit from the company. In January 2003 the OSS sent a copy of the agreement between the development company and the employee. In February 2009 the claimants commenced proceedings against the defendants based on a proprietary claim for secret profits, alleging no limitation period was applicable by virtue of s 21(1)(b) of the Limitation Act 1980; alternatively, the defendants had deliberately concealed some of the facts necessary to support the claim. The master dismissed the claim in summary proceedings brought by the defendants. The claimants appealed to the High Court.

Held: Dismissing the appeal on the following grounds:

1. The claimants' cause of action was in reality not a proprietary claim to recover trust property but a personal claim for an account which was subject to the limitation period, see *Sinclair v Versailles* (2011) (see Chapter 8).
2. The common law claim for damages for breach of trust and/or negligence was statute-barred for the time period started to run from the date that the claimants were aware of the gist of the claim.
3. In respect of the fiduciary claim, time commenced from the date that the claimants became aware of material evidence to support their claim. This was on the date of receipt of the letter from the OSS in January 2003. In the circumstances, this claim was also statute-barred and the extension of the time period in s 32(1) of the Limitation Act 1980 was not applicable.

JUDGMENT

'As regards the common law claims, in my judgment the Master was correct in holding that the breach of retainer/negligence claim was known to the Claimants by or after 25 November 2000 and that both this claim and the breach of fiduciary duty claim are both statute barred. I agree with the Master ... that the Claimants' letter to the OSS of 25 November 2000 shows that the Claimants knew sufficient facts to start time running in respect of these claims. At least the gist of the claim for damages for causing the Property to be sold at an undervalue appears to have been known to the Claimants by this date.'

Prevezer QC, Deputy Judge of the High Court

Likewise in *Cattley v Pollard* [2006] EWHC 3130 (Ch) (see earlier), the High Court decided that the limitation period for dishonest assistance claims ('class 2 actions') is the normal period of six years from the date of the accrual of the cause of action. These are, in essence, personal, as opposed to proprietary, claims against the defendant.

In *James v Williams* [2000] Ch 1, the Court of Appeal decided that where a beneficiary acted as if he were the sole owner of trust property, he would be treated as a constructive trustee and a claim against him would be exempt from the limitation period. In this case, the defendant's predecessor in title assumed ownership of her parents' house after their deaths. The claimant brought a claim to recover the property some 24 years after the cause of action accrued. The court held that the defendant had acquired title from a constructive trustee and the claim was not time-barred.

In *Gwembe Valley Development Co Ltd v Koshy* [2003] EWCA Civ 1048, the Court of Appeal clarified the law with regard to the limitation periods for claims for an account. In an action for an account based on breaches of fiduciary duties the existence or non-existence of a limitation period depended on:

(i) the nature and classification of the fiduciary relationship, as laid down by Millett LJ in *Paragon Finance plc v Thakerar* [1999] 1 All ER 400 (see Chapter 8). The first covers 'genuine' cases of constructive trusts concerning a pre-existing fiduciary relationship (proprietary claims) and the second use involves those cases where the breach of duties creates the fiduciary obligation (personal claims);

(ii) the nature of the conduct which gave rise to the duty to account. At one end of the spectrum would be a case in which a director has acted innocently, by failing to disclose an interest of which he was unaware, but is nonetheless liable to account for any profits. At the other end would be a case in which the non-disclosure of interest was deliberate and fraudulent. In the former, the limitation period of six years will apply but in the latter s 21(1)(a) of the 1980 Act will operate, and no limitation periods will apply to the claim.

CASE EXAMPLE

Gwembe Valley Development Co Ltd v Koshy and Others [2003] EWCA Civ 1048, CA

In 1986, a joint business venture was formed to develop a cotton and wheat farm of 2,500 hectares in Zambia. A group of investors funded the project. Each investor was allowed representation on the board of Gwembe Valley Development Co Ltd (GVDC) as the corporate vehicle for the project. Representation on the board was proportionate to the size of the investment. By far the largest investment in GVDC was made by a UK company, Lasco, controlled by Mr Koshy (Mr K). In 1987 Lasco made a loan of $5.8 million to GVDC, repayable to Lasco on demand. Mr K was a director and in de facto control of Lasco. At the same time he was the managing director of GVDC. Lasco stood to make a massive profit of $4.8 million on the deal. By 1993 the venture failed. The investors fell out and GVDC became insolvent and was put into receivership. In 1996 GVDC, through its receiver, commenced proceedings against Mr K and Lasco for an account of the profits made from the business transaction, equitable compensation for breaches of fiduciary duty and a declaration that Mr K and Lasco were liable as constructive trustees for all GVDC moneys received by them. The trial judge found that Mr K was dishonest and in breach of his fiduciary duties in procuring GVDC to enter into the loan transaction with Lasco without making proper disclosure to the other directors of GVDC of the extent of his personal interest in Lasco. The judge limited the account to the value of property, belonging in equity to GVDC, that Mr K had received, and refused a more general account of profits. The defendant appealed against these findings and alleged that the claims were statute-barred under the Limitation Act 1980. GVDC contended that the judge should have ordered an account of *all* of the unauthorised profits made by Mr K as a result of his breaches of fiduciary duties.

The Court of Appeal dismissed the appeal by Mr K and allowed GVDC's appeal on the following grounds:

1. Mr K acted in breach of his fiduciary duties as a director of GVDC in deliberately and dishonestly concealing from the other directors the nature and extent of the profits made by him in the loan transaction.
2. A claim by GVDC for an account of profits against Mr K is a claim for, or is treated for limitation purposes as analogous to an action for, 'fraud or fraudulent breach of trust' under s 21(1)(a) of the Limitation Act 1980.
3. The claim for an account of profits against Mr K was not a claim 'to recover from the trustee trust property ... in the possession of the trustee' within s 21(1)(b) of the Limitation Act 1980.
4. No limitation period applied to the claim by GDVC against Mr K.
5. The claim by GDVC was not barred by laches or acquiescence.
6. The judge was wrong to confine the scope of the account of profits. A general account of the profits was ordered.

JUDGMENT

'Claims for breach of fiduciary duty, in the special sense explained in *Bristol and West Building Society v Mothew* [1998] Ch 1 [see Chapter 8], will normally be covered by s 21. The six year time limit under s 21(3), will apply, directly or by analogy, unless excluded by sub-s 21(1)(a) (fraud) or (b) (Class 1 trusts).

In the present case, it is clear that these principles were applicable to a director in Mr Koshy's position. He had 'trustee-like responsibilities' in the exercise of the powers of management of the property of GVDC and in dealing with the application of its property for the purposes, and in the interests, of the company and of all its members. In our view, accordingly, the claim for an account, if it was based on a failure in the exercise of those responsibilities, was within the scope of s 21. It was in principle subject to a six year time limit under s 21(3). The question is whether it was excluded under either of the two statutory exceptions in s 21(1)(a) and (b).'

Mummery LJ

In accordance with s 22, the limitation period in respect of any claim to the estate of a deceased person is 12 years.

Furthermore, the limitation periods mentioned above do not apply to an action for an account brought by the Attorney General against a charitable trust, because charitable trusts do not have beneficiaries in a way similar to private trusts: *AG v Cocke* [1988] Ch 414.

Laches

Where no period of limitation has been specified under the Act (see s 21(1)), the doctrine of laches will apply to equitable claims. Section 36 of the Limitation Act 1980 enacts that nothing in the Act affects any equitable jurisdiction to refuse relief on the grounds of acquiescence or otherwise.

The doctrine of laches consists of a substantial lapse of time coupled with the existence of circumstances which make it inequitable to enforce the claim of the claimant. The doctrine is summarised in the maxim 'Equity aids the vigilant and not the indolent'. The rationale behind the doctrine was stated by Lord Camden LC in *Smith v Clay* (1767) 3 Bro CC 639, thus:

JUDGMENT

'A court of equity has always refused its aid to stale demands, where a party has slept upon his rights and acquiesced for a great length of time. Nothing can call forth this court into activity, but conscience, good faith and reasonable diligence; where these are wanting, the court is passive and does nothing.'

Lord Camden

It may be treated as inequitable to enforce the claimant's cause of action where the delay has led the defendant to change his position to his detriment in the reasonable belief that the claim has been abandoned, or the delay has led to the loss of evidence which might assist the defence or if the claim is to a business (for the claimant should not be allowed to wait and see if it prospers).

The jurisdiction of the court in respect of laches was summarised by Lord Selborne in *Lindsay Petroleum Co v Hurd* (1874) LR 5. The court decided that an essential ingredient of the defence of laches requires the defendant to establish that the delay in commencing proceedings by the claimant has caused the defendant to suffer detriment to such an extent that it would be unjust to allow the claimant's action to succeed:

JUDGMENT

'Now the doctrine of laches in courts of equity is not an arbitrary or technical doctrine. Where it could be practically unjust to give a remedy either because the party has, by his conduct, done that which might fairly be regarded as equivalent to a waiver of it or where by his conduct and neglect he has, though perhaps not waiving that remedy, yet put the other party in a situation in which it would not be reasonable to place him if the remedy were afterwards to be asserted, in either of these cases lapse of time and delay are most material.

… Two circumstances [that are] always important in such cases, are, the length of the delay and the nature of the acts done during the interval, which might affect either party and cause a balance of justice or injustice in taking the one course or the other, so far as relates to the remedy.'

Lord Selborne

A more flexible, modern and broad approach based on unconscionability was advocated by Aldous LJ in *Frawley v Neill* [2000] CP Reports 20, CA:

JUDGMENT

'In my view, the more modern approach should not require an inquiry as to whether the circumstances can be fitted within the confines of a preconceived formula derived from earlier cases. The inquiry should require a broad approach, directed to ascertaining whether it would in all the circumstances be unconscionable for a party to be permitted to assert his beneficial right. No doubt the circumstances which gave rise to a particular result in decided cases are relevant to the question whether or not it would be conscionable or unconscionable for the relief to be asserted, but each case has to be decided on its facts applying the broad approach.'

Aldous LJ

The applicability of the equitable doctrines of laches and acquiescence depend on the facts of each case. Unreasonable delay by the claimant, substantial prejudice and manifest injustice to the defendant are significant factors to be taken into consideration by the court. In order to raise a successful defence, the defendant is required to establish the following three elements:

1. that there has been unreasonable delay in bringing the action by the claimant;

2. that there has been consequent substantial prejudice or detriment to the defendant;

3. that the balance of justice requires the claimant's cause of action to be withheld.

In *Patel v Shah* [2005] EWCA Civ 157, the Court of Appeal endorsed the modern 'broad approach' to the defence of laches based on the test of unconscionability. The Court decided that the defence would be available to a defendant who could establish that it would be unconscionable for the claimant to assert his right to the property in question.

In *Fisher v Brooker and Others*, *The Times*, 12 August 2009, the House of Lords decided that a delay of almost 40 years in claiming a share of the copyright in a musical work was not defeated by the doctrine of laches. The defendants had failed to prove that they had suffered detriment from the claimant's delay, and in any event had derived a financial benefit which far outweighed any detriment that might have resulted from the delay.

CASE EXAMPLE

Fisher v Brooker and Others, The Times, 12 August 2009, HL

The music for the song, 'A Whiter Shade of Pale' was composed in early 1967 by Gary Brooker, the lead singer and pianist of the band Procul Harum. The lyrics were written by the band's manager, Keith Reid, and recorded as a demonstration tape. On 7 March 1967, Mr Brooker and Mr Reid assigned to Essex Music Ltd all the copyright in the words and music of the song in return for a specified percentage of the royalties and other fees. Shortly thereafter, Mr Fisher joined the band as an organist and composed the organ melody. The song was recorded and released on 12 May 1967 and became an instant success. Mr Fisher left the band in 1969. In 1993 Essex Music Ltd assigned its rights to the song to Onward Music Ltd. In May 2005 the claimant notified the defendants of his claim to a share of the musical copyright in the song. The defendants pleaded, *inter alia*, laches but could not establish that they had suffered any detriment as a result of the delay. The court upheld the claim and decided that the claimant was a joint owner of the copyright in the song and further, that the defendants' laches defence would be rejected for they (defendants) enjoyed benefits from the delay which far outweighed any prejudice suffered.

JUDGMENT

'The argument based on laches faces two problems. The first is that ... laches only can bar equitable relief, and a declaration as to the existence of a long-term property right, recognised as such by statute, is not equitable relief. It is arguable that a declaration should be refused on the ground of laches if it was sought solely for the purpose of seeking an injunction or other purely equitable relief. However, as already mentioned, that argument does not apply in this case. Secondly, in order to defeat Mr Fisher's claims on the ground of laches, the Respondents must demonstrate some acts during the course of the delay period which result in a balance of justice justifying the refusal of the relief to which Mr Fisher would otherwise be entitled ... the Respondents are unable to do that. They cannot show any prejudice resulting from the delay, and, even if they could have done so, they have no answer to the judge's finding at [2006] EWHC 3239 (Ch), para 81, that the benefit they obtained from the delay would out-weigh any such prejudice.'

Lord Neuberger

16.5 Proprietary remedies (tracing or the claim *in rem*)

The claimant beneficiary who suffers a loss as a result of a breach of trust is entitled to claim restitution of the trust estate in an action for an account against the wrongdoers, the trustees. Such an action is a claim against the trustees and is referred to as a claim *in personam*, i.e. the claim is against the trustees personally, who are required to satisfy the claim from their personal assets. Provided that the trustees are solvent and have sufficient assets to satisfy the claim of the innocent beneficiary, the claimant will not be out of pocket. But if the trustees are insolvent, the claimant's cause of action will rank with the claims of the trustees' other unsecured creditors. This may result in the order of the court remaining unsatisfied. An alternative process that is available to the beneficiary is to 'follow' or '**trace**' the trust assets in the hands of the trustees or third parties, not being *bona fide* transferees of the legal estate for value without notice, and recover such property or obtain a charging order in priority over the trustees' creditors. This is known as a proprietary remedy or a claim *in rem* or a 'tracing order'.

trace
Process of identifying and recovering the claimant's original or substituted property from the defendant.

'Following' the assets in the hands of the defendant involves the process of identifying the same asset (but not in any substituted form, such as the proceeds of sale of the asset) as it moves from hand to hand with the effect that the claimant may attach an order on the property. On the other hand, a tracing order is a process whereby the claimant establishes and protects his title to assets in the hands of another. The remedy is 'proprietary' in the sense that the order is attached to specific property under the control of another or may take the form of a charging order thereby treating the claimant as a secured creditor. The remedies at common law and equity are mainly 'personal' in the sense that they are remedies which force the defendant to do or refrain from doing something in order to compensate the claimant for the wrong suffered. But the proprietary remedy exists as a right to proceed against a particular asset in the hands of the defendant.

In *Boscawen v Bajwa* [1996] 1 WLR 328, Millett LJ explained the process of tracing thus:

JUDGMENT

'Equity lawyers habitually use the expressions the tracing claim and the tracing remedy to describe the proprietary claim and the proprietary remedy which equity makes available to the beneficial owner who seeks to recover his property *in specie* from those into whose hands it has come. Tracing so called, however, is neither a claim nor a remedy but a process ... It is the process by which the plaintiff traces what has happened to his property, identifies the persons who have handled or received it, and justifies his claim that the money which they handled or received (and, if necessary, which they still retain) can properly be regarded as representing his property.'

Millett LJ

If the claimant succeeds in tracing or following his property into the hands of the defendant he will be entitled to a remedy that may be fashioned to suit his circumstances and to give effect to his claim. The nature of the remedy will vary as to whether the claim is personal or proprietary. A proprietary remedy is based on the claimant proving ownership of the property in the hands of the defendant. In the case of land the remedy may be specific recovery of the property; constructive trust in favour of the claimant; in the case of personal property the remedy may take the form of a lien (a charging order); constructive trust; conversion under the Torts (Interference with Goods) Act 1977; or subrogation in favour of the claimant. Millett LJ echoed this principle in *Boscawen v Bajwa* (1996).

JUDGMENT

'The plaintiff will generally be entitled to a personal remedy; if he seeks a proprietary remedy he must usually prove that the property to which he lays claim is still in the ownership of the defendant. If he succeeds in doing this the court will treat the defendant as holding the property on a constructive trust for the plaintiff and will order the defendant to transfer it *in specie*, to the plaintiff. But this is only one of the proprietary remedies which are available to a court of equity. If the plaintiff's money has been applied by the defendant, for example, not in the acquisition of a landed property but in its improvement, then the court may treat the land as charged with the payment to the plaintiff of a sum representing the amount by which the value of the defendant's land has been enhanced by the use of the plaintiff's money. And if the plaintiff's money has been used to discharge a mortgage on the defendant's land, then the court may achieve a similar result by treating the land as subject to a charge by way of subrogation in favour of the plaintiff.'

Millett LJ

A personal claim for 'money had and received', on the other hand, is distinct from a proprietary claim. Such personal claims are based on the notion that the defendant, without authority, has received the claimant's money. It is immaterial whether or not the defendant has retained the claimant's money. The claim is complete when the defendant receives the money, subject to the defence of change of position. But this personal action will be of no benefit to the claimant if the defendant becomes bankrupt. The claim is essentially a quasi-contractual remedy based on the principle of reversing the unjust enrichment of the defendant at the expense of the claimant. In *Trustee of the Property of F C Jones v Jones* [1996] 3 WLR 703, the Court of Appeal decided that the common law right to trace property belonging to the claimant extends to profits accruing to such property. The justification for allowing the claimant to seek the profits made by the defendant lies in restitution, to prevent the defendant being unjustly enriched at the expense of the claimant, see Millett LJ's judgment below.

CASE EXAMPLE

Trustee of the Property of F C Jones v Jones [1996] 3 WLR 703

In 1984, the partners of F C Jones and Sons, potato growers, committed an act of bankruptcy and in due course were adjudicated bankrupt. Following the act of bankruptcy, but before the adjudication, the defendant, the wife of one of the partners, paid £11,700 of partnership money into the account of commodity brokers. The defendant subsequently dealt in potato futures which proved to be a success. She received cheques totalling £50,760 from the brokers and paid these sums into an account she had opened with R Raphael and Sons plc. The Official Receiver informed Raphaels of his claim to the money and, thereupon, the defendant demanded the release of it. On an interpleader summons, the sum was ordered to be paid into court. The defendant conceded to the trustee's claim to the original £11,700, but argued that his claim could not extend to the profits generated by the original sum. The trial judge held in favour of the claimant on the ground that the defendant had received the money in a fiduciary capacity and was a constructive trustee of the money, including the profit element. The defendant appealed. The Court of Appeal dismissed the appeal but decided the case on different grounds from the High Court. The case was treated as involving tracing at common law. The defendant had clearly not received the money as a fiduciary and was not a constructive trustee. She had no title to the money at law or in equity but was merely in possession of it. This was due to the bankruptcy doctrine of relation back. The effect of this doctrine was to vest the legal title in the trustee in bankruptcy. The trustee's claim to trace the money was not made in equity. There was no mixture of the funds and, as such, the trustee was required to bring his claim at common law. He was entitled to trace his funds (including the profits) by applying common law principles because the money and profits belonged to him at law.

JUDGMENT

'The defendant had no title at all, at law or in equity. If she became bankrupt, the money would not vest in her trustee. But this would not be because it was trust property; it would be because it was not her property at all. If she made a profit, how could she have any claim to the profit made by the use of someone else's money? In my judgment she could not. If she were to retain the profit made by the use of the trustee's money, then, in the language of the modern law of restitution, she would be unjustly enriched at the expense of the trustee.'

Millett LJ

However, Nourse LJ, in the same decision, extended the basis of the claim for money had and received to include the recovery of profits made by the defendant's use of the claimant's money. The justification here was based on the defendant's conscience:

JUDGMENT

'I also agree that the appeal must be dismissed. I recognise that our decision goes further than that of the House of Lords in *Lipkin Gorman v Karpnale Ltd* [1991] 2 AC 548, in that it holds that the action for money had and received entitles the legal owner to trace his property into its product, not only in the sense of property for which it is exchanged, but also in the sense of property representing the original and the profit made by the defendant's use of it.'

Nourse LJ

16.5.1 Advantages of the proprietary remedy over personal remedies

The proprietary remedy has a number of advantages over the personal remedy, namely:

- The effectiveness of the claimant's action is not dependent on the solvency of the defendant. Indeed, the claimant's action is based on an assertion of ownership of the asset in question. Third parties who purport to derive interests from the defendant take a risk that their interest in property may be postponed in favour of the claimant.

- The claimant may be able to take advantage of increases in the value of the property in appropriate cases.

- On a proprietary claim, interest accrues from the date the property was acquired by the defendant while claims *in personam* carry interest only from the date of the judgment.

- The limitation periods for commencing claims are not applicable to claimants who seek to trace and recover their property in the possession of the trustee.

16.5.2 Tracing at common law

To a limited extent the right to trace exists at common law. In order to pursue this course of action the claimant is required to establish legal ownership of the property. Before the Judicature Act 1873/75, the only ownership that was recognisable at common law was the legal title and this principle continues today. In *MCC v Lehman Bros* [1998] 4 All ER 675 (see Chapter 1), the beneficiaries under a trust did not have the capacity to pursue a claim at law. In addition the claimant is required to establish that the property is identifiable. The approach here is that provided that the claimant's property is 'identifiable', the process of tracing may continue through any number of transformations. The form which the property takes is irrelevant, provided that the claimant shows a direct connection between his property in its original form and the property in its altered form in the hands of the defendant.

The main restriction in the common law right to trace is that the property ceased to be 'identifiable' when it became comprised in a mixed fund or when the asset ceases to be wholly owned by the claimant.

CASE EXAMPLE

Taylor v Plumer (1815) 3 M & S 562

The defendant, Sir Thomas Plumer (later Master of the Rolls), had given money to Walsh, his stockbroker, in order to purchase Exchequer bills. Walsh, without authority, purchased American investments and bullion and attempted to abscond to America. There was a dramatic chase by the defendant's attorney and a police officer who caught up with Walsh at Falmouth where he was waiting for a boat bound for Lisbon. Walsh handed the property over to the defendant's agents and was later adjudicated bankrupt. His assignee in bankruptcy claimed to recover the property from the defendant. The court held in favour of the defendant because the property had belonged to him.

JUDGMENT

'It makes no difference in reason or in law into what other form, different from the original, the change may have been made, whether it be into that of promissory notes for the security of the money which was produced by the sale of the goods of the principal ... or into other merchandise, for the product of or substitute for the original thing still follows the nature of the thing itself, as long as it can be ascertained to be such and the right only ceases when the means of ascertainment fail which is the case when the subject is turned into money and mixed and confounded in a general mass of the same description.'

Lord Ellenborough CJ

More recently, in *Lipkin Gorman (a firm) v Karpnale Ltd* [1991] 3 WLR 10, Lord Goff said:

JUDGMENT

'It is well established that a legal owner is entitled to trace his property into its product, provided that the latter is indeed identifiable as the product of his property ... Of course, tracing or following property into its product involves a decision by the owner of the original property to assert his title to the product in place of his original property ... the bank was the debtor and the solicitors were its creditors. Such a debt constitutes a choice in action, which is a species of property; and since the debt was enforceable at common law, the choice in action was legal property belonging to the solicitors at common law. There is in my opinion no reason why the solicitors should not be able to trace their property at common law in that chose in action, or in any part of it, into its product i.e. cash drawn by loss from their client account at the bank. Such a claim is consistent with their assertion that the money so obtained by loss was their property at common law.'

Lord Goff

In *Lipkin Gorman* (1991) the claimant had not sought a tracing order (proprietary claim), but Lord Goff considered that such a claim might have had a reasonable chance of success. The relationship of banker and customer (debtor and creditor) created a chose in action in favour of the claimant. The customer was entitled to trace his property (chose) in its unconverted form or in its substituted form, such as the cash drawn by Cass from the client's account. Since the club had conceded that it had retained some of the solicitor's cash, namely, £154,695, the firm would have been entitled at common law to trace this sum into the hands of the defendant in accordance with the principle in *Taylor v Plumer*.

CASE EXAMPLE

Lipkin Gorman (a firm) v Karpnale Ltd [1991] 3 WLR 10

Mr Cass, a partner in the claimant's firm of solicitors, was a compulsive gambler, unbeknown to the other partners. He drew cheques on the firm's client account by making out cheques for cash and sending the firm's cashier to cash them. He withdrew a total of £323,222 from the account. From this amount, £100,313 was replaced, accounted for or recovered. The balance of £222,909 represented money which Cass stole from the firm and was irrecoverable from him. Cass used the relevant funds at the gaming tables of the Playboy Club, owned by the defendant. It was conceded that the club was still in possession of £154,695 which was derived from the firm's account. On one occasion, Cass procured a banker's draft for £3,735 drawn in favour of the firm which was paid for by a cheque drawn on the firm's account. He endorsed the draft on behalf of the firm (without authority) and proffered it to the club for 'chips' which Cass used for gambling. Within the club, 'chips' were treated as the currency, and Cass would redeem these for money whenever he chose to do so. The 'chips' were worthless outside the casino and at all times remained the property of the club. Cass was convicted of theft. The club at all times had acted in good faith and had no knowledge that Cass was using unauthorised funds.

The questions in issue were, first, whether the claimant was entitled to maintain an action against the defendant in quasi-contract for money had and received and, second, whether the defendant was entitled to retain the proceeds of the draft of £3,735.

The House of Lords decided as follows:

(a) The club, as the recipient in good faith of stolen money, was under an obligation to pay the equivalent to the claimant. The club had provided no valuable consideration to Cass and had been unjustly enriched at the expense of the claimant.

(b) The 'purchase' and use of 'chips' were convenient mechanisms for facilitating gambling. Gamblers did not make separate contracts to 'purchase' or acquire 'chips'. The property in the 'chips' remained in the club. No valuable consideration was provided by the club in exchanging cash for 'chips' or vice versa.

(c) Each bet placed by a gambler and accepted by the club created a separate contract, which was void by virtue of s 18 of the Gaming Act 1845. The club was under no legal obligation to honour bets. If it paid out funds in respect of winning bets, these payments were construed as gifts. Equally, gamblers who lost bets were treated as making gifts of their stakes to the club. Accordingly, the club did not provide any valuable consideration, despite running the risk of voluntarily paying out sums in respect of winning bets.

(d) The firm of solicitors was entitled to recover the amount as stated in the banker's draft (£3,735). The club did not become a holder in due course under s 29(1) of the Bills of Exchange Act 1882. The draft was made payable to the firm and the unauthorised endorsement by Cass, in favour of the club, was done on behalf of the firm of solicitors.

It should be noted that had Cass mixed his money with the firm's property, the right to trace would have been governed by equitable rules exclusively. The claimant would have been entitled to trace its property in the hands of Cass, who would be considered to be a constructive trustee. The effect would have been that the firm would have had a first charge on the mixed fund in the hands of Cass (see *Re Hallett's Estate* (1880) 13 Ch D 696, below). The onus would then have been on Cass to establish the extent of the amount of the mixed fund which belonged to him (see Ungoed-Thomas J in *Re Tilley* [1967] Ch 1179, below). The consequence would have been that the firm of solicitors would be entitled to trace its property in the hands of the club, an innocent volunteer, and effect a charge ranking in *'pari passu'* (see *Sinclair v Brougham* [1914] AC 398, below).

In *Trustee of the Property of F C Jones and Sons v Jones* [1996] 3 WLR 703, the Court of Appeal allowed the Official Receiver of a bankrupt firm to trace at law (£11,700) and recover the profits (£50,760) derived from the claimant's property.

16.5.3 Tracing in equity

Equity had developed a more realistic approach to tracing as opposed to the common law. The fact that the subject-matter of tracing did not exist in its original form, but subsists in a substituted form, was no bar to the process of tracing in equity. Equity had conceived the notion that once property was identifiable, recognition of the claimant's right could be given by attaching the order:

- to specific property; or
- by charging the asset for the amount of the claim.

Unmixed fund

Equity followed the common law and declared that where the property had been transferred in breach of trust but exists in its original form in the hands of the defendant the claimant will be entitled to follow the property and an order to give effect to his proprietary interest. This right may not be extended against a defendant who is a *bona fide* purchaser of the legal estate for value without notice. In appropriate cases the claimant will be entitled to compel the trustee to bring the claim at law, but where this is not possible the beneficiary may institute such a claim in equity. However, where the trust property has been transformed into property of a different form by the trustees and has been kept separate and distinct from the trustees' resources, the beneficiary may trace his interest and take the proceeds. If the proceeds of sale have been used to acquire further property, the beneficiary may elect:

 (i) to take the property which has been acquired wholly with the trust property; or

 (ii) to charge the property for the amount belonging to the trust.

JUDGMENT

'The modern doctrine of Equity as regards property disposed of by persons in a fiduciary position is a very clear and well-established doctrine. There is no distinction between a rightful or wrongful disposition of the property so far as the right of the beneficial owner to follow the proceeds. You can take the proceeds of sale if you can identify them. But it very often happens that you cannot identify the proceeds. The proceeds may have been invested together with money belonging to the person standing in a fiduciary position, in a purchase. He may have bought land with it. In that case, according to the now well-established doctrine of Equity, the beneficial owner has a right to elect either to take the property purchased, or to hold it as security for the amount of the purchase money, or, as we generally express it, he is entitled at his election either to take the property or to have a charge on the property for the amount of the trust money.'

Jessel MR in *Re Hallett's Estate* (1880) 13 Ch D 696

CASE EXAMPLE

Banque Belge pour L'Etranger v Hambrouck [1921] 1 KB 321

The defendant drew cheques from his employer's bank account which were paid into his own account. Sums were drawn out of this account and paid into the account of his mistress, Mlle Spanoghe. A claim to trace and recover the sum from her account succeeded.

JUDGMENT

'The case of *Re Hallett's Estate* (1880) 13 Ch D 696 makes it plain that the court will investigate a banking account into which another person's money has been wrongfully paid, and will impute all drawings out of the account in the first instance to the wrongdoer's own moneys, leaving the plaintiff's money intact so far as it remains in the account at all.'

Atkin LJ

Mixed fund

Where the trustee or fiduciary has mixed his funds with that of the beneficiary or has purchased further property with the mixed fund, the beneficiary loses his right to elect to take the property acquired. The reason is that the property would not have been bought with the beneficiary's money pure and simple but with the mixed fund. However, in the exercise of the exclusive jurisdiction of equity, the beneficiary would be entitled to have the property charged for the amount of the trust money.

JUDGMENT

'But where the trustee has mixed the money with his own the beneficiary can no longer elect to take the property, because it is no longer bought with the trust money but with a mixed fund. He is, however, still entitled to a charge on the property purchased for the amount of the trust money laid out in the purchase ... That is the modern doctrine of Equity.'

Jessel MR in *Re Hallett's Estate* (1880)

Where a trustee or fiduciary mixes trust funds with his own in breach of trust and withdraws part of the blended fund which is dissipated, he is presumed to withdraw his own funds before depleting the trust balance in the account. The effect is that the funds withdrawn, and possibly lost, are presumed to be the trustee's moneys. The justification for this principle is that where a person does an act which may be rightfully performed he cannot be heard to say that that act was intentionally done wrongfully, e.g. if a trustee pays £50,000 belonging to the trust into his bank account with a balance of £10,000 of the trustee's personal funds, and withdraws £5,000 which is used for his own purpose and is no longer identifiable, this amount is presumed to be the trustee's own funds, see *Re Hallett* (1880).

CASE EXAMPLE

Re Hallett's Estate [1880] 13 Ch D 696

Mr Hallett was a solicitor and a trustee of his own marriage settlement in favour of his wife for life and subject thereto for himself for life with remainder to the issue of the marriage. He paid the trust moneys into his bank account. As a solicitor he acted on behalf of Mrs Cotterill and paid a sum of money received on her behalf into his account. He made various payments into and out of the account. At the time of his death the account had sufficient funds to meet the claims of the trust and Mrs Cotterill but not, in addition, the claims of the general creditors. The personal representatives of Hallett sued to ascertain whether or not the trustees and Mrs Cotterill (collectively) had priority in satisfaction of their claim over the general creditors. The Court of Appeal held that the trustees and Mrs Cotterill had priority and were entitled to a charge on the bank account to the extent of their claim. The personal representatives had argued that the amounts withdrawn from the account were primarily trust moneys so that the balance remaining in the account belonged to the personal representatives. This argument was rejected by the Court of Appeal on the ground that an individual who controls funds belonging to an innocent person which have been mixed with his own and withdraws part of the fund which is dissipated is assessed to have withdrawn his own funds before depleting the innocent person's balance in the account

JUDGMENT

'Where a man does an act which may be rightfully performed, he cannot say that that act was intentionally and in fact done wrongly. When we come to apply that principle to the case of a trustee who has blended trust monies with his own, it seems to me perfectly plain that he cannot be heard to say that he took away the trust money when he had a right to take away his own money. The simplest case put is the mingling of trust monies in a bag with money of the trustee's own. Suppose he had 100 sovereigns in a bag and he adds to them another 100 sovereigns of his own, so that they are co-mingled in such a way that they cannot be distinguished and the next day he draws out for his own purposes 100, is it tolerable for anybody to allege that what he drew out was the first 100 of trust monies and that he misappropriated it and left his own 100 in the bag? It is obvious he must have taken away that which he had a right to take away, his own 100.'

Jessel MR

The rule in *Re Hallett's Estate* (1880) is to the effect that where a trustee or fiduciary mixes trust moneys with his own:

- the beneficiary is entitled in the first place to a charge on the amalgam of the fund in order to satisfy his claim;

- if the trustee or fiduciary withdraws moneys for his own purposes, he is presumed to draw out his own moneys so that the beneficiary may claim the balance of the fund as against the trustee's general creditors.

In *Space Investments Ltd v Canadian Imperial Bank of Commerce Trust Co* [1986] 1 WLR 1072, the Privy Council decided that a customer who deposits funds into a bank account acquires a chose in action which he is entitled to trace into the assets of the bank in the event of a liquidation of the bank. But where a bank trustee lawfully mixes the trust funds with its own funds and goes into liquidation, the funds become the bank's (including the trust funds) and the beneficiaries' proprietary right to trace is lost because the trust funds are no longer identifiable.

CASE EXAMPLE

Space Investments Ltd v Canadian Imperial Bank of Commerce Trust Co [1986] 1 WLR 1072

The defendant bank was trustee of a variety of settlements and had deposited the funds in deposit accounts at its bank. The bank went into liquidation. The beneficiaries of the trusts attempted to trace the trust funds into the bank's assets and recover in priority over the unsecured creditors. The court held that the claims failed because the bank was expressly authorised to deposit the funds into its account for the general purposes of the bank. The beneficiaries therefore were not entitled to identify their assets.

JUDGMENT

'A customer who deposits money with a bank authorises the bank to use that money for the benefit of the bank in any manner the bank pleases. The customer does not acquire any interest in or charge over any asset of the bank or over all the assets of the bank. The deposit account is an acknowledgement and record by the bank of the amount from time to time deposited and withdrawn and of the interest earned. The customer acquires a chose in action, namely the right on request to payment by the bank of the whole or any part of the aggregate amount of principal and interest which has been credited or ought to be credited to the account. If the bank becomes insolvent the customer can only prove in the liquidation of the bank as unsecured creditor for the amount which was, or ought to have been, credited to the account at the date when the bank went into liquidation.'

Lord Templeman

Lord Templeman's view (in *Space Investments*) of the termination of the proprietary right to trace is highly controversial. It is based on the assumption that if the bank trustee is entitled to mix trust funds with its own, it is entitled to treat the amalgamated fund as its own. This is clearly in direct contradiction of the principle in *Re Hallett* and has not generally been supported. In addition, Lord Templeman declared that where the beneficiaries are entitled to trace as against the bank trustee, but no specific asset is identifiable, the beneficiaries may be entitled to a charging order over all the assets of the bank. This is clearly an over-simplification of the tracing rules.

Where a trustee mixes his funds with the trust funds and acquires a new asset with the mixed fund, the beneficiary is entitled to choose whether to charge the asset with a proportionate share of his interest, or to sue the trustee for breach of trust and enforce a lien on the proceeds to secure restoration of the funds. Accordingly, where a trustee misappropriates trust funds in order to fund premiums on a life assurance policy created for his benefit, the beneficiaries (under the trust) become part owners of a chose in action, and thus the policy proceeds, and are entitled to a *pro rata* share of the sum assured.

pro rata
Proportionately.

CASE EXAMPLE

Foskett v McKeown [2001] 1 AC 102

Trustees held funds allegedly in pursuance of a land development deal which did not materialise. One of the trustees effected a whole life insurance policy in the sum of £1 million. The first two annual premiums were paid out of the trustee's funds, but the fourth and fifth premiums were paid out of the investors' funds. The trustee committed suicide and the insurance company duly paid the sum assured to the named beneficiaries under the policy. The claimant sued as a representative of the investors for a *pro rata* share of the policy proceeds. The House of Lords, by a majority, held in favour of the claimant on the ground that immediately before the payment of the fourth premium, the property, held in trust for the defendants, was a chose in action, i.e. the bundle of rights enforceable under the policy was held in trust against the insurers. The trustee, by paying the fourth premium out of the moneys of the claimants' trust fund, wrongly mixed the value of the premium with the value of the policy. Thereafter, the defendants held the same chose in action (i.e. the policy) but with the enhanced value of both contributions. The effect was that the proceeds of the policy were held in proportion to the contributions which the parties made to the five premiums.

JUDGMENT

'Where a trustee wrongfully uses trust money to provide part of the cost of acquiring an asset, the beneficiary is entitled at his option either to claim a proportionate share of the asset or to enforce a lien upon it to secure his personal claim against the trustee for the amount of the misapplied money. It does not matter whether the trustee mixed the trust money with his own in a single fund before using it to acquire the asset, or made separate payments (whether simultaneously or sequentially) out of the differently owned funds to acquire a single asset … if a claimant can show that premiums were paid with his money, he can claim a proportionate share of the policy. His interest arises by reason of and immediately upon the payment of the premiums, and the extent of his share is ascertainable at once. He does not have to wait until the policy matures in order to claim his property. His share in the policy and its proceeds may increase or decrease as further premiums are paid; but it is not affected by the realisation of the policy. In principle the plaintiffs are entitled to the insurance money which was paid on Mr Murphy's death in the same shares and proportions as they were entitled in the policy immediately before his death.'

Lord Millett

Assets purchased

The rule in *Re Hallett* is to the effect that as between the wrongdoing trustee and the beneficiaries the trustee of a mixed fund is presumed to withdraw his own funds before depleting the trust funds. The issue here is in respect of the ownership of the balance of funds in the account, or identifiable assets bought with the fund. If the balance of the funds remaining in the account has been depleted so that the beneficiary's right to trace into the account has been exhausted, the claimant may be entitled to trace into any identifiable assets bought by the trustee with the mixed fund. The justification for this rule is that since the beneficiaries are entitled to trace their property (including a charge) into a mixed fund, it follows that that right (to trace) may extend to property (assets) acquired with the mixed fund. Accordingly, if a part of the fund has been used to purchase an asset which is identifiable and the remainder of the fund has been exhausted (so that the right to trace against the fund becoming otiose), or is insufficient to satisfy the claim of the beneficiary, the latter may claim to trace against the asset acquired by the trustees, for as between the trustee and the beneficiary, the beneficiary's claim is required to be satisfied before the trustee may assert his interest in the property.

In short, from the point of view of the beneficiary, the trustee and his successors in title are prevented from denying the interest in the property deemed to be acquired with the mixed fund.

CASE EXAMPLE

Re Oatway [1903] 2 Ch 356

O, a trustee, paid trust moneys of £3,000 into his private bank account containing his own moneys. He later purchased shares in Oceana Ltd for £2,137. After this drawing out there was still more in the account than the amount of trust moneys paid in. O paid further sums into the account but his subsequent drawings for his own purposes exhausted the entire amount standing to his credit. The shares were later sold for £2,474. O died insolvent. The beneficiaries claimed that the proceeds of sale of the shares represented their moneys. The personal representatives claimed that as O had sufficient moneys in his account to satisfy the claim of the beneficiaries at the time of the purchase of the shares, that purchase was met by the trustee's own funds. The court held in favour of the beneficiaries.

JUDGMENT

'It is clear that when any of the money drawn out has been invested and the investment remains in the name or under the control of the trustee, the balance having been dissipated by him, he cannot maintain that the investment which remains represents his own money and that what was spent and can no longer be recovered was the money belonging to the trust. In other words, when private money of the trustee and that which he held in a fiduciary capacity have been mixed in the same banking account from which various payments have been made, then, in order to determine to whom any remaining balance or any investment paid for out of the account ought to be deemed to belong, the trustee must be debited with all the sums that have been withdrawn and applied to his own use so as to be no longer recoverable, and the trust money in like manner debited with any sums taken out and duly invested in the names of the proper trustees. The personal representatives have contended that the trustees were entitled to withdraw from the account and rightly applied the fund for his own purposes; and accordingly the shares belong to his estate. To this I answer that he never was entitled to withdraw the £2,137 from the account or, at all events, that *he could not be entitled to take that sum from the account and hold it or the investments made therewith, freed from the charge in favour of the trust, unless and until the trust money paid into the account had been first restored and the trust fund reinstated by due investment of the money in the joint names of the proper trustees, which was never done.*' [Emphasis added]

Joyce J

Scope of the charge

After some hesitation, it appears that a beneficiary, who has a right to trace into an asset bought by the trustees, would be permitted to claim any increase in the asset purchased. It makes no difference whether the asset was bought with an unmixed or a mixed fund. No difficulty arises if the asset was bought with an unmixed fund because the claimant is the sole owner of such asset. But the difficulty surrounds the claim to any increase in the asset bought with a mixed fund. One argument which has been put forward is that the charge on the asset ought to be limited to the amount of the trust moneys and no more, because the claimant is only seeking to recover his money and not claiming the asset bought with his funds. Supporters of this view refer to Jessel MR's judgment in *Re Hallett's Estate* (1880) as advancing this argument. However, Ungoed-Thomas J in *Re Tilley's Will Trust* [1967] Ch 1179 distinguished the statement by Jessel MR in *Re Hallett* (1880) on the ground that the judge was not considering the question of the 'proportion' of the property that would have been subject to the charge, but was only considering whether the charge existed or not. Furthermore, Ungoed-Thomas J declared *obiter* that the beneficiary's charge on the asset would be in respect of a proportionate part of the increase in value, because otherwise the trustee (and his successors in title who ought to be in no better position) may profit from the breach of trust.

CASE EXAMPLE

Re Tilley's Will Trust [1967] Ch 1179

A testator, who died in 1932, left property to his widow, as sole trustee, on trust to his widow for life, with the remainder to Charles and Mabel (his children by a former marriage) in equal shares. The trust properties were realised between 1933 and 1952 for a total of £2,237 (trust moneys). This amount was paid into the widow's bank account and was blended with her own

causa sine qua non

A cause without which a consequence would not have taken place. The expression is sometimes referred to as an indirect or historical cause for an event.

causa causans

The direct cause for an event.

moneys. Until 1951, the widow's bank account was at various times substantially overdrawn (in 1945, overdraft of £23,536). Investments were purchased by the widow, financed by overdraft facilities at the bank. From 1951 her account was sufficiently in credit from her own personal contributions, i.e. without regard to any trust moneys. In 1959, the widow died with an estate valued at £94,000. Mabel had predeceased the widow and her administrators sued the widow's personal representatives, claiming that Mabel's estate was entitled to one-half of the proportion of the profits made by the widow, i.e. on the assumption that the widow's personal representative failed to show that Mrs Tilley's investments were made out of her personal moneys, the claimant was entitled to a pro rata amount of the profits from the investments. The court held that the trust moneys were not used to purchase the investments made by Mrs Tilley (the trustee) but were used only to reduce her overdraft which was the source of the purchase moneys. In short, there was a **causa sine qua non** between the trust moneys and the investments, but the trust moneys were not the **causa causans** of the profit.

JUDGMENT

'[I]t seems to me, on a proper appraisal of all the facts of this case, that Mrs Tilley's breach halted at the mixing of the funds in her bank account. Although properties bought out of those funds would, like the bank account itself (at any rate if the monies in the bank account were inadequate) be charged with repayment of the trust monies which then would stand in the same position as the bank account, yet the trust monies were not invested in properties at all but merely went in reduction of Mrs Tilley's overdraft which was in reality the source of the purchase monies. The plaintiff's claim therefore failed and he was entitled to no more than repayment of half of £2,237.'

Ungoed-Thomas J

However, Ungoed-Thomas J considered *obiter* the scope of the charge on the assets bought had the claimant been entitled to trace into the investments. He expressed his view that the beneficiary is entitled to claim any increases in the value of the property that he is entitled to trace. He reasoned thus:

JUDGMENT

'In *Re Hallett* the claim was against a bank balance of mixed fiduciary and personal funds, and it is in the context of such a claim that it was held that the person in a fiduciary character drawing out money from the bank account must be taken to have drawn out his own money in preference to the trust money, so that the claim of the beneficiaries prevailed against the balance of the account.

Re Oatway (1903) was the converse of the decision in *Re Hallett* (1880). In that case the claim was not against the balance left in the bank of such mixed monies, but against the proceeds of sale of shares which the trustee had purchased with monies which, as in *Re Hallett* (1880), he had drawn from the bank account. But, unlike the situation in *Re Hallett* (1880), his later drawings had exhausted the account so that it was useless to proceed against the account. It was held that the beneficiary was entitled to the proceeds of sale of the shares which were more than their purchase price but less than the trust monies paid into the account. Further, *Re Oatway* (1903) did not raise the question whether the beneficiary is entitled to any profit made out of the purchase of property by the trustee out of a fund consisting of his personal monies which he mixed with the trust monies and so the judgment was not directed to, and did not deal with that question ... Lord Parker in *Sinclair v Brougham* (1914) had con sidered *Re Hallett* (1880) but he did not address his mind to the question of whether the beneficiary could claim a proportion of the property corresponding to his own contribution to the purchase. In *Snell's Principles of Equity* (26th edn, 1966) the law is thus stated at p. 315:

> Where the trustee purchases shares with part of a mixed fund and then dissipates the balance, the beneficiary's charge binds the shares; for although the trustee is presumed to have bought the shares out of his own money, the charge attaches to the entire fund and could be discharged only by restoring the trust monies. Where the property purchased has increased in value, the charge will not be merely for the amount of the trust monies but for a proportionate part of increased value.'

Ungoed-Thomas J

One of the issues raised in *FHR European Ventures v Mankarious* (2016) was whether the right to trace trust funds paid into separate accounts at the same bank ought to be treated as one. In other words, whether funds paid into one bank account (*euro* account), and no longer traceable, ought to be identified with mixed funds withdrawn from a *sterling* account at the same bank? The claimants contended that the defendants, as fiduciaries acting in breach of trust, were not entitled to claim to be able to withdraw any sum from any account without having first restored the trust money to its rightful owners. The effect was to treat the separate accounts at the same bank as effectively one mixed account including both the claimants' and defendants' funds. The claimants relied on the principle laid down in *Re Oatway* (1903). The defendants argued that the broad proposition put forward by the claimants was inconsistent with the nature of tracing and was not borne out by the decision in *Re Oatway*, which related to a single mixed account. The principles of tracing involve 'hard-nosed property rights' as distinct from whether it is fair, just and reasonable to allow the claimants to treat separate accounts at the same bank as one and without a direct link to the use of the claimants' money. Instead, in the context of this case, the principles that were applicable were laid down in *Re Hallett* (1880), to the effect that withdrawals by the trustee from a mixed fund which are then dissipated, are presumed to be withdrawals of the trustee's own funds before depleting the innocent beneficiary's funds. The justification for this rule has always been that, in the context of a mixed fund, the trustee is presumed to first withdraw funds which he is justified to withdraw, namely his personal funds.

CASE EXAMPLE

FHR European Ventures v Mankarious and others [2016] EWHC 359 (High Court)

The claimants commenced an action against three defendants, Mr Mankarious, Cedar LLC and Cedar Ltd (the latter two defendants were under the control of Mr Mankarious), in respect of the wrongful payment of commission. Cedar LLC entered into a brokerage agreement with the owners of the Monte Carlo Grand Hotel to facilitate its sale. At the same time the claimants engaged the services of Cedar LLC to negotiate the purchase of the hotel on its behalf in return for the payment of commission of €10 million. The defendants failed to disclose to the claimants the existence of the prior agreement. Following the purchase of the hotel for €211.5 million the claimants became aware of the secret commission and commenced proceedings to recover it. In *FHR European Ventures v Cedar Capital Partners* [2014] UKSC 45 (see Chapter 8), the Supreme Court decided that the secret commission was held by the defendants on constructive trust for the claimants. The commission was paid by the defendants into a Jersey bank account held in euros. Subsequently the funds from the euro account were transferred to Mr Mankarious and the third defendant so that the balance in this account was nil. However, £78,982 derived from the commission was paid into a sterling account with the same bank and became mixed with funds belonging to the defendants. The parties agreed that £180,000 from the sterling account (now reduced to zero) was transferred to Mr Mankarious and used to pay the deposit on a house bought in Hampstead in the joint names of Mr and Mrs Mankarious. Incidental costs of the purchase (such as stamp duty, solicitor's and surveyor's fees) amounted to £75,715. In addition, Cedar LLC purchased two term life assurance policies with a sum assured of $13 million in the event of Mr Mankarious's death before 14 March 2028. Cedar LLC paid the first premium but the remaining premiums were paid by Mr Mankarious.

The issues before the court were:

1. whether Mr Mankarious and the other defendants (Cedar Capital Partners) had breached their fiduciary duties owed to the claimants;
2. whether the claimants were entitled to trace the deposit on the Hampstead house of £180,000 paid out of the sterling account as money derived from the commission;
3. alternatively, whether they were entitled to claim a proportionate share of the Hampstead house equivalent to a contribution of £78,982 towards the purchase price;
4. whether the claimants were entitled to an increased interest in the property based on the provision of the incidental costs of acquisition of £75,715 paid out of the sterling account with funds derived from the commission;
5. whether Mr Mankarious's share of the unrealised profits in the Hampstead house was subject to the claim of the claimants;
6. whether the two life assurance policies were held on trust for the claimants absolutely or in proportion to the contribution derived from the commission;
7. whether Mr Mankarious was liable to account for the sums paid to him which were derived from the commission.

JUDGMENT

'I accept the defendants' counsel's submission. *Oatway* was concerned with a single account in which monies belonging to the trustee and to the beneficiary were mixed. In support of the claimants' counsel submission that it should be of broader application, he did not refer me to any statements of principle in the reported cases on this topic. To accept his submissions would be to extend the application of *Oatway*, but the only basis put forward for doing so was that the defendants' position was as unattractive as that of the trustee in *Oatway*. I conclude that *Oatway* does not apply on the facts of this case.'

Master Clark

Lowest intermediate balance

The rule in *Re Hallett's Estate* (1880) (vis-à-vis the 'balance' in a blended bank account) is to the effect that withdrawals from a mixed fund are presumed to take the order of the trustee's moneys before the beneficiary's funds. Accordingly, if the funds in the account fall below the amount of the trust funds originally paid in, that part of the trust fund (the depreciation) is presumed to have been spent. The right to trace into the balance held in the bank account will be depreciated to the extent of the lowest balance in the account. The lowest intermediate balance is presumed to be the trust property, but personal claims may be made against the trustee for this shortfall. Subsequent payments in are not *prima facie* treated as repayments to the trust fund in order to repair the breach, unless the trustee earmarks such repayments as having that effect.

CASE EXAMPLE

Roscoe v Winder [1915] 1 Ch 62

The purchaser of the goodwill of a business, Wigham, had agreed to collect the debt and pay it over to the company. He collected the debt (£623 8s 5d) and paid £455 18s 1d into his personal bank account. The remainder of the debt was unaccounted for. He drew out funds which were dissipated until the credit balance in his account was only £25 18s. Later, he paid in more of his own moneys and died leaving a balance in the account of £358 5s 5d. The question in issue was the extent to which the claimant could assert a charge under the rule in *Re Hallett's Estate* (1880). It was held that although Wigham had held the money as trustee, the charge was limited to £25 18s – the lowest intermediate balance subsequent to the appropriation.

JUDGMENT

'*Prima facie* under the second rule in *Re Hallett* any drawings out by the debtor ought to be attributed to the private monies which he had at the bank and not to the trust monies, yet, when the drawings out had revealed such an amount that the whole of his private money part had been exhausted, it necessarily followed that the rest of the drawings must have been against trust monies. Counsel for the plaintiff contended that the account ought to be treated as a whole and the balance from time to time standing to the credit of that account was subject to one continual charge or trust ... you must for the purpose of tracing put your finger on some definite fund which either remains in its original state or can be found in another shape. That is tracing and tracing seems to be excluded except as to £25 18s.

Certainly, after having heard *Re Hallett's Estate* stated over and over again, I should have thought that the general view of that decision was that it only applied to such an amount of the balance ultimately standing to the credit of the trustee as did not exceed the lowest balance of the account during the intervening period.'

Sargant J

The logical effect of this rule is that *prima facie* if the mixed account is left without funds after the appropriation by the trustee, the claimant will not be entitled to a charge under *Re Hallett* (1880). This is the position whether subsequent funds are paid in or not.

Similarly, where a company receives funds from a payer, subject to a stipulation that the funds are to be paid into a separate client account, and acts in breach of this promise and pays the fund into a deficit account to be used to settle the company's debts, the payer will lose his proprietary right to trace the funds. The Court of Appeal so held in *Moriarty v Atkinson and Others* (2009).

CASE EXAMPLE

Moriarty v Atkinson and Others, *The Times*, 14 January 2009, CA

The company sold boats and received £97,500 from the respondents to hold in a client account, but, instead, paid the funds into a deficit current account mixed with other funds which had been used to pay off debts. Later, the company went into liquidation. The applicants, as administrators, were required to secure the debts of the company. The respondents claimed to be entitled to a return of the funds as beneficiaries under a trust created in their favour. The court decided that the respondents had a good claim against the company for breach of trust, but despite the maxim, 'Equity regards as done that which ought to be done', that did not mean that they had a proprietary interest in that account. The proprietary claim therefore failed.

tutor tip

'Breach of trust involves a drawing together of a number of strands ranging from the extent and scope of the trustees' liability for breach of trust to the personal and proprietary remedies that are available to the beneficiaries.'

The court should not be too ready to extend the circumstances in which proprietary claims could be made, bearing in mind the consequences to unsecured creditors. In the case of an insolvent debtor, every time a proprietary claim was held to exist, the likely consequence was that one commercial creditor would get paid in full to the detriment of all the other commercial creditors.

The 'trust fund' in the present case was the client account, and there had been no breach of trust in relation to any money in that account. Unfortunately for the respondents, the breach of trust occurred before the money in question could become part of the trust fund. Indeed, the breach of trust had the consequence that the money had never become part of a trust fund, and it resulted in the money ceasing to exist.

JUDGMENT

'I prefer to rest my decision in this case on the simple point that the money, which was paid over by the appellants to the company, and then paid by the company into the current account, never formed part of the fund against which a claim is now sought to be made, namely the money in the client account.

The trust fund in the present case is the client account, and there has been no breach of trust in relation to any money in that account. Unfortunately for the appellants, for whom one must have sympathy, the breach of trust occurred before the money in question could become part of any trust fund. Indeed, the breach of trust complained of had the very consequence that the money never became part of the trust fund, as it resulted in the money ceasing to exist, to use the words of Lord Mustill in *Goldcorp*. In other words, this way of putting the appellants' cases also fails, as the breach of trust of which the appellants can complain did not relate to the trust fund in which they now claim a proprietary interest.'

Lord Neuberger in *Moriarty v Atkinson*

The same principle was applied in *Bishopsgate Investment v Homan* concerning an attempt to trace into a bank account which was overdrawn at one point in its history.

CASE EXAMPLE

Bishopsgate Investment Management Ltd v Homan [1994] 3 WLR 1270

BIM Ltd was a trustee of certain assets of pension schemes, held on trust for the benefit of employees and ex-employees of Maxwell Communication Corporation plc (MCC). MCC fraudulently paid these assets into its overdrawn account. The liquidator of BIM claimed to be entitled to an equitable charge in priority to all of the other unsecured creditors of MCC. The judge refused to make the order. The plaintiff appealed. The court decided equitable tracing did not extend to tracing through an overdrawn account, whether overdrawn at the time the money was paid into the account or subsequently. The court applied the principle in *Roscoe v Winder* and distinguished the *Space Investments* case:

JUDGMENT

'[I]n the absence of clear evidence of intention to make good the depredations on BIM, it is not possible to assume that the credit balance has been clothed with a trust in favour of BIM and its beneficiaries: see *James Roscoe (Bolton) Ltd v Winder*.'

Dillon LJ

Conversely, if the trustees, after the appropriation, deliberately earmark a repayment or purchase as belonging to the trust, the beneficiaries will be entitled to trace into that fund or asset. But this solution requires clear evidence of the intention to repair the breach.

CASE EXAMPLE

Robertson v Morrice (1845) 4 LTOS 430

A trustee who held stock subject to a trust, and additionally similar stock of his own, mixed both sets of properties and treated them as one holding. He sold parts of the mixed stock from time to time, so that, shortly before his death, the amount left was less than what he should have been holding on trust. On his deathbed, he instructed the clerk to buy more stock of a similar nature in order to replace that which he had misappropriated from the trust. This was done by the clerk. The beneficiaries claimed to be entitled to the stock as trust property. It was held that the entire portfolio of stock was subject to the trust, on the following grounds:

(i) the balance of the original mixed holding was subject to the charge that attached on the mixing;

(ii) the newly acquired holding was trust property because of the declaration by the trustee that such purchase was designed to replace the trust property.

Rule in *Clayton's case*

The rule in *Clayton's case* (*Devaynes v Noble* (1816 1 Mer 529)) is a rule of banking law and one of convenience which had been adopted in the early part of the nineteenth century to ascertain the respective interests in a bank account of two innocent parties *inter se*. Where a trustee mixes trust funds subsisting in an active current bank account belonging to two or more innocent beneficiaries, the amount of the balance in the account is determined by attributing withdrawals in the order of sums paid into the account ('first in first out' (FIFO)), e.g. if £50,000 belonging to the A trust was paid in by the trustees into an active current bank account and subsequently £20,000 belonging to the B trust was paid into the same account by the trustees, so that the account contained a mixture of £70,000 of funds belonging to two trusts. If the trustees withdraw £10,000 and spend it on some venture, the funds are deemed to be attributable to the A trust account. If this amount is no longer identifiable then the A trust alone will bear the loss.

The rule is applied as between beneficiaries (or innocent parties) *inter se* in order to ascertain:

(a) ownership of the balance of the fund; and

(b) ownership of specific items bought from funds withdrawn from the account.

The basis of the rule lies in the fact that as between the beneficiaries (or innocent parties) the 'equities are equal', i.e. there is no need to give one beneficiary any special treatment over the other. But it is worth noting that as between the trustee and beneficiary, the rule in *Re Hallett* (1880) and not *Clayton* (1816) applies. The wrongdoer may never take advantage of the FIFO rule.

CASE EXAMPLE

Clayton's case, Devaynes v Noble [1816] 1 Mer 529

Mr Clayton, a customer of a bank, had a balance of £1,713 in his favour at the time of the death of Devaynes, a partner in the bank. Clayton drew out more than £1,713 (thus creating an overdraft) and then paid in further sums totalling more. Later, the firm of bankers went bankrupt. Clayton sought to recover from Devaynes' estate. It was held that the sums withdrawn by Clayton, after Devaynes died, must have been appropriated to the earlier debt of £1,713 so that Devaynes' estate was free from liability. The sums which Clayton subsequently paid in constituted a 'new debt' for which the surviving partners alone were liable.

JUDGMENT

'[T]here is no room for any other appropriation than that which arises from the order in which the receipts and payments take place, and are carried into the account. Presumably, it is the sum first paid in, that is first drawn out. It is the first item on the debit side of the account, that is discharged, or reduced, by the first item on the credit side. The appropriation is made by the very act of setting the two items against each other. Upon that principle, all accounts current are settled, and particularly cash accounts.'

Lord Grant MR

The rule in *Clayton's case* (1816), as originally formulated, was a rule in banking law applicable in determining ownership of funds in an account. However, the rule has been extended to ascertain the interests of:

(a) beneficiaries *inter se* under two or more separate trusts; and

(b) competing claimants or beneficiaries under the same trust.

In *Re Stenning* [1895] 2 Ch 433, the court considered the application of the rule in *Clayton's case* (1816) in an *obiter* pronouncement.

CASE EXAMPLE

Re Stenning [1895] 2 Ch 433

A solicitor paid moneys belonging to a number of clients into his personal bank account. This money included £448 18s 6d due to Mrs Smith. There was often more than this amount in the account, but there was often less than the total of the clients' moneys paid in. On a claim made by Mrs Smith alleging that she was a beneficiary under a trust, the court held that no trust had been created on the facts but only a loan has been made by agreement. But if £448 18s 6d had been trust moneys, *Clayton's case* (1816) would have applied as between Mrs Smith and the other clients.

One criticism that has been levelled against the rule in *Clayton's case* (1816) is that it lacks justice and fairness as between claimants of equal standing. The rule exists as a rough and ready solution the outcome to which depends on a matter of chance, i.e. the application of the rule depends on the precise time when money from two trusts (or moneys from the same trust but belonging to two or more beneficiaries) was paid into a current account. A more equitable solution would have been to allow the two groups of innocent beneficiaries to share the balance in the account, rateably, in proportion to the sums originally placed in the account from the two trusts, i.e. the beneficiaries ought to be entitled to an order ranking in ***pari passu***.

pari passu
Equally, without preference.

In *Sinclair v Brougham* [1914] AC 398 the House of Lords adopted this equitable solution in respect of the claims of two innocent parties *inter se* to a fund, not being a current account, which had been mixed by a fiduciary.

CASE EXAMPLE

Sinclair v Brougham [1914] AC 398

The litigation arose when the Birkbeck Building Society, having borrowing power, established and developed, in addition to the legitimate business of a building society, a banking business which was admittedly *ultra vires*. In connection with this banking business, customers deposited sums of money. In 1911, the society was wound up. The assets were claimed *inter alia* by the ordinary shareholders and the depositors, each group claiming priority over the other. The House of Lords held that the two classes of claimants were entitled to the assets rateably, following the rule in *Re Hallett* (1880), i.e. an order was made entitling both groups of claimants to a charge ranking in *pari passu*, according to the proportion of their respective contribution.

JUDGMENT

'My Lords, I agree that the principle on which *Hallett's* case is founded justifies an order allowing the appellants to follow the assets, not merely to the verge of actual identification, but even somewhat further in a case like the present, where after a process of exclusion only two classes or groups of persons, having equal claims, are left in and all superior classes have been eliminated. Tracing in a sense it is not, for we know that the money coming from A went into one security and that coming from B into another and that the two securities did not probably depreciate exactly in the same percentage and we know further that no-one will ever know anymore. Still I think this well within the tracing equity, and that among persons making up these two groups the principle of rateable division of the assets is sound.'

Lord Sumner

Re Hallett *extended in* Sinclair v Brougham

Sinclair v Brougham (1914) was overruled in *Westdeutsche Landesbank v Islington BC* [1996] AC 669 on the ground that no single *ratio* could be detected. However, *Sinclair v Brougham* (1914) is mentioned here in order to demonstrate the application of the *Re Hallett* (1880) principle and the court's reluctance to follow *Clayton's case* (1816).

The litigation in *Re Hallett* (1880) was between persons of unequal standing, namely the innocent claimant and the wrongdoer (or successor). The wrongdoer is prevented from denying the interest acquired by the innocent claimant to the mixed fund.

On the other hand, the litigation in *Sinclair v Brougham* (1914) was between two groups of innocent claimants (of equal standing) whose moneys had been represented in assets available for distribution. Accordingly, the House of Lords extended the principle in *Re Hallett* (1880) in concluding that the claimants were entitled to the assets rateably.

JUDGMENT

'Each of the two classes of contributors claimed priority over the other. Until the case reached the House of Lords, the possibility that they might rank *pari passu* does not appear to have been considered … The House of Lords held that on the principle on which *Hallett's case* was founded, the two classes shared rateably. In one respect, no doubt, this application of the principle is an extension of it since, although the right of individuals to trace their own money (if they could) was preserved in the order of the House, the order provided for tracing the aggregate contributions of the two classes as classes ... the extension of the principle in *Sinclair v Brougham* was the obvious and, indeed on the facts, the only practical method of securing a first distribution of the assets.'

Lord Greene MR in Re Diplock [1948] Ch 465, CA

In *Barlow Clowes v Vaughan* [1992] 4 All ER 22, the Court of Appeal favoured the *pari passu* charge where the claimants were investors in a common fund, as opposed to the 'rough and ready' solution in *Clayton's case* (1816). The Court of Appeal recognised that the rule in *Clayton's case* (1816) was applicable when money belonging to several beneficiaries had been 'blended in one bank account'. The court was, however, satisfied that in the circumstances of the case, it was not appropriate to apply the rule because it was wholly inequitable to do so.

CASE EXAMPLE

Barlow Clowes v Vaughan [1992] 4 All ER 22

The companies promoted and managed certain investment plans in gilt-edged stock. Funds had been misapplied and the companies went into liquidation, and receivers were appointed. At the time of the collapse, the companies had a total liability of £115 million owed to around 11,000 investors. The amount available was far less than the amount of the investors' claims. The moneys and assets available for distribution to investors were contributed by three classes of claimants, namely:

(a) moneys paid by investors for investments in gilts which were acquired by the companies;
(b) moneys in bank accounts awaiting investment in gilts at the time the receivers were appointed;
(c) the net proceeds of sale of additional assets, including a yacht, *Boukephalos*.

The receivers brought proceedings for directions as to the basis on which the assets and moneys ought to be distributed. The judge (Peter Gibson J) decided that the distribution should be made in accordance with the rule in *Clayton's case* ('first in, first out'). Thus, the investors were to be paid in the reverse order to that in which they had made deposits, so that later investors were more likely to be repaid. The second defendant appealed.

The Court of Appeal decided that the moneys and assets were intended to form a common investment pool and the claimants ranked in *pari passu*. Thus, they were entitled to a charge on the common investment pool shared rateably, in proportion to their contributions, in accordance with the principles in *Sinclair v Brougham*. Where the rule in *Clayton* is impractical, or may cause injustice, or is contrary to the intention of the investors, the court is entitled to refuse to apply it, provided that an alternative method of distribution is available. *Clayton's* rule was considered to be time-consuming and expensive. In addition, the rule would cause injustice, because a relatively small number of investors would become entitled to most of the fund and the rule was, in any event, not applicable to tracing claims. An alternative method, known as the 'rolling charge', was rejected by the court. This solution regards a mixture of funds from different sources as a 'blend or cocktail'. The effect is that each withdrawal is treated as a depletion of an interest in the account in the same proportion as the interest bears to the fund immediately before the withdrawal is made. Thus, losses are borne proportionately, but later payments in the account are unaffected by earlier withdrawals. The court rejected this solution as complex, expensive and impractical.

JUDGMENT

'All the moneys which were provided by the investors were treated by BCI as a common pool to which they could have resort for their own purposes. Since all the investors have equitable charges, and their equities are equal, and they presumably intended their money to be dealt with collectively, they should share rateably what is left in the pool, as did the claimants in *Sinclair v Brougham* [1914] AC 398.'

Leggatt LJ

JUDGMENT

'The approach, in summary, which I would adopt to resolving the issues raised by this appeal are as follows:

(i) While the rule in *Clayton's Case* (1816) 1 Mer 529, is, *prima facie*, available to determine the interests of investors in a fund into which their investments have been paid, the use of the rule is a matter of convenience and if its application in particular circumstances would be impracticable or result in injustice between the investors it will not be applied if there is a preferable alternative.

(ii) Here, the rule will not be applied because this would be contrary to either the express or inferred or presumed intention of the investors. If the investments were required by the terms of the investment contract to be paid into a common pool, this indicates that the investors did not intend to apply the rule. If the investments were intended to be separately invested, as a result of the investments being collectively misapplied by BCI, a common pool of the investments was created. Because of their shared misfortune, the investors will be presumed to have intended the rule not to apply.

(iii) As the rule is inapplicable, the approach which should be adopted by the court depends on which of the possible alternative solutions is the most satisfactory in the circumstances. If the North American solution [rolling charge] is practical, this would probably have advantages over the *pari passu* solution. However, the complications of applying the North American solution in this case make the third solution the most satisfactory.

(iv) It must, however, be remembered that any solution depends on the ability to trace and if the fund had been exhausted (that is, the account became overdrawn) the investors whose moneys were in the fund prior to the fund being exhausted will not be able to claim against moneys which were subsequently paid into the fund. Their claims will be limited to following, if this is possible, any of the moneys paid out of the fund into other assets before it was exhausted.'

Woolf LJ

In *Commerzbank Aktiengesellschaft v IMB Morgan plc* [2004] EWHC 2771 (Ch), the High Court in reliance on the decision in *Barlow Clowes v Vaughan* concluded that the rule in *Clayton's case* ought to be resisted in the interest of fairness and justice.

JUDGMENT

'I am satisfied that the rule in *Clayton's Case* should not apply here, because it would be both impracticable and unjust to apply it. The only fair way to share the balances on each of the Accounts would be in proportion to the claims on the respective Accounts.

Where the rule in *Clayton's Case* does not apply, then (at least where the claimants have an equal right to be paid) it will normally be appropriate for the parties to be entitled to the mixed fund pari passu, i.e. the fund will be shared rateably amongst the beneficiaries according to the amount of their contributions.'

Collins J

In *Charity Commission for England and Wales v Framjee* [2014] EWHC 2507 (see Chapter 3), the High Court decided that surplus funds received by the Dove Trust, which were not distributed to charities of each donor's choice, were held on resulting trust for the relevant donors on a *pari passu* basis. In this respect the loss was apportioned between the relevant donors on a *pro rata* basis. The court refused to follow *Clayton's case* on the grounds that that principle is arbitrary and unfair to donors who had made earlier donations and, in any event, is treated as a default solution. Another alternative, the rolling charge method, was also rejected because it was considered to be impracticable.

JUDGMENT

'I think that the fairest solution is to regard all the unpaid recipients as participants in a common misfortune brought about by the way in which the donation scheme was managed by the trustees. If the matter is viewed in that way, there is no good reason to differentiate between victims depending on when their donations were made, or to seek to divide up the available pool of assets on the basis of a minute examination of changing beneficial entitlements as and when payments were made in and out of it. There is admittedly an element of rough justice involved for the most recent contributors to the pool, but this seems to me unavoidable once a decision has been taken in favour of pari passu distribution, which itself responds to a very basic human feeling that, when faced by a common misfortune, all those affected by it should bear the burden equally.'

Henderson J

Backward tracing

'Backward tracing' is a novel concept in English law and involves a fiduciary acquiring an asset with the assistance of a loan and repaying the loan with misappropriated trust funds. The issue is whether the innocent beneficiaries are entitled to recover or charge the asset even though it was acquired prior to the misappropriation. In *Bishopsgate Investment Ltd v Homan*, at first instance, Vinelott J stated the general rule that tracing is not possible through an overdrawn account, but he added a reservation to the effect that where there is a connection between the misappropriation and the acquisition of an asset, backward tracing may be possible. This would be the case where there was an inference that when the borrowing occurred it was the intention of the trustee that it would be repaid by a misappropriation of the trust funds. In the Court of Appeal Dillon LJ, in an *obiter* pronouncement, considered that it was arguable that backward tracing was permissible in the circumstances envisaged by Vinelott J. Leggatt LJ in the same case rejected the concept and held that 'there can be no equitable remedy against an asset acquired before misappropriation of money takes place, since *ex hypothesi* it cannot be followed into something which existed and so had been acquired before the money was received and therefore without its aid'. This view was endorsed by the majority of the Lords Justices of Appeal in *Foskett v McKeown* [1998] Ch 265. However, the third member of the Court of Appeal in *Foskett*, Scott VC, regarded the matter as still open and said:

> I do not regard the fact that an asset is paid for out of borrowed money with the borrowing subsequently repaid out of trust money as being necessarily fatal to an equitable tracing claim by the trust beneficiaries. The availability of equitable remedies ought, in my view, to depend upon the substance of the transaction in question and not upon the strict order in which the associated events happen.

The issue was not considered when the case reached the House of Lords.

Professor Conaglen, in an article entitled 'Difficulties with tracing backwards' (2011) 127 LQR 432, accepts that there is nothing conceptually impossible about the courts tracing trust funds through the payment of a debt into assets that the trustee had acquired, before the payment was made, by incurring the debt. But he argues that there is very little support for that view in case law. It is ultimately a matter of legal policy whether the law ought to allow backward tracing. He concludes that

> the unsecured creditors should not have their position worsened further by effectively making them insurers for the beneficiaries against trustee defalcations. Alternatively, if backward tracing is to be allowed, then the extent to which payment of the debt is considered attributable to acquisition of the asset should perhaps be limited in some way, such as by reference to the time when the asset was acquired, whether the trustee intended to misuse trust funds to pay for it. That would be consistent with equity's traditional concern for substance – meaning intention – over form.

In the *Federal Republic of Brazil v Durant International Corporation* (2015), the Royal Court in Jersey, after reviewing the relevant law and academic writings, concluded that the law on backward tracing was uncertain and English law on this issue was unlikely to be settled prior to consideration by the Supreme Court. But Jersey law ought not to set its face against accepting that backward tracing may be permissible. Accordingly, where the bank account remained in credit during the relevant period, so that there was no question of possible insolvency and prejudice to unsecured creditors, the question should be whether there was sufficient evidence to establish a clear link between credits and debits to an account. If such a link were established, the court may not consider that there was cause to diminish its effect by introducing the concept of 'a lowest intermediate balance rule'. Otherwise any sophisticated fraudster would be able to defeat an otherwise effective tracing claim, simply by manipulating the sequence in which credits and debits were made to his account. The Court of Appeal in Jersey upheld the reasoning and conclusion of the Royal Court. The Privy Council upheld the decision of the Court of Appeal and decided that in exceptional cases where the circumstances justify it, backward tracing may be a feasible solution in equity and is an appropriate solution provided that the claimant establishes a transactional link between the depletion of the trust fund and the acquisition of an asset which is the subject-matter of a tracing claim.

CASE EXAMPLE

Federal Republic of Brazil v Durant International Corporation [2015] UKPC 35, (Privy Council)

Owing to its constitution, the Republic of Brazil is required to be treated as a nominal party in respect of legal proceedings brought outside Brazil. The effective claimant is the Municipality of Sao Paulo ('the municipality'). The defendants ('Durant' and 'Kildare') are companies registered in the British Virgin Islands. Kildare is the wholly owned subsidiary of Durant and both companies, at the material time, were under the control of Mr Paulo Maluf and his son, Mr Flavio Maluf. Mr Maluf (senior) was the mayor of the municipality between 1993 and 1996. The Court of Appeal of Jersey upheld the decision of the Royal Court that the companies were liable to the municipality as constructive trustees for $10.5 million, representing bribes to Mr Maluf (senior) in connection with public road building contracts. On appeal, the defendants argued that they were liable to $7.7 million representing the bribes and not the full amount claimed. The basis of this appeal was on two grounds: first, that three payments into a bank account controlled by Mr Maluf (junior) (Chanani account) were made on a date following the final payment from that account to the Durant account. The appellants submitted that those three payments could not be traced back to the claimants' fund for there was no sound basis for backward tracing. Second, the Chanani account was a mixed account and drawings on that account reduced the balance to less than the amount representing the claimant's money. Accordingly, the amount which the claimant was allegedly able to recover was limited to the maximum that can be regarded as representing the bribes, i.e. the lowest intermediate balance. Thus the funds must have come from other sources.

The Royal Court and the Court of Appeal in Jersey rejected the appellants' argument and the Privy Council affirmed their decision. Backward tracing may be legitimate where there is a clear transactional link between credits and debits in an account. This is consistent with judicial policy and practicality and will thwart the efforts of sophisticated fraudsters who may otherwise be able to defeat effective tracing claims. The court recognised that this principle will operate where an account remained in credit during the relevant period so that there was no question of possible insolvency or prejudice to unsecured creditors, and no intervention of a *bona fide* purchaser for value.

JUDGMENT

'The development of increasingly sophisticated and elaborate methods of money laundering, often involving a web of credits and debits between intermediaries, makes it particularly important that a court should not allow a camouflage of interconnected transactions to obscure its vision of their overall purpose and effect. If the court is satisfied that the various steps are part of a co-ordinated scheme, it should not matter that, either as a deliberate part of the choreography or possibly because of the incidents of the banking system, a debit appears in the bank account of an intermediary before a reciprocal credit entry. The Board agrees with Sir Richard Scott VC's observation in *Foskett v McKeown* that the availability of equitable remedies ought to depend on the substance of the transaction in question and not upon the strict order in which the associated events occur.

The Board therefore rejects the argument that there can never be backward tracing, or that the court can never trace the value of an asset whose proceeds are paid into an overdrawn account. But the claimant has to establish a co-ordination between the depletion of the trust fund and the acquisition of the asset which is the subject of the tracing claim, looking at the whole transaction, such as to warrant the court attributing the value of the interest acquired to the misuse of the trust fund.'

Lord Toulson

Innocent volunteers

In *Sinclair v Brougham* (1914), the mixing of the funds of the two innocent claimants was effected by a fiduciary, namely the directors of the building society. This was consistent with the principle in *Hallett* (1880).

But a controversial issue was whether the proprietary remedy would be available to a claimant when the mixing was effected by an innocent volunteer and not by the fiduciary. The Court of Appeal in *Re Diplock* (1948) enunciated (*obiter*) that the remedy would be available.

For example: trustees hold property on trust for A for life, with remainder to B absolutely. The trustees, without authority, distribute £2,000 of the trust income to the remainderman, B, who pays the same into a bank account containing £3,000 of his personal moneys. The trust is later terminated (see *Saunders v Vautier* (1841)) and B becomes bankrupt. A may be entitled to a charge on B's bank account ranking *in pari passu*.

JUDGMENT

'Where an innocent volunteer (as distinct from a purchaser for value without notice) mixes money of his own with money which in equity belongs to another person, or is found in possession of such a mixture, although that other person cannot claim a charge on the mass superior to the claim of the volunteer ... it appears to us to be wrong to treat the principle which underlies *Hallett's* case as coming into operation only where the person who does the mixing is not only in a fiduciary position but is also a party to the tracing action. If he is a party to the action he is, of course, precluded from setting up a case inconsistent with the obligations of his fiduciary position. But supposing he is not a party? The result cannot surely depend on what equity would or would not have allowed him to say *if* he had been a party.'

Lord Greene MR in *Re Diplock* (1948)

CASE EXAMPLE

Re Diplock [1948] Ch 465

Caleb Diplock, by his will, directed his executors to apply the residue of his estate 'for such charitable institutions or other charitable or benevolent objects in England as they may select in their absolute discretion'. The executors assumed that the will created a valid charitable trust and distributed £203,000 among 139 different charities before the validity of the distribution was challenged by the next of kin. In earlier litigation in *Chichester Diocesan Fund v Simpson* [1944] AC 341, the House of Lords decided that the clause in Caleb Diplock's will failed to create a charitable trust for uncertainty of charitable objects. The next of kin sued the executors and charities. The claim against the executors was eventually compromised. But the claimants persisted in their action against the wrongly paid charities on two grounds, namely:

(i) claims *in personam* against the recipient institutions – see *Ministry of Health v Simpson* [1951] AC 251, affirming the decision of the Court of Appeal; and

(ii) claims *in rem* against the assets held by the institutions.

It was held by the Court of Appeal that the action *in rem* would not succeed because the next of kin's moneys were no longer identifiable and, in any event, the charge ranking *in pari passu* would have inflicted an injustice on the institutions in causing the institutions to sell such assets.

Limitations

The Court of Appeal in *Re Diplock* (1948) enunciated the limits surrounding the right to trace:

■ The equitable remedy does not affect rights obtained by a *bona fide* transferee of the legal estate for value without notice. All equitable claims are extinguished against such persons. The beneficiaries may be able to recover the proceeds of sale from the trustee if those funds are identifiable.

■ Tracing will not be permitted if the result will produce inequity, because 'he who comes to equity must do equity'. Accordingly, if an innocent volunteer spends money improving his land there can be no declaration of charge because the method of enforcing the charge would be by way of sale, thus forcing the volunteer to convert his property.

In *Lipkin Gorman (a firm) v Karpnale* [1991] 3 WLR 10, Lord Goff advocated a defence of *bona fide* change of position which ought to be adopted in English law in respect of restitutionary claims. This defence will be developed on a case-by-case basis:

JUDGMENT

'Whether change of position is, or should be, recognised as a defence to claims in restitution is a subject which has been much debated in the books. It is however a matter on which there is a remarkable unanimity of view, the consensus being to the effect that such a defence should be recognised in English law. I myself am under no doubt that this is right ... At present I do not wish to state the principle any less broadly than this: that the defence is available to a person whose position has so changed that it would be inequitable in all the circumstances to require him to make restitution or alternatively to make restitution in full.'

Lord Goff

In *Westdeutsche Landesbank v Islington BC* [1996] AC 669, Lord Goff revisited the principle, stating it concisely in terms of considering the fairness of outcomes. He said:

JUDGMENT

'Where an innocent defendant's position is so changed that he will suffer an injustice if called upon to repay or to repay in full, the injustice of requiring him so to repay outweighs the injustice of denying the plaintiff restitution.'

Lord Goff

The usual approach adopted by the courts is based on estoppel, which has limitations that make it unsuitable to restitutionary claims. The estoppel is based upon a representation by the claimant, whether express or implied, that the defendant is entitled to treat the money as his own. The mere payment of money under a mistake cannot, by itself, constitute a representation which will estop the payer from asserting his right to receive his payment.

The defence would be available to an innocent volunteer who, after receiving the claimant's money, has altered his position to such an extent that, having regard to all the circumstances, it would be inequitable to require him to make full restitution to the claimant: see *Abou-Ramah v Abacha* [2006] All ER (D) 80. On the other hand, the defence ought not to be available to a defendant who has changed his position in bad faith, that is, a defendant who spends the claimant's money after knowledge of facts entitling the claimant to restitution. Likewise, in *Cressman v Coys of Kensington* [2004] EWCA Civ 47, the Court of Appeal decided that the defence was not available to the defendant who acquired a personalised, cherished number plate by mistake and consciously disposed of it in order to avoid the claimant's action. Similarly, the defence will not be available to a wrongdoer. In *Barros Mattos v MacDaniels Ltd* [2004] 3 All ER 299, the High Court decided that the defence was not available to a person who had acted illegally, unless, of course, the illegality was *de minimis*.

In order to establish the defence, the defendant is required to establish that there is a causal link between the mistaken receipt of the overpayment and the recipient's change of position, which makes it inequitable for the recipient to be required to make restitution: see *Scottish Equitable plc v Derby* [2001] 3 All ER 818. The mere fact that the defendant has spent the money in whole or in part, in the ordinary course of things, does not, of itself, render it inequitable that he should be called upon to repay the claimant. In *Price-Jones v Commerzbank AG, The Times*, 26 November 2003, the Court of Appeal decided that a City banker who received an overpayment of £250,000 from his employer by mistake, and who had remained in employment rather than moving to another bank, was not a sufficient change of position to entitle him to retain the windfall payment.

It was for the claimant to demonstrate a sufficient causal connection between the change of position and the mistaken payment.

But if the defendant has spent the claimant's money on a venture which would not have been undertaken but for the gift or overpayment, such conduct would be capable of being construed as a change of position.

In *Credit Suisse (Monaco) SA v Attar* [2004] EWHC 374 (Comm), the court decided that dishonesty on the part of the defendant would deprive him of the defence of change of position. Likewise, the repayment of a debt which was required to be repaid sooner or later would not afford a defence to the defendant, for in such a case there is no causal connection between the mistaken receipt and the expenditure.

Wilful blindness with regard to a windfall amount received by the defendant followed by a payment out of his account will be insufficient to support the defence: see *Fea v Roberts* [2005] All ER (D) 69 (Sept).

 The right to trace is extinguished if the claimant's property is no longer identifiable, for example the trust moneys have been spent on a dinner or a cruise or in paying off a loan.

JUDGMENT

'The equitable remedies presuppose the continued existence of the money either as a separate fund or as part of a mixed fund or as latent in property acquired by means of such a fund. If, on the facts of any individual case, such continued existence is not established, equity is as helpless as the common law itself.'

Lord Greene MR in *Re Diplock* (1948)

 It is essential that the claimant proves that the property was held by another on his behalf in a fiduciary or quasi-fiduciary capacity in order to attract the jurisdiction of equity. This fiduciary need not be the person who mixes the funds or the assets. The mixture may be effected by an innocent volunteer, as in *Re Diplock* (1948).

CASE EXAMPLE

Agip (Africa) Ltd v Jackson and Others [1991] 3 WLR 116

The Court of Appeal decided that the claimant company was entitled to trace in equity a fraudulent payment of £518,822, which was received by the defendants.

JUDGMENT

'[I]n the present case, there is no difficulty about the mechanics of tracing in equity. The money can be traced through the various bank accounts to Baker Oil and onwards. It is, however, a prerequisite to the operation of the remedy in equity that there must be a fiduciary relationship which calls the equitable jurisdiction into being. There is no difficulty about that in the present case since Mr Zdiri must have been in a fiduciary relationship with Agip. He was the chief accountant of Agip and was entrusted with the signed drafts or orders.'

Fox LJ

CASE EXAMPLE

Chase Manhattan Bank v Israel-British Bank [1979] 3 All ER 1025

The claimant, Chase, a New York bank, acting on instructions, paid $2,000,687 to another New York bank, via the New York clearing house system, for the defendant's account. Later on the same day, owing to a clerical error on the part of an employee of Chase, a second payment of the same amount was made. The defendant, another bank based in London, received the funds and discovered the mistake two days later. Subsequently, the defendant company was wound up and was found to be insolvent. The claimant brought an action in equity to trace its funds in the hands of the defendant.

The High Court decided that the claimant had retained a proprietary right in the funds and was entitled to a charging order against the defendant. The fiduciary relationship had been created when the defendant received the windfall payment. In short, the mistake made by the paying bank affected the conscience of the recipient bank.

JUDGMENT

'[T]he fund to be traced need not (as was the case in *Re Diplock* itself) have been the subject of fiduciary obligations before it got into the wrong hands. It is enough that, as in *Sinclair v Brougham* [1914] AC 398, the payment into the wrong hands itself gave rise to a fiduciary relationship … *In the same way, I would suppose, a person who pays money to another under a factual mistake retains an equitable property in it and the conscience of that other is subjected to a fiduciary duty to respect his proprietary right.*' [Emphasis added]

Goulding J

Thus, Goulding J decided that the conscience of the recipient bank was affected *when it received the overpayment* and thus became a fiduciary at this time.

This decision was heavily criticised because of the unjustified way in which the recipient bank may be treated as a fiduciary, simply by virtue of receiving the windfall amount. In *Westdeutsche Landesbank Girozentrale v Islington Borough Council* [1996] 2 All ER 961, the House of Lords (Lord Browne-Wilkinson) reviewed the *Chase Manhattan* case and concluded that the decision may be justified but not for the reasons stated. Instead, the conscience of the recipient bank became affected when, with knowledge of the overpayment, it refused to return the surplus amount to the paying bank. It is at this stage that the bank became a fiduciary and was subject to the proprietary claim.

JUDGMENT

'[A]lthough I do not accept the reasoning of Goulding J, *Chase Manhattan* may well have been rightly decided. The defendant bank knew of the mistake made by the paying bank within two days of the receipt of the moneys. The judge treated this fact as irrelevant but in my judgment it may well provide a proper foundation for the decision. Although the mere receipt of the moneys, in ignorance of the mistake, gives rise to no trust, the retention of the moneys after the recipient bank learned of the mistake may well have given rise to a constructive trust.'

Lord Browne-Wilkinson

16.6 Tracing/subrogation

Tracing is a process that is involved where the claimant is capable of identifying his interest in property that is in the hands of the defendant. Appropriate remedies may be instituted to secure the claimant's interest in the property. Subrogation, on the other hand, is an equitable remedy that substitutes one claimant for another. The effect is that third party rights against the defendant are transferred to the claimant. Thus, the claimant (A) steps in the shoes of a third party (B) and makes a claim against the defendant (C), the rights and remedies to which the third party (B) was entitled. For example, if the A Co Ltd insures B's car under a comprehensive insurance policy and C, another motorist, negligently causes damage to B's car, A Co Ltd under the contract may compensate B for the damage but is entitled to bring proceedings against C (albeit in B's name); or A Co Ltd is subrogated to the rights of B to sue C in negligence and recover its loss. In the context of a marine insurance claim Lord Blackburn in *Burnand v Rodocanachi, Sons and Co* (1882) 7 App Cas 333, said:

JUDGMENT

'The general rule of law (and it is obvious justice) is that where there is a contract of indemnity … and a loss happens, anything which reduces or diminishes that loss reduces or diminishes the amount which the indemnifier is bound to pay; and if the indemnifier has already paid it, then, if anything which diminishes the loss comes into the hands of the person to whom he has paid it, it becomes an equity that the person who has already paid the full indemnity is entitled to be recouped by having that amount back.'

Lord Blackburn

The rationale for the creation of this remedy is based on principles that bind the conscience of the defendant. In appropriate cases whenever it would be unconscionable for the defendant to deny the proprietary interest of the claimant the court may grant the remedy of subrogation. In short, the underlying basis of subrogation is the reversal of unjust enrichment. In *Boscawen and Others v Bajwa and Others* [1995] All ER 769, the issue concerned the rights of a bank (Abbey National) to be subrogated to the rights of the mortgagee. The bank's fund intended for its customer for the purchase of property was released prematurely, through an error of judgment on the part of the purchaser's solicitor, to the vendor. This fund was then used to discharge the vendor's mortgage. The intended purchase by Abbey's customer fell through and the vendor became bankrupt.

Millett LJ explained the scope of a subrogation remedy in the following terms:

JUDGMENT

'Subrogation is a remedy, not a cause of action: see Goff and Jones, *Law of Restitution*, 4th edn, 1993, pp. 589 *et seq*; *Orakpo v Manson Investments Ltd* [1978] AC 95, p. 104, *per* Lord Diplock; and *In Re TH Knitwear (Wholesale) Ltd* [1988] Ch 275, p. 284. It is available in a wide variety of different factual situations in which it is required in order to reverse the defendant's unjust enrichment. Equity lawyers speak of a right of subrogation, or of an equity of subrogation, but this merely reflects the fact that it is not a remedy which the court has a general discretion to impose whenever it thinks it just to do so. The equity arises from the conduct of the parties on well settled principles and in defined circumstances, which make it unconscionable for the defendant to deny the proprietary interest claimed by the plaintiff. A constructive trust arises in the same way. Once the equity is established, the court satisfies it by declaring that the property in question is subject to a charge, by way of subrogation in the one case, or a constructive trust in the other.'

Millett LJ

In the *Banque Financière de la Cite v Parc (Battersea) Ltd and Others* [1998] 2 WLR 475, the House of Lords decided that, as a restitutionary remedy, subrogation is dependent on the following four principles:

(a) whether the defendant would be enriched;

(b) whether the enrichment was at the expense of the claimant;

(c) whether the enrichment would be unjust; and

(d) whether there are any policy reasons for denying the remedy.

Unmixed funds	Unmixed and mixed funds
Common law – *Lipkin Gorman v Karpnele*	Equity • charge on bank account (lowest intermediate funds) – *Roscoe v Winder* • withdrawals used to purchase assets – *Barlow Clowes* (*pari passu*) • innocent volunteers – *Re Diplock* First in, first out (FIFO) – *Clayton's case*

Figure 16.1 Tracing

KEY FACTS

Proprietary remedy (tracing)

Common law tracing	
The common law had recognised the right to trace to a limited extent, i.e. provided that the property had remained unmixed	*Taylor v Plumer* (1815); *Banque Belge pour L'Etranger v Hambrouck* (1921); *Lipkin Gorman v Karpnale* (1991); *F C Jones v Jones* (1996)
Tracing in equity	
This principle exists in both unmixed and mixed funds. However, it is crucial that the claimant establish the existence of a fiduciary relationship	
Mixed property	*Re Hallett* (1880)
Assets purchased by withdrawals from mixed fund	*Re Oatway* (1903); *FHR European Ventures v Mankarious* (2016)
Increases in the value of assets	*Re Tilley* (1967); *F C Jones v Jones* (1996); *Foskett v McKeown* (2001)
Lowest intermediate balance	*Roscoe v Winder* (1915); *Moriarty v Atkinson* (2009); *Bishopsgate v Homan* (1994); *Robertson v Morrice* (1845)
Tracing as between beneficiaries of two trusts	*Clayton's case* (1816); *Sinclair v Brougham* (1914); *Barlow Clowes Int v Vaughan* (1992); *Commerzbank Aktiengesellschaft v IMB Morgan* (2004)
Backward tracing	*Fed Republic of Brazil v Durant* (2015)

Limits regarding the right to trace in equity	
Tracing cannot affect rights acquired by a *bona fide* purchaser of the legal estate for value without notice	*Re Diplock* (1948)
Tracing is extinguished where property cannot be identified, e.g. the fund has been spent on a holiday	
Tracing is not allowed where it would lead to inequitable consequences, now called a 'change of position defence'	*Lipkin Gorman v Karpnale* (1991)
It is essential that the claimant establish that the property was held by a trustee or fiduciary, even though the mixing need not be effected by the fiduciary	*Chase Manhattan v Israel-British Bank* (1979); *Agip v Jackson* (1991); *Westdeutsche Landesbank Girozentrale v Islington Borough Council* (1996)
The rationale for the subrogation remedy is unjust enrichment	*Boscawen v Bajwa* (1995); *Banque Financière* (1998)

ACTIVITY

1. 'Equitable tracing claims are, in some respects, too narrow in their scope and in other respects too wide.' Discuss.
2. In January of this year, Harold, a trustee, paid £2,000 into his private account (the balance then was £500). The sum paid into his account represented the proceeds of sale of assets belonging to the Church of Belvedere, of which he was a trustee. The following day he withdrew £900 and used it to pay his debts.

    In February of this year, Harold paid into his account £300 representing the half-yearly dividends of trustees' stock belonging to the estate of his father, Charles. Harold was the sole trustee of this estate.

    In March of this year, Harold withdrew £1,000 and again spent it on his own affairs.

    In April of this year, he paid into the account £500 of his own money. Shortly afterwards, Harold became bankrupt.

    Explain the rights of Harold's trustee in bankruptcy and of the beneficiaries of the two trusts.

SUMMARY

▨ A breach of trust arises where, in purporting to carry out his duties, a trustee does an improper act or omits to perform an act which he ought to perform. Trustees' duties may be created by the trust instrument or by operation of law.

▨ The measure of the trustee's liability is the loss caused directly or indirectly to the trust estate. This is based on the principles of restitution to the trust estate concerning traditional trusts. The general rule is that the trustee's liability for any breach of his duties is strict. Each transaction is considered separately with the effect that a loss resulting in one transaction may not be set off against a profit from another transaction.

   ◉ Where the trustees commit a breach of trust and the trust comes to an end the beneficiary is entitled to compensation rather than restitution.

- Where the breach of trust is in respect of a commercial transaction, the remedy of equitable compensation is to put the claimant in the position he would have been in had the breach not occurred.

- The court is entitled to award simple interest under s35A of the Senior Courts Act 1981 (formerly the Supreme Court Act 1981) on monetary sums payable by trustees. The rate of interest is 1 per cent above the bank's base rate.

- The court has a discretion to award compound interest designed to require trustees to disgorge the benefit of the use of trust funds. This jurisdiction may be exercised where the trustees have been guilty of fraud. In other cases the court has a discretion as to the award of such interest against trustees and other fiduciaries. The governing principle here is to prevent a trustee from profiting from his breach.

- In general where a breach of trust has been committed by virtue of the actions of two or more trustees, their liability is considered to be joint and several. Accordingly, each is liable for the entire loss even though they are not all equally blameworthy. Constructive trustees are included in this rule. If a successful action is brought against one trustee he has a right of contribution against his co-trustees. The test is laid down in the Civil Liability (Contribution) Act 1978.

- In some cases a trustee may be entitled to claim a complete indemnity from his co-trustees. These are:
  - where one trustee has fraudulently obtained a benefit from the breach of trust;
  - where the trustee is also a beneficiary and has exclusively obtained a benefit from the breach of trust;
  - where one trustee is a solicitor and the breach has been committed solely as a result of acting on his advice.

- Section 21(3) of the Limitation Act 1980 lays down the general rule concerning the limitation period. This is six years from the date on which the cause of action accrued. Where a beneficiary is under a disability, e.g. infancy or of unsound mind, time runs from the ending of the disability. Where a beneficiary is entitled to a future interest time does not run until his interest falls into possession. In the case of fraud or the recovery of the trust property from the trustee no limitation period exists, see s21(1) of the 1980 Act.

- Section 32(1) of the Limitation Act 1980 declares that time does not start to run where the action is based on the fraud of the defendant, the deliberate concealment of facts relevant to the claimant's cause of action or where the action is based on relief from the consequences of a mistake, until the claimant discovers the fraud, concealment or mistake (or could with reasonable diligence have done so). In short, the limitation period may be postponed.

- Where no limitation period exists the equitable doctrine of laches operates to deny a claim for breach of trust. The doctrine of laches consists of a substantial lapse of time in bringing the claim coupled with the existence of circumstances that make it inequitable to enforce the claim.

- A beneficiary who has freely consented to or concurred in a breach of trust is not entitled to sue the trustees for breach of trust.

- Section 62 of the Trustee Act 1925 empowers the court to impound the interest of a beneficiary who instigates a breach of trust by the trustees.

- Section 61 of the Trustee Act 1925 enables the court in its discretion to grant relief to a defaulting trustee where he acts honestly, reasonably and ought fairly to be excused.

- Tracing is a process which allows a claimant to recover his property or its equivalent from the defendant. Tracing exists both at common law and in equity.
- At common law tracing does not exist where funds have become mixed with other funds.
- Tracing in equity exists where the trustee or fiduciary mixes trust moneys with his own. In these circumstances:
  - the beneficiary is entitled to a charge on the amalgam of the fund;
  - any withdrawals by the trustee or fiduciary for his own purposes is treated as a withdrawal of his own moneys;
  - but where the trustees withdraw funds from the mixed fund and purchase identifiable assets with the fund and the balance in the account has been dissipated, the right to trace may be extended to those assets.
- Limitations on the right to trace in equity include:
  - tracing into a bank account is subject to the 'lowest intermediate balance' in that account;
  - the rule in *Clayton's case* (1816). Where the trustee mixes two trust funds into a single account and withdraws funds, the order of withdrawals is 'first in first out';
  - however, where the rule in *Clayton* is impractical, or may cause injustice or is contrary to the intention of the claimants, the court may refuse to apply it and treat the claimants on a *pari passu* basis;
  - in exceptional circumstances, the court may permit backward tracing in respect of an asset where there is a transactional link between the depletion of the trust funds and the acquisition of the asset;
  - rights acquired by a *bona fide* transferee of the legal estate for value without notice are unaffected;
  - the defence of *bona fide* change of position;
  - the requirement of a fiduciary relationship in the history of the transaction;
  - where the property is no longer identifiable.
- Subrogation is an equitable remedy that substitutes one claimant for another so as to enable the claimant to acquire the rights of a third party in order to sue the defendant.

SAMPLE ESSAY QUESTION

Consider the following essay question:

Outline the advantages and limitations of a proprietary claim in equity.

Answer plan

> Consider when a tracing claim will subsist in equity.

> Explain the meaning of the expression 'proprietary claim'.
>
> Distinguish between 'following' and 'tracing'.

State the advantages of a tracing claim over a personal claim:

- a tracing claim is not dependent on the solvency of the defendant;
- the claimant may be entitled to take advantage of increases in the value of the property;
- interest accrues from the date of the breach of trust on the part of the trustee or fiduciary;
- no limitation periods are applicable in respect of a right to recover property from a trustee;
- consider the test laid down in *Re Hallett* (1880);
- identify the distinction between *Re Hallett* and *Re Oatway* (1903);
- would an equitable charge include increases in the value of assets? See *Re Tilley* (1967); *Foskett v McKeown* (2001)?;
- consider the lowest intermediate balance when tracing in to a bank account, see *Roscoe v Winder* (1915); *Moriarty v Atkinson* (2009); *Bishopsgate v Homan* (1994);
- the effect of the deliberate earmarking of funds repaid in to a bank acccount in order to repair a breach of trust, see *Robertson v Morrice* (1845);
- tracing in to a bank account containing the funds of two innocent parties, see *Clayton's case* (1816);
- distinguishing the rule in Clayton where manifest injustice may result or where the mixing does not accord with the intention of the claimants, see *Barlow Clowes v Vaughan* (1992); *Charity Commission for England and Wales v Framjee* (2014);
- backward tracing may be permitted in exceptional circumstances where the claimant may establish a transactional link between the asset and the depletion of the funds and the account remains in credit, *Fed. Republic of Brazil v Durant* (2015).

State the limitations that subsist in respect of tracing in equity:

- tracing is not available against a *bona fide* transferee of the legal estate for value without notice;
- in appropriate cases a defendant is entitled to plead the defence of *bona fide* change of position;
- tracing in equity is only available where a fiduciary relationship subsisted in respect of the history of the transaction;
- tracing will only subsist in respect of identifiable property;
- the right to trace is subject to the lowest intermediate balance in respect of mixed funds in a bank account.

CONCLUSION

Further reading

Beatson, J and Andrews, N, 'Common law tracing: springboard or swansong?' (1997) LQR 21.

Birks, P, 'Proprietary restitution: an intelligible approach' (1995) 9 Tru LI 43.

Birks, P, 'Tracing, subrogation and change of position' (1996) 9 Tru LI 124.

Capper, D, 'Compensation for breach of trust' (1997) 61 Conv 14.

Chambers, R, 'Tracing, trusts and liens' (1997) 11 Tru LI 86.

Clark, R and Taylor, A, 'Bankers trust orders: tracing misappropriated funds' (2009) 4 JIBFL 224.

Conaglen, M, 'Difficulties with tracing backward' (2011) 127 LQR 432.

Davies, P, 'Section 61 of the Trustee Act 1925: Deus Ex Machina? (2015) Conv 379.

Elliott, S, 'Rethinking interest on withheld and misapplied trust money' (2001) 65 Conv 313.

Elliott, S, 'Remoteness criteria in equity' (2002) 65 MLR 588.

Grantham, R and Rickett, C, 'Tracing and property rights: the categorical truth' (2000) MLR 905.

Halliwell, M, 'Restitutionary claims: a change of position defence?' (1992) Conv 124.

Hayton, D, 'Rights of creditors against trustees and trust funds' (1997) 11 Tru LI 58.

McBride, N, 'Trustees' exemption clauses' (1998) 57 CLJ 33.

Maudsley, R, 'Proprietary remedies for the recovery of money' (1959) 75 LQR 234.

Millett, P, 'Tracing and the proceeds of fraud' (1991) 107 LQR 71.

Oliver, P, 'The extent of equitable tracing' (1995) 9 Tru LI 78.

Pavlowski, M, 'The demise of the rule in *Clayton's Case*' (2003) Conv 339.

Rickett, C, 'Equitable compensation: the giant stirs' (1996) 112 LQR 2.

Scanlan, G and Prime, T, 'Limitation periods for breach of trust or fiduciary claims with reference to directors' duties' (2009) 5 JIBFL 256.

Smith, L, 'Tracing into payment of a debt' (1995) CLJ 290.

Stevens, J, 'Vindicating the proprietary nature of tracing' (2001) Conv 94.

17

Equitable remedies of injunctions and specific performance

AIMS AND OBJECTIVES

By the end of this chapter you should be able to:

- understand the original policy that led to the introduction of the various equitable remedies
- appreciate a number of features which underlie the granting of equitable remedies
- identify the prerequisites for the granting of an injunction and the various types of injunctions that exist
- to understand when an order for specific performance may be granted
- appreciate the existence of other equitable remedies such as rectification, rescission and account

17.1 Introduction

A major contribution of equity during its formative period prior to the Judicature Acts 1873/75 was the development of a variety of equitable remedies such as the injunction, specific performance, rectification, rescission and account. This was known as the concurrent jurisdiction of equity that gave effect to recognised legal or equitable rights by creating new remedies. Before examining these individual remedies it is worth identifying a number of features of equitable remedies in general.

The only common law remedy that may be claimed as of right is damages. All other remedies are equitable and are granted at the discretion of the court. This does not mean that the availability of equitable remedies is subject to the 'whim and fancy' of the court. Instead, the discretionary nature of the award is tantamount to the court taking into account all relevant matters that lean towards the justice or injustice of granting the remedy. In short, the court takes a holistic view of the circumstances before deciding whether or not to grant the remedy. Factors that are relevant to the court before deciding whether to grant an equitable remedy include whether the remedy at common law is inadequate, whether the conduct of the claimant has been inequitable, whether the availability of the remedy sought may cause undue hardship to the defendant, whether there has been considerable delay in bringing the claim, whether the imposition of the remedy may cause the defendant to suffer undue hardship. This requires the judge to conduct a balancing exercise. On the one hand the judge will weigh up the inconvenience or detriment that will be suffered by the claimant if he were left without an equitable remedy and determine whether this outweighs the hardship that may be suffered by the defendant. The effect is that the exercise of the discretion by the courts, in the context of equitable remedies, has been reduced to a structured set of principles in an effort to achieve justice for all the parties concerned. In *Haywood v Cope* (1858) 25 Beav 140, Romilly MR expressed the approach in the following manner:

JUDGMENT

'[T]he rule which is adopted in this and the other Courts, which is, that the discretion of the Court must be exercised according to fixed and settled rules; you cannot exercise a discretion by merely considering what, as between the parties, would be fair to be done; what one person may consider to be fair, another person may consider very unfair; you must have some settled rule and principle upon which to determine how that discretion is to be exercised.'

17.2 Injunctions

An injunction is an order of the court directing a party to the proceedings to do or refrain from doing a specified act. There are several different types of injunctions. An injunction may be 'prohibitory', i.e. forbidding the performance of a particular act; or 'mandatory', i.e. ordering the defendant to do a particular act. Injunctions could also be classified as 'perpetual', i.e. following the final determination of the rights of the parties or, until recently, as 'interlocutory' (now referred to as 'interim'), i.e. pending the determination of rights at the trial. In addition, a *'quia timet'* (literally, 'because he fears') injunction could be obtained where the claimant fears that damage may occur in the future.

Courts of equity have had the power to grant injunctions for a considerable period of time. Injunctions, like all equitable remedies, are discretionary, but the court will exercise its discretion according to well-established equitable principles. Originally, injunctions were unavailable in the common law courts but s 79 of the Common Law Procedure Act 1854 gave such courts the power to issue an injunction instead of awarding damages. Likewise, the Chancery Procedure Amendment Act 1858, known as Lord Cairns' Act, gave the courts of equity the power to award damages instead of granting an injunction. This power, entitling a court of equity to award damages, does not mean that the court will be more reluctant to issue an injunction when the circumstances warrant such a remedy.

Since the Judicature Acts 1873/75 both legal and equitable remedies have been available in the same court, but it seems that the template governing the principles that are applicable to injunctions remains the same. The jurisdiction today is laid down in s 37(1) of the Senior Courts Act 1981 (previously enacted as s 37(1) of the Supreme Courts Act 1981) which provides that: 'The High Court may by order (whether interlocutory or final) grant an injunction … in all cases in which it appears to the court to be just and convenient to do so.'

The power of the County Court to issue injunctions is now contained in the County Courts Act 1984 (as amended by the Courts and Legal Services Act 1990) and, subject to exceptions, its jurisdiction is similar to the High Court.

17.3 Underlying principles

In general, the court will take similar principles into account when considering applications for each type of injunction. These principles are:

▪ The claimant is required to prove the infringement or potential infringement (in the case of a *quia timet* injunction) of a right which is recognised either in equity or at common law as a precondition for the grant of an injunction.

CASE EXAMPLE

Day v Brownrigg [1878] 10 Ch D 294, (CA)

The claimants sought an injunction to prevent the defendant from naming his house, 'Ashford Lodge', a name used by the claimant for 60 years. The claimants alleged that the defendant's conduct caused them a great inconvenience and annoyance, and had materially diminished the value of their property. The court decided that the act of the defendant was not a violation of any legal right of the claimant and therefore the claim was dismissed.

JUDGMENT

'This Court can only interfere where there is an invasion of a legal or equitable right. No such legal or equitable right exists … I think it right to add that the power given to the Court by sect. 25, sub-sect. 8, of the *Judicature Act*, 1873, to grant an injunction in all cases in which it shall appear to the Court to be "just or convenient" to do so, does not in the least alter the principles on which the Court should act.'

James L

▪ The injunction will not be granted where damages will provide an appropriate remedy. For instance, where the damage had already occurred to the claimant and could be rectified by a monetary payment and was not likely to be repeated, an injunction may not be granted. But once the claimant has shown that the defendant has infringed his (claimant's) rights and intends to continue with such course of conduct, he will *prima facie* be entitled to an injunction.

CASE EXAMPLE

Pride of Derby and Derbyshire Angling Association v British Celanese [1953] Ch 149

An injunction was granted on behalf of the claimants in order to restrain the defendants from causing or permitting the pollution of the rivers Trent and Derwent, as a consequence of their business activities.

JUDGMENT

'[T]he question arises whether there should be any injunction in the circumstances or whether the plaintiffs, should content themselves with some less relief? Prima facie, a plaintiff, whose rights have been invaded … is entitled to relief from this court by way of injunction.'

Harman J

A similar approach was taken in *Shelfer v City of London Electric Lighting Co* [1895] 1 Ch 287. The courts are very reluctant in allowing a wealthy defendant to purchase from the claimant the right to continue to commit a wrong. On the other hand, the court may exercise its discretion not to grant an injunction but instead to award damages:

1. Where the damage to the claimant is small, and

2. The claimant's loss could be estimated in monetary terms, and

3. The damages will provide adequate compensation, and

4. The grant of an injunction may be unnecessarily oppressive on the defendant. This requires the court to balance the relative interests of the parties.

These guiding principles have been consistently applied by the courts over the years, save for occasions where there have been exceptional circumstances.

CASE EXAMPLE

Shelfer v City of London Electric Lighting Co [1895] 1 Ch 287

The operations of the defendant electricity company caused structural damage to a house and nuisance to its occupier. The owner and occupier sought relief by way of injunction. The trial judge refused injunctive relief and awarded damages. His decision was reversed by the Court of Appeal, which roundly rejected the view that wrongs should be permitted to continue simply because the wrongdoer was able and willing to pay damages. The court gave guidance:

JUDGMENT

'Many judges have stated, and I emphatically agree with them, that a person by committing a wrongful act (whether it be a public company for public purposes or a private individual) is not thereby entitled to ask the Court to sanction his doing so by purchasing his neighbour's rights, by assessing damages in that behalf, leaving his neighbour with the nuisance, or his lights dimmed, as the case may be. In such cases the well-known rule is not to accede to the application, but to grant the injunction sought, for the plaintiff's legal right has been invaded, and he is *prima facie* entitled to an injunction.'

Smith LJ

The court followed up with guidelines as to the circumstances in which damages may be awarded in lieu of an injunction. At the same time he emphasised that the discretionary nature of this limitation varies with the facts of each case:

JUDGMENT

'There are, however, cases in which this rule may be relaxed, and in which damages may be awarded in substitution for an injunction as authorized by this section. In any instance in which a case for an injunction has been made out, if the plaintiff by his acts or laches has disentitled himself to an injunction the Court may award damages in its place. So again, whether the case be for a mandatory injunction or to restrain a continuing nuisance, the appropriate remedy may be damages in lieu of an injunction, assuming a case for an injunction to be made out. In my opinion, it may be stated as a good working rule that – (1) If the injury to the plaintiff's legal rights is small, (2) and is one which is capable of being estimated in money, (3) and is one which can be adequately compensated by a small money payment, (4) and the case is one in which it would be oppressive to the defendant to grant an injunction: – then damages in substitution for an injunction may be given. There may also be cases in which, though the four above-mentioned requirements exist, the defendant by his conduct, as, for instance, hurrying up his buildings so as if possible to avoid an injunction, or otherwise acting with reckless disregard to the plaintiff's rights, has disentitled himself from asking that damages may be assessed in substitution for an injunction. In the present case it appears to me that the injury to the Plaintiff is certainly not small, nor is it in my judgment capable of being estimated in money, or of being adequately compensated by a small money payment.'

Smith LJ

In *Kennaway v Thompson* [1980] 3 WLR 361, the claimant was granted an injunction to restrain a motorboat racing club from committing a nuisance by excessive noise, where the first three principles in *Shelfer* had not been met.

In the seminal decision in *Regan v Paul Properties Ltd* (2006), the Court of Appeal took the opportunity to review the law and clarified the guidelines as to when damages may be awarded by the courts in lieu of an injunction. These guidelines include:

(i) *prima facie*, a claimant is entitled to an injunction against a defendant who commits a wrongful act;

(ii) the defendant is not entitled to request that the courts 'ratify' his wrongful actions by the payment of damages to the claimant;

(iii) damages in lieu of an injunction may be awarded at the discretion of the Court, but only in exceptional circumstances particularly when:

- the injury is small;
- it can be adequately compensated by a small money payment;
- it would be oppressive on the defendant if the injunction is granted to the claimant;
- the court has found that the claimant was only motivated by money;
- the claimant's conduct rendered it unjust to grant more than financial relief;
- other circumstances may justify the refusal of an injunction.

On the assumption that the claimant's right to light is not insubstantial and the enjoyment of his property is substantially reduced in value, an injunction ought to be granted. The defendant bears the burden of establishing that damages in lieu of an injunction is, on balance, a feasible alternative.

CASE EXAMPLE

Regan v Paul Property Ltd [2006] EWCA Civ 1391 (Court of Appeal)

The defendants proposed to develop a 16-unit property with a penthouse opposite the claimant's property. The claimant objected to the development on the ground that the penthouse will have the effect of infringing his right to light. The defendants took advice from their surveyor who assured them that the loss of light was likely to be insubstantial. The defendants went ahead with the development without modification. On the claimant applying to the court for an injunction, the Court of Appeal, reversing the decision of the trial judge, granted the order. The claimant's loss of light was not capable of being compensated by the defendants. The defendants had taken a risk that their advice was not incorrect. Furthermore, although an injunction would have a serious effect on the defendants, that was not determinative of the issue of oppressiveness and the choice of remedy. It was necessary to consider all the circumstances of the case.

JUDGMENT

'The defendants must take the natural consequences of their acts in interfering with the right to light. What matters is not so much the amount of light that is taken as the amount of light that is left as a result of the infringement. The consequence of the obstruction to the light in the middle of the living room was that Mr Regan would suffer a substantial interference with the enjoyment of natural light in his living room.

Whether an injunction would be oppressive to the defendants, would obviously be serious in its effect on cutting back the defendants' plans for unit 16 which would reduce the sale price, create extra costs in cutting back unit 16 and possibly cause planning and building regulation difficulties. In total the defendants' losses would be substantial and would probably exceed Mr Regan's losses, but those things on their own are not determinative of the issue of oppressiveness and of the choice of remedy. It is necessary to consider all the surrounding circumstances of the dispute and the conduct of the parties.'

Mummery LJ

More recently the Supreme Court in *Lawrence v Fen Tigers Ltd and Others* [2014] 3 WLR 555, considered the principles governing the award of damages in substitution for an injunction. The court formulated the view that the *Shelfer* principles ought not be construed as a fetter to the discretionary power of the judge in awarding damages as opposed to an injunction. In this case, the claimant, Mrs Lawrence, brought a claim against the defendants in noise nuisance created at a motor sports stadium. The court decided *inter alia* that the claimant was entitled to an injunction for a limited period of time, subject to the defendants applying for a modification of the remedy and an award of damages in lieu of the injunction. Further, in exercising its discretion to award damages in lieu of an injunction, the court is required to take into account the public interest and if the defendants' activities are subject to planning permission, that may be strong evidence against the imposition of an injunction. The court may also take into account other factors related to the public interest such as the effect of any injunction on the viability of the defendants' business and on the public's enjoyment of the activities carried on by that business.

JUDGMENT

'Where a claimant has established that the defendant's activities constitute a nuisance, prima facie the remedy to which she is entitled (in addition to damages for past nuisance) is an injunction to restrain the defendant from committing such nuisance in the future.

It seems to me that (i) an almost mechanical application of A L Smith LJ's four tests [in *Shelfer*], and (ii) an approach which involves damages being awarded only in "very exceptional circumstances", are each simply wrong in principle, and give rise to a serious risk of going wrong in practice. (Quite apart from this, exceptionality may be a questionable guide in any event.) The court's power to award damages in lieu of an injunction involves a classic exercise of discretion, which should not, as a matter of principle, be fettered, particularly in the very constrained way in which the Court of Appeal has suggested in *Regan* (2006). And, as a matter of practical fairness, each case is likely to be so fact-sensitive that any firm guidance is likely to do more harm than good. I would accept that the prima facie position is that an injunction should be granted, so the legal burden is on the defendant to show why it should not.

Where does that leave A L Smith LJ's four tests? While the application of any such series of tests cannot be mechanical, I would adopt a modified version of the view expressed by Romer LJ in *Fishenden* (1935) 153 LT 128. First, the application of the four tests must not be such as "to be a fetter on the exercise of the court's discretion". Secondly, it would, in the absence of additional relevant circumstances pointing the other way, normally be right to refuse an injunction if those four tests were satisfied. Thirdly, the fact that those tests are not all satisfied does not mean that an injunction should be granted.'

Lord Neuberger PSC

An injunction will not be granted where the injury to the claimant's rights is trivial and an alternative remedy, such as a declaration, is available.

CASE EXAMPLE

Llandudno UDC v Woods [1899] 2 Ch 705

The claimants sought an injunction to restrain the defendant from preaching on a beach at Llandudno and a declaration that he was a trespasser. The court decided that the complaint was 'too trivial' to justify the grant of an injunction but the claimants were entitled to a declaration to the effect that the defendant was a trespasser.

JUDGMENT

'It is no part of the duty of the council, as lessees from the Crown for an unexpired term of two years, to prevent a harmless user of the shore. There are persons who derive satisfaction from listening to the addresses of the defendant, and the defendant derives satisfaction from delivering these addresses. I cannot conceive why they should be deprived of this innocent pleasure. Nobody is obliged to listen. Nobody is molested … I cannot refuse to make a declaration that the defendant is not entitled, without the consent of the plaintiffs, to hold meetings or deliver addresses, lectures, or sermons on any part of the foreshore in lease from the Crown. But I decline to go further. I decline to grant an injunction. That is a formidable legal weapon which ought to be reserved for less trivial occasions.'

Cozens-Hardy J

The court will take into account the general equitable principles such as hardship to the parties, inordinate delay on the part of the claimant in initiating proceedings and whether the claimant comes to court 'with clean hands'. The relative importance of these factors may vary depending on the type of injunction sought by the claimant. The oppressive nature of the order on the defendant is required to be judged on the date of the application for the grant.

CASE EXAMPLE

Jaggard v Sawyer [1995] 1 WLR 269

The claimant sought an injunction to prevent the defendants trespassing over his property in breach of a restrictive covenant that prohibited building on the plot. The claimant delayed by about two years in seeking an injunction to prevent the defendants from building a house on the plot. At this time the building was at an advanced stage. The court refused the injunction on the ground that the injunction would have been unduly oppressive on the defendants. In reaching that conclusion, the court took into account the conduct of the claimant and defendants, the nature of the trespass and the relevant land. The Court of Appeal affirmed the trial judge's ruling that the claimant's failure to seek interlocutory relief at an early stage and the fact that the restrictive covenants were not absolute or perpetually inviolable, led to the conclusion that the grant of an injunction would be oppressive, and to award the claimant damages in lieu of an injunction.

JUDGMENT

'In considering whether the grant of an injunction would be oppressive to the defendant, all the circumstances of the case have to be considered. At one extreme, the defendant may have acted openly and in good faith and in ignorance of the plaintiff's rights, and thereby inadvertently placed himself in a position where the grant of an injunction would either force him to yield to the plaintiff's extortionate demands or expose him to substantial loss. At the other extreme, the defendant may have acted with his eyes open and in full knowledge that he was invading the plaintiff's rights, and hurried on his work in the hope that by presenting the court with a fait accompli he could compel the plaintiff to accept monetary compensation. Most cases, like the present, fall somewhere in between.

In the present case, the defendants acted openly and in good faith and in the not unreasonable belief that they were entitled to make use of Ashleigh Avenue for access to the house that they were building. At the same time, they had been warned by the plaintiff and her solicitors that Ashleigh Avenue was a private road, that they were not entitled to use it for access to the new house and that it would be a breach of covenant for them to use the garden of No 5 to gain access to No 5A. They went ahead, not with their eyes open, but at their own risk. On the other hand, the plaintiff did not seek interlocutory relief at a time when she would almost certainly have obtained it. She should not be criticised for that, but it follows that she also took a risk, viz that by the time her case came for trial the court would be presented with a fait accompli. The case was a difficult one, but in an exemplary judgment the judge took into account all the relevant considerations, both those which told in favour of granting an injunction and those which told against, and in the exercise of his discretion he decided to refuse it. In my judgment his conclusion cannot be faulted.'

Millett LJ

KEY FACTS

Injunctions – general principles

Infringement of a legal or equitable right	Day v Brownrigg (1878)
Damages inadequate Review of the *Shelfer* principles. The claimant is *prima facie* entitled to an injunction where his rights of enjoyment of property have been substantially depleted. The defendant bears the burden of showing that damages in lieu of an injunction is a feasible solution The Supreme Court declared that the *Shelfer* principles ought not to fetter the discretionary power of the court to award damages in lieu of an injunction	*Pride of Derby and Derbyshire Angling Association v British Celanese* (1953); *Shelfer v City of London Electric Lighting Co* (1895) *Regan v Paul* (2006) *Lawrence v Fen Tigers Ltd* (2014)
Trivial injury to the claimant and alternative remedy available	*Llandudno UDC v Woods* (1899)
Excessive hardship to the defendant if injunction granted	*Jaggard v Sawyer* (1995)

17.4 Types of injunctions

As indicated earlier, there are various types of injunctions – prohibitory, mandatory, *quia timet*, interim, freezing and search orders. Another classification of injunctions is into perpetual or interim. This section will outline the various types of injunction.

17.4.1 Perpetual injunctions

A perpetual or final injunction is one that is granted at the trial of the claim or other hearing in which final judgment is given. Whereas an interim injunction is one made prior to the trial and which is intended to last only until the trial at the latest. A perpetual injunction may be prohibitory, mandatory or *quia timet*.

17.4.2 Prohibitory injunctions

A prohibitory injunction is generally said to be easier to obtain than a mandatory one and is available to restrain the defendant from acting in a particular way, as in *Shelfer*'s case and *Pride of Derby v British Celanese*, see above.

Such an injunction would also be available to restrain the breach of a negative term of a contract. In such a case it has been said that the court must grant the injunction once it is satisfied that there has been a breach of the term. In *Doherty v Allman*, Lord Cairns explained that in such a case it was not necessary to consider factors like the balance of convenience as the parties had themselves freely contracted not to do a particular thing. The court, nonetheless, has a discretion to decide whether the injunction ought to be granted. In exercising that discretion the court will consider, among other things, whether the performance of the act sought to be restrained will produce an injury to the party seeking the injunction; whether that injury can be remedied or atoned for, and, if capable of being atoned for by damages, whether those damages must be sought in successive suits, or could be obtained once for all.

CASE EXAMPLE

Doherty v Allman [1878] 3 App Cas 709

Two leases of land were granted subject to positive covenants to maintain the premises in good order, but without a reservation of a power of re-entry for breaches of the covenants. The defendants were proposing to act in breach of the covenant and the claimants sought an injunction. The court refused the application in the exercise of its discretion and left the claimant to pursue his claim for damages.

JUDGMENT

'The Court of Equity ... will consider for example whether the injury which it is asked to restrain is an injury which if done cannot be remedied. It will consider whether, if done, it can or cannot be sufficiently atoned for by the payment of a sum of money in damages. It will ask also this question, – suppose the act to be done, would the right to damages for it be decided exhaustively, once and for all, by one action, or would there necessarily be a repetition of actions for the purpose of recovering damages from time to time? Those are matters which a Court of Equity would well look to, and on the other hand a Court of Equity would look to this: If we interfere and say, in aid of this affirmative covenant, that something shall not be done which would be a departure from it, no doubt we shall succour and help the Plaintiff who comes for our assistance. But shall we do that? Will the effect of our doing that be to cause possible damage to the Defendant, very much greater than any possible advantage we can give to the Plaintiff? Now, in a case of that kind, where there is an amount of discretion which the Court must exercise, those are all considerations which the Court will carefully entertain before it decides how it will exercise its discretion.'

Lord Cairns LC

The Attorney General may apply for a prohibitory injunction to restrain the continued commission of a criminal offence if he considers that such a course of action will be in the public interest. In *Gouriet v Union of Post Office Workers* [1977] 3 WLR 300, the House of Lords stressed that this procedure is restricted to the Attorney General in order to enforce public rights and is not available to individuals.

17.4.3 Mandatory injunctions

A mandatory injunction is one which orders the defendant to perform a specific act, such as taking down a hoarding that unlawfully infringes the claimant's rights. There is a striking similarity between this injunction and an order for specific performance (see later). However, there are certain contracts of which specific performance will not be granted and the claimant is usually left to his common law right of damages. Refusing an injunction in respect of a contract expressed in positive terms in *Bower v Bantam Investments Ltd* [1972] 1 WLR 1120, Goff J said:

JUDGMENT

'[T]o found a claim for relief by way of injunction it is necessary to point to something specific which a defendant has by implication agreed not to do. The mere fact that his conduct or proposed conduct is inconsistent with his obligations under the contract is not sufficient.'

Goff J

In recent times even the general principle seems to have been restricted. Mandatory injunctions have been granted to enforce contracts for the supply of goods, even though the contracts were not within the jurisdiction to grant specific performance, but where the failure to supply the claimants with petrol would have put them out of business, e.g. *Sky Petroleum Ltd v VIP Petroleum Ltd* [1974] 1 WLR 576, see later.

Moreover, the defendant must know exactly what it is that he has to do as disobedience to an injunction is a contempt of court.

The question of hardship to the defendant is of particular importance and public interest factors may be relevant in determining this question.

CASE EXAMPLE

Wrotham Park Estates Ltd v Parkside Homes Ltd [1974] 3 All ER 321

The claimants applied to the court for a mandatory injunction requiring the defendants to demolish houses which had been built in breach of a restrictive covenant. The grant of an injunction is always discretionary and in this case the court took the view that it would have been 'an unpardonable waste of much needed houses' to order their demolition. A just substitute for mandatory injunctions would be damages, i.e. a sum of money as might reasonably have been demanded by the claimants from defendants as a quid pro quo for relaxing the covenants.

JUDGMENT

'It is no answer to a claim for a mandatory injunction that the plaintiffs, having issued proceedings, deliberately held their hand and did not seek the assistance of the court for the purpose of preserving the status quo. On the other hand, it is, in my view, equally true that a plaintiff is not entitled 'as of course' to have everything pulled down that was built after the issue of the writ. The erection of the houses, whether one likes it or not, is a fait accompli and the houses are now the homes of people. I accept that this particular fait accompli is reversible and could be undone. But I cannot close my eyes to the fact that the houses now exist. It would, in my opinion, be an unpardonable waste of much needed houses to direct that they now be pulled down and I have never had a moment's doubt during the hearing of this case that such an order ought to be refused. No damage of a financial nature has been done to the plaintiffs by the breach of the layout stipulation. The plaintiffs' use of the Wrotham Park estate has not been and will not be impeded. It is totally unnecessary to demolish the houses in order to preserve the integrity of the restrictive covenants imposed ... Without hesitation I decline to grant a mandatory injunction.'

Brightman J

However, in *Charrington v Simons Co Ltd* [1971] 1 WLR 598, the Court of Appeal took a different view and granted a mandatory injunction requiring the defendant company to remedy its breach of a covenant contained in a deed of conveyance made between the parties where there had been a plain breach of covenant which resulted in interference with the claimant's business. The trial judge suspended the injunction for up to three years to enable the defendant to carry out works on the claimant's land, with a strong indication that if the claimant did not consent to this the injunction would be discharged. On appeal the court modified the order and deleted the suspension contained in the order.

JUDGMENT

'In our judgment the learned judge, in adopting the course which he did, travelled beyond the bounds within which discretion may be judicially exercised; for in effect he sought to force on a reluctant plaintiff something very like a settlement involving operations by the defendant company on the plaintiff's land which must lead to greatly increased harm to his business, as a condition or term of his obtaining a mandatory injunction should the works not prove a satisfactory solution. If the learned judge, in his judgment, had said to the plaintiff that he would not grant the injunction unless the plaintiff consented to submit to these works, and the plaintiff refused so to give consent, it would not in our judgment have been a proper ground on which to withhold the injunction to which the plaintiff was otherwise entitled. The course taken by the judge was, it seems to us, no different in substance. We accordingly allow the appeal on this point, with the result, we think, that so much of the order as suspends the operation of the injunction and is dependent on such suspension should be deleted.'

Russell LJ

17.4.4 *Quia timet* injunctions

This expression literally means 'because he fears'. A *quia timet* injunction is available to the claimant *before* the occurrence of an apprehended injury or damage to person or property, e.g. where the defendant threatened to demolish a building and the claimant alleged a right of support. To some extent, this type of injunction conflicted with the general principle that the claimant must show injury to a recognised right. Hence, a *quia timet* injunction requires strong evidence in support. Lord Upjohn in *Redland Bricks v Morris* [1970] AC 652, explained the nature of a *quia timet* injunction thus:

JUDGMENT

'My Lords, quia timet actions are broadly applicable to two types of cases: first, where the defendant has as yet done no hurt to the plaintiff but is threatening and intending (so the plaintiff alleges) to do works which will render irreparable harm to him or his property if carried to completion. Your Lordships are not concerned with that and those cases are normally, though not exclusively, concerned with negative injunctions. Secondly, the type of case where the plaintiff has been fully recompensed both at law and in equity for the damage he has suffered but where he alleges that the earlier actions of the defendant may lead to future causes of action.'

Lord Upjohn

CASE EXAMPLE

Redland Bricks v Morris [1970] AC 652

The claimants carried on the business of market gardeners and the defendant was involved in quarrying activities on adjoining land. Following land subsidence as a result of excavations carried out by the defendant the claimants applied for an injunction. The purpose of the injunction was to order the defendant to restore support to the claimants' market garden. The House of Lords refused the injunction on the grounds that it was not clear precisely what action the defendant was expected to take, the defendant had not behaved unreasonably, it was not clear that further damage would have occurred and the costs of restoring support to the building was out of all proportion to the value of the claimant's land.

It is particularly difficult to obtain a mandatory *quia timet* injunction. In *Redland Bricks v Morris*, Lord Upjohn stated that such injunctions would normally only be granted:

- where the claimant showed a strong possibility of damage occurring;
- where the remedy of damages would not be appropriate if such damage did occur;
- where the cost to the defendant was not disproportionate (as the claimant would retain his normal remedies if damage did occur).

17.4.5 Interim injunctions

An interim injunction is one made after the commencement of the proceedings but prior to the final determination of the court. As there is often some delay between the issue of the summons and the trial of the action, a claimant may apply for an interim injunction in order to ensure that the defendant does not continue in his injurious conduct during the period before the trial. Normally the claimant will be required to give an undertaking in damages, i.e. the claimant will undertake to reimburse the defendant for any losses which he may have suffered consequent upon the granting of the injunction if it is decided at the trial that he (defendant) did not act unlawfully.

The court's jurisdiction to grant an interim injunction is now governed by s 37 of the Senior Courts Act 1981 (originally enacted as the Supreme Court Act 1981). The claim to an interim injunction under s 37 is required to be incidental to and dependent upon the enforcement of a substantive right in the main proceedings. In *Newport Association Football Club Ltd v Football Association of Wales Ltd* [1995] 2 All ER 87, the court held that it had jurisdiction to grant an interim injunction even where the cause of action was a claim for a declaration.

The claimant applies for the interim injunction by filing an application notice. This must state the order sought, the date, time and place of the hearing. The application is required to be accompanied by evidence in support. This can be in the form of witness statements, statements of the case or application, verified by a statement of truth. These documents must be served on the defendant three days before the court hears the application. In the case of a freezing injunction or search order, there must be affidavit evidence. In the event of extremely urgent applications the application may be dealt with by telephone.

The principles applicable to the granting of interim injunctions have been the source of much judicial dispute. At one time the court would refuse to grant an interim injunction unless the claimant could show a strong probability of success at the trial of the action. This was the approach taken by the House of Lords in *Stratford v Lindley* [1965] AC 269. However, in *Hubbard v Vosper* [1972] 2 QB 84, Lord Denning stated that the remedy of an injunction should remain flexible and that the court should take into account all the circumstances of the case.

The principles governing the granting of interim injunctions were reviewed and restated by the House of Lords in *American Cyanamid Co v Ethicon Ltd* [1975] 2 WLR 316.

CASE EXAMPLE

American Cyanamid Co v Ethicon Ltd [1975] 2 WLR 316

The claimants, an American company, owned a patent covering certain sterile absorbable surgical sutures. The defendants, also an American company, which traded mainly in the United States, were about to launch on the British market a suture which the claimants alleged infringed their patent. The claimants applied for an interim injunction (originally called an interlocutory injunction) to restrain the defendants' conduct. The injunction was granted by the judge at first instance with the usual undertaking in damages by the claimants. The Court of Appeal reversed his decision on the ground that no *prima facie* case of infringement had been made out.

The House of Lords allowed the claimants' appeal on the following grounds:

1. That in all cases, including patent cases, the court must determine the matter on a balance of convenience, there being no rule that it could not do so unless first satisfied that, if the case went to trial on no other evidence than that available at the hearing of the application, the claimant would be entitled to a permanent injunction in the terms of the interlocutory injunction sought; where there was a doubt as to the parties' respective remedies in damages being adequate to compensate them for loss occasioned by any restraint imposed on them, it would be prudent to preserve the status quo.
2. That there was no ground for interfering with the judge's assessment of the balance of convenience or his exercise of discretion and the injunction should be granted accordingly.

In this case, Lord Diplock took the opportunity to modify the principles on which an interim injunction may be granted. The relevant principles, and the order in which they should be considered, are as follows:

- Is there a serious question to be tried? This means that the claim must not be frivolous or vexatious.

  If the answer is no, then the injunction should be refused.

  If the answer is yes, then the next question should be considered.
- Which way does the balance of convenience lie?
- Are damages an adequate remedy for the claimant and is the defendant able to pay such sum?

  If the answer is yes, then the injunction should be refused.

  If the answer is no, then the next question should be considered.
- Does the undertaking as to damages provided by the claimant constitute adequate protection for the defendant and will the claimant be able to honour it?

  If the answer is yes, then the injunction will be granted.

  If the answer is no, then the next question should be considered.

- The maintenance of the status quo.

  Where the other factors are evenly balanced, the court will prefer to maintain the status quo. The status quo is that state of affairs that existed before the last change of circumstances occurred. Normally this will work in the claimant's favour but it is not by itself conclusive. Where it is not, the court will go on to consider:

- Other factors.

  Where the court, having considered the circumstances as stated above and in that order, is still unable to arrive at a decision, it can then go on to consider other factors, including social and economic factors. In *American Cyanamid* the court took into account the fact that no jobs would be lost and no factories would be closed if the injunction was granted, see *Hubbard v Pitt* [1976] QB 142.

- The relative strength of the parties' cases.

  As a last resort, where the court, having considered all of the above, is still unable to arrive at a decision it can take into account the relative strength of the parties' cases.

Lord Diplock did not refer to *Stratford v Lindley* [1965] AC 269 in his judgment, accordingly, it is arguable that the two cases conflict. However, subsequent cases have suggested that the principles set out in *American Cyanamid* are only guidelines and that the point about not considering the relative strength of the parties' cases relate to those cases in which there are difficult issues of fact and law to decide. In *Series 5 Software Ltd v Clarke*, Laddie J suggested that Lord Diplock in *American Cyanamid* did not intend to exclude consideration of the relative strength of the parties' cases in most applications for interim injunctions. He suggested that what was intended was to avoid having to resolve difficult issues of fact or law on an interim application. The consideration of the relative strength of the parties' cases is thus not a matter of last resort but should be avoided in cases involving difficult disputes of fact or law.

CASE EXAMPLE

Series 5 Software Ltd v Clarke [1996] 1 All ER 853

The claimant company sought an interim injunction to restrain use of commercial information and company equipment by ex-employees. The High Court refused the application on the following grounds: the claimant's case, while arguable in the sense that the facts at trial could possibly support the allegations made, was weak in relation to some claims, and in relation to others it was impossible at an interlocutory stage to come to a conclusion as to whether there was substance in the claim or the defence. As far as the balance of convenience was concerned, while it was clear that the injunctions sought could effectively deprive the defendants of their means of earning a living, the claimant's assertion of substantial and immediate damage was unsubstantiated. The court also added that it was not precluded from considering the strength of each party's case when deciding whether to grant an application for interlocutory relief, but should rarely attempt to resolve difficult issues of fact or law, and any view as to the strength of the parties' cases should be reached only where it was apparent from the affidavit evidence and any exhibited contemporary documents that one party's case was much stronger than the other's.

JUDGMENT

'[I]t appears to me that in deciding whether to grant interlocutory relief, the court should bear the following matters in mind. (1) The grant of an interlocutory injunction is a matter of discretion and depends on all the facts of the case. (2) There are no fixed rules as to when an injunction should or should not be granted. The relief must be kept flexible. (3) Because of the practice adopted on the hearing of applications for interlocutory relief, the court should rarely attempt to resolve complex issues of disputed fact or law. (4) Major factors the court can bear in mind are (a) the extent to which damages are likely to be an adequate remedy for each party and the ability of the other party to pay, (b) the balance of convenience, (c) the maintenance of the status quo, and (d) any clear view the court may reach as to the relative strength of the parties' cases.'

Laddie J

Exceptions to American Cyanamid

American Cyanamid was a commercial case involving breach of copyright. In other types of cases it may be difficult to apply the same principles. Accordingly, the court will take the strength of the parties' case into account in certain exceptional circumstances (rather than apply the guidelines suggested in *American Cyanamid*), for example:

- Where the injunction will finally dispose of the matter. To obtain interim relief in such cases the claimant must show a strong *prima facie* case, or at least more than an arguable case, otherwise the court will permit the defendant's right to a trial.

- Where the defendant has no arguable defence. In such cases the court does not consider the principles in *American Cyanamid*, but it will consider the relative strengths of the parties' cases, see *Patel v WH Smith* [1987] 1 WLR 853.

- Cases involving public as opposed to private rights. Where an interim injunction affects public rights, the court will take into account the public interest when determining the balance of convenience. Hence, the principles in *American Cyanamid* will not be strictly adhered to, see *Lewis v Heffer* [1978] 1 WLR 1061.

- Interim mandatory injunctions. A mandatory injunction is concerned with undoing what has been done. Granting such an injunction might prove to be a waste of time and money if it transpires that the defendant's conduct was justified. Accordingly, the court may be reluctant to grant such interim injunctions. In *Shepherd Homes Ltd v Sandham* [1971] 1 Ch 340, Megarry J refused to grant an interim mandatory injunction where the defendant had erected a fence in breach of a restrictive covenant. He went on to say that the case has to be unusually strong and clear before the mandatory injunction will be granted.

- Where there is a likelihood of a defence (in respect of those acts which are done in contemplation or furtherance of a trade dispute) under s 221 of the Trade Union and Labour Relations (Consolidation) Act 1992.

- Article 10 of the European Convention on Human Rights protects freedom of expression, subject to exceptions. Section 12 of the Human Rights Act 1998 enacts that a restraint on this freedom requires the court to be 'satisfied that the applicant is likely to establish that publication should not be allowed'. This test requires the court to look at the relative strength of the case of the applicant.

Interim injunctions

American Cyanamid guidelines
Serious question to be tried
Balance of convenience in favour of the claimant
Is damages an adequate remedy?
Undertaking in damages adequate
Maintenance of status quo
Other relevant factors
Relative strength of each party's case

17.4.6 Freezing injunctions

In recent years the courts have developed new forms of interim injunctions that can be regarded as formidable weapons in the litigation armoury. One of these is the 'Mareva' injunction, which is now known as a freezing injunction.

CASE EXAMPLE

Mareva Compania Naviera SA v International Bulkcarriers SA [1975] 2 Lloyd's Rep 509

The claimants, Mareva Compania Naviera SA ('the shipowners'), issued a writ on 25 June 1975 claiming against the defendants, International Bulkcarriers SA ('the charterers'), unpaid hire and damages for repudiation of a charterparty. On an *ex parte* application Donaldson J granted an injunction until 17.00 hours on 23 June restraining the charterers from removing or disposing out of the jurisdiction moneys standing to the credit of the charterers' account at a London bank. The shipowners appealed against Donaldson J's refusal to extend the injunction beyond 17.00 hours on 23 June. The Court of Appeal dismissed the appeal and extended the injunction until the date of the judgment at the trial.

The original jurisdiction to grant 'freezing' orders was assumed by the court as part of its inherent jurisdiction, but today this jurisdiction is laid down in s 37 of the Senior Courts Act 1981 (originally named Supreme Court Act).

The criteria to be satisfied include the following:

- that the claimant has a good arguable case;
- that the claimant has satisfied the court that the defendant has control of assets within the jurisdiction and, where an extra territorial order is sought, assets exist outside the jurisdiction;
- that there is a real risk of dissipation or secretion of assets which would render nugatory any judgment which the claimant might obtain;
- that the applicant who seeks a freezing injunction *ex parte* must make full disclosure of all material facts, including any facts that he might reasonably discover;
- that the claimant has given an undertaking in damages;
- the defendant should not be prevented from using his assets for a purpose which does not conflict with the purpose of a freezing injunction;
- the order should not be used to prevent a defendant from living as he has always lived, or from paying legal costs to defend the proceedings;

the order should make reasonable provision for the protection of third parties and should include notice of their right to seek variation of the order.

Worldwide freezing injunctions

The court is entitled to make a freezing order that takes effect outside the jurisdiction of the United Kingdom where it is satisfied that the defendant's English assets are insufficient to satisfy the claim and that the defendant has control of foreign assets and that there is real risk of the disposal of the latter. In addition, the court must be satisfied that the defendant will not be oppressed by the exposure to a multiplicity of proceedings and will be protected against the misuse of any information gained, and that third parties will be protected.

17.4.7 Search orders (*Anton Piller* orders)

This order derives its name from the case *Anton Piller KG v Manufacturing Processes Ltd* [1976] 1 All ER 779. It was designed by the court for cases where there is a serious risk that the defendant may destroy material evidence before the date of the final hearing. It is a form of a mandatory, interim injunction with discoveries and enables the claimant to attend the defendant's premises and inspect and take copies of materials (documents and articles) specified in the order.

CASE EXAMPLE

Anton Piller KG v Manufacturing Processes Ltd [1976] 1 All ER 779

The claimants alleged a breach of confidentiality in that their copyright material for new machines was leaked to the defendants. Before the main hearing they applied *ex parte* for an order for discovery of the defendant's correspondence fearing that it may be destroyed and which was relevant to their claim. The court granted the order. The court laid down the following guidance as to when the order may be made:

- the claimant must have a strong *prima facie* case;
- the claimant must show actual or potential damage of a very serious nature;
- there is clear evidence that the defendant has incriminating documents or things and that there is a real possibility of these documents or things being destroyed before an *inter partes* application could be made;
- the search order is not to be used as a fishing expedition;
- the claimant is required to give an undertaking to the court as to damages at the time of making the application.

The jurisdiction and purpose for making the order was put on a statutory footing by s 7 of the Civil Procedure Act 1997. Thus the power to enter the defendant's premises and obtain discoveries of relevant documents and articles is no longer based on the fiction that the defendant had consented to the entry. The order, by itself, is the basis for entry.

The mode of execution was subject to a number of guidelines laid down in *Universal Thermosensors Ltd v Hibben* [1992] 3 All ER 257. These guidelines have been formalised in the Civil Procedure Rules 25. The applicant is required to follow these guidelines:

- that the order be served and supervised by a solicitor from a different firm from that acting for the claimant;
- that the solicitor supervising the search should be experienced and knowledgeable about the workings of search orders;

- that the solicitor should prepare a written report on the execution of the order;
- that a copy of the report should be served on the defendant and that the report should be presented to the court at an *inter partes* hearing;
- that the orders should be served on weekdays during office hours in order to give the defendants the opportunity to obtain legal advice;
- that the party serving the order should include a woman if it is likely that a woman might be alone at the premises.

Moreover, in *Columbia Picture Industries Inc v Robinson* [1987] Ch 38, the court ruled that the claimant, having obtained the search order, should not act oppressively or abuse its power in the execution of the order. In addition the court stated that the draconian and essentially unfair nature of a search order in its effect on a defendant requires that it be drawn so as to extend no further than the minimum extent necessary to achieve the purpose for which it was granted, namely the preservation of documents or articles which might otherwise be destroyed or concealed; anything beyond that is impossible to justify. Thus, an order that allows the claimant's solicitors to take and retain all relevant documentary material and correspondence cannot be justified. Once the claimant's solicitors have satisfied themselves what material exists and have had an opportunity to take copies thereof, the material ought to be returned to the owner, and should only be retained for a relatively short period for such purpose. It is inappropriate for seized material, the ownership of which is in dispute, such as alleged pirate tapes, to be retained by the claimant's solicitor pending trial. Although the solicitor is an officer of the court, the main role of the solicitor for the claimant is to act for the claimant. As soon as a solicitor for the defendant is on the record, the claimant's solicitor ought to deliver the material to the defendant's solicitor on his undertaking to keep it in safe custody and produce it, if required, in court.

Where these safeguards have been breached by either the claimant or his solicitor, the court may set aside the order. In the event of the order not being set aside, the court can award exemplary damages and the solicitor may be liable for contempt of court.

The effectiveness of the search order has been restricted by the application of the defendant's privilege against self-incrimination.

CASE EXAMPLE

Rank Film Distributors Ltd v Video Information Centre [1982] AC 380

The court upheld the defendant's claim to the privilege against self-incrimination in a case that involved breach of copyright.

Section 7(7) of the Civil Procedure Act 1997 (as amended) expressly enacts that the order does not affect the defendant's privilege against self-incrimination. However, s 72 of the Senior Courts Act 1981 now prohibits the defendant from relying on this privilege in cases involving passing off and/or cases relating to the infringement of intellectual property rights.

17.5 Specific performance

The remedy at common law for breach of contract is damages. But in some cases an award of damages would be inappropriate, e.g. where there is a contract for the sale of land or shares in a private company the claimant might want the land or shares for their unique value and would regard damages as a poor substitute. The equitable remedy of specific performance is an order addressed to a contracting party requiring him to perform what he promised to do.

In an action for specific performance the claimant is required to show that there is a contract which is enforceable at law. Hence, all the essential elements of a contract, such as agreement and consideration, must be present.

It has often been said that specific performance will not be available unless the remedy is 'mutual', i.e. mutually available to either party (see *Flight v Boland* (1882) 4 Russ 298, an infant was not entitled to specific performance because the remedy is not available against him). However, it seems that this may be an over-simplification. In fact one party may be disentitled to specific performance because he has either delayed in bringing the action or he does not come to the court with 'clean hands', e.g. he may have breached a term of the contract. However, the other party may still be entitled to specific performance if he so desires. Thus, the contract may be enforced despite an apparent lack of mutuality. In *Price v Strange* [1977] 3 All ER 371, it was held that mutuality was merely a factor to be considered in the exercise of the court's discretion. The relevant time for considering the defence of want of mutuality was not the date of the contract but the date of the trial.

17.6 Underlying principles for specific performance

Although the availability of the remedy is discretionary the court exercises its discretion, not in an unrestricted manner, but based on settled principles.

17.6.1 Damages inadequate

Courts of equity were originally prepared to grant decrees of specific performance because it was recognised that in some cases the common law remedy of damages was inadequate. This will be the position in the case of contracts for the sale of property that has a unique quality such as land, paintings, shares in a private company.

The reverse proposition that specific performance will not be ordered where damages would adequately compensate the claimant is an accurate statement of the law. This is especially so in the case of a contract for the sale of unascertained goods or goods which are freely available on the open market. In such a situation, the claimant would be left with his common law remedy of damages as this would enable him to purchase the goods elsewhere. However, in *Sky Petroleum Ltd v VIP Petroleum Ltd* [1974] 1 WLR 576 the court extended the jurisdiction to grant specific performance of a contract in exceptional circumstances where, but for the order, the claimant was in serious danger of being forced out of business. The court issued a mandatory injunction despite the clear link between this remedy and an order for specific performance.

CASE EXAMPLE

Sky Petroleum Ltd v VIP Petroleum Ltd [1974] 1 WLR 576

The claimant had entered into a contract whereby the defendant had agreed to supply to the claimant all the petrol it needed. The defendant purported to terminate the contract during a period of limited petrol supplies. The court granted an interim injunction restraining the defendant from refusing to supply the petrol. The court acknowledged that this amounted to specific performance of the contract but stated that it did have the jurisdiction to grant specific performance of a contract for the sale of chattels even though they were unascertained goods.

JUDGMENT

'There is, in my judgment, so far as I can make out on the evidence before me, a serious danger that unless the court interferes at this stage the plaintiff company will be forced out of business. In those circumstances, unless there is some specific reason which debars me from doing so, I should be disposed to grant an injunction to restore the former position under the contract until the rights and wrongs of the parties can be fully tried out. ... I am entirely unconvinced by counsel for the plaintiff company when he tells me that an injunction in the form sought by him would not be specific enforcement at all. The matter is one of substance and not of form and it is, in my judgment, quite plain that I am for the time being specifically enforcing the contract if I grant an injunction.'

Goulding J

17.6.2 Discretionary nature of the remedy

Like all equitable remedies, specific performance is discretionary. Accordingly, the courts will take many factors into account when considering whether or not to grant a decree, including laches, the conduct of the claimant and the question of hardship to the defendant. In *Patel v Ali*, it was held that, in considering the issue of hardship to the defendant, the court could take into account events which had occurred after the contract had been entered into, although this would be rare.

CASE EXAMPLE

Patel v Ali [1984] 1 All ER 978

The claimant applied for an order of specific performance for breach of a contract for the sale of a house. There was an unforeseen change in the defendant's circumstances subsequent to date of the contract of sale. The defendant, a young married woman with three young children, contracted bone cancer resulting in amputation of a leg subsequent to the date of contract. The defendant became dependent on assistance from family and friends living in the neighbourhood of the house contracted to be sold. The court decided that it would have inflicted hardship amounting to injustice on the defendant to order specific performance of the contract since that would have the effect of asking her to do what she had never bargained for, namely to complete the sale after more than four years and after all the unforeseeable changes that had taken place during that period. Moreover, after the long period of delay (for which neither party was to blame) it would have been just to leave the claimants to their remedy in damages.

The court may also take into account the conduct of the claimant, such as delay in bringing the claim or breach of a term of the contract as well as hardship that may be suffered by a third party in refusing to make an order for specific performance.

17.6.3 Contracts requiring supervision

The courts may refuse to make an order of specific performance in particular cases, such as those involving contracts which require constant supervision. The reason being to refrain from the possibility of repeated applications to the court in order to secure compliance with the contract. In *Dowty Boulton Paul Ltd v Wolverhampton Corp* [1971] 2 All ER 277, the court refused to order the defendant to carry on the business of running an airfield. Likewise, in *Co-Operative Insurance Society Ltd v Argyll Stores (Holdings) Ltd* [1997] 3 All ER 294, the House of Lords decided that the defendant would not be compelled to keep its supermarket open pursuant to a 'keep open' clause in the lease. In this case the court referred to a distinction between orders requiring the defendant to carry on an activity and orders directing him to achieve a result.

It is a question of degree to determine whether or not a contract requires continuous supervision. Even if continuous supervision of a contract should prove to be necessary, specific performance could still be granted provided that it is quite clear what the defendant is required to do. Thus, in *Beswick v Beswick* [1968] AC 58, all the Law Lords thought it unimportant that the obligation under the contract to pay an annuity to the claimant was a continuing one.

17.6.4 Contracts for personal services

The justification for not ordering specific performance for contracts for personal services are that such contracts may require continuous supervision and it was thought to be contrary to public policy to compel the parties to continue a working relationship where one of them was unwilling to do so. In *Lumley v Wagner* (1852) 1 De GM & G 604, the court refused to grant specific performance of a contract to sing at a theatre. In *Giles & Co v Morris* [1972] 1 All ER 960, Megarry J stated the rationale for the general rule thus:

JUDGMENT

'The reasons why the court is reluctant to decree specific performance of a contract for personal services (and I would regard it as a strong reluctance rather than the rule) are, I think, more complex, and more firmly bottomed on human nature. If a singer contracts to sing, there could no doubt be proceedings for committal if, ordered to sing, the singer remained obstinately dumb. But instead the singer sang sharp, or flat, or too fast or too slowly ... the threat of committal would reveal itself as a most unsatisfactory weapon.'

Megarry J

But not all contracts for personal services present such difficulties. The courts sometimes draw a distinction between contracts for personal services and contracts to achieve a result that had been agreed between the parties.

CASE EXAMPLE

Erskine McDonald Ltd v Eyles [1921] 1 Ch 631

The claimant signed a copyright agreement offering the defendant, an authoress, a publishing contract to write her next three books subject to certain royalty terms. In breach of this agreement the defendant attempted to sell her manuscripts to a rival publisher. The court granted an order of specific performance on the ground that such agreements were not contracts to render personal services, but contracts to sell the products of the labour or industry of the contracting party.

JUDGMENT

'This is not, in my opinion, a contract of personal service. It is a contract by Mrs. Eyles to hand over to the plaintiffs for a consideration the product of her labour; and I can see no difference in principle between this contract and a contract to transfer all future patents or improvements on an invention or a contract by a farmer for the sale of a future crop: see *Ward, Lock & Co. v. Long* [1906] 2 Ch 550.'

Peterson J

It should be noted that the courts are prepared to grant specific performance of restraint of trade covenants contained in contracts of employment. In *Awnayday & Co v D'Alphen* (1997), *The Times*, 24 June, the Court of Appeal enforced anti-solicitation and anti-competition covenants contained in an agreement against the defendants.

17.6.5 Agreements that are futile

As a general principle, specific performance will not be granted where it would be futile or impossible as 'equity does nothing in vain'. Thus, specific performance will not be ordered of a partnership agreement which is not for a fixed term as the partnership could be terminated anyway at will, see *Hercy v Birch* (1804) 9 Ves 357.

17.6.6 Mistake and misrepresentation

Both mistake and misrepresentation may give one party the right to rescind the contract. They may also be used as a 'defence' to an action for specific performance as it seems that the court may be more willing to refuse a decree of specific performance than to grant rescission.

CASE EXAMPLE

Denny v Hancock [1870] Ch App 1

The defendant bid for property at an auction, believing that it included 'three fine elm trees', whereas in fact it did not. His mistake was attributable to a plan provided by the claimant which the court found to be misleading. The defendant subsequently wished to withdraw from the contract and the claimant sued for specific performance. The court refused the claimant's application as it was felt that to grant it would be inequitable. The court also remarked that a unilateral mistake not induced by the claimant might be a ground for refusing specific performance although it would not entitle the defendant to rescind the contract.

KEY FACTS

Specific performance – general principles

Damages for breach of contract inadequate	*Sky Petroleum v VIP Petroleum* (1974)
Discretionary nature of equity's jurisdiction	*Patel v Ali* (1984)
Contracts not requiring constant supervision	*Dowty Boulton Paul Ltd v Wolverhampton Corp* (1971); *Co-Operative Insurance v Argyll Stores* (1997)
Orders which will be practical and effective	*Lumley v Wagner* (1852); *Erskine McDonald Ltd v Eyles* (1921); *Hercy v Birch* (1804)

SUMMARY

- Equitable remedies were originally created in accordance with principles of justice and fair play to the parties. The only common law remedy was damages but in appropriate cases this remedy may be inappropriate for the claimant. Equitable remedies act *in personam* and it is a contempt of court to wilfully refuse to comply with the court order.

An injunction is an order of the court directing a party to the proceedings to do or refrain from doing a specified act.

The claimant is required to prove that a right recognised in law or equity has been infringed by the defendant.

The jurisdiction of equity to grant an injunction was activated where the claimant establishes that the common law remedy of damages was an inappropriate remedy.

- In *Shelfer v City of London Electric Lighting Co* (1895) the Court of Appeal laid down a number of guidelines when it would exercise its discretion not to grant an injunction.
- In *Regan v Paul* (2006) the *Shelfer* guidelines were reviewed and regarded as too rigid. *Prima facie* the claimant is entitled to an injunction where his rights of enjoyment of property were substantially reduced by the conduct of the defendant. The latter bears the burden of proving that damages in lieu of an injunction is a feasible alternative.
- The Supreme Court in *Lawrence v Fen Tigers Ltd* (2014) declared that the *Shelfer* principles ought not to fetter the discretionary power of the court to award damages in lieu of an injunction.

Equity exercised its jurisdiction to grant an injunction in a discretionary manner by considering all the facts such as hardship to the defendant, inordinate delays and improprieties by the claimant.

There are a variety of injunctions that may be ordered by the courts including perpetual, prohibitory, mandatory, *quia timet*, interim, freezing injunctions and search orders.

A perpetual or final injunction is an order made following a trial. It is the ultimate remedy applied for by the claimant.

A prohibitory injunction restrains the defendant from doing something that he is not entitled to do.

A mandatory injunction is an order of the court requiring a defendant to perform an act that he ought to perform. Whether an injunction is prohibitory or mandatory is strictly speaking a matter of substance and not in the form of words used. Thus an order requiring the defendant to stop doing something is prohibitory. Whereas, an order restraining the defendant from not doing something is mandatory.

A *quia timet* injunction may be granted to restrain an apprehended breach of duty. Thus, the claimant is required to discharge a high degree of proof that the breach may occur which will result in the likelihood of substantial damage occurring.

An interim injunction is one that is ordered pending the trial of the substantive issues. Guidelines that need to be followed were laid down in *American Cyanamid Co v Ethicon Ltd* (1975).

A freezing injunction is a special interim injunction designed to prevent a defendant from removing assets from the jurisdiction of the British courts (or dissipating assets within the jurisdiction) which, if not prohibited, would defeat the whole purpose of litigation.

A search order is a form of an interim, mandatory injunction that may be ordered where there is a serious risk that the defendant may destroy material evidence before the date of the final hearing.

Specific performance is an order requiring a party to a contract to perform or complete the performance of his obligations under a contract. The effect of the order is to put the parties in the position they would have been had the contract been performed.

The claimant is required to establish that damages would not be an adequate remedy. This may be the case where the defendant's obligation is a continuing one.

- Specific performance may be ordered where the subject-matter of the contract has unique qualities (such as land, paintings, shares in a private company) and the defendant is shown to have acted in breach of his obligations under the contract.

- In exercising its jurisdiction to grant an order of specific performance the court will take into account the effect of the order on the defendant. If this may result in exceptional hardship the court has the discretion to refuse the order.

- The court may not order specific performance of contracts that require constant supervision. The purpose is to avoid the need to make repeated applications to the court in order to secure completion of the contract.

- Likewise, contracts for personal services may not be specifically enforced. Such contracts may require continuous supervision and it was thought to be contrary to public policy to compel the parties to continue a working relationship where one of them was unwilling to do so.

- The court will not make such an order where it would be futile in nature for 'equity does not act in vain', e.g. where the defendant may lawfully terminate a contract despite an order of specific performance.

- Mistake and misrepresentation may entitle a party to another equitable remedy of rescission and may be a ground for refusing to grant an order of specific performance.

ACTIVITY

Self-test questions

1. What factors should be considered by the court when deciding whether or not to grant an order for an interim injunction?
2. How true is it to say that there must be mutuality between the parties before the court will grant an order of specific performance?

SAMPLE ESSAY QUESTION

'The decision whether or not a [search order] should be granted requires a balance to be struck between the plaintiff's need that the remedies allowed by the civil law for the breach of his rights should be attainable and the requirements of justice that a defendant should not be deprived of his property without being heard.' *Per* Scott J in *Columbia Pictures Incorporation v Robinson* [1986] 3 All ER 338.

Consider what safeguards exist to prevent abuse by a claimant in granting a search order.

Answer plan

Definition of a search order (originally an *Anton Piller* order).

General constitutional right to property – *Entinck v Carrington*.

Anton Piller requirements:

- the claimant must have a strong *prima facie* case;
- the order may not be used as a fishing expedition;
- the claimant must show actual or potential damage of a very serious nature;
- there is clear evidence that the defendant has incriminating documents or things and that there is a real possibility of these documents or things being destroyed before an *inter partes* application could be made;
- the inspection on behalf of the claimant must do no real harm to the defendant or his case;
- the court will need to be satisfied that the claimant has the capacity to pay for any damages that may be ordered against him when the merits of the case are ultimately determined.

Application procedure.

Execution procedure.

Effect of breaches of safeguards.

Nature of the order including discharge and variation.

Privilege against self-incrimination.

Restriction within s 72 of the Senior Courts Act 1981.

Exceptional jurisdiction to issue after judgment.

CONCLUSION

Further reading

Buckley, R, 'Injunctions and the public interest' (1981) 44 MLR 212.

Capper, D, 'The trans-jurisdictional effects of Mareva injunctions' (1996) 15 CLQ 21.

Chynoweth, P, 'Rights to light: radical consequences of an orthodox decision' (2007) Conv 175.

Fox, D, 'Remedies for interference with a prescriptive right to light' (2007) CLJ 267.

Gee, S, 'The undertaking in damages' (2006) LMCLQ 181.

Gray, C, 'Interlocutory injunctions since Cyanamid' (1981) 40 CLJ 307.

Jones, G, 'Specific performance of a contract of service' (1987) 46 CLJ 21.

Keay, A, 'Whither American Cyanamid? Interim injunctions in the 21st century' (2004) CJQ 132.

McGrath, P, 'The freezing order: a constantly evolving jurisdiction' (2012) 31(1) CJQ 12.

Mason, A, 'Place of equity and equitable remedies in the contemporary common law world' (1994) LQR 238.

Reece-Thomas, K and Dockray, M, 'Anton Piller orders: the new statutory regime' (1998) CLQ 272.

Strong, B, 'Disclosure orders and the privilege against self-incrimination' (1992) 13 Comp Law 66.

Warwick, M, 'Final injunctions' (2005) 149 Sol J 823.

Wilson, J, 'Diva in dispute' (2012) 162 NLJ 690.

Zuckerman, A, 'Mareva and interlocutory injunctions disentangled' (1992) 108 LQR 559.

Glossary

A fortiori
More conclusively.

Ab initio
From the beginning.

Ad hoc
For this purpose or individual cases.

Ad litem
For the suit.

Affidavit
A written, signed statement made on oath or subject to a solemn affirmation.

Attesting witness
Witness who signs a document verifying the signature of a person who executes the document.

Attorney General
The legal adviser to the government; in addition, the legal representative of objects under a charitable trust.

Bona fide
In good faith.

Bona vacantia
Property without an apparent owner but which is acquired by the Crown.

Causa causans
The direct cause for an event.

Causa sine qua non
A cause without which a consequence would not have taken place. The expression is sometimes referred to as an indirect or historical cause for an event.

Cestui(s) que trust
An expression used originally to describe the beneficiary(ies) under a trust.

Chose(s) in action
These are personal, intangible property(ies) such as rights to have a loan repaid, the right to dividends from shares and intellectual property.

Common law
That part of the law of England and Wales formulated, developed and administered by the old common law courts. The rules that were originally applied by these courts were based on the common customs of this country.

Conscience
This expression denotes fairness, good faith and even-handedness.

Contempt of court
A disregard of the authority of the court. This is punishable by the immediate imprisonment of the offender.

Contingent interest
An estate or interest transferred but subject to the satisfaction of a precondition.

Cy-près
Nearest alternative gift.

Delegatus non potest delegare
A delegate cannot delegate his duties.

Donatio mortis causa
A deathbed gift or gift made *inter vivos* in contemplation of and conditional on the death of the donor.

Equity
That separate body of rules formulated and administered by the Court of Chancery prior to the Judicature Acts 1873/75 in order to supplement the deficiency in the rules and procedure at common law.

Ex parte
An interested person who is not a party; or, by one party in the absence of the other.

Execution of a will
The signature of a testator in the presence of two or more attesting witnesses.

Expectancy
These are rights that do not currently exist but may or may not exist in the future.

Feoffee
An expression that was used originally to describe the trustee. The full title was 'feoffee to use'.

Feudal incidents
Penalties or taxes that were payable in respect of the transfer of land.

Fiduciary
A person whose judgment and skill is relied on by another.

Gift over in default of appointment
An alternative gift in the event of a failure to distribute property under a power of appointment.

Hereditaments
Refers to the two types of real properties that exist, namely, corporeal and incorporeal. Corporeal hereditaments are visible and tangible objects such as houses and land, whereas incorporeal

hereditaments refer to intangible objects attached to the land, such as easements and restrictive covenants.

In personam
An act done or right existing with reference to a specific person as opposed to *in rem* (or in the thing).

In rem
A right that exists against the world at large as opposed to *in personam*.

In specie
In its original form.

Inter se
Between themselves.

Inter vivos
During the lifetime or before death.

Intestacy
A person who dies without making a valid will. His estate devolves on those specified under the intestacy rules.

Legatee
A person who inherits personal property under a valid will, as opposed to a 'devisee' who takes real property under a will.

Locus standi
The right to be heard in court or other proceedings.

Natural justice
Rules applied by the courts and other tribunals designed to ensure fairness and good faith and affording each party the opportunity to fairly state his case.

Obiter
A principle of law stated by a judge but not directly applicable to the facts of the case before him.

Pari passu
Equally, without preference.

Per se
By itself or on its own.

Perpetuity
Endless years. There is a rule against perpetuities which, if infringed, will make a gift void.

Personalty
Personal property.

Prima facie
At first appearance, or on the face of it.

Pro rata
Proportionately.

Probanda
Proof of specified elements.

Subpoena
The forerunner of the witness summons. It was a writ issued in an action requiring the addressee to be present in court at a specified date and time. Failure to attend without good cause is subject to a penalty.

Sui juris
A person who is under no disability, such as mental illness, affecting his power to own or transfer property.

Testator
A person who dies having made a valid will.

Trace
Process of identifying and recovering the claimant's original or substituted property from the defendant.

Trust instrument
The instrument setting out the terms of an express trust.

Trust today
The transfer of property to a trustee who holds the legal title for the benefit of a third party.

Trustee de son tort
Trustee of his own wrong, or one who intermeddles as a trustee without authority.

Virtute officio
By virtue of his office.

Vis-à-vis
In relation to.

Will
A document signed by the testator and attested by two or more witnesses which disposes of the testator's assets on his death.

Index

Page numbers in *italics* denote tables, those in **bold** denote figures.

of 493–5, 500; management powers of trustees, variation of 504–6, **506**; mortgages 491; not to make profits from the trust 482–90; other statutory provisions for the delegation of discretions 476–7; partitioning land under a trust of land 498; persons who may be appointed as nominees or custodians 475; and powers of appointment 58–9, 60–1, 475; receipts, giving of 497; remuneration and other financial benefits 212–20, 232–4, 485–9; self-dealing 210–11, 234–8, 483–4, 499; standard and duty of care at common law 466–9; standard of duty and care under the Trustee Act 2000 469–70, 500; trustees' discretion, control of 149–52: *see also* breach of trust

education 396–8, 406–10
enforcement theory 371
environmental protection 418
equitable obligation 20, 21
equitable remedies 593–618; award of damages in lieu of an injunction 596–9; contracts for personal services 613–14; contracts requiring supervision 612–13; discretionary nature of the remedy 612; freezing injunctions 13, 608–9; futile specific performance agreements 614; inadequate damages 611–12; injunctions 615; injunctions and their underlying principles 594–600, *600*; interim injunctions 604–7, *608*; mandatory injunctions 602–3, 607; mistake and misrepresentation in specific performance 614; perpetual injunctions 601; prohibitory injunctions 601–2; *Quia timet* injunctions 603–4; search orders 13, 609–10; specific performance 610–14, *614*; types of injunctions 600–10
equity 619; adaptability of equity today 12–14; Chancellor's intervention 5; contributions of equity to law development 7–8, 13; Court of Appeal in Chancery 8; definition 1–2; duality of ownership 5–6; injunctions 7; maxims of equity 14–15, 16; nineteenth-century reforms 8–12; petitions to the Lord Chancellor 2–3; procedure in Chancery 3–4; Statute of Uses 1535 6; terminology 2; tracing in equity 563–85; trusts as a product of equity 4–5; use upon a use 6–7
estoppel 133, 135, 583
evidential uncertainty 62, 71
ex parte 364, 619
exclusion clauses, and trustees' liability 477–80
executors 31–2
expectancy 23, 619
express trusts 30–1, 34, 35, 70; agreements enforceable by non-volunteers 95; and the certainties test 71; charitable purposes 390; commercial contexts 42–3; constitution of 75–122, *93*; Contracts (Right of Third Parties) Act 1999, effect of 97–8; covenants to create trusts before the Contracts (Right of Third Parties) Act 1999 96–7; debts enforceable at law 92–3; declarations of trusts 124–5; direction to trustees 129–30; disclaimers 137; dispositions under s 53(1)(c) of the Law of Property Act 1925 126–37; *donatio mortis causa* 103–11; donor's intention, nature of 100–3; equity will not assist a volunteer rule,

exceptions to 99–118, *118*; exclusion 125–6; fixed/discretionary trusts 33, 55–8, 61, 70–1; formalities for the creation of 123–40, *138*; future property, no trust of 89–90; incompletely constituted trusts 94–8; modes of creation 39–40, 75–6; multiple trustees including the settlor 87–9; no self-declaration following imperfect transfer 85–6; pension scheme nominations 137; perfect trusts, consequences of 94; proprietary estoppel 112–18; reasons for the creation of 34, 35; rule in *Milroy v Lord* [1862] 76–84, 88, 94, **97**; self-declaration of trusts 84–5, 136–7; settlors adoption of both modes of creation 86–7; signature 125, 128; *Strong v Bird* [1874] rule 99–100, 102–3; transfer and declaration mode 77; transfer of legal and equitable titles to a third party 131–2; transfer of shares in a private company 78–84; trust instrument 142; trust of land, declaration of 123–5; trusts of choses in action 90–3

fair dealing 210, 210–11, 211, 212, 235, 238, 484–5, 499
family home 13, 281–331; ante-nuptial and post-nuptial agreements, status of 322–5; date and method of valuation of the interest 314–19; domestic duties 308–9; express discussions between the parties, unwarranted requirement for 312–13; imputed intention 319–21; indirect contributions 309–12; investment properties 293–8; legal title in the joint names of the parties 282–93; legal title in the name of one party only 298–302; Matrimonial Proceedings and Property Act 1970, Section 37 321–2; nature of the trust 302–5; order of sale 322; proprietary rights in the family home 281–302, *326–7*; reliance and detriment 313
feoffee 4, 5–6, 14, 619
feudal incidents 4, 619
fiduciaries 20, 22, 196–7, 619; bribes or secret profits received by fiduciaries 221–30; constructive trusts, fiduciary relationship 211–12; fiduciary duties 45–6, 145, 148–9, 157, 164, 196–7; fiduciary power 58, 59, 145; unauthorised remuneration or financial benefit 212–20
fixed trusts 33, 55–7, 70, 142, **148**, 152, 157
forfeiture 155–6
Forfeiture Act 1882 238–43
a fortiori 334, 619
fraud 5–6, 9, 15, 244–5, 468–9, 547; fraudulent benefit from breach of trust 535; and secret trusts 336–8; and standard of proof 348–9

general charitable intention: existent/non-existent charitable body 439–40; form/substance 438; general/specific charitable intention 437–8; incorporated associations/unincorporated associations 440–1; initial failure 436–7; subsequent failure 433–6
gifts: *donatio mortis causa* 103–11; gift over in default of appointment 145, 619; imperfect transfers 85–6; invalidation of 63; legal titles 75–6; share transfers 78–84; subject to conditions precedent and subsequent 64–7; and trusts 30; to unincorporated associations 372–9

LIBRARY, UNIVERSITY OF CHESTER